TEST BANK

to accompany

Ronald J. Comer

Abnormal Psychology

Sixth Edition

Debra B. Hull
Wheeling Jesuit College

John H. Hull
Bethany College

Worth Publishers

Test Bank
by Debra B. Hull and John B. Hull
to accompany
Comer: Abnormal Psychology, Sixth Edition

Copyright © 2007 by Worth Publishers

ISBN 13: 978-0-7167-2447-6

ISBN 10: 0-7167-2447-2

Printed in the United States of America

First Printing

Worth Publishers
41 Madison Avenue
New York, NY 10010
www.worthpublishers.com

Contents

Preface

This Test Bank contains more than 2,500 questions, carefully constructed to help evaluate students' understanding of *Abnormal Psychology*, Sixth Edition. The questions are organized according to where the source of information can be found in each chapter. Each question is correlated to the relevant textbook topic, keyed to the page on which the information appears, labeled according to difficulty level, and identified as either factual or applied. All the answer information appears on the lines above the questions, formatted as in the example below:

Generalized Anxiety Disorder, p, 116
Diff: M, Type: Applied, Ans: b

A question is assigned a difficulty level of "E" (Easy) if, in the test bank authors' opinions, the question could be answered from knowledge obtained in another psychology course, or from general knowledge some students might have. A question is assigned a difficulty level of "M" (Medium) if answering it requires more specific attention to material in the text, or some degree of interpretation or integration of text material. A question is assigned a difficulty level of "H" (Hard) if it includes responding to subtle differences among alternatives, if it requires substantial integration of text material, or if it requires abstracting principles from the text material. As in the past, we have attempted to increase the difficulty level of items, and increase the range of item difficulty. Difficulty ratings are subjective, although both test bank authors agreed on all test question difficulty level ratings.

The factual/applied designation distinguishes between questions that may be answered directly from the textbook and questions that require the students to look for examples or implications. Fill-in and essay questions employ the same answer information format, except that most essay items include references to several pages on which relevant answer information may be found.

The questions and answers have been checked several times for accuracy. Wrong answers may have eluded us, for which we apologize in advance. In addition, some instructors may not agree with the test bank writers' views on particular questions. For these reasons, we encourage you to read over each question before using it.

The computerized versions of this test bank allow users to easily edit answers and/or questions. They also enable users to quickly add their own questions. For more information about the computerized version, please contact your Worth sales representative.

Your students can find multiple-choice practice questions in three places: on the *Abnormal Psychology*, 6e CD-ROM; in the Student Workbook available from Worth; and on the *Abnormal Psychology*, Web site (http://www.worthpublishers.com/comer). The web site and CD-ROM contain duplicate quizzes in the event that students don't have a fast Internet connection. The student workbook contains a different set of questions for each chapter so that students have two ways to review the material. All the questions also contain feedback and answer keys to help students in their studying and learning.

The questions in this test bank have been reviewed and updated to reflect the new edition of the textbook. The authors of this edition wish to acknowledge and thank those involved in earlier versions for their contributions. They are Melvyn King, Debra Clark, Steven Winshel, Jeffrey Gossett, Meath Bowen, Patty Nankervis, and Ronald J. Comer.

CHAPTER 1

Abnormal Psychology: Past and Present

MULTIPLE-CHOICE QUESTIONS

Abnormal Psychology: Past and Present, p. 2
Diff: E, Type: Factual, Ans: c

1. One who systematically gathers information in order to describe, predict, and explain abnormality is a clinical:
    a. mentalist.
    b. legalist.
    c. scientist.
    d. practitioner.

Abnormal Psychology: Past and Present, p. 2
Diff: M, Type: Applied, Ans: a

2. If you wanted a career in which you focus on detecting, assessing, and treating abnormal patterns of functioning, you should look into becoming a:
    a. clinical practitioner.
    b. clinical researcher.
    c. clinical historian.
    d. clinical statistician.

Deviance, p. 3
Diff: M, Type: Applied, Ans: b

3. A student in an abnormal psychology class receives the highest test grade in a class of 50 students. This behavior is considered abnormal because it is:
    a. dangerous to self or others.
    b. deviant.
    c. dysfunctional.
    d. distressful.

Deviance, p. 3
Diff: E, Type: Factual, Ans: a

4. The explicit and implicit rules for proper conduct that a society establishes are referred to as:
    a. norms.
    b. culture.
    c. morality.
    d. conventions.

Deviance, p. 3
Diff: M, Type: Factual, Ans: a
5.   Behavior that violates legal norms is:
      a.   deviant and criminal.
      b.   distressful and criminal.
      c.   deviant and psychopathological.
      d.   distressful and psychopathological.

Deviance, p. 3
Diff: E, Type: Factual, Ans: c
6.   The history, values, institutions, technology, and arts of a society make up that society's:
      a.   laws.
      b.   norms.
      c.   culture.
      d.   conventions.

Deviance, p. 3
Diff: M, Type: Applied, Ans: b
7.   Last week Elaine took an IQ test and scored extremely high. According to the definition of abnormality, her behavior is an example of:
      a.   distress.
      b.   deviance.
      c.   dysfunction.
      d.   danger to self or others.

Deviance, p. 3
Diff: H, Type: Applied, Ans: a
8.   Brilliant scholars or champion athletes are not considered clinically abnormal because:
      a.   their behaviors are valued by the culture.
      b.   their behaviors are not sufficiently deviant.
      c.   there are many people who exhibit these behaviors
      d.   people who exhibit these behaviors are not unhappy.

Deviance, p. 3
Diff: H, Type: Applied, Ans: b
9.   Which of the following depressed people would be the least likely to be diagnosed with a mental disorder—because of specific circumstances?
      a.   someone whose mother was depressed
      b.   someone whose husband was killed on 9/11
      c.   someone who was experiencing a chemical brain imbalance
      d.   someone who was also an alcoholic

Deviance, p. 3
Diff: H, Type: Applied, Ans: a
10.   Mario is so miserable that he can barely tolerate living. According to the definition of abnormality, this description is an example of:
      a.   distress.
      b.   deviance.
      c.   dysfunction.
      d.   danger to self or others.

Dysfunction, pp. 3, 4
Diff: H, Type: Applied, Ans: c

11. An individual has a 9-to-5 job. However, this person seldom gets up early enough to be at work on time, and expresses great distress over this fact. This individual's behavior would be considered abnormal because it is:
    a. dysfunctional.
    b. deviant.
    c. dysfunctional and deviant.
    d. dangerous.

Dysfunction, p. 4
Diff: M, Type: Factual, Ans: c

12. Which aspect of the definition of abnormality includes the inability to care for oneself and work productively?
    a. distress
    b. deviance
    c. dysfunction
    d. danger to self or others

Dysfunction, p. 4
Diff: H, Type: Applied, Ans: d

13. A Secret Service agent steps in front of the President of the United States, prepared to be killed or injured if the President's safety is threatened. Psychologically speaking, the Secret Service agent's behavior is:
    a. functional, but psychologically abnormal.
    b. functional, and not psychologically abnormal.
    c. dysfunctional, and psychologically abnormal.
    d. dysfunctional, but not psychologically abnormal.

Danger, p. 4
Diff: M, Type: Applied, Ans: c

14. Research shows that danger to self or others is found in:
    a. all cases of abnormal functioning.
    b. most cases of abnormal functioning.
    c. some cases of abnormal functioning.
    d. no cases of abnormal functioning.

Danger, p. 4
Diff: M, Type: Factual, Ans: b

15. Despite popular misconceptions, most people with psychological problems are not:
    a. dysfunctional.
    b. dangerous.
    c. distressing.
    d. deviant.

The Elusive Nature of Abnormality, p. 5
Diff: H, Type: Factual, Ans: d
16. Thomas Szasz's view about the idea of "mental illness" is that:
    a. most people suffer some form of psychological abnormality most of the time.
    b. most people suffer some form of psychological abnormality at some time.
    c. the majority of abnormalities are merely "eccentricities."
    d. most abnormalities are simply "problems in living."

The Elusive Nature of Abnormality, p. 5
Diff: M, Type: Factual, Ans: b
17. According to Thomas Szasz's views, the deviations that some call mental illness are really:
    a. mental illnesses.
    b. problems in living.
    c. caused by one's early childhood experiences.
    d. eccentric behaviors with a biological cause.

The Elusive Nature of Abnormality, p. 5
Diff: H, Type: Applied, Ans: a
18. A researcher spends 15 or more hours per day conducting experiments or doing library reading and records observations on color-coded index cards. This person lives alone in the country, but doesn't interfere with others' lives. The best description of the researcher's behavior is that it is:
    a. eccentric.
    b. abnormal.
    c. dangerous.
    d. dysfunctional.

What is Treatment?, p. 6
Diff: M, Type: Factual, Ans: c
19. Clinical theorist Jerome Frank would say that all forms of therapy include all of the following except a:
    a. series of contacts.
    b. healer.
    c. third-party payer.
    d. sufferer who seeks relief.

What is Treatment?, p. 6
Diff: M, Type: Applied, Ans: d
20. One who sees abnormality as a problem in living usually refers to those seeking help with their problems in living as:
    a. pupils.
    b. patients.
    c. trainees.
    d. clients.

How Was Abnormality Viewed and Treated in the Past?, p. 6
Diff: H, Type: Factual, Ans: d

21.   Several researchers have shown that in a typical year in the United States about what percentage of adults show disturbances severe enough to need clinical treatment?
   a.   less than 1%
   b.   5-10%
   c.   10-15%
   d.   more than 15%

How Was Abnormality Viewed and Treated in the Past?, p. 6
Diff: M, Type: Factual, Ans: a

22.   Which of the following statements is most accurate regarding the incidence of psychological abnormality, historically and worldwide?
   a.   It appears in all cultures during all time periods.
   b.   It appears in all cultures, but only during occasional time periods.
   c.   It appears in only some cultures, but during all time periods in those cultures.
   d.   It appears in only some cultures, and only occasionally in those cultures.

How Was Abnormality Viewed and Treated in the Past?, p. 6
Diff: H, Type: Factual, Ans: a

23.   Which of the following is estimated to occur most frequently in the adult population of the United States?
   a.   anxiety
   b.   schizophrenia
   c.   Alzheimer's
   d.   completed suicides

How Was Abnormality Viewed and Treated in the Past?, p. 6
Diff: H, Type: Applied, Ans: c

24.   The proportion of people who experience schizophrenia in the United States is nearest to the proportion who experience:
   a.   anxiety.
   b.   depression.
   c.   Alzheimers.
   d.   a personality disorder.

Ancient Views and Treatments, p. 8
Diff: E, Type: Factual, Ans: c

25.   The practice of trephination was probably used to:
   a.   remove a part of the brain.
   b.   relieve pressure on the brain.
   c.   allow the release of evil spirits.
   d.   restore the balance among the four humors.

Ancient Views and Treatments, p. 8
Diff: M, Type: Factual, Ans: c

26.   The use of exorcism suggests a belief that what we call mental illness was caused by:
   a.   germs.
   b.   poisons.
   c.   evil spirits.
   d.   psychological trauma.

Ancient Views and Treatments, p. 8
Diff: H, Type: Applied, Ans: a

27. A person seeking help for a psychological abnormality is made to drink bitter herbal potions and then submit to a beating, in the hope that "evil spirits" will be driven from the person's body. This form of "therapy" is called:
    a. exorcism.
    b. shaman.
    c. couvade.
    d. trephination.

Ancient Views and Treatments, p. 8
Diff: H, Type: Applied, Ans: d

28. If you were being treated by a shaman, you would most likely be undergoing:
    a. psychoanalysis.
    b. gender-sensitive therapy.
    c. community-based treatment.
    d. an exorcism.

Greek and Roman Views and Treatments, p. 9
Diff: E, Type: Factual, Ans: b

29. Greek and Roman physicians described a person with mania as having symptoms of:
    a. paranoia and aggression.
    b. euphoria and frenzied activity.
    c. heightened perception of surroundings.
    d. inflexible and maladaptive personality traits.

Greek and Roman Views and Treatments, p. 9
Diff: M, Type: Applied, Ans: d

30. Bob experiences unshakable sadness. His friends have given up trying to cheer him up because nothing works. An ancient Greek physician would have labeled his condition:
    a. mania.
    b. hysteria.
    c. delusional.
    d. melancholia.

Greek and Roman Views and Treatments, p. 9
Diff: M, Type: Factual, Ans: a

31. Roughly 2,000 years ago, a Greek or Roman physician would most likely diagnose a person experiencing an overall decline in intellectual functioning as suffering from:
    a. dementia.
    b. delusions.
    c. melancholia.
    d. hysteria.

Greek and Roman Views and Treatments, p. 9
Diff: E, Type: Factual, Ans: c

32. Dementia is a condition characterized by:
    a. general paresis.
    b. physical ailments.
    c. a general intellectual decline.
    d. loss of contact with reality

Greek and Roman Views and Treatments, p. 9
Diff: H, Type: Applied, Ans: c

33.   Margie's ability to think clearly and remember events has been deteriorating over the last several years. She now has difficulty even reading anything longer than a sentence because she cannot keep track of what she is reading. She is almost completely unable to function intellectually. According to Greek and Roman views, this is an example of:
   a.   amnesia.
   b.   hysteria.
   c.   dementia.
   d.   general paresis.

Greek and Roman Views and Treatments, p. 9
Diff: H, Type: Factual, Ans: a

34.   Jeff's left arm suddenly went numb. His physician was unable to find a physical cause of the problem. Jeff is apparently experiencing what the ancient Greek physicians called:
   a.   hysteria.
   b.   dementia.
   c.   paralysis.
   d.   hypochondriasis.

Greek and Roman Views and Treatments, p. 9
Diff: H, Type: Applied, Ans: c

35.   Sam once found a $100 bill on the sidewalk and did not turn it in to the police. Recently he has become more and more convinced that the police know this and have been following him and searching his house. He is certain that they mean to arrest him and put him in jail. His behavior involves what the ancient Greeks referred to as:
   a.   mania.
   b.   hysteria.
   c.   delusions.
   d.   hallucinations.

Greek and Roman Views and Treatments, p. 9
Diff: M, Type: Applied, Ans: c

36.   As you are talking to your advisor, he stares at the wall and asks you if you see the ants crawling on it (there are none). Your advisor is:
   a.   delusional.
   b.   displaying a neurosis.
   c.   having a hallucination.
   d.   displaying a hysterical symptom.

Greek and Roman Views and Treatments, p. 9
Diff: E, Type: Factual, Ans: c

37.   Hippocrates thought that abnormal behavior resulted from an imbalance in the four humors, one of which was:
   a.   water.
   b.   lymph gland fluid.
   c.   phlegm.
   d.   cerebrospinal fluid.

Greek and Roman Views and Treatments, p. 9
Diff: E, Type: Factual, Ans: b

38. Hippocrates's contribution to the development of our understanding of mental illness was the view that such conditions were the result of:
    a. stress.
    b. natural causes.
    c. brain pathology.
    d. spiritual deviations.

Greek and Roman Views and Treatments, p. 9
Diff: H, Type: Factual, Ans: c

39. Hippocrates attempted to treat mental disorders by:
    a. hypnotizing patients.
    b. chaining patients to walls.
    c. correcting underlying physical pathology.
    d. encouraging patients to speak about past traumas.

Greek and Roman Views and Treatments, p. 9
Diff: H, Type: Applied, Ans: b

40. "Abnormal behavior is a symptom of disease, and once the disease is cured, the abnormality will cease." Who would agree most strongly with this statement?
    a. St. Vitus
    b. Hippocrates
    c. demonologists
    d. clergy of the Middle Ages

Greek and Roman Views and Treatments, p. 9
Diff: H, Type: Applied, Ans: b

41. "What this person needs to be rid of abnormal behavior is a quiet life, a vegetarian diet, exercise, and celibacy." Who would agree most strongly with this statement?
    a. clergy of the Middle Ages
    b. ancient Roman physicians
    c. Henry VIII
    d. von Krafft-Ebing

Europe in the Middle Ages: Demonology Returns, p. 9
Diff: E, Type: Applied, Ans: d

42. What model of mental illness did most people hold during the Middle Ages?
    a. the moral model
    b. the medical model
    c. the psychogenic model
    d. the demonology model

Europe in the Middle Ages: Demonology Returns, p. 9
Diff: M, Type: Factual, Ans: b

43. Tarantism and lycanthropy are examples of:
    a. exorcism.
    b. mass madness.
    c. physical pathology causing mental illness.
    d. disorders that were treated with trephination.

Europe in the Middle Ages: Demonology Returns, p. 9
Diff: H, Type: Applied, Ans: a

44.   "The Devil made me do it!" would be a believable reason for abnormal behaviors for:
       a.   clergy of the Middle Ages.
       b.   ancient Roman physicians.
       c.   ancient Greek physicians.
       d.   von Krafft-Ebing.

Europe in the Middle Ages: Demonology Returns, p. 9
Diff: M, Type: Factual, Ans: d

45.   St. Vitus's dance, characterized by people suddenly going into convulsions, jumping around, and dancing, was also known as:
       a.   lycanthropy.
       b.   melancholia.
       c.   phlegmatism.
       d.   tarantism.

Europe in the Middle Ages: Demonology Returns, p. 9
Diff: M, Type: Factual, Ans: c

46.   "Mass madness" is a general term that includes which of the following disorders common in the Middle Ages in Europe?
       a.   tarantism
       b.   lycanthropy
       c.   exorcism
       d.   shamanism

Europe in the Middle Ages: Demonology Returns, p. 10
Diff: M, Type: Factual, Ans: d

47.   Those most often in charge of treating abnormality in the Middle Ages in Europe were the:
       a.   physicians.
       b.   nobility.
       c.   peasants.
       d.   clergy.

The Renaissance and the Rise of Asylums, p. 10
Diff: M, Type: Factual, Ans: a

48.   The first physician to specialize in mental illness was:
       a.   Johann Weyer.
       b.   William Tuke.
       c.   Benjamin Rush.
       d.   Sigmund Freud.

The Renaissance and the Rise of Asylums, p. 10
Diff: M, Type: Factual, Ans: b

49.   The individual considered to be the "parent" of the modern study of psychopathology is:
       a.   Hippocrates.
       b.   Johann Weyer.
       c.   Dorothea Dix.
       d.   Emil Kraepelin.

The Renaissance and the Rise of Asylums, p. 10
Diff: M, Type: Factual, Ans: b
50.   Johann Weyer, considered to be the founder of the modern study of psychopathology, was a
      physician in the:
      a.   1200s.
      b.   1500s.
      c.   1700s.
      d.   1800s.

The Renaissance and the Rise of Asylums, p. 10
Diff: H, Type: Factual, Ans: b
51.   Pilgrims in the 1500s would be most likely to go for "psychic healing" to:
      a.   Bethlehem Hospital in London.
      b.   Gheel, Belgium.
      c.   La Bicêtre in Paris.
      d.   Athens, Greece.

The Renaissance and the Rise of Asylums, p. 10
Diff: E, Type: Factual, Ans: b
52.   In many areas, asylums of the 1500s, such as Bethlehem asylum in London, became:
      a.   shrines.
      b.   tourist attractions.
      c.   sheltered workshops.
      d.   centers of moral treatment.

The Renaissance and the Rise of Asylums, p. 10
Diff: E, Type: Factual, Ans: b
53.   Treatment for mental illness in crowded asylums tended to be:
      a.   moral therapy.
      b.   harsh and cruel.
      c.   religiously based.
      d.   psychogenic therapy.

The Renaissance and the Rise of Asylums, p. 11
Diff: M, Type: Factual, Ans: b
54.   The first asylum was founded in:
      a.   Paris, France.
      b.   Muslim Spain.
      c.   New York.
      d.   London, England.

The Renaissance and the Rise of Asylums, p. 11
Diff: E, Type: Factual, Ans: a
55.   What is the distinction of Bethlehem Hospital, founded in London in 1547?
      a.   Popularly called "Bedlam," it came to represent deplorable conditions for patients.
      b.   It was the first asylum.
      c.   It was founded by Henry VIII as a place to house his numerous ex-wives.
      d.   It was the first asylum where the moral treatment of patients was practiced.

The Nineteenth Century: Reform and Moral Treatment, p. 12
Diff: H, Type: Applied, Ans: c
56.   Had they been able, male mental patients in the early 1800s probably would have chosen to
      be institutionalized in:
      a.   Bethlehem Hospital, London.
      b.   Lunatics' Tower, Vienna.
      c.   La Bicêtre, Paris.
      d.   Val d'Isère, France.

The Nineteenth Century: Reform and Moral Treatment, p. 12
Diff: E, Type: Factual, Ans: c
57.   The basis for moral treatment of asylum patients was the belief that:
      a.   mental problems had a biological basis.
      b.   demonology was a cause of mental illness.
      c.   mental illness should be treated with sympathy and kindness.
      d.   the cause of mental illness was immoral behavior.

The Nineteenth Century: Reform and Moral Treatment, p. 12
Diff: E, Type: Factual, Ans: d
58.   The person who cannot be given credit for the introduction of moral therapy was:
      a.   William Tuke.
      b.   Jean Esquirol.
      c.   Philippe Pinel.
      d.   Henry VIII.

The Nineteenth Century: Reform and Moral Treatment, p. 12
Diff: E, Type: Factual, Ans: c
59.   The man who brought about the reforms of moral therapy to northern England was:
      a.   John Dix.
      b.   Joseph Gall.
      c.   William Tuke.
      d.   Benjamin Rush.

The Nineteenth Century: Reform and Moral Treatment, p. 12
Diff: M, Type: Factual, Ans: d
60.   The man who brought the reforms of moral therapy to the United States was:
      a.   John Dix.
      b.   Joseph Gall.
      c.   William Tuke.
      d.   Benjamin Rush.

The Nineteenth Century: Reform and Moral Treatment, p. 12
Diff: H, Type: Applied, Ans: c
61.   "'Moral treatment' is the best way to deal with abnormality; even the best of us at some time
      may break under stress." Who of the following would agree most strongly with this
      statement?
      a.   Henry VIII
      b.   Emil Kraepelin
      c.   Philippe Pinel
      d.   Friedrich Anton Mesmer

The Nineteenth Century: Reform and Moral Treatment, p. 13
Diff: H, Type: Factual, Ans: b

62.   The "parent" of American psychiatry, who organized the first course in psychiatry in America, is:
    a.   Dorothea Dix.
    b.   Benjamin Rush.
    c.   William Tuke.
    d.   Sigmund Freud.

The Nineteenth Century: Reform and Moral Treatment, p. 13
Diff: M, Type: Factual, Ans: b

63.   The American schoolteacher who lobbied state legislatures for laws to mandate human treatment of people with mental disorders was:
    a.   William Tuke.
    b.   Dorothea Dix.
    c.   Clifford Beers.
    d.   Benjamin Rush.

The Nineteenth Century: Reform and Moral Treatment, p. 13
Diff: E, Type: Factual, Ans: b

64.   Which of the following is part of the legacy of Dorothea Dix?
    a.   deinstitutionalization
    b.   state mental hospitals
    c.   federal prisons
    d.   privatization of mental hospitals

The Nineteenth Century: Reform and Moral Treatment, p. 13
Diff: E, Type: Applied, Ans: d

65.   All of the following were advocates of "moral treatment" except for:
    a.   Dorothea Dix.
    b.   Benjamin Rush.
    c.   William Tuke.
    d.   Sigmund Freud.

The Nineteenth Century: Reform and Moral Treatment, p. 13
Diff: H, Type: Applied, Ans: d

66.   The "moral treatment" movement rapidly declined in the late nineteenth century because:
    a.   prejudice against those with mental disorders decreased.
    b.   fewer and fewer immigrants were being sent to mental hospitals.
    c.   all patients needing treatment had been helped.
    d.   hospitals became underfunded and overcrowded.

The Nineteenth Century: Reform and Moral Treatment, p. 13
Diff: E, Type: Factual, Ans: a

67.   Part of the downfall of moral therapy was that:
    a.   it did not work for everyone.
    b.   it was shown to be completely ineffective.
    c.   too few patients were hospitalized.
    d.   the development of psychogenic drugs replaced it.

The Early Twentieth Century: The Somatogenic and Psychogenic Perspectives, p. 13
Diff: H, Type: Applied, Ans: b
68.   Hippocrates' model of mental illness would be described as:
a. psychiatric.
b. somatogenic.
c. psychogenic.
d. supernatural.

The Early Twentieth Century: The Somatogenic and Psychogenic Perspectives, p. 14
Diff: M, Type: Factual, Ans: a
69.   Another term for a cluster of symptoms is:
a. syndrome.
b. somatogenesis.
c. psychogenesis.
d. general paresis.

The Early Twentieth Century: The Somatogenic and Psychogenic Perspectives, p. 14
Diff: H, Type: Applied, Ans: a
70.   The fact that some people in the advanced stages of AIDS experience neurological damage
that results in psychological abnormality supports what type of perspective about abnormal
psychological functioning?
a. somatogenic
b. psychogenic
c. moral
d. deterministic

The Early Twentieth Century: The Somatogenic and Psychogenic Perspectives, p. 14
Diff: M, Type: Factual, Ans: d
71.   The discovery of the link between general paresis and syphilis was made by:
a. Benjamin Rush.
b. Emil Kraepelin.
c. Fritz Schaudinn
d. Richard von Krafft-Ebing.

The Early Twentieth Century: The Somatogenic and Psychogenic Perspectives, p. 14
Diff: H, Type: Applied, Ans: b
72.   The finding that syphilis causes general paresis is important because it supports the idea that:
a. mental patients should be deinstitutionalized.
b. organic factors can cause mental illness.
c. antibiotics cannot "cure" viral diseases.
d. physicians should be the ones treating mental illnesses.

The Early Twentieth Century: The Somatogenic and Psychogenic Perspectives, p. 15
Diff: M, Type: Factual, Ans: c
73.   The German researcher who argued that physical factors may cause mental dysfunction, and
who developed the first modern classification system for abnormal behaviors, was:
a. Richard von Krafft-Ebing.
b. Friedrich Anton Mesmer.
c. Emil Kraepelin.
d. Fritz Schaudinn.

The Early Twentieth Century: The Somatogenic and Psychogenic Perspectives, p. 15
Diff: H, Type: Applied, Ans: a

74.   Eugenic sterilization reflects the _____ perspective on abnormality.
       a. somatogenic
       b. psychoanalytic
       c. cultural
       d. managed care

The Early Twentieth Century: The Somatogenic and Psychogenic Perspectives, p. 15
Diff: E, Type: Factual, Ans: c

75.   The somatogenic treatment for mental illness that seems to have been the most successful was
       the use of:
       a. psychosurgery.
       b. psychoanalysis.
       c. various medications.
       d. insulin shock therapy.

The Early Twentieth Century: The Somatogenic and Psychogenic Perspectives, p. 15
Diff: H, Type: Applied, Ans: b

76.   Hypnotism is associated with all of the following except:
       a. Mesmer.
       b. the somatogenic perspective.
       c. psychodynamic therapy.
       d. the late 1700s.

The Early Twentieth Century: The Somatogenic and Psychogenic Perspectives, p. 15
Diff: M, Type: Factual, Ans: b

77.   Mesmer became famous—or infamous—for his work with patients suffering from bodily
       problems with no physical basis. His patients' disorders are termed:
       a. somatogenic.
       b. hysterical.
       c. phlegmatic.
       d. bilious.

The Early Twentieth Century: The Somatogenic and Psychogenic Perspectives, p. 15
Diff: M, Type: Applied, Ans: a

78.   An otherwise "normal" person during hypnotic suggestion is made to bark, sit, and fetch like
       a dog. The occurrence of these "abnormal" behaviors lends support to which explanation for
       abnormality?
       a. psychogenic
       b. somatogenic
       c. parthenogenic
       d. schizophrenegenic

The Early Twentieth Century: The Somatogenic and Psychogenic Perspectives, p. 15
Diff: M, Type: Factual, Ans: a

79.   The nineteenth-century physician who argued that hysterical disorders were the result of degeneration in portions of the brain was:
   a.   Jean Charcot.
   b.   Josef Breuer.
   c.   Sigmund Freud.
   d.   Hippolyte-Marie Bernheim.

The Early Twentieth Century: The Somatogenic and Psychogenic Perspectives, p. 15
Diff: M, Type: Factual, Ans: a

80.   Which point of view was supported by the discovery that the symptoms of hysteria (e.g., mysterious paralysis) could be induced by hypnosis?
   a.   psychogenic
   b.   somatogenic
   c.   demonological
   d.   psychoanalytic

The Early Twentieth Century: The Somatogenic and Psychogenic Perspectives, p. 15
Diff: H, Type: Factual, Ans: a

81.   Bernheim and Liébault used hypnotic suggestion to induce hysterical disorders in "normal" people, providing support for which perspective of abnormality?
   a.   psychogenic
   b.   somatogenic
   c.   psychoanalytic
   d.   sociocultural

The Early Twentieth Century: The Somatogenic and Psychogenic Perspectives, p. 15
Diff: M, Type: Applied, Ans: c

82.   The early psychogenic treatment that was advocated by Jean Charcot, Josef Breuer, and even Sigmund Freud was:
   a.   prayer.
   b.   bleeding.
   c.   hypnotism.
   d.   trephining.

The Early Twentieth Century: The Somatogenic and Psychogenic Perspectives, p. 16
Diff: M, Type: Factual, Ans: b

83.   Acquiring insight about unconscious psychological processes is a feature of:
   a.   moral therapy.
   b.   psychoanalysis.
   c.   psychogenic therapy.
   d.   all psychological therapy.

The Early Twentieth Century: The Somatogenic and Psychogenic Perspectives, p. 16
Diff: M, Type: Factual, Ans: b

84.   Psychoanalysis is a form of:
   a.   moral therapy.
   b.   outpatient therapy.
   c.   behavioral therapy.
   d.   somatogenic therapy.

The Early Twentieth Century: The Somatogenic and Psychogenic Perspectives, p. 16
Diff: M, Type: Applied, Ans: d

85.   "Many people are not aware of the sources of their abnormality, because abnormality often arises from unconscious psychological processes; such people need insight about those processes." Who would agree most strongly with this statement?
       a.   Mesmer
       b.   Cicero
       c.   Galen
       d.   Freud

The Early Twentieth Century: The Somatogenic and Psychogenic Perspectives, p. 16
Diff: M, Type: Factual, Ans: b

86.   Psychoanalysis, as Freud developed it, was a form of what we now would call:
       a.   Mesmerism.
       b.   outpatient therapy.
       c.   community psychology.
       d.   Kraepelinism.

The Early Twentieth Century: The Somatogenic and Psychogenic Perspectives, p. 16
Diff: M, Type: Applied, Ans: c

87.   Which of the following patients is most likely to benefit most from psychoanalytic treatment?
       a.   a person who needs to make profound behavioral changes very quickly
       b.   a person who has difficulty expressing ideas and feelings verbally
       c.   someone who is insightful and thinks clearly
       d.   someone who is severely disturbed and in a mental hospital

The Early Twentieth Century: The Somatogenic and Psychogenic Perspectives, p. 16
Diff: H, Type: Applied, Ans: c

88.   Psychoanalysis is NOT very effective for hospitalized mental patients because:
       a.   there is not enough time for long-term therapy.
       b.   the ratio of caretaker to patient is too high.
       c.   patients lack the necessary insight and verbal skills.
       d.   there are not enough patients to form meaningful therapy groups.

Current Trends, p. 16
Diff: H, Type: Applied, Ans: d

89.   Regarding the cause of mental disorders, more people today believe that mental illness is caused by which of the following?
       a.   sinful behavior
       b.   lack of willpower
       c.   lack of self-discipline
       d.   something the person brought on him or herself

Multicultural Psychology, p. 21
Diff: H, Type: Applied, Ans: c

114.   If you were receiving multicultural therapy, you could expect all of the following except:
   a.   greater sensitivity to cultural issues in therapy.
   b.   a focus on the uniqueness of the issues you face.
   c.   a focus on healthy feelings and actions rather than on problems.
   d.   sensitivity to the traditions of the your particular culture.

Multicultural Psychology, p. 21
Diff: H, Type: Applied, Ans: d

115.   If a patient is a minority group member and has trouble affording treatment, feels uncomfortable with the therapist, and doesn't see results, the person is at risk for:
   a.   staying in therapy longer than recommended.
   b.   abandoning his or her ethnic traditions.
   c.   becoming more "Americanized."
   d.   dropping out of therapy.

Multicultural Psychology, p. 21
Diff: H, Type: Applied, Ans: a

116.   According to multicultural therapy, which of the following is the best recommendation for therapists who want to serve members of minority cultures?
   a.   learn about the minority culture
   b.   practice "traditional" rather than empirical treatments
   c.   focus on incorporating everyone into the dominant culture
   d.   hospitalize minority members together

The Growing Influence of Insurance Coverage, p. 21
Diff: H, Type: Applied, Ans: a

117.   "What the #%*$!! is going on? The insurance company says I have to stop my anger management program now!" The client who says this is most likely voicing concern about a:
   a.   managed care program.
   b.   private psychotherapist.
   c.   community mental health agency.
   d.   sociocultural resource center.

The Growing Influence of Insurance Coverage, p. 21
Diff: E, Type: Factual, Ans: d

118.   Which of the following is not a common feature of managed care programs?
   a.   limited pool of practitioners for patients to choose from
   b.   preapproval for treatment by the insurance company
   c.   ongoing reviews and assessments
   d.   patient choice in number of sessions therapy can last

The Growing Influence of Insurance Coverage, pp. 21-22
Diff: H, Type: Factual, Ans: b

119.   Parity laws for insurance coverage of mental health treatment mandate that:
   a.   physicians and psychologists must have the same level of education.
   b.   coverage for mental and physical problems must be reimbursed equally.
   c.   the number of sessions allowed for treatment of mental and physical treatment must be equal.
   d.   patients must be allowed to choose the therapist they want for treatment.

What Are Today's Leading Theories and Professions?, p. 22
Diff: H, Type: Applied, Ans: b

120. Which of the following sequences is correct in terms of prominence of mental health treatments in the United States during the twentieth century and beyond?
    a. sociocultural, biological, psychoanalytic, behavioral
    b. psychoanalytic, biological, cognitive, sociocultural
    c. humanistic, sociocultural, biological psychoanalytic
    d. biological, humanistic, psychoanalytic, sociocultural

What Are Today's Leading Theories and Professions?, p. 22
Diff: M, Type: Factual, Ans: a

121. A physician who offers psychotherapy is called a:
    a. psychiatrist.
    b. clinical psychologist.
    c. psychodiagnostician.
    d. psychoanalyst.

What Are Today's Leading Theories and Professions?, p. 22
Diff: M, Type: Factual, Ans: a

122. One major difference between psychiatrists and clinical psychologists is that psychiatrists:
    a. went to medical school.
    b. must work in a medical setting.
    c. are allowed to do psychotherapy.
    d. have more training in mental illness.

What Are Today's Leading Theories and Professions?, p. 22
Diff: M, Type: Factual, Ans: b

123. The specialty that presently has the largest number of practitioners is:
    a. counseling psychology.
    b. psychiatric social work.
    c. educational and school psychology.
    d. marriage therapy.

What Are Today's Leading Theories and Professions?, p. 22
Diff: E, Type: Factual, Ans: a

124. A psychiatrist receives three to four years of training in the treatment of abnormal functioning after medical school; this training is called a(n):
    a. residency.
    b. internship.
    c. practicum.
    d. community mental health tour.

What Are Today's Leading Theories and Professions?, p. 22
Diff: M, Type: Applied, Ans: a

125. A person is hard at work trying to discover which combination of environmental and genetic factors produces schizophrenia. Most likely, the person is a:
    a. clinical researcher.
    b. psychiatric social worker.
    c. family therapist.
    d. counseling psychologist.

What Are Today's Leading Theories and Professions?, p. 22
Diff: E, Type: Factual, Ans: d
126.   The largest group of providers of psychotherapy and related services is:
    a.   psychiatrists.
    b.   clinical psychologists.
    c.   counseling psychologists.
    d.   psychiatric social workers.

What Are Today's Leading Theories and Professions?, p. 22
Diff: H, Type: Applied, Ans: c
127.   If you were representing the current dominant theory of mental disorders, you would be:
    a.   a psychoanalyst.
    b.   a gender-sensitive therapist.
    c.   no single viewpoint dominates currently.
    d.   an existentialist.

What Are Today's Leading Theories and Professions?, p. 22
Diff: H, Type: Applied, Ans: d
128.   Clinical psychologists are unique among mental health professionals because they:
    a.   can prescribe medications.
    b.   can conduct group therapy.
    c.   work in outpatient centers.
    d.   use psychological tests and conduct research.

Putting It Together, p. 23
Diff: H, Type: Factual, Ans: d
129.   The most accurate summary of the field of abnormal psychology at the present time is that clinical psychologists generally:
    a.   accept one definition of abnormality, and practice one form of treatment.
    b.   do not accept one definition of abnormality, but practice one form of treatment.
    c.   accept one definition of abnormality, but practice more than one form of treatment.
    d.   do not accept one definition of abnormality, and practice more than one form of treatment.

Putting It Together, p. 23
Diff: H, Type: Applied, Ans: c
130.   One who studies the history of the field of abnormal psychology most likely would compare our current understanding of abnormal behavior with a book that:
    a.   hasn't even been begun.
    b.   has received a title, but no text.
    c.   is in the process of being written.
    d.   is completed, and needs only to be read to be understood.

Putting It Together, p. 23
Diff: H, Type: Factual, Ans: b
131.   The total economic cost of psychological disorders, including substance abuse, in the United States is closest to:
    a.   400 million.
    b.   400 billion.
    c.   400 trillion.
    d.   400 thousand.

FILL-IN QUESTIONS

Deviance, p. 3
Diff: E, Type: Factual, Ans: norms
1. The explicit and implicit rules that a society establishes to govern conduct are referred to as
    _____.

Deviance, p. 3
Diff: E, Type: Factual, Ans: deviance
2. The aspect of the definition of abnormality that characterizes behavior as different from the
    norm is _____.

Deviance, p. 3
Diff: M, Type: Applied, Ans: distress
3. Ken is so anxious that he is miserable. This represents the aspect of the definition of
    abnormality called _____.

Deviance, p. 3
Diff: M, Type: Applied, Ans: dysfunction
4. Colleen is so afraid of open spaces that she cannot leave her house to go to work. This
    represents the aspect of the definition of abnormality called _____.

Deviance, p. 3
Diff: E, Type: Applied, Ans: danger to self or others
5. Heather has been called to heaven and the only way to get there is to kill herself. Killing
    herself represents the aspect of the definition of abnormality called _____.

The Elusive Nature of Abnormality, p. 5
Diff: H, Type: Factual, Ans: Thomas Szasz
6. The idea that the behaviors we label abnormal are just problems in living has been proposed
    by _____.

What Is Treatment?, p. 6
Diff: M, Type: Factual, Ans: client
7. While some clinicians will refer to the person they are treating as a patient, others will refer
    to the person as a _____.

Ancient Views and Treatments, p. 8
Diff: H, Type: Factual, Ans: trephination
8. The crude early form of surgery in which a hole was made in the skull of a person
    presumably to allow evil spirits to escape was called _____.

Ancient Views and Treatments, p. 8
Diff: M, Type: Factual, Ans: exorcism
9. The procedure that a priest or other powerful person might perform to drive evil spirits from a
    person is called _____.

What Do Clinical Researchers Do?, p. 28
Diff: H, Type: Applied, Ans: a
10.   Which of the following is the best example of the idiographic approach?
      a.   Freud's study of Little Hans
      b.   a study of the most effective treatment for phobias
      c.   a study of the relative frequency of horse and rat phobias among adults
      d.   a review of all Freud's phobic patient cases

What Do Clinical Researchers Do?, p. 28
Diff: M, Type: Applied, Ans: b
11.   A case study of a patient includes a history, tests, and interviews with associates. A clear
      picture is constructed of this individual so that her behavior is understood. This approach is:
      a.   nomothetic.
      b.   idiographic.
      c.   experimental.
      d.   correlational.

What Do Clinical Researchers Do?, p. 28
Diff: E, Type: Factual, Ans: b
12.   True experiments involve the manipulation of some:
      a.   fact.
      b.   variable.
      c.   hypothesis.
      d.   observation.

What Do Clinical Researchers Do?, p. 28
Diff: H, Type: Applied, Ans: a
13.   Which of the following is an example of an idiographic approach to knowledge?
      a.   a clinical evaluation of an individual
      b.   an experiment on animals
      c.   a quasi-experimental study
      d.   a correlational study of the relationship between parental discipline practices and later
           psychopathology

What Do Clinical Researchers Do?, p. 28
Diff: H, Type: Applied, Ans: c
14.   If you were using the scientific method to conduct research in abnormal psychology, you
      would be seeking:
      a.   an idiographic understanding.
      b.   to advance conventional wisdom.
      c.   a nomothetic understanding.
      d.   to change current graduate training.

What Do Clinical Researchers Do?, p. 28
Diff: H, Type: Applied, Ans: d
15.   Which of the following is NOT considered a research method?
      a.   the case study
      b.   a correlation
      c.   an experiment
      d.   a treatment plan for an individual

What Do Clinical Researchers Do?, p. 28
Diff: H, Type: Applied, Ans: c

16.   In this research question, "Do children from single-parent families show more depression than those from two-parent families," there is(are) _____ known variable(s).
       a.   0
       b.   1
       c.   2
       d.   3

What Do Clinical Researchers Do?, p. 28
Diff: M, Type: Factual, Ans: d

17.   What is the problem with "conventional wisdom" (what people assume without scientific testing to be the cause of abnormal behavior)?
       a.   it doesn't deal with the serious mental illnesses
       b.   it fails to account for family influences on mental illness
       c.   it does not lead to medical intervention
       d.   it is not based on sound research

What Do Clinical Researchers Do?, p. 28
Diff: H, Type: Applied, Ans: b

18.   Experiments are consistent with the _____ approach.
       a.   theoretical
       b.   nomothetic
       c.   idiographic
       d.   correlational

What Do Clinical Researchers Do?, p. 28
Diff: M, Type: Applied, Ans: d

19.   The idea that children from single-parent families show more depression than those from two-parent families is a(n):
       a.   variable.
       b.   experiment.
       c.   correlation.
       d.   hypothesis.

The Case Study, p. 29
Diff: M, Type: Factual, Ans: a

20.   Freud's study of Little Hans is an example of:
       a.   a case study.
       b.   an experiment.
       c.   a phantasy.
       d.   a correlational study.

The Case Study, p. 29
Diff: M, Type: Applied, Ans: b

21.   A psychologist does a study of an individual involving a history, tests, and interviews of associates. A clear picture is constructed of this individual so that his behavior is better understood. This study is:
   a.   a hypothesis.
   b.   a case study.
   c.   an experimental study.
   d.   a correlation.

The Case Study, p. 29
Diff: M, Type: Applied, Ans: c

22.   Freud's study of Little Hans is an example of:
   a.   an experiment.
   b.   a correlational study.
   c.   the nomothetic approach.
   d.   the idiographic approach.

The Case Study, p. 29
Diff: E, Type: Factual, Ans: b

23.   Which of the following could be an example of a case study?
   a.   a study involving use of a control group
   b.   a long-term study of a clinical client
   c.   a study of all the cases of a disorder in a community
   d.   the creation of a disorder in a group of lab rats

The Case Study, pp. 29-30
Diff: H, Type: Factual, Ans: a

24.   Freud's study of Little Hans involved:
   a.   letters sent to Freud by Hans' father.
   b.   Freud's observation of Hans with horses.
   c.   use of antianxiety medication.
   d.   interviews with Hans' mother.

How Are Case Studies Helpful?, p. 31
Diff: H, Type: Applied, Ans: b

25.   Case studies are helpful for all of the following reasons except that:
   a.   their results may inspire new therapeutic techniques.
   b.   their results can be generalized.
   c.   they may be a source of new ideas about behavior.
   d.   they offer opportunities to study unusual problems.

How Are Case Studies Helpful?, p. 31
Diff: M, Type: Factual, Ans: b

26.   Case studies are useful for:
   a.   forming general laws of behavior.
   b.   studying unusual problems.
   c.   conducting scientific experiments.
   d.   eliminating observer bias.

What Are the Limitations of Case Studies?, p. 31
Diff: M, Type: Factual, Ans: d

27.   Case studies are useful for all of the following except:
      a.   studying unusual problems.
      b.   learning a great deal about a particular patient.
      c.   suggesting new areas for further study.
      d.   determining general laws of behavior.

What Are the Limitations of Case Studies?, p. 31
Diff: M, Type: Factual, Ans: a

28.   Which of the following is a limitation of the case study?
      a.   It does not result in high external validity.
      b.   It does not lead to an individualized approach.
      c.   It does not enable the therapist to understand the whole patient.
      d.   It does not allow the therapist to propose a course of treatment for a patient.

What Are the Limitations of Case Studies?, p. 31
Diff: H, Type: Factual, Ans: a

29.   Internal validity reflects how well a study:
      a.   rules out the effects of all variables except those being studied.
      b.   can be generalized to others that are not studied directly.
      c.   appears to be measuring what it is designed to measure.
      d.   predicts some future behavior.

What Are the Limitations of Case Studies?, p. 31
Diff: H, Type: Applied, Ans: b

30.   If a particular study of alcoholism failed to control for cultural patterns in drinking in the participants, the study would have low:
      a.   external validity.
      b.   internal validity.
      c.   face validity.
      d.   natural validity.

What Are the Limitations of Case Studies?, p. 32
Diff: M, Type: Applied, Ans: d

31.   The ability to generalize results from a study of certain individuals to other individuals not studied is called:
      a.   construct validity.
      b.   context validity.
      c.   internal validity.
      d.   external validity.

What Are the Limitations of Case Studies?, p. 32
Diff: E, Type: Factual, Ans: c

32.   External validity refers to the extent to which the results of a study:
      a.   rule out alternative explanations.
      b.   are the result of a single variable.
      c.   apply to subjects and situations other than the ones studied.
      d.   support the theory being tested.

What Are the Limitations of Case Studies?, p. 32
Diff: H, Type: Applied, Ans: b

33. A psychologist studies memory techniques in adult volunteers and learns how to facilitate memory. He applies what he learns to the new class of students in his freshman psychology course. He has faith in:
    a. the internal validity of his study.
    b. the external validity of his study.
    c. the content validity of his technique.
    d. the conceptual validity of memory.

What Are the Limitations of Case Studies?, p. 32
Diff: H, Type: Applied, Ans: c

34. One of the problems with animal research is the question of whether the results can apply to human beings. This is a question of:
    a. face validity.
    b. internal validity.
    c. external validity.
    d. content validity.

What Are the Limitations of Case Studies?, p. 32
Diff: M, Type: Applied, Ans: a

35. Which of the following is likely to have the lowest external validity?
    a. a case study
    b. an experiment
    c. a national survey
    d. a correlational study

What Are the Limitations of Case Studies?, p. 32
Diff: E, Type: Factual, Ans: c

36. If a study's findings generalize beyond the immediate study to other persons and situations, then the study has:
    a. external observer bias.
    b. internal observer bias.
    c. external validity.
    d. internal validity.

The Correlational Method, p. 32
Diff: H, Type: Applied, Ans: a

37. Correlations and experiments are preferred over case studies for all of the following reasons except:
    a. they offer rich detail that make the results extremely interesting.
    b. they typically observe many individuals.
    c. they are more easily replicable.
    d. they use statistical tests to analyze results.

The Correlational Method, p. 32
Diff: H, Type: Applied, Ans: b

38.   In a graph of a correlational study, the line of best fit:
       a.   inevitably runs from the lower left to the upper right.
       b.   is as close as possible to all points in the graph.
       c.   allows one to determine causality.
       d.   has no meaning unless it is positive.

The Correlational Method, p. 32
Diff: H, Type: Applied, Ans: a

39.   A researcher finds individuals who report large numbers of "hassles" in their lives usually
       also report higher levels of stress. Those who report fewer "hassles" generally report lower
       levels of stress. The correlation between number of "hassles" and stress level is:
       a.   positive.
       b.   negative.
       c.   curvilinear.
       d.   nonexistent.

The Correlational Method, p. 32
Diff: M, Type: Applied, Ans: c

40.   "The heavier you are, the more food you are likely to eat." If it is true, this statement
       expresses:
       a.   no correlation at all.
       b.   a causal relationship.
       c.   a positive correlation.
       d.   a negative correlation.

The Correlational Method, p. 33
Diff: H, Type: Applied, Ans: c

41.   If you were to graph the relationship between the number of negative life events experienced
       in the last month and that person's perception of stress, you would probably find:
       a.   a vertical line.
       b.   a horizontal line.
       c.   an upward-sloping line (to the right).
       d.   a downward-sloping line (to the right).

The Correlational Method, p. 34
Diff: H, Type: Factual, Ans: b

42.   Which of the following is true of the correlation coefficient?
       a.   It ranges from 0.00 to +1.00 and indicates the strength of the relationship between two
            variables.
       b.   It rangers from −1.00 to +1.00 and indicates the strength and the direction of the
            relationship between two variable.
       c.   It ranges from 0.00 to +1.00 and indicates the strength and the direction of the
            relationship between two variables.
       d.   It ranges from −1.00 to +1.00 and indicates the strength of the relationship between two
            variables and the total variability of those measurements.

The Correlational Method, p. 34
Diff: M, Type: Factual, Ans: a
43.   Correlation coefficients indicate:
   a.   the magnitude and direction of the relationship between variables.
   b.   the cause-and-effect relationship between variables.
   c.   the internal and external validity between variables.
   d.   the significance and variability between variables.

The Correlational Method, p. 34
Diff: H, Type: Applied, Ans: b
44.   Which of the following correlation coefficients is of the highest magnitude?
   a.   +.05
   b.   -.81
   c.   +.60
   d.   -.01

The Correlational Method, p. 34
Diff: H, Type: Applied, Ans: b
45.   Which of the following correlation coefficients represents the weakest relationship?
   a.   -.95
   b.   -.06
   c.   +.30
   d.   +.54

The Correlational Method, p. 34
Diff: H, Type: Applied, Ans: d
46.   If the correlation between severity of depression and age is -.05, it means that:
   a.   older people have more severe depression.
   b.   older people have less severe depression.
   c.   younger people have almost no depression.
   d.   there is no consistent relationship between age and severity of depression.

The Correlational Method, p. 34
Diff: H, Type: Applied, Ans: d
47.   Which of the following correlations is most likely to be statistically significant?
   a.   +.85, based on a sample of 10 people
   b.   -.08, based on a sample of 100 people
   c.   +.35, based on a sample of 10 people
   d.   -.80, based on a sample of 100 people

The Correlational Method, p. 34
Diff: E, Type: Factual, Ans: b
48.   Using generally accepted standards, what is the chance that a statistically significant result is
      due to chance?
   a.   0
   b.   5 percent
   c.   20 percent
   d.   It depends on the sample size.

The Correlational Method, p. 34
Diff: H, Type: Factual, Ans: c
49.   The major advantage of a correlational study over a case study is that it:
      a.   allows us to determine causation.
      b.   is more individualized.
      c.   has better external validity.
      d.   requires fewer participants.

The Correlational Method, p. 34
Diff: E, Type: Factual, Ans: d
50.   All of the following are merits of the correlational method *except*:
      a.   it allows for prediction.
      b.   it can be analyzed statistically.
      c.   results can be generalized.
      d.   it allows for in-depth study of an individual.

The Correlational Method, p. 35
Diff: H, Type: Applied, Ans: b
51.   If stress levels and physical health are negatively correlated, we know that:
      a.   stress causes people to have poor health.
      b.   as stress increases, health decreases.
      c.   poor health causes people to experience stress.
      d.   mental illness causes both stress and poor health.

The Correlational Method, p. 35
Diff: H, Type: Applied, Ans: d
52.   A researcher finds a strong positive correlation between ratings of life stress and symptoms of
      depression. Therefore, the researcher may be confident that:
      a.   life stress causes symptoms of depression.
      b.   symptoms of depression cause life stress.
      c.   both a and b.
      d.   neither a nor b.

The Correlational Method, p. 35
Diff: H, Type: Applied, Ans: d
53.   If the amount of stress people experience and their level of depression are positively
      correlated, we know that:
      a.   stress causes depression.
      b.   depression is a stressor.
      c.   poverty causes both stress and depression.
      d.   None of the answers are correct.

The Correlational Method, p. 35
Diff: H, Type: Applied, Ans: a
54.   Which of the following results most likely came from an epidemiological study?
      a.   The rate of suicide is higher in Ireland than in the United States.
      b.   Autism is caused by influenza vaccinations.
      c.   Child abuse is often found in the backgrounds of those with multiple personalities.
      d.   Alcoholism runs in families.

The Correlational Method, p. 35
Diff: E, Type: Factual, Ans: c
55. The form of correlational research that seeks to find how many new cases of a disorder occur in a group in a given time period is termed:
    a. longitudinal (incidence).
    b. longitudinal (prevalence).
    c. epidemiological (incidence).
    d. epidemiological (prevalence).

The Correlational Method, p. 35
Diff: M, Type: Applied, Ans: b
56. The incidence of HIV+ results on campus tells you:
    a. one's risk for becoming HIV+.
    b. the number of new HIV+ cases measured in a time period.
    c. the total number of HIV+ cases at a given point.
    d. the HIV+ rate compared to the national average.

The Correlational Method, p. 35
Diff: M, Type: Applied, Ans: a
57. The prevalence of sexual dysfunction in older men seen at a clinic tells you:
    a. the total number of older men with sexual dysfunction at the clinic.
    b. the risk of a man developing a sexual dysfunction.
    c. the number of new cases of sexual dysfunction over a period of time.
    d. the rate of sexual dysfunction in the community.

The Correlational Method, p. 35
Diff: E, Type: Factual, Ans: d
58. Studies that determine the incidence and prevalence of a disorder in a particular population are called:
    a. longitudinal studies.
    b. correlational studies.
    c. developmental studies.
    d. epidemiological studies.

The Correlational Method, p. 35
Diff: E, Type: Factual, Ans: a
59. The number of new cases of a disorder in the population that emerge in a particular time interval is called the:
    a. incidence.
    b. prevalence.
    c. correlation.
    d. epidemiology.

The Correlational Method, p. 35
Diff: M, Type: Applied, Ans: b
60. There were ten new cases of schizophrenia in a small town in the Midwest this week. This observation refers to the _____ of schizophrenia in this small population.
    a. risk
    b. incidence
    c. prevalence
    d. epidemiology

The Correlational Method, p. 35
Diff: E, Type: Factual, Ans: c
61.   The total number of cases of a disorder in the population is called the:
       a.   risk.
       b.   incidence.
       c.   prevalence.
       d.   rate of occurrence.

The Correlational Method, p. 35
Diff: H, Type: Applied, Ans: c
62.   The prevalence rate for a disorder will _____ the incidence rate.
       a.   always be the same as
       b.   always be higher than
       c.   always be the same or higher than
       d.   always be lower than

The Correlational Method, p. 35
Diff: H, Type: Applied, Ans: c
63.   Describing the number of cases of mental retardation in the children of older mothers in 2005
       would be a legitimate goal for a(n) _____ study:
       a.   case
       b.   experimental
       c.   epidemiological
       d.   correlational

The Correlational Method, p. 36
Diff: H, Type: Applied, Ans: d
64.   The finding that women have higher rates of anxiety and depression than men in the United
       States is most likely due to _____ research.
       a.   case study
       b.   longitudinal
       c.   analogue
       d.   epidemiological

The Correlational Method, p. 36
Diff: H, Type: Applied, Ans: a
65.   Imagine that a longitudinal study found that children raised by schizophrenics are more likely
       to commit crimes later. This result tells us:
       a.   that children of schizophrenics are at higher risk for criminal behavior.
       b.   that children of schizophrenics inherit a "criminal" gene.
       c.   that criminal children cause their parents to become schizophrenic.
       d.   that schizophrenics teach their children to become criminals.

The Correlational Method, p. 36
Diff: M, Type: Applied, Ans: b
66.   If researchers studied Vietnam veterans for 30 years after their return, the study would be:
       a.   epidemiological.
       b.   longitudinal.
       c.   incidental.
       d.   experimental.

The Experimental Method, p. 36
Diff: M, Type: Factual, Ans: d

67. In a scientific experiment, the variable manipulated or controlled by the experimenter is called the:
    a. confounding variable.
    b. alternative variable.
    c. dependent variable.
    d. independent variable.

The Experimental Method, p. 36
Diff: M, Type: Factual, Ans: d

68. Which of the following is an aspect of the experimental approach?
    a. the use of confounding variables
    b. observation of people over a period of time
    c. a detailed interpretive description of a subject
    d. the manipulation of a variable by the researcher

The Experimental Method, p. 36
Diff: E, Type: Factual, Ans: d

69. The variable manipulated in an experiment is called:
    a. a confound.
    b. the control variable.
    c. the dependent variable.
    d. the independent variable.

The Experimental Method, p. 36
Diff: H, Type: Factual, Ans: b

70. The statement or prediction that we make about a potential causal relationship in a proposed study is called the:
    a. theory.
    b. hypothesis.
    c. conclusion.
    d. explanation.

The Experimental Method, p. 36
Diff: H, Type: Applied, Ans: d

71. The following experiment is conducted to study the causes of aggression in children. Half the children eat a sugared cereal; the remaining half eat cornflakes. The number of aggressive acts displayed by the children in one-hour play period after breakfast is then recorded. In this experiment:
    a. sugared cereal is the dependent variable and cornflakes is the independent variable.
    b. breakfast is the independent variable, and the group of children is the dependent variable.
    c. the type of cereal is the dependent variable, and the number of aggressive responses is the independent variable.
    d. the type of cereal is the independent variable, and the number of aggressive responses is the dependent variable.

The Experimental Method, p. 36
Diff: M, Type: Applied, Ans: a

72.   A psychologist was interested in the effect of hunger on psychological disturbances. She food deprived half of a group of healthy volunteers for one day and fed the other half normally. She then administered the MMPI-2 to all the participants. What was the independent variable?
       a.   level of food deprivation
       b.   the MMPI-2
       c.   the results on the MMPI-2
       d.   There is no independent variable because this is a correlational study.

The Experimental Method, p. 36
Diff: H, Type: Applied, Ans: d

73.   Dr. Tim required half of a group of healthy volunteers to study a passage for 1 hour. The other half of the participants studied for 15 minutes. She then administered a test of their memory of details from the passage. What was the dependent variable?
       a.   the study time
       b.   the memory test
       c.   the reading passage
       d.   the results of the memory test

The Experimental Method, p. 36
Diff: H, Type: Applied, Ans: b

74.   We have 60 people suffering from ordinary headache. Twenty get aspiring, 20 get a sugar pill that looks like aspiring and 20 get nothing at all. In 65 percent of the aspirin group, the headache goes away. In the other two groups the "cure" rates are 35 and 5 percent, respectively. Other than the drug condition, the participants are treated identically. This study:
       a.   demonstrates a double-blind design.
       b.   is an experimental study.
       c.   contains an important confound.
       d.   has three dependent variables.

The Experimental Method, p. 36
Diff: H, Type: Applied, Ans: a

75.   In a study designed to test a new antidepressant, a large group of outpatient psychiatric patients was randomly assigned to one of two groups. One of the groups was given the drug as a pill. The other group was given identical-looking inert pills. All participants were tested in the morning. The level of depression of each subject was measured by three psychologists independently, using the Beck Depression Inventory. Which of the following was the independent variable in this study?
       a.   the drug
       b.   the level of agitation
       c.   the Beck Depression Inventory
       d.   the assignment of the participants to groups

The Experimental Method, p. 36
Diff: H, Type: Applied, Ans: a

76. Students are given a sensation-seeking test and then divided into two groups depending on their scores. A researcher observes how many times students in each group get out of their seats in 2 hours. The dependent variable is:
    a. number of times getting out of one's seat.
    b. scores on the sensation-seeking test.
    c. the group of students.
    d. There is no dependent variable.

The Experimental Method, p. 36
Diff: E, Type: Factual, Ans: c

77. A research procedure in which a variable is manipulated and the manipulation's effect on another variable is observed is called a(n):
    a. case study.
    b. correlation.
    c. experiment.
    d. independent variable.

The Experimental Method, p. 37
Diff: M, Type: Factual, Ans: b

78. Factors other than the independent variable may also act on the dependent variable. If these factors vary systematically with the independent variable, they are called _____ variables.
    a. irrelevant
    b. confounding
    c. blind variables
    d. controlled variables

The Control Group, p. 37
Diff: E, Type: Factual, Ans: a

79. The group of participants that is not exposed to the independent variable under investigation (in an experiment) is called the:
    a. control group.
    b. confound group.
    c. dependent group.
    d. experimental group.

Questions 80-81 refer to the paragraph below.
A researcher wishes to study the effect of a new drug on symptoms of depression. Research participants are randomly assigned to two groups. Participants in Group A receive the drug whenever they report depressive symptoms to the experimenter; participants in Group B receive nothing when they report depressive symptoms to the experimenter. After a month of this procedure, participants in Group A report significantly fewer symptoms of depression.

The Control Group, p. 37
Diff: M, Type: Applied, Ans: a

80. In the accompanying study, Group A is the:
    a. experimental group.
    b. control group.
    c. correlational group.
    d. cross-sectional group.

Blind Design, p. 38
Diff: H, Type: Applied, Ans: d

81.   A serious flaw of the accompanying study is that it:
       a.   involves placebo therapy.
       b.   is really a case study.
       c.   is not a natural experiment.
       d.   is not a double-blind design.

Random Assignment, p. 37
Diff: E, Type: Factual, Ans: c

82.   Not all participants are the same. Researchers use _____ to reduce the possibility that
       preexisting differences between groups are responsible for observed differences after
       experimental manipulation.
       a.   a control group
       b.   random selection
       c.   random assignment
       d.   an experimental group

Questions 83-85 refer to the paragraph below.
One hundred psychiatric patients were randomly assigned to one of two groups. One group
received a new drug in pill form. The other group was given identical-looking placebo pills.
All participants were evaluated for level of agitation by a panel of psychiatrists who didn't
know which pill they received.

The Control Group, p. 37
Diff: E, Type: Factual, Ans: c

83.   What is the control group?
       a.   the new drug
       b.   the level of agitation
       c.   the ones who got the placebo
       d.   the psychiatric evaluation

The Experimental Method, p. 36
Diff: H, Type: Applied, Ans: c

84.   What could be a potential confound in the above study?
       a.   Having some seriously ill and some moderately ill patients in both groups
       b.   Having all patients come from the same clinic
       c.   Having the drug group be inpatients and the placebo group be outpatients
       d.   Not previously testing the drug on primates

Blind Design, p. 38
Diff: H, Type: Applied, Ans: b

85.   In the study described above, how could experimenter bias be reduced?
       a.   by having experienced psychiatrists evaluate agitation
       b.   by having researchers who don't know who got which pill
       c.   by adding another placebo condition
       d.   by adding a therapy group

The Control Group, p. 37
Diff: H, Type: Applied, Ans: b

86.   As a general rule, if the sample is large, the difference between the groups is large, and the range of scores within a group is small, then:
    a.   the results are likely to be socially meaningful.
    b.   the results are likely to be statistically significant.
    c.   the results are likely to be due to chance.
    d.   the results are likely to be from a triple-blind study.

Random Assignment, p. 37
Diff: H, Type: Applied, Ans: c

87.   To accomplish random assignment, one could assign participants to groups by:
    a.   placing all the participants who share an important characteristic in the same group.
    b.   making sure there is only one participant in each group.
    c.   flipping a coin.
    d.   asking participants to choose the group they prefer.

Clear as a Bell?, p. 38, Box 2-2
Diff: E, Type: Factual, Ans: c

88.   For people to decide about participating in psychological research, they must be given full knowledge of the nature of the study and their rights. This principle is called:
    a.   risk disclosure.
    b.   benefit analysis.
    c.   informed consent.
    d.   privacy.

Clear as a Bell?, p. 38, Box 2-2
Diff: E, Type: Factual, Ans: c

89.   The principle of informed consent assumes that:
    a.   there is compensation.
    b.   the benefits outweigh the risks.
    c.   the participant can understand the explanation.
    d.   there are no risks in the study under consideration.

Blind Design, p. 38
Diff: M, Type: Factual, Ans: c

90.   The use of single-blind design is an attempt to reduce the influence of:
    a.   experimenter bias.
    b.   dependent variables.
    c.   participant bias.
    d.   confounding variables.

Blind Design, p. 38
Diff: M, Type: Applied, Ans: a

91.   Russ wants to be a good participant. He knows that his professor is an environmentalist, so his answers on the survey reflect a pro-environment position. This is an example of:
    a.   subject bias.
    b.   a placebo effect.
    c.   random variation.
    d.   experimenter bias.

Blind Design, p. 38
Diff: H, Type: Factual, Ans: a
92. Another term for experimenter bias caused by the experimenter unintentionally transmitting expectations to the research participants is the:
a.   Rosenthal effect.
b.   Triple-blind effect.
c.   Buffalo Creek effect.
d.   Quasi-experimental design.

Blind Design, p. 38
Diff: E, Type: Applied, Ans: a
93. A sugar pill used as the control condition in a drug study is a:
a.   placebo.
b.   confound.
c.   random variable.
d.   dependent variable.

Blind Design, p. 38
Diff: M, Type: Factual, Ans: d
94. A researcher's expectations about a study can affect its outcome. The type of research design used specifically to address this problem is:
a.   an experiment.
b.   a random-assignment design.
c.   a matched control group design.
d.   a double-blind procedure.

Blind Design, p. 38
Diff: H, Type: Applied, Ans: b
95. In preparation for a study of the effectiveness of an antischizophrenia drug, an assistant puts all drugs into capsules of the same color and codes them. The assistant will have no part in administering the drug. Neither the subjects nor the experimenter will know who gets which drug. This is an example of a:
a.   single-blind design.
b.   double-blind design.
c.   triple-blind design.
d.   quasi-experimental design.

Blind Design, p. 38
Diff: E, Type: Factual, Ans: a
96. The function of the double-blind design is to guard against:
a.   participant and experimenter expectancies.
b.   imitation therapies.
c.   subject bias.
d.   the Rosenthal effect.

Blind Design, p. 38
Diff: M, Type: Applied, Ans: b
97.   A therapist believes so strongly in her approach that she finds improvement even when none
       exists. Which design would prevent this problem?
       a.   longitudinal
       b.   double-blind
       c.   epidemiological
       d.   experimental

Blind Design, p. 39
Diff: M, Type: Applied, Ans: c
98.   In an experiment on the effects of two new drugs on mood, neither the patients, researchers,
       nor those who are evaluating mood know which drug the patients are getting. The study is
       _____ blind.
       a.   single
       b.   double
       c.   triple
       d.   quadruple

Alternative Experimental Designs, p. 39
Diff: E, Type: Factual, Ans: a
99.   What is the term for studies that have the structure of experiments except that they use groups
       that already exist, instead of randomly assigning participants to control and experimental
       groups?
       a.   quasi-experiments
       b.   natural experiments
       c.   correlational experiments
       d.   developmental experiments

Quasi-Experimental Design, p. 39
Diff: H, Type: Applied, Ans: d
100.   Which of the following distinguishes a quasi-experimental study from a true experiment?
       a.   The quasi-experiment does not use a control group.
       b.   The quasi-experiment uses multiple groups for comparison.
       c.   The quasi-experiment does not use any experimental control.
       d.   The quasi-experiment does not allow for manipulation of the independent variable.

Quasi-Experimental Design, p. 39
Diff: M, Type: Applied, Ans: d
101.   A researcher selected a group of 10 men and a group of 10 women to study some gender
       differences. She treated them exactly the same. Each participant was given a test of
       psychological function. This study is an example of:
       a.   an experiment.
       b.   an analogue study.
       c.   a correlational study.
       d.   a quasi-experimental study.

Quasi-Experimental Design, p. 39
Diff: H, Type: Applied, Ans: b

102.   Which of the following would most appropriately be studied using a quasi-experimental design?
       a.   the effects of running and weight lifting on mood
       b.   the effects of schizophrenic parents on children's adjustment
       c.   the effects of a parental training program on children's achievement
       d.   the effects of a support group in helping people lose weight

Quasi-Experimental Design, p. 39
Diff: H, Type: Applied, Ans: a

103.   If one were studying the hypothesis that people with high levels of stress are more likely to get cancer and wanted to include a matched control group, that group:
       a.   would have low levels of stress.
       b.   would have high levels of stress.
       c.   would have cancer.
       d.   would not have cancer.

Quasi-Experimental Design, p. 39
Diff: H, Type: Applied, Ans: d

104.   If researchers using matched control subjects find that abused children are sadder than nonabused children, we know that:
       a.   both groups of children showed equal levels of sadness before the study.
       b.   the nonabused group differed from the abused group in many important ways.
       c.   there were more girls than boys in the abused group because girls are more likely to be sad.
       d.   abuse is very likely what is causing the difference in sadness among these groups.

Natural Experiment, p. 39
Diff: H, Type: Factual, Ans: a

105.   The form of experiment used most often to study the psychological effects of unusual or unpredictable events is:
       a.   natural.
       b.   matched-control.
       c.   analogue.
       d.   single-subject.

Natural Experiment, p. 39
Diff: E, Type: Applied, Ans: c

106.   Which of the following would be the best design to study the effects of disasters on the survivors?
       a.   an experiment
       b.   a quasi-experiment
       c.   a natural experiment
       d.   a double-blind strategy

Natural Experiment, p. 39
Diff: M, Type: Applied, Ans: a
107.   Which of the following would be *least* appropriately studied using a natural experiment?
   a.   the effects of premarital abstinence on later sexual functioning
   b.   the effects of war on children in Kosova
   c.   the effects of a plant closing on community cohesiveness
   d.   the effects of a particularly harsh blizzard on depression

Questions 108-110 are based on the paragraph below.
A researcher randomly divides young women suffering from anorexia into two groups. Participants in Group A receive psychotherapy and drug treatments; participants in Group B receive attention (but no therapy) and a "sugar pill." The researcher then compares participants in the two groups on relief of anorexia symptoms.

Human Subjects Have Rights, Too, p. 40, Box 2-3
Diff: H, Type: Applied, Ans: a
108.   The above is an example of what research design?
   a.   experiment
   b.   natural experiment
   c.   correlational study
   d.   case study

Human Subjects Have Rights, Too, p. 40, Box 2-3
Diff: H, Type: Applied, Ans: d
109.   One important criticism of the above research is that it is a:
   a.   medication-withdrawal study.
   b.   symptom-exacerbation study.
   c.   multiple-baseline study.
   d.   placebo study.

Human Subjects Have Rights, Too, p. 40, Box 2-3
Diff: H, Type: Factual, Ans: b
110.   The ethical concern about placebo drug studies is that:
   a.   the experimental group gets an untried medication.
   b.   the placebo group gets no treatment at all.
   c.   the placebo group gets another medication that may not be as effective.
   d.   None of the answers are correct.

Analogue Experiment, p. 40
Diff: E, Type: Factual, Ans: b
111.   Which of the following types of research is most likely to involve nonhuman participants?
   a.   natural experiment
   b.   analogue experiment
   c.   multiple-baseline design
   d.   reversal design

Analogue Experiment, p. 40
Diff: M, Type: Applied, Ans: b
112. Which of the following is an analogue study?
      a. studying children in their classrooms
      b. studying the effects of stress in nonhumans
      c. studying the effects of metaphors on memory
      d. studying the elderly in nursing homes

Analogue Experiment, p. 40
Diff: M, Type: Applied, Ans: b
113. A researcher is interested in the effects of a new drug for treating anxiety. He decides to study it in rats by conditioning the fear of a high-pitched noise and then testing rats' reactions with and without the drug. This is an example of:
      a. a natural experiment.
      b. an analogue experiment.
      c. a quasi-experimental study.
      d. a correlation.

Analogue Experiment, p. 41
Diff: H, Type: Applied, Ans: a
114. Seligman's study in which he created learned helplessness in the lab is an example of a(n) _____ study:
      a. analogue
      b. case
      c. epidemiological
      d. quasi-experimental

Analogue Experiment, p. 41
Diff: H, Type: Factual, Ans: c
115. Experimenters are generally willing to:
      a. subject humans to more pain than animals.
      b. subject animals to excessive pain.
      c. subject animals to more discomfort than humans.
      d. do analogue studies with humans but not animals.

Single Subject Experiment, p. 42
Diff: H, Type: Applied, Ans: d
116. Imagine that you are doing an ABAB reversal design study in which you are measuring level of depression with and without the addition of an exercise program. What is the first "A" in the study?
      a. healthy eating habits
      b. exercise
      c. depression
      d. no exercise

Single Subject Experiment, p. 42
Diff: H, Type: Applied, Ans: b

117.   Imagine that you are doing an ABAB reversal design study in which you are measuring level of depression with and without the addition of an exercise program. What is the second "B" in the study?
   a.   healthy eating habits
   b.   exercise
   c.   no exercise
   d.   depression

Single Subject Experiment, p. 42
Diff: E, Type: Factual, Ans: b

118.   In single-subject experimental designs, the participant is observed and measured before the manipulation of an independent variable. This initial observation period is called the:
   a.   reversal period.
   b.   baseline period.
   c.   normalization period.
   d.   standardization period.

Single Subject Experiment, p. 42
Diff: M, Type: Factual, Ans: c

119.   In the ABAB (reversal) design, condition "A" is a(n):
   a.   independent variable application.
   b.   dependent variable application.
   c.   no-treatment condition.
   d.   experimental condition.

Single Subject Experiment, p. 42
Diff: M, Type: Applied, Ans: d

120.   If a participant's self-stimulation is observed, punished, observed again without punishment, and punished again, the design is:
   a.   a multiple baseline.
   b.   an analogue.
   c.   a correlation.
   d.   an ABAB reversal.

Single Subject Experiment, p. 42
Diff: H, Type: Applied, Ans: d

121.   A researcher works to reduce the amount of disruptive talking a child does in school. The researcher first measures the disruptive talking frequency, then institutes treatment, while continuing to measure the behavior. Later, treatment is removed, as measurement continues. Finally the researcher re-introduces the treatment. This type of study is a:
   a.   double-blind design.
   b.   triple-blind design.
   c.   multiple-baseline design.
   d.   reversal design.

Single Subject Experiment, p. 42
Diff: M, Type: Factual, Ans: a
122.   A case study differs from a single-subject experiment because single-subject experiments involve:
   a.   observation of a subject before and after independent variable manipulation.
   b.   extended observations of a particular individual.
   c.   more than one observation period.
   d.   statistical analyses.

Single Subject Experiment, p. 42
Diff: H, Type: Factual, Ans: a
123.   Which of the following is true about case studies and single-subject designs?
   a.   Single-subject designs have more internal validity.
   b.   Single-subject designs have more external validity.
   c.   Case studies have more external validity.
   d.   Case studies have more internal validity.

Putting It Together, p. 43
Diff: H, Type: Factual, Ans: b
124.   Which of the following is not true about the obstacles that clinical scientists face in studying psychological disorders?
   a.   The level of self-awareness that humans possess may influence the results.
   b.   Humans have unusually stable (unchanging) moods and behavior.
   c.   The causes of human functioning are complex.
   d.   Ethical considerations limit the kinds of studies that can be done.

Putting It Together, p. 43
Diff: H, Type: Applied, Ans: d
125.   The single-subject study has _____ internal validity and _____ external validity compared to the case study.
   a.   less; less
   b.   more; more
   c.   the same amount of; the same amount of
   d.   more; the same amount of

Putting It Together, p. 43
Diff: H, Type: Applied, Ans: a
126.   Various obstacles interfere with the study of abnormal psychology. All of the following are examples except:
   a.   Most clinicians oppose the scientific study of their discipline
   b.   Human beings are complex.
   c.   Self-awareness may influence the results of the study.
   d.   Clinicians often have a special relationship with their research subjects.

Putting It Together, p. 43
Diff: H, Type: Factual, Ans: c
127.   A design in which an experimenter selects two or more dependent variables and observes the effect that the manipulation of an independent variable has on those dependent variables in a single participant is called a(n) _____ design.
   a.   ABAB
   b.   reversal
   c.   multiple-baseline
   d.   all of the above

Putting It Together, p. 44
Diff: H, Type: Applied, Ans: b
128.   When more than one research method produces similar results, we:
   a.   are suspicious of the results
   b.   can have more confidence in the results
   c.   suspect that experimenter bias has occurred
   d.   conclude that our results are due to confounds

Putting It Together, p. 44
Diff: H, Type: Applied, Ans: b
129.   Which of the following is the best way for clinicians to come to an understanding of abnormal behavior?
   a.   to rely solely on experimental research studies
   b.   to rely on findings that have been supported by multiple research methods
   c.   to ignore studies that show conflicting results
   d.   to rely on the conventional wisdom of past ages

Putting It Together, p. 44
Diff: H, Type: Applied, Ans: b
130.   Once a study in abnormal psychology finds significant results:
   a.   we can conclude that the study is valid.
   b.   we must ask a number of questions about the details of the study.
   c.   we can apply the results to clinical practice.
   d.   we have good information about how to prevent the disorder from occurring.

Putting It Together, p. 44
Diff: H, Type: Applied, Ans: d
131.   In order to conclude that a clinical researcher's conclusions are justified, we must:
   a.   make sure the study was done by a psychiatrist if it involves drugs.
   b.   make sure the study has equal numbers of patients from each ethnic group.
   c.   make sure the researcher is not also a therapist.
   d.   make sure there is no legitimate alternative explanation for the results.

FILL-IN QUESTIONS

Research in Abnormal Psychology, p. 27
Diff: E, Type: Factual, Ans: research
1.   The systematic search for facts through observation and investigation is _____.

Research in Abnormal Psychology, p. 28
Diff: E, Type: Factual, Ans: scientific
2.   Sound research in abnormal psychology uses the _____ method.

What Do Clinical Researchers Do?, p. 28
Diff: M, Type: Factual, Ans: nomothetic
3.   Clinical researchers form general, or _____, knowledge about the nature, causes, and treatments of abnormal behavior.

What Do Clinical Researchers Do?, p. 28
Diff: M, Type: Factual, Ans: idiographic
4.   The understanding of human behavior that clinical practitioners seek is usually individual. The term for it is _____.

The Case Study, p. 29
Diff: E, Type: Applied, Ans: case study
5.   Jason met with a researcher several times. He was interviewed, he took tests, and he was physically evaluated. In addition the researcher studied his school and employment records and interviewed key people in his life. The type of study being done by the researcher is best called a(n) _____.

The Case Study, p. 29
Diff: E, Type: Factual, Ans: case study
6.   Freud's report on Little Hans is an example of a(n) _____.

What Are the Limitations of Case Studies?, p. 31
Diff: E, Type: Applied, Ans: internal validity
7.   A study has _____ when it controls for all variables except the ones being investigated.

What Are the Limitations of Case Studies?, p. 32
Diff: M, Type: Applied, Ans: nomothetic
8.   Results that have the greatest external validity are most likely derived from research that is _____.

What Are the Limitations of Case Studies?, p. 32
Diff: E, Type: Factual, Ans: external validity
9.   An investigation is said to have _____ when findings of the investigation can be generalized beyond the immediate study.

Describing a Correlation, p. 32
Diff: E, Type: Factual, Ans: positive
10. Tall people tend to have larger feet than short people. This statement indicates a(n) _____ correlation between foot size and height.

Describing a Correlation, p. 32
Diff: M, Type: Applied, Ans: negative
11. The more television you watch, the lower your grades in school are likely to be. This statement indicates a(n) _____ correlation between hours watching TV and grades.

Describing a Correlation, p. 34
Diff: E, Type: Factual, Ans: -1, +1
12.   The strength or magnitude of a correlation can vary from _____ to _____.

When Can Correlations Be Trusted?, p. 34
Diff: E, Type: Factual, Ans: chance
13.   If a result is statistically significant, it is unlikely to be the result of _____.

When Can Correlations Be Trusted?, p. 34
Diff: H, Type: Factual, Ans: statistically significant
14.   Any result that is unlikely to be a chance occurrence because calculations indicate that it will only occur one time in 20 by chance is _____.

When Can Correlations Be Trusted?, p. 34
Diff: E, Type: Factual, Ans: causal
15.   Correlations cannot be used to conclude that a _____ relationship exists between two variables.

Special Forms of Correlational Research, p. 35
Diff: H, Type: Factual, Ans: epidemiological
16.   Studies that determine the incidence and prevalence of a disorder in a given population are called _____ studies.

Special Forms of Correlational Research, p. 35
Diff: H, Type: Applied, Ans: incidence
17.   The number of new cases of a disorder that appear during a set period of time is the _____ of that disorder.

Special Forms of Correlational Research, p. 35
Diff: H, Type: Applied, Ans: prevalence
18.   If we knew that there were 500,000 total cases of schizophrenia in the United States as of now, we would know the _____ of schizophrenia in the United States.

Special Forms of Correlational Research, p. 36
Diff: M, Type: Applied, Ans: longitudinal, developmental, high-risk
19.   Sammy agreed to be in the study of memory, but he had not anticipated how he would feel about returning to the lab every other year for 10 years. He is involved in a _____, _____, and _____ study.

Special Forms of Correlational Research, p. 36
Diff: E, Type: Factual, Ans: longitudinal
20.   A study of the same individuals on many occasions over a period of time is a _____ study.

The Experimental Method, p. 36
Diff: E, Type: Factual, Ans: hypothesis
21.   A tentative explanation or hunch that provides a basis for study is a(n) _____.

The Experimental Method, p. 36
Diff: E, Type: Factual, Ans: experiment
22.   The type of study that allows a direct determination of a causal relationship between two variables is a(n) _____.

The Experimental Method, p. 36
Diff: H, Type: Applied, Ans: dependent variable

23.   Jack was doing a study on anxiety. One group was asked to estimate how many years each
       had to live. The other group was asked to estimate how many months to their next vacation.
       He then gave each of his participants the Taylor Manifest Anxiety Scale and scored them.
       The score on this test is an example of a(n) _____.

The Experimental Method, p. 37
Diff: H, Type: Applied, Ans: independent variable

24.   Ian made the participants in one of his groups anxious by making loud noises but kept the
       participants in the other group in quiet surroundings. The presence of noise in this case is an
       example of a(n) _____.

The Experimental Method, p. 37
Diff: H, Type: Applied, Ans: confounded

25.   Dr. Smith deprived the subjects in one group of water and gave water to the subjects in the
       other group. She tested the thirsty group at 9:00 A.M. and the water satiated group at 4:00
       P.M. Now she cannot interpret her results clearly because water deprivation and time of day
       were _____.

The Experimental Method, p. 37
Diff: H, Type: Applied, Ans: confound

26.   Dr. Han did his experimental manipulation and then tested his experimental group at 9 A.M.
       and his control group at 9 P.M. His study contains a _____.

The Control Group, p. 37
Diff: M, Type: Applied, Ans: control group

27.   The nontreated or comparison group that is not exposed to the independent variable in an
       experiment is called the _____.

Blind Design, p. 38
Diff: E, Type: Factual, Ans: single-blind

28.   If a participant does not know in which condition she is being tested, she is participating in a
       _____ design.

Blind Design, p. 38
Diff: M, Type: Factual, Ans: subject bias

29.   Dr. Pliny did not tell her subjects which group (what level of the independent variable) they
       were in. She did this to guard against _____.

Blind Design, p. 38
Diff: M, Type: Factual, Ans: experimenter bias

30.   In addition to subject bias, the double-blind design guards against _____.

Blind Design, p. 38
Diff: E, Type: Applied, Ans: placebo

31.   Lola took an antidepressant and it really made her feel better. She did not know it but it was
       just a sugar pill. The effect of this sugar pill is referred to as a _____ effect.

Alternative Experimental Designs, p. 39
Diff: H, Type: Applied, Ans: quasi-experimental

32.   Any study that compares the responses of men and women (the "independent variable") is
        best described as a(n) _____ design.

Alternative Experimental Designs, p. 39
Diff: H, Type: Applied, Ans: natural

33.   Genie was isolated from human contact and language by her (badly disturbed) parents for
        most of the first thirteen years of her life. The effects of early language deprivation could
        easily be seen and studied. This is an example of a(n) _____ experiment.

Alternative Experimental Designs, p. 40
Diff: H, Type: Applied, Ans: analogue

34.   If a researcher did a study of anxiety and used cats for subjects instead of people, she would
        be doing a(n) _____ study.

Alternative Experimental Designs, p. 42
Diff: H, Type: Applied, Ans: baseline

35.   The phase in a single-subject design that is comparable to a control group is the _____.

Alternative Experimental Designs, p. 42
Diff: H, Type: Factual, Ans: self (or same subject)

36.   The _____ serves as the control in a single-subject design.

ESSAY QUESTIONS

The Case Study: Alternative Experimental Designs, pp. 29ff
Diff: H, Type: Applied

1.   What are important differences between case studies and single-subject experiments? Be sure
        to mention advantages and disadvantages of each.

The Case Study, p. 29
Diff: H, Type: Factual

2.   Case studies can be used to help more than just the one being studied. Briefly describe three
        ways one could use information gathered from a case study and use it more broadly.

The Case Study, p. 31ff
Diff: H, Type: Applied

3.   Imagine you are designing a study to compare school achievement in children whose mothers
        did and did not drink alcohol during pregnancy. Briefly describe two ways you could ensure
        that the study has good internal validity and two ways you could ensure that it has good
        external validity.

The Correlational Method, p. 33
Diff: H, Type: Applied

4.   Using the variables age and reaction time, draw three hypothetical graphs, one illustrating no
        correlation, one illustrating a strong positive correlation, and one illustrating a weak negative
        correlation. Be sure to label the axes and indicate what each graph illustrates.

The Correlational Method, p. 34
Diff: H, Type: Factual

5.   A major shortcoming of a correlational study is that even when a correlation between two variables is statistically significant, one cannot infer causation. For example, a significant correlation exists between life stress and depression, yet one cannot say for sure that life stress causes depression. Given this major shortcoming, what are some specific reasons one might still wish to conduct a correlational study, as opposed to an experimental study (from which one might infer a cause-and-effect relationship)?

The Correlational Method, p. 35
Diff: H, Type: Applied

6.   Suppose you found a strong positive correlation between college GPA and self-esteem. Describe three possible and distinctly different causal explanations for this relationship.

The Correlational Method, p. 35
Diff: H, Type: Applied

7.   Assume that a researcher wishes to do research designed to pinpoint early-childhood events related to later development of eating disorders such as anorexia nervosa. What type of investigation might the researcher use? What would be potential strengths and weaknesses of the type of investigation you suggest? Finally, are there any ethical concerns the researcher ought to address?

The Experimental Method, p. 36
Diff: H, Type: Applied

8.   Design an experiment to test the hypothesis that older women who take estrogen are less likely to get Alzheimer's disease. Be sure to identify the control group, experimental group, independent variable, dependent variable, and ways to reduce subject and experimenter bias.

The Experimental Method, p. 36ff
Diff: H, Type: Applied

9.   A researcher wishes to use experimentation to study the effect of stress on the development of abnormal behaviors. Please describe how the researcher might conduct that study, using one of the three alternatives below:
     a.   an experiment involving experimental and control groups
     b.   a natural experiment
     c.   an analogue experiment

Human Subjects Have Rights, Too, pp. 40-41, Box 2-3
Diff: H, Type: Factual

10. Briefly describe the ethical issues involved in each of the following types of studies typically involving antipsychotic drug treatments for patients with psychoses:
     a.   new drug studies
     b.   placebo studies
     c.   symptom-exacerbation studies
     d.   medication-withdrawal studies

Putting It Together, p. 43
Diff: H, Type: Factual

11. The text discusses how clinical scientists conducting research in abnormal psychology might encounter some challenges particular to this field. Briefly describe three of these challenges.

CHAPTER 3   Models of Abnormality

MULTIPLE-CHOICE QUESTIONS

Models of Abnormality, p. 48
Diff: E, Type: Applied, Ans: d

1. The paradigm or model adopted by people in the Middle Ages to explain abnormal behavior would have been:
    a. sociocultural.
    b. biological.
    c. cognitive.
    d. demonological.

Models of Abnormality, p. 48
Diff: E, Type: Applied, Ans: c

2. In science, the perspectives used to explain phenomena are known as:
    a. facts.
    b. experiments.
    c. paradigms.
    d. hypotheses.

Models of Abnormality, p. 48
Diff: H, Type: Applied, Ans: c

3. The models or paradigm an investigator uses influences:
    a. the symptoms of a particular disorder.
    b. the treatment that is most effective for a disorder.
    c. the questions and observations the investigator uses.
    d. the culture in which the disorder is found.

Models of Abnormality, p. 48
Diff: E, Type: Factual, Ans: a

4. The model of abnormality that cites physical processes as being the key to behavior is the:
    a. biological model.
    b. sociocultural model.
    c. psychodynamic model.
    d. humanistic-existential model.

Models of Abnormality, p. 48
Diff: E, Type: Factual, Ans: b

5. The model of abnormality that examines the effects of society and culture is the:
    a. behavioral model.
    b. sociocultural model.
    c. psychodynamic model.
    d. humanistic-existential model.

Models of Abnormality, p. 48
Diff: E, Type: Factual, Ans: d

6.   The model of abnormality that focuses on unconscious internal processes and conflicts in behavior is the:
      a.   cognitive model.
      b.   behavioral model.
      c.   sociocultural model.
      d.   psychodynamic model.

Models of Abnormality, p. 48
Diff: E, Type: Applied, Ans: b

7.   "Understanding a person's unconscious processes is critical in explaining abnormality." Which model of abnormality does this quote most closely represent?
      a.   behavioral
      b.   psychodynamic
      c.   cognitive
      d.   humanistic-existential

Models of Abnormality, p. 48
Diff: E, Type: Factual, Ans: a

8.   The model of abnormality that focuses on learning is the:
      a.   behavioral model.
      b.   sociocultural model.
      c.   psychodynamic model.
      d.   humanistic-existential model.

Models of Abnormality, p. 48
Diff: E, Type: Factual, Ans: a

9.   The model of abnormality that concentrates on thinking is the:
      a.   cognitive model.
      b.   behavioral model.
      c.   sociocultural model.
      d.   psychodynamic model.

Models of Abnormality, p. 48
Diff: E, Type: Applied, Ans: a

10.   "Abnormal" behaviors—indeed, all behaviors—are acquired through learning." Which model of abnormality does this quote most closely represent?
      a.   behavioral
      b.   psychodynamic
      c.   cognitive
      d.   humanistic-existential

Models of Abnormality, p. 49
Diff: E, Type: Factual, Ans: d

11.   The model of abnormality that focuses on the roles in behavior is the:
      a.   cognitive model.
      b.   sociocultural model.
      c.   psychodynamic model.
      d.   humanistic-existential model.

How Do Biological Theorists Explain Abnormal Behavior?, p. 49
Diff: H, Type: Factual, Ans: b

12.   Huntington's disease, which has psychological as well as physical aspects, results from loss of cells in the:
   a.   corpus callosum.
   b.   basal ganglia.
   c.   hippocampus.
   d.   amygdala.

How Do Biological Theorists Explain Abnormal Behavior?, p. 49
Diff: H, Type: Applied, Ans: b

13.   According to the analogy used in your textbook, the amygdala is most like a:
   a.   state.
   b.   continent.
   c.   country.
   d.   hemisphere.

How Do Biological Theorists Explain Abnormal Behavior?, p. 50
Diff: E, Type: Factual, Ans: d

14.   Messages moving from neuron to neuron must cross tiny spaces called:
   a.   dendrites.
   b.   axons.
   c.   neurotransmitters.
   d.   synapses.

How Do Biological Theorists Explain Abnormal Behavior?, p. 50
Diff: M, Type: Applied, Ans: a

15.   If a person had an anxiety disorder, one would suspect a problem with which of these neurotransmitters?
   a.   gamma-aminobutyric acid
   b.   dopamine
   c.   serotonin
   d.   norepinephrine

How Do Biological Theorists Explain Abnormal Behavior?, p. 50
Diff: M, Type: Applied, Ans: b

16.   If a person had schizophrenia, one would suspect a problem with which of these neurotransmitters?
   a.   gamma-aminobutyric acid
   b.   dopamine
   c.   serotonin
   d.   norepinephrine

How Do Biological Theorists Explain Abnormal Behavior?, p. 50
Diff: H, Type: Factual, Ans: c

17.   Depression has been linked to which neurotransmitter abnormality?
   a.   low activity of GABA
   b.   excessive activity of GABA
   c.   low activity of serotonin
   d.   excessive activity of serotonin

How Do Biological Theorists Explain Abnormal Behavior?, p. 50
Diff: M, Type: Factual, Ans: a
18. Abnormal chemical activity in the body's endocrine system relates to the release of:
     a. hormones.
     b. neurotransmitter.
     c. neurons.
     d. genes.

How Do Biological Theorists Explain Abnormal Behavior?, p. 51
Diff: M, Type: Applied, Ans: d
19. In how many cases of psychological disorders does an individual gene appear to be responsible?
     a. virtually all
     b. most but not all
     c. about half
     d. virtually none

How Do Biological Theorists Explain Abnormal Behavior?, p. 51
Diff: M, Type: Applied, Ans: b
20. Identifying which genes help cause various human disorders rests with the ability to:
     a. clone individuals.
     b. map or sequence genes.
     c. insert RNA into genes.
     d. control mutations.

How Do Biological Theorists Explain Abnormal Behavior?, p. 52
Diff: M, Type: Factual, Ans: c
21. Current research suggests that schizophrenia may be related to:
     a. bacterial infections at the time of puberty.
     b. a resistance to antibiotics.
     c. viral infection in utero.
     d. hormonal imbalances.

Biological Treatments, p. 53
Diff: H, Type: Applied, Ans: c
22. Which of the following is an antipsychotic drug?
     a. Valium
     b. Zoloft
     c. Risperdal
     d. Lithium

Biological Treatments, p. 53
Diff: H, Type: Applied, Ans: d
23. A person reports experiencing tension and anxiety, but not mood swings. If a drug is prescribed as part of the treatment, the drug most likely would be:
     a. Prozac.
     b. Risperdal.
     c. lithium.
     d. Xanax.

Biological Treatments, p. 53
Diff: M, Type: Applied, Ans: a
24.   An important factor to consider in using drugs for the treatment of abnormality would be that:
       a.   some people do not benefit from drug treatments.
       b.   drugs cannot be combined with other forms of treatment.
       c.   drugs are not very effective in the treatment of schizophrenia.
       d.   drugs should not be used unless surgery has been unsuccessful.

Biological Treatments, p. 53
Diff: E, Type: Factual, Ans: c
25.   Electroconvulsive therapy (ECT) is used most often in the treatment of:
       a.   schizophrenia.
       b.   anxiety disorders.
       c.   depression.
       d.   bipolar disorder.

Biological Treatments, p. 53
Diff: E, Type: Factual, Ans: b
26.   The form of "psychosurgery" performed in prehistoric times is called:
       a.   lobotomy.
       b.   trephining.
       c.   ECT.
       d.   laparoscopy.

Biological Treatments, p. 54
Diff: E, Type: Factual, Ans: c
27.   The treatment a patient would be *least* likely to receive is:
       a.   drug therapy.
       b.   ECT.
       c.   psychosurgery.
       d.   "talk therapy."

The Psychodynamic Model, p. 54
Diff: E, Type: Factual, Ans: c
28.   The oldest of the following modern psychological models is the:
       a.   cognitive model.
       b.   behavioral model.
       c.   psychodynamic model.
       d.   humanistic-existential model.

The Psychodynamic Model, p. 54
Diff: M, Type: Applied, Ans: b
29.   An assumption of determinism is that abnormal behaviors:
       a.   are learned.
       b.   are not accidental.
       c.   have physiological bases.
       d.   are due to unconscious conflicts.

The Psychodynamic Model, p. 54
Diff: E, Type: Applied, Ans: b
30.   Which of the following is true of psychological conflicts according to psychoanalysis?
    a.   They are sexual in nature.
    b.   They are tied to experiences early in life.
    c.   They are only a problem when they reach consciousness.
    d.   They are unconscious, and therefore not a factor in conscious experience.

The Psychodynamic Model, p. 55
Diff: H, Type: Factual, Ans: a
31.   Which of the following would not subscribe to the psychodynamic model?
    a.   Joseph Wolpe
    b.   Alfred Adler
    c.   Sigmund Freud
    d.   Carl Gustav Jung

How Did Freud Explain Normal and Abnormal Functioning?, p. 55
Diff: M, Type: Factual, Ans: d
32.   Freud believed that the three central forces that shape the personality were the:
    a.   instincts, the ego, and the self.
    b.   biological forces, culture, and learning.
    c.   consciousness, unconsciousness, and instincts.
    d.   instinctual needs, rational thinking, and moral standards.

How Did Freud Explain Normal and Abnormal Functioning?, p. 55
Diff: M, Type: Applied, Ans: b
33.   Freud believed that the source of energy that fuels the id:
    a.   are defense mechanisms.
    b.   is the libido.
    c.   is conscious.
    d.   is learned.

How Did Freud Explain Normal and Abnormal Functioning?, p. 55
Diff: M, Type: Applied, Ans: a
34.   The _____ operates in accord with the pleasure principle.
    a.   id.
    b.   superego.
    c.   erogenous zone.
    d.   ego.

How Did Freud Explain Normal and Abnormal Functioning?, p. 55
Diff: E, Type: Applied, Ans: a
35.   According to Freud, pleasure from nursing your baby is reflected in which part of the
personality?
    a.   id
    b.   ego
    c.   superego
    d.   ego ideal

How Did Freud Explain Normal and Abnormal Functioning?, p. 55
Diff: E, Type: Applied, Ans: b

36.   Infants tend to do things that feel good. This is in accord with what Freud called:
       a.   reflex.
       b.   the pleasure principle.
       c.   primary process thought.
       d.   secondary process thought.

How Did Freud Explain Normal and Abnormal Functioning?, p. 55
Diff: M, Type: Applied, Ans: a

37.   Barney's mother is taking cookies out of the oven. Which of the following would suggest
       most strongly that the id is firmly in control of Barney's behavior?
       a.   Barney grabs some of the cookies and runs.
       b.   Barney wants the cookies desperately but asks his mother for a couple.
       c.   Barney waits for his mother to leave the room, takes a few cookies, and runs away.
       d.   Barney asks for some cookies in a whiney voice and throws a tantrum when he is denied.

How Did Freud Explain Normal and Abnormal Functioning?, p. 55
Diff: E, Type: Factual, Ans: c

38.   What is libido?
       a.   the same as the id
       b.   the source of pleasure
       c.   the sexual energy of the id
       d.   the sum of the id's instinctual needs

How Did Freud Explain Normal and Abnormal Functioning?, p. 55
Diff: E, Type: Factual, Ans: b

39.   The part of the personality that guides us to know when we can and cannot express our
       impulses is the:
       a.   id.
       b.   ego.
       c.   superego.
       d.   libido.

How Did Freud Explain Normal and Abnormal Functioning?, p. 55
Diff: H, Type: Applied, Ans: c

40.   Mara's mother is taking a chocolate pudding out of the refrigerator. Which of the following
       would suggest most strongly that the ego is successfully managing the id?
       a.   Mara asks for some pudding in a whiney voice and throws a tantrum when she is denied.
       b.   Mara dreams about eating some of the delicious-looking pudding.
       c.   Mara waits for her mother to leave the room, takes a cup of pudding, and sneaks away.
       d.   Mara reaches right in and grabs some pudding, without asking or waiting for her mother
            to leave.

How Did Freud Explain Normal and Abnormal Functioning?, p. 55
Diff: H, Type: Applied, Ans: d

41.   "The force that operates on the 'reality principle' is an independent, powerful force in human functioning." The kind of theorist who would agree most strongly with this statement would be a(n) _____ therapist.
       a.   classical Freudian
       b.   self
       c.   object relations
       d.   ego

How Did Freud Explain Normal and Abnormal Functioning?, p. 55
Diff: E, Type: Factual, Ans: c

42.   According to Freud's psychodynamic theory, the part of the personality that is the conscience is the:
       a.   id.
       b.   ego.
       c.   superego.
       d.   ego ideal.

How Did Freud Explain Normal and Abnormal Functioning?, p. 55
Diff: E, Type: Factual, Ans: b

43.   What we would call "conscience" is most like what Freud would call the:
       a.   defense mechanism.
       b.   superego.
       c.   ego.
       d.   erogenous zone.

How Did Freud Explain Normal and Abnormal Functioning?, p. 55
Diff: E, Type: Factual, Ans: a

44.   According to Freud's psychodynamic theory, ineffective interaction of the id, ego, and superego can lead to entrapment at a developmental level. This is called:
       a.   fixation.
       b.   neurosis.
       c.   repression.
       d.   displacement.

How Did Freud Explain Normal and Abnormal Functioning?, p. 56
Diff: H, Type: Applied, Ans: d

45.   A psychoanalyst says that a middle-aged patient appears to be extremely dependent, mistrustful, and depressed. The term the psychoanalyst would most likely use for this patient is:
       a.   repressed.
       b.   depressed.
       c.   experiencing latency.
       d.   fixated.

How Did Freud Explain Normal and Abnormal Functioning?, p. 56
Diff: E, Type: Factual, Ans: a

46.   According to Freud's psychodynamic theory, at birth the child is in the:
    a.   oral stage.
    b.   anal stage.
    c.   phallic stage.
    d.   latency stage.

How Do Other Psychodynamic Explanations Differ from Freud's?, p. 57
Diff: M, Type: Factual, Ans: d

47.   The motivation to form relationships with others is a central theme of:
    a.   ego theory.
    b.   self theory.
    c.   psychoanalytic theory.
    d.   object relations theory.

How Do Other Psychodynamic Explanations Differ from Freud's?, p. 57
Diff: M, Type: Factual, Ans: b

48.   The role of the unified personality is a central theme of:
    a.   ego theory.
    b.   self theory.
    c.   psychoanalytic theory.
    d.   object relations theory.

How Do Other Psychodynamic Explanations Differ from Freud's?, p. 57
Diff: E, Type: Factual, Ans: c

49.   A general term used for theories such as Freud's, Adler's, and Jung's is:
    a.   psychiatric.
    b.   biological.
    c.   psychodynamic.
    d.   psychophysical.

How Do Other Psychodynamic Explanations Differ from Freud's?, p. 57
Diff: E, Type: Applied, Ans: a

50.   The model most likely to suggest using free association to uncover unconscious processes is
    the _____ model.
    a.   psychodynamic
    b.   cognitive
    c.   humanistic-existential
    d.   behavioral

How Do Other Psychodynamic Explanations Differ from Freud's?, p. 58
Diff: H, Type: Applied, Ans: a

51.   The model most likely to predict that transference will occur during therapy is the _____
    model.
    a.   psychodynamic
    b.   cognitive
    c.   humanistic-existential
    d.   behavioral

How Do Other Psychodynamic Explanations Differ from Freud's?, p. 58
Diff: M, Type: Applied, Ans: b

52.   Colin is asked to "free associate" about his mother's new husband and he responds by changing the subject. A psychodynamic therapist would consider this an example of:
       a.   catharsis.
       b.   resistance.
       c.   transference.
       d.   countertransference.

How Do Other Psychodynamic Explanations Differ from Freud's?, p. 58
Diff: E, Type: Factual, Ans: a

53.   The model most likely to use terms such as "resistance" and "transference" is the _____ model.
       a.   psychodynamic
       b.   behavioral
       c.   humanist-existential
       d.   sociocultural

How Do Other Psychodynamic Explanations Differ from Freud's?, p. 58
Diff: E, Type: Factual, Ans: b

54.   According to psychoanalytic theory, which of the following is true regarding dreams?
       a.   They are without real importance.
       b.   They reflect our unconscious desires and needs.
       c.   They are a means of reprocessing information necessary for survival.
       d.   They are the brain's attempts to understand abnormal electrical activity.

How Do Other Psychodynamic Explanations Differ from Freud's?, p. 58
Diff: M, Type: Factual, Ans: d

55.   According to Freud, another term for the symbolic meaning of dreams is:
       a.   positive transference.
       b.   negative transference.
       c.   manifest content.
       d.   latent content.

How Do Other Psychodynamic Explanations Differ from Freud's?, p. 58
Diff: M, Type: Factual, Ans: d

56.   If a patient relives past repressed feelings, that patient is said to have experienced _____, according to psychoanalysts.
       a.   repression
       b.   transference
       c.   resistance
       d.   catharsis

How Do Other Psychodynamic Explanations Differ from Freud's?, p. 59
Diff: E, Type: Applied, Ans: b

57.   Teresa has been told that her course of therapy is likely to take a year or more because it
      involves the reshaping of her personality and that takes many sessions. Her therapy is most
      likely:
      a.   client-centered therapy.
      b.   psychodynamic therapy.
      c.   cognitive-behavioral therapy.
      d.   existential-humanistic therapy.

How Do Other Psychodynamic Explanations Differ from Freud's?, p. 59
Diff: H, Type: Applied, Ans: c

58.   A patient participates in weekly therapy for several years, gradually becoming aware of the
      impact of early life events on present functioning. The form of psychotherapy the patient is
      receiving is called:
      a.   cognitive therapy.
      b.   drug therapy.
      c.   psychodynamic therapy.
      d.   behavior therapy.

How Do Other Psychodynamic Explanations Differ from Freud's?, p. 59
Diff: H, Type: Applied, Ans: d

59.   If a patient chose a dynamic focus for therapy, the patient would most likely be receiving:
      a.   relational psychoanalytic therapy.
      b.   psychoanalysis.
      c.   extended psychoanalytic therapy.
      d.   short-term psychodynamic therapy.

Assessing the Psychodynamic Model, p. 60
Diff: H, Type: Factual, Ans: d

60.   Evidence in support of the psychodynamic model has come primarily from:
      a.   lab-based human experimentation.
      b.   experiments carried out in "real-world" settings.
      c.   surveys.
      d.   case studies.

Assessing the Psychodynamic Model, p. 60
Diff: M, Type: Factual, Ans: d

61.   Evidence of the effectiveness of psychodynamic therapy:
      a.   is research based.
      b.   comes from pharmaceutical companies.
      c.   comes from double-blind studies.
      d.   is limited to case studies.

Assessing the Psychodynamic Model, p. 60
Diff: E, Type: Factual, Ans: b
62.   Evidence that supports the effectiveness of psychodynamic therapies has come from:
       a.   longitudinal experimental studies.
       b.   individual case studies.
       c.   controlled correlational studies.
       d.   carefully controlled experiments.

The Behavioral Model, p. 61
Diff: M, Type: Applied, Ans: b
63.   Theory focused on learned responses to the environment is usually described as:
       a.   psychoanalytic.
       b.   behavioral.
       c.   sociocultural.
       d.   psychodynamic.

The Behavioral Model, p. 61
Diff: H, Type: Applied, Ans: b
64.   "When I was young, I met a large dog. I wasn't afraid of the dog, but as I tried to pet it, the
       dog snarled and jumped at me. I have been afraid of dogs ever since." A therapist who
       assumes that this sentence describes a phobia acquired from classical conditioning most likely
       favors which model of abnormality?
       a.   humanistic-existential
       b.   behavioral
       c.   cognitive
       d.   psychodynamic

How Do Behaviorists Explain Abnormal Functioning?, p. 61
Diff: H, Type: Applied, Ans: b
65.   When a young child yells and throws toys ("temper tantrum"), the parents give the child a
       good deal of attention. As time goes on, the temper tantrums become more and more
       common. A behavioral psychologist would say that the temper tantrums result from:
       a.   unresolved intrapsychic conflict.
       b.   operant conditioning.
       c.   unconditional positive regard.
       d.   neurotransmitter imbalances.

How Do Behaviorists Explain Abnormal Functioning?, p. 61
Diff: H, Type: Applied, Ans: c
66.   The only time that Timmy gets attention is when he misbehaves in a bizarre way. This is an
       example of:
       a.   shaping.
       b.   modeling.
       c.   operant conditioning.
       d.   classical conditioning.

How Do Behaviorists Explain Abnormal Functioning?, p. 61
Diff: E, Type: Applied, Ans: b

67.   Animals and humans learn without reinforcement. They learn just by watching. This form of learning is called:
   a.   shaping.
   b.   modeling.
   c.   operant conditioning.
   d.   classical conditioning.

How Do Behaviorists Explain Abnormal Functioning?, p. 61
Diff: M, Type: Applied, Ans: a

68.   Jamal observed his parents' generous behavior throughout his childhood. As a result, he developed a positive and generous attitude toward the world. According to the behavioral model, Jamal has acquired his lifestyle through the process of:
   a.   modeling.
   b.   self-actualization.
   c.   operant conditioning.
   d.   classical conditioning.

How Do Behaviorists Explain Abnormal Functioning?, p. 61
Diff: M, Type: Applied, Ans: b

69.   The model most likely to emphasize the importance of one's history of conditioning as the source of depression is the _____ model.
   a.   psychodynamic
   b.   behavioral
   c.   humanist-existential
   d.   sociocultural

How Do Behaviorists Explain Abnormal Functioning?, p. 61
Diff: H, Type: Factual, Ans: d

70.   The model emphasizing the importance of conditioning in determining human actions is the _____ model.
   a.   psychodynamic
   b.   cognitive
   c.   humanistic-existential
   d.   behavioral

How Do Behaviorists Explain Abnormal Functioning?, p. 62
Diff: M, Type: Applied, Ans: a

71.   A child is bitten by a vicious dog in front of a park. The child is later very afraid of the park. According to classical conditioning, the park is a(n):
   a.   conditioned stimulus.
   b.   unconditioned stimulus.
   c.   unconditioned response.
   d.   conditioned response.

How Do Behaviorists Explain Abnormal Functioning?, p. 62
Diff: E, Type: Factual, Ans: b
72.   A previously neutral environmental event that becomes associated with the unconditioned stimulus is called a:
    a.   learned stimulus.
    b.   conditioned stimulus.
    c.   unconditioned stimulus.
    d.   discriminative stimulus.

How Do Behaviorists Explain Abnormal Functioning?, p. 62
Diff: M, Type: Applied, Ans: c
73.   If you imagine biting into a big, juicy, sour lemon, you are likely to salivate. The lemon is an example of:
    a.   a conditioned stimulus.
    b.   a conditioned response.
    c.   an unconditioned stimulus.
    d.   an unconditioned response.

How Do Behaviorists Explain Abnormal Functioning?, p. 62
`   **Diff: M, Type: Applied, Ans: b**
74.   If you close your eyes and imagine biting into a big, sour lemon, you are likely to salivate. The salivation to this imagery is an example of:
    a.   a conditioned stimulus.
    b.   a conditioned response.
    c.   an unconditioned stimulus.
    d.   an unconditioned response.

How Do Behaviorists Explain Abnormal Functioning?, p. 62
Diff: E, Type: Factual, Ans: a
75.   If, after conditioning, the conditioned stimulus is repeatedly presented alone (without the unconditioned stimulus), it will eventually stop eliciting the conditioned response through a process called:
    a.   extinction.
    b.   habituation.
    c.   punishment.
    d.   unconditioning.

Behavior Therapies, p. 62
Diff: M, Type: Factual, Ans: d
76.   The first step in using the treatment called "systematic desensitization" is to:
    a.   construct a fear hierarchy.
    b.   construct a list of useful reinforcers.
    c.   confront the client with the feared stimulus or thought.
    d.   teach the skill of relaxation over the course of several sessions.

Behavior Therapies, p. 62
Diff: M, Type: Applied, Ans: c

77.   A client in a totally relaxed state vividly imagines formerly anxiety-arousing situations without feeling any lingering anxiety. Most likely, that client has just completed what type of therapy?
      a.   Freudian psychoanalysis
      b.   family systems
      c.   systematic desensitization
      d.   cognitive therapy

Assessing the Behavioral Model, p. 63
Diff: M, Type: Factual, Ans: a

78.   All of the following are true of the behavioral model except:
      a.   it cannot be tested in the laboratory.
      b.   it has been found to be helpful in treating disorders.
      c.   it is criticized as being too simplistic.
      d.   it can be used to create abnormal symptoms.

Assessing the Behavioral Model, p. 63
Diff: E, Type: Factual, Ans: c

79.   Systematic desensitization has been shown to be especially effective in the treatment of:
      a.   bipolar disorders.
      b.   schizophrenia.
      c.   phobias.
      d.   substance abuse disorders.

Assessing the Behavioral Model, p. 63
Diff: M, Type: Factual, Ans: a

80.   Behavior therapy:
      a.   can be tested in the lab.
      b.   cannot explain the origin of abnormal behavior.
      c.   does not have associated therapeutic techniques.
      d.   is not based on research.

Assessing the Behavioral Model, p. 64
Diff: H, Type: Applied, Ans: a

81.   "Thoughts, as well as overt behaviors, are acquired and modified by various forms of conditioning." The orientation of the author of this quote most likely would be:
      a.   cognitive-behavioral.
      b.   humanistic-existential.
      c.   psychodynamic-Gestalt.
      d.   self-efficacious.

Assessing the Behavioral Model, p. 64
Diff: H, Type: Applied, Ans: c

82.   If you believe that you can master and perform needed behaviors whenever necessary, Bandura would say that you had a positive sense of:
      a.   overgeneralization.
      b.   classical conditioning.
      c.   self-efficacy.
      d.   modeling.

The Cognitive Model, p. 64
Diff: H, Type: Applied, Ans: d

83.   An athlete who is in fact well prepared nevertheless thinks just before a contest, "I can't do this! I need to be perfect, and I know I'm going to fail!" The theorist who would emphasize the illogical thinking process of this athlete as a source of poor performance most likely would support which model of abnormality?
       a.   psychodynamic
       b.   behavioral
       c.   existential
       d.   cognitive

The Cognitive Model, p. 64
Diff: M, Type: Factual, Ans: c

84.   The form of therapy that helps clients recognize errors in logic, and try out new interpretations of events is:
       a.   psychodynamic.
       b.   Gestalt.
       c.   cognitive.
       d.   humanistic.

How Do Cognitive Theorists Explain Abnormal Functioning?, p. 64
Diff: M, Type: Applied, Ans: c

85.   Henry goes into a fit of depression and self-abuse when anyone criticizes or expresses disapproval. Much of what he does is for the purpose of getting people to like him. Cognitive theorists would say that Henry's depression results in large part from:
       a.   modeling.
       b.   self-efficacy.
       c.   illogical thinking.
       d.   unconscious feelings of loss.

How Do Cognitive Theorists Explain Abnormal Functioning?, p. 64
Diff: M, Type: Applied, Ans: c

86.   When Jose did not get the job he was sure that everything was going wrong, that his life was completely off track. This thought is an example of:
       a.   depression.
       b.   selective perception.
       c.   overgeneralization.
       d.   unconditional negative regard.

Cognitive Therapies, p. 65
Diff: M, Type: Applied, Ans: a

87.   If a patient is being guided to challenge irrational thinking and to try out new interpretations, the patient is most likely being treated by a follower of:
       a.   Beck.
       b.   Freud.
       c.   Bandura.
       d.   Wolpe.

Assessing the Cognitive Model, p. 66
Diff: M, Type: Applied, Ans: d

88.   Which of the following is the most legitimate criticism of cognitive therapy?
      a.   It is difficult to assess through research.
      b.   It is not effective as a means for treating patients.
      c.   Thinking is not an important human process to address.
      d.   It leaves out questions of the values and meaning of life.

The Humanistic-Existential Model, p. 66
Diff: M, Type: Applied, Ans: b

89.   "When we try to establish how abnormality develops, we need to consider how individuals deal with the meaning of life, and with the value they find in living." A psychologist from which background would agree most strongly with this statement?
      a.   cognitive-behavioral
      b.   humanistic-existential
      c.   psychodynamic
      d.   cognitive

The Humanistic-Existential Model, p. 66
Diff: E, Type: Factual, Ans: d

90.   According to _____, the self-actualization motive plays an important part in human functioning.
      a.   cognitive theorists
      b.   behaviorists
      c.   psychoanalysts
      d.   humanists

The Humanistic-Existential Model, p. 66
Diff: M, Type: Factual, Ans: b

91.   A therapist who believes people often hide from their responsibilities, and therefore often feel alienated, depressed, inauthentic—empty—would most likely be:
      a.   humanistic.
      b.   existential.
      c.   psychodynamic.
      d.   cognitive.

The Humanistic-Existential Model, p. 66
Diff: M, Type: Factual, Ans: c

92.   The model that proposes that humans strive to self-actualize is the _____ model.
      a.   psychodynamic
      b.   cognitive
      c.   humanistic-existential
      d.   behavioral

The Humanistic-Existential Model, p. 66
Diff: E, Type: Factual, Ans: b

93.   Humanists would say that an individual who cares about others, is spontaneous, courageous, and independent is:
      a.   authentic.
      b.   self-actualizing.
      c.   role playing.
      d.   experiencing catharsis.

The Humanistic-Existential Model, p. 66
Diff: H, Type: Applied, Ans: c

94.   "Humans are born with freedom, yet do not 'naturally' strive to reach their full growth potential." The psychologist who would most closely agree with this statement would be:
      a.   behavioral.
      b.   humanistic.
      c.   existential.
      d.   psychodynamic.

The Humanistic-Existential Model, p. 67
Diff: M, Type: Applied, Ans: b

95.   The social upheaval and soul searching of the 1960s and 1970s in Western society gave rise to which of the following approaches to therapy?
      a.   psychodynamic
      b.   humanist and existential
      c.   behavioral
      d.   cognitive

Rogers's Humanistic Theory and Therapy, p. 67
Diff: H, Type: Factual, Ans: b

96.   If you recognize your worth as a person, Carl Rogers would say that you have developed:
      a.   spontaneity.
      b.   unconditional self-regard.
      c.   unconditional positive regard.
      d.   conditions of worth.

Rogers's Humanistic Theory and Therapy, p. 67
Diff: E, Type: Factual, Ans: a

97.   The term for the form of psychotherapy pioneered by Carl Rogers is:
      a.   client-centered.
      b.   insight.
      c.   Gestalt.
      d.   existential.

Rogers's Humanistic Theory and Therapy, p. 67
Diff: E, Type: Applied, Ans: d

98.   A therapist listens carefully to a client's words, then attempts to show accurate empathy and genuineness. The hope is that the client will self-examine with acceptance and honesty. Most likely, the therapist is:
   a. behavioral.
   b. cognitive-behavioral.
   c. psychodynamic.
   d. humanistic.

Rogers's Humanistic Theory and Therapy, p. 68
Diff: H, Type: Factual, Ans: a

99.   In Rogers's therapy, the honesty and genuineness of the therapist allows clients to look at themselves with acceptance in a process called:
   a. experiencing.
   b. accurate empathy.
   c. conditions of worth.
   d. unconditional positive regard.

Rogers's Humanistic Theory and Therapy, p. 68
Diff: M, Type: Applied, Ans: d

100.   If a client-centered therapist were treating a very anxious woman, the therapist would try to:
   a. point out her misconceptions.
   b. give insightful interpretations of her statements.
   c. identify the client's unreasonable ideas and feelings.
   d. show unconditional positive regard for her statements.

Rogers's Humanistic Theory and Therapy, p. 68
Diff: M, Type: Applied, Ans: b

101.   "That's all right. You are doing your best, don't worry. I am here for you." A therapist who would say this as a primary part of the therapy process would most probably follow the _____ tradition.
   a. cognitive
   b. humanistic
   c. psychodynamic
   d. rational emotive

Rogers's Humanistic Theory and Therapy, p. 68
Diff: H, Type: Applied, Ans: a

102.   When clients are freed from the insecurities and doubts that prevent self-actualization, they are said to be exhibiting which of the following?
   a. experiencing
   b. conditions of worth
   c. resistance
   d. free association

Gestalt Theory and Therapy, p. 69
Diff: M, Type: Factual, Ans: b
103. When a gestalt therapist refuses to meet her patient's demands, the therapist is using:
      a. role-playing.
      b. skillful frustration.
      c. passive aggression.
      d. deliberate accurate refusal.

Existential Theories and Therapies, p. 69
Diff: M, Type: Applied, Ans: b
104. "You can do anything you want. You can lead a perfectly useless life. It is all up to you." A therapist who would say these frustrating statements as a primary part of the therapy process would follow the _____ tradition.
      a. cognitive
      b. existential
      c. humanistic
      d. psychodynamic

Existential Theories and Therapies, p. 69
Diff: H, Type: Applied, Ans: a
105. Which of the following would be most likely to use skillful frustration as a part of therapy?
      a. Fritz Perls
      b. Joseph Wolpe
      c. Abraham Maslow
      d. Karen Horney

Existential Theories and Therapies, p. 69
Diff: H, Type: Factual, Ans: a
106. Therapists who often deliberately frustrate and challenge their clients, and who often use role playing and a "here and now" orientation, are:
      a. gestalt.
      b. neo-Freudian.
      c. cognitive-behavioral.
      d. humanistic.

The Sociocultural Model, p. 71
Diff: E, Type: Factual, Ans: c
107. The model of abnormality that pays particular attention to a client's family structure, societal norms, and a client's roles in society is:
      a. existential.
      b. cognitive-behavioral.
      c. sociocultural.
      d. humanistic.

How Do Sociocultural Theorists Explain Abnormal Functioning?, p. 71
Diff: M, Type: Applied, Ans: c

108.   David Rosenhan sent "pseudopatients" to a mental hospital where they pretended to be
        disturbed. The results led him to conclude that _____ greatly impacts mental illness.
        a. an actual symptom
        b. the community mental health system
        c. labeling
        d. communication

How Do Sociocultural Theorists Explain Abnormal Functioning?, p. 71
Diff: H, Type: Applied, Ans: a

109.   If someone is isolated and lacks social support or intimacy in his or her life, that person is
        more likely to _____ than someone who has social support and intimacy.
        a. become depressed when under stress
        b. become depressed even when not under stress
        c. become depressed, but recover more quickly
        d. be a carrier of depression to later generations

How Do Sociocultural Theorists Explain Abnormal Functioning?, p. 71
Diff: E, Type: Factual, Ans: d

110.   Which model of abnormality would focus on factors such as norms, family structure and
        support systems, in particular?
        a. behavioral
        b. cognitive-behavioral
        c. gestalt
        d. sociocultural

How Do Sociocultural Theorists Explain Abnormal Functioning?, p. 72
Diff: H, Type: Factual, Ans: d

111.   According to family systems theory, families that show "disengagement" are characterized
        by:
        a. members who are overinvolved in one another's lives.
        b. parents who have a "laissez-faire" parenting style.
        c. children who very seldom fight.
        d. rigid boundaries between family members.

How Do Sociocultural Theorists Explain Abnormal Functioning?, p. 72
Diff: M, Type: Applied, Ans: c

112.   If a mother seems excessively involved in her child's life such that they do not seem to be
        independent people, their relationship is said to be:
        a. externalized.
        b. cultural.
        c. enmeshed.
        d. disengaged.

How Do Sociocultural Theorists Explain Abnormal Functioning?, p. 72
Diff: H, Type: Applied, Ans: d
113.   Current multicultural perspectives are most likely to focus on:
    a.   the inferiority of particular cultural groups.
    b.   the cultural deprivation that is characteristic of some groups.
    c.   the limitations of a focus on ethnicity.
    d.   the special external pressures faced by members of a culture.

How Do Sociocultural Theorists Explain Abnormal Functioning?, p. 73
Diff: M, Type: Applied, Ans: b
114.   Multicultural theorists would explain the higher levels of mental illness among poor people as most likely due to:
    a.   genetic make-up.
    b.   social factors leading to stress.
    c.   irrational patterns of thinking.
    d.   fixation at a lower level of ego functioning.

How Do Sociocultural Theorists Explain Abnormal Functioning?, p. 73
Diff: H, Type: Applied, Ans: c
115.   Which of the following explanations for the higher levels of anorexia nervosa in Western cultures is consistent with a multicultural model?
    a.   Thin people are subject to prejudice and discrimination in hiring.
    b.   The standards for male body types are more limited than for female body types.
    c.   The media set an unreasonably small ideal body type for women.
    d.   Obesity levels are rising among school children.

How Do Sociocultural Theorists Explain Abnormal Functioning?, p. 73
Diff: M, Type: Applied, Ans: a
116.   The fact that anorexia nervosa is more common in Western cultures supports which of the following aspects of the sociocultural model?
    a.   cultural
    b.   family systems
    c.   social network
    d.   communication

How Do Sociocultural Theorists Explain Abnormal Functioning?, p. 74
Diff: E, Type: Factual, Ans: d
117.   Recent research on the role of religion in mental health shows that religious people:
    a.   are more lonely and depressed than nonreligious people.
    b.   attempt suicide more than nonreligious people.
    c.   abuse drugs more than nonreligious people.
    d.   cope better with life stresses than nonreligious people.

Sociocultural Treatments, p. 75
Diff: M, Type: Applied, Ans: a
118.   A gender-sensitive therapy would:
    a.   be geared to the special pressures of being a woman in Western society.
    b.   make sure that women patients have women therapists.
    c.   reject a feminist approach to understanding mental disorders.
    d.   be inconsistent with a group-therapy approach.

Sociocultural Treatments, p. 75
Diff: M, Type: Applied, Ans: c

119.   Which of the following phrases would one be most likely to hear in a self-help group?
   a.   "I don't have any idea what you should do."
   b.   "The therapist will tell us what to do."
   c.   "Try this. It worked for me."
   d.   "Let's talk about our dreams."

Sociocultural Treatments, p. 76
Diff: H, Type: Applied, Ans: b

120.   If a therapist advised you to pay attention to how you were communicating with family members and to change harmful patterns, the therapist would most likely be practicing:
   a.   structural family therapy.
   b.   conjoint family therapy.
   c.   feminist therapy.
   d.   self-help therapy.

Sociocultural Treatments, p. 78
Diff: H, Type: Applied, Ans: a

121.   According to recent research, which of the following couples would be most likely to benefit from couples therapy?
   a.   younger couples with less rigid gender roles
   b.   couples with teenage children
   c.   couples with more serious problems
   d.   older couples with well-defined gender roles

Sociocultural Treatments, p. 79
Diff: M, Type: Factual, Ans: b

122.   A primary focus of the community treatment approach to abnormality is:
   a.   using drugs along with psychotherapy.
   b.   prevention.
   c.   homeostasis.
   d.   rejecting all conventional forms of explaining abnormality.

Sociocultural Treatments, p. 80
Diff: H, Type: Factual, Ans: c

123.   Providing treatment as soon as it is needed, so that problems that are moderate or worse do not become long-term, is called:
   a.   primary prevention.
   b.   secondary prevention.
   c.   tertiary prevention.
   d.   pre-prevention.

Putting It Together, p. 80
Diff: H, Type: Applied, Ans: d

124.   Which of the following statements is the best example of the biopsychosocial perspective?
   a.   There is one legitimate approach to understanding mental disorders.
   b.   Abnormality is best explained by sociocultural stresses a person experiences.
   c.   Eclectic approaches fail to take interactions of various models into account.
   d.   Abnormality results from the interaction of genetic, emotional, and cultural influences.

Putting It Together, p. 81
Diff: E, Type: Factual, Ans: a
125.   Combining any two or more treatment techniques results in an approach is called:
    a. eclectic.
    b. reciprocal.
    c. couple therapy.
    d. group therapy.

Putting It Together, p. 81
Diff: H, Type: Factual, Ans: d
126.   About what percent of clinicians today would describe their approach as "eclectic"?
    a. 5%
    b. 10%
    c. 20%
    d. more than 20%

Putting It Together, p. 81
Diff: M, Type: Applied, Ans: c
127.   Imagine that a man inherits the tendency to be socially awkward. That leads him to choose inappropriate romantic partners who increase his level of stress. A biopsychosocial therapist would use the _____ effects explanation of his functioning.
    a. cognitive
    b. cultural
    c. reciprocal
    d. deterministic

FILL-IN QUESTIONS

Models of Abnormality, p. 48
Diff: M, Type: Factual, Ans: paradigm or model
1.   The explicit set of basic assumptions that gives structure to the understanding and investigation of an area is called a(n) _____ .

Models of Abnormality, p. 48
Diff: E, Type: Factual, Ans: biological
2.   According to the _____ model, physical processes are the cause of all human behavior.

How Did Freud Explain Normal and Abnormal Functioning?, p. 55
Diff: E, Type: Factual, Ans: id
3.   According to psychoanalytic theory, the basic part of the personality focused on instinctual needs is the _____ .

How Did Freud Explain Normal and Abnormal Functioning?, p. 55
Diff: M, Type: Factual, Ans: conscience
4.   The superego can also be called the _____ .

How Did Freud Explain Normal and Abnormal Functioning?, p. 55
Diff: E, Type: Applied, Ans: superego
5.   Ramon tries not to do bad things (he feels guilty when he does) and to live up to his parents' expectations. According to psychoanalytic theory, he has a well-developed _____ .

How Did Freud Explain Normal and Abnormal Functioning?, p. 56
Diff: E, Type: Factual, Ans: repression
6.   The most basic defense mechanism is _____.

How Did Freud Explain Normal and Abnormal Functioning?, p. 56
Diff: E, Type: Applied, Ans: erogenous zone
7.   During the oral stage, the mouth is the important _____.

How Did Freud Explain Normal and Abnormal Functioning?, p. 56
Diff: E, Type: Factual, Ans: oral
8.   Infants are in the _____ stage, according to psychoanalytic theory.

How Did Freud Explain Normal and Abnormal Functioning?, p. 56
Diff: M, Type: Factual, Ans: genital
9.   Adolescents are in the _____ stage, according to psychoanalytic theory.

How Do Other Psychodynamic Explanations Differ from Freud's?, p. 57
Diff: M, Type: Factual, Ans: objects relations
10.   Relationships are the focus of the psychodynamic approach called _____ theory.

Psychodynamic Therapies, p. 57
Diff: E, Type: Applied, Ans: free association
11.   The patient says whatever comes into her mind in the psychodynamic technique called
_____.

Psychodynamic Therapies, p. 58
Diff: M, Type: Applied, Ans: resistance
12.   If a patient changes the subject during psychodynamic therapy, the therapist might interpret it
as _____.

Psychodynamic Therapies, p. 58
Diff: E, Type: Factual, Ans: latent
13.   The underlying symbolic meaning of a dream is its _____ content.

Psychodynamic Therapies, p. 58
Diff: E, Type: Applied, Ans: manifest
14.   When a person describes a dream, he or she is most likely describing the _____ content.

The Behavioral Model, p. 61
Diff: E, Type: Factual, Ans: behavioral
15.   Learned behaviors are the focus of the _____ approach.

The Behavioral Model, p. 61
Diff: M, Type: Applied, Ans: reward
16.   You have a slightly depressed child and decide to treat this condition by responding to the
child only when he does or says "happy" things. Your response to the child is a _____,
according to the behavioral model.

The Behavioral Model, p. 61
Diff: E, Type: Factual, Ans: modeling
17.   According to the behavioral model, learning through observation is called _____.

The Behavioral Model, p. 61
Diff: M, Type: Factual, Ans: modeling
18.   Learning without direct reinforcement but by watching others is part of the behavioral approach. It is called _____.

The Behavioral Model, p. 61
Diff: E, Type: Applied, Ans: modeling
19.   Two-year-old Carol watches a cooking show on television and then goes into the kitchen to "bake a cake." This is an example of _____.

The Behavioral Model, p. 62
Diff: M, Type: Applied, Ans: conditioned stimulus
20.   If a friend bites into a grapefruit in front of you, you are likely to salivate. The sight of the grapefruit is a _____.

Behavioral Therapies, p. 62
Diff: E, Type: Factual, Ans: systematic desensitization
21.   The most common technique used by behavioral therapists to treat phobias is _____.

Behavioral Therapies, p. 62
Diff: E, Type: Applied, Ans: extinction
22.   If a conditioned stimulus is repeatedly presented without the unconditioned stimulus, the response gradually declines. This is called _____.

Assessing the Behavioral Model, p. 64
Diff: H, Type: Applied, Ans: self-efficacy
23.   Self-confidence is similar to the concept of _____ in Bandura's behavioral approach.

The Cognitive Model, p. 64
Diff: E, Type: Factual, Ans: cognitive
24.   The _____ model focuses on the processes and content of thinking.

The Cognitive Model, p. 64
Diff: M, Type: Applied, Ans: cognitive
25.   "People get depressed because they have depressing thoughts." This statement is consistent with the _____ model.

The Cognitive Model, p. 64
Diff: E, Type: Factual, Ans: cognitive
26.   Challenging a client's inaccurate assumption is a specific feature of _____ therapy.

How Do Cognitive Theorists Explain Abnormal Functioning?, p. 64
Diff: H, Type: Factual, Ans: assumptions and attitudes
27.   Albert Ellis believes that abnormal behavior stems from a set of _____ that some people hold.

The Humanistic-Existential Model, p. 66
Diff: E, Type: Factual, Ans: humanistic-existential
28.   The role of values and free choice is the central focus of the _____ model.

The Humanistic-Existential Model, p. 66
Diff: E, Type: Factual, Ans: existential

29.   Living an authentic life is a goal of _____ therapy.

Rogers's Humanistic Theory and Therapy, p. 67
Diff: M, Type: Factual, Ans: unconditional positive regard

30.   According to Roger's humanistic approach, children need _____ to later self-actualize.

Rogers's Humanistic Theory and Therapy, p. 68
Diff: E, Type: Factual, Ans: unconditional positive regard

31.   Rogers's humanistic approach to therapy involves the use of support and acceptance for everything that the client says. This is called _____.

ESSAY QUESTIONS

No Specific Topic, No Specific Page
Diff: M, Type: Factual

1.   Discuss how the humanistic-existential model and the biological model differ in their understanding of causes of abnormality?

Biological Treatments, pp. 52-53
Diff: E, Type: Factual

2.   What are some advantages and disadvantages of using drugs in psychotherapy?

No Specific Topic, No Specific Page
Diff: H, Type: Factual

3.   Please choose any two of the following models, then say how each could explain an abnormal fear of dogs: psychodynamic, behavioral, sociocultural.

No Specific Topic, No Specific Page
Diff: H, Type: Applied

4.   If a friend of yours needed to be treated for depression, what would be advantages and disadvantages of your friend receiving either psychodynamic therapy, or cognitive therapy? Which of these two alternatives would you recommend to your friend?

Sociocultural Treatments, pp. 74-75
Diff: M, Type: Factual

5.   Discuss the reasons that culture-sensitive therapy arose and the challenges it seeks to address.

No Specific Topic, No Specific Page
Diff: H, Type: Applied

6.   Group therapy, family therapy, and couple therapy were described in the Sociocultural Model section of this chapter. However, these types of therapy often are done by therapists who follow other models. Please describe how a therapist following either a behavioral or a humanistic model might do therapy using one of the three forms of therapy named above.

Sociocultural Treatments, pp. 78-79
Diff: H, Type: Factual
7.   One unique part of the sociocultural model is the "community treatment" aspect, a key
      component of which is prevention. How do community treatment advocates accomplish
      prevention?

Sociocultural Treatments, pp. 78-79
Diff: H, Type: Applied
8.   Define primary, secondary, and tertiary prevention. Provide an example of each.

Putting It Together, p. 80
Diff: M, Type: Applied
9.   Explain the biopsychosocial approach to understanding the causes of abnormality. Provide an
      example of how this approach might be applied to the causes of depression.

Putting It Together, p. 81
Diff: E, Type: Factual
10.   Many clinicians describe their approach as "eclectic." What is an eclectic approach to
      abnormality? Please describe at least one example of an eclectic approach to abnormality.

Putting It Together, p. 81, Table 3-5
Diff: M, Type: Factual
11.   Please describe the origins of abnormality according to any three of these models of
      abnormality: sociocultural, psychodynamic, behavioral, cognitive, humanistic-existential,
      biological.

CHAPTER 4

Clinical Assessment, Diagnosis, and Treatment

MULTIPLE-CHOICE QUESTIONS

Clinical Assessment, Diagnosis, and Treatment, p. 85
Diff: M, Type: Factual, Ans: c

1. The major focus of a clinical practitioner when dealing with a new client is to gather what type of information?
   a. diagnostic
   b. nomothetic
   c. idiographic
   d. dispassionate

Clinical Assessment, Diagnosis, and Treatment, p. 85
Diff: E, Type: Factual, Ans: c

2. A mental health practitioner attempts to learn about the behavior and emotional state of each client. This approach to abnormal psychology is called:
   a. behavioral.
   b. nomothetic.
   c. idiographic.
   d. psychodynamic.

Clinical Assessment: How and Why Does the Client Behave Abnormally?, p. 85
Diff: M, Type: Applied, Ans: a

3. When graduate schools choose students based on test scores, college grades, and relevant experience, they are engaging in:
   a. assessment.
   b. diagnosis.
   c. treatment.
   d. classification.

Clinical Assessment: How and Why Does the Client Behave Abnormally?, p. 86
Diff: E, Type: Factual, Ans: b

4. A functional analysis involves:
   a. using projective tests.
   b. learning about a person's behaviors.
   c. learning about unconscious conflicts in the client.
   d. obtaining information about the components of a person's personality.

Clinical Assessment: How and Why Does the Client Behave Abnormally?, p. 86
Diff: E, Type: Applied, Ans: a

5.   One of the assumptions of a functional analysis is that:
        a. abnormal behaviors are learned.
        b. abnormal behaviors are maladaptive.
        c. learning about unconscious conflicts will explain a person's abnormal behavior.
        d. learning the structure of a person's personality will explain his or her abnormal behavior.

Clinical Assessment: How and Why Does the Client Behave Abnormally?, p. 86
Diff: M, Type: Applied, Ans: b

6.   A clinician gathers data about what things might be reinforcing to someone's abnormal behavior. This variety of assessment is called:
        a. psychodynamic.
        b. behavioral.
        c. structured.
        d. free-form.

Characteristics of Assessment Tools, p. 86
Diff: M, Type: Applied, Ans: d

7.   Another term for developing norms for an assessment tool is:
        a. reliability.
        b. face validity.
        c. predictive validity.
        d. standardization.

Characteristics of Assessment Tools, p. 86
Diff: H, Type: Applied, Ans: b

8.   If a new test for anxiety is normed on individuals who are waiting to take introductory psychology final exams, the new test is surely lacking:
        a. reliability.
        b. adequate standardization.
        c. validity.
        d. structure.

Characteristics of Assessment Tools, p. 86
Diff: H, Type: Applied, Ans: a

9.   A new test for anxiety shows consistent levels of anxiety across time for people, but very few people have taken the test, and accurate norms don't exist. The test has:
        a. high reliability, but inadequate standardization.
        b. high reliability, and adequate standardization.
        c. low reliability, and inadequate standardization.
        d. low reliability, but adequate standardization.

Characteristics of Assessment Tools, p. 86
Diff: H, Type: Applied, Ans: a
10.   A clinician has developed a new assessment tool. Clients write stories about their problems, then two different judges independently evaluate the stories in terms of how logically they are written. For this assessment technique to be useful, there must be:
a.   high interjudge reliability.
b.   low observer reliability.
c.   high split-half reliability.
d.   low test-retest reliability.

Characteristics of Assessment Tools, p. 86
Diff: M, Type: Applied, Ans: c
11.   A panel of psychologists and psychiatrists evaluates the test results and clinical interviews of a client in a sanity hearing. They all arrive at the same diagnosis. The panel has high:
a.   internal validity.
b.   predictive validity.
c.   interrater reliability.
d.   test-retest reliability.

Characteristics of Assessment Tools, p. 86
Diff: H, Type: Applied, Ans: d
12.   A campus newspaper publishes an "Exam Anxiety" test, which was put together by the newspaper staff one evening just before their publishing deadline. Despite its hasty construction, the test most likely has:
a.   standardization.
b.   predictive validity.
c.   face validity.
d.   a standardization sample.

Characteristics of Assessment Tools, p. 86
Diff: H, Type: Applied, Ans: c
13.   An assessment tool asks individuals to record all the times they feel sad, in order to try to measure tendencies toward depression. However, individuals report wide variation from day to day in terms of the number of "sad" episodes they record. This assessment tool has:
a.   high test–retest reliability, and high face validity.
b.   high test–retest reliability, and low face validity.
c.   low test–retest reliability, and high face validity.
d.   low test–retest reliability, and low face validity.

Characteristics of Assessment Tools, p. 86
Diff: M, Type: Applied, Ans: a
14.   Because people who are manic have very elevated moods, a new test for mania includes questions about how happy the person feels and how often he or she laughs. This test has:
a.   face validity.
b.   content validity.
c.   construct validity.
d.   concurrent validity.

Characteristics of Assessment Tools, p. 86
Diff: M, Type: Applied, Ans: b

15.   A test is constructed to identify people who will develop schizophrenia. Of the 100 people the test identifies, 93 show signs of schizophrenia within five years. The test may be said to have high:
   a.   internal reliability.
   b.   predictive validity.
   c.   concurrent validity.
   d.   test-retest reliability.

Characteristics of Assessment Tools, p. 87
Diff: M, Type: Factual, Ans: c

16.   A new assessment tool does a good job of differentiating those who later will be depressed and those who will not be depressed, and it produces results similar to those of other tools measuring depression. Therefore, the new assessment tool has good:
   a.   predictive validity.
   b.   face validity.
   c.   interjudge reliability.
   d.   test-release reliability.

Characteristics of Assessment Tools, p. 87
Diff: H, Type: Applied, Ans: c

17.   If a new test for assessing anorectic tendencies produces scores comparable to those of other tests for assessing anorectic tendencies, then the new test has high:
   a.   predictive validity.
   b.   standardization criteria.
   c.   concurrent validity.
   d.   performance criteria.

Clinical Interviews, p. 87
Diff: E, Type: Factual, Ans: c

18.   Clinical interviews are the preferred assessment technique of many practitioners. One particular strength of the interview process is:
   a.   validity.
   b.   the reliability of the technique.
   c.   the chance to get a general sense of the client.
   d.   that it asks only open-ended questions.

Clinical Interviews, p. 88
Diff: M, Type: Applied, Ans: b

19.   Dr. Martin has just asked a potential client to talk about herself. After she responds, the doctor's next question is based on some interesting point she brought up. There are few constraints on the conversation. Dr. Martin has just:
   a.   used free association.
   b.   conducted an unstructured interview.
   c.   used a behavioral assessment technique.
   d.   employed (Rogers's) nondirective therapy.

Clinical Interviews, p. 88
Diff: H, Type: Applied, Ans: d

20.   The clinical interviewer most interested in stimuli that trigger abnormal responses would have what orientation?
   a.   cognitive
   b.   psychodynamic
   c.   humanistic
   d.   behavioral

Clinical Interviews, p. 88
Diff: M, Type: Applied, Ans: d

21.   A clinical interviewer says, in part, "How do you feel about yourself today? How do you feel about what's going on in your life?" Most likely, that clinical interviewer's orientation is:
   a.   biological.
   b.   behavioral.
   c.   psychodynamic.
   d.   humanistic.

Clinical Interviews, p. 88
Diff: H, Type: Applied, Ans: a

22.   An interviewer who asks a client questions such as "Where are you now?" "Why do you think you're here?" or even "Who are you?" is probably conducting a(n):
   a.   mental status exam.
   b.   behavioral interview.
   c.   sociocultural interview.
   d.   intelligence test.

Clinical Interviews, p. 88
Diff: H, Type: Applied, Ans: d

23.   If a clinician begins by asking, "Would you tell me about yourself?" the clinician is most likely conducting:
   a.   a mental status exam.
   b.   an interview schedule.
   c.   a structured interview.
   d.   an unstructured interview.

Clinical Interviews, p. 89
Diff: H, Type: Applied, Ans: d

24.   Which of the following is a reason to question the *validity* of clinical interviews?
   a.   People respond differently to different interviewers.
   b.   People may respond differently to clinicians who are not of their race.
   c.   On different days, people might describe themselves differently.
   d.   Clinicians might overemphasize pathology.

Clinical Interviews, p. 89
Diff: H, Type: Applied, Ans: b
25.   A patient complains of a phobia. Two lines of questioning by the clinician concern the specific object of the phobia and what the person does when he or she confronts that object. This clinician's orientation is probably:
a.   biological.
b.   behavioral.
c.   humanistic.
d.   sociocultural.

Clinical Interviews, p. 89
Diff: M, Type: Factual, Ans: c
26.   One limit of the clinical interview as an assessment tool is that:
a.   each client is different.
b.   the approach is too rigid.
c.   the client may give an overly positive picture.
d.   the clinician sees the client too infrequently.

Clinical Tests, p. 89
Diff: M, Type: Factual, Ans: b
27.   Personality assessment using projective tests is designed to:
a.   perform a functional analysis of the client.
b.   learn about unconscious conflicts in the client.
c.   obtain detailed information about specific dysfunctional behaviors.
d.   obtain detailed information about specific dysfunctional cognitions.

Clinical Tests, p. 89
Diff: E, Type: Applied, Ans: b
28.   The assumption behind the use of projective tests as assessment tools is that:
a.   they are relatively easy to score.
b.   the responses come from the client's unconscious.
c.   they stimulate abnormal behaviors that the clinician can observe.
d.   patient responses to specific stimuli will uncover specific disorders.

Clinical Tests, p. 89
Diff: H, Type: Applied, Ans: d
29.   A clinician has developed a test that requires test takers to tell stories about a series of pictures of city skylines. Most likely, this new test is a:
a.   neuropsychological test.
b.   personality inventory.
c.   response inventory.
d.   projective test.

Clinical Tests, p. 90
Diff: H, Type: Factual, Ans: b
30.   The only test among the following that is *not* a projective test is the:
a.   Rorschach Test.
b.   Minnesota Multiphasic Personality Inventory.
c.   Draw-a-Person Test.
d.   Thematic Apperception Test.

Clinical Tests, p. 90
Diff: M, Type: Factual, Ans: b

31. A patient looks at a series of black-and-white pictures, making up a dramatic story about each. The patient is taking:
     a. the Rorschach Test.
     b. the Thematic Apperception Test.
     c. the Minnesota Multiphasic Personality Inventory.
     d. an affective inventory.

Clinical Tests, p. 90
Diff: H, Type: Applied, Ans: c

32. When Rorschach testers ask themselves questions like, "Did the person respond to the whole picture or to specific details, and to the colors or to the white spaces?" they are interested in the _____ of the response.
     a. theme
     b. content
     c. style
     d. images

Clinical Tests, p. 90
Diff: H, Type: Applied, Ans: b

33. Use of projective tests has decreased in the past few decades because projective tests often have:
     a. interrater reliability that is too high.
     b. poor concurrent validity.
     c. rigid scoring standards.
     d. bias in favor of minority groups.

Clinical Tests, p. 90
Diff: M, Type: Factual, Ans: b

34. Which of the following statements about the use of projective techniques by today's clinicians is true?
     a. Projective tests are not used any more.
     b. The centrality of projective tests has declined since their introduction.
     c. Current clinicians rely on projective tests as a primary source of insight about their patients.
     d. Projective tests have a more prominent place in the clinician's repertoire than they did 50 years ago.

Clinical Tests, p. 90
Diff: H, Type: Applied, Ans: b

35. When a clinician using the Rorschach focuses on the actual images that a person "sees," the clinician is emphasizing:
     a. style.
     b. theme.
     c. color.
     d. latency to respond.

Clinical Tests, p. 91
Diff: H, Type: Applied, Ans: c

36. If a person responds to a TAT card with his or her own concerns, the person is said to be identifying with the:
     a. theme.
     b. pathology.
     c. hero.
     d. ideal.

Clinical Tests, p. 91
Diff: E, Type: Applied, Ans: d

37. If a clinician focused on where you placed your drawing on the page, the size of the drawing, and the parts you omitted, you most likely took which of the following tests?
     a. Rorschach
     b. TAT
     c. MMPI
     d. Draw-a-Person

Clinical Tests, p. 93
Diff: E, Type: Factual, Ans: b

38. Which of the following tests is a personality inventory?
     a. Draw-a-Person
     b. MMPI-2
     c. Rorschach Test
     d. Thematic Apperception Test

Clinical Tests, p. 93
Diff: H, Type: Applied, Ans: b

39. Statements were presented to both mental patients and nonpatients. They were asked to indicate whether each statement was applicable to themselves. The questions that differentiated between the two groups comprised the final test. What is the term for this technique of test construction?
     a. standardizing
     b. criterion keying
     c. predictive validating
     d. reliability determination

Clinical Tests, p. 93
Diff: M, Type: Applied, Ans: d

40. Youssef is the kind of person who breaks laws and rules with no feeling of guilt and is emotionally shallow. He would probably score high on the MMPI-2 scale called:
     a. paranoia.
     b. schizophrenia.
     c. psychasthenia.
     d. psychopathic deviate.

Clinical Tests, p. 93
Diff: H, Type: Applied, Ans: b

41.   Clients check off either "Applies" or "Does Not Apply" to a series of 200 items dealing with what they do and what they think in a variety of situations. The kind of test they are taking most likely is a:
a.   projective test.
b.   personality inventory.
c.   neuropsychological battery.
d.   sentence-completion test.

Clinical Tests, p. 93
Diff: M, Type: Factual, Ans: d

42.   The test that reports one's results on clinical scales such as "hypochondriasis" (HS) and "Psychopathic deviate" (PD) is the:
a.   Sentence-Completion Test.
b.   Thematic Apperception Test.
c.   Bender Visual-Motor Gestalt Test.
d.   Minnesota Multiphasic Personality Inventory.

Clinical Tests, p. 94
Diff: H, Type: Factual, Ans: a

43.   The test with built-in items designed to detect things such as lying and carelessness is the:
a.   Minnesota Multiphasic Personality Inventory.
b.   Thematic Apperception Test.
c.   Draw-a-Person Test.
d.   Sentence Completion Test.

Clinical Tests, p. 94
Diff: H, Type: Factual, Ans: a

44.   The MMPI-2 is considered by many to be superior to the original MMPI because the MMPI-2:
a.   was tested on a more diverse group of people.
b.   produces results that are not comparable to the results of the original MMPI.
c.   has fewer items.
d.   produces only one score.

Clinical Tests, p. 94
Diff: H, Type: Applied, Ans: b

45.   George is consumed with concern that his house will burn down. Before he leaves, he makes sure that all his appliances are unplugged. He often has to go back home and check to make sure he did not leave any plugged in. Which MMPI-2 scale would he most likely score high on?
a.   schizophrenia
b.   psychasthenia
c.   social introversion
d.   psychopathic deviate

Clinical Tests, p. 94
Diff: E, Type: Factual, Ans: a
46. Compared to projective tests, personality inventories:
    a. have higher validity.
    b. are less standardized.
    c. have lower reliability.
    d. are more difficult to administer and evaluate.

Clinical Tests, p. 94
Diff: M, Type: Applied, Ans: b
47. The test with the highest validity in identifying psychological disturbances is the:
    a. Thematic Apperception Test.
    b. Minnesota Multiphasic Personality Test.
    c. Rorschach Test.
    d. Draw-a-Person Test.

Clinical Tests, p. 94
Diff: M, Type: Applied, Ans: b
48. Which of the following tests is likely to have the lowest reliability?
    a. the MMPI
    b. the Draw-a-Person Test
    c. a social skills inventory
    d. the Beck Depression Inventory

Clinical Tests, p. 94
Diff: H, Type: Factual, Ans: a
49. Compared to projective tests, personality inventories generally have:
    a. greater reliability and greater validity.
    b. greater reliability and poorer validity.
    c. poorer reliability but greater validity.
    d. poorer reliability and poorer validity.

Clinical Tests, p. 95
Diff: H, Type: Applied, Ans: a
50. If a clinician wanted to know more detailed information about a person's functioning in a specific area, the clinician would use:
    a. a response inventory.
    b. a validity assessment.
    c. a measure of reliability.
    d. standardization.

Clinical Tests, p. 95
Diff: M, Type: Applied, Ans: b
51. An inventory that asks about one's level of anxiety, depression, and anger is a(n) _____ inventory:
    a. cognitive
    b. affective
    c. social skills
    d. functional

Clinical Tests, p. 95
Diff: M, Type: Applied, Ans: c

52.   An inventory that asks about how one would act in a variety of situations is a(n) _____
      inventory:
      a.   cognitive
      b.   affective
      c.   social skills
      d.   functional

Clinical Tests, p. 95
Diff: M, Type: Factual, Ans: b

53.   A response inventory that asks individuals to provide detailed information about their typical
      thoughts and assumptions is a(n):
      a.   social skill inventory.
      b.   cognitive inventory.
      c.   affective inventory.
      d.   behavioral inventory.

Clinical Tests, p. 95
Diff: H, Type: Applied, Ans: c

54.   An example of a reasonably reliable, valid response inventory is the:
      a.   Minnesota Multiphasic Personality Inventory.
      b.   Rorschach Inkblot Test.
      c.   Beck Depression Inventory.
      d.   Draw-a-Person Test.

Clinical Tests, p. 96
Diff: M, Type: Factual, Ans: d

55.   Which of the following is designed to disclose a patient's thoughts and assumptions?
      a.   the MMPI-2
      b.   the Rorschach Test
      c.   an affective inventory
      d.   a cognitive inventory

Clinical Tests, p. 96
Diff: M, Type: Applied, Ans: b

56.   A person taking a polygraph test is suspected of lying when measures of physiological
      variables:
      a.   are higher for control than test questions.
      b.   are higher for test than control questions.
      c.   are evenly high for test and control questions.
      d.   are unchanging for test and control questions.

Clinical Tests, p. 96
Diff: E, Type: Applied, Ans: b

57.   A client is hooked up to an apparatus that measures galvanic skin response and blood pressure, after which the client verbally answers a series of questions. The type of clinical test being used is:
        a.   projective.
        b.   psychophysiological.
        c.   neuropsychological.
        d.   affective response inventory.

Clinical Tests, p. 97
Diff: H, Type: Applied, Ans: d

58.   If your friend had her brain waves recorded in order to measure electrical activity, she most likely had a(n):
        a.   PET scan.
        b.   MRI.
        c.   CAT scan.
        d.   EEG.

Clinical Tests, p. 97
Diff: M, Type: Factual, Ans: a

59.   The assessment instrument most likely to be used to detect subtle brain abnormalities is the:
        a.   neuropsychological test.
        b.   intelligence test.
        c.   psychophysiological test.
        d.   projective test.

Clinical Tests, p. 98
Diff: M, Type: Factual, Ans: d

60.   The technique that uses X-rays of the brain taken at different angles to create a static picture of the structure of the brain is called:
        a.   electroencephalography.
        b.   magnetic resonance imaging.
        c.   position emission tomography.
        d.   computerized axial tomography.

Clinical Tests, p. 98
Diff: E, Type: Factual, Ans: c

61.   How does an MRI make a picture of the brain?
        a.   It measures the degree of activity in the various areas scanned.
        b.   It uses X-rays, and pictures are taken at several different angles.
        c.   It relies on the magnetic properties of the atoms in the cells scanned.
        d.   It uses a recording of the electrical impulses produced by the neurons in the brain.

Clinical Tests, p. 98
Diff: H, Type: Factual, Ans: b
62.   If it were necessary to get the clearest and most accurate picture of the physical anatomy of
        the brain in order to aid in the diagnosis of a psychological disorder, the method of choice
        would be:
        a.   MMPI-2.
        b.   MRI.
        c.   DAP.
        d.   PET.

Clinical Tests, p. 98
Diff: H, Type: Factual, Ans: c
63.   Which of the following is not a form of neuroimaging?
        a.   MRI
        b.   CAT scan
        c.   GSR
        d.   PET

Clinical Tests, p. 98
Diff: H, Type: Applied, Ans: b
64.   An 18-year-old completing a neuropsychological test has difficulty remembering and
        drawing some designs. This person is performing at:
        a.   an average level on the Bender-Gestalt.
        b.   a poorer-than-average level on the Bender-Gestalt.
        c.   an average level on the Halstead-Reitan Neuropsychology Battery.
        d.   a poorer-than-average level on the Halstead-Reitan Neuropsychology Battery.

Clinical Tests, p. 98
Diff: E, Type: Factual, Ans: c
65.   When a person has organic brain impairment, that person would most likely have difficulty
        completing the/a:
        a.   CAT scan.
        b.   EEG.
        c.   Bender-Gestalt.
        d.   MRI.

Clinical Tests, p. 98
Diff: M, Type: Factual, Ans: b
66.   Which of the following is most likely to be used to assess *psychological* impairment
        following neurological damage?
        a.   the MMPI-2
        b.   Bender-Gestalt
        c.   magnetic resonance imagery (MRI)
        d.   the response inventory

Clinical Tests, p. 98
Diff: H, Type: Applied, Ans: d

67.   A clinical diagnostician is dissatisfied with tests that cannot specify the type of brain damage or brain impairment clients have. Your best suggestion for that diagnostician would be to use:
      a.   the Bender-Gestalt test.
      b.   the Wechsler Adult Intelligence Scale.
      c.   the Beck Inventory.
      d.   a battery of neuropsychological tests.

Clinical Tests, p. 98
Diff: E, Type: Applied, Ans: c

68.   Binet and Simon are know for their work in creating a:
      a.   projective test.
      b.   personality inventory.
      c.   intelligence test.
      d.   brain scan.

Clinical Tests, p. 98
Diff: H, Type: Applied, Ans: a

69.   A person with a mental age of 10 and a chronological age of 8 has an IQ of:
      a.   125.
      b.   80.
      c.   150.
      d.   40.

Clinical Tests, p. 99
Diff: M, Type: Applied, Ans: b

70.   Which category of clinical tests tends to have the best standardization, reliability, and validity?
      a.   projective tests
      b.   intelligence tests
      c.   response inventories
      d.   neuropsychological tests

Clinical Tests, p. 99
Diff: H, Type: Factual, Ans: d

71.   A strength of intelligence tests include their:
      a.   lack of racial or cultural bias.
      b.   accuracy even when test takers have high anxiety.
      c.   relatively low reliability.
      d.   large standardization sample.

Clinical Tests, p. 99
Diff: M, Type: Applied, Ans: b

72.   The most legitimate criticism of intelligence tests concerns their:
      a.   validity.
      b.   cultural fairness.
      c.   reliability.
      d.   standardization.

Clinical Observations, p. 99
Diff: E, Type: Factual, Ans: d

73.   A therapist's preferred method of assessing abnormal behavior is to watch clients in their everyday environments and record their activities and behaviors. This approach is known as:
   a.   self-monitoring.
   b.   battery observation.
   c.   structured observation.
   d.   naturalistic observation.

Clinical Observations, p. 100
Diff: E, Type: Applied, Ans: a

74.   Under the instructions of a psychologist, Tina's mother records the number of times Tina hits her brother at home, and what happens immediately prior to the hitting. In this situation, Tina's mother is:
   a.   a participant observer.
   b.   demonstrating observer bias.
   c.   conducting structured observations.
   d.   engaging in self-monitoring behavior.

Clinical Observations, p. 100
Diff: M, Type: Factual, Ans: b

75.   A clinician who is using naturalistic observation would be most likely to do which of the following?
   a.   observe parent-child interactions in an office setting
   b.   observe parent child interactions in the family's home
   c.   have a parent self-monitor family interactions in an office setting
   d.   have a parent self-monitor family interactions at home

Clinical Observations, p. 100
Diff: E, Type: Applied, Ans: b

76.   The knowledge that the person a clinician is about to interview has already been diagnosed as having an anxiety disorder could lead to:
   a.   reactivity.
   b.   observer bias.
   c.   observer drift.
   d.   increased accuracy of the diagnosis.

Clinical Observations, p. 100
Diff: H, Type: Applied, Ans: c

77.   One way a clinician might try to reduce observer drift would be to:
   a.   increase the number of different behaviors being monitored.
   b.   try to focus on different aspects of one behavior being monitored.
   c.   decrease the lengths of the observation periods.
   d.   try not to learn too much about a client before making observations.

Clinical Observations, p. 100
Diff: H, Type: Applied, Ans: a

78.   A client reports having infrequent, but extremely disturbing, tactile hallucinations. The most useful of the following ways to gather information about this person would involve:
      a.   self-monitoring.
      b.   naturalistic observations.
      c.   structured observations.
      d.   a neuropsychological battery.

Clinical Observations, p. 100
Diff: H, Type: Applied, Ans: a

79.   While someone is watching, Jennifer actually eats fewer sweets than usual. This tendency to decrease a behavior while being observed is an example of:
      a.   reactivity.
      b.   observer bias.
      c.   observer drift.
      d.   poor reliability.

Clinical Observations, p. 100
Diff: M, Type: Applied, Ans: d

80.   An adult frequently displays symptoms of depression at home, but seldom does so at work. In this case, clinical observations of this person at home would lack:
      a.   observer bias.
      b.   observer drift.
      c.   structure.
      d.   external validity.

Diagnosis: Does the Client's Syndrome Match a Known Disorder?, p. 101
Diff: E, Type: Factual, Ans: c

81.   Deciding that a client's psychological problems represent a particular disorder is called:
      a.   psychotherapy.
      b.   assessment.
      c.   diagnosis.
      d.   triage.

Diagnosis: Does the Client's Syndrome Match a Known Disorder?, p. 101
Diff: E, Type: Factual, Ans: d

82.   The term used to refer to a psychologist's comprehensive view of the causes and stimuli sustaining a person's abnormal behavior is:
      a.   a model.
      b.   a diagnosis.
      c.   an interpretation.
      d.   the clinical picture.

Diagnosis: Does the Client's Syndrome Match a Known Disorder?, p. 101
Diff: M, Type: Factual, Ans: d

83.   Which of the following is an inaccurate belief that many clinicians appear to have?
      a.   Disagreement in diagnoses can often occur and lead to poor reliability.
      b.   Personal biases can influence clinical judgment.
      c.   Clients can consult a therapist even if they do not have a clinical disorder.
      d.   Clinicians using their own logic are more accurate than statistical analyses.

Classification Systems, p. 101
Diff: M, Type: Applied, Ans: c

84. Symptoms such as sadness, loss of appetite, and low energy cluster together to form a:
    a. treatment.
    b. classification system.
    c. syndrome.
    d. medical condition.

Classification Systems, p. 101
Diff: M, Type: Factual, Ans: a

85. A cluster of symptoms that go together and define a mental disorder is called a:
    a. syndrome.
    b. classification system.
    c. DSM axis.
    d. treatment approach.

Classification Systems, p. 102
Diff: E, Type: Factual, Ans: b

86. The *Diagnostic and Statistical Manual of Mental Disorders* (presently DSM-IV-TR) was developed by:
    a. the American Psychoanalytic Association.
    b. the American Psychiatric Association.
    c. the American Psychological Association.
    d. the American Phrenological Association.

Classification Systems, p. 102
Diff: H, Type: Factual, Ans: b

87. DSM-IV-TR is the classification system for abnormal behaviors that is:
    a. used by the World Health Organization.
    b. most widely used in the United States.
    c. used for medical disorders.
    d. used exclusively for children.

Classification Systems, p. 102
Diff: M, Type: Applied, Ans: c

88. The DSM-IV-TR, the most widely used classification system of mental disorders, divides the categories along five separate axes. The Axis I disorders are disorders:
    a. that relate to a person's general level of functioning.
    b. related to physiological ailments from which the person is currently suffering.
    c. that cause significant impairment and that may emerge and end at various points in the life cycle.
    d. that are long-standing and usually begin in childhood or adolescence, persisting in stable form into adult life.

DSM-IV-TR, p. 104
Diff: E, Type: Factual, Ans: b
89. Under what axis do long-standing problems fall in DSM-IV-TR?
   a. Axis III
   b. Axis II
   c. Axis IV
   d. Axis V

DSM-IV-TR, p. 104
Diff: H, Type: Applied, Ans: c
90. A high school bully constantly ignores others' rights, and appears not even to realize that others *do* have rights. A likely DSM-IV-TR partial diagnosis for this bully would be:
   a. a GAF of 60 on Axis II.
   b. a GAF of 60 on Axis III.
   c. antisocial personality disorder on Axis II.
   d. antisocial personality disorder on Axis III.

DSM-IV-TR, p. 104
Diff: E, Type: Factual, Ans: b
91. Mental retardation is found in _____ of DSM-IV-TR.
   a. Axis I
   b. Axis II
   c. Axis III
   d. Axis IV

DSM-IV-TR, p. 104
Diff: E, Type: Factual, Ans: b
92. Axis III includes:
   a. long-standing problems.
   b. any relevant general medical condition.
   c. any relevant psychosocial or environmental problem.
   d. vivid clinical syndromes that typically cause significant impairment.

DSM-IV-TR, p. 104
Diff: H, Type: Applied, Ans: c
93. Racine has recently broken up with her boyfriend and at the same time lost her job. Which axis of DSM-IV-TR would these factors be included under?
   a. Axis II
   b. Axis III
   c. Axis IV
   d. Axis V

DSM-IV-TR, p. 104
Diff: E, Type: Factual, Ans: c
94. Axis IV includes:
   a. any global assessment of functioning.
   b. any relevant general medical condition.
   c. any relevant psychosocial or environmental problem.
   d. vivid clinical syndromes that typically cause significant impairment.

DSM-IV-TR, p. 104
Diff: E, Type: Factual, Ans: a
95.   Altogether, a DSM-IV-TR evaluation might involve diagnoses on a maximum of how many axes?
   a. 5
   b. 6
   c. 7
   d. 8

Is DSM-IV-TR an Effective Classification System?, p. 104
Diff: M, Type: Factual, Ans: a
96.   Dr. Ross and Dr. Carman agree that Suzette if suffering from posttraumatic stress disorder. Their judgment is said to have:
   a. reliability.
   b. generalizability.
   c. external validity.
   d. internal validity.

Is DSM-IV-TR an Effective Classification System?, p. 105
Diff: H, Type: Applied, Ans: d
97.   The greater reliability of the DSM-IV-TR is most likely because of:
   a. its ability to predict the outcome of disorders more accurately.
   b. its greater applicability to minority populations.
   c. its greater reliance on labeling mental disorders.
   d. its field trials of new criteria and categories.

Is DSM-IV-TR an Effective Classification System?, p. 105
Diff: H, Type: Applied, Ans: a
98.   If you received the diagnoses of both social phobia and agoraphobia, your diagnoses would be:
   a. comorbid.
   b. field tested.
   c. more reliable.
   d. valid only if you were an adolescent.

Is DSM-IV-TR an Effective Classification System?, p. 105
Diff: M, Type: Factual, Ans: d
99.   What kind of validity is most important to clinicians in evaluating the utility of a classification system?
   a. face validity
   b. internal validity
   c. external validity
   d. predictive validity

Is DSM-IV-TR an Effective Classification System?, p. 106
Diff: H, Type: Applied, Ans: b
100.   The concept of "negative affect" is an example of a:
   a. discrete diagnostic category.
   b. dimension of functioning.
   c. specific diagnosis.
   d. field tested category.

Can Diagnosis and Labeling Cause Harm?, p. 107
Diff: H, Type: Applied, Ans: d
101.   An institutionalized individual behaving abnormally says, "The doctor claims I'm schizophrenic! How *else* would you expect me to act?" The individual's comments reflect:
    a.   misdiagnosis.
    b.   reading-in-syndrome.
    c.   a misunderstanding of multiaxial diagnosis.
    d.   self-fulfilling prophesy.

Can Diagnosis and Labeling Cause Harm?, p. 107
Diff: M, Type: Factual, Ans: b
102.   Studies of diagnostic conclusions made by clinicians show that:
    a.   they overemphasis information gathered early in the assessment process.
    b.   they pay too much attention to some information and too little to other information.
    c.   they don't allow enough of their own expectations to enter into the decision.
    d.   they do not allow their own biases to play a role in their decisions.

Treatment Decisions, p. 108
Diff: M, Type: Factual, Ans: b
103.   Studies show that most therapists these days are *most* likely to learn about the latest information on treatment of psychological disorders from:
    a.   reading research articles.
    b.   talking with professional colleagues.
    c.   conducting their own research.
    d.   writing grants.

Treatment Decisions, p. 108
Diff: M, Type: Factual, Ans: c
104.   Therapies that have received clear research support are called:
    a.   meta-analyses.
    b.   idiographic.
    c.   evidence-based.
    d.   outcome complex.

The Effectiveness of Treatment, p. 109
Diff: M, Type: Factual, Ans: c
105.   The initial problem in studying the effectiveness of psychotherapy is:
    a.   defining what the treatment is.
    b.   the range and complexity of treatments available.
    c.   defining what it means for a treatment to be successful.
    d.   deciding how to measure improvement, whether to use self-report, behavioral observations, rating scales, or something else.

The Effectiveness of Treatment, p. 110
Diff: H, Type: Applied, Ans: b
106.   If you ask the question, "What type of therapy has been shown to be the most effective for my particular disorder?" you are asking a question about:
    a.   diagnosis reliability studies.
    b.   therapy outcome studies.
    c.   classification syndrome studies.
    d.   ethics of treatment studies.

The Effectiveness of Treatment, p. 110
Diff: M, Type: Factual, Ans: d
107.   Standardizing and combining the findings of many different studies is called:
    a.   outcome study.
    b.   rapprochement.
    c.   eclecticism.
    d.   meta-analysis.

The Effectiveness of Treatment, p. 110
Diff: M, Type: Factual, Ans: a
108.   In order to study the general effectiveness of treatment, Smith and Glass and their colleagues performed:
    a.   a meta-analysis of many studies.
    b.   an analysis of their clinical cases.
    c.   a survey of many clients who had received therapy.
    d.   a controlled study that involved random assignment of subjects to treatment conditions.

The Effectiveness of Treatment, p. 110
Diff: H, Type: Applied, Ans: c
109.   Freud's view of therapy was that it could:
    a.   never be harmful.
    b.   be harmful only if drugs were used.
    c.   not be helpful if it could not also be harmful.
    d.   only be harmful if a behavioral model was used.

The Effectiveness of Treatment, p. 110
Diff: H, Type: Applied, Ans: b
110.   "You know, it really doesn't matter. One kind of psychotherapy is generally just about as good as any other." One who agrees with this statement is:
    a.   making an accurate statement about what we know about psychotherapy.
    b.   falling victim to the uniformity myth.
    c.   accurately reflecting the findings of most meta-analyses.
    d.   failing to notice therapeutic rapprochement.

The Effectiveness of Treatment, p. 110
Diff: H, Type: Factual, Ans: c
111.   The movement that has tried to find the common strategies that effective therapists use is called:
    a.   uniformity.
    b.   particularity.
    c.   rapprochement.
    d.   idiosyncatics.

The Effectiveness of Treatment, p. 110
Diff: H, Type: Applied, Ans: d
112.   Therapy outcome studies show all of the following except:
    a.   people in therapy are generally better off than people with similar problems who receive no therapy.
    b.   the various therapies do not appear to differ dramatically in their effectiveness.
    c.   certain therapies appear to be more effective than other therapies for certain disorders.
    d.   most people report that therapy doesn't help them much, despite the fact that it does.

The Effectiveness of Treatment, p. 111
Diff: H, Type: Applied, Ans: c

113. Which of the following would be most likely to have been in therapy at some point in their lives?
    a. men with a high school education
    b. elderly people from the Northeast
    c. women with a postgraduate education
    d. young adults from the South

The Effectiveness of Treatment, p. 111
Diff: H, Type: Applied, Ans: d

114. Which of the following dimensions appears to be most related to the likelihood of receiving therapy?
    a. age
    b. gender
    c. region of the country
    d. education

The Effectiveness of Treatment, p. 111
Diff: M, Type: Applied, Ans: a

115. The most effective treatment for phobias is:
    a. behavioral therapy.
    b. drug therapy.
    c. a combination of humanistic and existential therapies.
    d. psychodynamic therapy.

The Effectiveness of Treatment, p. 111
Diff: M, Type: Factual, Ans: a

116. The single most effective treatment for schizophrenia is:
    a. drug therapy.
    b. behavior therapy.
    c. psychoanalysis.
    d. existential therapy.

The Effectiveness of Treatment, p. 111
Diff: E, Type: Factual, Ans: b

117. A person who primarily prescribes medication but does not conduct psychotherapy is called a:
    a. pharmacist.
    b. psychopharmacologist.
    c. clinical psychologist.
    d. family practice nurse.

The Effectiveness of Treatment, pp. 111-112
Diff: H, Type: Applied, Ans: a

118.   If a graph shows the years of the twentieth century along the horizontal axis, and confidence
in assessment of abnormality—from low confidence to high confidence—going up the
vertical axis, then confidence in assessment of abnormality over the past 50 years would be
a(n):
   a.   "U"-shaped function—high, then low, then high.
   b.   inverted "∩"-shaped function—low, then high, then low.
   c.   decreasing linear function (\)—steadily decreasing confidence.
   d.   increasing linear function (/)—steadily increasing confidence.

Putting It Together, p. 111
Diff: H, Type: Applied, Ans: b

119.   Which of the following is the best conclusion you could draw about the effectiveness of the
various assessment techniques?
   a.   There is one standard assessment battery used by all clinicians.
   b.   When all is said and done, no technique stands out as superior.
   c.   Clinicians have abandoned the use of assessment.
   d.   Assessment is used at the beginning of therapy but not thereafter.

Putting It Together, p. 112
Diff: M, Type: Applied, Ans: c

120.   Which of the following factors leads to increased respect for assessment and diagnosis?
   a.   the ability to identify disorders without assessment
   b.   more global and less precise DSM-IV-TR categories
   c.   increased assessment research
   d.   decreased emphasis on clinical studies involving "real" patients

Putting It Together, p. 112
Diff: H, Type: Applied, Ans: d

121.   The biggest social threat to the use of comprehensive assessment techniques today is:
   a.   concern about the cultural bias in tests.
   b.   concern about the gender bias in tests.
   c.   concern about low reliability and validity.
   d.   concern about cost—expressed by managed care companies.

FILL-IN QUESTIONS

Clinical Assessment, Diagnosis, and Treatment, p. 85
Diff: E, Type: Factual, Ans: nomothetic

1.   A researcher seeks information with which to generalize about abnormal functioning. This
approach to abnormal behavior is called _____.

Clinical Assessment, Diagnosis, and Treatment, p. 85
Diff: E, Type: Applied, Ans: idiographic

2.   A therapist evaluates a client prior to beginning therapy by compiling detailed information
about that individual. This approach is called _____.

Clinical Assessment: How and Why Does the Client Behave Abnormally?, p. 86
Diff: E, Type: Factual, Ans: functional

3.   An analysis of how a person's behaviors are learned and reinforced is called a(n) _____ analysis.

Clinical Assessment: How and Why Does the Client Behave Abnormally?, p. 86
Diff: M, Type: Factual, Ans: behavioral or cognitive

4.   The most likely theoretical orientation of a clinician who performs a functional analysis of a patient is _____.

Characteristics of Assessment Tools, p. 86
Diff: E, Type: Factual, Ans: reliability

5.   A test that has a high degree of consistency is said to have good _____.

Characteristics of Assessment Tools, p. 86
Diff: E, Type: Factual, Ans: reliability

6.   If an examiner administered the same test now and in a week and correlated the results, a low correlation coefficient would indicate poor _____ for the test.

Characteristics of Assessment Tools, p. 87
Diff: H, Type: Applied, Ans: concurrent

7.   If a test result indicates anxiety and there are also reports of anxiety from spouse, parents, and co-workers, that test shows _____ validity.

Clinical Interviews, p. 88
Diff: E, Type: Factual, Ans: structured

8.   A clinician who uses a published interview schedule is conducting a _____ interview.

Clinical Tests, p. 89
Diff: E, Type: Factual, Ans: projective test

9.   An assessment tool that consists of unstructured or ambiguous material to which people are asked to respond is called a(n) _____.

Clinical Tests, p. 90
Diff: M, Type: Factual, Ans: Thematic Apperception Test

10.   A projective test that requires the client to describe what is happening in the scene portrayed in a vague picture is the _____.

Clinical Tests, p. 93
Diff: E, Type: Applied, Ans: MMPI (or MMPI-2)

11.   A client has just responded true or false to several hundred statements that may or may not apply to her (e.g., "I certainly feel useless much of the time"). Minutes later, she receives a profile sheet that evaluates her on 10 clinical scales, including hypochondriasis, depression and psychopathic deviation. She has completed the _____.

Clinical Tests, p. 97
Diff: E, Type: Factual, Ans: electroencephalography (or EEG)

12.   The technique that records brain waves through the patient's scalp is _____.

Clinical Tests, p. 98
Diff: H, Type: Factual, Ans: neuroimaging

13. The method of assessing brain structure that involves taking pictures of brain structure and activity is _____.

Clinical Tests, p. 98
Diff: M, Type: Factual, Ans: magnetic resonance imaging (or MRI)

14. A person lies on a machine that creates a magnetic field around his head, exciting hydrogen atoms in the brain. The signals given off by these atoms are converted into a detailed picture of the brain. This procedure is called _____.

Clinical Observations, p. 100
Diff: E, Type: Factual, Ans: naturalistic observation

15. The assessment technique in which clinicians observe clients in their everyday environment, such as a school or home, is called _____.

Clinical Observations, p. 100
Diff: M, Type: Factual, Ans: overload

16. The inability to see or record all important behavior when making observations is called _____.

Clinical Observations, p. 100
Diff: M, Type: Factual, Ans: observer drift

17. During clinical observation, the observer becomes fatigued or changes the criteria that they have been using. This problem is known as _____.

Clinical Observations, p. 100
Diff: M, Type: Factual, Ans: observer bias

18. A disadvantage of using clinical observation to assess clients' behavior is that the clinician may be influenced by information and expectations that he or she already has about the client. This problem is known as _____.

Clinical Observations, p. 100
Diff: E, Type: Factual, Ans: self-monitoring

19. A clinician asks one of his patients to record the frequency of his hallucinations and the circumstances under which they occur. This technique is called _____.

Diagnosis: Does the Client's Syndrome Match a Known Disorder?, p. 101
Diff: E, Type: Factual, Ans: diagnosis

20. The clinician uses the interpreted assessment information to arrive at a technical description of a disorder called a _____.

DSM-IV-TR, p. 104
Diff: E, Type: Factual, Ans: reliability (or interrater reliability)

21. Developers of DSM-IV-TR hope that the categories they have chosen to include allow different clinicians to develop the same diagnosis for the same condition. That is, they hope they have a system with high _____.

The Effectiveness of Treatment, p. 111, Figure 4-7
Diff: H, Type: Factual, Ans: higher

22. People with _____ levels of education are more likely to receive therapy.

ESSAY QUESTIONS

Clinical Interviews, p. 87ff
Diff: M, Type: Applied

1.   If you had only 15 minutes to conduct a preliminary clinical interview, what information would you be sure to try to get, and why?

Clinical Tests, p. 90ff
Diff: H, Type: Applied

2.   Assume you had to do a clinical assessment, and the only tests you had available to you were the Rorschach Test, the Thematic Apperception Test, and The Minnesota Multiphasic Personality Inventory. Which *two* would you use, and why? What would be the strengths and weaknesses of the two tests you chose?

Clinical Tests, pp. 90, 93
Diff: M, Type: Factual

3.   Your choice: Please describe in detail either the MMPI-2 or the TAT, being sure to categorize the test of your choice, and describe its strengths, weaknesses, and applications.

Clinical Tests, p. 92, Table 4.1
Diff: H, Type: Applied

4.   Describe the potential negative impact on assessment and/or diagnosis of the following: ethnic minority client, immigrant client, and any particular classification system.

Clinical Tests, p. 96
Diff: M, Type: Factual

5.   Please distinguish between neurological tests and neuropsychological tests, giving examples of each, and describing in general how each type of test is used diagnostically.

Clinical Tests, p. 99
Diff: E, Type: Factual

6.   List and describe three important shortcomings of modern intelligence tests.

Clinical Observations, p. 103ff
Diff: H, Type: Factual

7.   Differentiate among naturalistic observation, analog observation, and self-monitoring. Be sure to indicate under what conditions each technique would work best.

DSM-IV-TR, p. 103
Diff: M, Type: Factual

8.   What are the important characteristics of DSM-IV-TR? Please be sure to include in your answer a description of its multiaxial form.

Can Diagnosis and Labeling Cause Harm?, p. 107
Diff: H, Type: Applied

9.   Despite the fact that using diagnostic labels for psychological disorders is extremely common, what are some ethical factors one ought to consider in the use of diagnostic labels?

The Effectiveness of Treatment, p. 110
Diff: H, Type: Factual

10.   Provide evidence that psychotherapy is effective. What elements need to be present for effectiveness?

Putting It Together, p. 111
Diff: H, Type: Applied

11.   What are the weaknesses in assessment? What can be done to address these weaknesses? Be sure to address reliability, validity, and bias issues.

CHAPTER 5   Anxiety Disorders

MULTIPLE-CHOICE QUESTIONS

Anxiety Disorders, p. 115
Diff: M, Type: Factual, Ans: a
1. Fear differs from anxiety in that:
    a. fear is to a specific threat and anxiety is more general.
    b. anxiety is more likely to lead to aggression than is fear.
    c. anxiety is to an interpersonal threat and fear is to an inanimate threat.
    d. anxiety is an immediate response; fear is more vague.

Anxiety Disorders, p. 116
Diff: E, Type: Factual, Ans: b
2. Anxiety disorders differ from everyday experiences of fear and anxiety in:
    a. severity.
    b. duration.
    c. that they have an adaptive function.
    d. that they are more unpleasant.

Anxiety Disorders, p. 116
Diff: M, Type: Factual, Ans: b
3. The most common mental disorders in the United States are the:
    a. mood disorders.
    b. anxiety disorders.
    c. personality disorders.
    d. sexual disorders.

Anxiety Disorders, p. 116
Diff: M, Type: Applied, Ans: d
4. A college student who is so anxious that he can't function unless his clothes are arranged by color and type in his closet is experiencing:
    a. a generalized anxiety disorder.
    b. a phobia.
    c. a panic disorder.
    d. an obsessive-compulsive disorder.

Anxiety Disorders, p. 116
Diff: M, Type: Applied, Ans: c

5.   A person who frequently experiences terror attacks, and goes to the emergency room complaining of shortness of breath, rapid heart rate, and feelings of impending death, although nothing is medically wrong is experiencing:
      a.   a generalized anxiety disorder.
      b.   a phobia.
      c.   a panic disorder.
      d.   an obsessive-compulsive disorder.

Anxiety Disorders, p. 116
Diff: H, Type: Applied, Ans: d

6.   A professor who becomes anxious unless students sit in alphabetical order, turn in their papers in alphabetical order, and leave tests in that same order is experiencing:
      a.   a generalized anxiety disorder.
      b.   a phobia.
      c.   a panic disorder.
      d.   an obsessive-compulsive disorder.

Anxiety Disorders, p. 116
Diff: M, Type: Applied, Ans: a

7.   A person who constantly feels upset and nervous, so much so that it interferes with work is experiencing:
      a.   a generalized anxiety disorder.
      b.   a phobia.
      c.   a panic disorder.
      d.   an obsessive-compulsive disorder.

Anxiety Disorders, p. 116
Diff: H, Type: Applied, Ans: b

8.   College students who always become so anxious when taking a test that they cannot remember even simple things that they know quite well are experiencing:
      a.   a generalized anxiety disorder.
      b.   a phobia.
      c.   a panic disorder.
      d.   an obsessive-compulsive disorder.

Anxiety Disorders, p. 116
Diff: E, Type: Factual, Ans: b

9.   A lasting and groundless fear of a specific object, activity, or situation is called:
      a.   a panic disorder.
      b.   a phobia.
      c.   a generalized anxiety disorder.
      d.   an obsessive-compulsive disorder.

Anxiety Disorders, p. 116
Diff: E, Type: Factual, Ans: d

10.   Which of the following is an anxiety disorder?
   a. schizophrenia
   b. bipolar disorder
   c. major depression
   d. obsessive-compulsive disorder

Anxiety Disorders, p. 116
Diff: M, Type: Applied, Ans: d

11.   Max is upset because he cannot stop thinking that he has forgotten something and is
       constantly going back to his apartment to check. It is interfering with his life because he does
       it so often. This behavior is an example of:
   a. panic disorder.
   b. phobic disorder.
   c. generalized anxiety disorder.
   d. obsessive-compulsive disorder.

Anxiety Disorders, p. 116
Diff: M, Type: Applied, Ans: a

12.   Every once in a while, Ona feels nervous to the point of terror. It seems to come on suddenly
       and randomly. Her experience is an example of:
   a. panic disorder.
   b. phobic disorder.
   c. generalized anxiety disorder.
   d. obsessive-compulsive disorder.

Anxiety Disorders, p. 116
Diff: M, Type: Applied, Ans: d

13.   Raphael was just outside the parking garage of the World Trade Center when the explosion
       occurred. At the time he was terrified and had visions of the building falling on him. Ever
       since the bombing he has had periods of anxiety and sleeplessness. This is an example of a:
   a. panic disorder.
   b. phobic disorder.
   c. generalized anxiety disorder.
   d. posttraumatic stress disorder.

Anxiety Disorders, p. 116
Diff: H, Type: Applied, Ans: a

14.   Leila always feels threatened and anxious—imagining something awful is about to happen.
       But she is able to work and care for her family, although not as well as she would like. Leila
       is probably experiencing:
   a. generalized anxiety disorder.
   b. a hormonal imbalance.
   c. no specific problem; she just likes to worry.
   d. a specific fear response.

Anxiety Disorders, p. 116
Diff: E, Type: Factual, Ans: a
15. People with one anxiety disorder are most likely to:
     a. experience another anxiety disorder, too.
     b. experience only that one anxiety disorder.
     c. experience another nonanxiety disorder.
     d. experience hallucinations.

Generalized Anxiety Disorder, p. 116
Diff: H, Type: Applied, Ans: a
16. A person who is restless, keyed up, and on edge for no apparent reason is experiencing:
     a. free-floating anxiety.
     b. specific anxiety.
     c. fearful anxiety.
     d. obsessions.

The Sociocultural Perspective, p. 117
Diff: M, Type: Applied, Ans: a
17. Someone interested in the effects of social change, poverty, and race on the risk for
     generalized anxiety disorders probably represents the _____ perspective.
     a. sociocultural
     b. psychodynamic
     c. humanistic-existential
     d. cognitive

The Sociocultural Perspective, p. 117
Diff: H, Type: Applied, Ans: c
18. "Who wouldn't be afraid all the time? We have the bomb, overpopulation, AIDS, and violent
     crime everywhere. It is difficult to get a good job unless you understand all that complicated
     computer junk." This complaint is consistent with a _____ explanation of generalized
     anxiety disorder.
     a. behavioral
     b. humanistic
     c. sociocultural
     d. psychodynamic

The Sociocultural Perspective, p. 117
Diff: M, Type: Factual, Ans: a
19. Generalized anxiety disorder is more common:
     a. in African-Americans than in white Americans.
     b. in men than in women.
     c. years after rather than immediately after traumatic events.
     d. in wealthy people than in poor people.

The Sociocultural Perspective, p. 117
Diff: H, Type: Factual, Ans: c

20. One limitation of the sociocultural approach to understanding generalized anxiety disorders is that:
    a. it cannot explain the paradox that as poverty gets worse, generalized anxiety declines.
    b. it cannot explain the relationship between race, poverty, and job opportunity.
    c. it cannot explain why everyone who experiences danger doesn't experience generalized anxiety.
    d. it cannot explain the differences in generalized anxiety in countries around the world.

The Psychodynamic Perspective, p. 117
Diff: H, Type: Applied, Ans: b

21. According to Freud, children who are prevented from expressing id impulses—making mud pies, playing war, and exploring their genitals—are at risk for developing:
    a. realistic anxiety.
    b. neurotic anxiety.
    c. moral anxiety.
    d. existential anxiety.

The Psychodynamic Perspective, p. 117
Diff: M, Type: Factual, Ans: d

22. Which theoretical position explains the origin of anxiety disorders as the overrun of defense mechanisms by neurotic or moral anxiety?
    a. the behavioral approach
    b. the humanistic approach
    c. the sociocultural approach
    d. the psychodynamic approach

The Psychodynamic Perspective, p. 117
Diff: H, Type: Factual, Ans: c

23. According to Freud, children who are severely and repeatedly punished for expressing their id impulses may develop:
    a. realistic anxiety.
    b. neurotic anxiety.
    c. moral anxiety.
    d. existential anxiety.

The Psychodynamic Perspective, p. 117
Diff: H, Type: Factual, Ans: b

24. According to Freud, generalized anxiety disorder is most likely to result when:
    a. a person does not dream, and thus has no outlet for anxiety.
    b. defense mechanisms are too weak to cope with anxiety.
    c. a person never has a chance to experience trauma.
    d. defense mechanisms are too strong.

The Psychodynamic Perspective, p. 119
Diff: H, Type: Factual, Ans: a
25.   Which of the following is least consistent with a psychodynamic explanation for the development of generalized anxiety?
      a.   People with generalized anxiety did not have excessive discipline or disturbed environments as children.
      b.   People with generalized anxiety tend to use repression and denial when asked to discuss their problems.
      c.   People with generalized anxiety had parents who were particularly protective of them as children.
      d.   People with generalized anxiety have difficulty remembering fear-arousing events they have experienced.

The Psychodynamic Perspective, p. 119
Diff: M, Type: Factual, Ans: b
26.   Psychodynamic theorists would predict that high levels of anxiety in adulthood would be positively related to earlier:
      a.   low levels of punishment or threat by parents during childhood.
      b.   extreme protectiveness by parents during childhood.
      c.   inability to forget unsettling experiences.
      d.   encouragement to express id impulses.

The Psychodynamic Perspective, p. 119
Diff: M, Type: Factual, Ans: b
27.   Object relations therapists:
      a.   use flooding to prompt patients to reexperience traumatic events.
      b.   use psychodynamic techniques to help patients work through childhood trauma.
      c.   use cognitive therapy to help patients identify their maladaptive patterns of thinking.
      d.   use sociocultural analysis of one's environment to understand generalized anxiety.

The Humanistic Perspective, p. 119
Diff: M, Type: Factual, Ans: d
28.   "Phobic and generalized anxiety disorders arise when people stop looking at themselves honestly and with acceptance and instead deny and distort their true thoughts, emotions, and behavior." This explanation for anxiety disorders would most likely be offered by:
      a.   behaviorists.
      b.   cognitive theorists.
      c.   sociocultural theorists.
      d.   humanistic theorists.

The Humanistic Perspective, p. 119
Diff: H, Type: Applied, Ans: c
29.   If you criticized everything you did, looking for flaws, and never could measure up to your personal standards, you would be exhibiting what Rogers called:
      a.   empathy.
      b.   unconditioned positive regard.
      c.   conditions of worth.
      d.   moral anxiety.

The Humanistic Perspective, p. 119
Diff: E, Type: Factual, Ans: c
30.   Which theory states that people develop generalized anxiety disorders because they failed to receive unconditional positive regard as children and evaluate themselves with conditions of worth?
    a.   Pavlov's conditioning theory
    b.   Freud's psychoanalytic theory
    c.   Rogers's client-centered theory
    d.   Ellis's rational-emotive theory

The Humanistic Perspective, p. 119
Diff: M, Type: Factual, Ans: d
31.   Which of the following is not an appropriate match?
    a.   Beck and cognitive therapy
    b.   Meichenbaum and stress inoculation training
    c.   Ellis and rational-emotive therapy
    d.   Rogers and sociocultural therapy

The Humanistic Perspective, p. 119
Diff: H, Type: Factual, Ans: d
32.   Using traditional research studies, which of the following has been shown to be a highly effective long-term treatment for generalized anxiety?
    a.   object relations therapy
    b.   client-centered therapy
    c.   Freudian psychoanalysis
    d.   antidepressant medication

The Humanistic Perspective, p. 120
Diff: H, Type: Factual, Ans: b
33.   Psychodynamic and humanistic therapies have in common:
    a.   their understanding of how generalized anxiety develops and can be treated.
    b.   their lack of strong support from controlled studies.
    c.   their reliance on a rather harsh, confrontational therapeutic style.
    d.   their use of multidisciplinary therapists who work exclusively in group settings.

The Cognitive Perspective, p. 120
Diff: H, Type: Applied, Ans: b
34.   If I believe that it is a dire necessity for me to be loved or approved by everyone and that it is catastrophic if things are not the way I want them, I am displaying basic:
    a.   existential anxiety.
    b.   irrational assumptions.
    c.   moral anxiety.
    d.   conditions of worth.

The Cognitive Perspective, p. 120
Diff: H, Type: Applied, Ans: b
35. A person who believes that it is awful and catastrophic when things are not the way he or she would like them to be is displaying:
    a. metaworry.
    b. irrational assumption.
    c. compulsion.
    d. condition of worth.

The Cognitive Perspective, p. 120
Diff: H, Type: Applied, Ans: b
36. A person who believes that one should be thoroughly competent, adequate, and achieving in all possible respects is displaying:
    a. metaworry.
    b. irrational assumption.
    c. compulsion.
    d. condition of worth.

The Cognitive Perspective, p. 120
Diff: H, Type: Factual, Ans: a
37. Cognitive therapists believe that generalized anxiety disorder is induced by:
    a. maladaptive assumptions.
    b. lack of empathy.
    c. interpersonal loss.
    d. overactive id impulses.

The Cognitive Perspective, p. 121
Diff: H, Type: Factual, Ans: c
38. Research on the cognitive explanation for the development of generalized anxiety shows that people with generalized anxiety symptoms:
    a. respond more fearfully to predictable than to unpredictable events.
    b. fail to pay attention to threatening cues.
    c. overestimate their chances of being harmed.
    d. show little physiological arousal to stress.

The Cognitive Perspective, p. 121
Diff: E, Type: Factual, Ans: d
39. Cognitive researchers have found that lives full of anxiety most often are associated with:
    a. predictable positive events.
    b. unpredictable positive events.
    c. predictable negative events.
    d. unpredictable negative events.

The Cognitive Perspective, p. 122
Diff: H, Type: Applied, Ans: d
40. Which of the following is an example of a metaworry?
    a. worry about all possible signs of danger
    b. worrying about not worrying enough
    c. thinking about worrying
    d. worrying about worrying

The Cognitive Perspective, p. 122
Diff: H, Type: Applied, Ans: a

41. Of the following, the best description of the "avoidance theory of generalized anxiety disorder" is:
    a. worrying serves to reduce bodily arousal.
    b. worrying interferes with our ability to cope with life.
    c. worrying keeps the focus on emotions, not cognitions.
    d. worrying is an uncontrollable part of life.

The Cognitive Perspective, p. 123
Diff: H, Type: Applied, Ans: c

42   If your therapist gave you homework that required you to challenge your faulty assumptions and replace them with healthier ones, the therapist would be using:
    a. cognitive-existential therapy.
    b. client-centered therapy.
    c. rational-emotive therapy.
    d. interpersonal-physiotherapy.

The Cognitive Perspective, p. 123
Diff: E, Type: Factual, Ans: b

43. The therapy for generalized anxiety disorder developed by Albert Ellis is called:
    a. behavior modification.
    b. rational-emotive therapy.
    c. self-instruction training.
    d. stress inoculation training.

The Cognitive Perspective, p. 123
Diff: M, Type: Factual, Ans: b

44. The therapist who developed a cognitive therapy for anxiety disorders that is based on his therapy for depression is:
    a. Albert Ellis.
    b. Aaron Beck.
    c. Joseph Wolpe.
    d. Donald Meichenbaum.

The Biological Perspective, p. 124
Diff: M, Type: Factual, Ans: c

45. Until recently, the evidence that generalized anxiety disorder is related to biological factors came largely from:
    a. drug studies.
    b. clinical interviews.
    c. family pedigree studies.
    d. neurological studies.

The Biological Perspective, p. 124
Diff: H, Type: Applied, Ans: a
46. Evidence in support of the biological understanding of generalized anxiety is supported by the finding that:
    a. relatives of people with generalized anxiety are more likely to have it than nonrelatives.
    b. distant relatives of those with generalized anxiety are more likely to have it than close relatives.
    c. relatives share not only biological characteristics, but also similar environments.
    d. identical twins have more similar environments than fraternal twins.

The Biological Perspective, p. 124
Diff: M, Type: Factual, Ans: a
47. Benzodiazepines are believed to be effective in treating generalized anxiety disorder because they mimic the effect of _____ at certain receptor sites in the limbic system and hypothalamus.
    a. GABA
    b. dopamine
    c. acetylcholine
    d. serotonin

The Biological Perspective, p. 124
Diff: M, Type: Factual, Ans: d
48. GABA, an inhibitory neurotransmitter believed to be involved in reducing the excitability of neurons in the limbic system, has been implicated in the etiology of:
    a. schizophrenia.
    b. panic disorder.
    c. conversion disorder.
    d. generalized anxiety disorder.

The Biological Perspective, p. 125
Diff: H, Type: Factual, Ans: d
49. GABA is related to:
    a. increased neuronal firing in the brain.
    b. doubling the speed of neuronal firing.
    c. intensifying the strength of neuronal firing.
    d. inhibiting neuronal firing in the brain.

The Biological Perspective, p. 125
Diff: H, Type: Applied, Ans: a
50. Which of the following statements is most accurate?
    a. Long-term anxiety is related to poor GABA reception.
    b. Long-term anxiety causes poor GABA reception.
    c. Poor GABA reception causes long-term anxiety.
    d. Neurotransmitter deficiencies cause long-term anxiety and poor GABA reception.

The Biological Perspective, p. 125
Diff: H, Type: Applied, Ans: b
51. If you wanted a drug to improve the functioning of GABA, you would choose:
   a.   a drug that increases neuronal firing speed.
   b.   a benzodiazepine.
   c.   any of the antidepressants.
   d.   a drug that works on the endocrine level rather than neuron level.

The Biological Perspective, p. 125
Diff: M, Type: Factual, Ans: b
52. All of the following are biological treatments for generalized anxiety except:
   a.   antianxiety drugs.
   b.   rational emotive therapy.
   c.   relaxation training.
   d.   biofeedback.

The Biological Perspective, p. 126
Diff: H, Type: Applied, Ans: c
53. If your friend asks you which of the following medications would be best to treat generalized anxiety disorder, you should say:
   a.   an antipsychotic.
   b.   an anti-GAMA drug.
   c.   an antidepressant.
   d.   an antiemetic.

The Biological Perspective, p. 126
Diff: H, Type: Factual, Ans: a
54. Disadvantages of taking benzodiazepines include all of the following except:
   a.   lack of sleep, increased anxiety, and passivity.
   b.   return of anxiety symptoms when the medication is withdrawn.
   c.   impairment in cognitive and psychomotor functioning.
   d.   physical dependence on the drug.

The Biological Perspective, p. 126
Diff: E, Type: Factual, Ans: b
55. Which of the following is a nondrug biological treatment for anxiety that is in general use today?
   a.   psychoanalysis
   b.   relaxation therapy
   c.   behavior modification
   d.   rational-emotive therapy

The Biological Perspective, p. 126
Diff: E, Type: Applied, Ans: c
56. "Please flex your biceps. Now release your biceps. Now flex your thigh. Now release it." These statements might be made by a therapist using:
   a.   biofeedback training.
   b.   EEG training.
   c.   relaxation therapy.
   d.   self-instruction therapy.

The Biological Perspective, p. 126
Diff: E, Type: Applied, Ans: a
57. Devon is being treated for anxiety. He is connected to an instrument that records muscle tension. His job is to try to reduce muscle tension. This is an example of:
    a. biofeedback training.
    b. EMG training.
    c. relaxation training.
    d. self-instruction training.

The Biological Perspective, p. 127
Diff: M, Type: Applied, Ans: b
58. A friend asks you whether to try relaxation training or biofeedback to reduce anxiety. Based upon present research, your best answer is:
    a. "Try something else; neither one works very well."
    b. "Try either one; they're both modestly effective."
    c. "Try relaxation training; biofeedback doesn't work."
    d. "Try biofeedback; relaxation doesn't work."

Phobias, p. 127
Diff: E, Type: Factual, Ans: b
59. An intense, persistent, and irrational fear that is accompanied by a compelling desire to avoid the object of the fear to the point of interfering with the life of the person is called:
    a. panic disorder.
    b. phobic disorder.
    c. obsessive-compulsive disorder.
    d. generalized anxiety disorder.

Phobias, p. 127
Diff: H, Type: Applied, Ans: d
60. How do phobias and common fear differ?
    a. A fear more dramatically interferes with one's life.
    b. A phobia is less intense.
    c. A fear lasts longer.
    d. A phobia leads to a greater desire to avoid the object.

Specific Phobias, p. 127
Diff: E, Type: Applied, Ans: d
61. Karla's phobia about small insects is:
    a. acrophobia.
    b. agoraphobia.
    c. social phobia.
    d. specific phobia.

Specific Phobias, p. 128
Diff: M, Type: Factual, Ans: a
62. Which of the following is true about specific phobias?
    a. Each year about 9% of people in the United States suffer from a phobia.
    b. Men are more likely than women to have phobias.
    c. There do not appear to be racial differences in the incidence of phobias.
    d. Most people with phobias seek treatment.

Specific Phobias, p. 128
Diff: H, Type: Applied, Ans: a

63.   Steve is afraid of eating in public, expecting to be judged negatively and to feel humiliated. As a result, he always makes up excuses when asked out to eat. He would most likely be diagnosed with:
   a.   a social phobia.
   b.   a specific phobia.
   c.   generalized anxiety disorder.
   d.   posttraumatic stress disorder.

Specific Phobias, p. 128
Diff: M, Type: Factual, Ans: b

64.   Of the following, those least likely to experience specific phobias are:
   a.   white American females.
   b.   white American males.
   c.   Hispanic American females.
   d.   Hispanic American males.

Social Phobias, p. 128
Diff: H, Type: Applied, Ans: a

65.   Which of the following is an example of a narrow social phobia?
   a.   fear of public speaking
   b.   fear of snakes
   c.   fear of tornados when a tornado warning is in effect
   d.   fear of generally functioning poorly in front of others

What Causes Phobias?, p. 129
Diff: E, Type: Factual, Ans: c

66.   Which theoretical position explains the origin of phobias as due to classical conditioning?
   a.   biological
   b.   sociocultural
   c.   behavioral
   d.   psychodynamic

What Causes Phobias?, p. 129
Diff: M, Type: Applied, Ans: c

67.   When he was five years old, Samir was almost struck by lightning while walking through a forest during a rainstorm. Today, he is extremely afraid of trees. A behaviorist would say that he has acquired this fear by:
   a.   operant conditioning.
   b.   modeling and imitation.
   c.   classical conditioning.
   d.   stimulus generalization.

What Causes Phobias?, p. 129
Diff: M, Type: Applied, Ans: a

68.   While walking through a forest during a rainstorm, 5-year-old Samir was almost struck by lightning. Today, as an adult, he is extremely afraid of trees. What is the conditioned stimulus in the example?
    a.   the trees
    b.   the lightning
    c.   the rain storm
    d.   the feelings of fear

What Causes Phobias?, p. 129
Diff: E, Type: Applied, Ans: a

69.   Davon watched his father recoil from a snake in fear. Now he is afraid of snakes. This apparent acquisition of fear of snakes is an example of:
    a.   modeling.
    b.   response discrimination.
    c.   escape response.
    d.   stimulus generalization.

What Causes Phobias?, p. 131
Diff: M, Type: Factual, Ans: b

70.   According to behavioral theory, specific learned fears become a generalized anxiety disorder through the process of:
    a.   modeling.
    b.   stimulus generalization.
    c.   stimulus discrimination.
    d.   response prevention.

What Causes Phobias?, p. 131
Diff: E, Type: Applied, Ans: c

71.   Little Karen was bitten by a tan pony she was riding at a carnival. It hurt and frightened her. The next month she was visiting her uncle, who had a tan Great Dane (dog). It frightened her even though she had never had a bad experience with a dog. Fear of this dog is an example of:
    a.   response discrimination.
    b.   modeling.
    c.   stimulus generalization.
    d.   vicarious reinforcement.

What Causes Phobias?, p. 131
Diff: E, Type: Factual, Ans: b

72.   Research has supported all of the following behavioral assumptions except that:
    a.   fear can be acquired through modeling.
    b.   phobias are always acquired through classical conditioning in humans.
    c.   animals can learn to make avoidance responses.
    d.   phobias can be acquired through classical conditioning in humans.

What Causes Phobias?, p. 131
Diff: M, Type: Applied, Ans: d

73.   Apparently, people develop phobias more readily to such objects as spiders and the dark than they do to such objects as computers and radios. This observation supports the idea of:
    a.   modeling.
    b.   stimulus generalization.
    c.   conditioning.
    d.   preparedness.

What Causes Phobias?, p. 131
Diff: M, Type: Applied, Ans: a

74.   If the idea of "preparedness" is accurate, then:
    a.   some phobias should be acquired more easily than others.
    b.   all phobias should diminish–with treatment–at about the same rate.
    c.   animals and humans should have the same phobias.
    d.   phobias should be less frequent in modern than ancient times.

What Causes Phobias?, p. 132
Diff: H, Type: Applied, Ans: b

75.   Someone who believes that among our ancestors, those who feared animals, darkness, and heights were more likely to survive long enough to reproduce, represents the _____ explanation of the development of phobias.
    a.   environmental
    b.   evolutionary
    c.   empirical
    d.   externalized

What Causes Phobias?, p. 132
Diff: H, Type: Applied, Ans: c

76.   Someone who believes that experiences teach us early in life that certain objects are legitimate sources of fear represents the _____ explanation of the development of phobias.
    a.   empirical
    b.   evolutionary
    c.   environmental
    d.   ecological

How Are Phobias Treated?, p. 132
Diff: H, Type: Applied, Ans: d

77.   A phobic person is taken to a snake-handling convention in order to actually confront snakes as part of desensitization training. This is an example of the _____ technique.
    a.   covert
    b.   modeling
    c.   fear hierarchical
    d.   in vivo

How Are Phobias Treated?, p. 132
Diff: H, Type: Applied, Ans: a

78.   A phobic person is taught to imagine the feared items as part of desensitization training. This is an example of the _____ technique.
      a.   covert
      b.   modeling
      c.   fear hierarchical flooding
      d.   in vivo

How Are Phobias Treated?, p. 132
Diff: M, Type: Applied, Ans: d

79.   You are suffering from arachnophobia. Your therapist first has you go through relaxation training, then has you construct a fear hierarchy and, finally, has you go through a phase of graded pairings of spiders and relaxation responses. This approach is called:
      a.   modeling.
      b.   flooding.
      c.   implosive therapy.
      d.   systematic desensitization.

How Are Phobias Treated?, p. 132
Diff: M, Type: Factual, Ans: b

80.   Pairing the thought of feared objects and relaxation training is:
      a.   implosive therapy.
      b.   systematic desensitization.
      c.   experimental extinction.
      d.   self-instruction training.

How Are Phobias Treated?, p. 132
Diff: E, Type: Factual, Ans: b

81.   The first step in treatment of systematic desensitization is:
      a.   role playing.
      b.   relaxation training.
      c.   construction of a fear hierarchy.
      d.   graded pairings with the phobic object.

How Are Phobias Treated?, p. 133
Diff: M, Type: Applied, Ans: b

82.   Your fear of spiders is debilitating because you are an entomologist. To treat this phobia, your therapist puts you in a room with spiders, even asking you to handle them. This technique might be used in:
      a.   modeling.
      b.   flooding.
      c.   covert desensitization.
      d.   systematic desensitization.

How Are Phobias Treated?, p. 133
Diff: E, Type: Applied, Ans: a

83.   If you were afraid of dogs and your therapist treated you by interacting with dogs while you watched, you would be receiving:
      a.   vicarious conditioning.
      b.   flooding.
      c.   systematic desensitization.
      d.   biofeedback.

How Are Phobias Treated?, p. 133
Diff: E, Type: Factual, Ans: b

84.   One procedure used to treat phobic disorders involves having the therapist confront the feared object or situation while the fearful client observes. This is called:
      a.   flooding.
      b.   modeling.
      c.   implosive therapy.
      d.   systematic desensitization.

How Are Phobias Treated?, p. 133
Diff: E, Type: Factual, Ans: b

85.   In vicarious conditioning, the client:
      a.   confronts the feared object directly.
      b.   observes the therapist confronting the feared object.
      c.   imagines the therapist confronting the feared object.
      d.   imagines himself or herself confronting the feared object.

How Are Phobias Treated?, p. 133
Diff: E, Type: Applied, Ans: b

86.   Harry is terrified of the snakes that his 8-year-old son brings home. During his therapy, his therapist demonstrated how to handle them. This is a form of therapy based on:
      a.   flooding.
      b.   modeling.
      c.   implosive techniques.
      d.   covert desensitization.

How Are Phobias Treated?, p. 133
Diff: H, Type: Applied, Ans: b

87.   A phobic person is exposed to computer graphics that simulate real-world situations. This is an example of the _____ technique.
      a.   covert
      b.   virtual reality
      c.   fear hierarchical flooding
      d.   in vivo

How Are Phobias Treated?, p. 134
Diff: H, Type: Applied, Ans: b

88.   Research indicates that the best therapy for treating a social phobia is:
      a.   benzodiazepines; they work better than antidepressants.
      b.   exposure therapy combined with group therapy.
      c.   implosive therapy.
      d.   psychodynamic therapy.

How Are Phobias Treated?, p. 135
Diff: H, Type: Factual, Ans: d

89.   The most accurate summary of the impact of the rational-emotive and other cognitive
       approaches on social fears is that these approaches usually:
       a.   have no long-term beneficial effects.
       b.   produce social fear elimination.
       c.   produce only short-term social fear reduction.
       d.   produce long-term social fear reduction.

Panic Disorder, p. 135
Diff: E, Type: Applied, Ans: a

90.   Rosa's heart was racing from the 4 cups of coffee she had just finished, but she thought she
       might be having a heart attack. Her fear seemed to be increasing without end. This might be
       the beginning of a:
       a.   panic attack.
       b.   manic episode.
       c.   specific phobia.
       d.   social phobia.

Panic Disorder, p. 135
Diff: M, Type: Applied, Ans: a

91.   You notice someone who is sweating, experiencing shortness of breath, choking, feeling
       dizzy, and is afraid of dying. If it is not a heart attack but an indicator of anxiety disorder, it is
       probably a:
       a.   panic attack.
       b.   phobia.
       c.   obsessive-compulsive response.
       d.   posttraumatic disorder.

Panic Disorder, p. 136
Diff: M, Type: Factual, Ans: b

92.   A person who experiences unpredictable panic attacks combined with dysfunctional behavior
       and thoughts is probably experiencing:
       a.   typical panic attacks.
       b.   panic disorder.
       c.   physiological damage.
       d.   a normal response to stress.

Panic Disorder, p. 136
Diff: M, Type: Factual, Ans: c

93.   The phobia most often associated with panic disorder is:
       a.   claustrophobia.
       b.   acrophobia.
       c.   agoraphobia.
       d.   metrophobia.

Panic Disorder, p. 136
Diff: M, Type: Applied, Ans: d
94.   One who is experiencing a panic disorder would most likely also be phobic about:
    a. high places.
    b. closed-in places.
    c. medical procedures.
    d. leaving home.

Panic Disorder, p. 136
Diff: H, Type: Factual, Ans: c
95.   Panic disorder develops most often in:
    a. younger men.
    b. older men.
    c. younger women.
    d. older women.

The Biological Perspective, p. 137
Diff: H, Type: Applied, Ans: b
96.   The drug treatment that is most effective in treating panic disorder is like that used to treat:
    a. schizophrenia.
    b. depression.
    c. bipolar disorder.
    d. generalized anxiety.

The Biological Perspective, p. 137
Diff: H, Type: Factual, Ans: a
97.   Panic disorder appears to be related to abnormal activity of which neurotransmitter?
    a. norepinephrine
    b. epinephrine
    c. serotonin
    d. endorphin

The Biological Perspective, p. 137
Diff: M, Type: Factual, Ans: d
98.   Antidepressant drugs are frequently effective in treating panic attacks. This may mean that the disorder is related to levels of the neurotransmitter:
    a. GABA.
    b. dopamine.
    c. acetylcholine.
    d. norepinephrine.

The Biological Perspective, p. 137
Diff: H, Type: Applied, Ans: c
99.   Which of the following convinces researchers that panic disorder is biologically different from generalized anxiety disorder?
    a. differences in the way the amygdala works in each disorder
    b. differences in the alarm and escape response in the brain
    c. differences in the brain circuitry in the two disorders
    d. differences in the heritability of the two disorders

The Biological Perspective, p. 138
Diff: M, Type: Factual, Ans: c
100.   The proportion of panic-attack sufferers who are helped at least somewhat by antidepressant
       drugs is about:
       a. 40%.
       b. 60%.
       c. 80%.
       d. almost 100%.

The Biological Perspective, p. 138
Diff: M, Type: Factual, Ans: b
101.   Antidepressants and alprazolam (Xanax) have been found to be successful in treating:
       a. phobias.
       b. panic disorders.
       c. generalized anxiety disorders.
       d. obsessive-compulsive disorders.

The Biological Perspective, p. 138
Diff: E, Type: Factual, Ans: c
102.   What type of drug is alprazolam (Xanax)?
       a. antipsychotic
       b. antidepressant
       c. benzodiazepine
       d. major tranquilizer

The Cognitive Perspective, p. 138
Diff: H, Type: Factual, Ans: c
103.   The cognitive explanation for panic disorders is that people who have them:
       a. have relatives who are atypically anxious.
       b. are prone to allergies and have immune deficiencies.
       c. misinterpret bodily sensations.
       d. experience more stress than average.

The Cognitive Perspective, p. 138
Diff: H, Type: Applied, Ans: d
104.   Imagine that researchers investigating panic disorder gave you a drug that caused you to
       hyperventilate and your heart to beat rapidly. You would have been given a(n):
       a. in vivo test.
       b. modeling test.
       c. covert sensitization test.
       d. biological challenge test.

The Cognitive Perspective, p. 139
Diff: E, Type: Factual, Ans: a
105.   Panic attacks are usually treated with cognitive therapy and/or:
       a. drug therapy.
       b. habituation training.
       c. classical conditioning.
       d. response prevention therapy.

What Are the Features of Obsessions and Compulsions?, p. 144
Diff: H, Type: Applied, Ans: c

126.   What is one important way obsessions and compulsions are related?
    a.   Compulsions are a way to prevent obsessions from occurring.
    b.   Obsessions generally lead to violent or immoral compulsions.
    c.   Compulsions help people control their obsessions.
    d.   Obsessions are not related to compulsions.

The Psychodynamic Perspective, p. 144
Diff: M, Type: Factual, Ans: d

127.   A psychodynamic theorist finds that a client is experiencing a battle between anxiety-provoking id impulses and anxiety-reducing ego defense mechanisms. She thinks that this usually unconscious conflict is being played out in an explicit and overt manner. She is sure this underlying conflict explains her client's:
    a.   fugue state.
    b.   schizophrenia.
    c.   generalized anxiety disorder.
    d.   obsessive-compulsive disorder.

The Psychodynamic Perspective, p. 144
Diff: E, Type: Factual, Ans: d

128.   Long-term studies of those with obsessive-compulsive disorder show that obsessive thoughts in many cases eventually lead to:
    a.   violent conduct.
    b.   immoral conduct.
    c.   lewd behavior.
    d.   cleaning or checking compulsions.

The Psychodynamic Perspective, p. 145
Diff: M, Type: Applied, Ans: b

129.   According to the psychodynamic perspective, if someone keeps engaging in immoral sexual behavior and repeatedly scrubs her face and hands in response to those thoughts:
    a.   the scrubbing represents a healthy coping response.
    b.   the immoral images represent id impulses.
    c.   the superego is helping the person to avoid id impulses.
    d.   ego defenses are not present.

The Psychodynamic Perspective, p. 145
Diff: M, Type: Applied, Ans: d

130.   If someone leads a life of service to others in order to counter his hatred and contempt for the poor and destitute, this person is exhibiting what psychodynamic theorists would call:
    a.   denial.
    b.   undoing.
    c.   isolation.
    d.   reaction formation.

The Psychodynamic Perspective, p. 145
Diff: H, Type: Applied, Ans: a
131.   The defense mechanism that involves doing good works in order to cancel out one's previous
       bad acts is called:
       a.   undoing.
       b.   isolation.
       c.   reaction formation.
       d.   denial.

The Psychodynamic Perspective, p. 145
Diff: H, Type: Applied, Ans: b
132.   The defense mechanism that involves not "owning" one's unwanted thoughts, but believing
       that they are "foreign" intrusions is called:
       a.   undoing.
       b.   isolation.
       c.   reaction formation.
       d.   denial.

The Psychodynamic Perspective, p. 145
Diff: E, Type: Factual, Ans: b
133.   According Freud, obsessive-compulsive disorders have their origin in the _____ stage of
       development:
       a.   oral
       b.   anal
       c.   phallic
       d.   genital

The Psychodynamic Perspective, p. 145
Diff: M, Type: Factual, Ans: a
134.   Psychodynamic therapies as a treatment for obsessive-compulsive disorders:
       a.   appear to work better when used in short-term rather than traditional ways.
       b.   must avoid pointing out the client's defense mechanisms.
       c.   work on intensifying the underlying conflict.
       d.   do not interpret the client's behavior.

The Behavioral Perspective, p. 145
Diff: H, Type: Factual, Ans: a
135.   Behaviorists believe that compulsive behavior:
       a.   is reinforced because engaging in it reduces anxiety.
       b.   originally is associated with an increase in anxiety.
       c.   is logically rather than randomly connected to fearful situations.
       d.   is exhibited by everyone.

The Behavioral Perspective, p. 146
Diff: M, Type: Factual, Ans: c
136.   The treatment of obsessive-compulsive disorder with exposure and response-prevention
       therapies has produced:
       a.   considerable improvement in less than half of those treated.
       b.   slight improvement in less than half of those treated.
       c.   considerable improvement in more than half of those treated.
       d.   slight improvement in more than half of those treated.

The Behavioral Perspective, p. 146
Diff: M, Type: Applied, Ans: b
137. An obsessive-compulsive person who was told that everyone was required to wear shoes at all times in the house and not to vacuum for a week, would be experiencing what therapy procedures?
    a. family therapy
    b. exposure and response prevention
    c. reinforcement for compulsive behavior
    d. free association

The Behavioral Perspective, p. 146
Diff: M, Type: Factual, Ans: b
138. Studies of the effectiveness of exposure and prevention therapy most often have focused on _____ compulsions.
    a. cooking
    b. cleaning
    c. depression
    d. ritual counting

The Behavioral Perspective, p. 147
Diff: M, Type: Factual, Ans: c
139. Exposure and response prevention as treatment for obsessive-compulsive disorder:
    a. changes behavior in the clinic, but don't carry over to home and the workplace.
    b. works only in about 25% of those who are treated with it.
    c. does not work as well for those who have obsessions but no compulsions.
    d. is only effective in a group setting.

The Behavioral Perspective, p. 147
Diff: M, Type: Factual, Ans: b
140. One of the drawbacks of exposure and response prevention as a therapy is that it:
    a. has a more than 50% relapse rate.
    b. is less effective with clients with obsessions but no compulsions.
    c. is less effective with clients who have both obsessions and compulsions.
    d. does not result in more improvement in obsessive-compulsive clients than do other cognitive-behavioral therapies.

The Cognitive Perspective, p. 147
Diff: E, Type: Applied, Ans: c
141. "Everyone has intrusive and unwanted thoughts. Most people ignore them. But some people blame themselves and expect terrible consequences, so they act in ways they hope will neutralize the thoughts." The type of theorist most likely to agree with this quote would be a:
    a. psychodynamic theorist.
    b. behaviorist.
    c. cognitive theorist.
    d. biologist.

The Cognitive Perspective, p. 147
Diff: M, Type: Factual, Ans: c
142.   According to cognitive theorists, compulsive acts serve to _____ obsessive thoughts.
        a. reinforce
        b. increase
        c. neutralize
        d. clarify

The Cognitive Perspective, p. 147
Diff: M, Type: Factual, Ans: d
143.   Cognitive theorists have found that people who develop obsessive-compulsive disorder also:
        a. have a lower rate of depression.
        b. have lower standards of conduct and morality.
        c. believe it is impossible and undesirable to have control over everything.
        d. believe their thoughts are capable of causing harm to themselves or others.

The Cognitive Perspective, p. 147
Diff: H, Type: Applied, Ans: a
144.   A friend of your says, "I'll try to see only the positive side of things, then everything will be OK." From a cognitive perspective, your friend is:
        a. neutralizing.
        b. habituating.
        c. exposing.
        d. engaging in response prevention.

The Cognitive Perspective, p. 147
Diff: E, Type: Applied, Ans: b
145.   If a client were instructed to tape-record obsessive thoughts and listen to them for two hours each day, the client would be experiencing what therapy technique?
        a. response prevention
        b. habituation training
        c. free association
        d. neutralization

The Biological Perspective, p. 149
Diff: H, Type: Factual, Ans: a
146.   Antidepressants that are effective in treating obsessive-compulsive disorder serve to:
        a. increase serotonin activity in the brain.
        b. increase norepinephrine activity in the brain.
        c. increase the level of all brain neurotransmitters.
        d. decrease serotonin activity in the brain.

The Biological Perspective, p. 149
Diff: H, Type: Applied, Ans: b
147.   A neurologist who was working with a person with obsessive-compulsive disorder would be suspicious of abnormality in what region of the brain?
        a. hypothalamus
        b. caudate nuclei
        c. cerebral cortex
        d. temporal lobe

The Biological Perspective, p. 149
Diff: E, Type: Factual, Ans: b
148.   The neurotransmitter implicated in the control of obsessive-compulsive disorder is:
   a. GABA.
   b. serotonin.
   c. norepinephrine.
   d. acetylcholine.

The Biological Perspective, p. 149
Diff: M, Type: Factual, Ans: d
149.   Which of the following brain areas have been implicated in obsessive-compulsive symptoms?
   a. the frontal lobes and the thalamus
   b. the thalamus and the hypothalamus
   c. the motor cortex and the caudate nuclei
   d. the orbital cortex and the caudate nuclei

The Biological Perspective, p. 149
Diff: H, Type: Factual, Ans: a
150.   For an antidepressant to be effective against obsessive-compulsive disorder, it must:
   a. increase serotonin activity.
   b. decrease serotonin activity.
   c. increase norepinephrine activity.
   d. decrease norepinephrine activity.

FILL-IN QUESTIONS

Anxiety Disorders, p. 116
Diff: E, Type: Factual, Ans: anxiety
1.   The ominous sense of being menaced by an unspecified threat is usually termed _____.

Anxiety Disorders, p. 116
Diff: E, Type: Factual, Ans: obsessive-compulsive disorder
2.   Recurrent and unwanted thoughts or the need to perform repetitive and ritualistic actions is characteristic of _____.

Generalized Anxiety Disorder, p. 116
Diff: M, Type: Applied, Ans: generalized anxiety disorder (or free-floating anxiety)
3.   Alan is always edgy and nervous and feels there is something to be afraid of but cannot name it. He is suffering from _____.

The Sociocultural Perspective, p. 117
Diff: E, Type: Factual, Ans: poverty
4.   One of the most powerful forms of societal stress is _____.

The Psychodynamic Perspective, p. 117
Diff: E, Type: Factual, Ans: realistic
5.   According to Freud, actual physical danger leads to _____ anxiety.

The Humanistic Perspective, p. 119
Diff: M, Type: Factual, Ans: conditions of worth
6.   Carl Rogers argued that anxiety disorders arise from the failure to receive unconditional positive regard during childhood. The person develops harsh self-standards, called _____, which he or she tries to meet by repeatedly distorting and denying his or her true experiences.

The Biological Perspective, p. 124
Diff: E, Type: Factual, Ans: GABA (gamma-aminobutyric acid)
7.   _____ is a neurotransmitter that carries an inhibitory message and has been implicated in anxiety disorders.

The Biological Perspective, p. 124
Diff: M, Type: Factual, Ans: GABA (gamma-aminobutyric acid)
8.   Benzodiazepines appear to reduce anxiety by acting on synapses that are mediated by the neurotransmitter _____.

The Biological Perspective, p. 126
Diff: E, Type: Factual, Ans: antidepressants
9.   Ironically, _____ help many people with anxiety disorders.

The Biological Perspective, p. 126
Diff: E, Type: Factual, Ans: biofeedback
10.   A bio-behavioral technique that allows clients to monitor and control their own physiological functions is called _____.

The Biological Perspective, p. 126
Diff: M, Type: Factual, Ans: biofeedback
11.   Anxiety can be reduced by teaching clients to use information about their bodies to eliminate certain physical responses and increase others. This approach, called _____, uses such techniques as EMG readings.

Phobias, p. 127
Diff: E, Type: Factual, Ans: specific phobia
12.   An uncontrollable and irrational fear of a chair is a _____.

Social Phobias, p. 128
Diff: M, Type: Factual, Ans: social phobia
13.   Performance anxiety is a form of _____.

Social Phobias, p. 128
Diff: E, Type: Factual, Ans: social
14.   A _____ phobia is a severe, persistent, and irrational fear of situations in which a person may be exposed to scrutiny, such as public speaking or performing.

What Causes Phobias?, p. 131
Diff: E, Type: Factual, Ans: preparedness
15.   It is possible that many common phobic reactions can be explained by human beings having a predisposition to develop certain fears. This idea is referred to as _____.

How Are Phobias Treated?, p. 132
Diff: E, Type: Factual, Ans: systematic desensitization

16.   After relaxation training, a therapist and client create a fear hierarchy of imagined situations that would provoke anxiety in the client. The next step in therapy is pairing of imagined situations with relaxation. This technique is best described as _____.

How Are Phobias Treated?, p. 133
Diff: M, Type: Factual, Ans: flooding

17.   Therapists who use the technique of _____ believe that people with phobic disorders must be forced to confront what they fear in its full intensity so they will see that no real danger exists.

How Are Phobias Treated?, p. 133
Diff: M, Type: Factual, Ans: flooding

18.   A technique for treating phobias in which the client is repeatedly exposed to the full effect of the fear-creating object without relaxation training is called _____.

How Are Phobias Treated?, p. 133
Diff: E, Type: Applied, Ans: participant modeling, modeling (or vicarious conditioning)

19.   To treat your fire phobia, your therapist lights a candle, holds it, and permits it to burn a bit. He then invites you to hold the candle. The name of the technique he is using is _____.

How Are Phobias Treated?, p. 134
Diff: M, Type: Applied, Ans: rational-emotive

20.   "The reason you are afraid to talk in public is because you believe that everyone must love and approve of you." This statement might be made by a therapist practicing _____ therapy.

Panic Disorder, p. 135
Diff: M, Type: Factual, Ans: panic attack

21.   A short-term anxiety reaction that accelerates into a smothering, horrifying ordeal in which one loses control, is practically unaware of what one is doing, and feels a sense of approaching doom, is called a _____.

Panic Disorder, p. 135
Diff: M, Type: Applied, Ans: panic attack

22.   Suddenly and without warning, and without apparent cause, Melissa acted as if there was a cataclysmic emergency, and she became paralyzed with fear for several minutes. She probably had a(n) _____.

The Biological Perspective, p. 138
Diff: M, Type: Factual, Ans: antidepressants

23.   Since the 1960s, the drugs most likely to be used against panic disorder have been the _____.

The Cognitive Perspective, p. 139
Diff: M, Type: Factual, Ans: panic disorder

24.   Cognitive therapists might train clients to label the sensation of the blood pounding in their veins as physical exertion. This is part of therapy for treating _____.

The Cognitive Perspective, p. 139
Diff: M, Type: Applied, Ans: anxiety sensitivity

25.   Nadia is generally not very anxious. She also does not react as much to bodily sensations that others find anxiety provoking. According to a cognitive explanation for panic attack, she probably has a low degree of _____.

Obsessive-Compulsive Disorder, p. 141
Diff: E, Type: Factual, Ans: obsessions

26.   Repetitive thoughts, ideas, impulses, or mental images that seem to invade a person's consciousness, are _____.

Obsessive-Compulsive Disorder, p. 141
Diff: E, Type: Factual, Ans: compulsions

27.   Repetitive and rigid activities that a person feels forced to perform are called _____.

What Are the Features of Obsessions and Compulsions?, p. 143
Diff: E, Type: Factual, Ans: compulsion (or compulsive ritual, or checking compulsion)

28.   Janet rarely has a calm moment. If she leaves the house, she must go to each window at least three times to be sure it is locked. Each appliance receives four passes, and doors are examined at least 10 times. Every aspect of her life, at home and away, is affected by her behavior. Janet suffers from a _____.

What Are the Features of Obsessions and Compulsions?, p. 146
Diff: H, Type: Factual, Ans: exposure and response prevention

29.   Meyer's technique, which involves instructing clients not to perform their compulsive behavior, is called _____.

The Behavioral Perspective, p. 146
Diff: E, Type: Factual, Ans: Self-help

30.   _____ procedures involve homework assignments in exposure and response prevention.

The Biological Perspective, p. 149
Diff: M, Type: Factual, Ans: serotonin

31.   The neurotransmitter involved in the brain's control of obsessive compulsive disorders appears to be _____.

The Biological Perspective, p. 149
Diff: H, Type: Factual, Ans: orbital region; caudate nucleus

32.   If metabolic activity is any indication, the part of the brain involved in obsessive-compulsive disorder is the _____ and the _____.

The Biological Perspective, p. 149
Diff: M, Type: Factual, Ans: serotonin

33.   Obsessive-compulsive disorder is improved by antidepressants that increase _____ activity in the brain.

ESSAY QUESTIONS

Anxiety Disorders, pp. 115-116
Diff: M, Type: Factual

1.   Distinguish between clinically significant fear and anxiety, and everyday fear and anxiety.

Generalized Anxiety Disorder, p. 116
Diff: H, Type: Applied

2.   Write a long paragraph modeled after the case descriptions in the textbook that illustrates generalized anxiety disorder. Indicate the symptoms of the disorder you are describing.

Generalized Anxiety Disorder, No Specific Page
Diff: H, Type: Factual

3.   Write a one- or two-sentence explanation for the development of generalized anxiety disorder from each of the following: a sociocultural, psychodynamic, humanistic, cognitive, and biological perspective.

The Cognitive Perspective, p. 120
Diff: M, Type: Applied

4.   Identify and provide examples of each of the following from the cognitive perspective: maladaptive assumptions, unpredictable negative events and metaworries.

The Biological Perspective, p. 125
Diff: H, Type: Factual

5.   Explain in detail, how GABA is related to the experience of anxiety. What are some limitations of this explanation?

What Causes Phobias?, p. 129
Diff: E, Type: Applied

6.   Using a diagram and accompanying description, illustrate how a behaviorist would explain the development of a dog phobia using classical conditioning principles. Be sure to identify the components of classical conditioning in your response.

How Are Phobias Treated?, p. 132
Diff: E, Type: Factual

7.   In the treatment of phobias, carefully describe the exposure therapies: systematic desensitization, flooding, and modeling.

The Biological Perspective, pp. 137-138
Diff: H, Type: Applied

8.   Imagine that a person has a diagnosed panic disorder. Based on the latest research, outline a treatment plan for this person that would have the greatest chance for both short-term and long-term success.

Obsessive-Compulsive Disorder, p. 141ff
Diff: H, Type: Applied

9.   Following the example of the case vignettes in the textbook, write a description of someone experiencing an obsessive-compulsive disorder. Be sure to include in your description the most common obsessive thoughts and compulsive behaviors.

Obsessive-Compulsive Disorder, No Specific Page
Diff: E, Type: Factual
10.   According to psychodynamic theorists, behaviorists, and cognitive theorists, what causes obsessive-compulsive disorders?

CHAPTER 6

Stress Disorders

MULTIPLE-CHOICE QUESTIONS

Stress Disorders, p. 155
Diff: H, Type: Applied, Ans: b
1. Poor health is best described as a:
    a. stress.
    b. stressor.
    c. stress response.
    d. stress model.

Stress Disorders, p. 155
Diff: M, Type: Applied, Ans: c
2. A person who copes well with a happy event in life is showing a positive:
    a. stress.
    b. stressor.
    c. stress response.
    d. stress model.

Stress Disorders, p. 155
Diff: M, Type: Applied, Ans: a
3. Having to walk the dog several times a day when it is raining is an example of a:
    a. stressor.
    b. stress response.
    c. stress disorder.
    d. psychophysical disorder.

Stress Disorders, p. 155
Diff: H, Type: Applied, Ans: b
4. Looking for rainbows while walking the dog in the rain is an example of a:
    a. stressor.
    b. stress response.
    c. social support system.
    d. potential stressor.

Stress Disorders, p. 156
Diff: H, Type: Applied, Ans: b
5. In the face of fear, someone is unable to concentrate and develops a distorted view of the world. This person is showing which of the following fear responses?
    a. physical
    b. emotional
    c. cognitive
    d. The person is showing all three responses.

Stress Disorders, p. 156
Diff: H, Type: Applied, Ans: c
6. A student who dreads being called on in class, and in fact panics at the thought of public speaking, is experiencing a(n) _____ response to stress.
    a. physical
    b. cognitive
    c. emotional
    d. developmental

Stress Disorders, p. 156
Diff: H, Type: Applied, Ans: d
7. A student who turns pale and feels nauseated when called on to speak in class is experiencing a(n) _____ response to stress.
    a. emotional
    b. cognitive
    c. developmental
    d. physical

Stress and Arousal: The Fight-or-Flight Response, p. 157
Diff: E, Type: Factual, Ans: c
8. The part of the body that releases hormones into the bloodstream is the _____ system.
    a. nervous
    b. exocrine
    c. endocrine
    d. autonomic

Stress and Arousal: The Fight-or-Flight Response, p. 158
Diff: H, Type: Applied, Ans: b
9. A coach who wants to produce high emotional anxiety in players would:
    a. make the team practice until they were really perspiring.
    b. threaten the players.
    c. change their pre-conceptions about the game.
    d. push players to regularly vomit before a game.

Stress and Arousal: The Fight-or-Flight Response, p. 158
Diff: H, Type: Applied, Ans: d
10. A teammate of a basketball player says, "Congratulations on making those game-winning free throws. Weren't you bothered by the fans waving their arms behind the basket?" The basketball player replies, "Thanks. I felt a little nervous, but to tell the truth, I didn't even notice the fans." Most likely, the player who made the foul shots has:
    a. high situational and trait anxiety.
    b. low trait anxiety, but high situational anxiety.
    c. high trait anxiety, but low situational anxiety.
    d. low situational and trait anxiety.

Stress and Arousal: The Fight-or-Flight Response, p. 158
Diff: M, Type: Applied, Ans: a

11. The athlete expected to experience the least situational anxiety would be the one who:
     a. experiences no difference between practice and a game.
     b. is generally an anxious person.
     c. is an inexperienced athlete playing on a team.
     d. is an inexperienced athlete participating in an individual sport.

Stress and Arousal: The Fight-or-Flight Response, p. 158
Diff: H, Type: Applied, Ans: c

12. In response to a threat, we perspire, breathe more quickly, get goose bumps, and feel nauseated. These responses are controlled by the:
     a. somatic nervous system.
     b. peripheral nervous system.
     c. sympathetic nervous system.
     d. parasympathetic nervous system.

Stress and Arousal: The Fight-or-Flight Response, p. 158
Diff: H, Type: Applied, Ans: d

13. Imagine that you just had a "close call" while driving, but now you feel your body returning to normal. Which part of your nervous system is controlling this return to normalcy?
     a. somatic nervous system
     b. peripheral nervous system
     c. sympathetic nervous system
     d. parasympathetic nervous system

Stress and Arousal: The Fight-or-Flight Response, p. 158
Diff: M, Type: Factual, Ans: c

14. The flight-or-fight system is controlled in part by the:
     a. somatic nervous system.
     b. peripheral nervous system.
     c. sympathetic nervous system.
     d. parasympathetic nervous system.

Stress and Arousal: The Fight-or-Flight Response, p. 158
Diff: H, Type: Factual, Ans: b

15. The group of hormones that appears to be most involved in arousal and fear reaction are the:
     a. prolactins.
     b. corticosteroids.
     c. adrenalaltoids.
     d. beta-blockers.

Stress and Arousal: The Fight-or-Flight Response, p. 158
Diff: E, Type: Factual, Ans: b

16. The gland that produces a hormone that is involved in the reaction to fearful and stressful situations is the:
     a. ganglion.
     b. adrenal.
     c. hippocampus.
     d. medulla.

Stress and Arousal: The Fight-or-Flight Response, p. 158
Diff: H, Type: Applied, Ans: a

17. Which of the following accurately describes the hypothalamic-pituitary-adrenal pathway of the stress response?
    a. The hypothalamus stimulates the pituitary to produce a stress hormone that causes the adrenal gland to release corticosteroids.
    b. The hypothalamus produces corticosteroids which stimulate the pituitary to produce a stress hormone that causes the adrenal gland to release adrenocorticotropic hormone.
    c. The hypothalamus stimulates the pituitary to produce corticosteroids that cause the adrenal gland to release adrenocorticotropic hormone.
    d. The hypothalamus stimulates the pituitary to produce a stress hormone that causes the adrenal gland to release hypothalamic hormone in a feedback loop.

Stress and Arousal: The Fight-or-Flight Response, p. 158
Diff: H, Type: Applied, Ans: a

18. Which of the following accurately describes the sympathetic nervous system pathway of the stress response?
    a. The hypothalamus excites the sympathetic nervous system which excites body organs to release hormones that serve as neurotransmitters, producing even more arousal.
    b. The parasympathetic nervous system excites the sympathetic nervous system which excites body organs to release hormones that serve as neurotransmitters, producing even more arousal.
    c. The hypothalamus excites the parasympathetic nervous system which excites body organs to release hormones that serve as neurotransmitters, producing even more arousal.
    d. The hypothalamus inhibits the sympathetic nervous system which inhibits body organs to release hormones that serve as neurotransmitters, producing a reduction in arousal.

Stress and Arousal: The Fight-or-Flight Response, p. 158
Diff: H, Type: Applied, Ans: c

19. The organ most related to controlling emotional memories and "turning off" the body's arousal is the:
    a. hypothalamus.
    b. adrenal gland.
    c. hippocampus.
    d. sympathetic nervous system.

Stress and Arousal: The Fight-or-Flight Response, p. 158
Diff: H, Type: Applied, Ans: a

20. I am generally a calm, relaxed person. If you are generally a tense, excitable person, we differ in:
    a. trait anxiety.
    b. state anxiety.
    c. situational anxiety.
    d. content anxiety.

Stress and Arousal: The Fight-or-Flight Response, p. 158
Diff: H, Type: Applied, Ans: c

21.   For me, crossing a bridge is terrifying. If you hardly notice crossing a bridge, we differ in:
   a.   trait anxiety.
   b.   cognitive anxiety.
   c.   situational anxiety.
   d.   physiological anxiety.

Stress and Arousal: The Fight-or-Flight Response, p. 158
Diff: M, Type: Factual, Ans: b

22.   Some people are stimulated by exciting, potentially dangerous activities that terrify others. These varying reactions represent differences in:
   a.   trait anxiety.
   b.   state anxiety.
   c.   neurotic anxiety.
   d.   existential anxiety.

The Psychological Stress Disorders: Acute and Posttraumatic Stress Disorders, p. 158
Diff: E, Type: Applied, Ans: d

23.   A person who witnessed a horrible accident and then became unusually anxious and depressed for 3 weeks is probably experiencing:
   a.   posttraumatic stress disorder.
   b.   pretraumatic stress disorder.
   c.   combat fatigue.
   d.   acute stress disorder.

The Psychological Stress Disorders: Acute and Posttraumatic Stress Disorders, p. 158
Diff: H, Type: Factual, Ans: d

24.   Posttraumatic stress disorders:
   a.   begin immediately after the stress occurs.
   b.   last between 1 and 3 weeks.
   c.   don't begin until years after the traumatic event.
   d.   last longer than a month.

The Psychological Stress Disorders: Acute and Posttraumatic Stress Disorders, p. 158
Diff: E, Type: Factual, Ans: b

25.   A pattern of anxiety, insomnia, depression, and flashbacks that begins shortly after a horrible event and persists for less than a month is called:
   a.   hysteria.
   b.   acute stress disorder.
   c.   generalized anxiety disorder.
   d.   posttraumatic stress disorder.

The Psychological Stress Disorders: Acute and Posttraumatic Stress Disorders, p. 158
Diff: M, Type: Factual, Ans: c

26.   One distinction that DSM-IV-TR makes between acute stress disorder and posttraumatic stress disorder is based on:
   a.   how intense the anxiety-linked symptoms are.
   b.   what the cause of the anxiety-linked symptoms was.
   c.   how long the anxiety symptoms last.
   d.   what sort of treatment is contemplated for the anxiety-linked symptoms.

The Psychological Stress Disorders: Acute and Posttraumatic Stress Disorders, p. 158
Diff: M, Type: Applied, Ans: d

27. Dorian was only 10 miles away when Mt. St. Helens exploded with one of the largest blasts in history. There was ash and lava everywhere, and he was sure he was going to die. He was terrified to the core of his being. When rescue teams found him a week later, he was cold, hungry, and scared. More than a year later he still has nightmares and wakes up in a cold sweat. This description best fits:
     a.   a phobia.
     b.   an acute stress disorder.
     c.   a generalized anxiety disorder.
     d.   a posttraumatic stress disorder.

The Psychological Stress Disorders: Acute and Posttraumatic Stress Disorders, p. 158
Diff: M, Type: Applied, Ans: c

28. Salina was terrified during the San Francisco earthquake of 1989 (who wouldn't be?). For a couple of weeks after, she did not sleep well or feel comfortable inside a building. However, gradually the fears diminished, and they disappeared within a month. Her reaction to the earthquake was:
     a.   a panic attack.
     b.   a phobic reaction.
     c.   an acute stress disorder.
     d.   a posttraumatic stress disorder.

The Psychological Stress Disorders: Acute and Posttraumatic Stress Disorders, p. 158
Diff: M, Type: Applied, Ans: d

29. Almost every night, Cara wakes up terrified and screaming for the boys to get off her. Two years later she still can't get the gang rape out of her mind. The fear, anxiety, and depression are ruining her life. This is an example of:
     a.   a phobia.
     b.   a panic reaction.
     c.   an acute stress reaction.
     d.   a posttraumatic stress reaction.

The Psychological Stress Disorders: Acute and Posttraumatic Stress Disorders, p. 158
Diff: E, Type: Factual, Ans: d

30. A pattern of anxiety, insomnia, depression, and flashbacks that persists for years after a horrible event is called:
     a.   hysteria.
     b.   acute stress disorder.
     c.   generalized anxiety disorder.
     d.   posttraumatic stress disorder.

The Psychological Stress Disorders: Acute and Posttraumatic Stress Disorders, p. 159
Diff: M, Type: Applied, Ans: a

31. Which of the following is the best example of "reduce responsiveness" as it relates to posttraumatic stress disorder?
     a.   feeling detached or estranged from others and loss of interest in activities
     b.   feelings of extreme guilt for surviving the traumatic event
     c.   reliving the event through day dreams and night dreams
     d.   excessive talking about the event in inappropriate settings

The Psychological Stress Disorders: Acute and Posttraumatic Stress Disorders, p. 159
Diff: E, Type: Applied, Ans: b

32.   Which of the following does not characterize stress disorders?
    a.   recurring memories, dreams, or nightmares about the event
    b.   a compulsive need to engage in activities that remind one of the event
    c.   reduced responsiveness to the world around one
    d.   signs of increased arousal, such as poor sleep and exaggerated startle reactions

The Psychological Stress Disorders: Acute and Posttraumatic Stress Disorders, p. 159
Diff: E, Type: Factual, Ans: a

33.   Which of the following typifies posttraumatic stress disorder?
    a.   increased arousal, anxiety, and guilt
    b.   inability to remember the event that led to the stress
    c.   increased responsiveness and emotion right after the event
    d.   a tendency to want to go back to see the site of the stress

The Psychological Stress Disorders: Acute and Posttraumatic Stress Disorders, p. 159
Diff: H, Type: Applied, Ans: d

34.   A person with posttraumatic stress disorder who is upset by what she or he had to do to survive and perhaps even feels unworthy of surviving is:
    a.   reexperiencing the traumatic event.
    b.   experiencing avoidance.
    c.   experiencing reduced responsiveness.
    d.   experiencing increased arousal, anxiety, and guilt.

The Psychological Stress Disorders: Acute and Posttraumatic Stress Disorders, p. 159
Diff: M, Type: Applied, Ans: a

35.   A person with posttraumatic stress disorder who is having "flashbacks" is:
    a.   reexperiencing the traumatic event.
    b.   experiencing avoidance.
    c.   experiencing reduced responsiveness.
    d.   experiencing increased arousal, anxiety, and guilt.

The Psychological Stress Disorders: Acute and Posttraumatic Stress Disorders, p. 159
Diff: M, Type: Applied, Ans: b

36.   A person with posttraumatic stress disorder who refuses to talk about it is:
    a.   reexperiencing the traumatic event.
    b.   experiencing avoidance.
    c.   experiencing reduced responsiveness.
    d.   experiencing increased arousal, anxiety, and guilt.

The Psychological Stress Disorders: Acute and Posttraumatic Stress Disorders, p. 159
Diff: H, Type: Applied, Ans: c

37.   A person with posttraumatic stress disorder who has symptoms of derealization and depersonalization is:
    a.   reexperiencing the traumatic event.
    b.   experiencing avoidance.
    c.   experiencing reduced responsiveness.
    d.   experiencing increased arousal, anxiety, and guilt.

What Triggers a Psychological Stress Disorder?, p. 160
Diff: M, Type: Factual, Ans: d
38.   Posttraumatic stress disorders:
    a.   occur in adults and not children.
    b.   are more common in men than in women.
    c.   are most often triggered by academic trauma.
    d.   often occur with depression and sleep difficulties.

What Triggers a Psychological Stress Disorder?, p. 160
Diff: M, Type: Factual, Ans: a
39.   When was acute stress disorder as a result of combat (called "shell shock") first recognized?
    a.   after World War I
    b.   after World War II
    c.   after the Vietnam War
    d.   during the Iraqi war.

What Triggers a Psychological Stress Disorder?, p. 160
Diff: M, Type: Factual, Ans: d
40.   About what proportion of Vietnam veterans suffered an acute or posttraumatic stress disorder?
    a.   8%
    b.   6-15%
    c.   20%
    d.   29%

What Triggers a Psychological Stress Disorder?, p. 161
Diff: H, Type: Applied, Ans: d
41.   Regarding disasters and stress, which of the following is not true?
    a.   Stress disorders follow both natural and accidental disasters.
    b.   About one-third of those in serious traffic accidents develop stress disorders.
    c.   Children who experience stress disorders typically have school problems and sleep difficulties.
    d.   The symptoms of disaster-induced stress disorders are different from those of combat-induced disorders.

What Triggers a Psychological Stress Disorder?, p. 161
Diff: E, Type: Factual, Ans: c
42.   What proportion of women are the victims of rape at some point during their lives?
    a.   1/3
    b.   1/5
    c.   1/7
    d.   1/4

What Triggers a Psychological Stress Disorder?, p. 162
Diff: M, Type: Factual, Ans: d
43.   Surveys suggest that about what percent of female rape victims in the U.S. are teenagers, or younger?
    a.   20%
    b.   40%
    c.   50%
    d.   over 60%

What Triggers a Psychological Stress Disorder?, p. 162
Diff: E, Type: Factual, Ans: c

44.   At what point is distress the greatest after a rape?
       a.   immediately after the assault
       b.   within one week after the assault
       c.   within one month after the assault
       d.   more than several months after the assault

What Triggers a Psychological Stress Disorder?, p. 162
Diff: M, Type: Factual, Ans: d

45.   What percentage of rape victims qualified for diagnosis of acute stress disorder in Rothbaum,
       et al.'s study (1992)?
       a.   12%
       b.   43%
       c.   76%
       d.   94%

What Triggers a Psychological Stress Disorder?, p. 163
Diff: M, Type: Factual, Ans: c

46.   Surveys show that in the U.S., the typical female victim of rape:
       a.   is not tested for HIV, and has no long-term health problems.
       b.   is tested for HIV, and has no long-term health problems.
       c.   is not tested for HIV, and has long-term health problems.
       d.   is tested for HIV, and has long-term health problems.

What Triggers a Psychological Stress Disorder?, p. 164
Diff: E, Type: Factual, Ans: c

47.   In the aftermath of the terrorist attacks in the U.S. on September 11, 2001, those living in
       New York City reported which of the following, compared to people living elsewhere in the
       U.S.?
       a.   the same amount of posttraumatic stress disorder, but more depression.
       b.   the same amount of posttraumatic stress disorder, and the same amount of depression.
       c.   more posttraumatic stress disorder, and more depression.
       d.   more posttraumatic stress disorder, but the same amount of depression.

What Triggers a Psychological Stress Disorder?, p. 165
Diff: E, Type: Factual, Ans: a

48.   Those most likely to experience substantial stress symptoms after the terrorist attacks in the
       U.S. on September 11, 2001:
       a.   lived near New York City.
       b.   lived near Washington DC.
       c.   lived far away from New York City.
       d.   lived on the West coast of the U.S.

What Triggers a Psychological Stress Disorder?, p. 165
Diff: M, Type: Factual, Ans: b

49. In response to the September 11, 2001, terrorist attacks in the United States, surveys show that New York children show:
     a. less PTSD than adults.
     b. more PTSD than adults.
     c. less PTSD than college students.
     d. less PTSD than children in other cities.

What Triggers a Psychological Stress Disorder?, p. 165
Diff: H, Type: Factual, Ans: a

50. Six months after the September 11, 2001, terrorist attacks on New York City, surveys showed that about 70% of New Yorkers:
     a. were concerned about another terrorist attack on their city.
     b. thought life was back to normal.
     c. report drinking more alcohol.
     d. feels less safe in their homes.

Why Do People Develop a Psychological Stress Disorder?, p. 166
Diff: M, Type: Factual, Ans: d

51. Investigators have shown that traumatic events are related to abnormal activity of the neurotransmitter:
     a. GABA.
     b. serotonin.
     c. epinephrine.
     d. norepinephrine.

Why Do People Develop a Psychological Stress Disorder?, p. 166
Diff: M, Type: Factual, Ans: a

52. Current research suggests that those who experience severe stress:
     a. have abnormal levels of norepinephrine and cortisol.
     b. are less anxious than the average person before the trauma.
     c. were likely to be wealthy as children.
     d. were not directly exposed to the trauma, but experienced it second-hand.

Why Do People Develop a Psychological Stress Disorder?, p. 166
Diff: H, Type: Applied, Ans: d

53. Research suggests that which of the following is best related to a person's risk for developing a stress disorder?
     a. good levels of adjustment prior to experiencing the trauma
     b. generally believing that negative events are under one's control
     c. being able to find something positive in a traumatic situation
     d. generally being described as lacking in resiliency

Why Do People Develop a Psychological Stress Disorder?, p. 166
Diff: H, Type: Applied, Ans: a

54.   Research suggests that which of the following people would be most immune to developing a stress disorder following trauma?
       a.   someone who believes that events are generally under his or her control
       b.   someone who has a poor level of psychological adjustment prior to the trauma
       c.   someone who is unable to find anything positive about a horrible situation
       d.   someone who could be described as not very hardy

Why Do People Develop a Psychological Stress Disorder?, p. 166
Diff: M, Type: Applied, Ans: d

55.   A person's levels of cortisol and norepinephrine are in the normal range. Most likely, that person is experiencing:
       a.   posttraumatic stress disorder.
       b.   the fight-or-flight syndrome.
       c.   severe stress response.
       d.   no stress disorder.

Why Do People Develop a Psychological Stress Disorder?, p. 167
Diff: M, Type: Factual, Ans: d

56.   Often those who respond to stress with a set of positive attitudes are less negatively affected by the stress, demonstrating what researchers call:
       a.   angst.
       b.   low perceived self-control.
       c.   the Rebound Effect.
       d.   hardiness or resiliency.

Why Do People Develop a Psychological Stress Disorder?, p. 167
Diff: E, Type: Applied, Ans: b

57.   After Marie's plane crashed, her mother came to stay with her. Her friends visited often, and went to lunch and dinner with her occasionally. This situation, which probably contributed to Marie's coping ability after the accident, relates to _____ as a factor in her response to the stress.
       a.   personality
       b.   social support
       c.   severity of the trauma
       d   the nature of her childhood experiences

Why Do People Develop a Psychological Stress Disorder?, p. 167
Diff: E, Type: Applied, Ans: c

58.   Kelly was in a passenger plane that had engine trouble. She watched as all four engines quit, one at a time. Then the plane exploded and she was thrown free 5,000 feet in the air. It was a miracle that she survived, though severely injured, because she landed in a thick pine forest covered with 10 feet or more of snow. When she regained consciousness several weeks later, she had a stress reaction that lasted for years, and she could never fly again. The factor that probably contributed most to her extreme posttraumatic stress reaction was:
       a.   her personality.
       b.   her social support.
       c.   the severity of the trauma.
       d.   the nature of her childhood experiences.

Why Do People Develop a Psychological Stress Disorder?, p. 167
Diff: E, Type: Applied, Ans: d
59.   We would expect posttraumatic stress disorder to be most common among military personnel
      who were prisoners of war for a:
      a.   short time, and who were welcomed home.
      b.   short time, and who were not welcomed home.
      c.   long time, and who were welcomed home.
      d.   long time, and who were not welcomed home.

How Do Clinicians Treat the Psychological Stress Disorders?, p. 168
Diff: M, Type: Applied, Ans: a
60.   A combat veteran undergoing "eye movement desensitization and reprocessing" is
      experiencing which general form of therapy?
      a.   exposure therapy
      b.   group therapy
      c.   insight therapy
      d.   drug therapy

How Do Clinicians Treat the Psychological Stress Disorders?, p. 168
Diff: M, Type: Applied, Ans: a
61.   A combat veteran receiving the best treatment for a stress disorder would be likely to
      experience all of the following except:
      a.   antipsychotic medication.
      b.   family therapy.
      c.   rap groups.
      d.   exposure therapy.

How Do Clinicians Treat the Psychological Stress Disorders?, p. 168
Diff: M, Type: Applied, Ans: b
62.   Combat veterans in a therapy group express a great deal of guilt and rage. Most likely, the
      veterans are in a:
      a.   desensitization and reprocessing group.
      b.   rap group.
      c.   "experience writing" group.
      d.   exposure group.

How Do Clinicians Treat the Psychological Stress Disorders?, p. 169
Diff: M, Type: Factual, Ans: d
63.   According to APA, the most common diagnosis for those receiving outpatient therapy is:
      a.   posttraumatic stress disorder.
      b.   insomnia.
      c.   acute stress disorder.
      d.   adjustment disorder.

How Do Clinicians Treat the Psychological Stress Disorders?, p. 171
Diff: H, Type: Factual, Ans: d

64. Educating survivors about symptoms they might develop in the aftermath of a huge disaster is relevant to:
    a. providing referrals.
    b. teaching self-help skills.
    c. diffusing anxiety, anger, and frustration.
    d. normalizing people's responses to the disaster.

How Do Clinicians Treat the Psychological Stress Disorders?, p. 171
Diff: H, Type: Factual, Ans: c

65. Helping survivors talk about their feelings and fears regarding a disaster is designed to:
    a. provide referrals.
    b. teach self-help skills.
    c. help people express anxiety, anger, and frustration.
    d. normalize people's responses to the disaster.

How Do Clinicians Treat the Psychological Stress Disorders?, p. 172
Diff: H, Type: Factual, Ans: b

66. Ideally, critical incident stress debriefing occurs:
    a. immediately, and is long-term.
    b. immediately, and is short-term.
    c. after a "recovery" period, and is long-term.
    d. after a "recovery" period, and is short-term.

How Do Clinicians Treat the Psychological Stress Disorders?, p. 172
Diff: H, Type: Applied, Ans: b

67. A flash flood hits a small Appalachian community. Those providing critical incident stress debriefing intervention would:
    a. provide long-term psychological therapy for flood survivors.
    b. provide short-term counseling services.
    c. keep their efforts separate from those of disaster relief agencies such as the Red Cross.
    d. focus first on the high-income, resilient citizens.

How Do Clinicians Treat the Psychological Stress Disorders?, p. 172
Diff: H, Type: Applied, Ans: b

68. If someone asked you about the effectiveness of psychological debriefing following a disaster, you would be most correct (based on the research) in saying that:
    a. there have been no controlled research studies on the topic of debriefing.
    b. there is little evidence that debriefing works.
    c. there is strong, convincing evidence that debriefing works well.
    d. there is evidence that debriefing works only if conducted by community members themselves.

How Do Clinicians Treat the Psychological Stress Disorders?, p. 172
Diff: H, Type: Applied, Ans: c
69.   The most accurate of the following statements about the effectiveness of psychological debriefing following a disaster (based on research studies) is:
       a. debriefing helps both rescuers and victims.
       b. debriefing by victims is more effective than debriefing by professionals.
       c. debriefing doesn't work too well; it might even make victims worse.
       d. debriefing is so ineffective that it is no longer done.

How Do Clinicians Treat the Psychological Stress Disorders?, p. 173
Diff: E, Type: Applied, Ans: c
70.   Crisis intervention techniques that work well with some groups of people may not work as well with other groups of people, raising concerns about:
       a. habituation effects.
       b. value self-helping skills.
       c. cultural competence of the counselors.
       d. the value of social support.

The Physical Stress Disorders: Psychophysiological Disorders, p. 173
Diff: M, Type: Factual, Ans: a
71.   Surveys show that people are least likely to do which of the following in order to relieve stress?
       a. drink alcoholic beverages
       b. watch TV
       c. go for a walk
       d. scream at others

The Physical Stress Disorders: Psychophysiological Disorders, p. 173
Diff: H, Type: Applied, Ans: d
72.   If you are similar to most other people, which of the following are you most likely to do to relieve stress?
       a. drink alcohol
       b. scream at others
       c. exercise
       d. watch TV

The Physical Stress Disorders: Psychophysiological Disorders, p. 173
Diff: E, Type: Factual, Ans: d
73.   Disorders that are thought to have both biological and psychosocial causes are:
       a. factitious.
       b. somatoform.
       c. psychogenic.
       d. psychophysical.

The Physical Stress Disorders: Psychophysiological Disorders, p. 173
Diff: H, Type: Applied, Ans: a

74.   René Descartes's mind-body dualism:
   a.   is inconsistent with modern views of the relationship between the mind and bodily
          illnesses.
   b.   is supported in diagnoses such as factitious and somatoform disorders.
   c.   is reflected in current research on the psychophysical disorders.
   d.   is supported by the idea that one's emotions can have an impact on physical health.

The Physical Stress Disorders: Psychophysiological Disorders, p. 174
Diff: M, Type: Factual, Ans: b

75.   If a physician believes that a patient's disorder due to hidden needs, repression, or
       reinforcement, then the patient may receive a diagnosis of:
   a.   malingering.
   b.   factitious disorder.
   c.   psychosomatic disorder.
   d.   psychophysiological disorder.

The Physical Stress Disorders: Psychophysiological Disorders, p. 174
Diff: M, Type: Factual, Ans: a

76.   A woman complains of an assortment of physiological ailments. You think that she is
       intentionally producing the physical symptoms in order to gain attention. You think that the
       ailment fills some psychological need. You would diagnose:
   a.   factitious disorder.
   b.   conversion disorder.
   c.   generalized anxiety disorder.
   d.   psychophysical disorder.

Traditional Psychophysiological Disorders, p. 174
Diff: M, Type: Applied, Ans: a

77.   An example of evidence for psychophysiological disorders is that:
   a.   ulcers, asthma, insomnia, and chronic headaches probably have physical and
          psychosocial causes.
   b.   disorders such as bacterial and viral infections have only physical causes.
   c.   disorders such as hypertension and coronary heart disease have only psychosocial causes.
   d.   cancer has been found to have a significant psychological cause.

Traditional Psychophysiological Disorders, p. 174
Diff: M, Type: Factual, Ans: c

78.   All of the following are considered traditional psychophysiological disorders except:
   a.   asthma.
   b.   insomnia.
   c.   cancer.
   d.   migraine headaches.

Traditional Psychophysiological Disorders, p. 174
Diff: E, Type: Factual, Ans: b
79.   About what proportion of the U.S. population experiences insomnia in a given year?
      a.   1/2
      b.   1/3
      c.   1/5
      d.   1/10

Traditional Psychophysiological Disorders, p. 174
Diff: M, Type: Applied, Ans: d
80.   A person feels well rested during the day, does not have burning sensations in the stomach, and appears to have normal breathing function. If you are told this person has a psychophysiological disorder, your best guess about what the disorder is would be:
      a.   insomnia.
      b.   asthma.
      c.   ulcers.
      d.   hypertension.

Traditional Psychophysiological Disorders, p. 175
Diff: E, Type: Applied, Ans: d
81.   The most common of the following psychophysiological disorders is:
      a.   ulcers.
      b.   chronic headaches.
      c.   asthma.
      d.   hypertension.

Traditional Psychophysiological Disorders, p. 175
Diff: E, Type: Applied, Ans: a
82.   Obesity and lack of exercise have been linked most closely to which of the following psychophysiological disorders?
      a.   coronary heart disease
      b.   ulcers
      c.   muscle contraction headaches
      d.   asthma

Traditional Psychophysiological Disorders, p. 175
Diff: M, Type: Applied, Ans: b
83.   Operating which of the following causes adults the most stress?
      a.   VCR
      b.   cell phone
      c.   TV
      d.   answering machine

Traditional Psychophysiological Disorders, p. 176
Diff: E, Type: Applied, Ans: a

84.   Hypertension is more common among African Americans than among white Americans. If someone believes this is because African Americans are more likely to live in dangerous areas, work at unsatisfying jobs, and suffer discrimination, one is emphasizing the role of _____ factors in the development of the disorder.
   a.   sociocultural
   b.   psychological
   c.   biological
   d.   interactive

Traditional Psychophysiological Disorders, p. 176
Diff: M, Type: Applied, Ans: d

85.   A person who has difficulty expressing unpleasant emotions such as anger or hostility is displaying a _____ and is at greater risk for heart disease/asthma.
   a.   sociocultural stressor
   b.   type A personality
   c.   type B personality
   d.   repressive coping style

Traditional Psychophysiological Disorders, p. 176
Diff: M, Type: Applied, Ans: b

86.   People who are consistently angry, impatient, competitive, driven, and ambitious are displaying a _____ and are at greater risk for heart disease.
   a.   sociocultural stressor
   b.   type A personality
   c.   type B personality
   d.   repressive coping style

Traditional Psychophysiological Disorders, p. 176
Diff: H, Type: Applied, Ans: a

87.   Which of the following aspects of Type A personality make a person most vulnerable to heart disease?
   a.   hostility and time urgency
   b.   ambition and competition
   c.   impatience and anger
   d.   cynicism and tension

Traditional Psychophysiological Disorders, p. 176
Diff: E, Type: Factual, Ans: c

88.   According to Selye, in the presence of stress, the body's initial response is in the _____ stage and involves primarily action of the _____.
   a.   resistance; parasympathetic nervous system
   b.   exhaustion; sympathetic nervous system
   c.   alarm; sympathetic nervous system
   d.   resistance; sympathetic nervous system

Traditional Psychophysiological Disorders, p. 176
Diff: E, Type: Factual, Ans: c
89.   Researchers have found a link between Type A personality and:
       a.   lack of aggressiveness.
       b.   somatoform disorder.
       c.   coronary heart disease.
       d.   generalized anxiety disorder.

Traditional Psychophysiological Disorders, p. 176
Diff: E, Type: Applied, Ans: c
90.   Stacey was out late at night when she came upon a group of men who appeared ready to
       attack her. She got scared and prepared to run. The part of her nervous system that was
       producing this reaction was the:
       a.   central nervous system.
       b.   peripheral nervous system.
       c.   sympathetic nervous system.
       d.   parasympathetic nervous system.

Traditional Psychophysiological Disorders, p. 176
Diff: E, Type: Factual, Ans: c
91.   The correct order for the general adaptation syndrome is:
       a.   danger, resistance, and collapse.
       b.   exhaustion, resistance, and alarm.
       c.   alarm, resistance, and exhaustion.
       d.   resistance, exhaustion, and collapse.

Traditional Psychophysiological Disorders, p. 176
Diff: E, Type: Factual, Ans: a
92.   Which phase of the general adaptation syndrome is assumed to involve activation of the
       sympathetic nervous system?
       a.   alarm
       b.   collapse
       c.   resistance
       d.   exhaustion

Traditional Psychophysiological Disorders, p. 176
Diff: M, Type: Factual, Ans: c
93.   Which phase of the general adaptation syndrome is assumed to involve activation of the
       parasympathetic nervous system?
       a.   alarm
       b.   collapse
       c.   resistance
       d.   exhaustion

Traditional Psychophysiological Disorders, p. 176
Diff: E, Type: Applied, Ans: a

94.   Suzanne is told that if she does not increase her work output significantly in the next week, she will be fired. According to Selye, her immediate reaction to this news is likely to be:
     a.   alarm.
     b.   collapse.
     c.   resistance.
     d.   exhaustion.

Traditional Psychophysiological Disorders, p. 176
Diff: E, Type: Applied, Ans: d

95.   Alberto has been working 18 hours a day trying to keep his business afloat. He has high blood pressure, an ulcer, and has just been taken to the hospital with chest pains. He is in Selye's stage of:
     a.   alarm.
     b.   collapse.
     c.   resistance.
     d.   exhaustion.

Traditional Psychophysiological Disorders, p. 176
Diff: M, Type: Applied, Ans: c

96.   Which of the following best reflects the correct order of Selye's stages of response to stress?
     a.   sympathetic arousal, sympathetic breakdown, exhaustion
     b.   sympathetic arousal, parasympathetic response, second sympathetic response
     c.   sympathetic arousal, parasympathetic response, exhaustion
     d.   parasympathetic response, sympathetic arousal, sympathetic breakdown

Traditional Psychophysiological Disorders, p. 176
Diff: E, Type: Applied, Ans: c

97.   Of the following, the individual with the highest risk of developing heart disease is:
     a.   Type A, with little concern about time.
     b.   Type B, with little concern about time.
     c.   Type A, hostile.
     d.   Type B, hostile.

New Psychophysiological Disorders, p. 177
Diff: H, Type: Applied, Ans: b

98.   If you were working in the field of psychoneuroimmunology, you would be studying:
     a.   the relationship between brain functioning and illness.
     b.   the links between psychosocial stress and physical illness.
     c.   the correlation between immune functioning and health.
     d.   the development of the neurological system when one is ill.

New Psychophysiological Disorders, p. 178
Diff: M, Type: Factual, Ans: d

99.   The Social Readjustment Rating Scale does all of the following except:
     a.   assigns a numerical value to stressful life events.
     b.   includes both positive and negative life events.
     c.   measures cumulative stress over a period of time.
     d.   reflects responses from many different ethnic groups.

New Psychophysiological Disorders, p. 178
Diff: H, Type: Applied, Ans: a

100.   If someone were to correlate scores on the Social Readjustment Rating Scale with the numbers of physical (health) complaints, one would most likely find:
    a.   a significant positive correlation.
    b.   a significant negative correlation.
    c.   no correlation.
    d.   the most illness for people experiencing very low and very high stress.

New Psychophysiological Disorders, p. 178
Diff: H, Type: Factual, Ans: c

101.   Of the following, the most serious limitation of the Social Readjustment Rating Scale is that it:
    a.   does not show a significant predictable relationship with physical illness.
    b.   has not been revised and is thus outdated.
    c.   does not take into account the stresses of diverse populations.
    d.   was normed only on college students.

New Psychophysiological Disorders, p. 178
Diff: M, Type: Factual, Ans: d

102.   One study of catastrophic stress effects in the months after the volcanic eruption of Mount St. Helens showed that emergency room visits at a nearby hospital:
    a.   stayed about the same, as did the hospital death rate.
    b.   increased, but the hospital death rate stayed about the same.
    c.   stayed about the same, but the hospital death rate increased.
    d.   increased, as did the hospital death rate.

New Psychophysiological Disorders, p. 178
Diff: E, Type: Factual, Ans: c

103.   African Americans rate all of the following as more stressful than white Americans do, except for:
    a.   major personal injury or illness.
    b.   major change in work responsibilities.
    c.   death of a spouse.
    d.   major change in living conditions.

New Psychophysiological Disorders, p. 179
Diff: E, Type: Factual, Ans: b

104.   The most stressful life event for a student on the Holmes and Rahe stress scale is:
    a.   unplanned pregnancy.
    b.   death of a family member (or friend).
    c.   being the victim of a crime.
    d.   breaking up with a boyfriend (or girlfriend).

New Psychophysiological Disorders, p. 179
Diff: E, Type: Factual, Ans: d

105.   Which of the following would you not find on the Social Readjustment Rating Scale?
    a.   death of spouse
    b.   jail term
    c.   pregnancy
    d.   exercise

New Psychophysiological Disorders, p. 179
Diff: E, Type: Applied, Ans: b

106. Which of the following people is experiencing the most stress as measured by the Social Readjustment Rating Scale?
   a. one who has just won the lottery
   b. one whose spouse has just died
   c. one who has just retired
   d. one whose child is seriously ill

New Psychophysiological Disorders, p. 179
Diff: M, Type: Applied, Ans: d

107. Those who report higher levels of stress related to a decrease in income or problems with one's credit are:
   a. young (college-age) men.
   b. young (college-age) women.
   c. men in general.
   d. women in general.

New Psychophysiological Disorders, p. 179
Diff: M, Type: Factual, Ans: c

108. Recent research suggests that stress interferes with human immune system functioning by:
   a. slowing lymphocyte reproduction.
   b. increasing lymphocyte effectiveness against antigens.
   c. triggering the production of immune cells.
   d. destroying antigens.

New Psychophysiological Disorders, p. 179
Diff: E, Type: Factual, Ans: a

109. Foreign invaders of the body that stimulate a response from the immune system are called:
   a. antigens.
   b. lymphocytes.
   c. killer T-cells.
   d. helper T-cells.

New Psychophysiological Disorders, p. 179
Diff: E, Type: Factual, Ans: b

110. The generic term for the white blood cells that react to foreign invaders in the body is:
   a. antigens.
   b. lymphocytes.
   c. killer T-cells.
   d. helper T-cells.

New Psychophysiological Disorders, p. 180
Diff: M, Type: Factual, Ans: d

111. The lymphocytes that identify foreign invaders and trigger the production of other kinds of immune cells are called:
   a. B-cells.
   b. antigens.
   c. killer T-cells.
   d. helper T-cells.

New Psychophysiological Disorders, p. 180
Diff: E, Type: Factual, Ans: c
112.   The white blood cells that destroy infected body cells are called:
       a.   B-cells.
       b.   antigens.
       c.   natural killer T-cells.
       d.   helper T-cells.

New Psychophysiological Disorders, p. 180
Diff: E, Type: Factual, Ans: d
113.   The reduction in activity of the immune system when a person is under stress is related to the
       activity of the neurotransmitter:
       a.   GABA.
       b.   dopamine.
       c.   acetylcholine.
       d.   norepinephrine.

New Psychophysiological Disorders, p. 180
Diff: H, Type: Factual, Ans: c
114.   The effect of norepinephrine and corticosteroids on a body experiencing stress is:
       a.   to keep the body's immune system functioning at a high level throughout the stress.
       b.   to keep the body's immune system functioning at a low level throughout the stress.
       c.   initially to stimulate the immune system, then to inhibit it.
       d.   initially to inhibit the immune system, then to stimulate it.

New Psychophysiological Disorders, p. 180
Diff: H, Type: Applied, Ans: b
115.   A person just subjected to very high stress immediately begins a long walk. Most likely, that
       person's overstressed body will begin to calm down—assuming that the stress hasn't
       continued—after about:
       a.   15 minutes.
       b.   30 minutes.
       c.   60 minutes.
       d.   120 minutes.

New Psychophysiological Disorders, p. 181
Diff: H, Type: Applied, Ans: b
116.   If you have a high level of C-reactive protein, we know that:
       a.   you have developed antibodies to protect you from infection.
       b.   you are at greater risk for heart disease, stroke, and other illness.
       c.   your liver is not producing cytokines.
       d.   your immune system is unusually healthy.

New Psychophysiological Disorders, p. 181
Diff: E, Type: Applied, Ans: a
117.   A friend says, "I feel like I'm stressed out and sick all the time. What kind of person is least
       likely to have an immune system messed up like mine?" Your best answer is:
       a.   "An optimist who is highly spiritual."
       b.   "An optimist who is not highly spiritual."
       c.   "A pessimist who is highly spiritual."
       d.   "A pessimist who is not highly spiritual."

New Psychophysiological Disorders, p. 181
Diff: E, Type: Factual, Ans: c
118. People with any psychological disorder are about how many times as likely to die of natural causes in a typical year, compared to people the same age without psychological disorders?
    a. half as likely
    b. as likely
    c. twice as likely
    d. three times as likely

New Psychophysiological Disorders, p. 181
Diff: H, Type: Applied, Ans: c
119. Which of the following is best supported by current research?
    a. Angry cancer patients have worse outcomes than those who do not express anger.
    b. No studies show any relationship between personality characteristics and cancer outcome.
    c. Social support seems to aid recovery in cancer patients.
    d. The chief cause of cancer is uncontrolled stress.

Psychological Treatments for Physical Disorders, p. 182
Diff: M, Type: Applied, Ans: d
120. If a friend was suffering from hypertension, the best advice you could give from the following alternatives is:
    a. combine relaxation training with biofeedback.
    b. combine biofeedback with medication.
    c. combine meditation with biofeedback.
    d. combine medication with relaxation training.

Psychological Treatments for Physical Disorders, p. 182
Diff: E, Type: Applied, Ans: c
121. Maureen is learning to warm her hands. She looks at a dial that reflects the output from a heat-sensitive device on her fingers. She simply tried to make the dial go up. This is a form of:
    a. meditation.
    b. relaxation training.
    c. biofeedback training.
    d. cognitive intervention.

Psychological Treatments for Physical Disorders, p. 182
Diff: M, Type: Applied, Ans: a
122. Relaxation training, biofeedback, meditation, and hypnosis all illustrate the use of:
    a. psychological treatments for physical illnesses.
    b. physical treatments for psychological illnesses.
    c. combinations of physical and psychological treatments.
    d. insight and social support therapies.

Psychological Treatments for Physical Disorders, p. 183
Diff: M, Type: Applied, Ans: b

123.   People who are coping with severe pain by telling themselves that they can get through it by focusing on the end of the pain, and by remembering that they have gotten through it before, are most likely to have received which of the following therapies?
   a.   insight therapy
   b.   cognitive intervention
   c.   behavioral medicine
   d.   psychotropic medication

Psychological Treatments for Physical Disorders, p. 184
Diff: H, Type: Applied, Ans: b

124.   People with stress-related problems write down their thoughts and feelings about their stressors several times in a procedure derived from:
   a.   cognitive-behavioral therapy.
   b.   insight therapy and support groups.
   c.   counseling and instruction training.
   d.   relaxing training.

FILL-IN QUESTIONS

Stress and Arousal: The Fight-or-Flight response, p. 158
Diff: E, Type: Factual, Ans: sympathetic nervous system (or autonomic nervous system)

1.   The portion of the nervous system which is responsible for changes in response to fear and arousal is the _____.

The Psychological Stress Disorders: Acute and Posttraumatic Stress Disorders, p. 158
Diff: E, Type: Factual, Ans: acute stress disorder

2.   Reactions to trauma that happen almost immediately and gradually go away in a month or so are likely to be diagnosed as _____.

The Psychological Stress Disorders: Acute and Posttraumatic Stress Disorders, p. 158
Diff: E, Type: Factual, Ans: posttraumatic stress disorder

3.   Reliving an event that happened months ago, avoidance of things associated with that event, and a generally reduced responsiveness, are symptoms of _____.

What Triggers a Psychological Stress Disorder?, p. 160
Diff: M, Type: Factual, Ans: posttraumatic stress disorder

4.   Clinicians eventually have come to realize that many soldiers also experienced serious psychological symptoms long after combat is over. The syndrome that can follow combat is called _____.

What Triggers a Psychological Stress Disorder?, p. 161
Diff: M, Type: Applied, Ans: posttraumatic stress disorder

5.   The mayor of Lockerbie, Scotland, still wakes up in a cold sweat thinking about a burning jetliner crashing into his town. This is an example of a _____.

What Triggers a Psychological Stress Disorder?, p. 161
Diff: E, Type: Factual, Ans: rape

6.   Forced sexual intercourse is called _____.

Why Do People Develop a Psychological Stress Disorder?, p. 166
Diff: H, Type: Factual, Ans: norepinephrine

7.   A biological explanation for the stress disorders involves the activity of the neurotransmitter/hormone _____.

Why Do People Develop a Psychological Stress Disorder?, p. 167
Diff: H, Type: Applied, Ans: hardy (or resilient)

8.   "The pressure's really getting to me!" says a friend of yours. "But I know I can cope." Your best reply is: "You're a _____ person."

Why Do People Develop a Psychological Stress Disorder?, p. 167
Diff: E, Type: Factual, Ans: social support

9.   The aspect of the response to or recovery from posttraumatic stress disorder or acute stress disorder that involves friends and family is _____.

How Do Clinicians Treat the Psychological Stress Disorders?, p. 168
Diff: M, Type: Factual, Ans: combat fatigue (or posttraumatic stress disorder)

10.   The "rap group" was invented to treat the psychological disorder called _____.

How Do Clinicians Treat the Psychological Stress Disorders?, p. 172
Diff: M, Type: Applied, Ans: psychological debriefing (or critical incident stress debriefing)

11.   A local psychologist goes with APA and Red Cross personnel to help firefighters deal with the stress they experience shortly after a disastrous fire. The psychologist is providing _____.

The Physical Stress Disorders: Psychophysiological Disorders, p. 174
Diff: E, Type: Factual, Ans: somatoform (or factitious)

12.   A disorder involving a "apparent" (but not actual) physical illness is called _____.

Traditional Psychophysiological Disorders, p. 174
Diff: E, Type: Factual, Ans: ulcers

13.   Lesions or holes that form in the lining of the stomach or duodenum and result in burning sensations or pain are called _____.

Traditional Psychophysiological Disorders, p. 175
Diff: E, Type: Factual, Ans: migraine

14.   Extremely severe and often immobilizing aches located on one side of the head, often preceded by an aura, are called _____ headaches.

Traditional Psychophysiological Disorders, p. 175
Diff: E, Type: Factual, Ans: hypertension

15.   High blood pressure is also called _____.

Traditional Psychophysiological Disorders, p. 176
Diff: H, Type: Factual, Ans: psychophysiological

16.   According to some theorists, wide-ranging stressors, chronic social circumstances, and transient stressors are types of sociocultural factors that may contribute to the development of _____ disorders.

Traditional Psychophysiological Disorders, p. 176
Diff: E, Type: Factual, Ans: Type A personality

17.   The personality type that is most likely to have heart disease is called the _____.

Traditional Psychophysiological Disorders, p. 176
Diff: M, Type: Applied, Ans: Type A

18.   Nadia never quits. She is always in quest of the "deal." She is aggressive, hard working, and not even a little fun loving. Her personality would be described as _____.

Traditional Psychophysiological Disorders, p. 176
Diff: M, Type: Applied, Ans: Type B

19.   Albert is relaxed and nothing seems to faze him for long. He is about as laid back as they come. His personality would be described as _____.

Traditional Psychophysiological Disorders, p. 176
Diff: E, Type: Factual, Ans: alarm

20.   The first stage of the general adaptation syndrome is _____.

Traditional Psychophysiological Disorders, p. 176
Diff: E, Type: Factual, Ans: stress

21.   Part of the point of the research conducted by Holmes and Rahe is that common daily adjustments can produce _____.

New Psychophysiological Disorders, p. 177
Diff: M, Type: Factual, Ans: immune system

22.   People are at risk after an enormously stressful life event because of the effect of stress on the _____.

ESSAY QUESTIONS

Stress and Arousal: The Fight-or-Flight response, p. 157
Diff: M, Type: Factual

1.   Explain how the autonomic nervous system responds in the face of fear and after the event has passed.

Stress and Arousal: The Fight-or-Flight response, pp. 157-158
Diff: H, Type: Applied

2.   Explain, using a diagram if you wish, either the sympathetic nervous system *or* the hypothalamic-pituitary-adrenal pathway as it relates to the stress response.

The Physiological Stress Disorders: Acute and Posttraumatic Stress Disorders, p. 158
Diff: E, Type: Factual

3.   Describe acute stress disorder and posttraumatic stress disorder. Carefully distinguish between the two.

What Triggers a Psychological Stress Disorder?, p. 161
Diff: H, Type: Applied

4.   Imagine that a friend of yours has been raped. What are the typical psychological reactions to rape that you might expect in your friend? That is, what is the course of her stress response to being raped likely to be?

What Triggers a Psychological Stress Disorder?, p. 164
Diff: M, Type: Factual

5.   Please discuss in some detail the factors related to higher rates of posttraumatic stress disorder in some groups following the September 11, 2001, terrorist attacks on New York City.

Why Do People Develop a Psychological Stress Disorder?, p. 166ff
Diff: H, Type: Factual

6.   Certain conditions make stress disorders more likely to occur. Briefly describe some of the biological/genetic, personality, childhood experiences, social support variables, and characteristics of the trauma that put people at risk for developing a stress disorder.

How Do Clinicians Treat the Psychological Stress Disorders?, p. 168ff
Diff: H, Type: Factual

7.   Describe three different treatments that have been effective in treating combat veterans experiencing stress disorders. Be sure to describe what actually happens in these treatments.

How Do Clinicians Treat the Psychological Stress Disorders?, p. 171ff
Diff: H, Type: Applied

8.   Imagine that there has been a dormitory fire on your campus that killed 5 people and injured 100 others. Using psychological debriefing principles, describe what you would do to help the victims.

The Physical Stress Disorders: Psychophysiological Disorders, p. 174ff
Diff: M, Type: Applied

9.   List four distinctly different psychophysiological disorders. For each discuss the interaction between psychological and physical causes. Please be very specific in your answer.

Psychological Treatments for Physical Disorders, p. 182ff
Diff: H, Type: Applied

10.   Describe any three of the following treatment techniques, then identify the specific psychophysical disorder for which each has been found most helpful: relaxation training, biofeedback, cognitive interventions, insight therapy, support groups.

CHAPTER 7   Somatoform and Dissociative Disorders

MULTIPLE-CHOICE QUESTIONS

What Are Hysterical Somatoform Disorders?, p. 190
Diff: M, Type: Applied, Ans: a

1. Just before debuting at Carnegie Hall, the pianist suffered paralysis of the left hand. Which of the following is the best diagnosis for this disorder?
   a. conversion disorder
   b. somatization disorder
   c. pain disorder associated with psychological factors
   d. preoccupation disorder

What Are Hysterical Somatoform Disorders?, p. 190
Diff: E, Type: Applied, Ans: c

2. A 35-year-old woman hobbles into the office of a physician complaining of a debilitating illness that has robbed her of the use of her left leg and right arm. The physician finds no physical basis for her symptoms. She appears totally unaware that the cause of her symptoms may be psychological. The diagnosis would be:
   a. malingering.
   b. factitious disorder.
   c. conversion disorder.
   d. preoccupation disorder.

What Are Hysterical Somatoform Disorders?, p. 190
Diff: E, Type: Applied, Ans: d

3. A person with conversion blindness, paralysis, or loss of feeling may also be said to be displaying:
   a. malingering.
   b. pain disorder.
   c. selective symptomatology.
   d. pseudoneurological symptom.

What Are Hysterical Somatoform Disorders?, p. 191
Diff: M, Type: Applied, Ans: a

4. Conversion disorders are more common in:
   a. women than men.
   b. men than women.
   c. the middle aged than the young.
   d. the elderly than the middle aged.

What Are Hysterical Somatoform Disorders?, p. 191
Diff: M, Type: Factual, Ans: b
5.   Conversion disorders most often appear in:
      a.   childhood.
      b.   adolescence.
      c.   middle adulthood.
      d.   late adulthood.

What Are Hysterical Somatoform Disorders?, p. 19
Diff: M, Type: Factual, Ans: b1
6.   If a person complains of a wide variety of physical symptoms over a period of time in the absence of a physical basis for the symptoms, the diagnosis would likely be:
      a.   conversion disorder.
      b.   somatization disorder.
      c.   body of dysmorphic disorder.
      d.   psychophysiological disorder.

What Are Hysterical Somatoform Disorders?, p. 191
Diff: M, Type: Applied, Ans: b
7.   Madeline appeared at the clinic complaining of pain in her knee, shoulder, and abdomen, nausea and vomiting, blurred vision, and exhaustion. The patient history revealed that she had been going to clinics for years trying to get treatment for these complaints and a host of other physical symptoms. The diagnostic consensus was that Madeline suffered from:
      a.   factitious disorder
      b.   somatization disorder.
      c.   preoccupation disorder.
      d.   body dysmorphic disorder.

What Are Hysterical Somatoform Disorders?, p. 191
Diff: H, Type: Applied, Ans: b
8.   The patient had several surgeries over the years for vague and nonspecific sexual reproductive problems, visiting many of the best hospitals in the East during the course of treatment. The best diagnosis for this disorder is:
      a.   conversion disorder.
      b.   somatization disorder.
      c.   pain disorder associated with psychological factors.
      d.   preoccupation disorder.

What Are Hysterical Somatoform Disorders?, p. 192
Diff: H, Type: Applied, Ans: a
9.   A somatization disorder differs from a conversion disorder in that:
      a.   conversion disorders usually last less time.
      b.   conversion disorders usually begin later in life than somatization disorders.
      c.   conversion disorders are more common than somatization disorders in the United States.
      d.   conversion disorders are more common in men and somatization disorders are more common in women.

What Are Hysterical Somatoform Disorders?, p. 192
Diff: M, Type: Applied, Ans: c

10.   The heart patient complained of adhesions from the scar, leg cramps, and joint stiffness, but no medical reason could be found to explain the symptoms. The best diagnosis for this disorder is:
      a.   conversion disorder.
      b.   somatization disorder.
      c.   pain disorder associated with psychological factors.
      d.   preoccupation disorder.

What Are Hysterical Somatoform Disorders?, p. 192
Diff: M, Type: Factual, Ans: a

11.   About what percentage of American men experience a somatization disorder in a given year?
      a.   less than 1%
      b.   1-2%
      c.   3-4%
      d.   over 5%

What Are Hysterical Somatoform Disorders?, p. 193
Diff: H, Type: Applied, Ans: a

12.   Which of the following is an example of malingering?
      a.   intentionally faking a tic in order to avoid military service
      b.   intentionally faking back problems because the person likes being a patient
      c.   experiencing chest pains in response to intense stress
      d.   enjoying unnecessary medical tests

What Are Hysterical Somatoform Disorders?, p. 193
Diff: M, Type: Applied, Ans: a

13.   Which of the following is true about malingering and factitious disorders?
      a.   Malingerers are trying to achieve some external gain by faking illness.
      b.   Those with factitious disorders do not intentionally create illness.
      c.   Malingerers and those with factitious disorders have no control over their behavior.
      d.   Hysterical and factitious disorders are identical.

What Are Hysterical Somatoform Disorders?, p. 193
Diff: M, Type: Applied, Ans: d

14.   A person appeared at the emergency room complaining of bloody diarrhea. When examined further, it was found that the person was intentionally creating the diarrhea through use of laxatives and anticoagulant medication, and liked being a patient. This person is most likely experiencing:
      a.   a psychophysical disorder.
      b.   malingering.
      c.   a somatoform disorder.
      d.   a factitious disorder.

What Are Hysterical Somatoform Disorders?, p. 193
Diff: E, Type: Applied, Ans: b

15. Which of the following is likely to be useful in distinguishing hysterical somatoform disorders from true medical problems?
   a. the particular body part showing the symptom
   b. the failure of a condition to develop as expected
   c. the patient's description of the source of the symptoms
   d. the usual course of development of the physical symptoms

What Are Hysterical Somatoform Disorders?, p. 193
Diff: H, Type: Applied, Ans: b

16. Which of the following would lead you to suspect hysterical rather than medical symptoms?
   a. muscle atrophy in the "paralyzed" body part
   b. uniform and even numbness in the "damaged" hand
   c. symptoms consistent with the way the neurological system is known to work
   d. a great number of accidents and an inability to get around in a "blind" person

What Are Hysterical Somatoform Disorders?, p. 194
Diff: H, Type: Applied, Ans: a

17. Having a background in medicine, but also a grudge against the profession puts a person at risk for:
   a. a factitious disorder.
   b. body dysmorphic disorder.
   c. dissociative amnesia.
   d. depersonalization.

What Are Hysterical Somatoform Disorders?, p. 194
Diff: H, Type: Applied, Ans: b

18. Someone who has Munchausen syndrome, also by definition, has:
   a. Munchausen by proxy.
   b. a factitious disorder.
   c. dissociative identity disorder.
   d. body dysmorphic disorder.

What Are Hysterical Somatoform Disorders?, p. 194
Diff: E, Type: Applied, Ans: d

19. Sarah brings her young daughter into the emergency room with internal bleeding. The attending physician later concludes that Sarah caused the symptoms in her daughter intentionally, to bring her to a doctor's attention. If this assessment is true, Sarah would be diagnosed as having:
   a. a factitious disorder.
   b. a conversion disorder.
   c. Munchausen syndrome.
   d. Munchausen syndrome by proxy.

What Are Hysterical Somatoform Disorders?, p. 194
Diff: M, Type: Applied, Ans: d

20.   If a chronically ill child was removed from home and placed in foster care, and then became quite healthy, one might suspect that the original parent was experiencing:
    a.   malingering.
    b.   a psychophysical disorder.
    c.   a somatoform disorder.
    d.   a factitious disorder.

What Are Hysterical Somatoform Disorders?, p. 194
Diff: M, Type: Factual, Ans: b

21.   Munchausen syndrome is a _____ disorder.
    a.   somatoform
    b.   factitious
    c.   psychophysical
    d.   conversion

What Are Hysterical Somatoform Disorders?, p. 194
Diff: E, Type: Applied, Ans: b

22.   Munchausen syndrome by proxy is most likely to adversely affect the physical well-being of:
    a.   the person experiencing it.
    b.   the child of the person experiencing it.
    c.   the spouse of the person experiencing it.
    d.   the medical personnel caring for the person experiencing it.

What Are Hysterical Somatoform Disorders?, p. 194
Diff: M, Type: Factual, Ans: c

23.   Which of the following is a primary characteristic of an individual with Munchausen syndrome by proxy?
    a.   psychotic
    b.   independent
    c.   emotionally needy
    d.   limited intelligence and education

What Are Preoccupation Somatoform Disorders?, p. 194
Diff: E, Type: Applied, Ans: d

24.   If you looked in Jeanette's medicine cabinet, you would find dozens of prescriptions and even more over-the-counter medications. Every time she sneezes, she is sure she has the latest deadly flu, although no physician has ever found anything wrong with her. She suffers from:
    a.   conversion disorder.
    b.   body dysmorphic disorder.
    c.   hysterical somatoform disorder.
    d.   preoccupation somatoform disorder.

What Are Preoccupation Somatoform Disorders?, p. 194
Diff: M, Type: Applied, Ans: d

25.   If a person were experiencing numerous physical complaints, visiting doctors frequently, and expressed great concern about normal bodily symptoms, one would most likely suspect:
       a.   somatization.
       b.   body dysmorphic disorder.
       c.   pain disorder associated with psychological factors.
       d.   hypochondriasis.

What Are Preoccupation Somatoform Disorders?, p. 194
Diff: H, Type: Applied, Ans: a

26.   Hypochondriasis differs from somatization disorder in that:
       a.   in hypochondriasis, anxiety is more pronounced than in somatization disorder.
       b.   hypochondriasis is a hysterical disorder rather than a preoccupation disorder.
       c.   more men than women experience somatization; more women than men experience hypochondriasis.
       d.   the symptoms are more pronounced in hypochondriasis than in somatization disorders.

What Are Preoccupation Somatoform Disorders?, p. 194
Diff: H, Type: Factual, Ans: c

27.   A key factor distinguishing between hypochondriasis and somatization disorder is that:
       a.   hypochondriasis is more common in women, and somatization disorder is more common in men.
       b.   somatization disorder is more common in women, and hypochondriasis is more common in men.
       c.   hypochondriasis involves minor ailments overshadowed by high anxiety, and somatization disorder involves significant symptoms that overshadow anxiety.
       d.   hypochondriasis involves minor ailments that overshadow anxiety, and somatization disorder involves significant ailments that are overshadowed by high anxiety.

What Are Preoccupation Somatoform Disorders?, p. 195
Diff: M, Type: Applied, Ans: b

28.   A person who is excessively concerned about genital odors and the shape and look of the genitals is most likely experiencing:
       a.   somatization.
       b.   body dysmorphic disorder.
       c.   pain disorder associated with psychological factors.
       d.   hypochondriasis.

What Are Preoccupation Somatoform Disorders?, p. 195
Diff: E, Type: Factual, Ans: d

29.   People who become preoccupied with some imagined or exaggerated defect in their appearance suffer from a:
       a.   conversion disorder.
       b.   somatization disorder.
       c.   hypochondriacal disorder.
       d.   body dysmorphic disorder.

What Are Preoccupation Somatoform Disorders?, p. 195
Diff: E, Type: Applied, Ans: c

30.   Martin was certain that his chin was too big and was misshapen. He was very anxious in public and tried to work at home whenever possible. His condition could best be diagnosed as:
    a.   somatization disorder.
    b.   hypochondriacal disorder.
    c.   body dysmorphic disorder.
    d.   factitious disorder with psychological symptoms.

What Are Preoccupation Somatoform Disorders?, p. 195
Diff: M, Type: Factual, Ans: d

31.   Dysmorphophobia is a somatoform disorder characterized by:
    a.   severe and prolonged pain in one area of the body.
    b.   significant dysfunctioning in one or more areas of the body.
    c.   overconcern with minor physical fluctuations in one's bodily state.
    d.   preoccupation with an imagined or exaggerated defect in appearance.

What Are Preoccupation Somatoform Disorders?, p. 196
Diff: M, Type: Applied, Ans: b

32.   A person who has repeated plastic surgeries in order to correct only very minor defects that no one else even notices is probably experiencing:
    a.   somatization.
    b.   body dysmorphic disorder.
    c.   pain disorder associated with psychological factors.
    d.   hypochondriasis.

What Causes Somatoform Disorders?, p. 196
Diff: M, Type: Applied, Ans: a

33.   Preoccupation somatoform disorders are typically explained by therapists in much the same way as _____ disorders are.
    a.   anxiety
    b.   substance abuse
    c.   mood
    d.   schizophrenic

What Causes Somatoform Disorders?, pp. 196-197
Diff: H, Type: Factual, Ans: d

34.   Ancient Greeks thought that hysterical disorders were caused by:
    a.   an unresolved wish to be a member of the other sex.
    b.   hypnotic suggestion.
    c.   classical conditioning.
    d.   the wandering uterus of a sexually ungratified woman.

What Causes Somatoform Disorders?, p. 197
Diff: M, Type: Factual, Ans: d
35.   Studies have shown that about what percent of women and men in the U.S. would change
       something about their appearance if they could?
       a.   less than 90% of women and of men
       b.   less than 90% of men, over 90% of women
       c.   less than 90% of women, over 90% of men
       d.   more than 90% of men and of women

What Causes Somatoform Disorders?, p. 198
Diff: H, Type: Applied, Ans: d
36.   With respect to the causes of somatoform disorders:
       a.   hysterical disorders are explained similarly to the way anxiety disorders are explained.
       b.   currently, hysterical disorders are thought to be due to a "wandering uterus."
       c.   hysterical symptoms appear to be particularly resistant to hypnosis.
       d.   the causes are poorly understood with no theory predominating.

What Causes Somatoform Disorders?, p. 198
Diff: M, Type: Factual, Ans: d
37.   Psychodynamic theorists propose that unconscious conflicts arouse anxiety. Disorders that
       represent the conversion of anxiety into physical symptoms are:
       a.   simple phobias.
       b.   dissociative disorders.
       c.   psychophysiological disorders.
       d.   hysterical somatoform disorders.

What Causes Somatoform Disorders?, p. 199
Diff: E, Type: Factual, Ans: b
38.   According to the psychodynamic view, conversion disorder symptoms function to keep
       unacceptable thoughts and conflicts out of consciousness. This is called:
       a.   sociocultural stress.
       b.   primary gain.
       c.   reinforcement.
       d.   secondary gain.

What Causes Somatoform Disorders?, p. 199
Diff: M, Type: Applied, Ans: d
39.   It was convenient when Rowena awoke blind. She had been terrified about testifying and
       now she did not have to. According to psychodynamic theory, this is an example of:
       a.   repression.
       b.   primary gain.
       c.   reinforcement.
       d.   secondary gain.

What Causes Somatoform Disorders?, p. 199
Diff: M, Type: Factual, Ans: b
40.   Freud believed that hysterical symptoms:
       a.   were rooted in the oral stage.
       b.   enabled people to avoid unpleasant activities.
       c.   were medical problems that needed medical, not psychological treatment.
       d.   were more common in men than women.

What Causes Somatoform Disorders?, p. 199
Diff: H, Type: Applied, Ans: a
41.   A woman who is particularly threatened by any display of anger becomes unable to speak
       when she is most angry with her husband, thereby keeping the anger out of her awareness.
       According to psychodynamic theorists, she is achieving _____ from her illness.
       a.   primary gain
       b.   secondary gain
       c.   tertiary gain
       d.   no gain

What Causes Somatoform Disorders?, p. 199
Diff: H, Type: Applied, Ans: b
42.   If the behavior of a man elicited kindness and sympathy from his wife when he was mute, he
       would be receiving _____ gains from his behavior.
       a.   primary
       b.   secondary
       c.   tertiary
       d.   no

What Causes Somatoform Disorders?, p. 199
Diff: M, Type: Applied, Ans: c
43.   Every time Miguel had a headache, his mother let him miss school. Now, as an adult, his
       headaches have become more frequent. His head pounds any time he is required to do
       something he would rather not. This is a _____ explanation of conversion symptoms.
       a.   cognitive
       b.   biological
       c.   behavioral
       d.   cultural

What Causes Somatoform Disorders?, p. 199
Diff: H, Type: Applied, Ans: c
44.   If a therapist believed that a person were displaying hysterical symptoms because the
       symptoms helped the person avoid unpleasant situations, without questioning the therapist
       about why the symptoms developed, you couldn't know for sure if the therapist were:
       a.   a cognitive theorist or a behaviorist.
       b.   a cognitive theorist or a psychoanalyst.
       c.   a psychoanalyst or a behaviorist.
       d.   a cognitive theorist, a behaviorist, or a psychoanalyst.

What Causes Somatoform Disorders?, p. 199
Diff: H, Type: Applied, Ans: c
45.   Behavioral therapists treating an hysterical disorder would be most likely to focus on:
       a.   identifying underlying emotional causes for the disorder.
       b.   helping the patient gain insight into how the disorder is reinforcing.
       c.   reducing the rewards available for displaying the disorder.
       d.   replacing the primary gain with a secondary gain.

What Causes Somatoform Disorders?, p. 199
Diff: H, Type: Applied, Ans: d

46. The chief criticism of the behavioral and psychodynamic explanations for the maintenance of hysterical disorders is that:
    a. they focus too much on the gains the disorder brings to the patient.
    b. they fail to take into account the gains the disorder brings to the patient.
    c. they confuse the ideas of gain and reward.
    d. they can't explain how the gains can outweigh the pain of the disorder.

What Causes Somatoform Disorders?, p. 200
Diff: M, Type: Factual, Ans: a

47. The perspective on hysterical disorders that suggest people use these symptoms to communicate emotions that they cannot easily express otherwise is the _____ view.
    a. cognitive
    b. behavioral
    c. humanistic
    d. psychodynamic

What Causes Somatoform Disorders?, p. 200
Diff: H, Type: Applied, Ans: d

48. A cognitive theorist would be most likely to say which of the following about hysterical disorders?
    a. The patient is receiving secondary gain from the symptoms.
    b. The patient is unable to express any emotion except anxiety.
    c. The patient is being rewarded for behaving in this way.
    d. The patient is otherwise unable to communicate difficult emotions.

What Causes Somatoform Disorders?, p. 200
Diff: M, Type: Applied, Ans: a

49. Which of the following is the best example of a placebo?
    a. someone suggesting that you will soon feel better
    b. an experimental treatment involving a new drug
    c. a treatment designed to produce a worsening of the symptoms
    d. treatment given by paraprofessionals

What Causes Somatoform Disorders?, p. 200
Diff: H, Type: Applied, Ans: a

50. The most current research suggests that expectations and suggestions work by:
    a. triggering chemical changes in the body.
    b. causing psychological but not biological changes in the body.
    c. blocking the release of endorphins.
    d. replacing one's logical cognitive skills.

How Are Somatoform Disorders Treated?, p. 201
Diff: H, Type: Factual, Ans: c

51. Those who are experiencing preoccupation somatoform disorders are likely to receive psychological treatment that is most like those who are experiencing _____ disorder.
    a. substance abuse
    b. mood
    c. generalized anxiety
    d. organic mental

How Are Somatoform Disorders Treated?, p. 201
Diff: H, Type: Applied, Ans: c

52. If you were receiving the most effective medication for body dysmorphic disorder, you would be receiving:
     a. an antianxiety medication.
     b. a weight control medication.
     c. an antidepressant medication.
     d. a medication designed to improve memory.

How Are Somatoform Disorders Treated?, p. 202
Diff: E, Type: Factual, Ans: a

53. Psychodynamic theorists propose that unconscious conflicts cause conversion disorders. Their remedy is to bring these to consciousness and work them through. Knowledge of the underlying problem will make the symptom disappear. This therapy is based on:
     a. insight.
     b. suggestion.
     c. confrontation.
     d. reinforcement.

How Are Somatoform Disorders Treated?, p. 202
Diff: H, Type: Applied, Ans: c

54. Albert had finally had enough of his inability to walk, and he went to a psychologist who told him there was nothing medically wrong. This therapy was based on:
     a. insight.
     b. suggestion.
     c. confrontation.
     d. exposure and response prevention.

How Are Somatoform Disorders Treated?, p. 202
Diff: H, Type: Applied, Ans: c

55. Based on evidence from case studies, the best advice you could give someone who was experiencing a hysterical disorder about seeking treatment is:
     a. be very wary of taking antidepressants; they don't work with this disorder.
     b. confrontation therapy is the treatment of choice.
     c. approaches using insight, suggestion, and reinforcement work best for physical symptoms.
     d. family therapy has been most heavily researched and seems to show the most promise.

Dissociative Disorders, p. 202
Diff: E, Type: Factual, Ans: c

56. Our preferences, needs, abilities, and characteristics combine to form our:
     a. memory.
     b. values.
     c. identity.
     d. ego ideal.

Dissociative Disorders, p. 203
Diff: H, Type: Applied, Ans: d

57.   If you had lost your sense of identity, which of the following would most likely be disrupted?
       a.   your relationships
       b.   your intellectual functioning
       c.   your attitudes toward your body
       d.   your memory

Dissociative Disorders, p. 203
Diff: H, Type: Factual, Ans: a

58.   Dissociative disorders:
       a.   involve major changes in memory.
       b.   usually have a precise physical cause.
       c.   are a type of anxiety disorder.
       d.   involve multiple personalities by definition.

Dissociative Disorders, p. 203
Diff: E, Type: Factual, Ans: c

59.   Which diagnosis includes a breakdown in sense of self, a significant alteration in memory or identity, and even a separation of one part of the identity from another part?
       a.   mood disorder
       b.   personality disorder
       c.   dissociative disorder
       d.   histrionic personality disorder

Dissociative Disorders, p. 203
Diff: H, Type: Applied, Ans: a

60.   Imagine that you are a therapist treating Iraqi war veterans. If you encountered a veteran with posttraumatic stress disorder, you would also be likely to find:
       a.   a dissociative disorder.
       b.   a body dysmorphic disorder.
       c.   a conversion disorder.
       d.   an hysterical disorder.

Dissociative Amnesia, p. 204
Diff: H, Type: Applied, Ans: b

61.   People who are unable to recall important information about themselves, especially of an upsetting nature, are most likely experiencing:
       a.   depersonalization.
       b.   dissociative amnesia.
       c.   body dysmorphic disorder.
       d.   the placebo response.

Dissociative Amnesia, p. 204
Diff: H, Type: Applied, Ans: b

62.   In the most common type of dissociative amnesia, a person loses memory for:
       a.   some but not all of the events surrounding the trauma.
       b.   all events beginning with the trauma but within a limited period of time.
       c.   all events from the trauma onward.
       d.   all events before and after the trauma.

Dissociative Amnesia, p. 204
Diff: H, Type: Applied, Ans: d

63.   After a major earthquake, television coverage showed survivors shuffling confusedly through the ruined buildings. If such victims later could not remember the days immediately after the earthquake, the victims would be suffering from what type of amnesia?
   a.   continuous
   b.   selective
   c.   posttraumatic
   d.   localized

Dissociative Amnesia, p. 204
Diff: E, Type: Factual, Ans: b

64.   What does dissociative amnesia affect?
   a.   personality
   b.   memory
   c.   intelligence
   d.   general cognitive functions

Dissociative Amnesia, p. 204
Diff: M, Type: Applied, Ans: b

65.   Mary Ann experiences a mugging and robbery in which her prized poodle is kidnapped. Eventually the dog is found and returned. However, she is unable to recall events immediately following the attack, up until the safe return of the dog. This is a classic example of:
   a.   selective amnesia.
   b.   localized amnesia.
   c.   continuous amnesia.
   d.   generalized amnesia.

Dissociative Amnesia, p. 205
Diff: M, Type: Applied, Ans: d

66.   Gwendolyn is held up at knifepoint and her young son is kidnapped. Eventually, her son is found and returned. However, she is unable to recall events that occurred since the attack, although she remembers some new experiences; worse still, she finds that she is forgetting events that occurred even before the attack. This is a classic example of:
   a.   selective amnesia.
   b.   localized amnesia.
   c.   continuous amnesia.
   d.   generalized amnesia.

Dissociative Amnesia, p. 205
Diff: M, Type: Applied, Ans: c

67.   Carlotta is attacked in the street and her young daughter is kidnapped. Eventually, the police
       find her daughter and she is returned to her mother. However, Carlotta is unable to recall
       events that have occurred since the attack. She is even unable to retain new information; she
       remembers what happened before the attack but cannot remember new and ongoing
       experiences. This is a classic example of:
       a.   localized amnesia.
       b.   selective amnesia.
       c.   continuous amnesia.
       d.   generalized amnesia.

Dissociative Amnesia, p. 205
Diff: H, Type: Applied, Ans: a

68.   Ever since the auto accident, during which Pat was miraculously unhurt, Pat has not been the
       same. Pat forgets appointments, friends' names, and even things done in the last few days.
       Pat's amnesia is termed:
       a.   continuous.
       b.   organic.
       c.   circumscribed.
       d.   selective.

Dissociative Amnesia, p. 205
Diff: M, Type: Applied, Ans: a

69.   Combat veterans are most likely to report symptoms of:
       a.   localized amnesia.
       b.   continuous amnesia.
       c.   generalized amnesia.
       d.   selective amnesia.

Dissociative Amnesia, p. 205
Diff: M, Type: Factual, Ans: b

70.   What is the term we use for the memory we have for abstract and categorical information?
       a.   episodic
       b.   semantic
       c.   short-term
       d.   procedural

Dissociative Amnesia, p. 205
Diff: M, Type: Factual, Ans: b

71.   All cases of dissociative amnesia generally involve:
       a.   interference with semantic memory.
       b.   interference with episodic memory.
       c.   interference with basic identity.
       d.   interference with sense of location.

Dissociative Fugue, p. 205
Diff: H, Type: Applied, Ans: d
72.   A person, years after committing a serious crime, is found living under a false identity over 1,000 miles from where the person used to live. The person's memory of the crime, and of other earlier events, is intact. Most likely this is a case of:
   a.   dissociative fugue.
   b.   dissociative amnesia.
   c.   dissociative identity (multiple personality) disorder.
   d.   no mental disorder.

Repressed Childhood Memories or False Memory Syndrome?, p. 206 (Box 7.4)
Diff: E, Type: Factual, Ans: c
73.   Which of the following is not an example of memory recovery techniques used by therapists?
   a.   hypnosis
   b.   journal writing
   c.   imagining the event
   d.   dream interpretation

Dissociative Fugue, p. 206
Diff: H, Type: Factual, Ans: d
74.   If recovered memories—of early childhood sexual abuse, for example—are *iatrogenic*, then the recovered memories:
   a.   are accurate, but are not supported by other forms of evidence.
   b.   are accurate, but are supported by other forms of evidence.
   c.   are intentionally created by the therapist.
   d.   are unintentionally created by the therapist.

Dissociative Fugue, p. 207
Diff: M, Type: Factual, Ans: b
75.   A personality change that often accompanies dissociative fugues is that people become:
   a.   more withdrawn.
   b.   more outgoing.
   c.   more inhibited.
   d.   more histrionic in their emotional reactions.

Dissociative Fugue, p. 207
Diff: H, Type: Factual, Ans: b
76.   Dissociative fugue states affect _____ memory but not _____ memory.
   a.   semantic; episodic
   b.   episodic; semantic
   c.   long-term; short-term
   d.   procedural; autobiographical

Dissociative Fugue, p. 207
Diff: E, Type: Factual, Ans: a
77.   Dissociative fugues usually:
   a.   follow a stressful event.
   b.   end very gradually.
   c.   have numerous recurrences.
   d.   involve irrecoverable memory loss.

Dissociative Fugue, p. 207
Diff: M, Type: Factual, Ans: b
78.   An individual who had suffered from dissociative fugue likely would have experienced all of the following except:
      a.   relatively few aftereffects.
      b.   a recurrence of the problem months or years later.
      c.   a fairly sudden ending to the dissociative fugue state.
      d.   a traumatic event.

Dissociative Identity Disorder (Multiple Personality Disorder), p. 208
Diff: M, Type: Factual, Ans: b
79.   One who suffers from dissociative identity disorder is most likely to be a:
      a.   man who was physically abused as a child.
      b.   woman who was physically abused as a child.
      c.   man who was not physically abused as a child.
      d.   woman who was not physically abused as a child.

Dissociative Identity Disorder (Multiple Personality Disorder), p. 208
Diff: H, Type: Applied, Ans: d
80.   A client who is talking calmly and rationally all of a sudden begins whining and complaining like a spoiled child. If that client suffers from true multiple personality disorder, the client just experienced:
      a.   host transfer.
      b.   mutual cognizance.
      c.   lability.
      d.   switching.

Dissociative Identity Disorder (Multiple Personality Disorder), p. 209
Diff: M, Type: Factual, Ans: d
81.   Alexis has multiple personality disorder. When one of her personalities, Jodi, is asked about another one, Tom, she claims ignorance. Tom has never heard of Jodi either. This would be called a:
      a.   co-conscious relationship.
      b.   mutually cognizant pattern.
      c.   one-way amnesic relationship.
      d.   mutually amnesic relationship.

Dissociative Identity Disorder (Multiple Personality Disorder), p. 209
Diff: M, Type: Factual, Ans: b
82.   When all of the subpersonalities in a person with dissociative identity disorder are aware of one another, it is termed a:
      a.   co-conscious relationship.
      b.   mutually cognizant pattern.
      c.   one-way amnesic relationship.
      d.   mutually amnesic relationship.

Dissociative Identity Disorder (Multiple Personality Disorder), p. 209
Diff: M, Type: Factual, Ans: b

83. Raymond has multiple personality disorder. All of his subpersonalities talk about and tattle on each other. This is called a:
    a. co-conscious relation.
    b. mutually cognizant pattern.
    c. one-way amnesic relationship.
    d. mutually amnesic relationship.

Dissociative Identity Disorder (Multiple Personality Disorder), p. 209
Diff: M, Type: Applied, Ans: a

84. In case of multiple personality, "Pat" is aware of the existence of "Jerry" and "Chris," but "Jerry" and "Chris" are not aware of the existence of the other personalities. This form of subpersonality relationship is called:
    a. one-way amnesic.
    b. mutually cognizant.
    c. mutually amnesic.
    d. co-conscious.

Dissociative Identity Disorder (Multiple Personality Disorder), p. 209
Diff: M, Type: Factual, Ans: c

85. Juanita has multiple personality disorder. Big Tony and Smart Alice are two personalities who are aware of all of the others. None of her other personalities are aware of each other. This would be called a:
    a. co-conscious relationship.
    b. mutually cognizant pattern.
    c. one-way amnesic relationship.
    d. mutually amnesic relationship.

Dissociative Identity Disorder (Multiple Personality Disorder), p. 209
Diff: M, Type: Factual, Ans: c

86. Jason has multiple personality disorder. Fat Freddy and Carmen are two personalities who are aware of all of the other, but do not interact with them. Fat Freddy and Carmen would be described as:
    a. self-reliant.
    b. co-occurring.
    c. co-conscious.
    d. mutually cognizant.

Dissociative Identity Disorder (Multiple Personality Disorder), p. 209
Diff: M, Type: Factual, Ans: c

87. Modern studies suggest that the average number of subpersonalities in cases of multiple personality in women is about:
    a. 8, and is lower for men.
    b. 8, and is higher for men.
    c. 15, and is lower for men.
    d. 15, and is higher for men.

Dissociative Identity Disorder (Multiple Personality Disorder), p. 209
Diff: M, Type: Applied, Ans: c

88.   An individual who formerly knew almost all the state and international capital cities can no
      longer remember them as a result of a dissociative disorder. That dissociative disorder most
      likely is:
      a.   dissociative fugue.
      b.   dissociative amnesia.
      c.   dissociative identity.
      d.   Such memories are affected about equally by the dissociative disorders.

Dissociative Identity Disorder (Multiple Personality Disorder), p. 210
Diff: H, Type: Factual, Ans: a

89.   Research on evoked potential with people with dissociative identity disorder has revealed
      that:
      a.   different subpersonalities have shown different brain response patterns.
      b.   people with dissociative identity disorder did not show different brain response patterns
           for subpersonalities.
      c.   no differences were found in brain activity between controls and individuals with
           dissociative identity disorder.
      d.   control subjects who were asked to pretend they had different personalities were able to
           create different brain response patterns for each subpersonality.

Dissociative Identity Disorder (Multiple Personality Disorder), p. 210
Diff: H, Type: Factual, Ans: b

90.   One very interesting study investigated the physiological responses of subpersonalities of
      those with dissociative identity disorder, and the physiological responses of the
      "subpersonalities" of those instructed to fake dissociative identity disorder. The study showed
      that the physiological responses of subpersonalities of those with dissociative identity
      disorder:
      a.   differed from one another, as did those of the subpersonalities of those faking dissociative
           identity disorder.
      b.   differed from one another, but the subpersonalities of those faking dissociative identity
           disorder did not.
      c.   did not differ from one another, although the subpersonalities of those faking dissociative
           identity disorder did differ.
      d.   did not differ from one another, nor did the subpersonalities of those faking dissociative
           identity disorder.

Dissociative Identity Disorder (Multiple Personality Disorder), p. 210
Diff: E, Type: Factual, Ans: a

91.   In the United States, the number of diagnosed cases per year of dissociative identity disorder:
      a.   has increased.
      b.   has decreased.
      c.   first increased, then decreased.
      d.   first decreased, then increased.

Dissociative Identity Disorder (Multiple Personality Disorder), p. 210
Diff: M, Type: Factual, Ans: c

92.   To what can we attribute much of the dramatic rise in the number of reported cases of dissociative identity disorder in recent years?
       a.   less strict criteria for defining schizophrenia
       b.   a growing belief that most cases of this disorder are iatrogenic
       c.   a growing belief by clinicians that this is an authentic disorder
       d.   the growing belief by clinicians that many women suffer from this disorder

Dissociative Identity Disorder (Multiple Personality Disorder), p. 210
Diff: M, Type: Applied, Ans: b

93.   A clinician says, "I've studied the literature carefully, and I really doubt the legitimacy of that particular diagnostic category." The "particular diagnostic category" to which that clinician refers probably is:
       a.   dissociative fugue.
       b.   dissociative identity disorder.
       c.   dissociative amnesia.
       d.   dementia.

Dissociative Identity Disorder (Multiple Personality Disorder), p. 210
Diff: H, Type: Applied, Ans: d

94.   The best example of the subpersonalities in dissociative identity disorder differing in their vital statistics occurs when:
       a.   one personality can drive or sew and another cannot.
       b.   one personality has asthma and another does not.
       c.   one personality has high blood pressure and another does not.
       d.   one personality is a woman and another is a man.

Dissociative Identity Disorder (Multiple Personality Disorder), p. 210
Diff: H, Type: Applied, Ans: a

95.   In the past, dissociative identity disorder was most likely "misdiagnosed" as:
       a.   schizophrenia.
       b.   mental retardation.
       c.   depersonalization.
       d.   body dysmorphic disorder.

How Do Theorists Explain Dissociative Disorders?, p. 211
Diff: M, Type: Factual, Ans: d

96.   A psychodynamic theorist would use repression as the chief explanation for all dissociative disorders except:
       a.   dissociative identity disorder.
       b.   dissociative fugue.
       c.   dissociative amnesia.
       d.   A psychodynamic theorist would use repression as the chief explanation for dissociative identity disorder, dissociative fugue, and dissociative amnesia.

How Do Theorists Explain Dissociative Disorders?, p. 211
Diff: E, Type: Factual, Ans: c

97.   Psychodynamic theorists believe that dissociative amnesias and fugues result from:
       a.   projection.
       b.   regression.
       c.   repression.
       d.   sublimation.

How Do Theorists Explain Dissociative Disorders?, p. 211
Diff: H, Type: Factual, Ans: a

98.   Which of the following hypotheses used to explain dissociative disorders is shared by
       psychodynamic and behavioral theorists?
       a.   They serve to help someone escape something unpleasant.
       b.   The attempts at forgetting are purposeful from the beginning.
       c.   The process involved in forgetting is supported by subtle reinforcement.
       d.   The individuals themselves are aware that their disorder is protecting them from facing a
            painful reality.

How Do Theorists Explain Dissociative Disorders?, p. 211
Diff: H, Type: Applied, Ans: c

99.   "An abused child's thoughts occasionally drift to other, less anxiety-arousing, topics; this
       anxiety reduction thus serves to strengthen 'other' thoughts, while weakening the thoughts
       about abuse." A psychologist with which theoretical background would be most likely to
       offer this quotation as an explanation for the development of dissociative disorders?
       a.   psychodynamic
       b.   biological
       c.   behavioral
       d.   sociocultural

How Do Theorists Explain Dissociative Disorders?, p. 212
Diff: E, Type: Applied, Ans: b

100.   Kevin studies his history notes and textbook while he is drinking beer. According to some
       theorists, Kevin would later do better on his history exam if he also had alcohol in his system
       while taking the exam. These theorists would be basing their claim on:
       a.   social learning theory.
       b.   state-dependent learning.
       c.   active-avoidance learning.
       d.   associative memory learning.

How Do Theorists Explain Dissociative Disorders?, p. 212
Diff: M, Type: Factual, Ans: c

101.   The chief sources of data used to support the theories of psychodynamic and behavioral
       clinicians are:
       a.   large-scale experimental studies.
       b.   biologically based.
       c.   case studies.
       d.   epidemiological.

How Do Theorists Explain Dissociative Disorders?, p. 212
Diff: M, Type: Applied, Ans: b

102. I was running down a familiar country lane when all of a sudden nothing looked familiar. It took me several seconds to realize where I was, and I continued my run without incident. What I experienced was:
    a. the tip-of-the-tongue phenomenon.
    b. jamais vu.
    c. déjà vu.
    d. absentmindedness.

How Do Theorists Explain Dissociative Disorders?, p. 212
Diff: H, Type: Applied, Ans: d

103. Just before 8 A.M. (when my first class meets), my young daughter did something that annoyed me as I was about to leave home for the short drive to campus. "Katie," I said, "what do I always say at a time like this?" She looked at the clock, then said to me, "What you say is, 'Where are my keys?'" My daughter was apparently familiar with my:
    a. visual memory deficit.
    b. jamais vu tendencies.
    c. nondisordered dissociative fugue.
    d. absentmindedness.

How Do Theorists Explain Dissociative Disorders?, p. 212
Diff: E, Type: Factual, Ans: d

104. A strong "feeling of knowing" is associated with which of the following?
    a. déjà vu
    b. jamais vu
    c. pseudopresentiment
    d. the tip-of-the-tongue phenomenon

How Do Theorists Explain Dissociative Disorders?, p. 212
Diff: E, Type: Factual, Ans: c

105. A visual image that is retained so vividly that one can continue to scan it for more information is called:
    a. déjà vu.
    b. jamais vu.
    c. an eidetic image.
    d. the tip-of-the-tongue phenomenon.

How Do Theorists Explain Dissociative Disorders?, p. 213
Diff: M, Type: Applied, Ans: b

106. Laurent has three subpersonalities. Jackie emerges when Laurent is in an awkward social situation, Grace surfaces during sporting events, and Carlos appears when Laurent is angry. The therapist believes that the mood and conditions under which each subpersonality appears are critical to understanding this disorder, demonstrating a belief in:
    a. avoidant dysmorphia.
    b. state-dependent learning.
    c. convergent variable learning.
    d. neurobiological concordance.

How Do Theorists Explain Dissociative Disorders?, p. 213
Diff: H, Type: Applied, Ans: b
107. If the state-dependent learning explanation of dissociative disorders is correct, a person may not remember stressful events because he or she is:
    a. simply too stressed at the time for memories to be laid down.
    b. at a different arousal level after the stress is over.
    c. a smoker.
    d. one who habitually drinks too much.

How Do Theorists Explain Dissociative Disorders?, p. 213
Diff: M, Type: Factual, Ans: b
108. Which of the following has been proposed as a cause of dissociative disorders?
    a. regression
    b. self-hypnosis
    c. lack of repression
    d. classical conditioning

How Do Theorists Explain Dissociative Disorders?, p. 213
Diff: H, Type: Applied, Ans: b
109. If you studied for this exam while you were unusually happy, you will probably do best taking it while you are:
    a. unusually sad.
    b. unusually happy.
    c. moderately happy.
    d. happy when you know the answers and sad when you don't.

How Do Theorists Explain Dissociative Disorders?, p. 213
Diff: M, Type: Factual, Ans: c
110. What characteristic is shared by both hypnotic amnesia and dissociative disorders?
    a. forgetting basic knowledge rather than events
    b. forgetting information that is specifically anxiety producing
    c. forgetting specific information for a period of time, yet later recalling it
    d. forgetting while retaining insight into why one is forgetting, or a feeling that something has been forgotten

How Do Theorists Explain Dissociative Disorders?, p. 213
Diff: E, Type: Factual, Ans: c
111. What disorder has been described as a use of self-hypnosis?
    a. catatonia
    b. schizophrenia
    c. multiple personality disorder
    d. paranoid personality disorder

How Do Theorists Explain Dissociative Disorders?, p. 213
Diff: M, Type: Factual, Ans: c
112. What conclusion does research on hypnosis and hypnotic amnesia support?
    a. People with multiple personalities may be faking their condition.
    b. Dissociative disorders are extremely odd and inexplicable events.
    c. Dissociative disorders are similar to behaviors seen in hypnotic amnesia.
    d. Self-hypnosis relies on different processes and produces different behavioral outcomes.

How Do Theorists Explain Dissociative Disorders?, p. 213
Diff: E, Type: Applied, Ans: a
113. Just after doing well in an intramural basketball game—something which left me very happy, and in a high state of excitement—I sat down and studied for my abnormal psychology test. Research shows I would perform best on that test if, at the time of the test, I was:
    a. happy and excited.
    b. happy but calm.
    c. neither happy nor sad, and excited.
    d. neither happy nor sad, and calm.

How Do Theorists Explain Dissociative Disorders?, p. 213
Diff: M, Type: Applied, Ans: a
114. A child in an extremely abusive family situation often seems to become deaf to the verbal abuse, and insensitive to the physical abuse, as if the child simply wasn't there experiencing the abuse. One explanation of this behavior is:
    a. self-hypnosis.
    b. state-dependent memory.
    c. eidetic imagery.
    d. memory while under simulated anesthesia.

How Do Theorists Explain Dissociative Disorders?, p. 214
Diff: M, Type: Factual, Ans: b
115. Theorists who accept the "special process" view of hypnosis and dissociative disorders believe that:
    a. hypnosis increases the capacity for rational thinking.
    b. people with dissociative disorders place themselves in internal trances.
    c. remembering during self-hypnosis can be automatic and complete for people with dissociative disorders.
    d. people with low levels of susceptibility to hypnosis are strong candidates for dissociative disorders.

How Do Theorists Explain Dissociative Disorders?, p. 214
Diff: H, Type: Applied, Ans: c
116. Someone who believes that hypnosis works because it increases motivation, focuses attention, and fulfills expectations, would also believe that hypnosis is due to:
    a. special processes.
    b. psychodynamic processes.
    c. common social and cognitive processes.
    d. the separation of body and mind.

How Are Dissociative Disorders Treated?, p. 214
Diff: M, Type: Factual, Ans: d
117. A person at which of the following ages probably would be least hypnotizable?
    a. 10
    b. 20
    c. 30
    d. 40

How Are Dissociative Disorders Treated?, p. 215
Diff: H, Type: Applied, Ans: d
118. The effectiveness of hypnosis in treating dissociative disorders suggests that:
    a. dissociative disorders can be caused by hypnosis as well.
    b. hypnosis works through special processes or extraordinary functioning.
    c. hypnosis works by normal social and cognitive processes.
    d. the mind might "cause" dissociative disorders as well as be used to treat them.

How Are Dissociative Disorders Treated?, p. 214
Diff: E, Type: Factual, Ans: a
119. What treatment approach is often used in cases of dissociative amnesia and fugue?
    a. hypnotherapy
    b. family therapy
    c. amphetamine injections
    d. electroconvulsive shock therapy

How Are Dissociative Disorders Treated?, p. 214
Diff: M, Type: Factual, Ans: a
120. Which of the following is *not* one of the leading forms of therapy for dissociative disorders?
    a. behavioral
    b. psychodynamic
    c. drug
    d. hypnotic

How Are Dissociative Disorders Treated?, p. 215
Diff: M, Type: Factual, Ans: c
121. Psychodynamic therapy may be particularly effective in the treatment of dissociative disorders because:
    a. most dissociative disorders involve some degree of fixation.
    b. most other forms of therapy take several years to improve functioning of those with these disorders.
    c. psychodynamic therapy often tries to recover lost memories.
    d. those with dissociative disorders generally do not respond well to drugs and hypnosis.

How Are Dissociative Disorders Treated?, p. 215
Diff: E, Type: Factual, Ans: a
122. People with which dissociative disorder typically do not eventually recover without receiving treatment?
    a. dissociative identity disorder
    b. dissociative fugue
    c. dissociative amnesia
    d. All dissociative disorders eventually resolve themselves successfully.

How Are Dissociative Disorders Treated?, p. 215
Diff: M, Type: Factual, Ans: d
123. What effect has the use of sodium amobarbital had in treating dissociative amnesia and fugue?
    a. Most clients recall past events easily with drugs.
    b. Recall is limited to the session itself.
    c. The patient's recollection doesn't begin until long after the session.
    d. Results are mixed, successful with some patients and not with others.

How Are Dissociative Disorders Treated?, p. 215
Diff: H, Type: Applied, Ans: a

124.   In the treatment of dissociative amnesia, sodium amobarbital and sodium pentobarbital work
       by:
       a.   freeing people from their inhibitions, thus allowing them to recall unpleasant events.
       b.   "forcing" people to tell the truth.
       c.   inducing a hypnotic state.
       d.   alleviating depression.

How Are Dissociative Disorders Treated?, p. 215
Diff: M, Type: Factual, Ans: d

125.   The usual goal of therapy for dissociative identity disorders is to:
       a.   have the subpersonalities develop equal "shares" of the person's functioning.
       b.   have the "other" subpersonalities become subject to the subpersonality that has the
            "protector" role.
       c.   gradually phase out all but one of the subpersonalities.
       d.   merge the subpersonalities into a single identity.

How Are Dissociative Disorders Treated?, p. 215
Diff: M, Type: Factual, Ans: a

126.   All of the following are true about hypnosis, except:
       a.   hypnosis involves a sleep-like state.
       b.   you can be hypnotized during exercise.
       c.   subjects can say "no" or stop hypnosis.
       d.   hypnotized subjects adhere to their usual values.

How Are Dissociative Disorders Treated?, p. 216
Diff: E, Type: Factual, Ans: a

127.   The first step in treating people with dissociative identity disorder is typically to:
       a.   bond with the primary personality.
       b.   integrate the subpersonalities into a unity.
       c.   establish a contract with the subpersonalities to prevent self-harm.
       d.   provide a forum for the subpersonalities to communicate with one another.

How Are Dissociative Disorders Treated?, p. 216
Diff: H, Type: Applied, Ans: d

128.   A client receiving treatment for dissociative identity disorder is progressing well through
       therapy; then, fusion occurs. Most likely, the client:
       a.   has experienced a significant, but short-term, setback.
       b.   has experienced a significant, and long-term, setback.
       c.   has merged the first two or more subpersonalities.
       d.   has merged the final two or more subpersonalities.

Depersonalization Disorder, p. 217
Diff: M, Type: Applied, Ans: c

129.   Someone who is experiencing "doubling" is:
       a.   showing two out of several multiple personalities at the same time.
       b.   suffering simultaneously from Munchausen syndrome and Munchausen syndrome by
            proxy.
       c.   feeling like his or her mind is floating above him or her.
       d.   malingering.

Depersonalization Disorder, p. 217
Diff: H, Type: Applied, Ans: b

130.   If a person's mental functioning or body feels unreal or foreign, the person is most likely suffering from:
        a.   body dysmorphic disorder.
        b.   depersonalization.
        c.   dissociative identity disorder.
        d.   dissociative amnesia.

Depersonalization Disorder, p. 217
Diff: H, Type: Applied, Ans: c

131.   Feeling that your hands and feet are smaller or bigger than usual or that you are in a dreamlike state is called:
        a.   doubting.
        b.   dumbing down.
        c.   doubling.
        d.   distrusting.

Depersonalization Disorder, p. 217
Diff: H, Type: Applied, Ans: d

132.   When a person feels that the external world is removed, mechanical, distorted, or even "dead," he or she is experiencing:
        a.   doubling.
        b.   depersonalization.
        c.   dissociative amnesia.
        d.   derealization.

Depersonalization Disorder, p. 217
Diff: H, Type: Applied, Ans: a

133.   I have just arrived in a city where I know no one, and English is not spoken by very many people. I feel as though my mind is separating from my body, that I am actually observing myself do things. What I am experiencing is:
        a.   temporary depersonalization.
        b.   depersonalization disorder.
        c.   posttraumatic stress disorder.
        d.   transient posttraumatic distress.

Depersonalization Disorder, p. 218
Diff: E, Type: Factual, Ans: b

134.   Depersonalization disorder is most common among those who are:
        a.   preadolescents.
        b.   adolescents and young adults.
        c.   adults between the ages of 40 and 60.
        d.   adults older than 60.

Depersonalization Disorder, p. 218
Diff: H, Type: Applied, Ans: b

135.   If I suffer from depersonalization disorder, but the symptoms disappear after a while, they
        most likely will reappear if I:
        a. get married to someone I really love.
        b. survive a bad car accident.
        c. travel on vacation near where I live.
        d. experience a sudden bout of mania.

Depersonalization Disorder, p. 218
Diff: M, Type: Factual, Ans: a

136.   Which of the following statements is most accurate?
        a. No therapy has emerged as particularly effective for treating depersonalization disorder.
        b. Most cases of depersonalization disorder are associated with changes in brain activity.
        c. The presence of severe stressors in one's life is not a predictor of depersonalization
            disorder.
        d. Depersonalization disorder rarely occurs transiently.

Depersonalization Disorder, p. 218
Diff: E, Type: Applied, Ans: d

137.   Depersonalization disorder was first identified and treated by:
        a. cognitive therapists.
        b. cognitive-behavioral therapists.
        c. biological therapists.
        d. psychodynamic therapists.

Putting It Together, p, 219
Diff: H, Type: Factual, Ans: d

138.   In the past 20 years, public interest in somatoform and dissociative disorders has:
        a. decreased, although therapy effectiveness has increased.
        b. decreased, and therapy effectiveness has not increased.
        c. increased, as has therapy effectiveness.
        d. increased, although therapy effectiveness has not increased.

FILL-IN QUESTIONS

What Are Somatoform Disorders?, p. 190
Diff: M, Type: Factual, Ans: hysterical

1.   The somatoform disorders that involve altered or lost physical functioning are collectively
        called _____ somatoform disorders.

What Are Somatoform Disorders?, p. 190
Diff: E, Type: Factual, Ans: genuine medical problems

2.   One of the dangers of diagnosing a hysterical disorder is that the mysterious origins of the
        patient's symptoms may actually be _____.

What Are Somatoform Disorders?, p. 190
Diff: M, Type: Applied, Ans: conversion disorder

3.   Beauregard saw his parents killed and the next morning he could not see. This is an example
        of a(n) _____.

What Are Somatoform Disorders?, p. 194
Diff: E, Type: Factual, Ans: factitious disorder (or Munchausen syndrome)

4.   People with _____ travel from hospital to hospital, gaining admission and receiving treatment for symptoms they caused intentionally.

What Are Preoccupation Somatoform Disorders?, p. 194
Diff: E, Type: Factual, Ans: hypochondriasis

5.   People who suffer from _____ unrealistically and fearfully interpret relatively minor physical discomforts as signs of serious illness.

What Are Preoccupation Somatoform Disorders?, p. 195
Diff: E, Type: Applied, Ans: body dysmorphic

6.   Eleanor thinks she has horribly ugly hair (in fact, she doesn't). She will not be seen in public without a scarf over her head. She suffers from _____ disorder.

What Causes Somatoform Disorders?, pp. 196-197
Diff: E, Type: Factual, Ans: uterus

7.   The ancient Greeks believed that the _____ of a sexually ungratified woman moved around in her body, lodging in different areas and causing physical symptoms.

What Causes Somatoform Disorders?, p. 199
Diff: M, Type: Factual, Ans: Electra complex

8.   Freud's view was that hysteria stemmed from an unresolved _____.

What Causes Somatoform Disorders?, p. 199
Diff: E, Type: Factual, Ans: primary

9.   A person whose symptoms keep their internal conflicts from emerging into consciousness achieves _____ gain.

What Causes Somatoform Disorders?, p. 199
Diff: E, Type: Factual, Ans: secondary

10.   A person whose symptoms fulfill some external need (such as avoiding something unpleasant) is achieving _____ gain.

Dissociative Disorders, p. 202
Diff: M, Type: Factual, Ans: identity

11.   Our _____ is our sense of who we are, our particular preferences, abilities, characteristics, and needs.

Dissociative Disorders?, p. 203
Diff: E, Type: Factual, Ans: memory

12.   One's identity is based in part on one's _____, which links the past, the present, and the future.

Dissociative Disorders, p. 203
Diff: E, Type: Factual, Ans: dissociative identity (or multiple personality disorder)

13.   An individual with _____ displays two or more distinct personalities and periodically switches from one to another.

Dissociative Amnesia, p. 204
Diff: E, Type: Factual, Ans: localized (or circumscribed)
14.   Dissociative amnesia characterized by forgetting, for a short time, all events following a
       traumatic episode is called _____ amnesia

Dissociative Amnesia, p. 204
Diff: E, Type: Factual, Ans: selective
15.   Dissociative amnesia characterized by forgetting, for a short time, some but not all events
       following a traumatic episode is called _____.

Dissociative Amnesia, p. 204
Diff: M, Type: Factual, Ans: generalized
16.   Dissociative amnesia characterized by forgetting, for a limited period of time, some but not
       all events both preceding and following a traumatic episode is called _____ amnesia.

Dissociative Amnesia, p. 204
Diff: E, Type: Factual, Ans: amnestic episode
17.   In dissociative amnesia, the forgotten period is called the _____.

Dissociative Amnesia, p. 205
Diff: M, Type: Factual, Ans: continuous
18.   Dissociative amnesia characterized by forgetting that extends indefinitely following a
       traumatic episode is called _____ amnesia.

Dissociative Fugue, p. 205
Diff: E, Type: Applied, Ans: dissociative fugue (or dissociative disorder)
19.   Quinn has forgotten who he is. He has fled to a different location from the one he has been
       living in and is wandering around aimlessly. After a few hours, he "comes to" and discovers
       his strange surrounding. Unable to recall how he got there or what he has been doing, Quinn
       appears to be suffering a _____.

Dissociative Fugue, p. 205
Diff: E, Type: Factual, Ans: physical flight
20.   The primary difference between dissociative amnesia and dissociative fugue is _____.

Repressed Memories or False Memory Syndrome?, p. 206 (Box 7-4)
Diff: M, Type: Factual, Ans: iatrogenic
21.   Some researchers argued that multiple personality disorder is caused by therapists who have
       subtly suggested the existence of alternative personalities during therapy. Such cases are
       called _____.

Dissociative Identity Disorder (Multiple Personality Disorder), p. 209
Diff: H, Type: Applied, Ans: one-way
22.   Calvin suffers from multiple personality disorder. He has three distinct identities: young
       Hank, Hermione, and middle-aged Cal. Hank knows about Hermione and Cal, but they do not
       know of the existence of each other or of Hank. This relationship is known as _____
       amnesic.

Dissociative Identity Disorder (Multiple Personality Disorder), p. 209
Diff: M, Type: Factual, Ans: co-conscious

23. In people with multiple personality disorder, there are sometimes personalities that are aware of the existence of the others, but they themselves remain unknown to some of the identities. The personalities that know of others are called _____.

Dissociative Identity Disorder (Multiple Personality Disorder), p. 211
Diff: E, Type: Factual, Ans: repression

24. Psychodynamic theorists believe that dissociative disorders represent an extreme use of the defense mechanism _____.

How Do Theorists Explain Dissociative Disorders?, p. 212
Diff: E, Type: Factual, Ans: state-dependent learning (or memory)

25. When people learn something in a particular situation or condition, they are more likely to recall this information when in the same situation or condition. This phenomenon is called _____.

How Do Theorists Explain Dissociative Disorders?, p. 212
Diff: E, Type: Factual, Ans: state-dependent

26. Dissociative amnesia is the result of experiencing an arousal state of extreme anxiety during an upsetting event and then being unable to recall the event during a later state of calm. This statement describes the _____ view of dissociative disorders.

How Are Dissociative Disorders Treated?, p. 215
Diff: E, Type: Factual, Ans: hypnotic therapy (or hypnotherapy)

27. The use of hypnosis to help people recall forgotten events is called _____.

Depersonalization Disorder, p. 217
Diff: E, Type: Factual, Ans: depersonalization disorder (or transient depersonalization experiences)

28. One who experiences a feeling of mind–body separation, and distorted senses, yet who remains in contact with reality, is experiencing _____.

ESSAY QUESTIONS

Somatoform Disorders, p. 190
Diff: H, Type: Applied

1. Imagine that a therapist is diagnosing a patient with a somatoform disorder. What are the symptoms the therapist has observed in coming up with this diagnosis? How should the therapist distinguish between hysterical and preoccupation disorders?

What Are Preoccupation Somatoform Disorders?, p. 195
Diff: M, Type: Factual

2. What is dysmorphophobia (body dysmorphic disorder)? What are the symptoms that someone experiencing this disorder would commonly have?

What Causes Somatoform Disorders?, p. 198ff
Diff: H, Type: Factual

3. Explain, in one sentence each, the psychodynamic, biological, and cognitive explanations for the development (cause) of somatoform disorders.

How Are Somatoform Disorders Treated?, p. 202
Diff: H, Type: Applied
4.   Sketch out a treatment plan for using exposure and response prevention to treat body dysmorphic disorder.

Dissociative Amnesia, p. 203ff
Diff: M, Type: Applied
5.   How are dissociative amnesia and dissociative fugue alike? How do they differ? Does the DSM-IV-TR really need both categories?

Repressed Memories or False Memory Syndrome?, p. 206 (Box 7-4)
Diff: M, Type: Applied
6.   From what you have studied in this course, do you think repressed childhood memories that supposedly are brought to light through intensive psychotherapy ought to be allowed as evidence in criminal trials involving, for example, physical or sexual child abuse? Or do you think that what is really involved is what some have called "false memory syndrome"? Please provide empirical evidence to support your answer.

Dissociative Identity Disorder (Multiple Personality Disorder), p. 208ff
Diff: H, Type: Applied
7.   Describe and provide examples of the variety of ways in which subpersonalities might interact in someone experiencing dissociative identity disorders.

How Do Theorists Explain Dissociative Disorders?, p. 211
Diff: H, Type: Applied
8.   Why might psychodynamic therapy be particularly effective in the treatment of dissociative disorders?

How Are Dissociative Disorders Treated?, p. 214ff
Diff: H, Type: Factual
9.   Please describe in some detail how treatment for dissociative identity disorder might differ from treatment for dissociative amnesia or dissociative fugue.

How Are Dissociative Disorders Treated?, p. 215 (Table 7-6)
Diff: H, Type: Applied
10.   Discuss at least 5 myths about hypnosis. For each myth, point out the actual reality.

Depersonalization Disorder, p. 217
Diff: M, Type: Applied
11.   Describe depersonalization disorder. What events are likely to cause it and why? When might "normal" people experience transient depersonalization disorder.

MULTIPLE-CHOICE QUESTIONS

Mood Disorders, p. 223
Diff: E, Type: Factual, Ans: a

1. A state of breathless euphoria, or frenzied energy, in which people have an exaggerated belief in their power describes:
    a. mania.
    b. dysthymia.
    c. depression.
    d. cyclothymia.

Mood Disorders, p. 223
Diff: E, Type: Factual, Ans: a

2. The most common form of mood disorder is:
    a. unipolar depression.
    b. bipolar disorder.
    c. mania.
    d. manic-depression.

Mood Disorders, p. 223
Diff: M, Type: Factual, Ans: a

3. The key emotions in mood disorders are:
    a. sadness and euphoria.
    b. helplessness and hopelessness.
    c. cyclothymia and dysthymia.
    d. self-denial and self-aggrandizement.

Mood Disorders, p. 223
Diff: M, Type: Factual, Ans: c

4. Which of the following is the least common form of a mood disorder?
    a. full manic and full depressive episodes
    b. swinging from manic to depressive symptoms on the same day
    c. full manic episodes with no depressive episodes
    d. full depressive episodes with no manic episodes

Mood Disorders, pp. 223-224
Diff: M, Type: Factual, Ans: c
5.   The chief difference between mood disorders and normal mood fluctuation is:
      a.   the particular medication used to treat the problem.
      b.   the cause of the problem.
      c.   the severity and duration of the problem.
      d.   the demographic characteristics of the person.

Mood Disorders, p. 224
Diff: M, Type: Factual, Ans: b
6.   What is the current annual incidence of severe unipolar depression in the United States?
      a.   1-5%
      b.   5-10%
      c.   8-15%
      d.   20-23%

How Common Is Unipolar Depression?, p. 224
Diff: H, Type: Applied, Ans: b
7.   Which person is at greatest risk for unipolar depression?
      a.   a poor child from a developing country
      b.   a middle-class American woman
      c.   an older African American man
      d.   a wealthy European college student

How Common Is Unipolar Depression?, p. 224
Diff: H, Type: Factual, Ans: d
8.   Which of the following is true about unipolar depression?
      a.   It is more common in men than women.
      b.   The risk of experiencing depression appears to be declining.
      c.   Poorer people are more likely to experience depression than wealthier people.
      d.   Most people recover from depression, but experience a recurrence.

What Are the Symptoms of Depression?, p. 225
Diff: E, Type: Factual, Ans: c
9.   Which of the following would be an emotional symptom of depression?
      a.   lack of desire to eat
      b.   a negative view of oneself
      c.   experiences of sadness and anger
      d.   staying in bed for hours during the day

What Are the Symptoms of Depression?, p. 225
Diff: M, Type: Factual, Ans: b
10.   The experience of feeling like weeping constantly would be considered a(n) _____ symptom
      of depression.
      a.   cognitive
      b.   emotional
      c.   behavioral
      d.   motivational

What Are the Symptoms of Depression?, p. 225
Diff: E, Type: Factual, Ans: a

11.   Which of the following would be a motivational symptom of depression?
       a.   lack of desire to eat
       b.   a negative view of oneself
       c.   experiences of sadness and anger
       d.   staying in bed for hours during the day

What Are the Symptoms of Depression?, p. 225
Diff: E, Type: Factual, Ans: d

12.   The experience of a lack of desire to engage in sexual activity with one's spouse would be
       considered a(n) _____ symptom of depression.
       a.   cognitive
       b.   emotional
       c.   behavioral
       d.   motivational

What Are the Symptoms of Depression?, p. 225
Diff: H, Type: Applied, Ans: c

13.   A person displaying sadness, lack of energy, headaches, and feelings of low self-worth is
       showing all of the following symptoms except _____ symptoms.
       a.   emotional
       b.   motivational
       c.   behavioral
       d.   cognitive

What Are the Symptoms of Depression?, p. 225
Diff: M, Type: Factual, Ans: d

14.   Which of the following would be a behavioral symptom of depression?
       a.   lack of desire to eat
       b.   a negative view of oneself
       c.   experiences of sadness and anger
       d.   staying in bed for hours during the day

What Are the Symptoms of Depression?, p. 226
Diff: E, Type: Factual, Ans: b

15.   A depressed person who is confused, unable to remember things, and unable to solve
       problems is suffering from _____symptoms.
       a.   emotional
       b.   cognitive
       c.   motivational
       d.   behavioral

What Are the Symptoms of Depression?, p. 226
Diff: E, Type: Factual, Ans: a

16.   Having frequent headaches is a(n) _____ symptom of depression.
       a.   physical
       b.   emotional
       c.   behavioral
       d.   motivational

What Are the Symptoms of Depression?, p. 226
Diff: E, Type: Factual, Ans: a
17.   Which of the following would be a physical symptom of depression?
      a.   sleeping poorly
      b.   lack of desire to go to work
      c.   decreased level of physical activity
      d.   experiences of sadness and dejection

What Are the Symptoms of Depression?, p. 226
Diff: E, Type: Factual, Ans: a
18.   The experience of dizziness and general unspecified pain would be considered _____
      symptoms of depression.
      a.   physical
      b.   emotional
      c.   behavioral
      d.   motivational

Diagnosing Unipolar Depression, p. 226
Diff: M, Type: Factual, Ans: a
19.   To be classified as having a major depressive episode, depression must last for a period
      of at least:
      a.   two weeks.
      b.   two months.
      c.   one year.
      d.   two years.

Diagnosing Unipolar Depression, p. 227
Diff: H, Type: Factual, Ans: c
20.   What would be the most appropriate diagnosis for a person who experienced a major
      depressive episode, without having any history of mania, and is either immobile or
      excessively active?
      a.   recurrent depression
      b.   seasonal depression
      c.   catatonic depression
      d.   melancholic depression

Diagnosing Unipolar Depression, p. 227
Diff: M, Type: Factual, Ans: d
21.   All of the following are types of major depressive disorders except:
      a.   recurrent.
      b.   seasonal.
      c.   melancholic.
      d.   posttraumatic.

Diagnosing Unipolar Depression, p. 227
Diff: E, Type: Applied, Ans: c

22.   Judith is currently experiencing a period of sadness that interferes with her ability to go to work and to take care of her children. It has lasted now for three weeks, and she has experienced similar episodes in the past. What type of major depression would she most likely be diagnosed with?
      a.   seasonal
      b.   catatonic
      c.   recurrent
      d.   melancholic

Diagnosing Unipolar Depression, p. 227
Diff: M, Type: Factual, Ans: c

23.   To receive a diagnosis of major depressive episode, catatonic, the individual must display:
      a.   repeated episodes.
      b.   fluctuation in mood during the year.
      c.   motor immobility or excessive activity.
      d.   onset within four weeks of giving birth.

Diagnosing Unipolar Depression, p. 227
Diff: E, Type: Factual, Ans: b

24.   Juan is currently experiencing a period of sadness that has resulted in almost total immobility. He sits in a chair all day and almost never moves. His wife has to assist him in getting into bed at night. What type of major depression would he most likely be diagnosed with?
      a.   seasonal
      b.   catatonic
      c.   recurrent
      d.   melancholic

Diagnosing Unipolar Depression, p. 227
Diff: E, Type: Factual, Ans: c

25.   Since immediately after the birth of her son, Maria has experienced a period of sadness that interferes with her ability to take care of him. She has never felt this way before, but this has been going on for several weeks. With what type of major depression would she most likely be diagnosed?
      a.   seasonal
      b.   catatonic
      c.   postpartum
      d.   melancholic

Diagnosing Unipolar Depression, p. 227
Diff: E, Type: Factual, Ans: d

26.   To receive a diagnosis of major depressive episode, melancholic, the individual must display:
      a.   repeated episodes.
      b.   fluctuation in mood during the year.
      c.   motor immobility or excessive activity.
      d.   almost no emotional response to pleasurable events.

Diagnosing Unipolar Depression, p. 227
Diff: M, Type: Applied, Ans: d

27.   All the pleasure has gone out of life for Trevor. Things he used to find fun and exciting no longer give him any joy. He finds he wakes up early in the morning and has no appetite. This has been going on for several weeks. What type of major depression would he most likely be diagnosed with?
      a.   seasonal
      b.   catatonic
      c.   recurrent
      d.   melancholic

Diagnosing Unipolar Depression, p. 227
Diff: M, Type: Factual, Ans: d

28.   To receive a diagnosis of dysthymic disorder, an individual must have experienced symptoms for at least:
      a.   two weeks.
      b.   two months.
      c.   one year.
      d.   two years.

What Causes Unipolar Depression?, p. 227
Diff: H, Type: Applied, Ans: d

29.   Jamal is experiencing a major depressive episode that appears to have begun three weeks ago. He is miserable and suffers from at least five symptoms of depression. No unusually stressful events have occurred in the past year. Based on these data, the diagnosis would be:
      a.   postpartum depression.
      b.   reactive depression.
      c.   exogenous depression.
      d.   endogenous depression.

What Causes Unipolar Depression?, p. 227
Diff: M, Type: Applied, Ans: b

30.   Jose just saw his best friend shot and killed by a gunman who was driving through his neighborhood. A month later he is in a psychologist's office complaining that he cannot work and it all seems hopeless. There are several other symptoms consistent with these. Based on these data, the diagnosis would be:
      a.   recurrent depression.
      b.   reactive depression.
      c.   endogenous depression.
      d.   melancholic depression.

What Causes Unipolar Depression?, p. 227
Diff: H, Type: Applied, Ans: d

31.   Sohila has been deteriorating for more than a year. She is always tired (she does not sleep), she is losing weight (she eats poorly), she is sad, feels terrible, and feels like it will never get any better. When asked, it is clear that nothing in particular has happened. Based on these data, the diagnosis would be:
      a.   manic depression.
      b.   reactive depression.
      c.   exogenous depression.
      d.   endogenous depression.

The Biological View, p. 227
Diff: M, Type: Factual, Ans: a
32. Dana is depressed and has been for a while. He, his twin brother, his mother, and his father all participate in a family pedigree study. Identify the proband(s) in this study.
    a. Dana
    b. Dana's twin
    c. both parents
    d. both Dana and his twin

The Biological View, p. 227
Diff: E, Type: Factual, Ans: b
33. Family pedigree and twin studies have been used to look for a predisposition for unipolar depression within families. Which theoretical framework encompasses these studies?
    a. humanist
    b. biological
    c. behavioral
    d. psychodynamic

The Biological View, p. 227
Diff: M, Type: Applied, Ans: b
34. A person who becomes depressed because of several recent tragic events would be experiencing _____ depression.
    a. endogenous
    b. exogenous
    c. experiential
    d. egocentric

The Biological View, p. 227
Diff: M, Type: Applied, Ans: a
35. If we were conducting a family pedigree study, we would be looking at:
    a. the number of depressed relatives a depressed person has.
    b. the cause of death of depressed peoples' twins.
    c. the influence of pets on depressed people.
    d. the depression rate in a person's neighborhood.

The Biological View, p. 227
Diff: E, Type: Factual, Ans: b
36. Family pedigree and twin studies have been used to look for a genetic predisposition for unipolar depression. These studies have found:
    a. a lower rate of unipolar depression among children of parents with this disorder.
    b. a higher than chance rate of depression among the families of depressed patients.
    c. high rates of unipolar depression among dizygotic twins but not among monozygotic twins.
    d. no compelling evidence for depression to be found in relatives of a depressed individual.

Sadness at the Happiest of Times, p. 228 (Box 8-1)
Diff: M, Type: Applied, Ans: d

37. A woman experiences recurrent thoughts of suicide, great sadness, and sleep disturbance. These symptoms began a week after she gave birth, and have lasted for over six months. The woman is experiencing:
    a. the "baby blues."
    b. postpartum psychosis.
    c. hormone withdrawal syndrome.
    d. postpartum depression.

Sadness at the Happiest of Times, p. 228 (Box 8-1)
Diff: M, Type: Applied, Ans: a

38. A woman who has just given birth is anxious, has trouble sleeping, and feels sad. These symptoms diminish in the next couple of weeks. What she has experienced is most likely:
    a. the "baby blues," something experienced by over half of new mothers.
    b. the "baby blues," something experienced by under half of new mothers.
    c. postpartum depression, something experienced by over half of new mothers.
    d. postpartum depression, something experienced by under half of new mothers.

The Biological View, p. 229 (Table 8-3)
Diff: E, Type: Factual, Ans: b

39. Recent studies show about what proportion of those experiencing major depressive disorder receive treatment for that disorder?
    a. 1/4
    b. 1/3
    c. 3/4
    d. 9/10

The Biological View, p. 229 (Table 8-3)
Diff: H, Type: Applied, Ans: d

40. A man diagnosed with major depressive disorder exhibited his first diagnosable symptoms when he was about 40 years old. Among those experiencing major depressive disorder, his case is:
    a. common: most people with this diagnosis are men in their early to mid 40s.
    b. uncommon: most people with this diagnosis are women in their early to mid 40s.
    c. uncommon: most people with this diagnosis are men in their mid to late 20s.
    d. very uncommon: most people with this diagnosis are women in their mid to late 20s.

The Biological View, p. 229
Diff: H, Type: Factual, Ans: a

41. If a biochemical imbalance were the cause of a person's depression, the latest research would lead us to expect that person to have:
    a. an abnormality in the activity of certain neurotransmitters, especially serotonin and norepinephrine.
    b. especially high levels of the neurotransmitters dopamine and acetylcholine, and their metabolites.
    c. particularly low levels of the neurotransmitters cortisol and melatonin, as measured by their metabolites.
    d. an absence of the neurotransmitters cortisol and serotonin.

The Biological View, p. 229
Diff: E, Type: Applied, Ans: b

42.   If people with unipolar depression were found to have higher levels of cortisol, it would support the _____ orientation.
    a.   behavioral
    b.   biochemical
    c.   psychoanalytic
    d.   sociocultural

The Rhythms of Depression, pp. 230-231 (Box 8-2)
Diff: H, Type: Applied, Ans: c

43.   An individual experiences proportionally more REM sleep toward morning, an average amount of deep sleep, and has a body temperature which typically peaks in the afternoon. Most likely, that individual is:
    a.   experiencing desynchronization, and probably will develop depression.
    b.   experiencing desynchronization, and probably will develop SAD.
    c.   normal, and will not develop depression.
    d.   particularly vulnerable to BDNF.

The Rhythms of Depression, pp. 230-231 (Box 8-2)
Diff: E, Type: Factual, Ans: b

44.   The hormone most closely associated with the onset of seasonal affective disorder is:
    a.   norepinephrine.
    b.   melatonin.
    c.   serotonin.
    d.   reserpine.

The Rhythms of Depression, pp. 230-231 (Box 8-2)
Diff: M, Type: Factual, Ans: a

45.   Researchers have found that the sleep cycle in depressed people is:
    a.   reversed.
    b.   extended.
    c.   devoid of REM sleep.
    d.   missing several steps.

The Rhythms of Depression, pp. 230-231 (Box 8-2)
Diff: M, Type: Factual, Ans: c

46.   Seasonal affective disorder is thought to be due to:
    a.   excessive neuronal GABA.
    b.   decreased levels of serotonin.
    c.   increased levels of melatonin.
    d.   decreased levels of norepinephrine.

The Rhythms of Depression, pp. 230-231 (Box 8-2)
Diff: M, Type: Factual, Ans: c

47.   The hormone that appears involved in seasonal affective disorder is:
    a.   serotonin.
    b.   dopamine.
    c.   melatonin.
    d.   norepinephrine.

The Rhythms of Depression, pp. 230-231 (Box 8-2)
Diff: E, Type: Factual, Ans: b
48. One of the most effective treatments for seasonal affective disorder has been shown to be:
    a. tricyclics.
    b. light therapy.
    c. a melatonin pill.
    d. monoamine oxidase inhibitors.

The Biological View, p. 231
Diff: H, Type: Factual, Ans: b
49. One problem with analogue studies of depression is that:
    a. people from different cultural backgrounds show different symptoms of depression.
    b. we cannot be sure depression-like symptoms in lab animals reflect human depression.
    c. computers are presently unable to simulate depressive symptoms as humans experience those symptoms.
    d. genetic correlational studies don't necessarily demonstrate causal links between genes and depression.

Psychological Views, p. 232
Diff: M, Type: Factual, Ans: c
50. According to Freudian theory, depression results in part from:
    a. learned helplessness.
    b. irrational expectations.
    c. regression to the oral stage.
    d. learned anxiety turned inward.

Psychological Views, p. 232
Diff: H, Type: Applied, Ans: c
51. Which of the following people is showing introjection?
    a. a parent who raises the child to be excessively dependent
    b. a spouse who relates in unsafe and insecure ways
    c. a person who directs feelings of grief for a lost loved one toward himself
    d. a student who feels her parents love her only when she achieves at a high level

Psychological Views, p. 232
Diff: E, Type: Factual, Ans: d
52. Depression occurs either when a loved one is lost or when a person experiences imagined or symbolic loss. This explanation for the onset of depression is proposed by:
    a. humanist theorists.
    b. cognitive theorists.
    c. behavioral theorists.
    d. psychodynamic theorists.

Psychological Views, p. 232
Diff: E, Type: Applied, Ans: a
53. The type of clinician who would be most likely to say, "Tell me about how your parents cared for and protected you" is a:
    a. psychoanalyst.
    b. behaviorist.
    c. cognitive clinician.
    d. sociocultural clinician.

Psychological Views, p. 232
Diff: E, Type: Applied, Ans: a

54.   The type of clinician who would be most likely to say, "Tell me about any early losses you experienced" is a:
   a. psychoanalyst.
   b. behaviorist.
   c. cognitive clinician.
   d. sociocultural clinician.

Psychological Views, p. 232
Diff: E, Type: Factual, Ans: d

55.   In general, object relations theorists follow which theoretical perspective?
   a. cognitive
   b. humanistic
   c. existential
   d. psychodynamic

Psychological Views, p. 233
Diff: H, Type: Applied, Ans: d

56.   Which theoretical orientation supports the finding that monkeys separated from their mothers at birth show signs of depression?
   a. behavioral
   b. biochemical
   c. cognitive
   d. psychodynamic

Psychological Views, p. 233
Diff: H, Type: Factual, Ans: d

57.   Children who were separated from their mothers at an early age are more likely than other children to experience weepiness, passivity, and withdrawal. This reaction, seen in children who are separated from their mothers up to the age of 6, has been called:
   a. dysthymia.
   b. detachment.
   c. insecure attachment.
   d. anaclitic depression.

Psychological Views, p. 233
Diff: H, Type: Applied, Ans: c

58.   A baby who was separated from its mother at birth, and who subsequently became withdrawn, sad, and tearful, could be experiencing:
   a. postpartum depression.
   b. posttraumatic depression syndrome.
   c. anaclitic depression.
   d. dysthymic depression.

Psychological Views, p. 234
Diff: M, Type: Applied, Ans: d

59.   An older person retires and begins experiencing health problems. Consequently, the person
       loses contact with old friends and becomes unpleasant to be around. A behaviorist would
       explain the resulting depression in terms of:
       a. learned helplessness.
       b. object relations loss.
       c. sociocultural changes.
       d. loss of positive social rewards.

Psychological Views, p. 234
Diff: H, Type: Factual, Ans: a

60.   Behaviorists explain the downward spiral of depression by theorizing that:
       a. depressed behavior leads to even fewer opportunities for social rewards.
       b. depressed people aren't responsive to normal social rewards.
       c. depressed family members give inaccurate self-reports.
       d. depressed mood cannot be alleviated by positive experiences.

Psychological Views, p. 234
Diff: E, Type: Applied, Ans: c

61.   Francoise is depressed. Her therapist asks her about her daily experiences, focusing on how
       often people say nice things to her. Her therapist most likely has a _____ orientation.
       a. cognitive
       b. biological
       c. behavioral
       d. psychoanalytic

Psychological Views, p. 234
Diff: H, Type: Applied, Ans: a

62.   Which theoretical orientation would support the finding that there is a significant relationship
       between positive life events and feelings of life satisfaction and happiness?
       a. behavioral
       b. biochemical
       c. cognitive
       d. psychodynamic

Psychological Views, p. 234
Diff: M, Type: Applied, Ans: b

63.   The type of clinician who would be most likely to say, "What are some things you enjoy
       doing, and how often do you do them?" would be a:
       a. psychoanalyst.
       b. behaviorist.
       c. cognitive clinician.
       d. sociocultural clinician.

Psychological Views, p. 234
Diff: M, Type: Factual, Ans: a

64.   Cognitive theorists explain depression in terms of a person's:
      a.   negative interpretation of events.
      b.   symbolic losses.
      c.   decrease in positive activities.
      d.   ethnic background.

Psychological Views, p. 234
Diff: H, Type: Applied, Ans: a

65.   Which of the following would provide the best evidence for the cognitive explanation for depression?
      a.   a finding that people show negative thoughts before they became depressed
      b.   a finding that people show negative thoughts only after they become depressed
      c.   a finding that biochemical imbalances lead to both depression and negative thoughts
      d.   a finding that social rewards are not related to happiness

Psychological Views, p. 234
Diff: H, Type: Applied, Ans: d

66.   Cognitive theorists and psychoanalysts have in common an emphasis on:
      a.   the components of the cognitive triad.
      b.   object relations theory as it relates to grief reactions.
      c.   methodologies for investigating mood disorders.
      d.   how early experiences shape one's risk for depression.

Psychological Views, p. 234
Diff: E, Type: Factual, Ans: a

67.   The person associated with developing a cognitive theory of depression based on negative and maladaptive thinking was:
      a.   Beck.
      b.   Freud.
      c.   Seligman.
      d.   Lewinsohn.

Psychological Views, p. 234
Diff: H, Type: Applied, Ans: c

68.   According to recent research, if you monitored young adults and their grandparents you would find that the number of young adults laughing in a typical hour would be about:
      a.   half the number of grandparents who would laugh in a typical hour.
      b.   equal to the number of grandparents who would laugh in a typical hour.
      c.   twice the number of grandparents who would laugh in a typical hour.
      d.   four times the number of grandparents who would laugh in a typical hour.

Psychological Views, p. 235
Diff: H, Type: Applied, Ans: b

69.   On any given day, Peggy, a clinically depressed parent, sings or plays music with her child, as well as reads to him. Compared with other clinically depressed parents, that parent is:
       a.   typical: more than half of clinically depressed parents do these things with their children daily.
       b.   less typical: more than half of clinically depressed parents sing or play music with their children daily, but under half read to their children.
       c.   less typical: less than half of clinically depressed parents sing or play music with their children daily, but over half read to their children.
       d.   least typical: less than half of clinically depressed parents do these things with their children daily.

Psychological Views, p. 235
Diff: M, Type: Applied, Ans: a

70.   A therapist describes a patient who believes her personal worth is tied to each task she performs. She draws negative conclusions from very little evidence, amplifies minor mistakes into major character flaws, and suffers from repetitive thoughts that remind her of her flaws. You conclude that the therapist holds which theoretical orientation?
       a.   cognitive
       b.   biological
       c.   behavioral
       d.   psychoanalytic

Psychological Views, p. 235
Diff: H, Type: Applied, Ans: b

71.   The dean of academic affairs visits a professor's class as part of a tenure review. At the conclusion of the lecture, the dean exits hurriedly, without saying a word to the professor. The professor, who is prone to depression, concludes, "The dean hated my class so much he was too embarrassed to speak to me." This is an example of a(n):
       a.   overgeneralization.
       b.   arbitrary inference.
       c.   selective abstraction.
       d.   magnification and minimization.

Psychological Views, p. 235
Diff: H, Type: Applied, Ans: a

72.   Which of these statements would not reflect a part of the cognitive triad?
       a.   Everyone is out to get me.
       b.   Life is just too overwhelming.
       c.   I don't even want to wake up tomorrow.
       d.   I just can't go on.

Psychological Views, p. 235
Diff: H, Type: Applied, Ans: c

73.   Which theoretical orientation would support the finding that depressed people choose more pessimistic and self-deprecating statements in a story-telling test?
       a.   behavioral
       b.   biochemical
       c.   cognitive
       d.   sociocultural

Psychological Views, p. 236
Diff: M, Type: Applied, Ans: b
74.   Which of the following concepts is not associated with the psychodynamic explanation for depression?
    a.   symbolic or imagined loss
    b.   learned helplessness
    c.   fixation at the oral stage
    d.   introjection

Psychological Views, p. 236
Diff: M, Type: Applied, Ans: a
75.   Which of these research findings provides the most direct support for Beck's cognitive theory of depression?
    a.   Depressed women make more errors in logic when interpreting a paragraph than do nondepressed women.
    b.   Lack of social rewards is related to the downward spiral of depression.
    c.   Both human infants and infant monkeys show depression-like symptoms when they are separated from their mothers.
    d.   Depression is related to an imbalance of neurotransmitters in the brain.

Psychological Views, p. 236
Diff: E, Type: Applied, Ans: c
76.   If I'm in a depressed mood and all I do is think about my mood, without trying to change it, I'm making what kind of response?
    a.   helplessness
    b.   hopelessness
    c.   ruminative
    d.   perseverative

Psychological Views, p. 236
Diff: E, Type: Factual, Ans: c
77.   The person associated with the learned helplessness theory of depression is:
    a.   Beck.
    b.   Freud.
    c.   Seligman.
    d.   Lewinsohn.

Psychological Views, p. 236
Diff: M, Type: Factual, Ans: d
78.   Seligman has developed a theory based on the idea that depression results from:
    a.   the loss of a loved one, real or symbolic.
    b.   negative thinking and maladaptive thoughts.
    c.   a decrease in the number of positive reinforcements.
    d.   a belief that one has no control over the events in one's life.

Psychological Views, p. 237
Diff: E, Type: Factual, Ans: c
79.   A group of naïve dogs quickly learns to avoid a shock by jumping over a barrier when a light
       dims. A second group that spent the previous day receiving inescapable shocks does not learn
       in this situation. This experimental procedures demonstrates:
       a.   depression.
       b.   escape learning.
       c.   learned helplessness.
       d.   approach-avoidance failure.

Psychological Views, p. 237
Diff: H, Type: Applied, Ans: b
80.   According to Seligman's theory, who of the following would be most likely to develop
       learned helplessness?
       a.   someone who had experienced no uncontrollable negative events, then experienced a
            controllable negative event
       b.   someone who had experienced uncontrollable negative events and then a controllable
            negative event
       c.   someone who had experienced controllable negative events, and then another controllable
            negative event
       d.   someone who had experienced a random sequence of controllable and uncontrollable
            events

Psychological Views, p. 237
Diff: M, Type: Applied, Ans: a
81.   A young woman believes that everything negative that happens to her is her own fault, that
       she ruins everything, and always will. The therapist diagnoses her as suffering from a learned
       helplessness-induced depression because she attributes negative events in her life to:
       a.   internal, global, stable factors.
       b.   internal specific, stable factors.
       c.   internal, global, unstable factors.
       d.   internal, specific, unstable factors.

Psychological Views, p. 237
Diff: M, Type: Applied, Ans: c
82.   Which theoretical orientation would support the that finding support that depressed people
       show an internal/global/stable pattern of attribution on a questionnaire?
       a.   behavioral
       b.   sociocultural
       c.   cognitive
       d.   psychoanalytic

Psychological Views, p. 237
Diff: H, Type: Applied, Ans: c
83.   The type of clinician who would be most likely to ask, "Do you believe you will always feel
       like this and in all situations?" is a:
       a.   psychoanalyst.
       b.   behaviorist.
       c.   cognitive clinician.
       d.   sociocultural clinician.

Psychological Views, pp. 237-238
Diff: M, Type: Applied, Ans: c

84.   A woman who was frequently but unpredictably beaten by her husband was finally taken to a shelter by the police. While there she did not take advantage of educational and job training opportunities. How would cognitive theorists explain her behavior?
      a.   automatic negative thoughts
      b.   faulty cognitive triad
      c.   learned helplessness
      d.   arbitrary attribution

Psychological Views, pp. 237-238
Diff: M, Type: Applied, Ans: d

85.   Darius thinks that his poor performance in math was due to a bad teacher, but he believes that he is good in language-based subjects. He is sure that he will do better next year. This is an example of _____ attribution.
      a.   internal, global, and stable
      b.   external, global, and stable
      c.   internal, specific, and stable
      d.   external, specific, and unstable

Psychological Views, p. 238
Diff: M, Type: Applied, Ans: c

86.   The type of clinician who would be most likely to ask, "In what circumstances do you feel hopeless? "is a:
      a.   psychoanalyst.
      b.   behaviorist.
      c.   cognitive clinician.
      d.   sociocultural clinician.

Psychological Views, p. 238
Diff: H, Type: Applied, Ans: a

87.   The chief difference between learned helplessness created in laboratory settings and real-life depression is that:
      a.   laboratory depression is more likely to be accompanied by anxiety.
      b.   laboratory depression is less easily treated.
      c.   real-life depression does not have a helplessness component.
      d.   lab animals do not show social withdrawal and passivity.

The Sociocultural View, p. 238
Diff: E, Type: Applied, Ans: c

88.   Someone who looks at the influence of race, living conditions, marital status, and roles on the development of depression would most likely represent which theoretical orientation?
      a.   behavioral
      b.   cognitive
      c.   sociocultural
      d.   psychoanalytical

The Sociocultural View, p. 238
Diff: M, Type: Applied, Ans: d
89. Which theoretical orientation would support the finding that Westerners experience more psychological symptoms of depression?
     a. biochemical
     b. cognitive
     c. psychoanalytic
     d. sociocultural

The Sociocultural View, p. 238
Diff: M, Type: Applied, Ans: d
90. Someone receiving treatment for depression periodically completes an Attributional Style Questionnaire, which is designed to measure the therapy's effectiveness. The theoretical orientation of the therapist is most likely:
     a. psychodynamic.
     b. behavioral.
     c. sociocultural.
     d. cognitive.

The Sociocultural View, p. 238
Diff: M, Type: Factual, Ans: c
91. As countries become Westernized, the symptoms of depressed people in those countries generally:
     a. stay as they already are—either predominantly physical or predominantly psychological.
     b. become more common and intense, whether they are predominantly physical or predominantly psychological.
     c. shift to become more psychological.
     d. shift to become more physical.

The Sociocultural View, p. 239
Diff: M, Type: Applied, Ans: d
92. The type of clinician who would be most likely to say, "Tell me about the quality of mutual support you receive from your marriage" is a:
     a. psychoanalyst.
     b. behaviorist.
     c. cognitive clinician.
     d. sociocultural clinician.

The Sociocultural View, p. 239
Diff: M, Type: Factual, Ans: a
93. In the United States, the highest depression rate is found in:
     a. divorced people.
     b. married people.
     c. widowed people.
     d. never-married people.

The Sociocultural View, **p. 239**
Diff: M, Type: Factual, Ans: d
94.   Which of the following is not true of the correlation between marriage and depression?
         a.   Depression is as common among widowed people as married people.
         b.   Those who are never married experience depression more often than those who are
              married.
         c.   Those who are separated or divorced experience depression more often than those who
              are never married.
         d.   Depression is about as common among those who are widowed as those who are
              separated or divorced.

The Sociocultural View, p. 239
Diff: M, Type: Applied, Ans: c
95.   After a couple has divorced, you learn that one of them is suffering from depression. Most
         likely:
         a.   the man's depression led to the divorce.
         b.   the woman's depression led to the divorce.
         c.   a troubled marriage led to the depression.
         d.   the depression developed after the divorce, due to the stress of starting to date again.

Sociocultural Landscape: Depressing News for Women, pp. 240-241 (Box 8-3)
Diff: H, Type: Factual, Ans: d
96.   Artifact, quality-of-life, and self-blame theories all can explain the fact that:
         a.   twice as many women as men are diagnosed with bipolar disorder.
         b.   twice as many men as women are diagnosed with bipolar disorder.
         c.   twice as many men as women are diagnosed with unipolar depression.
         d.   twice as many women as men are diagnosed with unipolar depression.

Sociocultural Landscape: Depressing News for Women, pp. 240-241 Box (8-3)
Diff: M, Type: Applied, Ans: b
97.   Pierre feels terrible. He is sad, tired, and depressed, but he refuses to show it. This is
         consistent with the:
         a.   hormone theory.
         b.   artifact theory.
         c.   quality-of-life theory.
         d.   social pressure.

Sociocultural Landscape: Depressing News for Women, pp. 240-241 Box (8-3)
Diff: E, Type: Factual, Ans: c
98.   Depression is more common in women because they experience more taxing life situations,
         such as poverty and menial jobs, than men. This is the:
         a.   self-blame theory.
         b.   artifact theory.
         c.   quality-of-life theory.
         d.   lack-of-control theory

Sociocultural Landscape: Depressing News for Women, pp. 240-241 Box (8-3)
Diff: H, Type: Applied, Ans: a
99. If a study demonstrated that concern about one's weight usually is caused by depression, that finding would provide strong evidence:
   a. against social pressure theory.
   b. for social pressure theory.
   c. against quality-of-life theory.
   d. for quality-of-life theory.

Sociocultural Landscape: Depressing News for Women, pp. 240-241 Box (8-3)
Diff: H, Type: Applied, Ans: a
100. Artifact theory differs importantly from other sociocultural theories of depression because it suggests:
   a. women and men are equally likely to develop depression.
   b. hormone changes mask the development of depression in women.
   c. concern about body weight can be both a cause and a result of depression.
   d. depression is caused by examining one's feelings too closely.

Sociocultural Landscape: Depressing News for Women, pp. 240-241 Box (8-3)
Diff: H, Type: Applied, Ans: b
101. A friend of yours has just finished a very good in-class speech. You say to her, "Nice job!" She replies, "Wow, I guess I got really lucky today." Her reply is best predicted by which sociocultural theory of depression?
   a. rumination
   b. self-blame
   c. lack-of-control
   d. social pressure

What Are the Symptoms of Mania?, p. 242
Diff: E, Type: Factual, Ans: b
102. People experiencing mania:
   a. are acutely aware of their domineering, excessive behaviors.
   b. want excitement and companionship.
   c. enthusiastically long for new friends, but ignore old friends.
   d. enthusiastically look for old friends, but ignore new friends.

What Are the Symptoms of Mania?, p. 242
Diff: E, Type: Applied, Ans: a
103. People who talk rapidly, dress flamboyantly, and get involved in dangerous activities are showing _____ symptoms of mania.
   a. behavioral
   b. motivational
   c. cognitive
   d. emotional

What Are the Symptoms of Mania?, p. 242
Diff: M, Type: Applied, Ans: b

104.   On an impulse, David decides to throw a huge party. It takes four days of round-the-clock work to get everything ready, then David welcomes over 200 guests. When the police stop by because David has blocked a public road to have room for the party, he flies into a rage. Most likely, David is experiencing:
   a.   a manic phase of bipolar II disorder.
   b.   a manic phase of bipolar I disorder.
   c.   a manic phase of cyclothymic disorder.
   d.   mania.

What Are the Symptoms of Mania?, p. 242
Diff: H, Type: Applied, Ans: d

105.   A good way to describe a typical manic episode would be to say that it's like:
   a.   a roller coaster—up and down, up and down.
   b.   a meteorite—a sudden burst of energy that's quickly gone.
   c.   a power plant's output—steady, regular energy being produced.
   d.   a flash flood—spreading out wherever there's room for it to go.

Diagnosing Bipolar Disorders, p. 243
Diff: M, Type: Factual, Ans: b

106.   Someone who experiences a half-dozen alternations between mild mania and major depression within a one-year timespan would be classified as:
   a.   bipolar II seasonal.
   b.   bipolar II rapid cycling.
   c.   bipolar I mixed episodes.
   d.   bipolar I.

Diagnosing Bipolar Disorders, p. 243
Diff: H, Type: Factual, Ans: b

107.   The difference between bipolar I disorder and bipolar II disorder is:
   a.   the number of depressive and manic episodes.
   b.   the severity of the manic episodes.
   c.   the number of depressive episodes.
   d.   the seasonal variation in the episodes.

Diagnosing Bipolar Disorders, p. 243
Diff: M, Type: Factual, Ans: a

108.   The most common cognitive description of someone exhibiting mania is that the person is:
   a.   excessively optimistic, with poor judgment.
   b.   excessively optimistic, with normal self-esteem.
   c.   very coherent, with good judgment.
   d.   very coherent, with abnormally high self-esteem.

Diagnosing Bipolar Disorders, p. 243
Diff: H, Type: Applied, Ans: d

109.   If a friend of yours experiences occasional hypomanic episodes, without having other mood
       disorder symptoms, one piece of relevant advice you might give is:
       a.   "Get help immediately; things probably will get much worse."
       b.   "See a psychodynamic therapist; you can work this out."
       c.   "Learn all you can about 'mixed episodes'."
       d.   "You might be able to accomplish a lot during those episodes."

Diagnosing Bipolar Disorders, p. 243-244
Diff: H, Type: Applied, Ans: b

110.   Of the following alternatives, which is usually the best advice you could give someone with
       bipolar disorder?
       a.   "Be especially concerned about the mania; that's a lot more common than the
            depression."
       b.   "Be especially concerned about the depression; that's a lot more common than the
            mania."
       c.   "Be equally concerned about mania and depression; they occur about equally often, and
            last about equally long."
       d.   "Don't worry too much; most people with bipolar disorder stop having mood episodes,
            even without therapy."

Abnormality and Creativity: A Delicate Balance, p. 244 (Box 8-4)
Diff: H, Type: Applied, Ans: d

111.   A friend of yours is a highly creative artist. What is the best advice you could give your
       friend regarding mood disorders?
       a.   "Avoid mood disorders, highly creative people have a lower than average incidence of
            them."
       b.   "Severe mania is related to long periods of high creativity."
       c.   "If you develop a mood disorder, don't get treated, or you'll lose your creative spark."
       d.   "Mild mood disorders are related to greater creativity than severe disorders."

Abnormality and Creativity: A Delicate Balance, p. 244 (Box 8-4)
Diff: M, Type: Applied, Ans: d

112.   A talented artist is experiencing severe bipolar disorder. In terms of artistic output only, the
       best thing that artist could do is:
       a.   decline all treatment: severe psychological disturbance is related to better artistic output.
       b.   decline all treatment: one might lose one's creativity if there were less psychological
            disturbance.
       c.   seek treatment, but only for the depression: mania is essential to better artistic output.
       d.   seek treatment: psychological disturbance is not necessary for good artistic output.

What Are the Symptoms of Depression?, p. 225
Diff: E, Type: Applied, Ans: depression

3.   Kareem is miserable. He has no desire to participate in his usual activities. "Leave me alone."
        Suicide sometimes seems attractive. He sees himself in a negative way. In addition, he has
        headaches, insomnia, and nausea. He is suffering from _____.

What Are the Symptoms of Depression?, p. 225
Diff: M, Type: Applied, Ans: behavioral

4.   Depressed people often move less often and more slowly. This is a(n) _____ symptom.

Diagnosing Unipolar Depression, p. 227
Diff: M, Type: Factual, Ans: dysthymic disorder

5.   An individual may receive a diagnosis of _____ if she displays less disabling symptoms of a
        depression over a period of at least two years.

Diagnosing Unipolar Depression, p. 227
Diff: M, Type: Factual, Ans: double depression

6.   Dysthymia is a milder form of depression that is distinguished from major depression. When
        dysthymia leads to a major episode, the sequence is called _____.

Diagnosing Unipolar Depression, p. 227
Diff: M, Type: Factual, Ans: reactive depression (or exogenous depression)

7.   When a clear-cut set of events appears to be responsible for the onset of a major depressive
        episode, clinicians refer to it as a _____.

Sadness at the Happiest of Times, p. 230 (Box 8-1)
Diff: E, Type: Factual, Ans: seasonal affective disorder (SAD)

8.   Some people exhibit unusually low energy levels, slow down, and oversleep during the
        winter. This condition is called _____.

The Rhythms of Depression, pp. 230-231 (Box 8-2)
Diff: M, Type: Factual, Ans: melatonin

9.   Seasonal affective disorder has been linked to the manufacture of _____ in the brain.

The Rhythms of Depression, pp. 230-231 (Box 8-2)
Diff: E, Type: Factual, Ans: light therapy (or phototherapy)

10.   One therapy that has been found to be successful in the treatment of seasonal affective
        disorder is _____.

Psychological Views, p. 232
Diff: H, Type: Factual, Ans: symbolic loss (or imagined loss)

11.   To maintain his underlying assumption of a relationship between loss and depression, Freud
        invoked the concept of _____, in which a person unconsciously interprets negative
        experiences as the loss of a loved one.

Psychological Views, p. 233
Diff: H, Type: Factual, Ans: psychodynamic

12.   Harlow's monkey studies have been used to support the _____ explanation of depression.

Psychological Views, p. 234
Diff: H, Type: Factual, Ans: positive reinforcements (or social rewards)

13.   Lewinsohn has developed a theory that depression results from a progressive decrease in the number of _____ that a person receives over a long period of time.

Psychological Views, p. 234
Diff: E, Type: Factual, Ans: Aaron Beck

14.   The theorist responsible for focusing attention on the negative aspects of thinking as an explanation of depression is _____.

Psychological Views, p. 235
Diff: M, Type: Factual, Ans: errors in thinking

15.   According to Beck, arbitrary inferences, minimization, and magnification are examples of _____ that lead to negativity.

Psychological Views, p. 236
Diff: M, Type: Factual, Ans: negative thinking (or cognition or maladaptive thinking or the cognitive triad)

16.   Aaron Beck's work led him to believe that _____ lies at the heart of unipolar depression.

Psychological Views, p. 236
Diff: E, Type: Applied, Ans: learned helplessness

17.   "I have no control over good things in my life." The _____ theory of depression most closely explains this statement.

Psychological Views, pp. 236-237
Diff: E, Type: Factual, Ans: learned helplessness

18.   People become depressed when they believe that they have no control over the events in their lives and that they cannot change this condition. This is known as the _____ view of depression.

The Sociocultural View, p. 239
Diff: M, Type: Applied, Ans: sociocultural (or social support)

19.   The fact that separated or divorced people are about three times as likely to experience depression than are married people provides the most direct support for _____ theory.

Sociocultural Landscape: Depressing News for Women, pp. 240-241 (Box 8.3)
Diff: M, Type: Factual, Ans: artifact theory (or hypothesis)

20.   "Women and men are equally likely to experience depression, but gender differences in the rate of diagnosing this disorder arise because clinicians often fail to detect this disorder in men." This is the _____.

What Are the Symptoms of Mania?, p. 242
Diff: M, Type: Applied, Ans: manic

21.   "I'm going out to convince the drug dealers of the errors of their ways. I'm going to start right now. Then I'll write a play about my work and put it on Broadway. But first, I need to go home and cook a gourmet meal." This patient is probably suffering from a _____ episode.

What Are the Symptoms of Mania?, p. 242
Diff: M, Type: Applied, Ans: hypomanic (or exhibiting hypomania)

22.   A person who exhibits mild euphoria, moderate feelings of well-being, and somewhat elevated levels of physical activity is _____.

Diagnosing Bipolar Disorders, p. 245
Diff: M, Type: Factual, Ans: cyclothymic disorder

23.   A milder pattern of mood swings that does not reach the severity of bipolar disorder but does include depressive and manic episodes has been identified as _____.

What Causes Bipolar Disorder?, p. 245
Diff: M, Type: Factual, Ans: reserpine

24.   A breakthrough occurred several years ago in the treatment of bipolar disorders with the discovery that _____ diminished the symptoms by reducing norepinephrine activity.

ESSAY QUESTIONS

No Specific Topic, No Specific Page
Diff: M, Type: Factual

1.   Carefully distinguish between bipolar disorder, unipolar depression, dysthymic disorder, and cyclothymic disorder.

No Specific Topic, No Specific Page
Diff: M, Type: Factual

2.   Describe the following categories of major depressive disorders: recurrent, catatonic, seasonal, postpartum, melancholic.

No Specific Topic, No Specific Page
Diff: H, Type: Applied

3.   Research that supports the various theoretical explanations for depression has a number of limitations. Provide examples of actual research that demonstrates: (a) application of animal research to human behavior, (b) correlational research that does not establish causation, and (c) limitations of physiological measurements.

No Specific Topic, No Specific Page
Diff: M, Type: Applied

4.   If you were trying to predict whether a person was more or less likely than average to develop severe unipolar depression, what are some data which would—and would not—be useful to you in making that prediction?

The Rhythms of Depression, pp. 230-231 (Box 8-2)
Diff: H, Type: Factual

5.   Explain how melatonin is related to the suspected cause and treatment of seasonal affective disorder.

Psychological Views, pp. 232-233
Diff: H, Type: Factual

6.   Briefly describe the psychodynamic explanation for the development of depression and the research that supports or refutes that explanation.

Psychological Views, p. 234
Diff: H, Type: Applied

7.   Imagine that you are a behaviorist. What are the types of questions you would ask your depressed patient? What sorts of questions would you not be likely to ask, given your theoretical orientation?

Psychological Views, pp. 234-236
Diff: M, Type: Factual

8.   Briefly describe the three parts of Beck's cognitive triad and give an example of each.

Psychological Views, pp. 234-236
Diff: H, Type: Applied

9.   Write five items that would be likely to be on a test that Aaron Beck might develop to measure depression.

Psychological Views, pp. 236-238
Diff: H, Type: Applied

10.   Imagine that a person had just had a minor fender-bender, caused when the person backed into a light pole. Using the concepts of attribution in learned helplessness, provide an example of what an individual at risk for depression and one not at risk for depression would say. Be sure to include all three attributional dimensions.

Abnormality and Creativity: A delicate Balance, p. 244 (Box 8-4)
Diff: M, Type: Applied

11.   Imagine you are going to give a talk to the Student Art Group on, "The Creative Frenzy." What are the major topics (for example, hypomania) that you would include, and why?

CHAPTER 9

Treatments for Mood Disorders

MULTIPLE-CHOICE QUESTIONS

Psychological Approaches, p. 252
Diff: E, Type: Factual, Ans: d

1. Free association, interpretation of associations, and dream interpretation are all techniques used primarily by:
    a. interpersonal therapists.
    b. cognitive therapists.
    c. couples therapists.
    d. psychodynamic therapists.

Psychological Approaches, p. 252
Diff: M, Type: Applied, Ans: a

2. If a therapist asked you to say whatever came to mind, then suggested interpretations designed to help you work through grief over real or imagined losses, your therapist would be using:
    a. psychodynamic therapy.
    b. cognitive therapy.
    c. behavioral therapy.
    d. sociocultural therapy.

Psychological Approaches, p. 252
Diff: H, Type: Applied, Ans: a

3. If you are like most people, you are more likely to _____ than to _____ in order to improve your mood.
    a. pray; exercise
    b. go out with friends; listen to music
    c. have sex; help others in need
    d. eat; take a shower

Psychological Approaches, p. 252
Diff: M, Type: Factual, Ans: b

4. About what percentage of clients with unipolar depression receive treatment from a mental health professional each year?
    a. 50%
    b. 35%
    c. 75%
    d. almost all

Psychological Approaches, p. 252
Diff: M, Type: Factual, Ans: c
5.   What do psychodynamic therapists believe is the cause of unipolar depression?
      a.   repression of feelings of inadequacy
      b.   a biological imbalance in neurotransmitters
      c.   unconscious grieving over real or imagined loss
      d.   projection of internal anxiety onto a loved object

Psychological Approaches, p. 252
Diff: M, Type: Factual, Ans: c
6.   From whom are depressed people most likely first to seek help?
      a.   self-help books
      b.   therapists
      c.   physicians
      d.   clergy

Psychological Approaches, p. 252 (Figure 9.1)
Diff: M, Type: Applied, Ans: c
7.   Which of the following are people most likely to do to improve their mood?
      a.   exercise
      b.   drink alcohol
      c.   talk to friends/family
      d.   help others in need

Psychological Approaches, pp. 252-253
Diff: H, Type: Applied, Ans: b
8.   A therapist using free association and dream interpretation discovers that as a small child her
      patient had been left alone by her mother on several occasions, and concludes that the patient
      is experiencing unipolar depression. The therapist is most likely from which orientation?
      a.   cognitive
      b.   psychodynamic
      c.   behavioral
      d.   humanistic

Psychological Approaches, p. 253
Diff: M, Type: Applied, Ans: a
9.   Which of the following is an example of an aspect of psychodynamic therapy for depression?
      a.   A therapist questions a client about losses she may have suffered in her past.
      b.   Every time Keith says anything even a little positive to his therapist, the therapist smiles.
      c.   The therapist questions a client about the frequency and nature of her daily activities,
            including those that give her pleasure.
      d.   The therapist attacks the irrationality of a client's beliefs about himself.

Psychological Approaches, p. 254
Diff: M, Type: Applied, Ans: d
10.   Which statement about the treatment of mood disorders is the least accurate?
      a.   Mood disorders respond to a wide variety of treatment techniques.
      b.   Behavioral therapies appear to work best for mild to moderate depression.
      c.   Electroconvulsive shock therapy is still used to treat mood disorders.
      d.   Research shows that psychodynamic therapy is highly effective in treating mood
            disorders.

Psychological Approaches, p. 254
Diff: H, Type: Applied, Ans: b

11.   The effectiveness of psychodynamic therapy for unipolar depression is limited because:
   a.   it lasts for a shorter amount of time than other therapies giving patients less time to make progress.
   b.   depressed patients may not have the energy to engage in a verbal approach that depends on the development of insight.
   c.   very few depressed people have experienced a real or imagined (symbolic) loss.
   d.   psychodynamic therapists do not believe that they are able to evaluate whether their patients are making progress or not.

Psychological Approaches, p. 254
Diff: H, Type: Applied, Ans: b

12.   The best evidence for the effectiveness of the psychodynamic approach comes from:
   a.   work with seriously depressed people.
   b.   case study reports.
   c.   large-scale research projects conducted by the APA.
   d.   situations when the childhood loss is less obvious.

Psychological Approaches, p. 254
Diff: M, Type: Applied, Ans: b

13.   If your therapist tried to reintroduce you to pleasurable activities, reinforced nondepressive actions, and improved your social skills, your therapist would be using:
   a.   psychodynamic therapy.
   b.   behavioral therapy.
   c.   cognitive therapy.
   d.   sociocultural therapy.

Psychological Approaches, p. 254
Diff: M, Type: Factual, Ans: c

14.   Modern direct-to-consumer drug advertising began in the:
   a.   1940s.
   b.   1960s.
   c.   1980s.
   d.   2000s.

Psychological Approaches, p. 255
Diff: E, Type: Applied, Ans: b

15.   The instrument called the "Pleasant Events Schedule" is most likely to be a part of a _____ therapy program.
   a.   cognitive
   b.   behavioral
   c.   interpersonal
   d.   psychoanalytic

Psychological Approaches, p. 255
Diff: E, Type: Applied, Ans: a
16. A therapist treating a patient for depression first finds out what activities the client once found pleasurable. These activities are then reintroduced into the patient's daily schedule. Which type of therapy is this therapist using?
    a. behavioral therapy
    b. humanistic therapy
    c. interpersonal therapy
    d. psychodynamic therapy

Psychological Approaches, p. 256
Diff: H, Type: Applied, Ans: b
17. Which of the following is important in using contingency management effectively?
    a. Increase the total number of activities, both positive and negative, so the person can learn to tell the difference.
    b. Make sure that the person receives reinforcement for engaging in positive activities.
    c. Be sure the person receives feedback from a group regarding which activities are positive and which are negative.
    d. Develop ways for the person to express depressed feelings through journal writing.

Psychological Approaches, p. 256
Diff: E, Type: Factual, Ans: d
18. Behavioral therapy for the treatment of unipolar depression is most likely to include:
    a. changing irrational thoughts.
    b. interpreting dreams.
    c. uncovering conflicts over loss.
    d. reinforcing nondepressed behavior.

Psychological Approaches, p. 256
Diff: M, Type: Factual, Ans: b
19. A behavioral therapist is most likely to use which of the following in treating a patient with unipolar depression?
    a. electroconvulsive treatments
    b. praise for engaging in positive activities
    c. insight into the underlying problem
    d. identification of distorted thinking and negative biases

Psychological Approaches, p. 256
Diff: H, Type: Factual, Ans: d
20. According to Lewinsohn, depressed people must improve their social skills because:
    a. the performance of socially unacceptable behavior is irrational.
    b. it is important to reinforce the client's depressive behavior.
    c. depressed people may be experiencing interpersonal role transition.
    d. positive reinforcement is given to people who exhibit positive social behavior.

Psychological Approaches, p. 256
Diff: H, Type: Applied, Ans: b
21.   A therapist turns on a buzzer when a client speaks slowly and laboriously. She turns it off when the client speaks more rapidly. In other cases the therapist instructs the client's spouse to ignore his mate when she complains or acts in a self-deprecating manner. This is an example of:
      a.   cognitive therapy.
      b.   behavioral therapy.
      c.   humanistic therapy.
      d.   psychodynamic therapy.

Psychological Approaches, p. 256
Diff: M, Type: Applied, Ans: b
22.   Arron's persistent feelings of sadness and impending doom dominate his life. Every time he says anything even a little positive to his therapist, the therapist smiles. Otherwise the therapist has a stone face. This therapist is probably using some variation of:
      a.   cognitive therapy.
      b.   behavioral therapy.
      c.   psychoanalytic therapy.
      d.   interpersonal psychotherapy.

Psychological Approaches, p. 256
Diff: M, Type: Factual, Ans: d
23.   What kind of unipolar depression is Lewinsohn's behavioral treatment most effective in treating?
      a.   severe depression
      b.   depression of sudden onset
      c.   depression of gradual onset
      d.   mild to moderate depression

Psychological Approaches, p. 256
Diff: H, Type: Applied, Ans: c
24.   The contingency management approach is an example of the application of _____ to the treatment of depression.
      a.   business principles
      b.   role playing
      c.   reinforcement
      d.   imitation (modeling)

Psychological Approaches, p. 256
Diff: M, Type: Applied, Ans: b
25.   Which one of the following is most consistent with a contingency management approach?
      a.   providing sympathy when the person talks about depressed feelings
      b.   praising the person for engaging in nondepressed activities
      c.   limiting the contact family members have with the person
      d.   analyzing the person's irrational thoughts

Psychological Approaches, p. 256
Diff: H, Type: Applied, Ans: a
26.   Jose is depressed. His therapist told him that reading a book each month would help. He should also visit friends, go bowling, do the laundry, mow the lawn, and eat meals with his wife. In short, he should increase his positive activity. His therapist most likely reflects the _____ orientation.
    a.   behavioral
    b.   psychodynamic
    c.   humanistic
    d.   interpersonal

Psychological Approaches, p. 256
Diff: H, Type: Applied, Ans: b
27.   Which of the following is a correct match of person and approach?
    a.   Lewinsohn and psychodynamic therapy
    b.   Beck and cognitive therapy
    c.   Seligman and behavioral therapy
    d.   Weissman and learned helplessness

Psychological Approaches, p. 256
Diff: E, Type: Applied, Ans: c
28.   If your therapist concentrated on helping you recognize and change negative thoughts and thus improve your mood, your therapist would be using:
    a.   psychodynamic therapy.
    b.   behavioral therapy.
    c.   cognitive therapy.
    d.   sociocultural therapy.

Psychological Approaches, p. 256
Diff: M, Type: Applied, Ans: b
29.   A depressed individual receiving therapy is told that many—even most—of the negative thoughts that individual experiences and records have no basis in fact. Most likely, the therapist is:
    a.   changing primary attitudes.
    b.   challenging automatic thoughts.
    c.   training the individual in dichotomous thinking.
    d.   negatively reinforcing verbal avoidance responses.

Psychological Approaches, p. 257
Diff: H, Type: Applied, Ans: b
30.   Typically, people who are in the loss and separation stage of grief:
    a.   have difficulty believing that the person has died.
    b.   dream that the person is still alive or "see" the person.
    c.   are irritable and feel guilty.
    d.   experience deteriorating social relationships.

Psychological Approaches, p. 257
Diff: E, Type: Applied, Ans: d
31.   Someone who feels much sadder than usual on the first anniversary of a close friend's death
        is experiencing:
        a.   shock.
        b.   pathological bereavement.
        c.   denial of the grief response.
        d.   a normal grief reaction.

Psychological Approaches, p. 258
Diff: H, Type: Applied, Ans: b
32.   A person experiencing unipolar depression writes the following in an activity schedule, "Go
        to store; doctor's appointment; visit museum; read novel; clean room." What treatment
        approach is this person most likely receiving?
        a.   psychodynamic therapy
        b.   cognitive therapy
        c.   interpersonal therapy
        d.   adjunctive therapy

Psychological Approaches, p. 258
Diff: H, Type: Applied, Ans: c
33.   The "increasing activities and elevating mood" phase of Beck's treatment for depression:
        a.   requires the use of antidepressant medication to be effective.
        b.   is the phase most related to cognitions.
        c.   makes the therapy cognitive-behavioral rather than purely cognitive.
        d.   deals with the problem of dichotomous thinking.

Psychological Approaches, p. 258
Diff: M, Type: Applied, Ans: c
34.   Which of the following is not a part of Beck's cognitive therapy for unipolar depression?
        a.   encouraging people to become more active and confident
        b.   education about what automatic thoughts are
        c.   discussion with family members about their maladaptive thoughts
        d.   prompting people to test their attitudes and thoughts

Psychological Approaches, p. 258
Diff: H, Type: Applied, Ans: c
35.   Which of the following would a cognitive therapist be least likely to say to you?
        a.   Please prepare a detailed schedule of your activities for the week.
        b.   Write down your automatic thoughts as they occur to you.
        c.   Try to evaluate what happens to you in "black and white" terms.
        d.   Let's do a little experiment to test that attitude.

Psychological Approaches, p. 258
Diff: M, Type: Applied, Ans: a

36.   "I do not know why you think you are a terrible surgeon. You have not lost a patient during an operation in two years. No one else in the city has that kind of record." Which of the following orientations is most likely to describe the therapist who made this statement?
      a.   cognitive
      b.   behavioral
      c.   humanistic
      d.   interpersonal

Psychological Approaches, p. 258
Diff: H, Type: Applied, Ans: b

37.   In cognitive behavior therapy, the process of altering or challenging primary attitudes is similar to:
      a.   increasing daily activities.
      b.   conducting an experiment.
      c.   identifying distorted thinking.
      d.   increasing positive reinforcements.

Psychological Approaches, p. 258
Diff: H, Type: Applied, Ans: c

38.   Clients who tend to see everything that occurs as either all right or all wrong, with nothing in between, need to focus on which phase of Beck's treatment for depression?
      a.   increasing activities and elevating mood
      b.   challenging automatic thoughts
      c.   identifying negative thinking and biases
      d.   changing primary attitudes

Psychological Approaches, pp. 258-259
Diff: H, Type: Applied, Ans: a

39.   Clients who test their assumptions about what is causing their depression are working in which phase of Beck's treatment program?
      a.   changing primary attitudes
      b.   challenging automatic thoughts
      c.   identifying negative thinking and biases
      d.   increasing activities and elevating mood

Psychological Approaches, p. 259 (Table 9-1)
Diff: E, Type: Factual, Ans: d

40.   Extensive research shows that the mood disorder for which there is the highest improvement rate after therapy is:
      a.   major depressive disorder.
      b.   bipolar I disorder.
      c.   bipolar II disorder.
      d.   the improvement rate is about the same for major depressive disorder, bipolar I disorder, and bipolar II disorder.

Psychological Approaches, p. 259
Diff: E, Type: Factual, Ans: d
41.	Which of the following is true about the research on the effectiveness of cognitive therapy in treating unipolar depression?
	a.	It is less effective than placebo treatments.
	b.	The research has not provided consistent results on this issue.
	c.	It is more effective in group than in individual therapy sessions.
	d.	It nearly eliminates depressive symptoms in 50-60% of the cases.

Psychological Approaches, p. 259
Diff: H, Type: Factual, Ans: a
42.	Which of the following is true about research on the effectiveness of cognitive therapy for treating unipolar depression?
	a.	Hundreds of studies show its effectiveness.
	b.	It is no more effective than placebo therapy.
	c.	80-90% of depressed people show almost total elimination of symptoms.
	d.	Although people become less depressed, their thought patterns don't change.

Sociocultural Approaches, p. 260
Diff: H, Type: Applied, Ans: b
43.	Which of the following is the best example of interpersonal role transition?
	a.	taking a very important exam
	b.	going away to college for the first time
	c.	exploring the spiritual dimensions of one's life
	d.	planting a garden

Sociocultural Approaches, p. 260
Diff: H, Type: Applied, Ans: a
44.	Why is interpersonal psychotherapy considered to be a sociocultural approach?
	a.	Depression is thought to result from disrupted social interactions and role expectations.
	b.	Depression is thought to result from individual pathology.
	c.	Depression is thought to be best treated within the family and in the real world rather than in the clinic.
	d.	Depression is thought to be best treated by use of a multidisciplinary treatment team.

Sociocultural Approaches, p. 260
Diff: M, Type: Applied, Ans: c
45.	If your therapist encouraged you to explore your roles in life—how they might be changing, or how your expectations might be different from someone else's—your therapist would be using:
	a.	cognitive therapy.
	b.	behavioral therapy.
	c.	interpersonal therapy.
	d.	psychodynamic therapy.

Sociocultural Approaches, p. 260
Diff: E, Type: Applied, Ans: b
46. A woman who is in conflict with her husband over whether she should have a career or stay at home full-time to care for their children is experiencing:
a. interpersonal loss.
b. interpersonal role dispute.
c. interpersonal role transition.
d. interpersonal deficits.

Sociocultural Approaches, p. 260
Diff: E, Type: Applied, Ans: d
47. A person who displays extreme shyness and insensitivity to others is showing signs of:
a. interpersonal loss.
b. interpersonal role dispute.
c. interpersonal role transition.
d. interpersonal deficits.

Sociocultural Approaches, p. 260
Diff: M, Type: Applied, Ans: a
48. Which interpersonal problem area identified by interpersonal psychotherapists is most like the cause of depression suggested by psychodynamic therapists?
a. interpersonal loss
b. interpersonal deficits
c. interpersonal role dispute
d. interpersonal role transition

Sociocultural Approaches, p. 260
Diff: E, Type: Factual, Ans: c
49. Interpersonal psychotherapists believe that therapy must address:
a. maladaptive attitudes.
b. ego-superego conflicts.
c. role transitions in relationships.
d. developing social skills to elicit reinforcement from others.

Sociocultural Approaches, p. 260
Diff: M, Type: Applied, Ans: c
50. Tomas has withdrawn from most social contacts because he never seems to be able to say the right thing. He just doesn't seem to fit in. His comments are always misinterpreted. He feels alone and is depressed. This is an example of what interpersonal psychotherapists refer to as:
a. an interpersonal loss.
b. an interpersonal role transition.
c. an interpersonal deficit.
d. an interpersonal role dispute.

Sociocultural Approaches, p. 260
Diff: M, Type: Applied, Ans: c
51.   Tony just does not feel close to anyone. He feels alone because although he can get to know someone (a woman) quite well on a friendship level, he doesn't know how to get beyond that to a more intimate level. This is depressing him. This is an example of what interpersonal psychotherapists refer to as:
   a.   an interpersonal role transition.
   b.   an interpersonal loss.
   c.   an interpersonal deficit.
   d.   an interpersonal role dispute.

Sociocultural Approaches, p. 260
Diff: E, Type: Factual, Ans: d
52.   Which of the following is true about the research on the effectiveness of interpersonal psychotherapy in treating unipolar depression?
   a.   It is less effective than placebo treatments.
   b.   The research has not provided consistent results on this issue.
   c.   It is more effective in group than in individual therapy sessions.
   d.   It nearly eliminates depressive symptoms in 50-60% of cases.

Sociocultural Approaches, p. 260
Diff: H, Type: Applied, Ans: a
53.   According to research studies, the success rate for interpersonal therapy is about the same as that for:
   a.   cognitive therapy.
   b.   psychodynamic therapy.
   c.   placebo therapy.
   d.   no therapy.

Sociocultural Approaches, p. 260
Diff: M, Type: Factual, Ans: b
54.   About what percentage of people receiving treatment for depression are in dysfunctional relationships?
   a.   25%
   b.   50%
   c.   75%
   d.   90%

Sociocultural Approaches, p. 260
Diff: E, Type: Applied, Ans: d
55.   If the focus of your therapy is primarily on how communication and problem-solving difficulties with your partner are contributing to your depression, your therapist is using:
   a.   cognitive therapy.
   b.   cognitive-behavioral therapy.
   c.   interpersonal therapy.
   d.   couple therapy.

Biological Approaches, p. 261
Diff: M, Type: Factual, Ans: a
56.   What is the average length of time for the treatment of major depressive disorder with ECT?
       a.   2-4 weeks
       b.   15 weeks
       c.   20 weeks
       d.   indefinite

Biological Approaches, p. 261
Diff: H, Type: Applied, Ans: c
57.   Which of the following is not an example of a biological treatment for depression?
       a.   electroconvulsive shock
       b.   antidepressant medication
       c.   contingency management
       d.   herbal remedies

Biological Approaches, p. 261
Diff: H, Type: Applied, Ans: d
58.   If you were treated with ECT, you would experience:
       a.   a reuptake of serotonin.
       b.   an insulin-induced coma.
       c.   an increase in energy and creativity.
       d.   a brain seizure.

Biological Approaches, p. 262
Diff: E, Type: Factual, Ans: a
59.   In the bilateral ECT, the electrical current passes through:
       a.   both sides of the brain.
       b.   only the left side of the brain.
       c.   only the right side of the brain.
       d.   the brain and the spinal cord.

Biological Approaches, p. 262
Diff: H, Type: Applied, Ans: a
60.   The use of ECT was prompted by the discovery that psychotic people:
       a.   rarely had epilepsy.
       b.   rarely experienced depression.
       c.   were very likely to experience convulsions.
       d.   were unable to eat pork without having a convulsion.

Biological Approaches, p. 262
Diff: H, Type: Applied, Ans: b
61.   Cerletti, the first psychiatrist to use ECT effectively, later abandoned the procedure, most
       likely because of:
       a.   the advent of antipsychotic medications.
       b.   the likelihood that convulsions caused by it would result in broken bones and dislocated
            joints.
       c.   the trend toward using bilateral rather than unilateral shock.
       d.   better results from using insulin.

Biological Approaches, p. 262
Diff: M, Type: Factual, Ans: c
62. Which patient group was the first treated with ECT?
     a. manic patients
     b. phobic patients
     c. psychotic patients
     d. hysterical patients

Biological Approaches, p. 262
Diff: M, Type: Factual, Ans: b
63. ECT (electroconvulsive therapy) has changed over the years. Patients given this treatment now may receive:
     a. higher levels of current.
     b. anesthetics.
     c. oxygen to prevent memory loss.
     d. insulin.

Biological Approaches, p. 262
Diff: M, Type: Factual, Ans: b
64. Today, electroconvulsive therapy:
     a. is more likely to involve the use of insulin than shock.
     b. also involves the use of muscle relaxants.
     c. is given without anesthetic to reduce memory loss.
     d. is more likely to involve bilateral shock.

Biological Approaches, p. 262
Diff: E, Type: Factual, Ans: c
65. One of the side effects of ECT is:
     a. mania.
     b. psychosis.
     c. memory loss.
     d. intensification of the depression.

Biological Approaches, p. 263
Diff: E, Type: Factual, Ans: a
66. Electroconvulsive therapy:
     a. appears to be most effective in treating severe depression.
     b. no longer causes memory loss and neurological damage.
     c. prevents brain seizures.
     d. commonly results in broken bones.

Biological Approaches, p. 263
Diff: M, Type: Factual, Ans: c
67. Which of the following is the most important reason for the decline in the use of electroconvulsive therapy since the 1950s?
     a. It was shown not to be effective in cases of severe depression with delusions.
     b. It is too expensive and not covered by medical insurance.
     c. Antidepressant drugs were developed.
     d. Most memory loss appeared to be permanent.

Biological Approaches, p. 263
Diff: E, Type: Factual, Ans: b

68.   The treatment of what disease led to the development of MAO inhibitors?
       a. epilepsy
       b. tuberculosis
       c. schizophrenia
       d. high blood pressure

Biological Approaches, p. 264
Diff: H, Type: Applied, Ans: c

69.   If you had high blood pressure, you would want to be especially careful when using:
       a. selective serotonin reuptake inhibitors.
       b. tricyclics.
       c. MAO inhibitors.
       d. second generation antidepressants.

Biological Approaches, p. 264
Diff: H, Type: Factual, Ans: a

70.   MAO inhibitors work by:
       a. blocking MAO from breaking down norepinephrine.
       b. raising the level of MAO.
       c. lowering the level of tyramine, found in cheese and wine.
       d. interacting with the production of amphetamines.

Biological Approaches, p. 264
Diff: H, Type: Factual, Ans: c

71.   MAO inhibitors are biochemical agents that alleviate depressive symptoms in approximately
       half of the clinically depressed patients who take them. What is the mechanism of action of
       these drugs?
       a. They stimulate serotonin production.
       b. They block synapses that release norepinephrine.
       c. They interfere with the destruction of norepinephrine.
       d. They raise the levels of monoamine oxidase in the brain.

Biological Approaches, p. 264
Diff: M, Type: Applied, Ans: c

72.   Which of the following is most likely to elevate the mood in a depressed person?
       a. inhibition of serotonin synthesis
       b. a decrease in the levels of brain serotonin
       c. an increase in the levels of brain norepinephrine
       d. blocking synaptic transmission at norepinephrine synapses

Biological Approaches, p. 264
Diff: H, Type: Factual, Ans: d

73.   How do monoamine oxidase (MAO) inhibitors work?
       a. They increase the levels of reserpine in the blood.
       b. They decrease supplies of serotonin in neurons.
       c. They decrease supplies of dopamine in neurons.
       d. They increase supplies of norepinephrine in neurons.

Biological Approaches, p. 264
Diff: H, Type: Applied, Ans: a

74.   People who take MAO inhibitors and want to decrease the risk of negative side effects would make the greatest changes in which aspect of life?
    a.   what they eat
    b.   the type and amount of exercise they get
    c.   their sex lives
    d.   the amount of time they could spend in the sun

Biological Approaches, p. 264
Diff: E, Type: Applied, Ans: d

75.   Corrina took an antidepressant and then ate a meal. Shortly thereafter her blood pressure skyrocketed and she felt faint. Which of the following is most likely to be true?
    a.   She took an overdose.
    b.   She took a tricyclic antidepressant.
    c.   She did not need the antidepressant.
    d.   She ate something containing tyramine.

Biological Approaches, p. 264
Diff: M, Type: Factual, Ans: a

76.   The nutraceutical SAM-e:
    a.   starts working faster than more traditional antidepressants.
    b.   has more severe side effects than traditional antidepressants.
    c.   is much less expensive than pharmaceuticals..
    d.   was tested first in the United States, then in Italy and other countries.

Biological Approaches, p. 265
Diff: H, Type: Applied, Ans: d

77.   If a friend is considering nutraceuticals for the treatment of depression, your best advice would be:
    a.   "Don't: nutraceuticals don't work."
    b.   "Black cohosh should help with practically any kind of mood disorder."
    c.   "Melatonin is effective only with severe depression."
    d.   "St. John's wort should only be used for mild depression."

Biological Approaches, p. 265
Diff: E, Type: Factual, Ans: d

78.   St. John's wort:
    a.   has been shown to be effective in treating severe depression.
    b.   produces undesirable side effects.
    c.   is available only with a prescription.
    d.   is inexpensive compared to pharmaceuticals.

Biological Approaches, p. 265
Diff: E, Type: Factual, Ans: b

79.   Researchers were searching for drugs to treat schizophrenia when they came across imipramine, which alleviated the symptoms of depression, although it was not effective against schizophrenia. It became the first of a class of drugs, all sharing a similar molecular structure, called:
      a.   tyramine.
      b.   tricyclics.
      c.   neuroleptics.
      d.   MAO inhibitors.

Biological Approaches, p. 266
Diff: H, Type: Factual, Ans: c

80.   The mechanism of action of imipramine is to:
      a.   destroy monoamine oxidase.
      b.   mimic the action of norepinephrine and serotonin.
      c.   block the reuptake of norepinephrine and serotonin.
      d.   block the receptor sites for norepinephrine and serotonin on the postsynaptic neuron.

Biological Approaches, p. 266
Diff: H, Type: Applied, Ans: b

81.   In order to effectively reduce the chances of relapse of depressive symptoms, patients should:
      a.   take a larger dose of tricyclics than necessary for relief of symptoms.
      b.   continue to take tricyclics after they are symptom free.
      c.   gradually taper the dose of tricyclics once they are symptom free.
      d.   take MAO inhibitors along with tricyclics.

Biological Approaches, p. 266
Diff: H, Type: Factual, Ans: d

82.   Apparently tricyclics work by:
      a.   blocking the production of norepinephrine and serotonin.
      b.   blocking the reuptake of the tricyclic by the neurotransmitter.
      c.   blocking the ingestion of the tricyclic.
      d.   blocking the reuptake of norepinephrine and serotonin.

Biological Approaches, p. 266
Diff: H, Type: Applied, Ans: c

83.   Critics of the "reuptake theory" of tricyclic antidepressant action focus on _____ to explain the mechanism by which tricyclics alleviate depressive symptoms.
      a.   the molecular similarity of norepinephrine and imipramine
      b.   the decline in the norepinephrine and serotonin levels of people taking tricyclics
      c.   the 7- to 14-day lag between the start of its blocking reuptake and its effect on depressive symptoms
      d.   the inconsistency between reuptake theory and the known mechanism of action of monoamine oxidase inhibitors

Biological Approaches, p. 267 (Table 9-2)
Diff: H, Type: Factual, Ans: a

84.   Which of the following is a correct match?
    a.   MAO inhibitor and Parnate
    b.   tricyclic and Nardil
    c.   tricyclic and Prozac
    d.   second-generation antidepressants and Tofranil

Biological Approaches, p. 267 (Table 9-2)
Diff: H, Type: Factual, Ans: a

85.   Which of the following is a second-generation antidepressant?
    a.   Zoloft
    b.   Nardil
    c.   Elavil
    d.   Tofranil

Biological Approaches, p. 267
Diff: H, Type: Applied, Ans: d

86.   The trade name for the tricyclic first tested as a treatment for tuberculosis is:
    a.   Elavil.
    b.   Prozac.
    c.   Wellbutrin.
    d.   Tofranil.

Biological Approaches, p. 267
Diff: H, Type: Applied, Ans: a

87.   Which of the following is an example of a second-generation antidepressant?
    a.   Straterra
    b.   Parnate
    c.   Aventil
    d.   Sinequan

Biological Approaches, p. 267
Diff: H, Type: Factual, Ans: c

88.   Some so-called second-generation antidepressants appear to act by:
    a.   destroying MAO.
    b.   facilitating the reuptake process.
    c.   selectively blocking the reuptake of serotonin.
    d.   blocking the reuptake processes of all neurotransmitters more completely.

Biological Approaches, p. 267
Diff: M, Type: Factual, Ans: b

89.   Second-generation antidepressants:
    a.   mimic MAO inhibitors and tricyclics.
    b.   target specific neurotransmission reuptake.
    c.   increase the sex drive of depressed people.
    d.   are yet to be widely prescribed.

Biological Approaches, p. 267
Diff: H, Type: Factual, Ans: c
90.   Second-generation antidepressants:
    a.   are significantly more effective than tricyclics.
    b.   are easier to overdose on than tricyclics.
    c.   produce fewer unpleasant side effects than tricyclics.
    d.   are less often prescribed than tricyclics.

Biological Approaches, p. 267
Diff: E, Type: Factual, Ans: a
91.   Which of the following is a side effect of tricyclic antidepressants?
    a.   dry mouth
    b.   depression
    c.   heightened suicide risk
    d.   dizziness after eating bananas

How Do the Treatments for Unipolar Depression Compare?, pp. 268-269
Diff: E, Type: Applied, Ans: d
92.   Your best advice to a friend who is experiencing severe depression would be:
    a.   "Try behavior therapy; it's the best therapy for severe depression."
    b.   "Couple therapy works better than other therapies if you have no marital problems."
    c.   "Psychodynamic therapy or behavior therapy should work better than anything else."
    d.   "Try combining cognitive therapy with drug therapy."

How Do the Treatments for Unipolar Depression Compare?, p. 269
Diff: H, Type: Factual, Ans: d
93.   A large-scale NIMH comparison study of cognitive therapy, interpersonal therapy and
       antidepressant drug therapy showed that:
    a.   cognitive therapy works more quickly than drug therapy.
    b.   drug therapy was better than cognitive therapy at preventing relapse.
    c.   interpersonal therapy was the least effective.
    d.   the three therapies were about equally effective at reducing depressive symptoms.

How Do the Treatments for Unipolar Depression Compare?, p. 269
Diff: H, Type: Applied, Ans: c
94.   A large-scale NIMH comparison study of cognitive therapy, interpersonal therapy, and
       antidepressant drug therapy showed that:
    a.   placebo therapy (attention from a therapist) was as effective as the other therapies tested.
    b.   about 75% of patients who completed treatment showed marked improvement.
    c.   during the final four weeks of treatment, the therapies were about equally effective.
    d.   psychodynamic therapists were criticized for failing to participate in the study.

How Do the Treatments for Unipolar Depression Compare?, p. 269
Diff: E, Type: Factual, Ans: a
95.   Which of the following is the fastest acting treatment for unipolar depression?
    a.   drug therapy
    b.   cognitive therapy
    c.   behavioral therapy
    d.   psychodynamic therapy

How Do the Treatments for Unipolar Depression Compare?, p. 269
Diff: M, Type: Applied, Ans: a

96.   A key to preventing relapse of unipolar depression appears to be:
       a.   continue the therapy, no matter its type, after the symptoms have gone.
       b.   receiving drug therapy in combination with a psychological therapy.
       c.   receiving individual attention from a therapist, no matter the therapy.
       d.   family support.

How Do the Treatments for Unipolar Depression Compare?, p. 269
Diff: H, Type: Applied, Ans: b

97.   There has been a significant increase in the number of physicians prescribing antidepressants
       in the past few decades:
       a.   because the results of drug therapy are vastly superior to those of cognitive therapy.
       b.   despite the success of cognitive therapy.
       c.   even though behavior therapy shows better results.
       d.   because successful drug therapy is only effective in the short term.

How Do the Treatments for Unipolar Depression Compare?, p. 269
Diff: H, Type: Applied, Ans: c

98.   Research now suggests that once someone has been successfully treated for depression he or
       she:
       a.   can safely stop treatment.
       b.   needs to begin drug treatment if it has not already been tried.
       c.   needs some type of continuation or maintenance therapy.
       d.   needs to follow up with the same type of therapy.

How Do the Treatments for Unipolar Depression Compare?, p. 269
Diff: H, Type: Applied, Ans: d

99.   Recent research indicates that behavioral therapy is the treatment of choice:
       a.   for serious but not mild forms of depression.
       b.   over drug and cognitive therapies.
       c.   when interpersonal therapy is the only other alternative.
       d.   over placebo treatment.

How Do the Treatments for Unipolar Depression Compare?, p. 269
Diff: H, Type: Applied, Ans: a

100.   Which of the following would a psychodynamic therapist be most likely to say about studies
       regarding the effectiveness of psychodynamic therapy for depression?
       a.   The therapy does not lend itself to empirical research.
       b.   Therapists' reports of individual recovery and progress should be disregarded.
       c.   The therapy is less effective than other methods.
       d.   More empirical studies need to be done before drawing conclusions.

How Do the Treatments for Unipolar Depression Compare?, p. 270
Diff: H, Type: Applied, Ans: b

101.   The most recent studies of treatment for depressed children and adolescents would lead you
       to recommend that:
       a.   medications should not be used.
       b.   medications and cognitive treatments should be used in combination.
       c.   cognitive therapy is ineffective because children are irrational thinkers.
       d.   either drug or cognitive therapy should be used, but not both.

How Do the Treatments for Unipolar Depression Compare?, p. 270
Diff: M, Type: Factual, Ans: b

102.   Which of the following treatments produces the fastest results in the biological treatment for
       unipolar depression?
       a.   MAO inhibitors
       b.   electroconvulsive therapy (ECT)
       c.   tricyclic antidepressant medication
       d.   second-generation antidepressant drugs

How Do the Treatments for Unipolar Depression Compare?, p. 270
Diff: M, Type: Factual, Ans: c

103.   The major present-day indication for the use of ECT as a treatment for depression is:
       a.   when the patient requests it.
       b.   when the patient is judged not competent to refuse it.
       c.   when a severely depressed patient does not respond to other therapies.
       d.   when a severely depressed patient suggests the possibility of suicide.

How Do the Treatments for Unipolar Depression Compare?, p. 270
Diff: H, Type: Applied, Ans: c

104.   Which of the following is the best advice (that is, most supported by research) you could give
       a person experiencing depression?
       a.   Even if you are experiencing severe discord in your marriage, couple therapy should not
            be your first choice.
       b.   If you are severely depressed, behavioral therapy is your best bet.
       c.   If you receive electroconvulsive therapy, you should follow that with drug treatment.
       d.   There is no faster-acting or more effective therapy than psychodynamic therapy.

How Do the Treatments for Unipolar Depression Compare?, p. 270
Diff: M, Type: Applied, Ans: b

105.   Electroconvulsive therapy would be most legitimately recommended when:
       a.   depression is mild to moderate.
       b.   the patient has not responded to antidepressant drugs.
       c.   suicide is not judged to be a significant risk.
       d.   the patient first comes to therapy.

Lithium Therapy, p. 271
Diff: M, Type: Applied, Ans: b

106.   If a person taking lithium began experiencing nausea, vomiting, sluggishness, tremors, and
       seizures, one would suspect:
       a.   the person was not experiencing bipolar disorder.
       b.   the person was experiencing lithium intoxication.
       c.   the dose was too low.
       d.   the person needs adjunctive therapy.

Lithium Therapy, p. 274
Diff: M, Type: Factual, Ans: d

107.   The effects of lithium were discovered during the investigation of:
       a.   a drug to treat tuberculosis.
       b.   a drug to treat schizophrenia.
       c.   the effects of camphor on psychosis.
       d.   the effect of toxic levels of uric acid.

Lithium Therapy, p. 274
Diff: H, Type: Applied, Ans: b
108.   Which of the following is an example of a prophylactic drug?
    a.   one that helps a person maintain gains made previously
    b.   one that helps prevent symptoms from developing
    c.   one that eliminates current symptoms
    d.   one that reverses negative side effects caused by previous treatment

Lithium Therapy, p. 274
Diff: E, Type: Applied, Ans: b
109.   Rosita swings between periods of bottomless depressions and high-flying enthusiasm. She never hits the middle. Her physician is most likely to recommend treatment with:
    a.   ECT.
    b.   lithium.
    c.   imipramine.
    d.   tranquilizers.

Lithium Therapy, p. 274
Diff: E, Type: Factual, Ans: c
110.   At least _____ of manic patients treated with lithium improve.
    a.   25%
    b.   50%
    c.   60%
    d.   75%

Lithium Therapy, p. 274
Diff: M, Type: Factual, Ans: b
111.   Lithium has been found to:
    a.   be useful in the treatment of posttraumatic stress disorder.
    b.   enhance the effectiveness of antidepressant drugs in treating unipolar depression.
    c.   increase the effectiveness of drugs used to treat obsessive-compulsive disorder.
    d.   be more effective in treating bipolar disorder when used in conjunction with ECT than when used alone.

Lithium Therapy, p. 274
Diff: E, Type: Factual, Ans: d
112.   All of the following about lithium as a treatment for bipolar disorder are true, except that it:
    a.   is highly effective at eliminating manic symptoms.
    b.   also alleviates depressive symptoms, though to a lesser degree.
    c.   appears to help prevent relapse.
    d.   interferes with the effectiveness of antidepressant medications.

Lithium Therapy, p. 274
Diff: H, Type: Factual, Ans: a
113.   Lithium appears to affect:
    a.   synaptic activity.
    b.   absorption of salt.
    c.   brain seizure activity.
    d.   reuptake of serotonin.

Lithium Therapy, p. 274
Diff: H, Type: Factual, Ans: a

114. Second messengers are:
    a. related to the action of lithium on neurotransmitters.
    b. the same as neurotransmitters.
    c. important in increasing the effectiveness of tricyclics.
    d. used by therapists when treating couples.

Adjunctive Psychotherapy, p. 275
Diff: M, Type: Factual, Ans: c

115. The combination of lithium and psychotherapy is better than lithium treatment alone. This therapeutic addition is called:
    a. conjoint ego analysis.
    b. sociodynamic training.
    c. adjunctive psychotherapy.
    d. chemo-behavioral treatment.

Adjunctive Psychotherapy, p. 275
Diff: H, Type: Applied, Ans: c

116. The best treatment recommendation you could give someone experiencing bipolar disorder is:
    a. complex, due to conflicting experimental results.
    b. broad; a number of different therapies work equally well.
    c. drug therapy, perhaps accompanied by psychotherapy.
    d. no therapy has been shown to be effective.

Adjunctive Psychotherapy, p. 275
Diff: H, Type: Applied, Ans: d

117. Of the following, the treatment that is the most effective with different types of depression is:
    a. couple therapy.
    b. behavioral therapy.
    c. ECT.
    d. cognitive therapy.

Adjunctive Psychotherapy, p. 275
Diff: H, Type: Applied, Ans: a

118. Which of the following is true about effective treatments for mild and severe forms of depression?
    a. Antidepressant drugs work well for both types.
    b. ECT works equally well for both types.
    c. Couple therapy works only when there is marital harmony in the relationship.
    d. Interpersonal therapy is best for severe depression; drugs are best for mild depression.

Adjunctive Psychotherapy, p. 275
Diff: M, Type: Factual, Ans: c
119.   Which one of the following is a likely reason for using adjunctive therapy to treat bipolar disorder?
   a.   People stop taking lithium because they dislike the euphoria it causes.
   b.   People stop taking lithium because they miss the depression.
   c.   People stop taking lithium because they feel more productive and creative without it.
   d.   People take overdoses of lithium because it makes them feel so good.

Adjunctive Psychotherapy, p. 275
Diff: M, Type: Applied, Ans: b
120.   Which of the following is an example of effective adjunctive therapy for bipolar disorder?
   a.   electroconvulsive therapy
   b.   individual or group therapy
   c.   hospitalization of the patient
   d.   Prozac in combination with lithium

Putting It Together, p. 276
Diff: H, Type: Applied, Ans: c
121.   The percentage of depressed patients who currently use antidepressant drugs as all or part of their treatment is:
   a.   10-20% lower than the percent who receive psychotherapy as all or part of their treatment.
   b.   about the same as the percent who receive psychotherapy as all or part of their treatment.
   c.   10-20% higher than the percent who receive psychotherapy as all or part of their treatment.
   d.   30-40% higher than the percent who receive psychotherapy as all or part of their treatment.

Putting It Together, p. 276
Diff: M, Type: Applied, Ans: c
122.   About what percentage of people with mood disorders do not improve with treatment?
   a.   60%
   b.   10%
   c.   40%
   d.   25%

Putting It Together, p. 276
Diff: H, Type: Applied, Ans: b
123.   When depression is marked by appetite and sleep problems:
   a.   interpersonal therapy appears to work best.
   b.   antidepressant drugs appear to work best.
   c.   there is no difference in the effectiveness of various treatments.
   d.   no treatment method seems to work very well.

Putting It Together, p. 276
Diff: H, Type: Applied, Ans: c
124.   If you were to receive effective therapy for depression, your chances of recovery would be:
    a. no better than chance.
    b. about 50–50.
    c. about 60%.
    d. about 40%.

FILL-IN QUESTIONS

Psychological Approaches, p. 252
Diff: E, Type: Applied, Ans: dependence
1.   According to psychoanalytic theory, depression is in part caused by the patient's excessive _____ on others.

Psychological Approaches, p. 252
Diff: E, Type: Applied, Ans: dream interpretation
2.   An example of a basic psychodynamic procedure is _____.

Psychological Approaches, p. 255
Diff: E, Type: Factual, Ans: behavioral
3.   Determining what a patient truly likes to do is part of a therapy for depression based on _____ principles.

Psychological Approaches, p. 256
Diff: M, Type: Factual, Ans: contingency management
4.   The therapeutic term for ignoring depressive behavior while reinforcing nondepressive behaviors is _____.

Psychological Approaches, p. 256
Diff: M, Type: Factual, Ans: the cognitive triad
5.   Aaron Beck has argued that a person suffering from unipolar depression must correct a group of cognitive errors, generally known as _____.

Psychological Approaches, p. 257
Diff: E, Type: Factual, Ans: a grief reaction, grief (or the grieving process)
6.   One of the possible antecedents to depression, according to interpersonal psychotherapists, is produced by the loss of a loved one. They refer to this as _____.

Sociocultural Approaches, p. 260
Diff: E, Type: Factual, Ans: interpersonal role transition
7.   Margarette is not getting what she expected out of her new marriage. Her husband is demanding but often absent. This situation is leading to depression for her. This is what interpersonal psychotherapists call a(n) _____.

Biological Approaches, p. 261
Diff: E, Type: Factual, Ans: memory (or neurological damage)
8.   One problem with ECT is that it may lead to problems with _____.

Biological Approaches, p. 262
Diff: E, Type: Factual, Ans: metrazol (or insulin)

9.   A chemical alternative that was replaced by the electricity used in ECT is _____.

Biological Approaches, p. 263
Diff: M, Type: Factual, Ans: tuberculosis

10.   Experience with patients being treated for _____ eventually led to the discovery of MAO inhibitors.

Biological Approaches, p. 264
Diff: M, Type: Factual, Ans: monoamine oxidase inhibitor

11.   The type of antidepressant drug that works by interfering with the enzyme that normally destroys norepinephrine is a _____.

Biological Approaches, p. 264
Diff: M, Type: Factual, Ans: tyramine

12.   People being treated for depression with MAO inhibitors should avoid foods containing _____.

Biological Approaches, p. 264
Diff: E, Type: Factual, Ans: high blood pressure

13.   Tyramine, a chemical in many foods, can cause _____ if allowed to accumulate.

Biological Approaches, p. 264
Diff: M, Type: Factual, Ans: tyramine

14.   MAO inhibitors should not be mixed with certain foods because the MAO inhibitors make it difficult for our bodies to break down _____.

Biological Approaches, p. 264
Diff: M, Type: Factual, Ans: nutraceuticals

15.   Another name for dietary supplements taken as drugs is _____.

Biological Approaches, p. 265
Diff: E, Type: Factual, Ans: depression

16.   Matthew is taking imipramine. He is probably being treated for _____.

Biological Approaches, p. 265
Diff: E, Type: Factual, Ans: tricyclic antidepressant

17.   The drug imipramine is a(n) _____.

Biological Approaches, p. 267
Diff: E, Type: Factual, Ans: depression

18.   Desyrel, Prozac, Marplan, Nardil, and Parnate are all trade names of drugs that reduce _____.

Biological Approaches, p. 267
Diff: E, Type: Factual, Ans: depression

19.   Amoxapine, fluoxetine, clomipramine, phenelzine, and tranylcypromine are all generic names of drugs that reduce _____.

Biological Approaches, p. 267
Diff: E, Type: Factual, Ans: SSRIs (or second-generation antidepressants)

20. Antidepressant drugs which target only one neurotransmitter are called _____.

Lithium Therapy, p. 270
Diff: E, Type: Factual, Ans: lithium

21. The most effective drug for the treatment of bipolar disorders is _____.

Lithium Therapy, p. 274
Diff: E, Type: Factual, Ans: prophylactic

22. A drug that actually helps prevent symptoms from developing is called a _____ drug.

Adjunctive Therapy, p. 275
Diff: E, Type: Factual, Ans: adjunctive psychotherapy (or adjunctive or an adjunct)

23. Bipolar disorders respond better to a combination of lithium treatment and psychotherapy than to either therapy alone. The psychotherapy component of this combination is called _____.

ESSAY QUESTIONS

Psychological Approaches, p. 252ff
Diff: H, Type: Applied

1. Write a one-paragraph treatment summary that reflects the psychodynamic understanding of depression. Be sure to include common causation factors, treatment techniques, and evidence of improvement.

Psychological Approaches, p. 254
Diff: E, Type: Applied

2. List and provide examples of the three parts of Levinsohn's behavior therapy for depression.

Psychological Approaches, p. 256
Diff: M, Type: Applied

3. Identify the parts of the cognitive triad and provide an example of each part.

Psychological Approaches, p. 258ff
Diff: H, Type: Applied

4. During therapy, a high school girl says to her therapist, "I can't stand that I don't have a date for the prom." Write a half-page dialogue between the girl and the therapist that illustrates cognitive principles of therapy. In parentheses, indicate what cognitive principles the therapist's statements reflect.

Sociocultural Approaches, p. 260
Diff: E, Type: Applied

5. Interpersonal therapists believe that any of four interpersonal problem areas can lead to depression and must be addressed in therapy. Briefly describe each of these areas and provide an example of each.

Biological Approaches, p. 262
Diff: H, Type: Factual

6. Discuss the history of the use of electroconvulsive therapy. What observation led to its development as a treatment? How has its use evolved over the years?

Biological Approaches, p. 263
Diff: H, Type: Applied

7. Suppose you were going to give a presentation on electroconvulsive therapy. What are the four most important points you would make to a group of people considering approving the use of electroconvulsive therapy for one of their loved ones?

Biological Approaches, p. 265ff
Diff: H, Type: Applied

8. The physician of one of my friends has prescribed a tricyclic to treat her depression. My friend is hesitating to take the medication. How would you help her make this decision? That is, what are the advantages and disadvantages of using tricyclics? When are they most effective?

How Do Treatments For Unipolar Depression Compare?, p. 268ff
Diff: H, Type: Factual

9. A recent NIMH study compared cognitive therapy, interpersonal therapy, and antidepressant drug therapy. Briefly discuss at least three of the major conclusions from that study.

Lithium Therapy, p. 275
Diff: H, Type: Applied

10. One of the difficulties with the use of lithium to treat bipolar disorder is that patients often stop taking the medication. Briefly discuss at least three reasons a person who is experiencing bipolar disorder would stop taking this highly effective medication, and what a therapist might do to improve treatment compliance.

CHAPTER **10** **Suicide**

MULTIPLE-CHOICE QUESTIONS

Suicide, p. 280
Diff: E, Type: Factual, Ans: b
1. About how many suicides are committed annually in the United States?
    a. 10,000
    b. 30,000
    c. 120,000
    d. 700,000

Suicide, p. 280
Diff: M, Type: Factual, Ans: d
2. About how many deaths occur by suicide each year around the world?
    a. 10,000
    b. 30,000
    c. 160,000
    d. 700,000

Suicide, p. 280
Diff: M, Type: Factual, Ans: c
3. About how many suicides are attempted annually in the United States?
    a. 30,000
    b. 120,000
    c. 600,000
    d. 2 million

Suicide, p. 280
Diff: M, Type: Factual, Ans: c
4. Which of the following is not true about suicide?
    a. More people attempt than actually succeed in committing suicide.
    b. Many apparent accidents are probably really intentional suicides.
    c. Suicide is more often associated with Alzheimer's than with depression.
    d. Suicide estimates are probably low, in part because of the stigma associated with it.

Suicide, p. 280
Diff: H, Type: Applied, Ans: c
5.   Why do many people feel that estimates of the rates of suicide are inaccurate?
     a.   Insurance companies pay extra life insurance in cases of suicide.
     b.   Many reported suicides are probably really accidents.
     c.   The stigma associated with suicide make people hesitate to report it.
     d.   Suicide is not a DSM-IV-TR category.

Suicide, p. 280
Diff: E, Type: Factual, Ans: a
6.   What is a parasuicide?
     a.   a failed attempt to commit suicide
     b.   a murder followed by a successful suicide
     c.   a successfully committed suicide on the first try
     d.   a successfully committed suicide after many tries

What is Suicide?, p. 282
Diff: M, Type: Applied, Ans: a
7.   Sylvia shot herself by placing the gun barrel in her mouth, in the middle of a dense woods, where she knew she wouldn't be heard or found. Sylvia is an example of what Shneidman refers to as a _____.
     a.   death seeker
     b.   death initiator
     c.   death ignorer
     d.   death darer

What is Suicide?, p. 282
Diff: M, Type: Applied, Ans: b
8.   Gloria has been contemplating suicide for several weeks. She decides one day, with great intention, clarity, and commitment, that she will kill herself. Within minutes, she has successfully committed suicide. According to Shneidman, Gloria is a:
     a.   death darer.
     b.   death seeker.
     c.   death ignorer.
     d.   death initiator.

What is Suicide?, p. 282
Diff: E, Type: Factual, Ans: c
9.   What is the critical way in which the death seeker differs from the death darer, according to Shneidman? Death seekers:
     a.   speed along a death sure to occur naturally.
     b.   are ambivalent about their death.
     c.   intend to end their lives with their action.
     d.   believe that death will not end their existence.

What is Suicide?, p. 283
Diff: M, Type: Applied, Ans: d
10. Ambivalent about dying, Jay repeatedly played a dangerous game involving gas and a cigarette lighter. Jay is an example of what Shneidman refers to as a _____.
    a. death seeker
    b. death initiator
    c. death ignorer
    d. death darer

What is Suicide?, p. 283
Diff: M, Type: Applied, Ans: d
11. Bobby plays chicken by aiming his car at a bridge abutment, then veering off at the last second. Bobby is an example of what Shneidman refers to as a _____.
    a. death seeker
    b. death initiator
    c. death ignorer
    d. death darer

What is Suicide?, p. 283
Diff: H, Type: Applied, Ans: c
12. Cecil and Jeanne, teenagers, made a love pact, jumping from a cliff in order to be with each other for eternity. Cecil and Jeanne are examples of what Shneidman refers to as _____.
    a. death seekers
    b. death initiators
    c. death ignorers
    d. death darers

What is Suicide?, p. 283
Diff: M, Type: Factual, Ans: d
13. According to Edwin Shneidman, people who commit suicide with clarity and commitment, yet who believe that they are simply facilitating a process that is already under way, are called:
    a. death darers.
    b. death seekers.
    c. death ignorers.
    d. death initiators.

What is Suicide?, p. 283
Diff: M, Type: Factual, Ans: d
14. Ernest Hemingway was a physically strong, proud man who developed grave concerns about his failing body. Depressed about his progressive illness, he intentionally ended his life. Edwin Shneidman would term Hemingway a:
    a. death darer.
    b. death seeker.
    c. death ignorer.
    d. death initiator.

What is Suicide?, p. 283
Diff: H, Type: Applied, Ans: d

15.   Daniel has received a diagnosis of terminal cancer. He organizes his financial and personal affairs, tells his wife and children good-bye, and takes an overdose of sleeping pills to avoid a prolonged, painful death. According to Shneidman, Daniel would be classified as a:
       a. death darer.
       b. death seeker.
       c. death ignorer.
       d. death initiator.

What is Suicide?, p. 283
Diff: E, Type: Factual, Ans: d

16.   What is the critical way in which death initiators differ from other categories, according to Shneidman?
       a. They employ more lethal means.
       b. They do not intend to end their lives with their action.
       c. They believe that death will not end their existence.
       d. They believe they are merely speeding up an ongoing process.

What is Suicide?, p. 283
Diff: E, Type: Factual, Ans: c

17.   According to Shneidman, how do death ignorers primarily differ from other categories?
       a. They employ more lethal means.
       b. They intend to end their lives with their action.
       c. They believe death will not end their existence.
       d. They believe they are merely speeding up an ongoing process.

What is Suicide?, p. 283
Diff: M, Type: Applied, Ans: c

18.   Miguel lost all of his family when his village was bombed. He throws himself off a cliff to die, in order to be reunited with them. Shneidman would classify Miguel as a:
       a. death darer.
       b. death seeker.
       c. death ignorer.
       d. death initiator.

What is Suicide?, p. 283
Diff: E, Type: Factual, Ans: a

19.   According to Shneidman, people who are ambivalent about their intent to die and whose actions leading to death do not guarantee death (e.g., swimming in shark-infested waters) are called:
       a. death darers.
       b. death seekers.
       c. death ignorers.
       d. death initiators.

What is Suicide?, p. 283
Diff: M, Type: Factual, Ans: a

20.   According to Shneidman, how do death darers primarily differ from other categories?
       a.   They are ambivalent about their deaths.
       b.   They intend to end their lives with their actions.
       c.   They believe that death will not end their existence.
       d.   They believe they are merely speeding up an ongoing process.

What is Suicide?, p. 283
Diff: H, Type: Factual, Ans: b

21.   Karl Menninger has distinguished a category called chronic suicide, in which people's
       actions lead to their own deaths. People in this category:
       a.   repeatedly try to commit suicide, but are in fact calling for help.
       b.   behave in life-endangering ways over an extended period of time.
       c.   do not believe that their self-inflicted death will mean the end of their existence.
       d.   actively and intently pursue the means to their death and are committed to completing the
            act.

What is Suicide?, p. 283
Diff: H, Type: Factual, Ans: d

22.   Menninger's category of chronic suicide is most like Shneidman's concept of:
       a.   a death seeker.
       b.   a death ignorer.
       c.   a death initiator.
       d.   subintentioned death.

How is Suicide Studied?, p. 283
Diff: H, Type: Applied, Ans: d

23.   Retrospective analysis involves:
       a.   interviewing those thought to be at high risk for suicide.
       b.   developing a suicide profile, especially for mental patients and prisoners.
       c.   studying people who survive suicide attempts.
       d.   gathering information about a suicide victim's past.

How is Suicide Studied?, p. 283
Diff: H, Type: Applied, Ans: b

24.   Which of the following is an example of retrospective analysis?
       a.   Researchers ask college students to write suicide notes in order to study what they think
            is the motivation for suicide.
       b.   Therapists who have patients who committed suicide are interviewed to look for
            commonalties.
       c.   Adolescents at high risk for suicide are treated through a suicide prevention center.
       d.   Those who have made suicide attempts are part of a suicide education program.

How is Suicide Studied?, p. 283
Diff: M, Type: Applied, Ans: b

25.   Knowing she was terminally ill, Bonnie swallowed a handful of barbiturates in order to save herself and her family from the final painful months of life. Bonnie is an example of what Shneidman refers to as a _____.
   a.   death seeker
   b.   death initiator
   c.   death ignorer
   d.   death darer

How is Suicide Studied?, p. 283
Diff: H, Type: Applied, Ans: d

26.   At the time of the suicide, a suicide victim was receiving psychotherapy, and left a clear suicide note. This suicide victim is:
   a.   the most common kind; most suicide victims are in psychotherapy, and leave a suicide note.
   b.   a somewhat uncommon kind; most suicide victims are in psychotherapy, but do not leave a suicide note.
   c.   a somewhat uncommon kind; about half of suicide victims have never received psychotherapy, but do leave a suicide note.
   d.   the least common kind; about half of suicide victims have never received psychotherapy, and do not leave a suicide note.

How is Suicide Studied?, pp. 283-284
Diff: H, Type: Applied, Ans: d

27.   Limitations that make research on suicide difficult include all but which of the following?
   a.   Good sources of information (suicide notes, therapy reports on those who have committed suicide) are often not available.
   b.   Grieving family members probably are not able to provide especially objective information to researchers.
   c.   People who survive suicide might be very different from those who don't.
   d.   Suicide is probably such a personal decision that there are few commonalties among those who kill themselves.

How is Suicide Studied?, p. 284
Diff: H, Type: Applied, Ans: c

28.   Someone who has committed suicide leaves the following suicide note: "I remember with great fondness the family vacations we used to take. I can picture us now, driving down the road into the great unknown." Most likely, the writer of this note is how old?
   a.   under 40
   b.   40–49
   c.   50–59
   d.   60 and over

How is Suicide Studied?, p. 284
Diff: H, Type: Applied, Ans: a

29. A poet writes,   "Just listen to the birds, as darkness falls,
                       They talk together, mingling their calls."
     Based only on what you know from these two lines, what is the comparative suicide risk for
     this poet?
     a. minimal, since it lacks self-references and uses communication terms
     b. moderate, since lack of self-references is correlated with suicide
     c. moderate, since using communication terms is correlated with suicide
     d. high, since lack of self-references and using communication terms both correlate with
         suicide

How is Suicide Studied?, p. 284 (Box)
Diff: H, Type: Factual, Ans: b

30. A suicide note cites an inability to cope with life as the reason for the suicide. The writer is
     most likely:
     a. younger than 40.
     b. 40 to 49 years old.
     c. 50 to 59 years old.
     d. over 60 years of age.

How is Suicide Studied?, p. 284 (Box)
Diff: H, Type: Factual, Ans: c

31. A suicide note provides no reason for the suicide. The writer is most likely:
     a. younger than 40.
     b. 40 to 49 years old.
     c. 50 to 59 years old.
     d. over 60 years of age.

How is Suicide Studied?, p. 284 (Box)
Diff: M, Type: Factual, Ans: d

32. A suicide note cites ill health and loneliness as the reason for the suicide. The writer is most
     likely:
     a. younger than 40.
     b. 40 to 49 years old.
     c. 50 to 59 years old.
     d. over 60 years of age.

Patterns and Statistics, p. 285
Diff: H, Type: Applied, Ans: d

33. Someone in the world has just committed suicide. The percent chance that the suicide victim
     is a Chinese woman is:
     a. about 1%.
     b. about 5%.
     c. about 10%.
     d. over 20%.

Patterns and Statistics, p. 285
Diff: H, Type: Applied, Ans: a

34.   Which of the following is arranged in order of suicide rate from highest to lowest?
       a. Japan, United States, Mexico
       b. United States, Spain, Germany
       c. England, Canada, United States
       d. Egypt, Mexico, Russia

Patterns and Statistics, p. 285
Diff: M, Type: Factual, Ans: b

35.   One of the factors that is believed to account for differences in the suicide rates of different
       countries is:
       a. climate.
       b. religious affiliation and beliefs.
       c. prevalence of mental disorders.
       d. governmental regulations regarding suicide.

Patterns and Statistics, p. 285
Diff: E, Type: Factual, Ans: c

36.   Which of the following aspects of religion is most closely linked to suicide?
       a. doctrine
       b. fellowship
       c. devoutness
       d. denomination

Patterns and Statistics, p. 285
Diff: E, Type: Factual, Ans: d

37.   What is the cause of death in the majority of male suicides?
       a. hanging
       b. car accidents
       c. drug overdose
       d. use of firearms

Patterns and Statistics, p. 285
Diff: H, Type: Applied, Ans: b

38.   Which of the following statements is most accurate about the relationship between religion
       and suicide?
       a. A country's economic status is a more important predictor of suicide rates than its major
           religion.
       b. The degree of one's devoutness is a more important predictor of suicide than one's
           specific religion.
       c. Countries that have high Jewish and Muslim populations also have high suicide rates.
       d. Religion is a more important predictor of suicide risk for women than it is for men,
           especially in Catholic countries.

Patterns and Statistics, p. 285
Diff: E, Type: Applied, Ans: a
39.   Given the research on suicide, which of the following would be the most surprising
       (inconsistent with research results) case?
       a.   a woman who stabbed and then hanged herself
       b.   a woman who attempted suicide but did not succeed
       c.   a man who shot himself
       d.   a woman who killed herself with a drug overdose

Patterns and Statistics, p. 285
Diff: H, Type: Factual, Ans: d
40.   Who of the following has two positive risk factors for suicide?
       a.   a devout woman
       b.   a married man
       c.   a divorced woman
       d.   an atheist man

Patterns and Statistics, p. 285
Diff: H, Type: Applied, Ans: d
41.   Which of the following is most likely to be associated with suicide risk?
       a.   being Mexican versus being American
       b.   being married versus being divorced
       c.   being a woman versus being a man
       d.   being an atheist versus being devout

Patterns and Statistics, pp. 285-286
Diff: H, Type: Factual, Ans: c
42.   Which of the following statements is not true regarding gender and suicide?
       a.   Women attempt suicide more often than men.
       b.   Men use more lethal means to commit suicide than women.
       c.   Women succeed at committing suicide more often than men.
       d.   the elderly are more likely to commit suicide than children.

Patterns and Statistics, p. 286
Diff: H, Type: Applied, Ans: d
43.   Which of the following statements is true regarding suicide rates for people 65 or older in the
       United States, taking into account gender and race?
       a.   Only African American males have a substantially higher suicide rate after the age of 65
            than they did between the ages of 35 and 44.
       b.   Only White American males have a substantially higher suicide rate after the age of 65
            than they did between the ages of 35 and 44.
       c.   Only White American females and males have substantially higher suicide rates beyond
            the age of 65 than they did between the ages of 35 and 44.
       d.   Only females have a substantially higher suicide rate after the age of 65 than they did
            between the ages of 35 and 44.

Patterns and Statistics, p. 286
Diff: H, Type: Factual, Ans: c

44. The group that has its highest suicide rate in the 25–34-year-old age range, with a rate of 20 per 100,000 population, is:
     a. African American females.
     b. white American females.
     c. African American males.
     d. white American males.

Patterns and Statistics, p. 286
Diff: M, Type: Factual, Ans: a

45. Which of the following statements regarding suicide is true?
     a. Native Americans have the highest suicide rate of any racial group in the United States.
     b. The suicide rate for whites in the United States is the same as that for blacks.
     c. Married people are more likely to commit suicide than adults who are single.
     d. Men are more likely to attempt suicide than women.

Patterns and Statistics, p. 286
Diff: M, Type: Factual, Ans: c

46. According to current estimates, the suicide rate is highest in the United States among:
     a. African Americans.
     b. Euro-Americans.
     c. Native Americans.
     d. Asian Americans.

Patterns and Statistics, p. 287
Diff: M, Type: Factual, Ans: a

47. Short-term stressors particularly common among those who attempt suicide include all the following except:
     a. occupational stress.
     b. divorce.
     c. death of a loved one.
     d. stress from a flood.

Patterns and Statistics, p. 287
Diff: M, Type: Factual, Ans: c

48. Long-term stressors particularly common among those who attempt suicide include all the following except:
     a. serious illness.
     b. occupational stress.
     c. divorce.
     d. an abusive environment.

Patterns and Statistics, p. 287
Diff: M, Type: Applied, Ans: a

49. Which of the following people would be at greatest risk of suicide?
     a. someone who had been in poor health for years and is now terminal
     b. someone who recently escaped from an abusive environment and is enrolled in school
     c. someone who has had fewer than the average number of stressors in life
     d. someone who is a devout Muslim

Patterns and Statistics, p. 287
Diff: H, Type: Applied, Ans: d

50.   All of the following are examples of immediate stress except:
      a.   loss of a loved one through death.
      b.   natural disaster.
      c.   loss of a job.
      d.   serious illness

Patterns and Statistics, p. 288
Diff: M, Type: Applied, Ans: b

51.   A person who sees life in "right or wrong" "all or none" terms is engaging in:
      a.   hopelessness.
      b.   dichotomous thinking.
      c.   psychache.
      d.   blaming.

Patterns and Statistics, p. 288
Diff: E, Type: Applied, Ans: b

52.   Which of the following occupations has a particularly high rate of suicide?
      a.   used-car salespeople
      b.   psychologists
      c.   priests
      d.   gourmet chefs

Mood and Thought Changes, p. 288
Diff: M, Type: Factual, Ans: c

53.   The mood and thoughts of suicidal people are most often characterized as:
      a.   anxious and irrational.
      b.   angry and aggressive.
      c.   sad and hopeless.
      d.   tense and manic.

Mood and Thought Changes, p. 288
Diff: E, Type: Factual, Ans: d

54.   An increase in which emotion is most often linked to suicide?
      a.   guilt
      b.   anger
      c.   anxiety
      d.   sadness

Alcohol and Other Drug Use, p. 288
Diff: E, Type: Factual, Ans: d

55.   About what percentage of people who commit suicide use alcohol just prior to the act?
      a.   10%
      b.   20%
      c.   35%
      d.   60%

Alcohol and Other Drug Use, p. 288
Diff: H, Type: Factual, Ans: c
56.   Of people who use alcohol just prior to committing suicide, what percentage are actually intoxicated?
       a.   10%
       b.   15%
       c.   25%
       d.   35%

Alcohol and Other Drug Use, pp. 288-289
Diff: H, Type: Factual, Ans: d
57.   Which is true about alcohol use and suicide?
       a.   Most people who attempt suicide drink alcohol just before the act.
       b.   About one-fourth of people who commit suicide are legally drunk.
       c.   Alcohol impairs judgment and lowers inhibitions.
       d.   All of the above are true.

Alcohol and Other Drug Use, pp. 288-289
Diff: H, Type: Applied, Ans: c
58.   Which one of the following is the most likely reason for the relationship between alcohol use and suicide?
       a.   There is a chemical in alcohol that triggers a suicide response in the brain.
       b.   Alcohol is less well metabolized by those who are depressed.
       c.   Alcohol lowers inhibitions and impairs judgment.
       d.   Pound for pound, women get drunk on less alcohol than men.

Alcohol and Other Drug Use, pp. 288-289
Diff: H, Type: Applied, Ans: a
59.   A coroner finds a high level of alcohol in the body of someone who has just died, and who may have committed suicide. If the coroner rules like most coroners would on the cause of death, the ruling will be:
       a.   "accidental," because of the high alcohol level.
       b.   "accidental," in spite of the high alcohol level.
       c.   "suicide," because of the high alcohol level.
       d.   "suicide," in spite of the high alcohol level.

Alcohol and Other Drug Use, pp. 288, 290
Diff: E, Type: Applied, Ans: b
60.   Which of the following does not make one at higher risk for suicide?
       a.   experiencing mood and thought changes.
       b.   learning about suicide in abnormal psychology.
       c.   having an alcohol abuse problem.
       d.   experiencing uncontrollable and repeated stressful events.

Alcohol and Other Drug Use, p. 289
Diff: H, Type: Applied, Ans: d

61.   A friend of yours wants certain heavy metal songs banned because, your friend says, listening to them will encourage suicidal tendencies. Your best reply, based on research, would be:
   a. "You're right—experts and the courts agree about the potential dangers."
   b. "It depends—experts agree with you, although the courts have not found musicians liable."
   c. "It depends—experts don't agree with you, although the courts have found musicians liable.
   d. "It probably won't work—experts don't agree with you, and the courts have not found musicians liable."

Mental Disorders, p. 290
Diff: H, Type: Applied, Ans: b

62.   A clinically depressed individual who has been threatening suicide finally shows diminishing of depressive symptoms. This person's risk of committing suicide:
   a. has increased dramatically; almost no one who is depressed commits suicide until she or he is recovering.
   b. may have increased, since the person may have the energy to act on the suicidal impulse.
   c. probably has decreased, although a slight risk remains.
   d. has decreased substantially; almost no one who is depressed commits suicide once recovery from depression is under way.

Mental Disorders, p. 290
Diff: M, Type: Applied, Ans: b

63.   "Why is there such a strong connection between alcohol abuse and suicide risk?" asks a friend of yours. Based on the best available research, you reply,
   a. "Being trapped in substance abuse leads to suicidal ideation."
   b. "No one really knows for sure."
   c. "Actually, being suicidal most often leads to alcohol abuse, and not the other way around."
   d. "Actually, the connection is weak, at best."

Mental Disorders, p. 290
Diff: M, Type: Applied, Ans: a

64.   Commonly observed triggers for suicide include all of the following except:
   a. being in therapy.
   b. heavy alcohol use.
   c. modeling of someone who committed suicide.
   d. stressful life events.

Mental Disorders, p. 290
Diff: H, Type: Applied, Ans: b

65.   Who of the following is most at risk for suicide?
   a. someone with a panic or other anxiety disorder
   b. someone who is depressed and dependent on alcohol
   c. someone who is schizophrenic and developmentally disabled
   d. someone without a diagnosable mental disorder

Mental Disorders, p. 290
Diff: M, Type: Factual, Ans: a
66.   Which mental disorders have been found to contribute to the greatest number of suicides?
      a.   mood disorders
      b.   sexual disorders
      c.   personality disorders
      d.   psychophysiological disorders

Mental Disorders, p. 290
Diff: M, Type: Factual, Ans: b
67.   Research indicates that suicides by people with schizophrenia are in response to:
      a.   voices commanding them to kill themselves.
      b.   feelings of demoralization.
      c.   overdoses of antipsychotic drugs.
      d.   feeling of invincibility.

Modeling: The Contagion of Suicide, p. 291
Diff: E, Type: Factual, Ans: a
68.   When a rash of suicides occurs in the aftermath of a celebrity's suicide or a case that has been
      highly publicized by the media, behavioral theorists believe it is attributable to:
      a.   modeling.
      b.   helplessness.
      c.   folie a deux
      d.   hopelessness.

Modeling: The Contagion of Suicide, p. 291
Diff: M, Type: Applied, Ans: b
69.   Assume that a recent local suicide attempt was clearly a case of modeling. The person who
      would most likely model another's suicide would be a(n):
      a.   preteen.
      b.   teenager.
      c.   adult in her or his 30s.
      d.   adult in his or her 50s.

Modeling: The Contagion of Suicide, p. 292
Diff: H, Type: Applied, Ans: a
70.   "How can we reduce suicide risk for our kids?" asks the high school counselor, the day after
      one of the school's star athletes commits suicide. Your best answer, based on research, is:
      a.   "Prevention often helps."
      b.   "There really is little you can do, other than watch the students carefully."
      c.   "Close the school for a week, and let the students' parents help them deal with the loss."
      d.   "Reverse modeling works best."

Modeling: The Contagion of Suicide, p. 292
Diff: H, Type: Applied, Ans: d
71.   As a political protest, two activists leap from a bridge in a highly publicized double suicide.
      Those most at risk for modeling these suicides are:
      a.   people with similar political points of view.
      b.   people with the opposite political point of view.
      c.   people in an unstable relationship with a significant other.
      d.   people with a history of emotional problems.

Modeling: The Contagion of Suicide, p. 292
Diff: E, Type: Factual, Ans: d

72. Media coverage that included the "don't do it" message, numbers for suicide prevention centers, and interviews with suicide experts followed the suicide of:
    a. Marilyn Monroe.
    b. the Jonestown members.
    c. James Dean.
    d. Kurt Cobain.

Modeling: The Contagion of Suicide, p. 292
Diff: E, Type: Factual, Ans: a

73. Which network was particularly helpful in preventing a large number of copycat suicides after the death of Kurt Cobain?
    a. MTV
    b. PBS
    c. ESPN
    d. CNN

What Are the Underlying Causes of Suicide?, p. 292
Diff: E, Type: Applied, Ans: d

74. The leading theories designed to explain suicide:
    a. are supported by a significant body of research.
    b. address the full range of suicide acts.
    c. satisfactorily explain suicidal behavior in the elderly but not the young.
    d. None of the above

The Psychodynamic View, p. 292
Diff: M, Type: Applied, Ans: d

75. The explanation of suicide as due to loss of loved ones and self-directed aggression is consistent with which theoretical perspective?
    a. cognitive
    b. humanist
    c. behavioral
    d. psychodynamic

The Psychodynamic View, p. 293
Diff: M, Type: Applied, Ans: c

76. "You must redirect your Thanatos," is a remark most likely made by a therapist with what theoretical point of view?
    a. sociocultural
    b. biological
    c. psychodynamic
    d. cognitive-behavioral

The Psychodynamic View, p. 293
Diff: H, Type: Applied, Ans: b

77. If the psychodynamic explanation for suicide is correct, then suicide rates should:
    a. increase in a nation which is at war.
    b. be higher in nations with low murder rates.
    c. be lower in those who experienced symbolic loss as children.
    d. be lower in those who experienced actual (real) loss as children.

The Psychodynamic View, p. 293
Diff: H, Type: Applied, Ans: c
78.   The fact that very angry people are not significantly more suicidal than other people argues most strongly against which explanation for suicide?
      a.   sociocultural
      b.   modeling
      c.   psychodynamic
      d.   biological

The Sociocultural View, p. 293
Diff: M, Type: Factual, Ans: c
79.   What kind of theory is Durkheim's theory of suicide?
      a.   cognitive
      b.   biological
      c.   sociocultural
      d.   psychodynamic

The Sociocultural View, p. 294
Diff: E, Type: Factual, Ans: b
80.   According to Durkheim, suicides by people over whom society has little or no control and who are not concerned with the norms and rules of society are called:
      a.   anomic suicides.
      b.   egoistic suicides.
      c.   imitative suicides.
      d.   altruistic suicides.

The Sociocultural View, p. 294
Diff: H, Type: Applied, Ans: c
81.   A society that loses its basic family and religious core values, experiences large-scale immigration of people with very different values, and fails to provide meaning for the life of its people is in danger of an increase in what Durkheim calls:
      a.   egoistic suicide.
      b.   altruistic suicide.
      c.   anomic suicide.
      d.   intragroup suicide.

The Sociocultural View, p. 294
Diff: H, Type: Applied, Ans: b
82.   A society that honors those who kill themselves to defend their families or country, or because of a value they hold dear, would have a higher rate of what Durkheim calls:
      a.   egoistic suicide.
      b.   altruistic suicide.
      c.   anomic suicide.
      d.   intragroup suicide.

The Sociocultural View, p. 294
Diff: M, Type: Applied, Ans: b

83. Juan is a loner and an atheist. He does what he wants and is alienated from others. He feels life isn't worth living and kills himself. According to Durkheim, he would be classified as an:
    a. anomic suicide.
    b. egoistic suicide.
    c. imitative suicide.
    d. altruistic suicide.

The Sociocultural View, p. 294
Diff: E, Type: Factual, Ans: d

84. According to Durkheim, suicides by people who give up their lives so that another person they love may live would be classified as:
    a. anomic suicides.
    b. egoistic suicides.
    c. imitative suicides.
    d. altruistic suicides.

The Sociocultural View, p. 294
Diff: M, Type: Applied, Ans: d

85. Carlos died by intentionally stepping in front of a bullet that was intended for another young man, for whom Carlos, as head of a platoon of soldiers in the Persian Gulf War, was responsible. Durkheim would call this an example of:
    a. anomic suicide.
    b. egoistic suicide.
    c. imitative suicide.
    d. altruistic suicide.

The Sociocultural View, p. 294
Diff: M, Type: Applied, Ans: b

86. Altruistic suicide is most likely to occur in a country that:
    a. is experiencing great upheaval, disruption of values, and immigration.
    b. honors those who kill themselves for a higher good.
    c. has a number of ethnic minorities who are very religious.
    d. has a high level of substance abuse.

The Sociocultural View, p. 295
Diff: H, Type: Applied, Ans: a

87. "It can be makoto—how we react to shame," might be said by a:
    a. Japanese to explain Japan's high suicide rate.
    b. Japanese to explain Japan's low suicide rate.
    c. Native American to explain the high suicide rate among Native Americans.
    d. Native American to explain the low suicide rate among Native Americans.

The Biological View, p. 296
Diff: H, Type: Applied, Ans: d
88.   If a biological explanation for suicide is valid, then doing which of the following ought to lower the possibility of a person attempting suicide?
      a.   removing the person from contact with a suicidal biological parent
      b.   removing the person from contact with a suicidal adoptive parent
      c.   gene-splicing to remove the "suicide" gene
      d.   raising the person's serotonin level

The Biological View, p. 296
Diff: M, Type: Applied, Ans: c
89.   A young man whose father and uncle committed suicide at about his age also commits suicide. Which explanation of suicide most easily explains the young man's suicide?
      a.   psychodynamic
      b.   sociocultural
      c.   biological
      d.   immediate trigger

The Biological View, p. 296
Diff: H, Type: Factual, Ans: a
90.   In research on the relationship between serotonin and suicide, serotonin seems most related to:
      a.   aggression.
      b.   introversion.
      c.   selfishness.
      d.   shame.

The Biological View, p. 296
Diff: H, Type: Factual, Ans: a
91.   Biological researchers have found a link between suicide and:
      a.   low levels of serotonin.
      b.   high levels of serotonin dopamine
      c.   high levels of 5-hydroxyindoleactic acid.
      d.   elevated number of serotonin receptor sites.

The Biological View, p. 296
Diff: H, Type: Factual, Ans: d
92.   Biological researchers have found a link between suicide and:
      a.   high levels of serotonin.
      b.   high levels of serotonin dopamine.
      c.   high levels of 5-hydroxyindoleactic acid.
      d.   a reduced number of serotonin receptor sites.

Children, p. 297
Diff: H, Type: Applied, Ans: b

93.   You are asked to speak before a local elementary school's PTA about suicide attempts by the very young. You should be sure to mention that suicide attempts by the very young often come right after the very young have:
       a.   shown a sudden drop in interest in death in general.
       b.   run away from home.
       c.   experienced the birth of a sibling.
       d.   begun to ignore criticism from others.

Children, p. 297
Diff: M, Type: Applied, Ans: a

94.   The "typical" child who commits suicide is a::
       a.   boy who understands what death really is.
       b.   girl who understands what death really is.
       c.   boy who does not understand what death really is.
       d.   girl who does not understand what death really is.

Children, p. 297
Diff: M, Type: Factual, Ans: a

95.   The age group least likely to commit suicide in the United States is:
       a.   children.
       b.   adolescents.
       c.   young adults.
       d.   the elderly.

Children, p. 297
Diff: H, Type: Applied, Ans: c

96.   Based on studies of suicide in children, the following case would be the most surprising (inconsistent with research results):
       a.   a child who had previously run away and tried to take an overdose.
       b.   a child who had experienced family stress—loss of a loved one, parental unemployment, abuse.
       c.   a child who had no understanding of death.
       d.   a child who was especially withdrawn and lonely.

Children, p. 297
Diff: H, Type: Factual, Ans: c

97.   Which of Shneidman's categories do most people generally believe that the majority of children who commit suicide belong in?
       a.   death darers
       b.   death seekers
       c.   death ignorers
       d.   death initiators

Adolescents, p. 298
Diff: H, Type: Factual, Ans: d
98.   Which of the following is true?
       a.   More teenagers than people at any other age group commit suicide.
       b.   Suicide is the leading cause of death among teenagers.
       c.   African-American teenage boys commit suicide at a higher rate than European-American
            boys.
       d.   None of the above

Adolescents, p. 298
Diff: H, Type: Factual, Ans: b
99.   Adolescent suicides differ from suicides at other age levels in all of the following ways
       except that:
       a.   in addition to depression, many also experience anger and impulsiveness.
       b.   many experience significant loss before the suicide.
       c.   suicides may be triggered by more immediate stress, especially at school.
       d.   adolescents may be more suggestible and eager to imitate others.

Adolescents, pp. 298-299
Diff: M, Type: Applied, Ans: a
100.   Most theories which seek to explain why the rate of teenage suicide is increasing focus on:
       a.   social changes.
       b.   factors unique to individual countries.
       c.   earlier puberty and other biological factors.
       d.   lack of prevention emphases.

Adolescents, p. 299
Diff: M, Type: Applied, Ans: a
101.   The finding that more than 90% of adolescents who attempt suicide know someone else who
       has attempted it provides a case for what process in suicidal actions?
       a.   modeling
       b.   reinforcement
       c.   unconscious conflicts
       d.   maladaptive thinking

Adolescents, p. 299
Diff: H, Type: Applied, Ans: a
102.   In a city that contains 10,000 "average" teenagers, about how many would be expected to
       commit suicide in a typical year?
       a.   one
       b.   three
       c.   five
       d.   over 5

Adolescents, p. 299
Diff: H, Type: Applied, Ans: b

103.	A friend says to you, "You're studying abnormal psychology; what do the media have to do with suicide among younger people (under 25 years old)?" Your best data-based answer is:
   a.	"Almost nothing, really."
   b.	"Media coverage probably affects about 10% of those who commit suicide."
   c.	"About half of those who commit suicide get the idea from the media."
   d.	"About half of those who commit suicide get the specific method from the media."

Adolescents, p. 299
Diff: M, Type: Applied, Ans: c

104.	Among teenagers who attempt suicide:
   a.	about 3% succeed the first time, and about half will try again.
   b.	about 3% succeed the first time, and about 10% will try again.
   c.	less than 1% succeed the first time, and about half will try again.
   d.	less than 1% succeed the first time, and about 10% will try again.

The Elderly, pp. 299, 301
Diff: H, Type: Applied, Ans: d

105.	The percentage of successful suicide attempts among the elderly is about:
   a.	equal to the percentage of successful suicide attempts among adolescents.
   b.	twice as high as the percentage of successful suicide attempts among adolescents.
   c.	10 times as high as the percentage of successful suicide attempts among adolescents.
   d.	50 times as high as the percentage of successful suicide attempts among adolescents.

The Elderly, p. 300
Diff: H, Type: Applied, Ans: c

106.	An elderly person reports being extremely concerned about the prospect of ending up in a nursing home. This kind of concern is:
   a.	rare; only about 5% of the elderly who commit suicide express this concern.
   b.	unusual; only about 10% of the elderly who commit suicide express this concern.
   c.	common; almost half of the elderly who commit suicide express this concern.
   d.	nearly universal; over 80% of the elderly who commit suicide express this concern.

The Elderly, p. 300
Diff: M, Type: Factual, Ans: d

107.	The age group most likely to commit suicide in the United States is:
   a.	children.
   b.	adolescents.
   c.	young adults.
   d.	the elderly.

The Elderly, p. 300
Diff: M, Type: Factual, Ans: c

108.	Why might the suicide rate among elderly Native Americans be low?
   a.	religious fervor
   b.	overcoming the rage of youth
   c.	the value the culture places on the elderly
   d.	This group overall has a very low suicide rate compared to whites.

What Therapies Are Used After Suicide Attempts?, 301
Diff: H, Type: Applied, Ans: d

109.   Someone who has attempted suicide is refusing therapy. Your best advice to this person, based on research, would be,
   a.   "Do the drug therapy; it has by far the highest success rate."
   b.   "Talk things over with a friend; friends help at least as much as therapists do, although nothing helps very much."
   c.   "Therapy—cognitive-behavioral therapy—only seems to work if the underlying problem is depression."
   d.   "Get therapy; the odds are lower that you'll try again after therapy."

What Therapies Are Used After Suicide Attempts?, p. 301
Diff: H, Type: Factual, Ans: b

110.   Treatment for suicide attempters:
   a.   appears not to be effective.
   b.   typically involves medical and psychological care.
   c.   is provided in about 90% of the cases.
   d.   shows that the cognitive group method is most successful.

The Right to Commit Suicide, p. 302 (Box 10-6)
Diff: H, Type: Applied, Ans: d

111.   A friend of yours thinks that someone suffering from terminal cancer ought to have the right to commit suicide. Your friend's opinion is
   a.   very uncommon—only about 5% of people in the United States would agree.
   b.   uncommon—about 10% of people in the United States would agree.
   c.   uncommon—about 25% of people in the United States would agree.
   d.   common—about 50% of people in the Unites States would agree.

What Is Suicide Prevention?, p. 303
Diff: H, Type: Factual, Ans: d

112.   Suicide prevention programs:
   a.   involve the use of paraprofessionals.
   b.   offer crisis interventions.
   c.   are often found in emergency rooms as well as clinics.
   d.   include paraprofessionals, crisis interventions, and are found in emergency rooms and clinics.

What Is Suicide Prevention?, p. 303
Diff: M, Type: Factual, Ans: c

113.   Suicide prevention centers:
   a.   are run on the AA model, using suicide survivors.
   b.   are hospitals for those who have attempted suicide.
   c.   may deliver services over the phone using paraprofessionals.
   d.   are declining in number in the United States.

What Is Suicide Prevention?, p. 303
Diff: H, Type: Applied, Ans: d
114. At a suicide prevention center, you hear the following from the counselor: "Hello. I am interested in you as a person and am going to stay on the phone with you as long as you want—all night, maybe." Which one of the goals and techniques does it best represent?
   a. formulating a plan
   b. assessing suicide potential
   c. understanding and clarifying the problem
   d. establishing a positive relationship

What Is Suicide Prevention?, p. 303
Diff: H, Type: Applied, Ans: c
115. At a suicide prevention center, you hear the following from the counselor: "Can you tell me what you think are the most important factors that are making you feel hopeless right now? If you could change three things about your life, what would they be?" Which of the goals and techniques of suicide prevention does this quote best represent?
   a. formulating a plan
   b. assessing suicide potential
   c. understanding and clarifying the problem
   d. assessing and mobilizing the caller's resources

What Is Suicide Prevention?, p. 303
Diff: M, Type: Applied, Ans: a
116. At a suicide prevention center, you hear the following from the counselor: "Do you have a gun? Is it loaded and do you know how to use it?" Which of the goals and techniques of suicide prevention does this quote best represent?
   a. assessing suicidal potential
   b. understanding and clarifying the problem
   c. establishing a positive relationship
   d. assessing and mobilizing the caller's resources

What Is Suicide Prevention?, p. 303
Diff: H, Type: Applied, Ans: b
117. At a suicide prevention center, you hear the following from the counselor: "Have you ever tried to commit suicide in the past? [If yes] How did you try to do it?" Which of the goals and techniques of suicide prevention does the quote best represent?
   a. formulating a plan
   b. assessing suicide potential
   c. establishing a positive relationship
   d. assessing and mobilizing the caller's resources

What Is Suicide Prevention?, p. 303
Diff: M, Type: Applied, Ans: d
118. At a suicide prevention center, you hear the following from the counselor: "Who can you think of who might be able to come over and stay with you for a few hours?" Which of the goals and techniques of suicide prevention does the quote best represent?
   a. assessing suicide potential
   b. understanding and clarifying the problem
   c. establishing a positive relationship
   d. assessing and mobilizing the caller's resources

What Is Suicide Prevention?, p. 303
Diff: H, Type: Applied, Ans: a

119. At a suicide prevention center, you hear the following from the counselor: Which of the goals and techniques of suicide prevention does this quote best represent? "Will you promise me that you will call again if you ever feel like killing yourself again?"
   a. formulating a plan
   b. assessing suicide potential
   c. understanding and clarifying the problem
   d. assessing and mobilizing the caller's resources

What Is Suicide Prevention?, p. 303
Diff: E, Type: Factual, Ans: b

120. When answering the telephone of a suicide hot line, the first step for the counselor is to:
   a. formulate a plan.
   b. establish a positive relationship.
   c. understand and clarify the problem.
   d. assess the caller's suicide potential

What Is Suicide Prevention?, p. 303
Diff: E, Type: Factual, Ans: a

121. When talking with a potential suicidal individual on a suicide hot line, the final step for the counselor is to:
   a. formulate a plan.
   b. establish a positive relationship.
   c. understand and clarify the problem.
   d. assess the caller's suicide potential.

What Is Suicide Prevention?, p. 304
Diff: M, Type: Factual, Ans: d

122. A typical caller to an urban suicide prevention center is:
   a. elderly, male, white.
   b. elderly, female, white.
   c. young, male, African American.
   d. young, female, African American.

Do Suicide Prevention Programs Work?, p. 304
Diff: H, Type: Factual, Ans: b

123. Because of the success of crisis intervention for dealing with suicidal people:
   a. a long-term therapy is no longer needed for suicidal people.
   b. crisis intervention techniques have been applied to other problems.
   c. suicide rates among teenagers around the world are dropping.
   d. All the answers are correct.

Do Suicide Prevention Programs Work?, p. 304
Diff: M, Type: Factual, Ans: a

124. One study showed that about what percentage of high-risk suicidal people who contact a suicide crisis hot line later commit suicide?
   a. 2%
   b. 10%
   c. 30%
   d. 50%

Do Suicide Prevention Programs Work?, pp. 304-305
Diff: H, Type: Factual, Ans: b

125.   Which statement about the successes of suicide prevention programs is most accurate?
    a.   People at greatest risk for suicide are most likely to call prevention centers.
    b.   Of those who call, fewer later commit suicide than would be expected by chance.
    c.   Suicide rates are consistently lower in communities that have centers.
    d.   People thinking of suicide know about and readily call centers.

Putting It Together, p. 305
Diff: E, Type: Applied, Ans: d

126.   The most well-developed insights on the causes of suicide come from the _____ model.
    a.   biological
    b.   psychoanalytic
    c.   behavioral
    d.   sociocultural

Putting It Together, p. 305
Diff: M, Type: Factual, Ans: c

127.   Suicide education programs typically focus on:
    a.   those who have previously attempted suicide.
    b.   clergy who are often contacted by suicidal people.
    c.   students and teachers.
    d.   high-risk people who call hot lines.

Putting It Together, p. 305
Diff: H, Type: Factual, Ans: d

128.   The most helpful explanation for suicide, particularly regarding the general background factors and triggers of suicides, come from the _____ perspective.
    a.   psychodynamic
    b.   behavioral
    c.   cognitive
    d.   sociocultural

FILL-IN QUESTIONS

What Is Suicide?, p. 282
Diff: M, Type: Factual, Ans: death seekers

1.   According to Shneidman, people who have a clear intention of ending their lives at the time they attempt suicide, and who are sufficiently clear-minded and committed to performing the act, are called _____.

What Is Suicide?, p. 283
Diff: E, Type: Factual, Ans: death initiators

2.   According to Edwin Shneidman, people who clearly intend to end their lives, but act out of a conviction that the process is already under way and that they are simply hastening the process, are called _____.

What Is Suicide?, p. 283
Diff: E, Type: Factual, Ans: death ignorers

3.   According to Shneidman, people who believe that their self-inflicted deaths will not mean the end of their existence are called _____ .

What Is Suicide?, p. 283
Diff: M, Type: Factual, Ans: subintentional death

4.   According to Shneidman, individuals who play an indirect, covert, partial, or unconscious role in their own deaths may belong to the category called _____ .

What Is Suicide?, p. 283
Diff: E, Type: Factual, Ans: death darer

5.   A person who commits suicide but shows ambivalence in the act would be classified as a _____ , according to Shneidman.

What Is Suicide?, p. 283
Diff: E, Type: Factual, Ans: chronic suicide

6.   The term Menninger used to refer to people who die as a result of behaving in life-endangering ways for a long time was _____ .

How Is Suicide Studied?, p. 283
Diff: M, Type: Factual, Ans: retrospective analysis

7.   The piecing together of data from people's pasts to understand their suicides is termed _____ .

Patterns and Statistics, p. 285
Diff: E, Type: Factual, Ans: devoutness

8.   The aspect of religion that is most highly related to suicide is _____ .

Patterns and Statistics, p. 286
Diff: E, Type: Factual, Ans: Native American

9.   In both the United States and Canada, _____ is the ethnic group with the highest suicide rate.

Mood and Thought Changes, p. 288
Diff: M, Type: Factual, Ans: hopelessness

10.   When people feel that their present circumstances, problems, and negative moods will not change, and this pessimistic belief contributes to suicide, the belief is called a sense of _____ .

Mood and Thought Changes, p. 288
Diff: M, Type: Factual, Ans: dichotomous thinking

11.   Cognitive theorists believe that suicide may be linked to _____ , in which people develop a pattern of viewing their problems and solutions in either/or terms.

Modeling: The Contagion of Suicide, p. 291
Diff: M, Type: Factual, Ans: modeling

12.   There is evidence that the likelihood of other suicides goes up when a celebrity commits suicide, the media focus on a particular case of suicide, or a co-worker or colleague of a suicide-prone person commits suicide. This "contagious" form of suicide has been attributed to the behavioral principle of _____ .

The Psychodynamic View, p. 292
Diff: E, Type: Factual, Ans: psychodynamic

13.   According to the _____ view, suicide usually results from a state of depression and a process of self-directed anger.

The Sociocultural View, p. 293
Diff: M, Type: Applied, Ans: sociocultural

14.   Dr. Alberto focuses on social relationships and connections with other people in understanding the suicide of an individual. Dr. Alberto seems to accept a _____ theoretical position.

The Sociocultural View, p. 294
Diff: M, Type: Factual, Ans: egoistic

15.   Durkheim defined _____ suicides as those committed by people who are not concerned with the norms or rules of society and who are not integrated into the social fabric.

The Sociocultural View, p. 294
Diff: M, Type: Applied, Ans: altruistic

16.   Darlene starves to death because she gives her meager food to her little sister. Durkheim would classify Darlene as an _____ suicide.

The Sociocultural View, p. 294
Diff: H, Type: Factual, Ans: anomic

17.   According to Durkheim, a person who commits suicide because his or her social environment fails to provide stable structures to support and give meaning to life has committed _____ suicide.

The Biological View, p. 296
Diff: M, Type: Factual, Ans: serotonin

18.   Recent research on biological factors in suicide has linked it to low levels of the neurotransmitter _____ in the brain.

The Biological View, p. 296
Diff: M, Type: Factual, Ans: aggressive

19.   The mediating factor between serotonin deficiency and suicide is thought to be _____ tendencies, which have been linked to low levels of serotonin, rather than to depression.

Children, p. 297
Diff: E, Type: Factual, Ans: rising

20.   Over the past several decades, the suicide rate for children in the United States has been _____.

The Elderly, p. 300
Diff: E, Type: Factual, Ans: the elderly

21.   The age group most at risk for committing suicide in the United States is _____.

What Is Suicide Prevention?, p. 301
Diff: E, Type: Factual, Ans: prevention (or education)

22.   During the past 50 years the emphasis has shifted from suicide treatment to _____.

What Is Suicide Prevention?, p. 303
Diff: M, Type: Factual, Ans: paraprofessionals

23.   Suicide prevention centers are often staffed by counselors called _____, who have no previous training but are under the supervision of a mental health professional.

ESSAY QUESTIONS

What Is Suicide?, pp. 282-283
Diff: M, Type: Applied

1.   Briefly describe the four types of people who end their lives, according to Shneidman. Then provide an example of each type of suicide.

How Is Suicide Studied?, p. 283
Diff: H, Type: Applied

2.   Imagine that you are responsible for conducting a retrospective analysis of someone who has committed suicide. Sketch out the method you would use and the types of information you would try to gather. What are some disadvantages of this type of analysis?

Suicide Notes, p. 284 (Box 10-2)
Diff: M, Type: Factual

3.   What do we know from studying suicide notes? Be as complete as you can in your answer.

Patterns and Statistics, pp. 285-291
Diff: H, Type: Applied

4.   Suicide education might reasonably involve discussion of risk factors. Imagine that you are talking with a group of resident assistants on a college campus. What are the five most important points about suicide risk that you would want to make with them?

What Are the Underlying Causes of Suicide?, pp. 292-297
Diff: H, Type: Applied

5.   Suicide appears to run in families. Why might this be the case? Be sure to discuss biological, psychological, and sociocultural explanations.

Children, p. 297
Diff: H, Type: Applied

6.   In a paragraph, describe a child who would be at great risk for suicide. Be sure to indicate which characteristics make the child at risk.

Adolescents, p. 298
Diff: H, Type: Factual

7.   Discuss at least three distinct ways in which the explanations for suicide in adolescents differ from the explanations for suicide in adults. What factors make adolescents particularly at risk for suicide.

The Elderly, pp. 300-301
Diff: M, Type: Applied

8.   Some maintain that the suicide rate for the elderly is higher among white Americans than among Native Americans because of the way the two groups value (or don't value) the elderly. Discuss at least three distinct differences in the way the two groups treat the elderly that might legitimately be related to the suicide risk.

The Right to Commit Suicide, p. 302 (Box 10-6)
Diff: H, Type: Applied

9.   Imagine that you were judging a debate on the right to commit suicide. What are the three
        most important points you would like for the debaters to make on both sides of this question
        (pro and con)?

What is Suicide Prevention?, p. 303
Diff: H, Type: Applied

10.   The Los Angeles Suicide Prevention Center has five goals for each call. List these and then
        provide responses a counselor might make that reflect each goal (one counselor response for
        each goal).

CHAPTER 11   Eating Disorders

MULTIPLE-CHOICE QUESTIONS

Anorexia Nervosa, p. 310
Diff: M, Type: Factual, Ans: c

1. Characteristics of anorexia nervosa include all the following except:
    a. body weight of 85 percent or less of normal.
    b. fear of becoming overweight.
    c. a view that one is currently unattractively thin.
    d. loss of menstrual periods.

Anorexia Nervosa, p. 310
Diff: E, Type: Applied, Ans: d

2. The disorder that is characterized by eating binges followed by forced vomiting is called:
    a. obesity.
    b. obsession.
    c. anorexia nervosa.
    d. bulimia nervosa.

Anorexia Nervosa, p. 310
Diff: E, Type: Applied, Ans: b

3. Carol has become very afraid of being overweight. She has recently reduced her food intake although she feels hungry all the time. As a result, her weight has dropped sharply below average, but she still believes that she is overweight. Carol is most likely experiencing:
    a. bulimia nervosa.
    b. anorexia nervosa.
    c. Carpenter's syndrome.
    d. carbohydrate deprivation.

Anorexia Nervosa, p. 310
Diff: M, Type: Applied, Ans: b

4. According to the DSM-IV-TR, to be diagnosed with anorexia nervosa, a person's weight loss must be at least _____ percent below normal.
    a. 10
    b. 15
    c. 25
    d. 30

Anorexia Nervosa, p. 310
Diff: M, Type: Applied, Ans: c
5.   A person who stopped eating candy and other sweets, then gradually eliminated other foods until the person was eating almost nothing could be experiencing:
      a.   binge-purge type of anorexia nervosa.
      b.   sweet-phobia type of anorexia nervosa.
      c.   restricting-type anorexia nervosa.
      d.   exercise-induced anorexia nervosa.

Anorexia Nervosa, p. 310
Diff: E, Type: Factual, Ans: b
6.   What is the first type of food usually eliminated from the diet of the developing anorexic person?
      a.   meat
      b.   sweets
      c.   breads
      d.   nuts and grains

Anorexia Nervosa, p. 310
Diff: E, Type: Applied, Ans: a
7.   A person who loses weight by forcing herself to vomit after meals or by using laxatives, and who otherwise fits the definition of anorexia is experiencing:
      a.   binge-eating/purging anorexia nervosa.
      b.   food-phobia anorexia nervosa.
      c.   restricted-type anorexia nervosa.
      d.   variable limited anorexia nervosa.

Anorexia Nervosa, p. 311
Diff: E, Type: Factual, Ans: a
8.   Which of the following would be most at risk for anorexia nervosa?
      a.   a 16-year-old girl
      b.   a 12-year-old girl
      c.   a 20-year-old young man
      d.   a 25-year-old young woman

Anorexia Nervosa, p. 311
Diff: M, Type: Factual, Ans: d
9.   Which of the following is not true about anorexia nervosa?
      a.   It usually follows a diet in someone who is of normal weight or slightly overweight.
      b.   It can follow a stressful event such as divorce, a move from home, or a personal failure.
      c.   Fatalities are brought on by suicide or serious medical problems due to starvation.
      d.   About 25 percent of people who experience anorexia nervosa are men.

Anorexia Nervosa, p. 311
Diff: H, Type: Factual, Ans: a
10.   What is the most common outcome for individuals with anorexia nervosa?
      a.   recovery
      b.   starving to death
      c.   suffering irreversible physical harm
      d.   suffering lifelong physiological trauma

Anorexia Nervosa, p. 311
Diff: M, Type: Factual, Ans: b
11.   What percentage of individuals with anorexia die from medical complications?
      a.   less than 2%
      b.   2-6%
      c.   10-20%
      d.   almost 25%

Anorexia Nervosa, p. 311
Diff: E, Type: Factual, Ans: c
12.   The peak age for the onset of anorexia nervosa is:
      a.   7-10.
      b.   10-13.
      c.   14-18.
      d.   20-25.

The Clinical Picture, p. 312
Diff: M, Type: Factual, Ans: a
13.   The primary motivating emotion a person with anorexia experiences is:
      a.   fear.
      b.   anger.
      c.   shame.
      d.   hate.

The Clinical Picture, p. 312
Diff: M, Type: Factual, Ans: a
14.   The preoccupation with food characteristic of anorexia nervosa is thought to:
      a.   result from starvation.
      b.   be the cause of the disorder.
      c.   be more pronounced in younger children with anorexia.
      d.   result from overeating.

The Clinical Picture, p. 312
Diff: M, Type: Factual, Ans: b
15.   In the 1940s a group of volunteers was put on a semistarvation diet for 6 months. During the
      latter part of the study:
      a.   several of the volunteers became anorexic.
      b.   the volunteers thought about food all the time.
      c.   they never thought about food because it made them hungry.
      d.   they tended to avoid meals because they did not get enough food.

The Clinical Picture, p. 312
Diff: M, Type: Factual, Ans: d
16.   A modern explanation of why many anorexic people continually have food-related thoughts
      and dreams is that:
      a.   thoughts of food occur in order to avoid eating.
      b.   fantasy about food fulfills basic needs of the id.
      c.   such thoughts and dreams are the cause of food deprivation.
      d.   such thoughts and dreams are the result of food deprivation.

The Clinical Picture, p. 312
Diff: M, Type: Factual, Ans: a
17.   The most common cognitive disturbance in anorexia nervosa is:
       a.   a distorted body image.
       b.   a revulsion toward food.
       c.   a major clinical depression.
       d.   views of others.

The Clinical Picture, p. 312
Diff: E, Type: Factual, Ans: a
18.   People suffering from anorexia nervosa tend to:
       a.   overestimate their body size.
       b.   underestimate their body size.
       c.   correctly estimate their body size.
       d.   vary in accuracy in estimating their body size.

The Clinical Picture, p. 312
Diff: M, Type: Applied, Ans: a
19.   Megan is anorexic. She believes that weight and body shape are the only true criteria on
       which self-worth can be judged. Her thought process in this regard illustrates:
       a.   distorted thinking.
       b.   distorted body image.
       c.   body dysmorphic disorder.
       d.   distorted internal perception.

The Clinical Picture, p. 312
Diff: H, Type: Applied, Ans: c
20.   Which of these characteristics is most consistent with anorexia nervosa?
       a.   a refusal to think about food at all
       b.   a view that one's body is too thin
       c.   body size overestimation
       d.   distorted perception of others' sizes

The Clinical Picture, p. 312
Diff: H, Type: Applied, Ans: d
21.   Which one of the following would be least likely to characterize the behavior of one
       experiencing anorexia nervosa?
       a.   careful preparation and planning of the food one eats during the day
       b.   feeling oneself to be unattractively overweight
       c.   a view that food deprivation makes one a better person
       d.   a hesitancy to think and talk about food

The Clinical Picture, p. 312
Diff: E, Type: Factual, Ans: c
22.   Nonanorexic people who are placed on a starvation diet:
       a.   lose weight much more slowly than anorexic people.
       b.   have more severe medical problems than anorexic people do.
       c.   show many of the cognitive problems of anorexia nervosa.
       d.   lose weight in the same way that anorexic people do, but do not suffer the same cognitive
             changes.

The Clinical Picture, p. 312
Diff: E, Type: Factual, Ans: a
23. Anorexic individuals often show which of the following personality factors?
     a. obsessions
     b. low anxiety
     c. multiple phobias
     d. episodes of mania

The Clinical Picture, p. 312
Diff: M, Type: Applied, Ans: d
24. Of the following, the psychological disorder that anorexia nervosa most resembles is:
     a. a simple phobia.
     b. narcissistic personality disorder.
     c. borderline personality disorder.
     d. obsessive-compulsive disorder.

The Clinical Picture, p. 312
Diff: M, Type: Factual, Ans: c
25. Which of the following psychological problems is least likely to be associated with anorexia nervosa?
     a. depression
     b. obsessive-compulsive disorder
     c. schizophrenia
     d. substance abuse

The Clinical Picture, p. 312
Diff: H, Type: Applied, Ans: a
26. If you were looking at a photograph of yourself and adjusting the size until you thought the picture looked like you, you would most likely be participating in an assessment of your:
     a. accuracy in estimating body size.
     b. self-esteem.
     c. readiness for therapy.
     d. susceptibility to societal stereotypes.

The Clinical Picture, p. 312
Diff: H, Type: Applied, Ans: b
27. If a friend were experiencing anorexia nervosa, you wouldn't be surprised to find that the friend was also experiencing all of the following except:
     a. substance abuse.
     b. a personality disorder.
     c. low self-esteem.
     d. anxiety.

The Clinical Picture, p. 312
Diff: H, Type: Applied, Ans: c
28. A patient in therapy who eats exactly eight pieces of bread that he or she has carefully made into balls of equal diameter is displaying a symptom of anorexia nervosa related to:
     a. schizophrenia.
     b. depression.
     c. obsessive-compulsive disorder.
     d. substance abuse.

Bulimia Nervosa, p. 313
Diff: H, Type: Applied, Ans: d

29.   Misusing diuretics and laxatives following a binge is a symptom of the _____ type of bulimia nervosa.
       a. adolescent-
       b. late-onset
       c. substance abuse
       d. purging-

Bulimia Nervosa, p. 313
Diff: H, Type: Applied, Ans: a

30.   Someone who fasts or exercises strenuously following a binge is engaging in:
       a. compensation.
       b. purging.
       c. enmeshment.
       d. exposure and response prevention.

Bulimia Nervosa, p. 313
Diff: H, Type: Factual, Ans: c

31.   Consequences of anorexia nervosa include all of the following except:
       a. amenorrhea.
       b. dry, rough, cracked skin.
       c. fever and high blood pressure.
       d. development of the silky hair that covers newborns.

Bulimia Nervosa, p. 313
Diff: E, Type: Factual, Ans: a

32.   Which of the following problems is common in anorexia nervosa?
       a. amenorrhea
       b. increased heart rate
       c. high blood pressure
       d. elevated body temperature

Bulimia Nervosa, p. 313
Diff: M, Type: Factual, Ans: b

33.   Which of the following problems is a possible medical complication of anorexia nervosa?
       a. high blood pressure
       b. decreased heart rate
       c. elevated body temperature
       d. increased bone mineral density

Bulimia Nervosa, p. 313
Diff: M, Type: Factual, Ans: a

34.   Bulimia is always characterized by:
       a. uncontrollable overeating.
       b. forced vomiting, and misuse of laxatives and enemas.
       c. fasting and frantic exercise.
       d. being underweight.

Bulimia Nervosa, p. 313
Diff: H, Type: Factual, Ans: b
35.   All of the following are compensatory behaviors for someone with bulimia except:
    a.   excessive exercise.
    b.   preoccupation with food.
    c.   forced vomiting.
    d.   use of diuretics.

Bulimia Nervosa, p. 313
Diff: M, Type: Factual, Ans: d
36.   If an anorexic woman has lanugo, what has happened?
    a.   She has lost body hair.
    b.   She has developed double vision.
    c.   Her menstrual cycle has become irregular.
    d.   She has grown fine silky hair on her body.

Bulimia Nervosa, p. 313
Diff: M, Type: Factual, Ans: d
37.   The central feature of bulimia nervosa is:
    a.   excessive dieting and weight loss.
    b.   fanatic exercising preceded by binge eating.
    c.   purging either by vomiting or use of laxatives.
    d.   binge eating followed by a compensatory behavior.

Bulimia Nervosa, p. 313
Diff: M, Type: Factual, Ans: b
38.   The best diagnosis for a woman who regularly eats a whole pizza, a carton of ice cream, and a box of donuts at one sitting, then forces herself to throw it all up is:
    a.   compulsive-type bulimia nervosa.
    b.   purging-type bulimia nervosa.
    c.   depressive-type bulimia nervosa.
    d.   anorexia-type bulimia.

Bulimia Nervosa, p. 313
Diff: M, Type: Applied, Ans: b
39.   Flora binges almost every day. Cookies, cake, ice cream, and almost anything else that is sweet goes down her throat. Sometime during the binge she takes a huge dose of a laxative so that she will "empty out" the food. This set of assumptions would lead to a diagnosis of:
    a.   binge-eating disorder.
    b.   purging-type bulimia nervosa.
    c.   nonpurging-type bulimia nervosa.
    d.   eating disorder not otherwise specified.

Bulimia Nervosa, p. 313
Diff: M, Type: Factual, Ans: c
40.   Which of the following is a diagnostic criterion for bulimia nervosa?
    a.   obsessive thoughts about cleanliness
    b.   weight at least 15 percent below normal
    c.   lack of control over eating during binging
    d.   one episode of binge eating followed by purging

Bulimia Nervosa, p. 313
Diff: M, Type: Applied, Ans: c

41.   Glenda binges almost every day. She eats chips and dips, burgers and fries, and a couple of
       shakes. After her eating she goes to the gym and does 90 minutes of aerobics, spends an hour
       on the stairstepper, and then does weights for another hour. She also does not eat for 72
       hours. This set of assumptions would lead to a diagnosis of:
       a.   binge-eating disorder.
       b.   purging-type bulimia nervosa.
       c.   nonpurging-type bulimia nervosa.
       d.   eating disorder not otherwise specified.

Bulimia Nervosa, p. 313
Diff: M, Type: Factual, Ans: c

42.   If binge eating is followed by a period of strenuous exercise to compensate for the food, the
       diagnosis is probably:
       a.   binge-eating disorder.
       b.   purging-type bulimia nervosa.
       c.   nonpurging-type bulimia nervosa.
       d.   eating disorder not otherwise specified.

Bulimia Nervosa, p. 313
Diff: H, Type: Factual, Ans: a

43.   To qualify for a diagnosis of bulimia nervosa, what must be true of the compensatory
       behaviors displayed?
       a.   They must occur.
       b.   They must involve vomiting.
       c.   They must effectively cause weight loss.
       d.   They must cause pathological changes in the body.

Bulimia Nervosa, p. 314
Diff: E, Type: Factual, Ans: c

44.   Most people with bulimia nervosa _____ compared to people with anorexia nervosa.
       a.   are younger
       b.   have less education
       c.   are of more normal weight
       d.   have obsessive thoughts about food

Bulimia Nervosa, p. 314
Diff: H, Type: Applied, Ans: c

45.   People who are often overweight and regularly binge eat without compensatory behaviors are
       experiencing:
       a.   binge-purge disorder.
       b.   anorexia-bulimia disorder.
       c.   binge-eating disorder.
       d.   noncompensatory binge disorder.

Bulimia Nervosa, p. 314
Diff: M, Type: Factual, Ans: c

46.   Many teenagers go on occasional eating binges. Which of the following is true?
    a.   The behavior is perfectly normal.
    b.   The behavior inevitably leads to bulimia.
    c.   Most people who engage in the behavior are not bulimic.
    d.   The behavior inevitably leads to excessive exercise.

Binges, p. 314
Diff: H, Type: Applied, Ans: b

47.   If a friend of yours had bulimia nervosa and engaged in frequent binges, about how many of his or her binges per week would you expect to witness yourself?
    a.   ten
    b.   none
    c.   seven
    d.   40

Binges, p. 315
Diff: H, Type: Applied, Ans: c

48.   In terms of emotions, the pattern common in bulimia from prebinge, through binge, to postbinge is best described as:
    a.   control, enjoyment, shame.
    b.   relaxation, pleasure, enjoyment.
    c.   tension, powerlessness, shame.
    d.   shame, doubt, guilt.

Binges, p. 315
Diff: H, Type: Applied, Ans: d

49.   Immediately preceding the onset of an eating disorder, one would most likely find that the patient:
    a.   had been unsuccessful in trying to lose weight.
    b.   had gone through a period of intense criticism from family.
    c.   had experienced a growth spurt.
    d.   had been successful in losing weight and had been praised by family.

Binges, p. 315
Diff: E, Type: Factual, Ans: d

50.   For people with bulimia nervosa, binge episodes produce feelings of:
    a.   control.
    b.   satisfaction.
    c.   anxiety and mania.
    d.   guilt and depression.

Binges, p. 315
Diff: M, Type: Factual, Ans: b

51.   People who binge:
    a.   like to eat high protein foods such as steak and nuts.
    b.   feel great tension before the binge.
    c.   are usually calm and rational just before and during a binge.
    d.   generally consume about 10,000 calories during a binge.

Compensatory Behaviors, p. 315
Diff: M, Type: Factual, Ans: b
52.   Vomiting as a compensatory behavior for those experiencing bulimia:
   a.   prevents the absorption of about 90% of calories consumed.
   b.   ironically, leads to greater hunger and more frequent binges.
   c.   helps one to feel full quicker during the next binge.
   d.   is often done in public with no attempt to hide the behavior.

Compensatory Behaviors, p. 315
Diff: M, Type: Factual, Ans: b
53.   How successful are compensatory behaviors in controlling weight?
   a.   Vomiting prevents the absorption of 90% of calories consumed.
   b.   Repeated vomiting affects one's ability to feel satiated.
   c.   Using laxatives almost completely undoes the caloric effects of bingeing.
   d.   Using diuretics almost completely undoes the caloric effects of bingeing.

Compensatory Behaviors, p. 316
Diff: H, Type: Applied, Ans: a
54.   Following a very low-calorie weight-loss program, participants would be at greatest risk for:
   a.   bingeing.
   b.   anorexia.
   c.   substance abuse.
   d.   family problems.

Not for Women Only, pp. 316-317 (Box 11-2)
Diff: H, Type: Factual, Ans: c
55.   A study of college men showed that they describe the ideal male as _____ and the ideal female as _____.
   a.   slim and trim; slim and trim
   b.   muscular; muscular
   c.   muscular; thin
   d.   athletic; strong

Not for Women Only, pp. 316-317 (Box 11-2)
Diff: H, Type: Applied, Ans: d
56.   What is the most likely explanation for the different explanations of eating disorders in men and women?
   a.   Men are judged by a harsher cultural standard of attractiveness.
   b.   Eating disorders may be overdiagnosed in women.
   c.   Men restrict their caloric intake more severely when dieting.
   d.   Male eating disorders are more likely to be tied to work or sports.

Not for Women Only, pp. 316-317 (Box 11-2)
Diff: M, Type: Factual, Ans: a
57.   Which of the following men are at greatest risk for an eating disorder?
   a.   jockeys
   b.   football players
   c.   gymnasts
   d.   divers

Bulimia Nervosa vs. Anorexia Nervosa, p. 317
Diff: H, Type: Factual, Ans: a

58.   Similarities between bulimia and anorexia include:
   a.   both tend to begin after a period of dieting among people afraid of becoming obese.
   b.   both involve a reluctance to think about food, weight, or appearance.
   c.   both involve an underestimation of one's weight and body size.
   d.   both tend to be related to personality disorders.

Bulimia Nervosa vs. Anorexia Nervosa, p. 317
Diff: H, Type: Applied, Ans: b

59.   A young woman who is very concerned about being attractive to others, is more sexually experienced, and has relatively few obsessive qualities is:
   a.   more likely to be experiencing anorexia than bulimia.
   b.   more likely to be experiencing bulimia than anorexia.
   c.   equally likely to be experiencing bulimia or anorexia.
   d.   showing no symptoms that have been found to be related to eating disorders.

Bulimia Nervosa vs. Anorexia Nervosa, p. 317
Diff: M, Type: Applied, Ans: b

60.   Which of the following would be at most risk of developing an eating disorder:
   a.   someone who had successfully completed a diet.
   b.   someone who is a habitual dieter with no success.
   c.   a yo-yo dieter (lots of losses and gains.)
   d.   someone who is morbidly obese.

What Causes Eating Disorders?, p. 318
Diff: H, Type: Applied, Ans: b

61.   If a therapist thought that eating disorders were best explained by an interaction of factors—sociocultural, psychological, and biological—that therapist would be taking a _____ perspective.
   a.   monodimentional
   b.   multidimentional
   c.   cognitive-behavioral
   d.   outdated

What Causes Eating Disorders?, p. 318
Diff: H, Type: Applied, Ans: c

62.   Someone who is experiencing bulimia is more likely to _____ than someone experiencing anorexia.
   a.   show obsessive tendencies
   b.   believe their body size is larger than it actually is
   c.   display characteristics of a personality disorder
   d.   have serious medical consequences from the disorder

What Causes Eating Disorders?, p. 318
Diff: M, Type: Factual, Ans: b

63.   Which one of the following is a medical condition more common in bulimia than anorexia?
   a.   amenorrhea
   b.   dental problems
   c.   high potassium levels in the blood
   d.   growth of immature body hair

What Causes Eating Disorders?, p. 318
Diff: M, Type: Factual, Ans: c
64.   One medical problem linked to bulimia nervosa is:
      a.   hair loss.
      b.   hypermania.
      c.   tooth loss.
      d.   sodium deficiency.

What Causes Eating Disorders?, p. 318
Diff: M, Type: Factual, Ans: b
65.   The medical problem that is about twice as frequent in anorexic women as it is in bulimic
      women is:
      a.   hair loss.
      b.   amenorrhea.
      c.   hypokalemia.
      d.   esophageal bleeding.

What Causes Eating Disorders?, p. 318
Diff: E, Type: Factual, Ans: d
66.   The currently accepted view of anorexia is that its cause is:
      a.   cognitive.
      b.   biological.
      c.   behavioral.
      d.   multidimensional.

Societal Pressures, p. 319
Diff: H, Type: Applied, Ans: c
67.   Based on past results, one would predict that women who win the Miss America contest in
      the future, will:
      a.   be larger than those who lose.
      b.   be about a pound heavier than the previous year's winner.
      c.   be smaller than those who lose.
      d.   have larger chests, but smaller hips than current winners.

Societal Pressures, p. 319
Diff: H, Type: Applied, Ans: d
68.   Recent research on eating disorders is most consistent with which of the following
      statements?
      a.   White American women have better body images and fewer problems with eating
           disorders than African American women.
      b.   African American women have better body images and fewer problems with eating
           disorders than white American women.
      c.   Both white American women and African American women have better body images and
           fewer problems with eating disorders these days than they did in the past.
      d.   The rates of eating disorders are increasing in minority women—approaching rates found
           in white American women.

Societal Pressures, p. 319
Diff: E, Type: Applied, Ans: a
69. If one found that the average weight and size of cheerleaders had declined significantly over the years, and that those who aspired to be cheerleaders had a high level of eating disorders, one would have evidence for _____ causes of eating disorders.
     a. societal
     b. family
     c. psychological
     d. biological

Societal Pressures, p. 319
Diff: M, Type: Factual, Ans: c
70. Which professionals are most at risk for an eating disorder?
     a. psychologists and psychiatrists
     b. doctors and nurses
     c. actors and athletes
     d. dress designers and make-up artists

Societal Pressures, p. 319
Diff: M, Type: Applied, Ans: d
71. Which one of the following is most at risk for an eating disorder?
     a. a college woman who is a non-athlete
     b. a woman lower on the socioeconomic scale
     c. an African-American woman
     d. a gymnast

Societal Pressures, p. 320
Diff: H, Type: Applied, Ans: a
72. One would be most likely to hear cruel jokes on TV related to:
     a. obesity.
     b. anorexia.
     c. bulimia.
     d. gender.

Societal Pressures, p. 321
Diff: H, Type: Factual, Ans: a
73. In one study, prospective parents rated a picture of a chubby child as less _____ than an average-weight child.
     a. friendly and intelligent
     b. masculine
     c. emotionally stable
     d. likely to succeed

Societal Pressures, p. 321
Diff: M, Type: Applied, Ans: d
74. A person who believes that obese people have no self control and are lazy is engaging in a belief that is:
     a. prejudiced.
     b. common in Western society.
     c. applied to obese children as well as adults.
     d. All the answers are correct.

Societal Pressures, p. 321
Diff: H, Type: Applied, Ans: b
75.   Research on doll choice in preschoolers shows that:
       a.   children choose the doll that looks most like they do.
       b.   children choose the thin doll rather than the chubby doll but don't seem to know why.
       c.   children choose the thin doll and say they want to be thin themselves.
       d.   children choose the chubby doll but don't seem to know why.

Societal Pressures, p. 322
Diff: H, Type: Applied, Ans: c
76.   If you had a friend with an eating disorder, research suggests that the friend's family would
       most likely:
       a.   be enmeshed.
       b.   encourage your friend to seek therapy.
       c.   it would be hard to say; families vary widely.
       d.   have ineffective parenting styles.

Family Environment, p. 322
Diff: H, Type: Applied, Ans: d
77.   Which one of the following is not characteristic of the mother of one with an eating disorder?
       a.   a mother who emphasizes thinness
       b.   a perfectionist mother
       c.   a mother who is concerned herself about dieting
       d.   a mother who was herself a gymnast

Family Environment, p. 322
Diff: M, Type: Applied, Ans: c
78.   Family members are overinvolved in each other's lives, but are affectionate and loyal. This
       description fits Minuchin's definition of an:
       a.   autonomous family pattern.
       b.   underfunctioning family pattern.
       c.   enmeshed family pattern.
       d.   institutionalized family pattern.

Family Environment, p. 322
Diff: E, Type: Factual, Ans: b
79.   Salvador Minuchin describes a family system in which members are overly involved in each
       other's affairs. It is known as the:
       a.   interrelationary pattern.
       b.   enmeshed family pattern.
       c.   homeostatic family system.
       d.   dysfunctionally interdependent system.

Family Environment, p. 322
Diff: H, Type: Factual, Ans: c
80.   The adolescent push for independence threatens the enmeshed family pattern. In these cases:
       a.   the child becomes anxious and this produces anorexia nervosa.
       b.   the stress of the situation leads to psychological (eating) disorders.
       c.   the child takes on a sick role to allow the family to live in harmony.
       d.   the child tries harder to adhere to the social view of physical perfection.

Ego Deficiencies and Cognitive Disturbances, p. 322
Diff: H, Type: Factual, Ans: d

81.   The important contribution to the treatment of eating disorders made by Hilde Bruch combines which theoretical frameworks?
        a. cognitive and behavioral
        b. humanistic and existential
        c. biological and psychoanalytic
        d. psychodynamic and cognitive

Ego Deficiencies and Cognitive Disturbances, p. 322
Diff: H, Type: Applied, Ans: c

82.   According to Hilde Bruch, which of the following would characterize ineffective parents whose children are prone to eating disorders?
        a. They feed children crying from hunger and comfort ones crying from fear.
        b. They feed children too much, regardless of whether they are crying or not.
        c. They feed anxious children and comfort tired ones.
        d. They fail to comfort their children at all.

Ego Deficiencies and Cognitive Disturbances, p. 322
Diff: H, Type: Applied, Ans: c

83.   Children who cannot accurately interpret their internal condition (that is, are not able to tell if they are upset because they are tired, hungry, afraid, or cold) are at risk of developing _____, according to Hilde Bruch.
        a. self-control and autonomy
        b. an ability to anticipate the needs of others
        c. ego deficiencies and cognitive disturbances
        d. a strong confidence in their own opinions

Ego Deficiencies and Cognitive Disturbances, p. 323
Diff: H, Type: Applied, Ans: a

84.   What underlies Bruch's ego deficiency view of eating disorders is a sense of:
        a. lack of control over their lives and a misperception of internal cues.
        b. parents who failed to anticipate and meet their needs, especially for food.
        c. hypersensitivity to and accuracy in interpreting internal cues.
        d. hostile and abusive parents.

Ego Deficiencies and Cognitive Disturbances, p. 323
Diff: H, Type: Applied, Ans: d

85.   Bruch's research suggests that when people with eating disorders are anxious or upset, they think they are:
        a. anxious or upset.
        b. worthless.
        c. depressed.
        d. hungry.

Mood Disorders, p. 324
Diff: H, Type: Applied, Ans: d

86.   If we find that many people with eating disorders also have symptoms of depression, we
       know that:
       a.   eating disorders cause depression.
       b.   depression causes one to have an eating disorder.
       c.   something else causes both eating disorders and depression.
       d.   eating disorders and depression are somehow related.

Mood Disorders, p. 324
Diff: H, Type: Applied, Ans: c

87.   Support for the idea that mood disorders set the stage for eating disorders comes from
       evidence that shows:
       a.   high levels of serotonin in the brain.
       b.   that eating disorders have been successfully treated using anti-anxiety medication.
       c.   that close relatives of people with eating disorders have a high rate of mood disorders.
       d.   that people with eating disorders are *not* more likely themselves to be diagnosed with
             depression.

Mood Disorders, p. 324
Diff: M, Type: Factual, Ans: b

88.   The levels of brain _____ are low in many people with depression and in eating disorders.
       a.   GABA
       b.   serotonin
       c.   dopamine
       d.   norepinephrine

Biological Factors, p. 324
Diff: M, Type: Factual, Ans: a

89.   Compared to the general public, people with eating disorders are more likely to:
       a.   be depressed.
       b.   suffer from mania.
       c.   experience panic attacks.
       d.   have higher serotonin levels.

Biological Factors, p. 324
Diff: E, Type: Factual, Ans: c

90.   The part of the brain most closely associated with the control of eating and body weight is
       the:
       a.   thalamus.
       b.   brain stem.
       c.   hypothalamus.
       d.   cerebral cortex.

Biological Factors, p. 324
Diff: H, Type: Factual, Ans: a

91.   When an experimenter stimulates a rat's lateral hypothalamus, the most likely result is:
       a.   eating.
       b.   loss of appetite.
       c.   death by starvation.
       d.   intense sexual desire.

How Are Eating Disorders Treated?, p. 330
Diff: M, Type: Factual, Ans: c

116.   All the treatment methods for bulimia nervosa share the immediate goal of:
    a.   changing distorted self-perceptions.
    b.   addressing the underlying causes of the bulimic patterns.
    c.   assisting the clients to eliminate their binge-purge patterns.
    d.   forcing the patient to accept the responsibility for his or her actions.

How Are Eating Disorders Treated?, p. 330
Diff: H, Type: Applied, Ans: d

117.   People receiving individual insight therapy for bulimia would:
    a.   be encouraged to suppress the reasons for their feelings of powerlessness, lack of self-trust, and need for control.
    b.   not be much helped, according to a large body of research that fails to support this approach to treatment.
    c.   be taught to repeat the negative thoughts that precede bingeing so as to habituate to them.
    d.   change perfectionistic standards and low self-concept.

How Are Eating Disorders Treated?, p. 331
Diff: M, Type: Factual, Ans: c

118.   The use of a food diary to keep track of eating behavior in the treatment of bulimic patients is most likely to be used by a therapist from the:
    a.   cognitive perspective.
    b.   humanist perspective.
    c.   behavioral perspective.
    d.   psychodynamic perspective.

How Are Eating Disorders Treated?, p. 331
Diff: M, Type: Applied, Ans: d

119.   Tanya is a behavioral therapist who exposes bulimic patients to situations that usually cause binge episodes and then prevents them from binge eating. The technique that she is using is called:
    a.   skillful frustration.
    b.   temptation-restriction.
    c.   willpower reinforcement.
    d.   exposure and response prevention.

How Are Eating Disorders Treated?, p. 331
Diff: H, Type: Applied, Ans: a

120.   A therapist who sat with the bulimic patient while the patient ate appropriate quantities of "forbidden" foods, and then stayed until the patient no longer had the urge to purge would be practicing:
    a.   exposure and response prevention.
    b.   group insight-oriented therapy.
    c.   correction and cognitive misperceptions.
    d.   supportive nursing care.

How Are Eating Disorders Treated?, p. 331
Diff: M, Type: Factual, Ans: b

121.   One of the therapy methods commonly used to treat bulimia nervosa is:
       a.   flooding.
       b.   exposure and response prevention.
       c.   aversive therapy.
       d.   systematic desensitization.

How Are Eating Disorders Treated?, p. 332
Diff: H, Type: Factual, Ans: b

122.   The medication most helpful in the treatment of bulimia is an:
       a.   antianxiety drug.
       b.   antidepressant drug.
       c.   antipsychotic drug.
       d.   antiemetic drug (to eliminate vomiting.)

How Are Eating Disorders Treated?, p. 333
Diff: M, Type: Factual, Ans: b

123.   Relapse for both bulimia and anorexia is most likely triggered by:
       a.   weight gain.
       b.   life stresses.
       c.   media exposure.
       d.   medication withdrawal.

How Are Eating Disorders Treated?, p. 333
Diff: H, Type: Applied, Ans: b

124.   Relapses of bulimia are most likely to occur following:
       a.   exposure to other bulimics.
       b.   life stresses.
       c.   periods of stomach sickness.
       d.   Christmas and other holidays.

How Are Eating Disorders Treated?, p. 333
Diff: E, Type: Factual, Ans: d

125.   The prognosis for recovery from bulimia nervosa is worse as a function of:
       a.   length of time in treatment.
       b.   age at onset of the disorder.
       c.   age at which treatment is implemented.
       d.   development of a pattern of frequent vomiting.

Putting It Together, p. 333
Diff: H, Type: Factual, Ans: c

126.   National telephone hot lines, Web sites, professional referrals, newsletters, workshops, and
       conferences designed to help people deal with eating disorders tend to:
       a.   be organized by medical researchers.
       b.   be led by nurses and other medical personnel.
       c.   be patient-run.
       d.   be sponsored by pharmaceutical companies.

FILL-IN QUESTIONS

Anorexia Nervosa, p. 310
Diff: E, Type: Factual, Ans: anorexia nervosa

1.   The disorder characterized by body weight 15 percent below normal and a disturbed body image is called _____.

Anorexia Nervosa, p. 310
Diff: M, Type: Factual, Ans: restricting

2.   Anorexia nervosa that is characterized exclusively by controlling the intake of food is called _____-type anorexia nervosa.

Anorexia Nervosa, p. 310
Diff: M, Type: Factual, Ans: bulimia nervosa (or binge/purge anorexia nervosa)

3.   Overeating and vomiting characterize _____.

The Clinical Picture, p. 312
Diff: H, Type: Factual, Ans: distorted thinking

4.   An emaciated woman who perceives herself as too fat illustrates _____.

The Clinical Picture, p. 312
Diff: M, Type: Factual, Ans: distorted thinking

5.   People with _____ have a low opinion of their body shape and physical attractiveness.

The Clinical Picture, p. 312
Diff: H, Type: Factual, Ans: obsessive-compulsive disorder

6.   The ritualistic behaviors surrounding food that are characteristic of anorexia nervosa are similar to _____.

Medical Problems, p. 313
Diff: M, Type: Factual, Ans: amenorrhea

7.   The cessation of menstruation common to anorexic women is known as _____.

Bulimia Nervosa, p. 313
Diff: M, Type: Factual, Ans: nonpurging

8.   Bulimia nervosa that is characterized by binge eating and then frantic exercise to work off the food is called _____ bulimia nervosa.

Bulimia Nervosa vs. Anorexia Nervosa, p. 318
Diff: E, Type: Factual, Ans: bulimia nervosa

9.   Dental problems are a possible medical complication of long-term _____.

What Causes Eating Disorders?, p. 318
Diff: M, Type: Factual, Ans: sociocultural

10.   Society's emphasis on female thinness helps create a strong predisposition toward eating disorders, according to _____ theorists.

Sociocultural Landscape: Is Body Image a Matter of Race?, pp. 320-321 (Box 11-3)
Diff: H, Type: Factual, Ans: white; African American
11.   In pre-1995 studies of eighth- and ninth-grade girls, 90 percent of the _____ respondents were unhappy with their bodies, while 70 percent of the _____ respondents were satisfied with their bodies.

Family Environment, p. 322
Diff: H, Type: Factual, Ans: enmeshed
12.   According to Minuchin, a(n) _____ family system is one in which members are overly concerned with each other's affairs.

Biological Factors, p. 325
Diff: M, Type: Factual, Ans: appetite suppressants
13.   The function in the body of glucagonlike peptide-1 is to act as natural _____.

Biological Factors, p. 325
Diff: E, Type: Factual, Ans: weight set point
14.   The weight to which a person's body naturally returns after a diet is known as his or her _____.

How Are Eating Disorders Treated?, p. 325
Diff: M, Type: Factual, Ans: Supportive nursing care
15.   _____ is a therapy program conducted in a hospital ward. It emphasizes educating anorexic patients, encouraging them, and providing a structured program for weight gain.

Obesity: To Lose or Not to Lose, pp. 326-327 (Box 11-4)
Diff: E, Type: Factual, Ans: rebound effect
16.   Gaining weight after a diet is over is called the _____.

Treatments for Bulimia Nervosa, p. 331
Diff: H, Type: Factual, Ans: exposure and response prevention
17.   In the therapy approach called _____, a therapist exposes a bulimic patient to binge-inducing stimuli and then prevents binge eating.

Treatments for Bulimia Nervosa, p. 332
Diff: M, Type: Factual, Ans: Antidepressant
18.   _____ medication has been shown to be particularly effective with bulimia nervosa.

ESSAY QUESTIONS

No Specific Topic, No Specific Page
Diff: M, Type: Factual
1.   Identify the similarities and differences in anorexia and bulimia.

Bulimia Nervosa, p. 313
Diff: M, Type: Applied
2.   Describe the behaviors a purging-type bulimic and a nonpurging-type bulimic would display.

Societal Pressures, p. 319
Diff: E, Type: Applied

3.   Some people feel that our society has become obsessed with thinness. What are three distinctly different types of evidence you could use to support this claim?

Societal Pressures, p. 319
Diff: H, Type: Applied

4.   If you were developing an educational eating disorders prevention program for 10- to 13-year-old-girls, what would be your goals? Be sure to think about all of the areas that are suspected causes of eating disorders.

No Specific Topic, No Specific Page
Diff: H, Type: Applied

5.   Give examples of at least two societal, familial, and biological conditions (six in all) that put one at risk for an eating disorder.

Sociocultural Landscape: Is Body Image a Matter of Race?, pp. 320-321 (Box 11-3)
Diff: H, Type: Applied

6.   Is body image a matter of race? Outline how someone might answer this question pre-1955 and post-1955, according to your textbook.

Mood Disorders, p. 324
Diff: H, Type: Applied

7.   It might be that bulimia causes depression or that depression helps cause bulimia. It might also be that both depression and bulimia are caused by something else. What might that "something else" be from a biological point of view?

How Are Eating Disorders Treated?, p. 325ff
Diff: M, Type: Applied

8.   Sketch out a treatment plan for one experiencing anorexia. Make sure to take into account both the immediate and long-term treatment needs.

How Are Eating Disorders Treated?, p. 329ff
Diff: H, Type: Applied

9.   How successful is treatment for anorexia? What can we anticipate about the long-term adjustment of one who has had anorexia, both medically and psychologically?

How Are Eating Disorders Treated?, p. 331
Diff: H, Type: Applied

10.   Imagine that you are a behavioral clinician treating someone with bulimia. What would be your treatment goals and what techniques would you use?

CHAPTER 12   Substance-Related Disorders

MULTIPLE-CHOICE QUESTIONS

Substance-Related Disorders, p. 338
Diff: M, Type: Factual, Ans: d
1. The hallucinations and distortions of perception some drugs produce are called:
   a. intoxication.
   b. substance dependence.
   c. substance abuse.
   d. hallucinosis.

Substance-Related Disorders, p. 338
Diff: H, Type: Factual, Ans: c
2. Which of the following would be considered a "drug"?
   a. heroin
   b. caffeine
   c. both caffeine and heroin
   d. neither caffeine nor heroin

Substance-Related Disorders, p. 338
Diff: H, Type: Applied, Ans: b
3. A college professor's work performance recently has deteriorated, and the professor's colleagues find the professor difficult to talk to. If this is due to a problem with drugs, the best description of this professor's behavior as detailed above would be:
   a. substance dependence.
   b. substance abuse.
   c. tolerance.
   d. withdrawal.

Substance-Related Disorders, p. 338
Diff: E, Type: Factual, Ans: b
4. A frequent drug user finds that more and more drug is necessary to produce the same "high" that much lower doses once produced. That drug user is developing:
   a. withdrawal symptoms.
   b. tolerance.
   c. hallucinosis.
   d. intoxication.

Substance-Related Disorders, p. 338
Diff: M, Type: Factual, Ans: c

5.   The long-term pattern of maladaptive behavior caused by the regular use of some chemical or
      drug is called:
      a.   tolerance.
      b.   addiction.
      c.   substance abuse.
      d.   hallucinosis.

Substance-Related Disorders, p. 338
Diff: E, Type: Applied, Ans: b

6.   Melanie has taken a lot of the drug that she was offered and in spite of being obviously
      uncoordinated and under the influence she wants to drive her car. Her condition is an
      example of:
      a.   addiction.
      b.   intoxication.
      c.   hallucinosis.
      d.   physical dependence.

Substance-Related Disorders, p. 338
Diff: E, Type: Factual, Ans: b

7.   Intoxication is actually a form of:
      a.   tolerance.
      b.   poisoning.
      c.   hallucination.
      d.   substance dependence.

Substance-Related Disorders, p. 338
Diff: E, Type: Applied, Ans: a

8.   Mendon began by taking one amphetamine a day to control his appetite. After a month or so
      it did not work as well but two pills did. This is an example of:
      a.   tolerance.
      b.   resistance.
      c.   withdrawal.
      d.   dependence.

Substance-Related Disorders, p. 338
Diff: E, Type: Applied, Ans: b

9.   Jenny simply cannot get up in the morning without her uppers, those little amphetamine pills
      her friend gave her. She feels she must take them every day. She has:
      a.   a drug tolerance.
      b.   a substance dependence.
      c.   an organic mental syndrome.
      d.   developed a tolerance for the drug.

Substance-Related Disorders, p. 339
Diff: M, Type: Applied, Ans: a

10.   Which of the following is a depressant?
   a.   opioids
   b.   cocaine
   c.   LSD
   d.   amphetamines

Depressants, p. 339
Diff: E, Type: Applied, Ans: a

11.   A newly developed drug causes users to lose some muscle control, slurring their speech and slowing central nervous system activity. Most likely this new drug is a:
   a.   depressant.
   b.   hallucinogen.
   c.   stimulant.
   d.   polydrug.

Depressants, p. 339
Diff: H, Type: Factual, Ans: b

12.   Hallucinogens would include which of the following?
   a.   cocaine
   b.   LSD
   c.   both LSD and cocaine
   d.   neither LSD nor cocaine

Alcohol, p. 339
Diff: M, Type: Factual, Ans: d

13.   Alcohol works as a central nervous system depressant by:
   a.   stimulating the release of inhibitory neurotransmitters.
   b.   blocking the release of inhibitory neurotransmitters.
   c.   unbinding receptors on neurons.
   d.   binding to receptors on neurons.

Alcohol, p. 339
Diff: H, Type: applied, Ans: a

14.   If all you know about someone is that the person has been binge drinking in the past month, then you know the person had at least:
   a.   five drinks at a time at least once, and probably is a male.
   b.   five drinks at a time at least once, and probably is female.
   c.   five drinks at a time at least twice, and probably is a male.
   d.   ten drinks at a time at least twice and probably is a male.

Alcohol, p. 340
Diff: H, Type: applied, Ans: b

15.   Of the following people, the one who would probably have the highest blood alcohol level after an hour of drinking would be a:
   a.   100-pound man who had drunk two cans of beer.
   b.   200-pound woman who had drunk six cans of beer.
   c.   200-pound man who had drunk six cans of beer.
   d.   150-pound woman who had drunk three cans of beer.

Alcohol, p. 340
Diff: E, Type: Applied, Ans: c

16. Pat and Jody each have 5 screwdrivers (OJ and vodka). Pat gets very drunk. Jody does not. Which of the following is most likely to be true?
     a.   Pat is older than Jody.
     b.   Pat is healthier than Jody.
     c.   Pat is a woman, Jody is a man.
     d.   Pat is Caucasian, Jody is African American.

Alcohol, p. 340
Diff: H, Type: Factual, Ans: c

17. Women tolerate alcohol less well than men because:
     a.   they have a higher proportion of body fat.
     b.   they drink alcohol in more concentrated forms.
     c.   their stomachs break down alcohol less well.
     d.   they metabolize alcohol in the liver less well.

Alcohol, pp. 340-341
Diff: M, Type: Factual, Ans: c

18. The blood-alcohol level that typically produces the symptoms of intoxication is _____ of the blood volume.
     a.   .01%
     b.   .06%
     c.   .09%
     d.   .55%

Alcohol, p. 341
Diff: H, Type: Applied, Ans: c

19. A person has ingested enough ethyl alcohol to lose consciousness, but not enough to produce death. The most probable alcohol concentration in that person, expressed as a percent of blood volume is:
     a.   .03.
     b.   .09.
     c.   .40.
     d.   .70.

Alcohol, p. 341
Diff: M, Type: Applied, Ans: b

20. A friend of yours who has been doing some recent heavy drinking asks you what to do to "sober up" as quickly as possible. Your best answer would be:
     a.   "drink hot coffee, with or without cream or sugar."
     b.   "stop drinking."
     c.   "rest with a cold towel wrapped around your head."
     d.   "drink carbonated soda."

Alcohol, p. 341
Diff: M, Type: Factual, Ans: a

21.   Of the following, the one most likely to be alcoholic would be a young adult:
       a.   white male.
       b.   African American male.
       c.   white female.
       d.   African American female.

Alcohol, p. 341
Diff: H, Type: Applied, Ans: c

22.   Two people of the same gender and weight consume the same amount of alcohol in the same amount of time. Nevertheless, one of them sobers up substantially sooner than the other. Most likely, this difference is due to:
       a.   the form in which they consumed the alcohol: beer versus wine, for instance.
       b.   personality: for example, Type B people usually sober up quicker than Type A people.
       c.   liver function: some people's livers metabolize alcohol faster than those of others'.
       d.   breathing rate: those who breathe more often can exhale the carbon-dioxide byproduct of alcohol metabolism faster.

Alcohol, p. 342
Diff: M, Type: Applied, Ans: c

23.   A full-time college student has just become a college dropout. The chances that alcohol was a factor in the dropout is about:
       a.   one in twenty.
       b.   one in ten.
       c.   one in four.
       d.   one in two.

Alcohol, p. 342
Diff: H, Type: Applied, Ans: d

24.   One study shows that, in "substance-free" dorms, the percent of students who are binge drinkers is:
       a.   less than one-tenth the percent of students, nationwide, who are binge drinkers.
       b.   about one-quarter the percent of students, nationwide, who are binge drinkers.
       c.   about one-half the percent of students, nationwide, who are binge drinkers.
       d.   well over one-half the percent of students, nationwide, who are binge drinkers.

Alcohol, p. 342
Diff: H, Type: Applied, Ans: a

25.   Perhaps the most important criticism of studies of binge drinking is that they:
       a.   rely on students' self-reports.
       b.   are based on very small sample sizes (usually fewer than 100 participants).
       c.   include only those who are 18 (the age of consent) or older.
       d.   are conducted by those who oppose drinking on campus.

Alcohol, Box, p. 342
Diff: E, Type: Factual, Ans: d

26. According to a recent study by Henry Wechsler and his colleagues at the Harvard School of Public Health, the best predictor of college binge drinking is:
    a. being an athlete.
    b. being a white male.
    c. having a business major.
    d. living in a fraternity or sorority house.

Alcohol, p. 343
Diff: E, Type: Applied, Ans: b

27 Wes has a drink in the morning upon rising. He has a cocktail with breakfast. He usually sneaks a snort during the morning ("just to get through the day") and then drinks during his lunch. When he gets home after work he goes to a singles bar and immediately has a drink to ease his nerves about approaching the women there. Later, at home, he generally has a small dinner and then sits in front of the TV watching sports and drinking beer (as many as 12 cans). Somehow he manages to get up and go to work the next morning. Wes is displaying:
    a. withdrawal.
    b. alcohol abuse.
    c. binge drinking.
    d. delirium tremens.

Alcohol, p. 343
Diff: M, Type: Applied, Ans: c

28. A person's hands and eyelids are shaking, and that person is experiencing visual and tactile hallucinations. Of the following, that person is most likely experiencing:
    a. Korsakoff's syndrome.
    b. narcotic attraction.
    c. delirium tremens.
    d. cannabis toxicity.

Alcohol, p. 343
Diff: E, Type: Factual, Ans: b

29. The severe withdrawal symptoms seen in alcohol withdrawal are known as:
    a. intoxication.
    b. delirium tremens.
    c. deleterious tremors.
    d. alcohol-induced psychotic disorder.

Alcohol, p. 343
Diff: H, Type: Applied, Ans: d

30. An individual who is dependent on alcohol is experiencing delirium tremens. This reaction is:
    a. common, starting about a week after an individual stops drinking.
    b. common, starting within three days after an individual stops drinking.
    c. uncommon, starting about a week after an individual stops drinking.
    d. uncommon, starting within three days after an individual stops drinking.

Alcohol, p. 343
Diff: H, Type: Applied, Ans: b

31.   A person you know has just started experiencing delirium tremens. Probably they will last:
        a.   two or three days, with no significant health risk.
        b.   two or three days, with a significant risk of problems like seizure or stroke.
        c.   about a week, with no significant health risk.
        d.   about a week, with a significant risk of problems like seizure or stroke.

Alcohol, p. 344
Diff: H, Type: Factual, Ans: c

32.   In what proportion of suicides and rapes in the U.S. does alcoholism play a role?
        a.   one-tenth
        b.   one-quarter
        c.   one-third
        d.   over one half

Alcohol, p. 344
Diff: E, Type: Factual, Ans: a

33.   The scarring of the liver caused by alcohol consumption is known as:
        a.   cirrhosis.
        b.   hemorrhaging.
        c.   vasoconstriction.
        d.   Korsakoff's syndrome.

Alcohol, p. 344
Diff: H, Type: Applied, Ans: d

34.   A patient in an alcohol rehabilitation center tells you a detailed story about growing up in the
        mountains of Tennessee. Later, you find out that the person in fact never even visited
        Tennessee. A day later you visit the patient again, and the patient does not recognize you.
        Most likely, the patient is suffering from:
        a.   fetal alcohol syndrome.
        b.   cirrhosis.
        c.   withdrawal of delirium.
        d.   Korsakoff's syndrome.

Alcohol, p. 344
Diff: M, Type: Factual, Ans: c

35.   A combination of alcohol abuse and a vitamin-B deficiency can lead to:
        a.   delirium tremens.
        b.   Tourette's syndrome.
        c.   Korsakoff's Syndrome.
        d.   alcohol-induced psychotic disorder.

Alcohol, p. 344
Diff: M, Type: Applied, Ans: a

36. Kelly is a long-time serious drinker. In the last year she has started having huge memory lapses. When this happens she makes up wild stories to help her fill in what she does not remember. This syndrome is called:
    a. confabulation.
    b. Korsakoff's syndrome.
    c. Wernicke's encephalospathy.
    d. alcohol-induced psychotic disorder.

Alcohol, p. 344
Diff: E, Type: Factual, Ans: c

37. Drinking alcohol during pregnancy can damage the developing embryo and fetus, resulting in:
    a. excessively large babies.
    b. Sudden Infant Death Syndrome.
    c. fetal alcohol syndrome.
    d. neonatal Korsakoff's syndrome.

Sedative-Hypnotic Drugs, p. 344
Diff: M, Type: Factual, Ans: d

38. Nan took the drug she was handed and in a few minutes felt calm and drowsy, and then went to sleep. She probably took:
    a. heroin.
    b. cocaine.
    c. cannabis.
    d. a barbiturate.

Sedative-Hypnotic Drugs, p. 344
Diff: M, Type: Applied, Ans: b

39. A pattern of mental retardation, head and facial deformities, heart defects, and slow growth characterizes one with:
    a. Korsakoff's syndrome.
    b. fetal alcohol syndrome.
    c. alcohol abuse syndrome.
    d. substance abuse syndrome.

Sedative-Hypnotic Drugs, p. 344
Diff: M, Type: Factual, Ans: c

40. Barbiturates were first prescribed to help people:
    a. diet.
    b. deal with the stresses of war.
    c. sleep.
    d. deal with pain.

Sedative-Hypnotic Drugs, pp. 344-345
Diff: E, Type: Factual, Ans: c
41.   All of the following are sedative-hypnotic drugs except:
    a.   barbiturates.
    b.   benzodiazepines.
    c.   opiates.
    d.   Xanax and Valium.

Sedative-Hypnotic Drugs, p. 345
Diff: H, Type: Factual, Ans: d
42.   The part of the brain that appears to be affected by high doses of barbiturates is the:
    a.   pons.
    b.   septum.
    c.   cerebellum.
    d.   reticular formation.

Sedative-Hypnotic Drugs, p. 345
Diff: H, Type: Factual, Ans: a
43.   Barbiturates primarily affect the neurotransmitter:
    a.   GABA.
    b.   serotonin.
    c.   dopamine.
    d.   norepinephrine.

Sedative-Hypnotic Drugs, p. 345
Diff: H, Type: Factual, Ans: c
44.   Because of the likelihood of convulsions, withdrawal from _____ is especially dangerous.
    a.   heroin
    b.   cocaine
    c.   barbiturates
    d.   amphetamine

Opioids, p. 345
Diff: H, Type: Applied, Ans: a
45.   A wounded veteran of the U.S. Civil War suffering from "soldiers' disease" most likely was suffering from:
    a.   morphine dependence.
    b.   THC-induced symptoms from wound binding made of hemp cloth.
    c.   alcohol dependence.
    d.   cirrhosis caused by drinking medicine dissolved in ethyl alcohol.

Opioids, p. 345
Diff: M, Type: Applied, Ans: c
46.   If a physician wanted to relieve anxiety with a lesser risk of drowsiness, overdose, and slowed breathing, the physician would prescribe:
    a.   barbiturates.
    b.   alcohol.
    c.   benzodiazepines.
    d.   cocaine.

Opioids, p. 345
Diff: H, Type: Applied, Ans: d

47.   "A powerful remedy for coughs," stated an advertisement in a 1903 medical journal, referring to a drug developed by the Elberfeld Company, called:
      a.   morphine.
      b.   benzodiazepine.
      c.   cocaine.
      d.   heroin.

Opioids, p. 346
Diff: H, Type: Applied, Ans: a

48.   A friend says, "I want to minimize my risks of organ damage and long-lasting mental change," and then asks, " What kind of drug should I most avoid?" Your best answer is:
      a.   "Alcohol."
      b.   "Opioids."
      c.   "Stimulants, especially amphetamines."
      d.   "Barbiturates."

Opioids, p. 346
Diff: H, Type: Applied, Ans: c

49.   The drug with the lowest risks for drug dependency and long-term behavioral change is:
      a.   amphetamines.
      b.   alcohol.
      c.   cannabis.
      d.   barbiturates.

Opioids, p. 346
Diff: M, Type: Applied, Ans: a

50.   After the accident, Kendra was taken to the hospital with broken legs and arms. They almost immediately gave her a shot that reduced her pain. The shot was probably:
      a.   morphine.
      b.   a sedative.
      c.   a barbiturate.
      d.   an amphetamine.

Opioids, p. 346
Diff: M, Type: Factual, Ans: a

51.   All the opioid drugs are known as:
      a.   narcotics.
      b.   endorphins.
      c.   depressants.
      d.   hallucinogens.

Opioids, p. 346
Diff: H, Type: Applied, Ans: d
52. Unlike the opioid drugs morphine and heroin, methadone:
     a. is not a narcotic.
     b. is a central nervous system depressor.
     c. causes nausea.
     d. is synthetic.

Opioids, p. 346
Diff: E, Type: Applied, Ans: b
53. Serina has just had a shot of heroin. She feels intense pleasure very quickly. This is:
     a. a nod.
     b. a rush.
     c. a high.
     d. intoxication.

Opioids, p. 346
Diff: E, Type: Factual, Ans: b
54. The drug which, when misused, would most quickly result in dependence or addiction would be:
     a. Xanax.
     b. opium.
     c. cannabis.
     d. ethyl alcohol.

Opioids, p. 346
Diff: E, Type: Factual, Ans: a
55. The drug which would produce effects similar to what the neurotransmitters called endorphins produce—pleasurable, calming feelings—is:
     a. heroin.
     b. LSD.
     c. Benzedrine.
     d. methamphetamine.

Opioids, p. 346
Diff: M, Type: Applied, Ans: a
56. During his first night in the detoxification unit, Quent developed what seemed like a case of the flu. He ached all over and had diarrhea. He was probably withdrawing from:
     a. heroin.
     b. alcohol.
     c. cocaine.
     d. cannabis.

Opioids, p. 346
Diff: E, Type: Applied, Ans: b
57. A person who has injected a narcotic feels relaxed, happy, and unconcerned about food, sex, or other bodily needs. This person is experiencing what is known as:
     a. a rush.
     b. a high.
     c. free-basing.
     d. endorphin release.

Opioids, p. 347
Diff: H, Type: Applied, Ans: a
58.   A heroin overdose is likely to occur when:
    a.   one has been without heroin for a period of time and takes one's usual dose.
    b.   one consistently takes the same dose of heroin.
    c.   one gradually, but consistently takes larger doses of heroin.
    d.   one has been without heroin for a period of time and takes a lower than usual dose.

Opioids, p. 347
Diff: H, Type: Factual, Ans: d
59.   Why is the risk of transmitting AIDS an important factor for heroin users?
    a.   because heroin facilitates the body's receptivity to AIDS
    b.   because heroin lowers immune system function
    c.   because heroin is a good medium in which viruses can grow
    d.   because heroin users often share dirty needles infected with the AIDS virus

Stimulants, p. 347
Diff: E, Type: Applied, Ans: c
60.   A person would be least likely to feel drowsy soon after taking a moderate dose of which type of drug?
    a.   barbiturates
    b.   ethyl alcohol
    c.   amphetamines
    d.   opium

Stimulants, p. 347
Diff: H, Type: Factual, Ans: a
61.   Cocaine and amphetamines produce:
    a.   similar behavioral effects, and similar emotional effects.
    b.   similar behavioral effects, but different emotional effects.
    c.   different behavioral effects, but similar emotional effects.
    d.   different behavioral effects, and different emotional effects.

Stimulants, p. 347
Diff: m, Type: Applied, Ans: d
62.   In the past 25 years, the rate of opioid addiction in the United States has:
    a.   increased steadily.
    b.   decreased steadily.
    c.   remained relatively constant.
    d.   gone down and up at least twice.

Stimulants, p. 348
Diff: H, Type: Applied, Ans: b
63.   A person who recently injected cocaine reports reaching the peak of subjective euphoria. Usually, that euphoria:
    a.   precedes the peak of dopamine-using neuron activity by about five minutes.
    b.   occurs at about the same time as the peak of dopamine-using neuron activity.
    c.   follows the peak of dopamine-using neuron activity by about five minutes.
    d.   follows the peak of dopamine-using neuron activity by at least ten minutes.

Stimulants, p 348
Diff: H, Type: Applied, Ans: b

64. An individual who has recently taken a drug angrily grabs some car keys and attempts to drive home. The person appears anxious, and keeps bragging that driving the car won't really be that difficult. Most likely, that person is experiencing:
   a. delirium tremens.
   b. cocaine intoxication.
   c. decreasing cross-tolerance.
   d. hallucinosis.

Stimulants, p. 348
Diff: M, Type: Applied, Ans: c

65. Mario felt awake and alive and as though he could conquer the world after taking:
   a. heroin.
   b. alcohol.
   c. cocaine.
   d. a barbiturate.

Stimulants, p. 348
Diff: M, Type: Factual, Ans: b

66. About what percent of the population becomes dependent on cocaine at some point in their lives?
   a. 1%
   b. 3%
   c. 5%
   d. 10%

Stimulants, p. 349
Diff: M, Type: Factual, Ans: b

67. The withdrawal symptoms that persist for more than a few weeks are likely to result from addiction to:
   a. heroin.
   b. cocaine.
   c. marijuana.
   d. barbiturates.

Stimulants, p. 349
Diff: M, Type: Applied, Ans: a

68. Ellen stopped taking her regular amount of cocaine after using it for months. She will probably experience:
   a. letdown, depressed feelings, and fatigue.
   b. pain, sweating, mania, and nausea.
   c. excitement, insomnia, and hallucinations.
   d. dramatic tremors of the hands and face, very rapid heart rate, and convulsions.

Stimulants, p. 349
Diff: H, Type: Applied, Ans: a
69. Free-basing has the effect of making cocaine:
     a. more concentrated.
     b. able to be injected.
     c. cheaper.
     d. condense into a liquid.

Stimulants, p. 349
Diff: H, Type: Applied, Ans: a
70. "Why is crack becoming more popular in the high schools?" a friend asks. Your best data-based reply is:
     a. "Because it's relatively cheap and fast acting."
     b. "Because it's relatively cheap, with a prolonged effect."
     c. "Because it's less addictive than snorted or injected cocaine."
     d. "Because it's less likely to produce overdose effects than snorted or injected cocaine."

Stimulants, p. 350
Diff: H, Type: Applied, Ans: d
71. If you were trying to convince a friend not to be a cocaine user, what would you cite as the greatest risk coming from cocaine use?
     a. being assaulted in drug-related crimes
     b. contracting AIDS
     c. damage to mucus membranes
     d. overdose effects

Amphetamines, p. 350
Diff: E, Type: Factual, Ans: d
72. Lola's physician prescribed diet pills. Which of the following drugs are they most likely to have contained?
     a. cocaine
     b. morphine
     c. barbiturates
     d. amphetamines

Amphetamines, p. 350
Diff: H, Type: Factual, Ans: d
73. Amphetamine users run an unusually high risk of becoming dependent because amphetamines:
     a. inhibit the release of neurotransmitters.
     b. prevent the body from experiencing identifiable withdrawal effects.
     c. produce feelings of euphoria, along with pleasant auditory distortions.
     d. produce drug tolerance very quickly.

Tobacco, Nicotine, and Addiction, p. 351 (Box 12-2)
Diff: M, Type: Factual, Ans: b
74. The proportion of Americans over the age of 12 who smoke is about:
     a. 10%.
     b. 25%.
     c. 50%.
     d. 60%.

Tobacco, Nicotine, and Addiction, p. 351
Diff: H, Type, Applied, Ans: c

75.   A friend asks you for advice about how to stop smoking. Based on the data, your best advice
        to your friend would be:
        a.   "Try a self-help kit, and stick with it. Most people who try to quit smoking succeed only
             if they can quit on their first try."
        b.   "Try a self-help kit, then try it again and again. Most people who try to quit smoking
             succeed only after they've failed to quit several times."
        c.   "Try aversion therapy, for example, rapid smoking."
        d.   "Support groups have the best long-term results."

Tobacco, Nicotine, and Addiction, p. 351
Diff: M, Type: Applied, Ans: b

76.   Methods of supplying nicotine to those who are trying to quit smoking include all of the
        following except:
        a.   nicotine nasal spray.
        b.   the subcutaneous nicotine pump.
        c.   the nicotine patch.
        d.   nicotine gum.

Caffeine, p. 352
Diff: H, Type: Applied, Ans: c

77.   A drug in pill form, designed to promote "alertness," has as its only active ingredient 100
        milligrams of caffeine. If brewed coffee sells at a local convenience store for $1 per cup, how
        much would you have to spend to get the same amount of caffeine as in two pills of the
        "alertness" drug?
        a. $.50¢ (if they let you buy a half-cup of coffee!)
        b. $1
        c. $2
        d. $4

Caffeine, p. 352
Diff: E, Type: Factual, Ans: d

78.   The stimulant used by more people in the world than any other is:
        a.   nicotine.
        b.   cocaine (including free-based and crack forms).
        c.   amphetamines.
        d.   caffeine.

Caffeine, p. 352
Diff: M, Type: Applied, Ans: d

79.   How many cups of coffee would one have to drink to produce seizures and respiratory or
        circulatory failure?
        a.   10
        b.   25
        c.   50
        d.   100

Caffeine, p. 352
Diff: M, Type: Factual, Ans: c
80.   Consumption of which drug has decreased among Americans since the mid-1980s?
       a.   cocaine
       b.   ethyl alcohol
       c.   caffeine
       d.   LSD

Hallucinogens, p. 353
Diff: M, Type: Applied, Ans: a
81.   A person who took a drug an hour or two ago sits alone, quietly and intensely listening—so
       the person says—to the sap running in a tree, the leaves of which appear a brilliant purple to
       the drug user. Most likely, the person has recently used:
       a.   LSD.
       b.   cocaine.
       c.   marijuana.
       d.   methamphetamine.

Hallucinogens, p. 353
Diff: M, Type: Applied, Ans: a
82.   While under the influence of LSD, Matilda believes that she can feel the sounds around her.
       This effect is known as:
       a.   synesthesia.
       b.   intoxication.
       c.   hallucination.
       d.   the psychedelic effect.

Hallucinogens, p. 353
Diff: M, Type: Applied, Ans: a
83.   What is the risk of tolerance and physical addiction to hallucinogens as compared to other
       addictive drugs?
       a.   minimal
       b.   more than most
       c.   about the same as the depressants
       d.   about the same as the stimulants

Hallucinogens, p. 353
Diff: H, Type: Factual, Ans: b
84.   The chief danger of LSD use is:
       a.   the risk of developing drug tolerance.
       b.   the possibility of very powerful, sometimes negative, reactions.
       c.   the severity of withdrawal symptoms among even occasional users.
       d.   the universal occurrence of "flashbacks" among former users.

Hallucinogens, p. 353
Diff: H, Type: Applied, Ans: b

85.   A person takes a drug at noon. Although remaining awake and alert, the person experiences poor coordination, palpitations, and greatly enhanced visual perceptions. By dinner, the symptoms have pretty well subsided. Most likely, that person:
   a.   had at least four beers.
   b.   took LSD.
   c.   injected heroin.
   d.   took a dose of barbiturates.

X Marks the (Wrong) Spot, pp. 354-355 (Box 12-3)
Diff: M, Type: Applied, Ans: d

86.   At the "rave," a student took a drug which caused a great burst of energy, along with badly distorted visual experiences. Most likely, the drug the student took was:
   a.   cannabis (smoked).
   b.   cannabis (ingested).
   c.   Xanax.
   d.   Ecstasy.

X Marks the (Wrong) Spot, pp. 354-355 (Box 12-3)
Diff: H, Type: Applied, Ans: a

87.   Months after last taking a drug, a former drug abuser still produces very little serotonin. The person is depressed and anxious, and has great difficulty remembering new material. Most likely, the abused drug–if it were a single drug–was:
   a.   Ecstasy.
   b.   cannabis.
   c.   LSD.
   d.   benzodiazepine.

Cannabis, p. 355
Diff: E, Type: Factual, Ans: b

88.   The most powerful form of cannabis is:
   a.   ganja.
   b.   hashish.
   c.   marijuana.
   d.   free-based THC.

Cannabis, p. 356
Diff: M, Type: Factual, Ans: b

89.   The duration of most of the effects of cannabis is about:
   a.   1 hour.
   b.   3-6 hours.
   c.   1-2 days.
   d.   a week.

Cannabis, p. 356
Diff: E, Type: Factual, Ans: a

90.   Those who used marijuana in the 1960s were less likely to develop drug dependence than
      users around the year 2000 because marijuana available in the 1960s had:
      a.   much less THC.
      b.   much more THC.
      c.   no hallucinogenic effects.
      d.   more powerful hallucinogenic effects.

Cannabis, p. 356
Diff: M, Type: Applied, Ans: a

91.   A high school student says to you, "What's the big deal about using pot? How can it hurt
      me?" The most accurate reply you could make is:
      a.   "If you're high, you won't be able to remember what you just learned."
      b.   "THC in your body can produce dangerous flashbacks when you get older."
      c.   "Even a moderate dose of THC can produce perceptual distortions and coma."
      d.   "You're right—it really won't affect you much in school."

Cannabis, p. 357
Diff: E, Type: Applied, Ans: a

92.   Which of the following is a negative effect of cannabis use?
      a.   decrease in fertility
      b.   the possibility of stroke
      c.   the possibility of heart attack
      d.   strong withdrawal symptoms upon stopping

Cannabis, p. 357
Diff: H, Type: Applied, Ans: c

93.   Three chronic marijuana users–a "light" user, a "moderate" user, and a "heavy" user–stop
      using marijuana. Several weeks later, the higher-than-normal blood flow, which had occurred
      in the brains of all three prior to quitting, had most likely:
      a.   returned to normal flow levels for all three.
      b.   returned to normal flow levels for the light and moderate users only.
      c.   dropped somewhat for the light and moderate users only, but still remained at too high
           levels.
      d.   dropped somewhat for all three, but remained at too high levels.

Cannabis, p. 357
Diff: M, Type: Applied, Ans: a

94.   Among U.S. teenagers, the percent using cocaine dropped in the late 1980s, then rose again
      through the mid-1990s. This same usage pattern occurred with:
      a.   both alcohol and marijuana.
      b.   alcohol, but not marijuana.
      c.   marijuana, but not alcohol.
      d.   neither marijuana nor alcohol.

Cannabis, p. 358
Diff: H, Type: Applied, Ans: d
95.   If someone opposes the medical use of THC, most likely they do so because:
   a.   scientific research shows no legitimate medical application of THC.
   b.   the physiological side effects substantially outweigh the known medical benefits.
   c.   "medical use" is just a euphemism for "legalized pot."
   d.   of legal or moral reasons.

Cannabis, p. 358
Diff: M, Type: Factual, Ans: b
96.   Opponents of the medical use of THC in the U.S. include:
   a.   the federal government and the American Medical Association.
   b.   the federal government, but not the American Medical Association.
   c.   the American Medical Association, but not the federal government.
   d.   neither the federal government nor the American Medical Association.

Combination of Substances, p. 359
Diff: H, Type: Applied, Ans: c
97.   An alcoholic in the midst of delirium tremens is given benzodiazepine to help deal with alcohol withdrawal. The alcoholic has experienced:
   a.   a synergistic effect.
   b.   polysubstance abuse.
   c.   cross-tolerance.
   d.   "compassionate use."

Combination of Substances, p. 359
Diff: M, Type: Applied, Ans: d
98.   Probably the worst thing someone who has "partied hard" with alcohol could do right after drinking would be to:
   a.   drink 4 or more cups of coffee.
   b.   eat a small to medium-sized meal.
   c.   sleep it off without taking drugs to minimize aftereffects.
   d.   take some barbiturates to fall asleep.

Combination of Substances, p. 359
Diff: H, Type: Applied, Ans: a
99.   Barry drank quite a lot at the biggest party of the year. Later, he had trouble falling asleep, so he took a barbiturate. If he dies from respiratory failure during the night, it is probably because the alcohol and barbiturate had:
   a.   a synergistic effect.
   b.   antagonistic actions.
   c.   complementary actions.
   d.   a cross-tolerance effect.

Combination of Substances, p. 359
Diff: H, Type: Applied, Ans: c
100.   Which of the following combinations is most likely to result in cross-tolerant effects?
   a.   cocaine and heroin
   b.   cannabis and cocaine
   c.   alcohol and barbiturates
   d.   LSD and benzodiazepines

Combination of Substances, p. 360
Diff: H, Type: Applied, Ans: d
101. Which of the following combinations is most likely to result in antagonistic effects?
      a. LSD and cocaine
      b. alcohol and barbiturates
      c. cocaine and amphetamine
      d. barbiturates and cocaine

Combination of Substances, p. 360
Diff: H, Type: Factual, Ans: d
102. Polysubstance use involving illegal drugs occurs in about what percent of U.S. illegal drug users?
      a. 20%
      b. 40%
      c. 60%
      d. over 60%

The Sociocultural View, p. 360
Diff: H, Type: Applied, Ans: a
103. Which of the following persons would be most likely to be alcoholic?
      a. a lower socioeconomic class person living in a high unemployment area
      b. a lower socioeconomic class person living in a low unemployment area
      c. a higher socioeconomic class person living in a high unemployment area
      d. a higher socioeconomic class person living in a low unemployment area

The Psychodynamic View, p. 361
Diff: M, Type: Factual, Ans: c
104. One longitudinal study found that men who become alcoholics were initially more:
      a. antisocial as adults.
      b. aggressive as children.
      c. impulsive in adolescence.
      d. depressed in adolescence.

The Psychodynamic View, pp. 361-362
Diff: H, Type: Factual, Ans: d
105. Studies attempting to relate personality traits to potential for developing substance abuse show that:
      a. one key personality trait—impulsivity—predicts substance abuse.
      b. one key personality trait—dependence—predicts substance abuse.
      c. a specific group of traits predicts substance abuse.
      d. no single trait or combination of traits predicts substance abuse.

The Behavioral and Cognitive Views, p. 362
Diff: E, Type: Applied, Ans: c
106. "Drug dependence may develop because one finds drug use rewarding when it reduces tension." Which view of substance abuse would applaud this statement most enthusiastically?
      a. biological
      b. sociocultural
      c. behavioral
      d. psychodynamic

The Behavioral and Cognitive Views, p. 362
Diff: H, Type: Applied, Ans: c

107.   A manager who feels anxious about speaking in front of large groups frequently has a couple of glasses of wine to "relax" before beginning to speak. This "medicinal" use of alcohol can be explained most easily:
    a.   by opponent-process theory.
    b.   through molecular biological analysis.
    c.   by reward theory.
    d.   as genetic predisposition.

The Behavioral and Cognitive Views, p. 362
Diff: H, Type: Applied, Ans: d

108.   Assume you have a 14-year-old child who says to you, "Why can't I start drinking? A lot of my friends drink. What's the big deal?" Based on the most up-to-date research, your best answer is:
    a.   "You're right; it really isn't a big deal."
    b.   "It's sort of a big deal; those who start drinking before they're 15 are more likely to develop alcohol abuse, but not alcohol dependence, later in life."
    c.   "It's sort of a big deal; those who start drinking before they're 15 are more likely to develop alcohol dependence, but not alcohol abuse, later in life."
    d.   "It's a big deal; those who start drinking before they're 15 are more likely to develop alcohol abuse and alcohol dependence later in life."

The Behavioral and Cognitive Views, p. 362
Diff: H, Type: Factual, Ans: d

109.   The fastest way to get a drug to the brain is:
    a.   snorting.
    b.   injection.
    c.   ingestion.
    d.   inhalation.

The Behavioral and Cognitive Views, p. 363
Diff: H, Type: Applied, Ans: c

110.   Daniel, an intravenous heroin user, feels intense cravings when he sees hypodermic needles. This might be an example of:
    a.   modeling.
    b.   operant conditioning.
    c.   classical conditioning.
    d.   observational learning.

The Behavioral and Cognitive Views, p. 363
Diff: H, Type: Factual, Ans: a

111.   The ideal that stimuli that gives pleasure lead to brain processes that counteract the effects of that pleasure is consistent with an explanation for drug use based on:
    a.   opponent processes.
    b.   operant conditioning.
    c.   classical conditioning.
    d.   psychodynamic principles.

The Biological View, pp. 363-364
Diff: H, Type: Applied, Ans: a

112. If genetics plays a strong role in the development of cocaine abuse, we would expect to find the lowest concordance rates for cocaine abuse among:
     a. genetically unrelated pairs of people.
     b. parents and their children.
     c. identical twins.
     d. siblings of the same gender.

The Biological View, p. 364
Diff: M, Type: Factual, Ans: b

113. Adoption studies of alcoholics' children have uncovered:
     a. no genetic predisposition to alcohol.
     b. a significant genetic component to alcohol.
     c. a significant environmental component to alcoholism.
     d. a significant genetic-environment interaction in the etiology of alcoholism.

The Biological View, p. 364
Diff: M, Type: Factual, Ans: b

114. Chronic and excessive use of benzodiazepines may cause the:
     a. increased production of GABA.
     b. decreased production of GABA.
     c. decreased breakdown of GABA.
     d. increased growth of GABA-producing cells.

The Biological View, p. 364
Diff: H, Type: Applied, Ans: b

115. Assume a researcher finds that overuse of a drug reduces the body's production of neurotransmitters. Thus, if an abuser of this drug stops taking the drug, withdrawal symptoms occur until the brain begins producing normal levels of neurotransmitters again. Such a finding would most directly support which view of the cause of substance-abuse disorders?
     a. sociocultural
     b. biochemical
     c. opponent-process
     d. behavioral

The Biological View, p. 364
Diff: H, Type: Factual, Ans: c

116. Research indicates that the most important neurotransmitter in the "pleasure pathway" of the brain is probably:
     a. acetylcholine.
     b. anandamide.
     c. dopamine.
     d. one of the endorphins.

How Are Substance-Related Disorders Treated?, p. 365
Diff: M, Type: Applied, Ans: c

117. Which of the following has been identified as a problem in designing and evaluating treatment methods for substance abuse?
    a. Virtually all patients relapse.
    b. Antagonistic drugs are not legal.
    c. It has been difficult to precisely define treatment success.
    d. The problem is a biological one and does not respond to psychological treatment.

Behavioral Therapies, p. 365
Diff: H, Type: Applied, Ans: a

118. Vivian is required to imagine feces in her glass each time she thinks she would like a drink. This is most like:
    a. covert sensitization.
    b. relapse-prevention training.
    c. self-help response training.
    d. behavioral self-control training.

Behavioral Therapies, p. 365
Diff: H, Type: Applied, Ans: d

119. A client being treated for alcohol abuse receives just enough of a drug called curare to produce temporary paralysis just as that client takes a swig of beer. Presumably, sufficient pairings of paralysis and alcohol will reduce the client's desire for alcohol. This procedure is called:
    a. covert sensitization.
    b. contingency training.
    c. relapse-prevention training.
    d. aversion therapy.

Behavioral Therapies, p. 365
Diff: H, Type: Applied, Ans: c

120. Psychodynamic therapies may not be very effective in the treatment of substance-related disorders because:
    a. they teach only new behaviors, not new thought patterns.
    b. they teach only new thought patterns, not new behaviors.
    c. finding the cause of a substance-related disorder is less important than treating the abuse as an independent problem.
    d. psychodynamic therapists unilaterally reject any use of multidimensional treatment programs.

Behavioral Therapies, p. 366
Diff: H, Type: Applied, Ans: b

121. Cocaine abusers on an inpatient ward earn rewards—and eventual release from the program—if they produce periodic urine samples that are free of the drug. The program they are in is a form of:
    a. behavioral self-control training (BSCT).
    b. contingency management.
    c. relapse-prevention training.
    d. detoxification.

Cognitive-Behavioral Therapies / Sociocultural Therapies, pp. 367, 370
Diff: H, Type: Applied, Ans: a

122.   A 25-year-old friend of yours is convinced that abstinence is the only way to get binge drinking under control. With that in mind, you might suggest using:
   a.   Alcoholics Anonymous, but not behavioral self-control training.
   b.   behavioral self-control training, but not Alcoholics Anonymous.
   c.   either Alcoholics Anonymous or behavioral self-control training.
   d.   neither Alcoholics Anonymous nor behavioral self-control training.

Cognitive-Behavioral Therapies, p. 367
Diff: E, Type: Factual, Ans: a

123.   In behavioral self-control training, patients are taught to:
   a.   monitor their own drug intake.
   b.   chastise themselves for relapsing.
   c.   share their feelings with their families.
   d.   mentally pair aversive stimuli with drug intake.

Cognitive-Behavioral Therapies, pp. 367-368
Diff: M, Type: Applied, Ans: c

124.   Jason, a recovering heavy drinker, has been trained to identify the situations that might cause him to drink and to be aware of when he should stop drinking. This approach is known as:
   a.   aversive therapy.
   b.   ego-control therapy.
   c.   relapse prevention training.
   d.   behavioral self-control training.

Biological Treatments, p. 368
Diff: M, Type: Applied, Ans: b

125.   Jess thought she was taking an aspirin. But later when she had a glass of wine and became very nauseated she realized the pill was:
   a.   naloxone.
   b.   disulfiram.
   c.   naltrexone.
   d.   methadone.

Biological Treatments, p. 368
Diff: M, Type: Factual, Ans: b

126.   The purpose of an antagonist drug is to:
   a.   stimulate the client to care about becoming drug-free.
   b.   block the effect of an addictive drug.
   c.   reduce withdrawal effects as one goes off a drug.
   d.   provide a placebo effect to replace the drug effect.

Biological Treatments, p. 369
Diff: M, Type: Factual, Ans: b

127.   The use of narcotic antagonists can be dangerous. This is based on their ability to initiate:
   a.   respiratory failure.
   b.   severe withdrawal.
   c.   neurological damage.
   d.   addiction to the antagonist.

Biological Treatments, p. 369
Diff: H, Type: Factual, Ans: c

128.   The use of methadone in drug maintenance programs is controversial because methadone:
   a.   use increases the risk of contracting AIDS.
   b.   costs over $50 a day per person treated.
   c.   produces withdrawal more difficult than heroin withdrawal.
   d.   needs to be taken several times per day in a rigid schedule.

Sociocultural Therapies, p. 370
Diff: M, Type: Factual, Ans: a

129.   The fact that a self-help group like Alcoholics Anonymous, which provides peer support and specific guidelines, helps many in their struggle with alcoholism, supports most directly which form of therapy?
   a.   sociocultural
   b.   cognitive-behavioral
   c.   psychodynamic
   d.   biological

Sociocultural Therapies, p. 370
Diff: E, Type: Factual, Ans: a

130.   One of the features of Alcoholics Anonymous is:
   a.   peer support.
   b.   residential services.
   c.   alcohol maintenance
   d.   antagonistic medication

Sociocultural Therapies, p. 370
Diff: E, Type: Factual, Ans: a

131.   Hanna goes to a meeting because her husband is an alcoholic who only occasionally can abstain from alcohol. The meetings with other people in similar situations helps her cope. She probably attends meetings of:
   a.   Al Anon.
   b.   Alcoholics Anonymous.
   c.   alcohol maintenance.
   d.   antagonistic medication.

Sociocultural Therapies, p. 370
Diff: E, Type: Factual, Ans: a

132.   Alcoholics Anonymous supports the belief that alcoholics should:
   a.   cease drinking entirely.
   b.   learn to stop after one drink.
   c.   be taught to drink more moderately.
   d.   admit that they are morally reprehensible for drinking.

"In the Beginning," p. 371 (Box 12-5)
Diff: H, Type: Applied, Ans: b

133.   Of the following, the greatest strength of Alcoholics Anonymous is the organization's:
   a.   successful lobbying for more severe penalties for the distribution of alcohol to minors.
   b.   very low cost to its members.
   c.   multimillion-dollar annual support for alcohol dependency research grants.
   d.   endorsement and support of "drying-out" facilities.

"In the Beginning," p. 372
Diff: M, Type: Applied, Ans: d
134.   Recent studies show that gender-sensitive programs for treating substance abuse:
    a.   may not be necessary; substance abusers of different genders have about the same physical and psychological reactions to drugs.
    b.   have some usefulness; substance abusers of different genders have the same physical, but different psychological, reactions to drugs.
    c.   have some usefulness; substance abusers of different genders have different physical, but the same psychological, reactions to drugs.
    d.   may be very useful; substance abusers of different genders have different physical and psychological reactions to drugs.

"In the Beginning," p. 372
Diff: E, Type: Factual, Ans: d
135.   Most evidence for the effectiveness of self-help programs comes from:
    a.   carefully monitored longitudinal studies.
    b.   laboratory experimentation and generalization of findings.
    c.   cross-sectional surveys of self-help program participants.
    d.   testimonials from those who have gone through such a program.

"In the Beginning," p. 373
Diff: H, Type: Factual, Ans: c
136.   A clinician wishes to begin a drug abuse prevention campaign in a community. The most important thing the clinician can do is to:
    a.   concentrate on radio and TV public service announcements.
    b.   enlist the help of those who are admired in the community.
    c.   provide a consistent message across the media about drug abuse.
    d.   obtain permission to focus the campaign in the local high school.

FILL-IN QUESTIONS

Substance-Related Disorders, p. 338
Diff: M, Type: Factual, Ans: dependence
1.   Tom uses alcohol to the point that it is central to his life. As a result, he develops a physical need for the drug. Tom's disorder is known as substance _____.

Alcohol, p. 339
Diff: E, Type: Factual, Ans: depressant
2.   The actual effect of alcohol on the nervous system is that of a(n) _____.

Alcohol, p. 340
Diff: H, Type: Factual, Ans: alcohol dehydrogenase
3.   The enzyme that breaks down ethyl alcohol in the body is _____.

College Binge Drinking: An Extracurricular Crisis, p. 342 (Box 12-1)
Diff: E, Type: Factual, Ans: binge drinking
4.   According to some educators, the number one public health hazard for college students is _____.

Alcohol, p. 344
Diff: M, Type: Factual, Ans: Korsakoff's syndrome
5.   Alcoholism sometimes leads to a disease marked by confusion and extreme memory impairment. This disease is called _____.

Sedative-Hypnotic Drugs, p. 345
Diff: M, Type: Factual, Ans: barbiturates
6.   Withdrawal from any one of the class of drugs called _____ is dangerous because of the possibility of convulsions.

Sedative-Hypnotic Drugs, p. 345
Diff: E, Type: Applied, Ans: withdrawal
7.   When Melody stopped taking barbiturates, she suffered a period of nausea, anxiety, and sleep problems. This phenomenon is known as _____.

Opioids, p. 346
Diff: E, Type: Factual, Ans: rush
8.   After the injection of heroin, a narcotic abuser feels an intense feeling called a _____.

Opioids, p. 346
Diff: E, Type: Factual, Ans: a high (or a nod)
9.   The relatively long-lasting effect of an injection of heroin is called _____.

Opioids, p. 346
Diff: E, Type: Factual, Ans: endorphins
10.   The brain's neurotransmitters that relieve pain are called _____,

Stimulants, p. 347
Diff: M, Type: Applied, Ans: amphetamines
11.   The effects of cocaine are most like those of_____.

Stimulants, p. 349
Diff: E, Type: Factual, Ans: cocaine
12.   Crack is a form of _____.

Stimulants, p. 352
Diff: M, Type: Factual, Ans: depression
13.   The major symptom present after stopping long-term cocaine or amphetamine use is _____.

Caffeine, p. 352
Diff: E, Type: Factual, Ans: caffeine
14.   The most widely used stimulant in the world is _____.

Hallucinogens, p. 353
Diff: E, Type: Applied, Ans: bad trip
15.   Several minutes after Lannie took the sugar cube she began to see horrible and scary things like black bugs eating her finger. She was experiencing a(n) _____.

Hallucinogens, pp. 354-355
Diff: D, Type: Factual, Ans: flashbacks
16.   Even years after taking LSD for the last time, a user may randomly experience _____.

Hallucinogens, pp. 354-355
Diff: E, Type: Applied, Ans: flashback
17.   Willa was watching television when she suddenly saw pretty wavy colors that looked just like her last LSD trip, two years ago. Her experience is an example of a(n) _____.

Cannabis, p. 355
Diff: M, Type: Factual, Ans: THC (or tetrahydrocannabinol)
18.   The most powerful active ingredient in marijuana is _____.

Combination of Substances, p. 359
Diff: H, Type: Factual, Ans: cross-tolerance
19.   While being treated for alcohol dependency, Hilda was given antianxiety drugs to ease her withdrawal symptoms. Helen's physician was using the principle of _____.

Combination of Substances, p. 359
Diff: H, Type: Factual, Ans: synergistic effect
20.   The effect of taking two different drugs may be more than the sum of the two effects. This is called a _____.

The Psychodynamic View, p. 361
Diff: E, Type: Applied, Ans: psychodynamic
21.   Jodi's therapist believes that her drug problem stems from dependence resulting from unresolved conflicts over early relationships with her parents. Her therapist's point of view is _____.

The Behavioral and Cognitive Views, p. 363
Diff: M, Type: Factual, Ans: opponent-process
22.   According to Richard Solomon's _____ theory, drug-induced euphoria leads, upon extensive use, to negative aftereffects that include cravings and withdrawal symptoms.

Behavior Therapies, p. 365
Diff: H, Type: Factual, Ans: aversion therapy
23.   Pairing the craving for a drug with an electric shock is an example of _____.

Cognitive-Behavior Therapies, pp. 367-368
Diff: M, Type: Factual, Ans: relapse-prevention
24.   Learning coping strategies to deal with situations known to stimulate drinking is part of _____ training.

Biological Treatments, p. 368
Diff: M, Type: Applied, Ans: detoxification
25.   When Tod arrived at the center, they gave him a physical and then allowed time for him to go through withdrawal symptoms. This process is called _____.

Biological Treatments, p. 369
Diff: M, Type: Factual, Ans: Methadone
26.   _____ is a drug that has been used as a substitute for heroin in the treatment of addiction.

Biological Treatments, p. 369
Diff: H, Type: Applied, Ans: narcotic antagonist (or naloxone, or cyclazocine)

27.   Within seconds of getting the injection, Glenda (a relatively new heroin user) was in the middle of withdrawal symptoms. The injection was probably a(n) _____.

Sociocultural Treatments, p. 370
Diff: E, Type: Factual, Ans: Alcoholics Anonymous

28.   The best known of the self-help groups for ethyl alcohol abusers is _____.

Sociocultural Treatments, p. 370
Diff: E, Type: Factual, Ans: Al Anon (or Alateen)

29.   The organization that was formed to offer guidance and support to the family members of alcoholics is called _____.

ESSAY QUESTIONS

No Specific Topic, No Specific Pages
Diff: H, Type: Factual

1.   Alcohol is certainly misused or abused in the U.S. more than any other drug. What about alcohol promotes physical and psychological dependence? What are the long-term problems associated with alcohol abuse? Finally, please describe one widely used form of therapy for those struggling with alcohol abuse.

Opioids/Stimulants, pp. 346-349
Diff: M, Type: Factual

2.   Please compare and contrast heroin and cocaine in the following ways: The physiological properties of the drugs; the forms in which the drugs are normally taken; the prevalence of abuse of each.

Tobacco, Nicotine, and Addiction, p. 351 (Box 12-2)
Diff: E, Type: Factual

3.   Why is nicotine abuse so difficult to treat? What are at least two reasonably successful treatments for nicotine abuse (or smoking cigarettes, if you prefer), and why is smoking cessation so desirable, from a purely physical standpoint?

Caffeine, p. 352
Diff: E, Type: Applied

4.   A friend says to you, "Why worry about caffeine abuse? The drug isn't very powerful, and besides, it's legal!" Please refute your friend's nonchalance about caffeine, being sure to describe relevant studies.

Hallucinogens/Cannabis, pp. 353, 355-357
Diff: H, Type: Factual

5.   Why is there a separate listing for "cannabis substances" in DSM-IV-TR? Why aren't marijuana products simply listed in the "hallucinogens" category? In answering these questions, please use smoked marijuana and LSD to make your comparisons between the two categories.

Hallucinogens, pp. 353-355
Diff: H, Type: Applied

6.   Assume a totally new drug, assumed to be hallucinogenic, has just hit the streets, and you are part of a research team charged with investigating the new drug. What information would you want to gather? How might you begin to assess the impact of the new drug on society? Assume (unrealistically, of course) your budget is practically limitless.

Cannabis, pp. 355-359
Diff: H, Type: Applied

7.   Occasionally, one hears a call for the legalization of marijuana. What do you think? From a psychological perspective, what would be the advantages and disadvantages of legalizing marijuana?

What Causes Substance-Related Disorders?, pp. 360-364
Diff: E, Type: Factual

8.   Please choose any *two* of the views below, and describe how they explain the causes of substance abuse disorders.

>   sociocultural
>   behavioral
>   ~~biological~~

How Are Substance-Related Disorders Treated?, pp. 365-368
Diff: H, Type: Applied

9.   Some behavioral and cognitive-behavioral procedures for treating substance-related disorders involve exposing clients to frightening or sickening stimuli or thoughts. Please describe in detail at least one of these procedures, and comment on the ethical issues involved in using such a procedure.

No Specific Topic, No Specific Pages
Diff: E, Type: Applied

10. A 20-year-old friend of yours expresses a desire to receive treatment for alcohol abuse. What form of treatment would you recommend your friend look into, and why? Please detail the strengths of the form of treatment you would recommend, along with its possible weaknesses.

Sociocultural Therapies, p. 372
Diff: H, Type: Factual

11. Describe the particular concerns embodied in culture and gender-sensitive substance abuse treatment programs.

CHAPTER 13   Sexual Disorders and Gender Identity Disorder

MULTIPLE-CHOICE QUESTIONS

Sexual Disorders and Gender Identity Disorder, p. 377
Diff: E, Type: Factual, Ans: b

1. A paraphilia:
    a. usually involves rape.
    b. is a response to a socially inappropriate object.
    c. is an inability to experience sexual arousal.
    d. is an inability to achieve sexual satisfaction.

Sexual Disorders and Gender Identity Disorder, p. 377
Diff: E, Type: Applied, Ans: c

2. A person who becomes sexually aroused in the presence of stimuli most people in that person's society would not think appropriate is experiencing:
    a. sexual dysfunction.
    b. gender identity disorder.
    c. paraphilia.
    d. hyperactive sexual desire.

Sexual Disorders and Gender Identity Disorder, p. 377
Diff: H, Type: Applied, Ans: a

3. If someone felt assigned to the wrong sex and identified with the other gender, that person would most likely receive a diagnosis of:
    a. gender identity disorder.
    b. homosexuality.
    c. fetishism.
    d. sexual dysfunction.

Sexual Dysfunctions, p. 378
Diff: M, Type: Factual, Ans: d

4. Research shows that sexual dysfunctions among homosexual couples:
    a. are virtually nonexistent.
    b. generally are more severe than among heterosexual couples.
    c. include two distinct categories not included among heterosexual dysfunctions.
    d. are the same as those seen in heterosexual couples.

Sexual Dysfunctions, p. 378
Diff: H, Type: Applied, Ans: b

5. If someone had a sexual dysfunction, we know that this person would not be having difficulty in which of the following phases of the sexual response cycle?
    a. excitement
    b. resolution
    c. orgasm
    d. desire

Sexual Dysfunctions, p. 378
Diff: E, Type: Applied, Ans: b

6. A man who has never been able to achieve or maintain an erection for sexual intercourse would most likely be diagnosed with what type of erectile disorder?
    a. acquired
    b. lifelong
    c. situational
    d. generalized

Sexual Dysfunctions, p. 378
Diff: H, Type: Applied, Ans: d

7. A woman is perfectly capable of masturbating herself to orgasm, yet is unable to reach orgasm with a partner, either through sexual intercourse or through being masturbated. Most likely, this type of orgasmic disorder would be called:
    a. lifelong.
    b. acquired.
    c. generalized.
    d. situational.

Sexual Dysfunctions, p. 378
Diff: M, Type: Applied, Ans: d

8. If an individual had experienced normal sexual functioning for years and gradually developed a problem with becoming aroused under any conditions, the DSM-IV-TR diagnosis would be:
    a. lifelong and situational.
    b. acquired and situational.
    c. lifelong and generalized.
    d. acquired and generalized.

Sexual Dysfunctions, p. 378
Diff: M, Type: Applied, Ans: b

9. If an individual had experienced normal sexual functioning for years and then had a problem with becoming aroused only when with her husband as a partner, the DSM-IV-TR diagnosis would be:
    a. lifelong and situational.
    b. acquired and situational.
    c. lifelong and generalized.
    d. acquired and generalized.

Sexual Dysfunctions, p. 378
Diff: M, Type: Applied, Ans: a

10.   If a woman had never experienced normal sexual functioning with her husband and had a problem with becoming aroused with him, but found she could be aroused with other men, the DSM-IV-TR diagnosis would be:
   a.   lifelong and situational.
   b.   acquired and situational.
   c.   lifelong and generalized.
   d.   acquired and generalized.

Sexual Dysfunctions, p. 378
Diff: M, Type: Applied, Ans: b

11.   A person who once experienced normal to above normal levels of sexual desire recently has begun to feel much less than normal sexual desire. A sexual dysfunction following this pattern would be called what type?
   a.   situational
   b.   acquired
   c.   lifelong
   d.   generalized

Sexual Dysfunctions, p. 378
Diff: E, Type: Factual, Ans: d

12.   Sexual aversion is considered a disorder of which phase of the human sexual response cycle?
   a.   excitement
   b.   resolution
   c.   orgasm
   d.   desire

Sexual Dysfunctions, p. 378 (Figure 13-1)
Diff: M, Type: Factual, Ans: a

13.   According to Masters and Johnson, the resolution phase is more gradual and less abrupt in women when:
   a.   they do not experience orgasm.
   b.   they do not experience arousal.
   c.   they experience a sexual aversion.
   d.   they have experienced multiple orgasms.

Disorders of Desire, p. 379
Diff: H, Type: Applied, Ans: a

14.   An otherwise healthy individual reports almost no interest in sexual activity, and has had very few sexual experiences in the past several years. That person most likely is experiencing:
   a.   hypoactive sexual desire.
   b.   paraphilia.
   c.   sexual aversion.
   d.   sexual repulsion.

Disorders of Desire, p. 379
Diff: M, Type: Factual, Ans: b
15. Hypoactive sexual desire may include all of the following except:
    a. a low level of sexual activity.
    b. finding sexual activity repulsive.
    c. a lack of interest in sexual activity.
    d. normal physical sexual responses.

Disorders of Desire, p. 379
Diff: H, Type: Factual, Ans: b
16. To be classified as having hypoactive sexual desire, one would desire sex less than once:
    a. a week.
    b. every two weeks.
    c. a month.
    d. a year.

Disorders of Desire, p. 379
Diff: M, Type: Factual, Ans: a
17. Which of the following is least likely in men?
    a. sexual aversion
    b. premature ejaculation
    c. male orgasmic disorder
    d. hypoactive sexual desire

Disorders of Desire, p. 380
Diff: E, Type: Factual, Ans: c
18. Which hormone can cause decreased sexual desire when present in low, but not high levels?
    a. estrogen
    b. prolactin
    c. testosterone
    d. progesterone

Disorders of Desire, p. 380
Diff: M, Type: Factual, Ans: a
19. Which hormone can cause decreased sexual desire when present in either low or high levels?
    a. estrogen
    b. prolactin
    c. testosterone
    d. progesterone

Disorders of Desire, p. 380
Diff: H, Type: Applied, Ans: b
20. A young woman who formerly had a fairly high sex drive, and who reports no new medical problems, nonetheless experiences an unexpected drop in sex drive. What would be an important question to ask her, before recommending some sort of psychotherapy?
    a. "Have you been exposed to high levels of testosterone lately?"
    b. "Have you recently started taking birth control pills?"
    c. "Have you recently stopped using marijuana?"
    d. "Have you experienced lower levels of prolactin lately?"

Disorders of Desire, p. 380
Diff: M, Type: Factual, Ans: c

21. Which of the following is least likely to be a source of either low sexual desire, or sexual aversion?
    a. sociocultural causes
    b. psychological causes
    c. biological causes
    d. sexual trauma

Disorders of Desire, p. 380
Diff: M, Type: Factual, Ans: c

22. Studies show hypoactive sexual desire is related to:
    a. exercise.
    b. normal prolactin levels.
    c. high level of alcohol use.
    d. low level of alcohol use.

Disorders of Desire, p. 380
Diff: M, Type: Applied, Ans: a

23. Obsessive-compulsive symptoms may contribute to hypoactive sexual desire because someone with this disorder:
    a. finds contact with body fluids and odors unpleasant.
    b. compulsively seeks sexual partners.
    c. obsesses about having no sexual partners.
    d. is too afraid of germs to enjoy sexual activity.

Disorders of Desire, p. 380
Diff: H, Type: Applied, Ans: c

24. If a therapist were seeing patients for treatment of hypoactive sexual desire, the therapist would be most likely to find which of the following disorders as well?
    a. schizophrenia and eating disorders
    b. substance abuse and anxiety disorder
    c. depression and obsessive-compulsive disorder
    d. organic brain dysfunction and personality disorders

Disorders of Desire, p. 380
Diff: H, Type: Applied, Ans: d

25. The following are all examples of sociocultural causes of hypoactive sexual disorder except:
    a. having a partner lacking in sexual skills.
    b. loss of a job.
    c. infertility problems.
    d. pain medication.

Lifetime Patterns of Sexual Behavior, p. 381 (Box 13-1)
Diff: H, Type: Factual, Ans: d

26. If grandma is 90 and healthy, what is the percent chance she still masturbates at least occasionally?
    a. less than 1%
    b. about 10%
    c. about 20%
    d. over 20%

Lifetime Patterns of Sexual Behavior, p. 381 (Box 13-1)
Diff: H, Type: Factual, Ans: d
27.   If grandpa is 90 and healthy, what is the percent chance he still masturbates at least occasionally?
    a.   less than 5%
    b.   about 20%
    c.   about 40%
    d.   over 40%

Lifetime Patterns of Sexual Behavior, p. 381 (Box 13-1)
Diff: M, Type: Factual, Ans: a
28.   Studies of patterns of teenage sexual behavior today compared to such behavior a generation ago show today's teens having:
    a.   intercourse younger, and using condoms more.
    b.   intercourse younger, and using condoms less.
    c.   intercourse at about the same age, and using condoms more.
    d.   intercourse at about the same age, and using condoms less.

Disorders of Excitement, p. 382
Diff: E, Type: Factual, Ans: a
29.   In females, the labia swells during which phase of the sexual response cycle?
    a.   excitement
    b.   arousal
    c.   orgasm
    d.   resolution

Disorders of Excitement, p. 382
Diff: H, Type: Applied, Ans: a
30.   A recently married, physically healthy man expresses great love for his new spouse, yet feels almost no sexual desire for her. One likely cause of his condition is:
    a.   belief in cultural double standard about women.
    b.   decreased testosterone output due to drinking on his wedding night.
    c.   increased estrogen output now that he has "settled down."
    d.   a relationship that is too positive and healthy.

Disorders of Excitement, p. 382
Diff: E, Type: Factual, Ans: b
31.   In males, the penis becomes erect during which phase of the sexual response cycle?
    a.   excitement
    b.   arousal
    c.   orgasm
    d.   resolution

Disorders of Excitement, p. 382
Diff: E, Type: Factual, Ans: a
32.   The event which is very likely to result in sexual aversion or hypoactive sexual desire is:
    a.   sexual molestation.
    b.   the birth of a child.
    c.   infertility difficulties.
    d.   conflict in a relationship.

Disorders of Excitement, p. 382
Diff: M, Type: Factual, Ans: c
33.   Women with sexual arousal disorder have difficulty with:
      a.   painful intercourse.
      b.   vaginal spasms.
      c.   maintaining proper lubrication.
      d.   stereotypical female sex roles.

Disorders of Excitement, p. 382
Diff: H, Type: Applied, Ans: a
34.   Studies have shown that the rate of female sexual arousal disorder is about:
      a.   10%, or about the same as the rate of male erectile disorder.
      b.   10%, or about twice the rate of male erectile disorder.
      c.   20%, or about the same as the rate of male erectile disorder.
      d.   20%, or about twice the rate of male erectile disorder.

Disorders of Excitement, p. 382
Diff: M, Type: Applied, Ans: d
35.   A woman reports having vivid sexual fantasies, yet is unable to experience either clitoral or labial swelling, or vaginal lubrication. The most likely diagnosis for this woman would be:
      a.   sexual aversion.
      b.   hypoactive sexual desire.
      c.   female orgasmic disorder.
      d.   sexual arousal disorder.

Disorders of Excitement, p. 382
Diff: M, Type: Factual, Ans: c
36.   Which of the following is a symptom of female sexual arousal disorder?
      a.   pain during penetration
      b.   lack of interest in sexual activity
      c.   inadequate lubrication during sexual activity
      d.   vaginal contractions that prevent penetration

Disorders of Excitement, p. 382
Diff: H, Type: Applied, Ans: c
37.   Studies have shown that the rate of male erectile disorder is about:
      a.   5%, or about the same as the rate of female arousal disorder.
      b.   5%, or about half the rate of female sexual arousal disorder.
      c.   10%, or about the same as the rate of female sexual arousal disorder.
      d.   10%, or about half the rate of female sexual arousal disorder.

Disorders of Excitement, p. 382
Diff: E, Type: Factual, Ans: c
38.   A recent study of erectile disorder showed that most cases of erectile disorder are caused by:
      a.   psychosocial factors.
      b.   physical impairment.
      c.   a combination of psychosocial and physical causes.
      d.   causes other than psychosocial or physical ones.

Disorders of Excitement, p. 383
Diff: H, Type: Applied, Ans: a

39.   A man awakens after eight hours of normal sleep, and has an unbroken "snap gauge" band. There's a pretty good chance that the man has:
    a.   not experienced nocturnal penile tumescence.
    b.   a case of socioculturally related erectile disorder.
    c.   a case of psychologically related erectile disorder.
    d.   a normal sex life.

Disorders of Excitement, p. 383
Diff: H, Type: Applied, Ans: a

40.   A person who (unfortunately) had the following disorders—clogged arteries, diabetes, kidney failure—would be at special risk for:
    a.   erectile disorder.
    b.   sexual aversion.
    c.   dyspareunia.
    d.   vaginismus.

Disorders of Excitement, p. 383
Diff: M, Type: Factual, Ans: d

41.   A normal healthy man experiences:
    a.   20 to 30 minutes of penile erection per night of sleep.
    b.   most nocturnal tumescence during deep (delta) sleep.
    c.   brief, fleeting nighttime erections.
    d.   erections during dream cycles.

Disorders of Excitement, p. 383
Diff: E, Type: Factual, Ans: c

42.   What is the most common biological cause of erectile failure in men?
    a.   diabetes
    b.   performance anxiety
    c.   vascular problems
    d.   abnormal hormone levels

Disorders of Excitement, p. 384
Diff: M, Type: Factual, Ans: d

43.   According to Masters and Johnson, performance anxiety may result in a man:
    a.   failing to break a "snap gauge" band.
    b.   breaking a "snap gauge" band.
    c.   experiencing severe depression after sexual activity.
    d.   adopting a spectator role during sexual activity.

Disorders of Excitement, p. 384
Diff: E, Type: Factual, Ans: b

44.   Which of the following is a sociocultural cause for male erectile disorder?
    a.   diabetes
    b.   loss of a job
    c.   mild depression
    d.   performance anxiety

Disorders of Orgasm, p. 385
Diff: M, Type: Factual, Ans: c
45.   Which is the most common male sexual dysfunction in the orgasm phase?
        a. dyspareunia
        b. sexual aversion
        c. premature ejaculation
        d. inhibited male orgasm

Disorders of Orgasm, p. 385
Diff: H, Type: Factual, Ans: d
46.   Compared to erectile disorder, premature ejaculation is:
        a. more common among older men.
        b. more likely to have a physical explanation.
        c. more likely related to a low testosterone level.
        d. more likely related to fear of "being caught."

Disorders of Orgasm, p. 385
Diff: H, Type: Factual, Ans: a
47.   In the United States, since the mid-20th century, the typical duration of sexual intercourse
        has:
        a. increased, as has the distress of those suffering from premature ejaculation.
        b. increased, while the distress of those suffering from premature ejaculation has decreased.
        c. decreased, while the distress of those suffering from premature ejaculation has increased.
        d. decreased, as has the distress of those suffering from premature ejaculation.

Disorders of Orgasm, p. 385
Diff: E, Type: Factual, Ans: d
48.   From what does premature ejaculation usually result?
        a. sexual aversion
        b. sexual impotence
        c. organic problems
        d. sexual inexperience

Disorders of Orgasm, p. 385
Diff: H, Type: Applied, Ans: c
49.   William, who is having his first affair, is a 20-year-old man who has gone to see a sex
        therapist about a sexual dysfunction problem. What is William most likely suffering from?
        a. sexual aversion
        b. inhibited ejaculation
        c. premature ejaculation
        d. hypoactive sexual desire

Disorders of Orgasm, p. 385
Diff: M, Type: Applied, Ans: c
50.   A male diagnosed with a sexual dysfunction is most likely to be diagnosed with:
        a. erectile disorder.
        b. orgasmic disorder.
        c. premature ejaculation.
        d. dyspareunia.

Disorders of Orgasm, p. 386
Diff: E, Type: Factual, Ans: a

51.   Male orgasmic disorder has been linked most clearly to:
       a.   Prozac.
       b.   overactive sexual desire.
       c.   overconfidence.
       d.   failure to focus clearly on one's performance.

Disorders of Orgasm, p. 386
Diff: M, Type: Factual, Ans: b

52.   Which sexual dysfunction in males is most likely to be caused by spinal cord injuries?
       a.   sexual aversion
       b.   male orgasmic disorder
       c.   premature ejaculation
       d.   hypoactive sexual desire

Disorders of Orgasm, p. 386
Diff: M, Type: Factual, Ans: a

53.   A woman who can masturbate or be masturbated to orgasm cannot reach orgasm during
       sexual intercourse. Most clinicians would diagnose this woman's condition as:
       a.   normal and healthy.
       b.   orgasmic disorder.
       c.   vaginismus.
       d.   dyspareunia.

Disorders of Orgasm, p. 386
Diff: M, Type: Applied, Ans: b

54.   Which of the following is most common among women?
       a.   failure to experience orgasm
       b.   very delayed orgasms among premenopausal women
       c.   rarely experiencing orgasm
       d.   very delayed orgasms among menopausal women

Disorders of Orgasm, p. 387
Diff: M, Type: Applied, Ans: a

55.   Research shows that parents who want to decrease the likelihood that their young daughters
       will experience orgasmic disorder as adults should:
       a.   be affectionate with each other.
       b.   expose them to strict religious training,.
       c.   make sure they have early sexual experiences.
       d.   punish them for masturbation.

Disorders of Orgasm, p. 387
Diff: M, Type: Factual, Ans: a

56.   Having a positive relationship with one's mother is associated with _____ in women.
       a.   orgasm
       b.   hypoactive desire
       c.   hyperactive desire
       d.   paraphilia

Disorders of Orgasm, p. 387
Diff: E, Type: Factual, Ans: a
57.   The view that modern researchers hold about clitoral orgasms is that they are:
      a.   as healthy as vaginal orgasms.
      b.   felt only by sexually dysfunctional women.
      c.   the result of fixation on neurotic infantile needs.
      d.   superior to vaginal orgasms in sexual gratification.

Disorders of Orgasm, p. 387
Diff: H, Type: Factual, Ans: a
58.   Surveys show that women agree more strongly than men with which of the following statements?
      a.   Casual sex is unacceptable.
      b.   Sex after engagement is acceptable.
      c.   Sex before marriage is unacceptable.
      d.   Casual sex is acceptable for women but not men.

Disorders of Orgasm, p. 388
Diff: E, Type: Factual, Ans: d
59.   Women are more likely to be orgasmic when they have:
      a.   unhappy marriages.
      b.   a weak emotional attachment to their first sex partner.
      c.   an attraction to their current partner's occupation.
      d.   had a relatively long relationship with one's first sex partner.

Disorders of Orgasm, p. 388
Diff: H, Type: Applied, Ans: b
60.   Which of the following findings would argue against the idea that hypoactive sexual desire in women is caused by societal treatment of women?
      a.   The same drugs that interfere with ejaculation in men cause hypoactive sexual desire in women.
      b.   A sexually restrictive history is just as common among women with and without hypoactive sexual desire.
      c.   Clitoral orgasms are just as common and pleasurable as vaginal orgasms.
      d.   Erotic fantasies are more common is women with hypoactive sexual desire than in those without it.

Disorders of Sexual Pain, p. 388
Diff: M, Type: Factual, Ans: a
61.   What is thought to be the cause of vaginismus (the involuntary contraction of vaginal muscles)?
      a.   conditioning of a fear response
      b.   nervous system damage from diabetes
      c.   neurological damage in the cerebellum
      d.   a learned aversion to sexual behavior in general

Disorders of Sexual Pain, p. 388
Diff: M, Type: Factual, Ans: b
62.   Of those listed below, the least common variety of sexual dysfunction for women is:
       a.   dyspareunia.
       b.   vaginismus.
       c.   orgasmic disorder.
       d.   sexual arousal disorder.

Disorders of Sexual Pain, p. 388
Diff: H, Type: Factual, Ans: b
63.   Symptoms of vaginismus always include:
       a.   an inability to experience orgasm.
       b.   involuntary contraction of vaginal muscles.
       c.   a dislike for and distrust of sexual relationships.
       d.   an emotional detachment from the partner.

Disorders of Sexual Pain, p. 388
Diff: M, Type: Applied, Ans: b
64.   One who experiences dyspareunia most likely is a:
       a.   male with physical problems.
       b.   female with physical problems.
       c.   male with psychological problems.
       d.   female with psychological problems.

Disorders of Sexual Pain, p. 388
Diff: M, Type: Factual, Ans: a
65.   What is another name for genital pain during sexual activity?
       a.   dyspareunia
       b.   premature ejaculation
       c.   post mature ejaculation
       d.   male orgasmic disorder

Disorders of Sexual Pain, p. 388
Diff: M, Type: Factual, Ans: d
66.   The most common cause of dyspareunia is:
       a.   adult rape.
       b.   childhood sexual abuse.
       c.   testosterone deprivation.
       d.   damage incurred during childbirth.

Treatments for Sexual Dysfunctions, p. 389
Diff: H, Type: Factual, Ans: a
67   In psychoanalytic theory, the therapeutic goal in treating sexual dysfunction is:
       a.   causing broad personality changes.
       b.   the systematic use of free association.
       c.   overcoming learned aversion to sexual material.
       d.   keeping a dream diary for dream interpretation.

Treatments for Sexual Dysfunctions, p. 389
Diff: M, Type: Factual, Ans: a
68.   What problem do behavioral therapists focus on when treating sexual dysfunction?
       a.   fear
       b.   depression
       c.   aggression
       d.   conflict resolution

Treatments for Sexual Dysfunctions, p. 389
Diff: E, Type: Factual, Ans: c
69.   The study of sexuality that led to a revolution in the field of understanding sexual dysfunction
       and treatment was done by:
       a.   Kaplan.
       b.   Freud and Jung.
       c.   Masters and Johnson.
       d.   Friedman and LoPiccolo.

Treatments for Sexual Dysfunctions, p. 389
Diff: M, Type: Factual, Ans: a
70.   If someone receives "modern" sex therapy, chances are that the course of therapy will last:
       a.   no more than 20 sessions, and center on specific sexual problems.
       b.   more than 20 sessions, and center on specific sexual problems.
       c.   no more than 20 sessions, and deal with broad personality issues.
       d.   more than 20 sessions, and deal with broad personality issues.

Treatments for Sexual Dysfunctions, p. 390
Diff: E, Type: Factual, Ans: b
71.   The idea that both partners share the accountability for sexual dysfunction is known as:
       a.   couples therapy.
       b.   mutual responsibility.
       c.   nondemand pleasuring.
       d.   interactionary dysfunction.

Treatments for Sexual Dysfunctions, p. 390
Diff: E, Type: Factual, Ans: b
72.   One of the most problematic aspects of treating sexual dysfunction is:
       a.   the limited success possible.
       b.   the prevalence of myths and sexual ignorance.
       c.   the lack of available treatment programs for people with disorders.
       d.   the failure of patients with sexual dysfunctions to achieve a healthy transference.

Treatments for Sexual Dysfunctions, p. 390
Diff: M, Type: Factual, Ans: d
73.   "Sensate focus" refers to the technique in which:
       a.   sexual intercourse is encouraged daily.
       b.   eye contact is maintained during sexual activity.
       c.   the genitals are focused on during sexual activity.
       d.   the sexual repertoire is rebuilt, concentrating on pleasure.

Treatments for Sexual Dysfunctions, p. 390
Diff: M, Type: Applied, Ans: d

74.   Which of the following statements about modern sex therapy is most accurate?
      a.   Most sex therapy deals directly with the person who has the dysfunction, and does not involved the person's sexual partner.
      b.   Most sex therapy involves only techniques useful for specific dysfunctions.
      c.   The psychodynamic approach is still the one most often used.
      d.   Anxiety elimination and increasing communication skills are almost always included.

Treatments for Sexual Dysfunctions, p. 391
Diff: H, Type: Applied, Ans: c

75.   Couples in sex therapy who are working on eliminating the spectator role, are generally advised:
      a.   to have sex in as many different settings as they can manage.
      b.   to videotape their sexual encounters in order to increase fantasy material.
      c.   to refrain from having intercourse and focus on other body pleasure instead.
      d.   to drink small quantities of alcohol in order to relax.

What Techniques Are Applied to Particular Dysfunctions?, p. 392
Diff: H, Type: Applied, Ans: c

76.   A client suffering from sexual aversion learns to think thoughts like, "It's OK to enjoy intercourse; sharing love with my spouse is a good thing, not a sin" whenever negative thoughts about sexual activity occur. Most likely, the therapist treating this client is using:
      a.   affectual awareness.
      b.   the tease technique.
      c.   self-instruction training.
      d.   sildenafil.

What Techniques Are Applied to Particular Dysfunctions?, p. 392
Diff: H, Type: Applied, Ans: d

77.   According to your textbook, which of the following is a sex-role myth?
      a.   A woman's sex life continues after menopause.
      b.   Contraception is an issue for the couple.
      c.   Some touching is just that, and not sexual.
      d.   Fantasizing about someone else during sex means the relationship is not good.

What Techniques Are Applied to Particular Dysfunctions?, p. 392
Diff: H, Type: Applied, Ans: a

78.   If you were instructed to imagine sexual scenes in order to identify when in the sexual encounter your anxiety about sex first arose, you would be engaging in a therapeutic technique called:
      a.   affectional awareness.
      b.   systematic desensitization.
      c.   orgasmic reorientation.
      d.   sexual satiation.

What Techniques Are Applied to Particular Dysfunctions?, p. 392
Diff: M, Type: Applied, Ans: b

79.   In therapy, a patient is taught to visualize sexual scenes and uncover any negative emotions that occur. This patient is being treated using:
      a.   self-instruction training.
      b.   affectual awareness.
      c.   aversion therapy.
      d.   performance anxiety.

What Techniques Are Applied to Particular Dysfunctions?, p. 393
Diff: M, Type: Factual, Ans: b

80.   In treating premature ejaculation, the "pause" technique involves:
      a.   three or more episodes of intercourse each night for a month.
      b.   stimulating the penis, but stimulation is stopped before ejaculation can be reached.
      c.   stimulating the penis until ejaculation, followed by a pause and then another period of stimulation.
      d.   stimulation of the penis, but before ejaculation can occur, the woman squeezes the penis below the head to prevent ejaculation.

What Techniques Are Applied to Particular Dysfunctions?, p. 393
Diff: H, Type: Factual, Ans: a

81.   How does Viagra work?
      a.   It increases blood flow into the penis.
      b.   It draws blood flow out of the penis to create a vacuum.
      c.   It increases testosterone levels.
      d.   It creates new cognitions about sex.

What Techniques Are Applied to Particular Dysfunctions?, p. 393
Diff: H, Type: Applied, Ans: d

82.   Erectile disorder may be treated with all of the following except:
      a.   sildenafil.
      b.   penile prosthesis.
      c.   a vacuum erection device.
      d.   nitroglycerin.

What Techniques Are Applied to Particular Dysfunctions?, p. 393
Diff: E, Type: Factual, Ans: a

83.   A penile prosthesis may be used in the treatment of:
      a.   erectile disorder.
      b.   sexual aversion.
      c.   premature ejaculation.
      d.   hypoactive sexual drive.

What Techniques Are Applied to Particular Dysfunctions?, p. 393
Diff: M, Type: Applied, Ans: c

84.   A man's sexual partner repeatedly stimulates him to erection, then allows the erection to
      subside without the man experiencing an ejaculation. The sexual technique is called the:
      a.   phase technique.
      b.   sneeze technique.
      c.   tease technique.
      d.   squeeze technique.

What Techniques Are Applied to Particular Dysfunctions?, p. 393
Diff: H, Type: Applied, Ans: b

85.   EMTs in the back of an ambulance need to be sure to ask someone who is taking
      nitroglycerin if that person also has taken:
      a.   estrogen.
      b.   sildenafil.
      c.   testosterone.
      d.   antidepressants.

What Techniques Are Applied to Particular Dysfunctions?, p. 393
Diff: H, Type: Applied, Ans: c

86.   If a man has been taught to masturbate almost to orgasm, and then to insert his penis for
      intercourse, the man is most probably being treated for:
      a.   premature ejaculation.
      b.   dyspareunia.
      c.   orgasmic disorder.
      d.   gender identity disorder.

What Techniques Are Applied to Particular Dysfunctions?, p. 395
Diff: M, Type: Applied, Ans: a

87.   A client receives directed masturbation training and self-exploration instruction as part of the
      client's sex therapy. Most likely, the client is a:
      a.   woman being treated for orgasmic disorder.
      b.   woman being treated for vaginismus.
      c.   man being treated for erectile dysfunction.
      d.   man being treated for premature ejaculation.

What Techniques Are Applied to Particular Dysfunctions?, p. 395
Diff: E, Type: Factual, Ans: b

88.   The first step of the directed masturbation technique for female arousal and orgasmic
      disorders is:
      a.   masturbation.
      b.   learning about her body.
      c.   oral stimulation by a partner.
      d.   intercourse followed by masturbation.

What Techniques Are Applied to Particular Dysfunctions?, p. 395
Diff: E, Type: Factual, Ans: b
89.   The percentage of women treated for vaginismus who eventually report experiencing pain-free intercourse is:
      a.   about 50%.
      b.   about 75%.
      c.   about 85%.
      d.   over 90%.

What Techniques Are Applied to Particular Dysfunctions?, p. 395
Diff: M, Type: Applied, Ans: c
90.   A physical treatment program involving a minimum of psychological intervention most often would be used for which dysfunction:
      a.   orgasmic disorder.
      b.   erectile dysfunction.
      c.   dyspareunia.
      d.   vaginismus.

What Are the Current Trends in Sex Therapy?, p. 395
Diff: H, Type: Applied, Ans: d
91.   All of the following are examples of current trends in sex therapy except:
      a.   treating partners who are living together but not married.
      b.   treating the elderly who have sexual dysfunctions.
      c.   treating homosexual people with sexual dysfunctions.
      d.   treating only those who do not have other serious psychological problems.

What Are the Current Trends in Sex Therapy?, p. 396
Diff: H, Type: Applied, Ans: a
92.   Most sex therapists are uneasy about recent reliance on drug treatments for sexual dysfunctions because:
      a.   the integrated approach to therapy might be abandoned.
      b.   drug treatment is generally not effective.
      c.   of the risk of drug dependence.
      d.   it makes the treatment of sexual disorders more complex than it needs to be.

What Are the Current Trends in Sex Therapy?, p. 396
Diff: E, Type: Factual, Ans: a
93.   DSM-IV-TR recommends a diagnosis of paraphilia only when associated behaviors, fantasies, or urges last at least:
      a.   six months.
      b.   one year.
      c.   two years.
      d.   three years.

Paraphilias, p. 396
Diff: H, Type: Applied, Ans: c
94.   Most clinicians would agree that paraphiliac activities should only be considered a disorder
       when they:
       a.   involve pornography.
       b.   are illegal.
       c.   are the exclusive means of achieving orgasm.
       d.   are related to drug use.

Paraphilias, p. 397
Diff: H, Type: Applied, Ans: b
95.   An antiandrogen would be most appropriate if a disorder is caused by:
       a.   too much estrogen in the body.
       b.   an inappropriate sex drive.
       c.   a deficiency in the production of testosterone.
       d.   a hormonal imbalance that occurred during the prenatal period.

Fetishism, p. 397
Diff: H, Type: Applied, Ans: b
96.   The campus "bra bandit" steals women's underwear from the campus laundry, then
       masturbates into the underwear. The most appropriate diagnosis would be:
       a.   no diagnosis: the behavior falls with "normal" limits.
       b.   fetishism.
       c.   transvestic fetishism.
       d.   exhibitionistic fetishism.

Fetishism, p. 397
Diff: E, Type: Factual, Ans: a
97.   What is the term for the use of and attraction to inanimate objects as a preferred method of
       achieving sexual excitement?
       a.   fetishism
       b.   pedophilia
       c.   voyeurism
       d.   exhibitionism

Fetishism, p. 397
Diff: M, Type: Factual, Ans: b
98.   What does the process of covert sensitization for fetishism involve?
       a.   masturbation while thinking of the fetish object
       b.   mentally pairing a fetish object with an aversive stimulus
       c.   pairing electric shock to the arm or leg with the fetish object
       d.   creating a hierarchy of arousing objects and teaching the patient to relax while thinking
            of each in turn

Fetishism, p. 397
Diff: M, Type: Factual, Ans: a
99.   When a fetishist imagines the object of the fetish, then immediately imagines an aversive stimulus, the behavioral approach being used is:
   a.   covert sensitization.
   b.   relapse-prevention training.
   c.   aversion therapy via classical conditioning.
   d.   aversion therapy via operant conditioning.

Fetishism, p. 398
Diff: H, Type: Applied, Ans: c
100.   Which of the following men would most likely be treated with masturbatory satiation? One experiencing:
   a.   transvestism.
   b.   premature ejaculation.
   c.   a fetish.
   d.   erectile dysfunction.

Fetishism, p. 398
Diff: H, Type: Applied, Ans: c
101   A man being treated for a fetish to women's hats first obtains an erection from looking at women's hats, then begins to masturbate while looking at a picture of a nude woman. At the moment of orgasm, he makes sure to be looking at the picture of the nude woman. The behavioral approach being used is:
   a.   covert sensitization.
   b.   masturbatory satiation.
   c.   orgasmic reorientation.
   d.   relapse-prevention training.

Transvestic Fetishism, p. 398
Diff: E, Type: Factual, Ans: b
102.   "Cross-dressing" is another term for:
   a.   homosexuality.
   b.   transvestism.
   c.   orgasmic reorientation.
   d.   satiation.

Transvestic Fetishism, p. 398
Diff: M, Type: Factual, Ans: c
103.   A man derives sexual arousal exclusively from dressing in women's clothing. Most likely, that person would be diagnosed as:
   a.   normal and healthy.
   b.   an exhibitionist.
   c.   a transvestite.
   d.   a homosexual.

Transvestic Fetishism, p. 398
Diff: M, Type: Applied, Ans: a
104. Terry has been diagnosed as having a paraphilia, specifically transvestic fetishism. Terry is most likely to be:
    a. male.
    b. feminine.
    c. female.
    d. elderly.

Exhibitionism, p. 399
Diff: E, Type: Factual, Ans: d
105. Exhibitionists engage in that behavior because they:
    a. were sexually abused as children.
    b. are trying to solicit sexual contact.
    c. are unable to experience sexual relations.
    d. desire a shock reaction from their victim.

Exhibitionism, p. 399
Diff: H, Type: Applied, Ans: c
106. Which of the following responses from the person he exposed himself to would be least satisfying to an exhibitionist?
    a. "I'm shocked. You really surprised me."
    b. screaming
    c. ignoring the exhibitionist
    d. hiding one's eyes and gasping

Voyeurism, p. 399
Diff: H, Type: Applied, Ans: d
107. Which of the following thoughts would likely be most arousing to a voyeur in the act of secretly watching a couple have sex?
    a. I wish those people knew I was watching them.
    b. I know I am doing this in a way that I can't get caught.
    c. I'll probably never think about this again.
    d. The people would be humiliated if they knew I was watching.

Voyeurism, p. 400
Diff: M, Type: Applied, Ans: b
108. Many people derive sexual arousal from watching others undress or have intercourse, but are not diagnosed as voyeurs because those whom voyeurs watch:
    a. are under the statutory age.
    b. know they are being watched.
    c. are sexually aroused as well because they know they are being watched.
    d. are usually of the same sex as the voyeur.

Voyeurism, p. 400
Diff: M, Type: Applied, Ans: d

109.   Dr. Washington argues that voyeurism occurs as a result of the attempt to reduce fear of having the penis cut off, and is therefore found in males, not in females. Which theoretical perspective is Dr. Washington using?
   a. cognitive
   b. humanist
   c. behavioral
   d. psychodynamic

Frotteurism, p. 400
Diff: M, Type: Applied, Ans: b

110.   In a very crowded department store during the Christmas rush, a woman suddenly feels a stranger rubbing his genital area against her thigh. He continues until the crowd begins to break up, then moves away. The most likely diagnosis for this man is:
   a. pedophilia.
   b. frotteurism.
   c. sexual masochism.
   d. hypoxyphilia.

Frotteurism, p. 400
Diff: H, Type: Factual, Ans: a

111.   During which period does frotteurism typically develop?
   a. adolescence
   b. early adulthood
   c. middle adulthood
   d. late adulthood

Pedophilia, p. 400
Diff: M, Type: Factual, Ans: a

112.   During which period does pedophilia typically develop?
   a. adolescence
   b. early adulthood
   c. middle adulthood
   d. late adulthood

Pedophilia, p. 400
Diff: M, Type: Factual, Ans: a

113.   Recent studies of pedophiliacs show that:
   a. most have at least one other psychological disorder.
   b. relapse-prevention training is unsuccessful.
   c. most victims are boys.
   d. there is a clear biological cause.

Pedophilia, p. 401
Diff: M, Type: Factual, Ans: d

114. The technique of having a client with pedophilia identify situations in which he performs
      inappropriate behavior and teaching more appropriate coping strategies is called:
      a. aversion therapy.
      b. masturbatory satiation.
      c. orgasmic reorientation.
      d. relapse prevention training.

Sexual Masochism, p. 401
Diff: E, Type: Applied, Ans: d

115. Arnold cannot enjoy sexual intercourse unless he is tied up by his partner and beaten. His
      behavior is typical of:
      a. voyeurism.
      b. frotteurism.
      c. sexual sadism.
      d. sexual masochism.

Sexual Masochism, p. 402
Diff: M, Type: Applied, Ans: b

116. Autoerotic asphyxia is a fatal side effect of:
      a. taking Viagra.
      b. a masochistic practice.
      c. cross-dressing.
      d. a rope fetish.

Sexual Sadism, p. 403
Diff: E, Type: Factual, Ans: a

117. What is the primary source of sexual excitement for sexual sadists?
      a. the victim's suffering
      b. a specific part of the victim's body
      c. the use of leather to cause suffering
      d. the intense pain they receive from their partner

Sexual Sadism, p. 403
Diff: H, Type: Applied, Ans: a

118. While inflicting pain, perhaps unintentionally, on an animal or person, a teenager may
      become sexually aroused and later turn out to be a sadist. The theory that best describes this
      example of the development of sadism is:
      a. behavioral.
      b. psychodynamic.
      c. sociocultural.
      d. biological.

Homosexuality and Society, p. 404 (Box 13-5)
Diff: E, Type: Factual, Ans: c

119. The current view of homosexuality by the psychiatric community is that it:
      a. co-occurs with transsexualism.
      b. develops from transvestic fetishism.
      c. is a variant of normal sexual behavior.
      d. is preceded by childhood gender identity disorder.

Homosexuality and Society, p. 404 (Box 13-5)
Diff: E, Type: Factual, Ans: c

120.   Which of the following is not a DSM-IV-TR diagnostic category?
        a. voyeurism
        b. transvestism
        c. homosexuality
        d. frotteurism

Homosexuality and Society, p. 404 (Box 13-5)
Diff: M, Type: Factual, Ans: b

121.   Twin studies of homosexuality have demonstrated that the concordance rate for identical
        twins for homosexuality is about:
        a. 80%.
        b. 50%.
        c. 20%.
        d. 10%.

Gender Identity Disorder, p. 404
Diff: E, Type: Applied, Ans: b

122.   A man who is biologically male but considers himself a woman and would like to live as a
        woman is a:
        a. pedophile.
        b. transsexual.
        c. transvestite.
        d. homosexual.

Gender Identity Disorder, p. 405
Diff: M, Type: Applied, Ans: d

123.   A person feels most comfortable wearing clothes preferred by the other gender, strongly
        wishes to be the other gender, and is considering a surgical solution. The most likely
        diagnosis for this person is:
        a. transvestite.
        b. sexual masochist.
        c. sexual sadist.
        d. transsexual.

Gender Identity Disorder, p. 405
Diff: M, Type: Factual, Ans: b

124.   What is the most common outcome of gender identity disorder in childhood?
        a. It develops into pedophilia.
        b. It disappears with no ill effects.
        c. It is a precursor to transsexualism.
        d. It is a precursor to transvestite fetishism.

Gender Identity Disorder, p. 405
Diff: M, Type: Factual, Ans: b

125.   One treatment often sought by male transsexuals is:
    a.   aversion therapy.
    b.   estrogen treatment.
    c.   testosterone treatment.
    d.   psychoanalytic therapy.

Gender Identity Disorder, p. 405
Diff: H, Type: Applied, Ans: b

126.   Which of the following theoretical orientations is most helpful in understanding the origin of gender identity disorder?
    a.   sociocultural
    b.   biological
    c.   family systems
    d.   cognitive

Gender Identity Disorder, p. 405
Diff: M, Type: Applied, Ans: b

127.   When people with gender identity disorder take hormones it is in an attempt to:
    a.   enhance their gender of birth.
    b.   facilitate their living as the other gender.
    c.   reduce their sex drives.
    d.   change their external genitals.

Gender Identity Disorder, p. 406
Diff: H, Type: Applied, Ans: c

128.   Who is most likely to receive phalloplasty?
    a.   someone experiencing premature ejaculation
    b.   someone experiencing erectile dysfunction
    c.   someone experiencing gender identity disorder
    d.   someone who has a homosexual orientation

Putting It Together, p. 407
Diff: H, Type: Applied, Ans: d

129.   Of the following, which is the best advice you could give someone who wanted to prevent his or her sexual dysfunctions from occurring in the future?
    a.   Get therapy now.
    b.   Start taking preventative medications.
    c.   Have as much sexual experience as you possibly can.
    d.   Learn as much as you can about sexual functioning.

FILL-IN QUESTIONS

Disorders of Desire, p. 380
Diff: E, Type: Factual, Ans: testosterone; estrogen

1.   The sex hormones, _____ and _____, influence the sex drives of men and women.

Disorders of Excitement, p. 382
Diff: E, Type: Factual, Ans: male erectile disorder

2.   Jonathon suffers from _____, which is the inability to achieve an erection.

Disorders of Excitement, p. 383
Diff: M, Type: Factual, Ans: vascular

3.   The cause of male erectile disorder is most frequently _____ abnormalities.

Disorders of Excitement, p. 383
Diff: H, Type: Factual, Ans: snap gauge band

4.   Nocturnal penile erections are measured through a rough screen device called a _____.

Disorders of Excitement, p. 384
Diff: M, Type: Factual, Ans: performance

5.   Masters and Johnson state that sexual disorders are often maintained because during intercourse one or both partners adopt a spectator role or have crippling fears about _____.

Disorders of Orgasm, p. 384
Diff: E, Type: Factual, Ans: male orgasmic disorder

6.   Difficulty in achieving orgasm in the male, even after adequate stimulation, is termed _____.

Disorders of Sexual Pain, p. 388
Diff: E, Type: Factual, Ans: vaginismus

7.   A woman suffering from _____ has vaginal muscle spasms that prevent comfortable entry of a penis.

Disorders of Sexual Pain, p. 388
Diff: E, Type: Factual, Ans: dyspareunia

8.   Pain in the genitals during intercourse is called _____.

What Are the General Features of Sex Therapy?, p. 390
Diff: E, Type: Factual, Ans: mutual responsibility

9.   In sex therapy, _____ refers to the belief that both partners in a relationship share responsibility for the sexual problem.

What Are the General Features of Sex Therapy?, p. 390
Diff: M, Type: Factual, Ans: sensate focus (or nondemand pleasuring)

10.   The technique _____ is a graded set of sexual exercises in which partners explore each other's body but with no demand to have intercourse.

What Techniques Are Applied to Particular Dysfunctions?, p. 393
Diff: E, Type: Factual, Ans: erectile failure

11.   A vacuum erection device sometimes is used to treat _____ in males.

Transvestic Fetishism, p. 398
Diff: M, Type: Factual, Ans: adolescence (or childhood)

12.   The time of life during which transvestite fetishism usually appears is _____.

Frotteurism, p. 400
Diff: E, Type: Factual, Ans: frotteurism
13.   A person who has _____ may rub his genitals against an unsuspecting person in a crowded theater.

Frotteurism, p. 400
Diff: H, Type: Factual, Ans: 25
14.   The disorder frotteurism usually disappears by _____.

Sexual Masochism, p. 402
Diff: M, Type: Factual, Ans: childhood
15.   Sexual sadism and sexual masochism fantasies usually first appear during _____.

Gender Identity Disorder, p. 405
Diff: E, Type: Factual, Ans: gender identity disorder (or transsexualism)
16.   An individual who feels that they have been assigned to the wrong sex would be diagnosed with _____.

Gender Identity Disorder, p. 406
Diff: H, Type: Factual, Ans: phalloplasty
17.   The procedure of constructing a functioning penis in a sex change operation is called _____.

Putting It Together, p. 407
Diff: M, Type: Factual, Ans: education
18.   Recent insights show that _____ about sexual dysfunction can be as important as therapy.

ESSAY QUESTIONS

Disorders of Desire, p. 379ff
Diff: E, Type: Factual
1.   First, differentiate hypoactive sexual desire and sexual aversion. Second, describe some of the probable psychological and sociocultural causes of these disorders.

No Specific Topic, p. 384ff
Diff: H, Type: Applied
2.   Your choice: Please select any three of the following sexual dysfunctions and define them, then describe possible causes of them. Finally describe in detail a course of therapy that would likely be successful for one of the three dysfunctions you choose.
        male erectile disorder
        premature ejaculation
        female orgasmic disorder
        vaginismus

No Specific Topic, p. 384ff
Diff: M, Type: Applied

3.   Assume by some fantastic twist of fate that you had to experience one of the following sexual dysfunctions (appropriate to your gender, of course) for the next year. Which one would you choose? Why would you choose to experience it, and not the other gender appropriate option? Finally, what kind of therapy would you seek after a year, and why. Please choose from among: premature ejaculation, male erectile disorder, female orgasmic disorder, and dyspareunia.

What Are the General Features of Sex Therapy?, p. 389
Diff: M, Type: Factual

4.   There are many principles and techniques common to most forms of sex therapy. Please name at least five of them, and say why they are so commonly used.

Sex-Role Myths, p. 392 (Box 13-2)
Diff: M, Type: Factual

5.   Please list at least four sex-role myths which may disturb normal sexual functioning, then provide accurate counter-statements for those myths.

What Techniques Are Applied to Particular Dysfunctions?, p. 393
Diff: M, Type: Applied

6.   Please discuss three different approaches for treating erectile disorder and how each works.

Fetishism, p. 397
Diff: M, Type: Factual

7.   Forms of behavior therapy frequently are used in the treatment of fetishes. Please choose any three of the following forms of behavior therapy, define them, and describe which paraphilias they are used to treat. Please choose from among: covert sensitization, masturbatory satiation, orgasmic reorientation, and aversion therapy

Serving the Public Good, p. 401 (Box 13-4)
Diff: M, Type: Applied

8.   A pedophiliac says, "What's the big deal? I don't really hurt the kids, and I always ask them first if they want to get involved." What *is* the big deal? First define pedophilia, being sure to describe the "typical" individual with this disorder. Second, describe a reasonably successful form of therapy, which has been used with pedophiliacs.

Homosexuality and Society, p. 404 (Box 13-5)
Diff: H, Type: Applied

9.   What is homosexuality? How does it differ from transvestism and gender identity disorder? Finally, what has been the history of the inclusion or noninclusion of homosexuality in the DSM-IV-TR, and why?

Gender Identity Disorder, p. 405ff
Diff: M, Type: Applied

10.   What do you think ought to be done in the treatment of gender identity disorder (transsexualism)? Please begin your answer by defining gender identity disorder, and then describe the issues involved in determining an appropriate course of treatment.

MULTIPLE-CHOICE QUESTIONS

Schizophrenia, p. 411
Diff: E, Type: Factual, Ans: a
1. The psychiatrist who coined the term schizophrenia was:
    a. Eugen Bleuler.
    b. Emil Kraepelin.
    c. Benedict Morel.
    d. Sigmund Freud.

Schizophrenia, p. 411
Diff: E, Type: Factual, Ans: b
2. What percentage of the world population is estimated to have schizophrenia?
    a. .05%
    b. 1%
    c. 5%
    d. 10%

Schizophrenia, p. 411
Diff: E, Type: Factual, Ans: b
3. Psychosis means:
    a. split personality.
    b. loss of contact with reality.
    c. brain seizures.
    d. drug abuse.

Schizophrenia, p. 411
Diff: M, Type: Factual, Ans: d
4. Bleuler, who coined the term "schizophrenia," meant the name to imply all of the following except:
    a. a spilt between thoughts and emotions.
    b. a fragmentation of thought processes.
    c. a withdrawal from reality.
    d. a division between mind and body.

Schizophrenia, p. 411
Diff: E, Type: Factual, Ans: a

5.   The term "schizophrenia" is derived from the Greek for:
     a.   split mind.
     b.   frantic mind.
     c.   multiple personality.
     d.   hysterical demeanor.

Schizophrenia, p. 411
Diff: E, Type: Factual, Ans: b

6.   Which of the following is not a necessary characteristic of schizophrenia, according to
     Bleuler?
     a.   withdrawal from reality
     b.   general intellectual decline
     c.   fragmented thought processes
     d.   split between emotion and thought

Schizophrenia, p. 412
Diff: H, Type: Factual, Ans: a

7.   Which of the following is not consistent with the most common pattern of schizophrenia?
     a.   Women develop the disorder earlier and more severely than men.
     b.   A significant risk of suicide—about 15%.
     c.   A higher incidence in lower than upper socioeconomic groups.
     d.   About a 1% risk of developing schizophrenia in a lifetime, worldwide.

Schizophrenia, p. 412
Diff: M, Type: Factual, Ans: b

8.   Downward drift is best reflected in which of the following statements?
     a.   Poverty and social disruption cause schizophrenia.
     b.   Schizophrenia causes people to fall into poverty and social disruption.
     c.   Genetic factors cause both schizophrenia and poverty.
     d.   Schizophrenia causes marital disruption, which causes poverty.

Schizophrenia, p. 412
Diff: E, Type: Factual, Ans: a

9.   Schizophrenia is found in all socioeconomic classes. However, it is more likely to be found in
     someone from a _____ background.
     a.   lower level
     b.   middle level
     c.   professional level
     d.   privileged (wealthy)

Schizophrenia, p. 412
Diff: H, Type: Applied, Ans: c

10.   Which of the following would give us the most convincing evidence for a racial difference in the incidence of schizophrenia?
   a.   Differences in the overall rate of schizophrenia between racial groups.
   b.   Differences in the socioeconomic levels between racial groups.
   c.   Differences in the rate of schizophrenia do not completely disappear when other factors thought to be related are controlled.
   d.   Differences in the rate of schizophrenia among married and unmarried people of different racial groups.

Schizophrenia, p. 412
Diff: H, Type: Applied, Ans: a

11.   A person diagnosed with schizophrenia is not hospitalized, yet eventually shows complete remission of symptoms. This pattern is:
   a.   typical of what happens in developing countries.
   b.   typical of what happens in developed countries.
   c.   unusual: not being hospitalized is typical in developing countries, but remission of symptoms is typical in developed countries.
   d.   unusual: not being hospitalized is typical in developed countries, but remission of symptoms is typical in developing countries.

The Clinical Picture of Schizophrenia, p. 413
Diff: H, Type: Applied, Ans: b

12.   Of the following statements, which best summarizes the clinical picture of schizophrenia in the early 21st century?
   a.   Schizophrenia is a "catchall" category; the diagnosis is assigned simply because someone acts "crazy."
   b.   Schizophrenic symptoms show a lot of variability, but schizophrenia is diagnosed less vaguely than it used to be.
   c.   The worldwide incidence of schizophrenia has declined by about 50 percent in recent years, due mainly to more stringent criteria for diagnosing the disorder.
   d.   Mounting evidence shows that "schizophrenia" is in fact several very different disorders, all of which have a nearly-exclusively genetic basis.

A Beautiful Mind: Movies vs. Reality, pp. 415, 412 (Box 14-1)
Diff: H, Type: Applied, Ans: c

13.   The film *A Beautiful Mind* describes the life of Nobel Prize winner and schizophrenic John Nash. In the movie, Nash develops symptoms at age 20, prominent among them visual hallucinations. In actual fact, Nash developed symptoms when he was 30, prominent among them auditory hallucinations. Whose experience is more like that of "typical" schizophrenics, "movie" Nash, or "real" Nash?
   a.   "movie" Nash
   b.   "real" Nash
   c.   some of both: symptom onset age from "movie" Nash, and auditory hallucinations from "real" Nash, are typical
   d.   some of both: visual hallucinations from "movie" Nash, and symptom onset age from "real" Nash, are typical

What Are the Symptoms of Schizophrenia?, p. 416
Diff: E, Type: Applied, Ans: c
14.   Armond does not feel much emotion and does not really want to do anything. He has also
       completely withdrawn from his friends and family. The presence of these behaviors illustrates
       _____ symptoms of schizophrenia.
       a.   active
       b.   positive
       c.   negative
       d.   psychomotor

What Are the Symptoms of Schizophrenia?, p. 416
Diff: M, Type: Applied, Ans: a
15.   Delusions, disorganized thinking and speech, heightened perceptions and hallucinations, and
       inappropriate affect are examples of _____ symptoms of schizophrenia.
       a.   positive
       b.   negative
       c.   cognitive
       d.   ineffective

What Are the Symptoms of Schizophrenia?, p. 416
Diff: M, Type: Applied, Ans: d
16.   Rosa is sure that her family is planning to kidnap her and take her inheritance. She has found
       her husband talking on the phone in whispers and has seen her children looking at her
       strangely. She is most likely suffering from:
       a.   delusions of grandeur.
       b.   delusions of reference.
       c.   delusions of control.
       d.   delusions of persecution.

What Are the Symptoms of Schizophrenia?, p. 416
Diff: M, Type: Applied, Ans: c
17.   Antonio believes that the anchor on the evening news (TV) is speaking directly (and
       personally) to him. He even goes to the television studio to talk to the man. He is suffering
       from:
       a.   delusions of persecution.
       b.   delusions of grandeur.
       c.   delusions of reference.
       d.   delusions of control.

What Are the Symptoms of Schizophrenia?, p. 416
Diff: M, Type: Applied, Ans: b
18.   One who believes that government agents have planted "bugs" in his car and are watching
       him from the trees in his backyard is experiencing:
       a.   delusions of reference.
       b.   delusions of persecution.
       c.   delusions of grandeur.
       d.   delusions of control.

What Are the Symptoms of Schizophrenia?, p. 416
Diff: M, Type: Applied, Ans: c
19.   One who believes herself to be the Virgin Mary, come to give birth to a new savior, would be experiencing:
   a.   delusions of reference.
   b.   delusions of persecution.
   c.   delusions of grandeur.
   d.   delusions of control.

What Are the Symptoms of Schizophrenia?, p. 416
Diff: M, Type: Applied, Ans: d
20.   A man who believes his thought are being influenced by the disc jockey on the radio is experiencing:
   a.   delusions of reference.
   b.   delusions of persecution.
   c.   delusions of grandeur.
   d.   delusions of control.

What Are the Symptoms of Schizophrenia?, p. 416
Diff: M, Type: Applied, Ans: a
21.   A woman who believed that the newspaper stories on political scandals were specific messages for her is experiencing:
   a.   delusions of reference.
   b.   delusions of persecution.
   c.   delusions of grandeur.
   d.   delusions of control.

What Are the Symptoms of Schizophrenia?, p. 416
Diff: E, Type: Applied, Ans: b
22.   Millie sees pretty colored butterflies on all the walls. She also hears gentle music (that is not there). The presence of these behaviors illustrates _____ symptoms of schizophrenia.
   a.   active
   b.   positive
   c.   negative
   d.   psychomotor

What Are the Symptoms of Schizophrenia?, p. 416
Diff: H, Type: Applied, Ans: d
23.   The "erotomanic delusions" of many stalkers—that they are loved by the ones they stalk (even though those they stalk do not know them)—are most similar to which kind of schizophrenic delusion?
   a.   reference
   b.   persecution
   c.   control
   d.   grandeur

What Are the Symptoms of Schizophrenia?, p. 418
Diff: M, Type: Applied, Ans: a

24. A schizophrenic who said, "It's cold today. My cold is better but I got it from the nurse. She is a big blonde who lives in Manhattan. I live in Manhattan with Jimmy Carter," is experiencing:
     a. loose associations.
     b. neologisms.
     c. perseveration.
     d. clang.

What Are the Symptoms of Schizophrenia?, p. 418
Diff: H, Type: Applied, Ans: d

25. "The rain in Spain stays mainly in the plain," is an example of:
     a. loose associations.
     b. neologisms.
     c. perseveration.
     d. clang.

What Are the Symptoms of Schizophrenia?, p. 418
Diff: M, Type: Applied, Ans: c

26. A schizophrenic who said, "It's time for supper, supper, supper. Supper is on in the supper room" is experiencing:
     a. loose associations.
     b. neologisms.
     c. perseveration.
     d. clang.

What Are the Symptoms of Schizophrenia?, p. 418
Diff: H, Type: Applied, Ans: b

27. "Jabberwocky" is an example of a:
     a. loose association.
     b. neologism.
     c. perseveration.
     d. clang.

What Are the Symptoms of Schizophrenia?, p. 418
Diff: E, Type: Applied, Ans: c

28. "I like to read books. I read a book about a gilzbok… but they have nothing to interest me… it is just amudence all over again." This type of talk illustrates:
     a. clang.
     b. derailment.
     c. neologisms.
     d. perseveration.

What Are the Symptoms of Schizophrenia?, p. 418
Diff: M, Type: Factual, Ans: d
29.   Schizophrenic research participants who were asked to listen for a particular syllable against a background of speech performed:
        a.   as well as nonschizophrenics with both simple and more distracting background speech.
        b.   poorer than nonschizophrenics with both simple and more distracting background speech.
        c.   poorer than nonschizophrenics with simple background speech, but as well as nonschizophrenics with more distracting background speech.
        d.   as well as nonschizophrenics with simple background speech, but poorer than nonschizophrenics with more distracting background speech.

What Are the Symptoms of Schizophrenia?, p. 418
Diff: M, Type: Applied, Ans: d
30.   In the middle of a crowded room with talking, music, laughing, and street noises, schizophrenics experiencing heightened perceptions would be most likely to:
        a.   focus intently on the conversation.
        b.   imitate an ambulance sound.
        c.   sing along with the music.
        d.   feel that their senses are overstimulated.

What Are the Symptoms of Schizophrenia?, pp. 418-419
Diff: H, Type: Applied, Ans: b
31.   People with deficiencies in smooth pursuit eye movement would be less able to:
        a.   focus on an object.
        b.   track an object with their eyes.
        c.   turn their heads from side to side.
        d.   blink in response to strong light.

What Are the Symptoms of Schizophrenia?, pp. 419, 416
Diff: M, Type: Applied, Ans: d
32.   A schizophrenic who tastes chlorine in untreated natural water, and then thinks that his wife is trying to slowly poison him is experiencing a(n) _____ hallucination and a delusion of
        _____.
        a.   auditory, grandeur
        b.   tactile, control
        c.   olfactory, reference
        d.   gustatory, persecution

What Are the Symptoms of Schizophrenia?, pp. 419, 416
Diff: M, Type: Applied, Ans: a
33.   A schizophrenic who hears all the animals around her making plans to get her ready for the ball, and comes to think she is Cinderella is experiencing a(n) _____ hallucination and a delusion of _____.
        a.   auditory, grandeur
        b.   tactile, control
        c.   olfactory, reference
        d.   gustatory, persecution

What Are the Symptoms of Schizophrenia?, pp. 419, 416
Diff: M, Type: Applied, Ans: b
34.   The chief difference between hallucinations and delusions is that:
      a.   hallucinations are more serious than delusions.
      b.   hallucinations involve perception and delusions belief.
      c.   hallucinations are more common early in the disorder and delusions more common later.
      d.   hallucinations are auditory and delusions are visual.

What Are the Symptoms of Schizophrenia?, p. 419
Diff: H, Type: Applied, Ans: a
35.   Which of the following would be the most common type of hallucination?
      a.   That dog is singing to me and asking me to sing along.
      b.   That butterfly is growing so much it is as big as the house.
      c.   There are invisible bugs crawling on my skin.
      d.   My intestines are a mass of wiggling worms.

What Are the Symptoms of Schizophrenia?, p. 419
Diff: E, Type: Factual, Ans: c
36.   The most common type of hallucination in schizophrenia is:
      a.   visual.
      b.   tactile.
      c.   auditory.
      d.   olfactory.

What Are the Symptoms of Schizophrenia?, p. 419
Diff: E, Type: Factual, Ans: c
37.   Research with those experiencing auditory hallucinations has demonstrated all of the following except:
      a.   increased blood flow in Broca's area.
      b.   increased activity in the brain's hearing center.
      c.   movement of the oval window of the cochlea.
      d.   increased activity near the brain's surface.

What Are the Symptoms of Schizophrenia?, p. 419
Diff: H, Type: Applied, Ans: d
38.   Which of the following is a somatic hallucination?
      a.   That dog is singing to me and asking me to sing along.
      b.   That butterfly is growing so much it is as big as the house.
      c.   There are invisible bugs crawling on my skin.
      d.   My intestines are a mass of wiggling worms.

What Are the Symptoms of Schizophrenia?, p. 419
Diff: H, Type: Applied, Ans: c
39.   Which of the following is a tactile hallucination?
      a.   That dog is singing to me and asking me to sing along.
      b.   That butterfly is growing so much it is as big as the house.
      c.   There are invisible bugs crawling on my tingling skin.
      d.   My intestines are a mass of wriggling worms.

What Are the Symptoms of Schizophrenia?, p. 419
Diff: E, Type: Applied, Ans: d

40. When Janice drinks her milk, she is sure from the taste that someone put salt in it. Janice is most likely experiencing a(n) _____ hallucination.
    a. somatic
    b. auditory
    c. olfactory
    d. gustatory

What Are the Symptoms of Schizophrenia?, p. 420
Diff: H, Type: Applied, Ans: a

41. A schizophrenic who is experiencing alogia is displaying:
    a. poverty of speech.
    b. blunted or flat affect.
    c. loss of volition.
    d. social withdrawal.

What Are the Symptoms of Schizophrenia?, p. 420
Diff: E, Type: Applied, Ans: c

42. A schizophrenic who laughs when told sad news and screams in situations that most people see as warm and tender is experiencing:
    a. cognitive distortion.
    b. delusions of control.
    c. inappropriate affect.
    d. olfactory hallucinations.

What Are the Symptoms of Schizophrenia?, p. 420
Diff: M, Type: Factual, Ans: b

43. Poverty of speech, blunted and flat affect, loss of volition, and social withdrawal are all examples of _____ symptoms of schizophrenia.
    a. positive
    b. negative
    c. hallucinatory
    d. psychomotor

What Are the Symptoms of Schizophrenia?, p. 420
Diff: M, Type: Factual, Ans: a

44. A decrease in the fluency and productivity of speech, seen in schizophrenia, is termed:
    a. alogia.
    b. blocking.
    c. avolition.
    d. catatonia.

What Are the Symptoms of Schizophrenia?, p. 420
Diff: H, Type: Factual, Ans: c

45. Alogia is a(n):
    a. example of inappropriate affect.
    b. positive symptom of schizophrenia.
    c. negative symptom of schizophrenia.
    d. psychomotor symptom of schizophrenia.

What Are the Symptoms of Schizophrenia?, p. 420
Diff: H, Type: Applied, Ans: b

46.   In the middle of a normal, calm conversation, a person with Tourette's syndrome might suddenly begin shouting, then follow that with a string of obscenities. This is similar to the symptom of schizophrenia called:
       a.   blunted and flat affect.
       b.   inappropriate affect.
       c.   poverty of speech.
       d.   loss of volition.

What Are the Symptoms of Schizophrenia?, p. 420
Diff: H, Type: Applied, Ans: c

47.   An emergency medical technician (EMT) arrives at the scene of a bad car accident, and calmly prepares a severely injured passenger for transport to a hospital while others at the scene are screaming and crying with fear and grief. The EMT's training has resulted in behavior similar to the symptom of schizophrenia called:
       a.   ahedonia.
       b.   poverty of speech.
       c.   blunted affect.
       d.   loss of volition.

What Are the Symptoms of Schizophrenia?, p. 420
Diff: H, Type: Applied, Ans: a

48.   I sit, staring at a blank page, unable to make myself write a new multiple-choice test item; I just don't seem to care. My behavior is like that of schizophrenics displaying the symptom called:
       a.   avolition.
       b.   ahedonia.
       c.   inappropriate affect.
       d.   flat affect.

What Are the Symptoms of Schizophrenia?, p. 421
Diff: H, Type: Applied, Ans: d

49.   A schizophrenic exhibiting social withdrawal appears to be unusually up-to-date on contemporary political issues. This is:
       a.   very common; social withdrawal usually includes spending more time on less personal issues, such as political issues.
       b.   common; about half the time social withdrawal includes spending more time on less personal issues, such as political issues.
       c.   uncommon; social withdrawal usually is independent of time spent on less personal issues, such as political issues.
       d.   very uncommon; those showing social withdrawal typically know less than usual about nonpersonal issues, such as political issues.

What Are the Symptoms of Schizophrenia?, p. 421
Diff: M, Type: Applied, Ans: b

50.   Martin is a schizophrenic person who feels ambivalent about most issues. He has no goals
      and does not seem to have the energy or interest to think about them. He certainly cannot
      make decisions. He is suffering from:
      a.   disturbances in affect.
      b.   disturbances in volition.
      c.   a disturbed sense of self.
      d.   a disturbed relationship with the outside world.

What Are the Symptoms of Schizophrenia?, p. 421
Diff: H, Type: Applied, Ans: b

51.   A schizophrenic who is experiencing anhedonia is displaying:
      a.   poverty of speech.
      b.   blunted or flat affect.
      c.   loss of volition.
      d.   social withdrawal.

What Are the Symptoms of Schizophrenia?, p. 421
Diff: H, Type: Applied, Ans: c

52.   A schizophrenic who is feeling apathetic, drained, and unable to start or follow through on
      any projects is displaying:
      a.   poverty of speech.
      b.   blunted or flat affect.
      c.   loss of volition.
      d.   social withdrawal.

What Are the Symptoms of Schizophrenia?, p. 421
Diff: H, Type: Applied, Ans: d

53.   A schizophrenic who is unable to recognize other people's needs and emotions and who
      doesn't know much about everyday events and issues is displaying:
      a.   poverty of speech.
      b.   blunted or flat affect.
      c.   loss of volition.
      d.   social withdrawal.

Howling for Attention, p. 421 (Box 14-3), p. 416
Diff: M, Type: Applied, Ans: c

54.   A person experiencing lycanthropy derives special meaning from the phases of the moon, and
      believes the moon indicates when to have lycanthropic episodes. This is most similar to
      which symptom of schizophrenia?
      a.   clang
      b.   neologisms
      c.   delusions of reference
      d.   blunted or flat affect

Howling for Attention, p. 421 (Box 14-3)
Diff: M, Type: Applied, Ans: b
55.   A person experiencing lycanthropy derives special meaning from the phases of the moon, and believes the moon indicates when to have lycanthropic episodes. Those lycanthropic episodes are most likely to include:
      a.   delusions of grandeur involving a religious savior.
      b.   acting like a werewolf.
      c.   behaving like a giant or a dwarf.
      d.   eating normally disgusting substances.

What Are the Symptoms of Schizophrenia?, p. 422
Diff: E, Type: Factual, Ans: d
56.   The inability to move the limbs in catatonic schizophrenia illustrates _____ symptoms of schizophrenia.
      a.   active
      b.   positive
      c.   negative
      d.   psychomotor

What Are the Symptoms of Schizophrenia?, p. 422
Diff: M, Type: Applied, Ans: a
57.   Schizophrenics who remain motionless and silent for long periods of time are experiencing:
      a.   catatonic stupor.
      b.   catatonic excitement.
      c.   catatonic rigidity.
      d.   catatonic posturing.

What Are the Symptoms of Schizophrenia?, p. 422
Diff: M, Type: Applied, Ans: a
58.   Noreen has been diagnosed as schizophrenic. She is totally unresponsive to her environment. She does not move for hours on end and never responds to contacts from others. This is an example of:
      a.   catatonic stupor.
      b.   general dysphoria.
      c.   inappropriate affect.
      d.   catatonic excitement.

What Are the Symptoms of Schizophrenia?, p. 422
Diff: M, Type: Applied, Ans: c
59.   Lester is schizophrenic. He has not moved for several hours and when the nurse tried to get him to go back to his room, she could not budge him. Lester is displaying:
      a.   waxy flexibility.
      b.   catatonic stupor.
      c.   catatonic rigidity.
      d.   catatonic posturing.

What Are the Symptoms of Schizophrenia?, p. 422
Diff: M, Type: Applied, Ans: d

60. Schizophrenics who hold awkward and bizarre positions for long periods of time are experiencing:
     a. catatonic stupor.
     b. catatonic excitement.
     c. catatonic rigidity.
     d. catatonic posturing.

What Are the Symptoms of Schizophrenia?, p. 422
Diff: M, Type: Applied, Ans: c

61. Schizophrenics who remain standing for hours and resist efforts to be moved are experiencing:
     a. catatonic stupor.
     b. catatonic excitement.
     c. catatonic rigidity.
     d. catatonic posturing.

What Are the Symptoms of Schizophrenia?, p. 422
Diff: M, Type: Applied, Ans: b

62. Schizophrenics who wave their arms around in wild motions and make kicking motions with their legs are experiencing:
     a. catatonic stupor.
     b. catatonic excitement.
     c. catatonic rigidity.
     d. catatonic posturing.

What is the Course of Schizophrenia?, p. 422
Diff: M, Type: Factual, Ans: c

63. The stage of the development of schizophrenia marked by deterioration of functioning and the display of some mild symptoms is called the:
     a. active phase.
     b. residual phase.
     c. prodromal phase.
     d. premorbid phase.

What is the Course of Schizophrenia?, p. 422
Diff: H, Type: Applied, Ans: d

64. A person is socially withdrawn, speaks in odd ways, has strange ideas, and expresses little emotion, but is not displaying full-blown schizophrenic symptoms. What phase of schizophrenia is this person in?
     a. prodromal
     b. active
     c. residual
     d. either prodromal or residual

What is the Course of Schizophrenia?, p. 422
Diff: M, Type: Factual, Ans: c

65.   Patients are more likely to recover from schizophrenia if they:
      a.   had hallucinations but no delusions.
      b.   showed delusions but no hallucinations.
      c.   demonstrated good premorbid functioning.
      d.   had primarily negative rather than positive signs.

What is the Course of Schizophrenia?, p. 422
Diff: M, Type: Applied, Ans: a

66.   Delia does not display all the full-blown schizophrenia symptoms any more. Occasionally, a shadow of a symptom appears. She is a bit withdrawn and not entirely clear all the time, but she can marginally function in the world. This is an example of _____ schizophrenia.
      a.   residual
      b.   catatonic
      c.   paranoid
      d.   undifferentiated

What is the Course of Schizophrenia, p. 422
Diff: H, Type: Applied, Ans: c

67.   Which of the following is not related to a fuller recovery from schizophrenia?
      a.   good prodromal functioning
      b.   schizophrenia initially triggered by stress
      c.   schizophrenia developing in early life
      d.   an abrupt beginning to the disorder

Diagnosing Schizophrenia, p. 423
Diff: M, Type: Applied, Ans: b

68.   A schizophrenic who was mute, statuelike, and failed to participate in the hospital routine is most likely experiencing _____ schizophrenia.
      a.   disorganized
      b.   catatonic
      c.   paranoid
      d.   undifferentiated

Diagnosing Schizophrenia, p. 423
Diff: H, Type: Applied, Ans: a

69.   A schizophrenic who is unusually silly, engages in odd mannerisms, and grimaces is most likely experiencing _____ schizophrenia.
      a.   disorganized
      b.   catatonic
      c.   paranoid
      d.   undifferentiated

Diagnosing Schizophrenia, p. 423
Diff: H, Type: Applied, Ans: c

70. A schizophrenic whose life is taken over by an elaborate system of delusions and auditory hallucinations is most likely experiencing _____ schizophrenia.
    a. disorganized
    b. catatonic
    c. paranoid
    d. undifferentiated

Diagnosing Schizophrenia, p. 423
Diff: M, Type: Applied, Ans: d

71. Jerry suffers from extremely disrupted thought processes and severe perceptual disturbances. He also displays odd mannerisms, silliness, and has difficulty communicating. He is most likely suffering from _____ schizophrenia.
    a. residual
    b. paranoid
    c. catatonic
    d. disorganized

Diagnosing Schizophrenia, p. 423
Diff: E, Type: Applied, Ans: a

72. Olive is hospitalized. She spends most of her time frozen in place. When she is moved by a nurse or physician, she remains in the position she is put into. This is an example of _____ schizophrenia.
    a. catatonic
    b. paranoid
    c. disorganized
    d. undifferentiated

Diagnosing Schizophrenia, p. 423
Diff: M, Type: Factual, Ans: a

73. A common symptom of paranoid schizophrenia is:
    a. auditory hallucinations.
    b. psychomotor disturbance.
    c. affect that is cool and aloof.
    d. loose associations and neologisms.

Diagnosing Schizophrenia, p. 423
Diff: M, Type: Applied, Ans: b

74. A person with schizophrenia experiences less frequent emotional outbursts than before, and is beginning to participate somewhat in family get-togethers; however, some symptoms persist. Most likely, this person's diagnosis is:
    a. paranoid type.
    b. residual type.
    c. undifferentiated type.
    d. unorganized type.

How Do Theorists Explain Schizophrenia?, p. 422
Diff: H, Type: Applied, Ans: a
75.   According to the diathesis-stress model of schizophrenia:
      a. people with a biological predisposition for schizophrenia will develop it if certain
          psychosocial stressors are also present.
      b. people with certain psychosocial stressors will develop schizophrenia in the absence of a
          biological predisposition.
      c. biological predispositions for schizophrenia override any evidence for the importance of
          psychosocial stressors.
      d. people with certain biological predispositions will develop schizophrenia in the absence
          of psychosocial stressors.

Biological Views, pp. 423-424
Diff: M, Type: Applied, Ans: a
76.   Which of the following statements about genetic factors in schizophrenia is accurate?
      a. Close relatives of schizophrenics are more likely to be schizophrenic than distant
          relatives of schizophrenics.
      b. Fraternal twins have a higher concordance rate for schizophrenia than do identical twins.
      c. Schizophrenics who have been adopted are more like their adoptive parents than like
          their biological parents.
      d. Recent family studies eliminate the confounding of environment and genetics.

Biological Views, p. 424
Diff: M, Type: Factual, Ans: c
77.   The data from twin studies have revealed that:
      a. schizophrenia is 100% genetically transmitted.
      b. there is no important genetic component in schizophrenia.
      c. schizophrenia has a strong genetic component.
      d. all types of twins have a relatively low concordance rate for schizophrenia.

Biological Views, p. 424
Diff: M, Type: Applied, Ans: c
78.   Recent research shows that if one identical twin develops schizophrenia, there is about a 50%
      chance the other twin will develop schizophrenia. If future research confirms this finding, we
      will have evidence of:
      a. a strong genetic component of schizophrenia.
      b. a strong environmental component of schizophrenia.
      c. strong environmental and strong genetic components of schizophrenia.
      d. a single, strong "schizophrenia gene."

Biological Views, p. 424
Diff: E, Type: Factual, Ans: b
79.   Based on family pedigree studies, which relative of an individual with a diagnosis of
      schizophrenia would be most at risk for developing the disorder?
      a. niece
      b. sister
      c. father
      d. grandson

Biological Views, p. 424
Diff: M, Type: Factual, Ans: c
80.   What is the rate of concordance for schizophrenia in identical twins?
      a.   2-5%
      b.   15-18%
      c.   40-50%
      d.   70-80%

Biological Views, p. 424
Diff: M, Type: Factual, Ans: b
81.   What is the rate of concordance for schizophrenia in fraternal twins?
      a.   2-5%
      b.   15-18%
      c.   40-50%
      d.   70-80%

Biological Views, p. 424
Diff: H, Type: Applied, Ans: c
82.   If schizophrenia depended solely on genetic make-up, then compared to siblings in general, "fraternal" twins should have:
      a.   four times the concordance rate for schizophrenia.
      b.   twice the concordance rate for schizophrenia.
      c.   the same concordance rate for schizophrenia.
      d.   half the concordance rate for schizophrenia.

Biological Views, pp. 424-425
Diff: M, Type: Factual, Ans: b
83.   The data from studies of the biological and adoptive parents of children who receive a diagnosis of schizophrenia as adults show that the concordance rate of schizophrenia with biological relatives is:
      a.   lower than with adoptive relatives.
      b.   higher than with adoptive relatives.
      c.   a direct function of the age of adoption.
      d.   equally low with both biological and adoptive relatives.

Biological Views, p. 425
Diff: H, Type: Applied, Ans: d
84.   For the first two weeks after starting college, a student can't seem to talk coherently, and is generally unresponsive to the moods of other students in the same dorm. Soon thereafter, the student resumes normal patterns of speaking and social interaction. This is an example of:
      a.   schizoaffective disorder.
      b.   catatonic schizophrenia.
      c.   schizophreniform disorder.
      d.   brief psychotic disorder.

Biological Views, p. 425
Diff: H, Type: Applied, Ans: d
85.   A middle-aged individual shows many of the negative symptoms of schizophrenia, and at the
      same time, often appears profoundly depressed. The symptoms have lasted almost a year.
      This is an example of:
      a.   shared psychotic disorder.
      b.   undifferentiated type of schizophrenia.
      c.   schizophreniform disorder.
      d.   schizoaffective disorder.

Biological Views, p. 425
Diff: H, Type: Applied, Ans: a
86.   A person acts extremely jealous all the time, and complains bitterly whenever other people
      appear to be getting more attention. This had been going on for a couple of months, and the
      person shows no other substantial symptoms. The best diagnosis—assuming, of course, the
      extreme jealousy has no basis in fact—is:
      a.   delusional disorder.
      b.   schizophreniform disorder.
      c.   paranoid schizophrenia.
      d.   brief psychotic disorder.

Biological Views, p. 425
Diff: H, Type: Applied, Ans: c
87.   Which of the following is the best example of a finding from genetic linkage and molecular
      biology studies?
      a.   The brains of schizophrenics are structured differently from the brains of those without
           schizophrenia.
      b.   Schizophrenics process certain neurotransmitters differently from those without
           schizophrenia.
      c.   Defects of certain chromosomes predispose one to schizophrenia.
      d.   Biological relatives of schizophrenics are at greatest risk for schizophrenia.

Biological Views, pp. 426-427
Diff: H, Type: Applied, Ans: c
88.   If the dopamine hypothesis provides an accurate explanation of the cause of schizophrenia,
      one would expect that a drug that was effective against Parkinson's disease symptoms might:
      a.   be an antipsychotic.
      b.   have no effect on psychotic behavior.
      c.   put the patient at risk for psychotic symptoms.
      d.   decrease the amount of dopamine in certain areas of the brain.

Biological Views, pp. 426-427
Diff: H, Type: Applied, Ans: b
89.   Which of the following best supports the dopamine hypothesis for schizophrenia?
      a.   Like those with Parkinsonism, schizophrenics have unusually low levels of dopamine.
      b.   Antipsychotic drugs often produce Parkinson-like symptoms.
      c.   Antipsychotic drugs increase the rate of firing at dopamine receptor sites.
      d.   Dopamine levels vary across the different kinds of schizophrenia.

Biological Views, pp. 426-427
Diff: M, Type: Applied, Ans: b
90.   Researchers found that phenothiazines reduced psychotic symptoms but also caused
      Parkinsonian symptoms (e.g., tremor). This discovery suggests that:
      a. schizophrenia masks Parkinson's disease.
      b. schizophrenia is tied to excessive dopamine.
      c. excessive dopamine is tied to Parkinson's disease.
      d. schizophrenia causes the synthesis of excessive amounts of dopamine.

Biological Views, pp. 426-427
Diff: H, Type: Applied, Ans: d
91.   A mother experiences "baby blues" shortly after delivering a child. The chances that she later
      will develop postpartum psychosis are closest to:
      a. 1 in 2.
      b. 1 in 10.
      c. 1 in 100.
      d. 1 in 1,000.

Postpartum Psychosis: The Case of Andrea Yates, pp. 426-427 (Box 14-4)
Diff: H, Type: Applied, Ans: a
92.   A woman has just been diagnosed with postpartum depression. Most likely, she will:
      a. neither progress to postpartum psychosis, nor physically harm her child.
      b. progress to postpartum psychosis, but will not physically harm her child.
      c. not progress to postpartum psychosis, but will physically harm her child.
      d. progress to postpartum psychosis, and will physically harm her child.

Postpartum Psychosis: The Case of Andrea Yates, pp. 426-427 (Box 14-4)
Diff: H, Type: Applied, Ans: b
93.   Which of the following statements about postpartum psychosis is most accurate?
      a. It affects less than 1% of women who have given birth, and is unpredictable.
      b. It affects less than 1% of women who have given birth, and is more common among
          women with a history of affective disorder.
      c. It affects about 2% of women who have given birth, and is unpredictable.
      d. It affects about 2% of women who have given birth, and is more common among women
          with a history of affective disorder.

Postpartum Psychosis: The Case of Andrea Yates, p. 427 (Box 14-4)
Diff: M, Type: Factual, Ans: a
94.   Postpartum psychosis occurs:
      a. in less than 1% of women, beginning soon after childbirth.
      b. in about 2% of women, beginning soon after childbirth.
      c. in less than 1% of women beginning 1-2 years after childbirth.
      d. in about 2% of women, beginning 1-2 years after childbirth.

Biological Views, p. 427
Diff: M, Type: Applied, Ans: b
95.   If a person receives the chemical L-dopa, a precursor of dopamine, it reduces the symptoms
        of Parkinson's disease. It also sometimes increases symptoms of schizophrenia. What might
        one conclude from this?
        a.   L-dopa causes schizophrenia.
        b.   Excessive dopamine produces schizophrenic symptoms.
        c.   Antipsychotic medication decreases the amount of L-dopa in the brain.
        d.   Antipsychotic medication increases the amount of dopamine in the brain.

Biological Views, pp. 427-428
Diff: M, Type: Factual, Ans: a
96.   The link between dopamine and schizophrenia is supported by the finding that:
        a.   antipsychotic drugs bind to dopamine receptors.
        b.   the use of L-dopa can reduce schizophrenic symptoms.
        c.   anitpsychotic drugs can block Parkinsonian symptoms.
        d.   dopamine-receiving synapses in schizophrenic persons are apparently inactive.

Biological Views, p. 428
Diff: H, Type: Applied, Ans: a
97.   Recently the dopamine hypothesis for schizophrenia has been challenged because it has been
        discovered that:
        a.   effective new drugs suggest abnormal neurotransmitter activity of serotonin as well as
             dopamine.
        b.   excessive dopamine activity contributes to only some kinds of schizophrenia.
        c.   atypical antipsychotic drugs work exclusively on dopamine receptors.
        d.   catatonic schizophrenics respond better to atypical than to traditional antipsychotic drugs.

Biological Views, p. 428
Diff: H, Type: Applied, Ans: b
98.   Francis behaves in a bizarre and ridiculous way. She has hallucinations and impossible leaps
        of logic and is generally unable to function outside an institution. Her schizophrenia is most
        likely related to:
        a.   serotonin.
        b.   dopamine.
        c.   norepinephrine.
        d.   acetylcholine.

Biological Views, p. 428
Diff: M, Type: Applied, Ans: c
99.   You have found enlarged ventricles during a postmortem analysis on a sample of brain tissue.
        This is most likely to be evidence of:
        a.   conversion disorder.
        b.   schizophrenia involving mainly positive symptoms.
        c.   schizophrenia involving mainly negative symptoms.
        d.   schizophreniform disorder.

Biological Views, p. 428
Diff: H, Type: Factual, Ans: c
100.   Regarding brain structure, schizophrenics have been found to have all of the following
       except:
       a.   abnormal blood flow to the brain.
       b.   smaller frontal lobes than nonschizophrenics.
       c.   larger amounts of cortical gray matter.
       d.   enlarged ventricles.

Biological Views, p. 428
Diff: M, Type: Applied, Ans: b
101.   A new medication for schizophrenia appears to work because it blocks dopamine from
       binding to a receptor. The new medication functions as:
       a.   a dopamine production inhibitor.
       b.   a dopamine antagonist.
       c.   a D-1 enhancer.
       d.   a D-2 enhancer.

Biological Views, p. 428
Diff: H, Type: Applied, Ans: c
102.   An individual's brain contains more than the average amount of cerebrospinal fluid. This is a
       sign associated with:
       a.   an unusually low likelihood of experiencing schizophrenia.
       b.   an average likelihood of experiencing schizophrenia.
       c.   an above-average likelihood of experiencing schizophrenia.
       d.   a virtual certainty of experiencing schizophrenia.

Psychological Views, p. 429
Diff: M, Type: Applied, Ans: a
103.   Since 1950, interest in psychological explanations for schizophrenia (as opposed to genetic
       and biological explanations) has:
       a.   decreased, then increased.
       b.   increased, then decreased.
       c.   decreased steadily.
       d.   stayed about the same.

Psychological Views, p. 429
Diff: M, Type: Factual, Ans: a
104.   The finding that the highest rates of schizophrenia are found among people who are born
       during the winter supports which theory of schizophrenia?
       a.   viral theory
       b.   genetic theory
       c.   dopamine theory
       d.   biochemical theory

Psychological Views, p. 429
Diff: H, Type: Applied, Ans: b

105.   Support for the idea that prenatal exposure to viruses causes (or at least contributes to) schizophrenia comes from studies that show:
     a.   more schizophrenics are conceived during the viral-laden winter than the summer.
     b.   fingerprint differences suggesting second trimester exposure to viruses.
     c.   mothers of schizophrenics have bacterial infections during pregnancy.
     d.   schizophrenics have antibodies to bacterial infections.

Psychological Views, p. 429
Diff: E, Type: Factual, Ans: a

106.   The viral explanation for schizophrenia suggests that brain abnormalities, and therefore schizophrenia, result from viral exposure:
     a.   before birth.
     b.   between birth and two years old.
     c.   during puberty.
     d.   during the two years just after puberty.

Psychological Views, p. 429
Diff: H, Type: Applied, Ans: d

107.   If schizophrenia results from prenatal exposure to viruses which cause brain abnormalities, then one would expect what kind of correlation between schizophrenic birth rates and stillbirth rates?
     a.   strong negative
     b.   weak negative
     c.   weak positive
     d.   strong positive

Psychological Views, p. 429
Diff: H, Type: Applied, Ans: a

108.   Freud thought that schizophrenia developed because inadequate parents caused their children to:
     a.   regress to a state of primary narcissism.
     b.   develop unnecessarily harsh superego control.
     c.   give up any attempts to reestablish ego control.
     d.   become excessively concerned with the needs of others.

Psychological Views, p. 429
Diff: M, Type: Factual, Ans: c

109.   According to Freud, schizophrenic people:
     a.   regress to the anal period.
     b.   are the victims of double-bind communication.
     c.   regress to a pre-ego state of primary narcissism.
     d.   receive a label that influences them to behave in a schizophrenic manner.

Psychological Views, p. 429
Diff: H, Type: Factual, Ans: b
110. According to Freudian psychodynamic interpretation, people who develop schizophrenia regress to a state of:
   a. secondary denial.
   b. primary narcissism.
   c. primary process thought.
   d. secondary thought processing.

Psychological Views, p. 430
Diff: H, Type: Applied, Ans: c
111. According to Fromm-Reichmann, schizophrenogenic mothers would be most likely to:
   a. genuinely self-sacrifice for their children.
   b. regress to a pre-ego level of functioning.
   c. be both overprotecting and rejecting of their children.
   d. be schizophrenic themselves.

Psychological Views, p. 430
Diff: M, Type: Factual, Ans: b
112. According to Frieda Fromm-Reichmann, schizophrenia is caused by:
   a. an excess of dopamine.
   b. a schizophrenegenic mother.
   c. regression to a stage of primary narcissism.
   d. an inadequately learned discrimination for cues that convey emotion.

Psychological Views, p. 430
Diff: H, Type: Applied, Ans: d
113. A psychodynamic theorist of the 21st century is most likely to say:
   a. "Fromm-Reichmann was right; schizophrenegenic mothers cause most cases of schizophrenia."
   b. "Fromm-Reichmann was wrong; schizophrenegenic teachers cause most cases of schizophrenia."
   c. "Extreme regression can lead to biological abnormalities."
   d. "Biological abnormalities can lead to extreme regression."

Psychological Views, p. 430
Diff: M, Type: Applied, Ans: b
114. "If one receives a good deal of attention for unusual behaviors, is it any surprise those behaviors are strengthened?" is a question most likely asked by what kind of theorist?
   a. cognitive
   b. behavioral
   c. psychodynamic
   d. sociocultural

Psychological Views, p. 430
Diff: H, Type: Applied, Ans: c
115. The behavioral approach to understanding schizophrenia is based on the observation that:
   a. parents of schizophrenics often reward their children's appropriate behavior to no avail.
   b. schizophrenics seem unusually responsive to rewards and punishments.
   c. schizophrenics can learn some appropriate behaviors.
   d. parents of schizophrenics don't know what is appropriate behavior for their children.

Psychological Views, p. 430
Diff: H, Type: Applied, Ans: b

116.   You hear a professor use the term "schizophrenogenic family" in a discussion of causes of schizophrenia. You can be pretty sure that the professor is describing a:
   a.   psychodynamic factor strongly supported by research.
   b.   psychodynamic factor largely unsupported by research.
   c.   cognitive-behavioral factor strongly supported by research.
   d.   cognitive-behavioral factor largely unsupported by research.

Psychological Views, p. 430
Diff: M, Type: Applied, Ans: d

117.   A behaviorist is able, using operant conditioning, to eliminate most of a schizophrenic's unusual behaviors. The behaviorist has demonstrated that those particular unusual behaviors:
   a.   were not acquired through classical conditioning.
   b.   were not acquired through operant conditioning.
   c.   were acquired through operant conditioning.
   d.   might have been acquired through operant conditioning.

Psychological Views, p. 430
Diff: H, Type: Applied, Ans: c

118.   A good summary of the behavioral view's explanation for schizophrenia is that the behavioral view does a:
   a.   reasonably good job of accounting for both the origins and the situational aspects of schizophrenic behaviors.
   b.   reasonably good job of accounting for the origins, but not the situational aspects, of schizophrenic behaviors.
   c.   reasonably good job of accounting for the situational aspects, but not the origins, of schizophrenic behaviors.
   d.   poor job of accounting for either the situational aspects or the origins of schizophrenic behaviors.

Psychological Views, p. 431
Diff: H, Type: Applied, Ans: c

119.   A person begins exhibiting early symptoms of schizophrenia; for example, hearing voices. Family members decide to discuss the voices with the person, to try to understand what is going on. This action by family members should:
   a.   increase the likelihood of future symptoms, according to both the behavioral and the cognitive viewpoints.
   b.   decrease the likelihood of future symptoms, according to both the behavioral and the cognitive viewpoints.
   c.   increase the likelihood of future symptoms, according to the behavioral viewpoint only.
   d.   increase the likelihood of future symptoms, according to the cognitive viewpoint only.

Psychological Views, p. 431
Diff: H, Type: Applied, Ans: a

120.   The cognitive view of schizophrenia is based on the assumption that schizophrenics experience strange and unreal sensations:
   a.   then tell their friends and family, who deny the reality of the sensations.
   b.   and misinterpret them as "normal."
   c.   that have no basis in biology.
   d.   confirmed by their schizophrenic mothers.

Psychological Views, p. 431
Diff: M, Type: Applied, Ans: a
121.   Occasionally, you see or hear things. Your friends tell you it's your imagination. Eventually you come to think your friends are hiding something and you develop delusions of persecution to explain their behavior. This thinking leads you down the "rational road to madness." This scenario is consistent with the _____ view.
   a.   cognitive
   b.   behavioral
   c.   existential
   d.   psychodynamic

Psychological Views, p. 431
Diff: M, Type: Factual, Ans: d
122.   The "rational path to madness" is most consistent with a _____ orientation.
   a.   behavioral
   b.   family systems
   c.   psychoanalytic
   d.   cognitive

Sociocultural Views, p. 431
Diff: M, Type: Applied, Ans: d
123.   People around those who have been diagnosed as schizophrenic begin to treat them as if they are "crazy," expecting and overreacting to odd behaviors that they might not even notice in others. This observation is most consistent with the _____ understanding of schizophrenia.
   a.   psychodynamic
   b.   family systems
   c.   cognitive
   d.   sociocultural

Sociocultural Views, p. 432
Diff: M, Type: Factual, Ans: b
124.   David Rosenhan sent eight normal people to various psychiatric hospitals complaining of hearing voices that said "empty," "hollow," and "thud." All eight people acted normally after being admitted to the hospital, yet all were diagnosed as schizophrenic. One of the conclusions from this study is that:
   a.   clinicians are unable to detect "real" schizophrenia.
   b.   the expectations produced by labeling can alter perception.
   c.   hospitals can produce schizophrenic behavior in normal people.
   d.   auditory hallucinations are sufficient for diagnosis as schizophrenic.

Sociocultural Views, p. 432
Diff: M, Type: Factual, Ans: a
125.   The idea of "metacommunication" is most important to one who thinks schizophrenia arises from:
   a.   double-bind messages.
   b.   operant conditioning contingencies.
   c.   expressed emotion.
   d.   a "rational path to madness."

Sociocultural Views, p. 432
Diff: H, Type: Applied, Ans: b
126.   Which of the following is the best example of a double-bind communication?
       a.   saying "Get away from me" while frowning and crossing one's arms
       b.   saying "I love you" but refusing to allow the child in your lap
       c.   saying "I love you" and cuddling the child
       d.   saying "Get away from me. You are not my child when you act like that."

Sociocultural Views, p. 432
Diff: M, Type: Applied, Ans: d
127.   Iphi glowered, and when her son did not come over to say hello, she said, "What's wrong?
       Don't you love your old mom anymore?" This is a(n):
       a.   distorted message.
       b.   existential message.
       c.   narcissistic message.
       d.   double-bind message.

Sociocultural Views, p. 432
Diff: M, Type: Factual, Ans: d
128.   Families that display high levels of expressed emotion do all of the following except:
       a.   intrude on one another's privacy.
       b.   frequently express negative emotions toward each other.
       c.   show hostility toward each other.
       d.   indicate approval of one another's actions.

Sociocultural Views, p. 432
Diff: H, Type: Applied, Ans: a
129.   In 1949, Eddy Howard wrote song lyrics which included, "Your lips tell me no, no/But
       there's yes, yes in your eye. . . ." If Mr. Howard were correct in his observations, then he
       described:
       a.   a double-bind message (and something a "schizophrenogenic mother" might do).
       b.   a double-bind message (but not something a "schizophrenogenic mother" might do).
       c.   something a "schizophrenogenic mother" might do, but not a double-bind message.
       d.   neither something a "schizophrenogenic mother" might do, nor a double-bind message.

Sociocultural Views, pp. 432-433
Diff: H, Type: Applied, Ans: d
130.   If observations of a relationship between "expressed emotion" in families and recovery from
       schizophrenia demonstrate cause-and-effect, one would predict that relapse would be least
       common in schizophrenics whose families:
       a.   frequently express criticism, and do not allow much privacy.
       b.   frequently express criticism, and allow a good deal of privacy.
       c.   infrequently express criticism, and do not allow much privacy.
       d.   infrequently express criticism, and allow a good deal of privacy.

Sociocultural Views, p. 433
Diff: M, Type: Applied, Ans: c

131.   Which theoretical orientation holds the perspective that schizophrenia is a constructive
        process designed to cure the individual of unhappiness and confusion produced by the family
        or society?
        a. cognitive
        b. behavioral
        c. sociocultural-existential
        d. psychodynamic

Sociocultural Views, p. 433
Diff: M, Type: Applied, Ans: c

132.   Which one of the following would be most likely to say that schizophrenia is a constructive
        process through which people try to find their "true" selves?
        a. psychodynamic theorists
        b. behaviorists
        c. sociocultural-existential theorists
        d. cognitive theorists

Putting It Together, p. 434
Diff: M, Type: Factual, Ans: b

133.   Schizophrenia researchers have been:
        a. about equally successful in identifying biological and psychological origins of
            schizophrenia.
        b. more successful in identifying biological origins than psychological origins of
            schizophrenia.
        c. more successful in identifying psychological origins than biological origins of
            schizophrenia.
        d. frustratingly unsuccessful in identifying either biological or psychological origins of
            schizophrenia.

FILL-IN QUESTIONS

Schizophrenia, p. 411
Diff: M, Type: Factual, Ans: dementia praecox

1.   The term that Emil Kraepelin used for what we now call schizophrenia was _____.

What Are the Symptoms of Schizophrenia?, p. 416
**Diff: E, Type: Factual, Ans: delusions (or: hallucination, disorganized thinking and
speech, heightened perceptions, or inappropriate affect)**

2.   A positive symptom in schizophrenia is _____.

What Are the Symptoms of Schizophrenia?, p. 416
Diff: E, Type: Applied, Ans: reference

3.   If you think the radio announcer is talking directly and personally to you and to you alone,
        this is a delusion of _____.

What Are the Symptoms of Schizophrenia?, p. 416
Diff: E, Type: Applied, Ans: control

4.   If you think you are being manipulated by a power on the moon, this is a delusion of _____.

What Are the Symptoms of Schizophrenia?, p. 416
Diff: E, Type: Applied, Ans: grandeur

5.   If you think you are the Majority Leader of the Senate, this is a delusion of _____.

Relationships of the Mind, p. 417 (Box 14-2)
Diff: H, Type: Applied, Ans: erotomanic delusions

6.   "I know he loves me!" shouts the stalker about an individual the stalker never actually met. The stalker is experiencing _____.

What Are the Symptoms of Schizophrenia?, p. 418
Diff: M, Type: Applied, Ans: clang (or rhyme)

7.   "You know, so, go, show all your thorough status quo," says a schizophrenic who is demonstrating _____.

What Are the Symptoms of Schizophrenia?, p. 418
Diff: E, Type: Factual, Ans: perseveration

8.   Schizophrenic individuals who repeat words and statements again and again are displaying the symptoms of _____.

What Are the Symptoms of Schizophrenia?, p. 419
Diff: E, Type: Applied, Ans: hallucination (or positive symptom)

9.   Karin, who has a diagnosis of schizophrenia, frequently sees hundreds of beautiful hummingbirds swarming around her. This symptom is an example of a(n)_____.

What Are the Symptoms of Schizophrenia?, p. 420
Diff: E, Type: Factual, Ans: flat affect (or: poverty of speech, social withdrawal, blunted affect, loss of volition)

10.   A negative symptom in schizophrenia is _____.

What Are the Symptoms of Schizophrenia?, p. 419
Diff: M, Type: Applied, Ans: somatic

11.   A schizophrenic client says, "It's happening again! The lizards are crawling in my guts." This form of hallucination—assuming, of course, that there are no lizards are in the client's guts—is _____.

What Are the Symptoms of Schizophrenia?, p. 420
Diff: E, Type: Factual, Ans: flat affect

12.   A schizophrenic person who shows almost no emotion at all is exhibiting _____.

Howling for Attention, p. 421 (Box 14-3)
Diff: H, Type: Applied, Ans: lycanthropy

13.   If a friend of yours howls at the moon, runs around at night biting people, and believes this condition originated because of being bitten by someone (something?) else with the same condition, your friend most likely would be diagnosed as having _____.

What Are the Symptoms of Schizophrenia?, p. 421
Diff: M, Type: Applied, Ans: avolition (or apathy)

14.   A schizophrenic cannot complete even the simplest of tasks, is extremely listless, and has no short- or long-term goals. This person is exhibiting _____.

What Is the Course of Schizophrenia?, p. 422
Diff: E, Type: Factual, Ans: prodromal

15.   Bill does not exhibit any signs of schizophrenia but his level of functioning has begun to deteriorate. If Bill later develops schizophrenia, this earlier period is referred to as the _____ phase.

Diagnosing Schizophrenia, p. 423
Diff: E, Type: Factual, Ans: catatonic

16.   Psychomotor disturbances are the central feature of _____ type of schizophrenia.

Diagnosing Schizophrenia, p. 423
Diff: E, Type: Factual, Ans: catatonic

17.   According to DSM-IV-TR, when the dominant symptoms of schizophrenia are near-total immobility or wild excitement, their schizophrenic disorder would be classified as _____ type.

How Do Theorists Explain Schizophrenia?, p. 423
Diff: M, Type: Factual, Ans: diathesis-stress

18.   One view of schizophrenia is that it results from some sort of psychological stimulus in individuals with a biological weakness. This is known as the _____ perspective or view.

Biological Views, p. 424
Diff: H, Type: Factual, Ans: concordant

19.   If both members of a twin pair have a particular trait, they are said to be _____ for that trait.

Biological Views, p. 426
Diff: M, Type: Factual, Ans: molecular biology (or genetic linkage)

20.   Blood samples are taken from members of a family. The DNA in the blood cells is isolated and used for identifying genetic factors. This approach is known as _____.

Biological Views, p. 426
Diff: M, Type: Factual, Ans: dopamine

21.   The neurotransmitter most strongly implicated as a biological factor in schizophrenia is _____.

Biological Views, p. 426
Diff: E, Type: Factual, Ans: Parkinson's disease

22.   One of the unfortunate side effects of the phenothiazines is a disorder like _____.

Biological Views, p. 427
Diff: H, Type: Factual, Ans: amphetamine psychosis

23.   Excessive use of amphetamines may lead to schizophrenia-like symptoms known as _____.

Psychological Views, p. 429
Diff: H, Type: Factual, Ans: regression ; restore (or reestablish)

24.   Psychodynamic theorists view the development of schizophrenia as a two-part psychological process: a _____ to pre-ego functioning, followed by an effort to _____ ego function.

Psychological Views, p. 430
Diff: H, Type: Factual, Ans: schizophrenegenic
25.   According to Frieda Fromm-Reichmann's view of the development of schizophrenia, an apparently self-sacrificing mother who is actually cold and domineering and uses her children for her own needs is a _____ mother.

Psychological Views, p. 430
Diff: E, Type: Factual, Ans: operant conditioning (or reinforcement)
26.   Behaviorists most often suggest _____ as the cause of schizophrenia.

Sociocultural Views, p. 432
Diff: M, Type: Factual, Ans: labeling (or social labeling or diagnostic labeling)
27.   Rosenhan (1973) did a study of schizophrenia that demonstrated the power of _____ in determining how schizophrenic patients are evaluated and treated.

Sociocultural Views, p. 432
Diff: M, Type: Factual, Ans: nonverbal (or meta)
28.   A double-bind message involves a contradiction between the message's primary communication and its _____ communication.

ESSAY QUESTIONS

What Are the Symptoms of Schizophrenia?, pp. 416-420
Diff: E, Type: Factual
1.   Describe the positive symptoms of schizophrenia.

What Are the Symptoms of Schizophrenia?, pp. 417-418
Diff: M, Type: Applied
2.   Provide an example of these various patterns of disorganized speech and thought in schizophrenia: derailment (loose associations), neologism, perseveration, and clang.

What Are the Symptoms of Schizophrenia?, pp. 420-422
Diff: M, Type: Factual
3.   Describe the negative symptoms of schizophrenia.

Diagnosing Schizophrenia, p. 423
Diff: H, Type: Applied
4.   Write a paragraph on the topic "What I Did on My Summer Vacation" as if you were a paranoid schizophrenic.

Diagnosing Schizophrenia, p. 423
Diff: H, Type: Applied
5.   Write a short letter to your parents asking for money as if you were a disorganized schizophrenic.

How Do Theorists Explain Schizophrenia?, p. 423
Diff: H, Type: Applied
6.   Explain the diathesis-stress model of schizophrenia and provide an example of how it might apply in the development of schizophrenia in a given individual.

Biological Views, pp. 423-425
Diff: H, Type: Factual

7.   Discuss evidence that supports the view of a genetic predisposition for schizophrenia.

Biological Views, pp. 426-428
Diff: H, Type: Factual

8.   Provide evidence from scientific studies that supports the dopamine hypothesis of
       schizophrenia and evidence that critiques it.

Psychological Views, pp. 430-431
Diff: H, Type: Applied

9.   Imagine that a person has just begun to have unusual (strange and unreal) sensations.
       Naturally, the person turns to friends and family to discuss these. From a cognitive point of
       view, explain how schizophrenia might develop from this point on.

Putting It Together, pp. 433-434
Diff: H, Type: Applied

10.   A psychology major friend of yours says, "I want to do cutting-edge research on the causes of
       schizophrenia when I finish grad school." Based on what is known today about the causes of
       schizophrenia, what advice would you give your friend, and why?

CHAPTER 15   Treatments for Schizophrenia and Other Severe Mental Disorders

MULTIPLE-CHOICE QUESTIONS

Treatments for Schizophrenia and Other Severe mental Disorders, p. 437
Diff: M, Type: Applied, Ans: c

1. In reality, the person labeled "schizophrenic" was suffering from a major depressive disorder. Most likely, this misdiagnosis occurred in the United States in the:
   a. mid-1800s.
   b. late-1800s.
   c. mid-1900s.
   d. late 1900s.

Institutional Care in the Past, p. 438
Diff: H, Type: Applied, Ans: a

2. A mental hospital, abandoned since the late 1900s, decays near the Appalachian Trail in rural New York, miles from the nearest city. In the early 1900s, when the hospital was built, that kind of location was:
   a. common, since land was cheap and wages were low in rural areas.
   b. a bit uncommon; land was cheap, but workers were hard to get, in rural areas.
   c. a bit uncommon; wages were low in rural areas, but land was expensive because of "suburban sprawl."
   d. very uncommon; workers were hard to get in rural areas, and land was expensive because of "suburban sprawl."

Institutional Care in the Past, p. 438
Diff: E, Type: Factual, Ans: a

3. What was the dominant way of dealing with schizophrenic people during the first half of the 20th century?
   a. institutionalization
   b. outpatient services
   c. individual psychotherapy
   d. treatment with neuroleptic drugs

Institutional Care in the Past, p. 438
Diff: E, Type: Applied, Ans: c

4. The chief contribution of Philippe Pinel to the care of those with severe mental illnesses was to:
   a. develop state hospitals for those who couldn't afford private care.
   b. use antipsychotic drugs in highly controlled settings.
   c. treat patients with sympathy and kindness.
   d. promote deinstitutionalization.

Lobotomy: How Could It Happen?, pp. 438-439 (Box 15-1)
Diff: M, Type: Factual, Ans: a

5.   Who was the first physician responsible for developing the prefrontal lobotomy for use on human patients?
      a. Egas Moniz
      b. Eliot Valenstein
      c. Walter Freeman
      d. Carlyle Jacobsen

Lobotomy: How Could It Happen?, p. 438
Diff: E, Type: Factual, Ans: b

6.   The technique for treating mental patients that was pioneered by Egas Moniz was:
      a. ECS therapy.
      b. the lobotomy.
      c. the use of drugs.
      d. the cingulotomy.

Lobotomy: How Could It Happen?, p. 439
Diff: M, Type: Factual, Ans: c

7.   The Americans Walter Freeman and James Watts "improved" the procedure developed by Egas Moniz by developing the:
      a. prefrontal lobotomy.
      b. prefrontal leucotomy.
      c. transorbital lobotomy.
      d. complete prefrontal lobectomy.

Lobotomy: How Could It Happen?, p. 439
Diff: H, Type: Factual, Ans: b

8.   One who had a needle inserted into the brain through the eye socket and then rotated in order to destroy brain tissue, experienced a:
      a. prefrontal lobotomy.
      b. transorbital lobotomy.
      c. singular nigra lobotomy.
      d. facial-cranial lobotomy.

Lobotomy: How Could It Happen?, p. 439
Diff: H, Type: Factual, Ans: b

9.   Why was lobotomy so enthusiastically accepted by the medical community in the 1940s and 1950s?
      a. it was based on sound experimental studies with animals
      b. it was practiced by eminent physicians
      c. it had relatively few and mild side effects
      d. it could be used to control criminals as well as mental patients

Institutional Care in the Past, p. 439
Diff: H, Type: Applied, Ans: c
10.   "Most schizophrenics were institutionalized in public hospitals and received only the basic necessities of life. Mostly patients were ignored, but sometimes abused." These statements are most characteristic of treatment in the U.S. in the year:
    a.   1750.
    b.   1845.
    c.   1945.
    d.   1990.

Institutional Care in the Past, p. 439
Diff: M, Type: Applied, Ans: c
11.   Which of the following is true of state mental hospitals in the U.S. in the mid-20th century?
    a.   They were built as places to warehouse, isolate, and punish mental patients.
    b.   They were built in large cities so patients could stay in contact with the "real" world.
    c.   They were overcrowded and understaffed.
    d.   Although successful treatments were available, they were too expensive to be used.

Institutional Care in the Past, p. 439
Diff: M, Type: Factual, Ans: a
12.   Most patients who lived on the back wards of state mental hospitals in the mid-1900's:
    a.   were schizophrenics.
    b.   were given individual "talk" therapy to no avail.
    c.   interacted well with each other but not with staff members.
    d.   were in fact violent criminals.

Institutional Care in the Past, p. 439
Diff: H, Type: Factual, Ans: b
13.   Patients who developed extreme withdrawal, anger, physical aggressiveness, and loss of personal hygiene as a result of poor institutional care were showing a pattern known as:
    a.   institutional deterioration.
    b.   social breakdown syndrome.
    c.   chronic back ward syndrome.
    d.   schizophrenic failure to thrive.

Institutional Care in the Past, p. 439
Diff: E, Type: Applied, Ans: d
14.   The usual way of dealing with troublesome or violent schizophrenic people in institutions in the first half of the 20th century was to:
    a.   use drugs.
    b.   beat them.
    c.   ignore them.
    d.   use physical restraint.

Institutional Care in the Past, p. 439
Diff: E, Type: Factual, Ans: c
15.   Long-term mental patients frequently developed anger, aggressiveness, and loss of interest in personal appearance. This condition has been called:
   a.   psychosis.
   b.   schizophrenia.
   c.   social breakdown syndrome.
   d.   neuroleptic malignant syndrome.

Institutional Care in the Past, p. 439
Diff: M, Type: Factual, Ans: d
16.   In the past the most common pattern of deterioration in patients that apparently resulted from institutionalization was:
   a.   movement disorder.
   b.   paranoid delusions.
   c.   auditory hallucinations.
   d.   social breakdown syndrome.

Institutional Care in the Past, p. 439
Diff: H, Type: Applied, Ans: d
17.   In 1950, a state mental hospital patient confined to a back ward initially made good progress in therapy, and was diagnosed as suffering from major depressive disorder. Compared to others confined in back wards in the 1950s, this patient was:
   a.   typical: most back ward patients then were not schizophrenic, and made good initial progress in therapy.
   b.   a bit atypical: most back ward patients then were not schizophrenic, and did not make good initial progress in therapy.
   c.   a bit atypical: most back ward patients then made good initial progress in therapy, and were schizophrenic.
   d.   very atypical: most back ward patients then did not make good initial progress in therapy, and were schizophrenic.

Milieu Therapy, p. 440
Diff: E, Type: Factual, Ans: c
18.   Humanistic theorists propose that institutionalized patients deteriorate because they are deprived of opportunities to develop self-respect and independence. The therapy that counters this effect by creating an environment that encourages self-respect and responsibility is known as:
   a.   token therapy.
   b.   social therapy.
   c.   milieu therapy.
   d.   environmental enhancement.

Milieu Therapy, p. 440
Diff: M, Type: Applied, Ans: a
19.   Which (humanistic) therapy is based on the premise that when you change the social environment you change the patient?
   a.   milieu therapy
   b.   insight therapy
   c.   family therapy
   d.   the token economy

Milieu Therapy, p. 440
Diff: M, Type: Applied, Ans: d

20. Maxwell Jones created an approach to psychotherapy of the institutionalized in London called:
    a. oral therapy.
    b. group therapy.
    c. a token economy.
    d. the therapeutic community.

Milieu Therapy, p. 440
Diff: E, Type: Applied, Ans: c

21. Milieu therapy is based primarily on the principles of _____ psychology.
    a. cognitive
    b. behavioral
    c. humanistic
    d. psychodynamic

Milieu Therapy, p. 440
Diff: H, Type: Applied, Ans: d

22. If one were treated by therapists who believed that patients needed to live in a social climate that promoted productive activity, self-respect, and individual responsibility, one would be likely to be living in the:
    a. 1920s.
    b. 1930s.
    c. 1940s.
    d. 1950s.

Milieu Therapy, p. 440
Diff: M, Type: Applied, Ans: c

23. A patient (called a resident) who lives in a therapeutic community and actively works with staff members to create a life that is as much like that outside the hospital as possible, is probably receiving _____ therapy.
    a. token economy
    b. custodial
    c. milieu
    d. lobotomy

Milieu Therapy, p. 440
Diff: M, Type: Factual, Ans: c

24. Maxwell Jones is best known as the one who:
    a. unchained the insane in Paris.
    b. established public mental hospitals in the U.S.
    c. developed a therapeutic community in London.
    d. opened up the back wards in Philadelphia.

The Token Economy, p. 440
Diff: H, Type: Factual, Ans: a

25.   Token economies developed initially because:
   a.   behaviorists were only allowed to work with patients whose problems seemed hopeless.
   b.   behaviorists were invited to mental hospitals because they held high status in the psychiatric community.
   c.   behaviorists, who were mostly nurses, wanted a way to get patients to take better care of their personal hygiene.
   d.   behaviorists had tried the new antipsychotic medications with their patients and found them to be ineffective.

The Token Economy, p. 440
Diff: E, Type: Applied, Ans: c

26.   A token economy approach to treatment is based on principles from the _____ view of abnormal behavior.
   a.   cognitive
   b.   biological
   c.   behavioral
   d.   humanistic

The Token Economy, p. 440
Diff: E, Type: Applied, Ans: c

27.   What is the token in behavioral terms?
   a.   a stimulus
   b.   motivation
   c.   a reinforcer
   d.   punishment

The Token Economy, p. 440
Diff: M, Type: Applied, Ans: b

28.   What is the best example of a token in everyday life?
   a.   food
   b.   money
   c.   power
   d.   shelter

The Token Economy, pp. 440-441
Diff: M, Type: Factual, Ans: b

29.   Tokens:
   a.   are given by patients to other patients whom they admire.
   b.   can be exchanged for a variety of reinforcers.
   c.   are given as punishment when one behaves unacceptably.
   d.   have a great street value.

The Token Economy, pp. 440-441
Diff: H, Type: Applied, Ans: c

30.   A third-grade teacher gives students stickers throughout the day when they engage in appropriate behaviors. At the end of the day, students can trade in their stickers for treats from the class "treasure chest." This program is most similar to which form of therapy used for institutionalized people with schizophrenia?
   a.   milieu therapy
   b.   insight therapy
   c.   token economy
   d.   partial hospitalization

The Token Economy, p. 441
Diff: H, Type: Applied, Ans: c

31.   If you wanted the therapy that would be most likely to reduce your psychotic symptoms and get you out of the mental hospital, you would want:
   a.   custodial care.
   b.   milieu therapy.
   c.   a token economy program.
   d.   insight therapy.

The Token Economy, p. 441
Diff: H, Type: Applied, Ans: b

32.   If researchers/therapists said they wanted to give patients food and a comfortable bed only when they behaved appropriately, the researchers/therapists would probably be told by hospital administrators:
   a.   ok, if you have a control group.
   b.   that's illegal.
   c.   tokens can be used for anything the patient chooses.
   d.   ok, if you continue to do that once the patient is released to a halfway house.

The Token Economy, p. 441
Diff: H, Type: Applied, Ans: c

33.   Which of the following is not a criticism of the token economy approach?
   a.   Many studies of effectiveness do not include a control group, confounding the treatment with attention.
   b.   Although token economy programs can change patients' delusional statements, they may not be changing delusional thoughts.
   c.   Token economy programs do not change the behavior of the most severely ill patients.
   d.   It is difficult for patients to make the transition from a token economy program to the community.

The Token Economy, p. 441
Diff: M, Type: Factual, Ans: c

34.   Which of the following best describes the effectiveness of token economy strategies?
   a.   They are ineffective in the long run.
   b.   They are reversing the progress of schizophrenia.
   c.   They are successful at changing the patient's behavior.
   d.   They are successful in altering the patient's distorted thinking.

The Token Economy, p. 441
Diff: M, Type: Factual, Ans: d

35.   What is the concern over the quality of the changes produced by token economies?
    a.   Many studies of token economies are methodologically flawed.
    b.   Some patients can function in normal life but deteriorate in the hospital.
    c.   The skills learned in the hospital may not generalize to the outside world.
    d.   The person may have learned new behaviors without changing his or her distorted thinking.

The Token Economy, p. 441
Diff: H, Type: Applied, Ans: b

36.   Recent questions raised about the use of token economy programs in mental hospitals have been:
    a.   theoretical questions about whether operant conditioning actually works.
    b.   legal and ethical questions about depriving patients of rewards used in the token economy.
    c.   economic questions about the cost of maintaining programs that have only a minimal effect on actual behaviors.
    d.   theoretical questions about why patients' thoughts often change while their behaviors don't.

The Token Economy, pp. 441-442
Diff: H, Type: Applied, Ans: d

37.   In the late 1950s, patients diagnosed with schizophrenia on one ward in a state mental hospital began making substantial progress. They became more active, their symptoms decreased, and within a few years, almost all of them had moved on to sheltered-care facilities, or other care outside the hospital. Most likely, they had been:
    a.   receiving atypical antipsychotic drugs.
    b.   participants in a well-controlled lobotomy study.
    c.   in milieu therapy.
    d.   in a token economy.

Antipsychotic Drugs, p. 442
Diff: E, Type: Factual, Ans: b

38.   The first of the important group of antipsychotic drugs, the phenothiazines, was developed during the:
    a.   1940s.
    b.   1950s.
    c.   1960s.
    d.   1970s.

Antipsychotic Drugs, p. 442
Diff: M, Type: Factual, Ans: c

39.   The first antipsychotic drug to be approved for use in the U.S. was:
    a.   Haldol.
    b.   Prozac.
    c.   Thorazine.
    d.   Mellaril.

Antipsychotic Drugs, p. 442
Diff: M, Type: Factual, Ans: a
40.   Antipsychotic drugs were discovered accidentally when researchers were trying to develop:
   a.   antihistamines.
   b.   analgesics.
   c.   sedatives.
   d.   antibiotics.

Antipsychotic Drugs, p. 442
Diff: E, Type: Factual, Ans: c
41.   The discovery of antihistamine drugs in the 1940s indirectly led to the development of:
   a.   lithium.
   b.   antianxiety drugs.
   c.   antipsychotic drugs.
   d.   antidepressant drugs.

Antipsychotic Drugs, p. 442
Diff: E, Type: Factual, Ans: d
42.   The term neuroleptic is applied to drugs that:
   a.   cure psychosis.
   b.   cure schizophrenia.
   c.   have potency against depression.
   d.   can mimic symptoms of neurological disorders.

Antipsychotic Drugs, p. 442
Diff: H, Type: Factual, Ans: d
43.   Which of the following drugs has antipsychotic properties?
   a.   Prozac
   b.   Valium
   c.   imipramine
   d.   haloperidol

Antipsychotic Drugs, p. 442
Diff: E, Type: Applied, Ans: d
44.   Very high dopamine activity is related to:
   a.   anxiety disorders.
   b.   addictive behavior.
   c.   Parkinson's disease.
   d.   schizophrenic disorders.

Antipsychotic Drugs, p. 442
Diff: E, Type: Factual, Ans: b
45.   The neuroleptic action of many drugs appears to depend on the ability to interfere with the activity of:
   a.   GABA.
   b.   dopamine.
   c.   serotonin.
   d.   norepinephrine.

Antipsychotic Drugs, p. 442
Diff: H, Type: Applied, Ans: a
46.   Antipsychotic drugs reduce symptoms by:
   a.   blocking transmission of the neurotransmitter dopamine.
   b.   enabling the body to decrease the number of dopamine receptor sites.
   c.   causing serotonin and other neurotransmitters to occupy dopamine sites.
   d.   reducing the total amount of dopamine circulating in the body.

How Effective Are Antipsychotic Drugs?, p. 443
Diff: H, Type: Applied, Ans: d
47.   If one were taking antipsychotic drugs for schizophrenia, one would expect the drugs to:
   a.   be most effective against the negative symptoms of schizophrenia.
   b.   be most effective after about six months.
   c.   be given in higher doses to women than to men.
   d.   need to be taken even after symptoms have been alleviated.

How Effective Are Antipsychotic Drugs?, p. 443
Diff: M, Type: Applied, Ans: a
48.   The schizophrenic symptom most likely to be relieved by antipsychotic drugs is:
   a.   delusions.
   b.   flat affect.
   c.   lack of speech.
   d.   lack of purpose.

How Effective Are Antipsychotic Drugs?, p. 443
Diff: M, Type: Applied, Ans: a
49.   If you could use only one treatment for schizophrenia and wanted the most effective treatment, you should choose:
   a.   antipsychotic drugs.
   b.   psychodynamic therapy.
   c.   milieu therapy.
   d.   electroconvulsive therapy.

The Unwanted Effects of Conventional Antipsychotic Drugs, p. 443
Diff: M, Type: Applied, Ans: a
50.   If a patient's chart said the patient had extrapyramidal side effects, you would expect to see the patient showing primarily _____ dysfunction.
   a.   motor
   b.   cognitive
   c.   emotional
   d.   language

The Unwanted Effects of Conventional Antipsychotic Drugs, p. 443
Diff: H, Type: Applied, Ans: b

51. A well-controlled clinical study of a commonly-used antipsychotic drug shows improvement in about 70% of those taking the drug after about six months of treatment. Those running the study:
     a. can stop the study, since most improvement with antipsychotic drugs occurs within six months.
     b. can stop the study, since most improvement with antipsychotic drugs occurs within six months, although participants should keep taking the drug, to prevent relapse.
     c. should continue the study for at least another six months, since much of the improvement with antipsychotic drugs occurs only after six or more months of the drug.
     d. must stop the study, since six months is far too long to take most antipsychotic drugs continuously.

The Unwanted Effects of Conventional Antipsychotic Drugs, p. 443
Diff: H, Type: Applied, Ans: a

52. Studies of the effectiveness of antipsychotic drugs indicate that:
     a. most recipients show substantial improvement, and almost no one gets worse.
     b. most recipients show substantial improvement, but about 10% get worse.
     c. about half of recipients show substantial improvement, and almost no one gets worse.
     d. about half of recipients show substantial improvement, but about 10% get worse.

The Unwanted Effects of Conventional Antipsychotic Drugs, p. 444
Diff: M, Type: Factual, Ans: c

53. The side effect of antipsychotic drugs, known as akathisia, is marked by:
     a. delusions.
     b. shouting obscenities.
     c. restlessness and agitation.
     d. bizarre movements of the tongue and neck.

The Unwanted Effects of Conventional Antipsychotic Drugs, p. 444
Diff: H, Type: Applied, Ans: b

54. Parkinson-like symptoms in someone taking antipsychotic medication:
     a. mean that one must stop taking the medication.
     b. can usually be successfully treated with an anti-Parkinsonian drug.
     c. unfortunately cannot be successfully treated at this time.
     d. lead to neuroleptic malignant syndrome.

The Unwanted Effects of Conventional Antipsychotic Drugs, p. 444
Diff: H, Type: Applied, Ans: b

55. Karen has been taking chlorpromazine for 25 years. Lately, she has been quite restless and agitated. She complains of soreness in her joints and fatigue from moving all the time. Her condition would probably be diagnosed as:
     a. dystonia.
     b. akathisia.
     c. tardive dyskinesia.
     d. neuroleptic malignant syndrome.

The Unwanted Effects of Conventional Antipsychotic Drugs, p. 444
Diff: E, Type: Factual, Ans: c
56.   Very low dopamine activity is related to:
    a.   anxiety disorders.
    b.   addictive behavior.
    c.   Parkinson's disease.
    d.   schizophrenic disorders.

The Unwanted Effects of Conventional Antipsychotic Drugs, p. 444
Diff: H, Type: Factual, Ans: c
57.   Of the following, which part of the brain is involved in Parkinson's disease?
    a.   limbic system
    b.   cerebral cortex
    c.   substantia nigra
    d.   the reticular activating system

The Unwanted Effects of Conventional Antipsychotic Drugs, p. 444
Diff: M, Type: Factual, Ans: c
58.   One of the unwanted and delayed side effects of antipsychotic medications is:
    a.   paralysis.
    b.   hyperactivity.
    c.   tardive dyskinesia.
    d.   Parkinson's disease.

The Unwanted Effects of Conventional Antipsychotic Drugs, p. 444
Diff: M, Type: Factual, Ans: d
59.   The neuroleptic side effect marked by muscle rigidity, fever, altered consciousness, and autonomic dysfunction is called:
    a.   dystonia.
    b.   akathisia.
    c.   tardive dyskinesia.
    d.   neuroleptic malignant syndrome.

The Unwanted Effects of Conventional Antipsychotic Drugs, p. 444
Diff: M, Type: Factual, Ans: c
60.   After starting treatment with antipsychotic drugs, tardive dyskinesia typically requires at least _____ to develop.
    a.   a week
    b.   a month
    c.   a year
    d.   a decade

The Unwanted Effects of Conventional Antipsychotic Drugs, p. 444
Diff: E, Type: Applied, Ans: c
61.   Donna has been treated with chlorpromazine for several years. Lately she seems to be chewing gum all the time and her arms are always in motion. She has begun to display twitches and she has a facial tic. This is an example of:
    a.   dystonia.
    b.   akathisia
    c.   tardive dyskinesia.
    d.   neuroleptic malignant syndrome.

The Unwanted Effects of Conventional Antipsychotic Drugs, p. 444
Diff: M, Type: Factual, Ans: b

62.   The proportion of patients taking antipsychotic medication who eventually develop tardive dyskinesia is closet to:
   a.   1%.
   b.   10%.
   c.   20%.
   d.   50%.

The Unwanted Effects of Conventional Antipsychotic Drugs, p. 444
Diff: H, Type: Applied, Ans: b

63.   A person who is experiencing a potentially fatal reaction to an antipsychotic drug involving muscle rigidity and autonomic nervous system dysfunction is displaying:
   a.   Parkinson-like symptoms.
   b.   neuroleptic malignant syndrome.
   c.   tardive dyskinesia.
   d.   akathisia.

The Unwanted Effects of Conventional Antipsychotic Drugs, p. 444
Diff: M, Type: Applied, Ans: d

64.   If a schizophrenic was making involuntary ticlike movements of the tongue, mouth, face, or whole body, smacking the lips, and making sucking and chewing movements, one would suspect the patient:
   a.   was taking too much antipsychotic medication.
   b.   was taking too little antipsychotic medication.
   c.   had been taking antipsychotic medication for a short time.
   d.   had been taking antipsychotic medication for a long time.

The Unwanted Effects of Conventional Antipsychotic Drugs, p. 444
Diff: H, Type: Factual, Ans: a

65.   The most successful way to eliminate tardive dyskinesia is:
   a.   to stop the antipsychotic medication.
   b.   to use anti-Parkinsonian drugs to treat the side effects.
   c.   to ignore it; it will go away eventually.
   d.   to increase the dose of antipsychotic medication.

The Unwanted Effects of Conventional Antipsychotic Drugs, p. 444
Diff: M, Type: Factual, Ans: b

66.   Tardive dyskinesia can be overlooked because:
   a.   its symptoms are always very subtle.
   b.   it has symptoms that are similar to schizophrenia.
   c.   the symptoms are manifest in different ways in different patients.
   d.   the symptoms do not begin until after the actual brain damage has taken place.

The Unwanted Effects of Conventional Antipsychotic Drugs, p. 444
Diff: H, Type: Applied, Ans: b

67.   If you were working with a patient who displayed muscle tremors and rigidity, dystonia, and akathisia, you would suspect that the person was receiving:
    a.   electroconvulsive therapy.
    b.   antipsychotic drugs.
    c.   milieu therapy.
    d.   psychodynamic therapy.

The Unwanted Effects of Conventional Antipsychotic Drugs, p. 444
Diff: H, Type: Applied, Ans: c

68.   An elderly patient who is taking antipsychotic drugs and shows signs of muscle rigidity, fever, altered state of consciousness, and improper autonomic functioning is probably experiencing:
    a.   Parkinsonism.
    b.   tardive dyskenesia.
    c.   neuroleptic malignant syndrome.
    d.   new antipsychotic drugs.

New Antipsychotic Drugs, p. 445
Diff: M, Type: Applied, Ans: a

69.   Which of the following drugs appears to act more at D-1 dopamine receptors than D-2 dopamine receptors?
    a.   clozapine
    b.   Thorazine
    c.   haloperidol
    d.   chlorpromazine

New Antipsychotic Drugs, p. 445
Diff: H, Type: Factual, Ans: b

70.   Which of the following antipsychotic drugs appears to work at serotonin receptors?
    a.   Haldol
    b.   clozapine
    c.   chlorpromazine
    d.   the phenothiazines

New Antipsychotic Drugs, p. 445
Diff: H, Type: Factual, Ans: a

71.   The most widely used atypical antipsychotic drug is:
    a.   Clozaril.
    b.   Xanac.
    c.   Thorazine.
    d.   Prozac.

New Antipsychotic Drugs, p. 445
Diff: H, Type: Applied, Ans: a

72.   The lowest number of extrapyramidal side effects is seen after taking:
    a.   clozapine.
    b.   haloperidol.
    c.   thioridazine.
    d.   chlorpromazine.

New Antipsychotic Drugs, p. 445
Diff: H, Type: Applied, Ans: d
73. Researchers study a group of people with schizophrenia who receive just enough of a conventional antipsychotic drug to receive about 90% of the drug's positive effect. About how much of the drug's extrapyramidal side effects also will emerge?
    a. almost none
    b. about 10%
    c. about 30%
    d. over 50%

New Antipsychotic Drugs, p. 445
Diff: H, Type: Applied, Ans: a
74. Researchers study a group of people with schizophrenia who receive just enough of an atypical antipsychotic drug to receive about 90% of the drug's positive effect. About how much of the drug's extrapyramidal side effects also will emerge?
    a. almost none
    b. about 10%
    c. about 30%
    d. over 50%

New Antipsychotic Drugs, p. 445
Diff: H, Type: Applied, Ans: d
75. "I want to maximize the antipsychotic effect of a drug while minimizing its undesirable side effects," says a doctor. What's the best advice you can give the doctor?
    a. "Unfortunately, effective doses of conventional and atypical antipsychotic drugs both produce a lot of undesirable side effects."
    b. "Fortunately, effective doses of both conventional and atypical antipsychotic drugs do not produce a lot of undesirable side effects."
    c. "Use a conventional antipsychotic drug."
    d. "Use an atypical antipsychotic drug."

New Antipsychotic Drugs, p. 446
Diff: M, Type: Applied, Ans: d
76. Why aren't atypical antipsychotic drugs universally prescribed for people with schizophrenia? After all, more people with schizophrenia show improvement with atypical antipsychotic drugs than with conventional antipsychotics.
    a. On average, atypicals produce more cases of tardive dyskinesia.
    b. On average, atypicals cause more extrapyramidal symptoms.
    c. Most atypicals produce life-threatening agranulocytosis.
    d. On average, atypicals cost more.

New Antipsychotic Drugs, p. 446
Diff: M, Type: Factual, Ans: a
77. Which of the following drugs can cause a dangerous drop in the number of white blood cells in the body?
    a. clozapine
    b. Thorazine
    c. haloperidol
    d. chlorpromazine

New Antipsychotic Drugs, p. 446
Diff: E, Type: Factual, Ans: b

78. Clozapine has one potentially dangerous side effect. It is:
    a. tolerance.
    b. agranulocytosis.
    c. Parkinson's disease.
    d. extrapyramidal motor symptoms.

Psychotherapy, p. 446
Diff: H, Type: Applied, Ans: b

79. "Stay in your own private world as long as you need to, until you want to come out and share the world with me," would most likely be said by which therapist?
    a. Minuchin
    b. Fromm-Reichmann
    c. Baucom
    d. Dixon

Psychotherapy, p. 446
Diff: M, Type: Factual, Ans: c

80. Why do some therapists believe psychotherapy is unsuccessful in treating schizophrenia?
    a. Schizophrenia increases the strength of most ego defense mechanism.
    b. Insurance does not cover psychotherapy for patients diagnosed as schizophrenic.
    c. Unmedicated schizophrenics are too far removed from reality to form the relationship needed.
    d. Excessive dopamine interferes with the process of free association that is requisite to the success of psychotherapy.

Psychotherapy, p. 446
Diff: M, Type: Applied, Ans: b

81. Frieda Fromm-Reichmann's approach to psychotherapy with schizophrenic patients was to
    a. challenge patients' statements.
    b. build a sense of trust in the patient.
    c. alter the psychotic person's behavior.
    d. encourage specific life adjustments by providing community support services.

Insight Therapy, p. 447
Diff: M, Type: Factual, Ans: a

82. What is a primary technique that insight therapists use to treat schizophrenia?
    a. challenging patients' statements
    b. altering the psychotic person's behavior
    c. using medication to reduce thought disturbances
    d. encouraging specific life adjustments by providing community support services

Family Therapy, p. 447
Diff: M, Type: Factual, Ans: b

83. A family with a high level of expressed emotion would display a great deal of:
    a. concern.
    b. criticism.
    c. joyfulness.
    d. underinvolvement.

Family Therapy, p. 447
Diff: H, Type: Applied, Ans: a

84.   You have just learned that an acquaintance who is diagnosed with schizophrenia will receive a combination of drug and family therapies. What do you think?
   a.   This is good; family therapy works well along with drug therapy.
   b.   It's wasting money; only the drug therapy will be effective.
   c.   It's wasting money; either form of therapy alone is as effective as the combination.
   d.   The drug therapy is good, but would work better with milieu therapy.

Family Therapy, p. 447
Diff: H, Type: Applied, Ans: b

85.   If a person is going to receive insight therapy for schizophrenia, the chance of a positive outcome (assuming, of course, drug therapy also is used):
   a.   depends greatly on the kind of insight therapy used.
   b.   is greater if the therapist challenges the client, and provides guidance.
   c.   is greater if the therapist is nondirective and comforting.
   d.   is minimal; insight therapy simply doesn't work with schizophrenia.

Family Therapy, p. 447
Diff: M, Type: Applied, Ans: b

86.   Family therapy is an important therapy option for people with schizophrenia because:
   a.   people with schizophrenia from families who display low levels of expressed emotion do comparatively poorly in therapy.
   b.   about a quarter of people recovering from schizophrenia live with family.
   c.   family members need to express very high expectations in order to promote recovery.
   d.   it works better in most cases than drug therapy.

Family Therapy, p. 448
Diff: H, Type: Applied, Ans: d

87.   Every time you hear about a person who is schizophrenic being arrested for committing a violent crime, remind yourself that, according to the research, people who are schizophrenic are:
   a.   over twice as likely to commit violent crimes as they are to be victims of violent crimes.
   b.   about as likely to commit violent crimes as they are to be victims of violent crimes.
   c.   about half as likely to commit violent crimes as they are to be victims of violent crimes.
   d.   less than one-fifth as likely to commit violent crimes as they are to be victims of violent crimes.

Family Therapy, p. 448
Diff: M, Type: Factual, Ans: a

88.   The goal of family therapy is to:
   a.   help the family better support the schizophrenic patient.
   b.   help the patient move out of the family home and live on his or her own.
   c.   help the family display higher levels of expressed emotion.
   d.   help patients return to the hospital more quickly.

Family Therapy, p. 448
Diff: E, Type: Applied, Ans: c
89. If relatives of a schizophrenic come to have more realistic expectations, reduce their guilt, and work on establishing better communication, they are probably receiving:
    a. milieu therapy.
    b. social therapy.
    c. family therapy.
    d. insight therapy.

Family Therapy, p. 448
Diff: H, Type: Factual, Ans: d
90. Research on therapy for schizophrenics and their families has been shown to:
    a. increase tension and relapse rates.
    b. work only in the absence of drug treatment.
    c. increase feelings of guilt for family members.
    d. help the schizophrenic avoid troublesome interactions with family members.

Family Therapy, p. 448
Diff: E, Type: Applied, Ans: a
91. If you and your family were receiving support, encouragement, and advice from other families with schizophrenic members, you would most likely be participating in:
    a. family psychoeducational programs.
    b. family milieu therapy.
    c. joint drug treatment.
    d. All the answers are correct.

Social Therapy, p. 449
Diff: M, Type: Factual, Ans: b
92. What's the focus of social therapy in treating schizophrenia?
    a. placing the patient in a halfway house
    b. finding work and housing for the patient
    c. finding a community mental health center for the patient
    d. helping the patient interact more effectively in the family environment

Social Therapy, p. 449
Diff: M, Type: Applied, Ans: b
93. A patient who receives help in finding work, in finding a place to live, and in taking medication correctly is probably receiving:
    a. milieu therapy.
    b. social therapy.
    c. family therapy.
    d. insight therapy.

Social Therapy, p. 449
Diff: M, Type: Applied, Ans: b
94. Of the following alternatives, which would be most effective for schizophrenic patients who have been hospitalized and released to avoid being re-hospitalized?
    a. see their family physician monthly
    b. take their medication and attend social therapy
    c. go to church
    d. exercise and eat healthily

What Are the Features of Effective Community Care?, p. 449
Diff: M, Type: Factual, Ans: b

95.   Programs designed to help people recovering from schizophrenia to handle daily pressures, make proper decisions, handle social situations, and make residential and vocational adjustments are called:
        a.   deinstitutionalization programs.
        b.   assertive community treatment.
        c.   rehabilitation services.
        d.   re-hospitalization programs.

What Are the Features of Effective Community Care?, p. 449
Diff: M, Type: Factual, Ans: d

96.   The Community Mental Health Act stipulated that patients with mental disorders should receive all of the following except _____ without leaving their communities.
        a.   inpatient treatment
        b.   preventative care
        c.   outpatient therapy
        d.   research opportunities

What Are the Features of Effective Community Care?, p. 449
Diff: M, Type: Factual, Ans: b

97.   Deinstitutionalization:
        a.   did not reduce substantially the number of people in state mental hospitals.
        b.   was aimed at returning patients with mental disorders to their communities.
        c.   resulted in a high level of community care being offered throughout the U.S.
        d.   provided medication to schizophrenics, but not to other mental patients.

What Are the Features of Effective Community Care?, p. 449
Diff: H, Type: Factual, Ans: c

98.   According to your textbook, which of the following is a key feature of effective community care programs?
        a.   long term hospitalization
        b.   self-help groups for family members
        c.   occupational training
        d.   exercise programs

What Are the Features of Effective Community Care?, p. 449
Diff: M, Type: Factual, Ans: c

99.   The approximate number of patients in state mental institutions in the early 1950s was about:
        a.   80,000.
        b.   250,000.
        c.   600,000.
        d.   1,000,000.

What Are the Features of Effective Community Care?, p. 449
Diff: M, Type: Factual, Ans: b
100. The "revolving door" syndrome in the treatment of mental illness refers to:
   a. deinstitutionalization.
   b. repeatedly releasing and readmitting patients.
   c. the inability to treat mental patients effectively.
   d. an open door policy in which patients may come and go as they please.

What Are the Features of Effective Community Care?, p. 449
Diff: M, Type: Factual, Ans: a
101. Since the 1950s, deinstitutionalization has led to a significant change in the number of patients in state institutions. The approximate number is now:
   a. 60,000.
   b. 250,000.
   c. 600,000.
   d. 1,000,000.

What Are the Features of Effective Community Care?, p. 450
Diff: E, Type: Factual, Ans: d
102. In the original Community Mental Health Act, the coordinating agency was supposed to be the:
   a. day center.
   b. halfway house.
   c. sheltered workshop.
   d. community mental health center.

What Are the Features of Effective Community Care?, p. 450
Diff: M, Type: Factual, Ans: c
103. Community mental health centers are designed to provide all of the following except:
   a. inpatient emergency care.
   b. medication and psychotherapy.
   c. vocational rehabilitation.
   d. coordination of other community services.

What Are the Features of Effective Community Care?, p. 450
Diff: M, Type: Applied, Ans: c
104. Schizophrenics who receive 24-hour supervision in a community setting, usually following a milieu approach, are receiving:
   a. coordinated services.
   b. partial hospitalization.
   c. halfway house services.
   d. occupational training.

What Are the Features of Effective Community Care?, p. 450
Diff: E, Type: Applied, Ans: c
105. Tory lives at home but spends his day at a mental health facility. The facility might be described as providing:
   a. aftercare.
   b. coordinated services.
   c. partial hospitalization.
   d. short-term hospitalization.

What Are the Features of Effective Community Care?, p. 450
Diff: E, Type: Applied, Ans: b
106.   Helen was just discharged from a public mental health facility. She went to live with a group
       of other former patients in a group-living arrangement. There were staff members to help out
       but the former patients controlled most of the day-to-day activities. Helen's living
       arrangement is a:
       a.   day center.
       b.   halfway house.
       c.   short-term hospital.
       d.   sheltered workshop.

What Are the Features of Effective Community Care?, p. 450
Diff: E, Type: Factual, Ans: d
107.   The staff that work in halfway houses are usually:
       a.   psychiatrists.
       b.   psychologists.
       c.   social workers.
       d.   paraprofessionals.

What Are the Features of Effective Community Care?, p. 450
Diff: H, Type: Applied, Ans: c
108.   When the Community Mental Health Act was passed, a county with 400,000 residents could
       have expected to end up with how many community mental health centers?
       a.   only 1
       b.   between 1 and 4
       c.   between 2 and 8
       d.   at least 10

Sociocultural Landscape: First Dibs on Atypical Antipsychotic Drugs,
p. 451 (Box 15-3)
Diff: H, Type: Applied, Ans: c
109.   Compared to African Americans, white Americans are:
       a.   more likely to receive conventional antipsychotic drugs for both schizophrenia and other
            psychotic disorders.
       b.   more likely to receive conventional antipsychotic drugs for schizophrenia, and more
            likely to receive atypical antipsychotic drugs for other psychotic disorders.
       c.   more likely to receive atypical antipsychotic drugs for both schizophrenia and other
            psychotic disorders.
       d.   more likely to receive atypical antipsychotic drugs for schizophrenia, and more likely to
            receive conventional antipsychotic drugs for other psychotic disorders.

What Are the Features of Effective Community Care?, p. 452
Diff: M, Type: Applied, Ans: c
110.   Several people with schizophrenia work at a recycling center, where on-time behavior is
       expected, and payment is made solely for work completed. The people do not compete with
       each other. Most likely, this work takes place at a:
       a.   halfway house.
       b.   community mental health center.
       c.   sheltered workshop.
       d.   community employment center.

What Are the Features of Effective Community Care?, p. 452
Diff: H, Type: Applied, Ans: c
111.   A person with a severe psychological disorder—schizophrenia, for example—says, "I've just got to get a job; that's really important to me." That person is:
   a. rare—less than 10% of those with severe psychological disorders want to work.
   b. uncommon—only about 20% of those with severe psychological disorders want to work.
   c. common—about 70% of those with severe psychological disorders want to work.
   d. almost universal—virtually all of those with severe psychological disorders want to work.

How Has Community Treatment Failed?, p. 452
Diff: H, Type: Applied, Ans: b
112.   According to the research, what should be done to improve community treatment for people with schizophrenia? Your best answer is:
   a. "Nothing much, really; almost everybody has access to the services they need."
   b. "Provide more services, and do a better job of getting them to those who need them."
   c. "Provide more services; we have adequate infrastructure to get the services to those who need them."
   d. "Provide better infrastructure; we have the services people need already."

How Has Community Treatment Failed?, p. 452
Diff: M, Type: Applied, Ans: a
113.   Schizophrenics who also have substance-abuse disorders are assigned a case worker who makes sure they know about and can use whatever is available to support them. They are receiving:
   a. coordinated services.
   b. partial hospitalization.
   c. halfway house services.
   d. occupational training.

How Has Community Treatment Failed?, p. 452
Diff: E, Type: Applied, Ans: d
114.   Schizophrenics who are working in a sheltered workshop are receiving:
   a. coordinated services.
   b. partial hospitalization.
   c. halfway house services.
   d. occupational training.

How Has Community Treatment Failed?, p. 452
Diff: H, Type: Factual, Ans: b
115.   About what percent of schizophrenics receive treatment in a given year?
   a. 25%–40%
   b. 40%–60%
   c. 60%–80%
   d. 80%–100%

How Has Community Treatment Failed?, p. 452
Diff: M, Type: Factual, Ans: d
116.   The person most responsible for coordinating community service and providing practical help
        with problem-solving social skills, and medication is a:
        a.   psychiatrist.
        b.   clinical psychologist.
        c.   nurse practitioner.
        d.   case manager.

Mentally Ill Chemical Abusers: A Challenge for Treatment, p. 453 (Box 15-4)
Diff: H, Type: Factual, Ans: c
117.   MICA stands for:
        a.   mentally ill child or adult.
        b.   mentally ill chronic alcoholic.
        c.   mentally ill chemical abuser.
        d.   mentally ill cocaine addict.

Mentally Ill Chemical Abusers: A Challenge for Treatment, p. 453 (Box 15-4)
Diff: H, Type: Factual, Ans: a
118.   MICA's tend to be:
        a.   young and male.
        b.   good students.
        c.   people who have good levels of social functioning.
        d.   people with fewer than average contacts with the criminal justice system.

Mentally Ill Chemical Abusers: A Challenge for Treatment, p. 453 (Box 15-4)
Diff: H, Type: Applied, Ans: d
119.   If we know that people with schizophrenia and substance abuse disorders are more likely to
        be homeless and to be victimized on the street, we know that:
        a.   schizophrenia causes substance abuse.
        b.   homelessness causes schizophrenia.
        c.   substance abuse causes one to be victimized.
        d.   therapists must tailor treatment programs to their unique combination of problems.

How Has Community Treatment Failed?, p. 454
Diff: M, Type: Factual, Ans: a
120.   Today the financial burden of providing community treatment for persons with long-term
        severe disorders often falls on:
        a.   local governments and nonprofit agencies.
        b.   the federal government.
        c.   state government.
        d.   international organizations.

How Has Community Treatment Failed?, p. 454
Diff: H, Type: Applied, Ans: d
121.   Which of the following is least likely to be a reason there is such a shortage of services for
        people with schizophrenia?
        a.   Health professionals prefer to work with people who are less seriously ill.
        b.   Neighbors often object to having schizophrenics near them in the community.
        c.   It is very costly to treat schizophrenics.
        d.   There are no laws regarding the treatment rights of schizophrenics.

How Has Community Treatment Failed?, p. 454
Diff: M, Type: Factual, Ans: b
122.   One of the problems that community-based programs face goes by the acronym of "NIMBY."
        What problem does this represent?
        a.   many community based programs are not effective
        b.   schizophrenic people will live in local neighborhoods
        c.   most community based programs cost too much
        d.   most therapists do not like to work with schizophrenic people

How Has Community Treatment Failed?, p. 454
Diff: H, Type: Applied, Ans: b
123.   Which of the following provides the best support for the statement that "people with
        schizophrenia are now dumped in the community rather than warehoused in institutions?"
        a.   Almost all schizophrenics are medicated, even though many experience serious side
             effects.
        b.   Many schizophrenics live in single-room occupancy hotels or are homeless.
        c.   Government disability payments support many schizophrenics.
        d.   Most institutions are now closed or used for other types of patients.

How Has Community Treatment Failed?, p. 454
Diff: M, Type: Applied, Ans: a
124.   SRO—"standing room only"—may be a good thing for a play producer on opening night,
        but to many people with schizophrenia, SRO means:
        a.   living alone in a single room.
        b.   having a job involving doing the same thing over and over again.
        c.   having access to a safe place to exercise outdoors.
        d.   a building housing only those with schizophrenia.

How Has Community Treatment Failed?, p. 455
Diff: H, Type: Applied, Ans: c
125.   A person with schizophrenia is living in a halfway house. This person's experience is:
        a.   very rare—only 1-2% of those with schizophrenia live in halfway houses.
        b.   rare—between 5% and 10% of those with schizophrenia live in halfway houses.
        c.   uncommon—between 10% and 20% of those with schizophrenia live in halfway houses.
        d.   the norm—almost half of those with schizophrenia live in halfway houses.

How Has Community Treatment Failed?, p. 456
Diff: M, Type: Applied, Ans: b
126.   A homeless person approaches you on a city street corner. The chance it is a person with
        schizophrenia is about:
        a.   50%
        b.   33%
        c.   15%
        d.   5%

The Promise of Community Treatment, p. 456
Diff: M, Type: Applied, Ans: a

127.   If you went to a meeting of a group lobbying for better care for the mentally ill and made up primarily of family members of people with severe mental disorders, you would probably be attending:
   a.   the National Alliance for the Mentally Ill.
   b.   the Association for Retarded Citizens.
   c.   the Society for Social Workers and Case Managers.
   d.   the Halfway House Paraprofessional Affiliates.

The Promise of Community Treatment, p. 456
Diff: M, Type: Factual, Ans: c

128.   What proportion of homeless persons are estimated to suffer from severe mental disorders?
   a.   most
   b.   about half
   c.   about a third
   d.   about a quarter

Putting It Together, p. 457
Diff: M, Type: Factual, Ans: a

129.   About what percent of people who experience schizophrenia recover permanently and completely from the disorder?
   a.   25%
   b.   40%
   c.   50%
   d.   75%

Putting It Together, p. 457
Diff: H, Type: Applied, Ans: b

130.   A little over a hundred years ago, Kraepelin guessed that about one in eight of those with schizophrenia improved. Today, the number of those who recover completely, plus the number of those who return to relatively independent lives, is about:
   a.   one in four (twice Kraepelin's estimate).
   b.   one in two (four times Kraepelin's estimate).
   c.   three in four (six times Kraepelin's estimate).
   d.   nine in ten (about seven times Kraepelin's estimate).

FILL-IN QUESTIONS

Institutional Care in the Past, p. 439
Diff: M, Type: Factual, Ans: social breakdown syndrome

1.   The symptoms developed because of the experience of long-term mental institutionalization itself are called _____.

Milieu Therapy, p. 440
Diff: E, Type: Applied, Ans: milieu

2.   Maxwell Jones's therapeutic community is a form of _____ therapy.

Antipsychotic Drugs, p. 442
Diff: M, Type: Factual, Ans: neuroleptics

3.   Because of the sort of damage they can cause, most conventional antipsychotic drugs are known as _____.

Antipsychotic Drugs, p. 442
Diff: E, Type: Factual, Ans: neuroleptic (or antipsychotic)

4.   Chlorpromazine and haloperidol are examples of _____ drugs.

How Effective Are Antipsychotic Drugs?, p. 443
Diff: E, Type: Factual, Ans: positive

5.   Hallucinations, delusions, or formal thought disorders are _____ symptoms of schizophrenia.

How Effective Are Antipsychotic Drugs?, p. 443
Diff: E, Type: Factual, Ans: flat affect (or poverty of speech, or loss of volition)

6.   The negative symptoms of schizophrenia include _____.

The Unwanted Effects of Conventional Antipsychotic Drugs, p. 443
Diff: M, Type: Applied, Ans: Parkinson's disease

7.   Thorazine can cause muscle tremors, rigidity, and shaking, which are common signs of _____.

The Unwanted Effects of Conventional Antipsychotic Drugs, p. 444
Diff: H, Type: Applied, Ans: dystonia

8.   After several treatments with Thorazine, Paula begins to exhibit bizarre and uncontrollable movements of the face, neck, tongue, and back. These undesirable effects are collectively known as _____.

The Unwanted Effects of Conventional Antipsychotic Drugs, p. 444
Diff: H, Type: Factual, Ans: substantia nigra (or basal ganglia)

9.   Parkinsonian symptoms are produced by impairment of the _____.

The Unwanted Effects of Conventional Antipsychotic Drugs, p. 444
Diff: M, Type: Applied, Ans: tardive dyskinesia

10.   A movement disorder associated with antipsychotic medication that may not appear until a year after a person begins taking neuroleptic drugs and which includes involuntary chewing, sucking, lip smacking, and jerky, purposeless movements of the arms, legs, and body is called _____.

New Antipsychotic Drugs, p. 446
Diff: H, Type: Factual, Ans: agranulocytosis

11.   The new neuroleptic called clozapine has a dangerous side effect called _____.

Psychotherapy, p. 447
Diff: E, Type: Applied, Ans: neuroleptics (or antipsychotic medication)

12.   Psychotherapy can often be effective in treating schizophrenia when it is used in conjunction with _____.

Family Therapy, p. 448
Diff: E, Type: Factual, Ans: family therapy

13.   The attempt to support the family of the schizophrenic to help them cope and provide the best environment for continued recovery is called _____.

Family Therapy, p. 448
Diff: E, Type: Factual, Ans: family support groups

14.   The family therapy approach to the treatment of schizophrenia includes bringing the members of the schizophrenic person's family together with other families who are in the same situation to share their thoughts and emotions in a format called _____.

Social Therapy, pp. 448-449
Diff: E, Type: Factual, Ans: social therapy

15.   Interventions for schizophrenia that make sure clients take their medications and help clients with self-management, problem solving, decision making, and the development of interpersonal skills have been labeled _____.

The Community Approach. p. 449
Diff: E, Type: Factual, Ans: deinstitutionalization

16.   The 1960s policy of releasing patients from mental health hospitals to community-based mental health facilities is called _____.

The Community Approach. p. 449
Diff: E, Type: Applied, Ans: deinstitutionalization

17.   One contributor to the increase in homeless individuals is the mental health policy of _____.

What Are the Features of Effective Community Care?, p. 450
Diff: E, Type: Factual, Ans: community mental health center

18.   The institution that is supposed to provide the coordination among posthospitalization services is the _____.

What Are the Features of Effective Community Care?, p. 450
Diff: M, Type: Applied, Ans: aftercare

19.   If patients with schizophrenia show improvement during short-term hospitalization, the follow-up treatment they receive in the community later is called _____.

What Are the Features of Effective Community Care?, p. 450
Diff: E, Type: Applied, Ans: halfway house

20.   Harry was released from the hospital to a dormitory-like facility that gives him considerable freedom during the day. It is probably a _____.

What Are the Features of Effective Community Care?, p. 452
Diff: E, Type: Factual, Ans: sheltered workshop

21.   A protected and partially supported factory that employs disabled people is called a _____.

ESSAY QUESTIONS

Institutional Care in the Past, pp. 438-441
Diff: M, Type: Applied

1.   Describe a typical public state hospital in the United States in the mid-20th century.

Lobotomy: How Could It Happen?, pp. 438-439 (Box 15-1)
~~**Diff: H, Type: Factual**~~

2.   Why was lobotomy briefly considered to be a "miracle" cure for schizophrenia? In fact what were the usual results of lobotomies?

Milieu Therapy/The Token Economy, pp. 440-442
Diff: H, Type: Applied

3.   How are milieu therapy and token economy programs alike and how are they different?

No Specific Topic, No Specific Page
Diff: H, Type: Applied

4.   Imagine that you are advising someone who is a relative of a schizophrenic and asking you about the proper medication. What would you tell the person that would help them make the best decision for their relative. Be sure to address issues such as types of symptoms, dosage level, and potential side effects.

Family Therapy, pp. 447-448
Diff: M, Type: Factual

5.   What does the typical family go through when they have a family member who is experiencing schizophrenia, both immediately and over time?

The Community Approach, pp. 449-452
Diff: M, Type: Factual

6.   List and briefly describe the 5 key features of effective community care, according to the text.

The Community Approach, pp. 450-452
Diff: M, Type: Applied

7.   Why is work so important to those experiencing schizophrenia? What type of work are schizophrenics most likely to be able to do and what sort of treatments have been developed to support them.

How Has Community Treatment Failed?, pp. 452-454
Diff: M, Type: Factual

8.   In large part, community treatment has failed those with schizophrenia. Why?

How Has Community Treatment Failed?, pp. 454-456
Diff: M, Type: Factual

9.   What happens to people with serious mental disorders who are not treated effectively? Please be comprehensive in your answer.

The Promise of Community Treatment, pp. 456-457
Diff: H, Type: Factual

10.   Describe the latest trends in meeting the needs of those with serious mental disorders.

CHAPTER 16   Personality Disorders

MULTIPLE-CHOICE QUESTIONS

Personality Disorders, p. 461
Diff: E, Type: Factual, Ans: c

1. The enduring pattern of inner experiences and outward behavior that is unique to each individual is termed:
    a. a trait.
    b. character.
    c. personality.
    d. individuality.

Personality Disorders, p. 461
Diff: E, Type: Factual, Ans: c

2. The consistencies of one's personality are called:
    a. inherited characteristics.
    b. learned responses.
    c. personality traits.
    d. personality typologies.

Personality Disorders, pp. 461-462
Diff: M, Type: Applied, Ans: d

3. What differentiates normal personality characteristics from personality disorders?
    a. the specific characteristics
    b. the degree of inflexibility and maladaptiveness
    c. the length of time one possesses the characteristics
    d. All of the answers are correct.

Personality Disorders, p. 462
Diff: M, Type: Factual, Ans: c

4. The most important similarity among the personality disorders listed in the text is that:
    a. disorders of thought, perception, and attention are present.
    b. the personality traits are limited to discrete periods of illness.
    c. they are inflexible, maladaptive, and related to impaired functioning or distress.
    d. they are social in that they involve an inability to form lasting relationships with other people.

Personality Disorders, p. 462
Diff: E, Type: Factual, Ans: b
5. By the DSM-IV-TR classification system, personality disorders are disorders on which axis?
   a. Axis I
   b. Axis II
   c. Axis III
   d. Axis IV

Personality Disorders, p. 462
Diff: M, Type: Applied, Ans: a
6. A person suffering from a personality disorder also suffers from an Axis I disorder; this is called:
   a. comorbidity.
   b. co-axiality.
   c. biaxial disorder.
   d. predisposition.

Personality Disorders, p. 462
Diff: M, Type: Factual, Ans: b
7. One reason that the personality disorders are difficult to treat is that the afflicted individuals:
   a. enjoy their symptoms and do not seek change.
   b. are frequently unaware that they have a problem.
   c. experience no distress and do not want treatment.
   d. have accompanying mood disorders that must be treated first.

Personality Disorders, p. 462
Diff: E, Type: Factual, Ans: c
8. The term comorbidity means that:
   a. one disorder may develop into another.
   b. one disorder automatically implies the other.
   c. two disorders may occur together in an individual.
   d. the appearance of one disorder implies the disappearance of the one that preceded it.

Personality Disorders, p. 462
Diff: H, Type: Applied, Ans: d
9. Based on a structured interview, Diagnostician A classifies an individual's personality disorder in the "odd" cluster! Based on another structured interview of the same type, Diagnostician B classifies an individual's personality disorder in the "dramatic" cluster. If what is described here is typical of what happens when that variety of structured interview is used, one would say the structured interview has:
   a. high reliability and high validity.
   b. high reliability and low validity.
   c. low reliability and high validity.
   d. low reliability and low validity.

Personality Disorders, p. 462
Diff: E, Type: Factual, Ans: d
10. Personality disorders are categorized by clusters that include all of the following except:
a. odd.
b. dramatic.
c. anxiety.
d. schizophrenic.

"Odd" Personality Disorders, p. 463
Diff: H, Type: Applied, Ans: b
11. An individual has just received a diagnosis of paranoid personality disorder. That individual is most likely to have a parent or sibling who has:
a. bipolar disorder.
b. schizophrenia.
c. one of the paraphilias.
d. alcoholism.

"Odd" Personality Disorders, p. 463
Diff: M, Type: Applied, Ans: c
12. Which of the following statements is most accurate, in terms of present research findings?
a. "Odd" personality disorders cause schizophrenia.
b. "Odd" personality disorders are caused by schizophrenia.
c. "Odd" personality disorders and schizophrenia are related to one another.
d. "Odd" personality disorders and schizophrenia are not related to one another.

"Odd" Personality Disorders, p. 463
Diff: M, Type: Factual, Ans: d
13. The category of "odd" personality disorders includes the traits of:
a. anxiety and fearfulness.
b. being highly dramatic, emotional, or erratic.
c. inflexibility and total loss of contact with reality.
d. extreme suspiciousness, social withdrawal, and cognitive and perceptual peculiarities.

"Odd" Personality Disorders, p. 463
Diff: H, Type: Applied, Ans: d
14. An individual with a diagnosed personality disorder is jealous and sensitive, as well as extremely self-critical. This person's diagnosis is likely to be which of the following personality disorders?
a. borderline
b. histrionic
c. narcissistic
d. antisocial

"Odd" Personality Disorders, p. 463
Diff: H, Type: Applied, Ans: a

15.   An individual with a diagnosed personality disorder is emotionally unstable, as well as impulsive and reckless. This person's diagnosis is most likely to be which of the following personality disorders?
   a.   borderline
   b.   schizotypal
   c.   obsessive-compulsive
   d.   avoidant

Paranoid Personality Disorder, p. 464
Diff: M, Type: Applied, Ans: b

16.   Reese is distrustful of others and reacts quickly to perceived threats. Even though he has no evidence, he is sure his wife is unfaithful. He finds it almost impossible to forgive those he thinks have wronged him. Reese displays the characteristic of the _____ personality disorder.
   a.   avoidant
   b.   paranoid
   c.   narcissistic
   d.   obsessive-compulsive

Paranoid Personality Disorder, pp. 464-465
Diff: M, Type: Factual, Ans: b

17.   In role-playing situations, subjects with paranoid personality disorder generally interpret ambiguous behavior as:
   a.   angry.
   b.   hostile.
   c.   confusing.
   d.   contradictory.

Paranoid Personality Disorder, p. 465
Diff: M, Type: Factual, Ans: b

18.   Although those with paranoid personality disorder often are deeply suspicious, their suspicions usually do not:
   a.   threaten their interpersonal relationships.
   b.   become delusional.
   c.   result in anger.
   d.   involve those with whom they work.

Paranoid Personality Disorder, p. 465
Diff: E, Type: Applied, Ans: d

19.   "It is clear that very demanding parents caused this person to develop paranoid personality disorder." This quote most likely would come from one with which theoretical position?
   a.   cognitive
   b.   behavioral
   c.   sociocultural
   d.   psychodynamic

Paranoid Personality Disorder, p. 465
Diff: H, Type: Applied, Ans: a

20.   A person experiencing paranoid personality disorder frequently says things like "You've got
       to get them before they get you," and "People have been sinners since the Garden of Eden."
       If these sayings reflect maladaptive assumptions the person has about people in general, the
       theorist who would be least surprised would have which theoretical position?
       a. cognitive
       b. biological
       c. sociocultural
       d. psychodynamic

Paranoid Personality Disorder, p. 465
Diff: M, Type: Applied, Ans: d

21.   Which of the following statements regarding the treatment of paranoid personality disorder is
       most accurate?
       a. Drug therapy generally works best.
       b. Psychodynamic therapy involving hypnotic regression is often effective.
       c. Behavioral therapy usually works well, and in relatively few sessions.
       d. Most therapies are of limited effectiveness, and progress slowly.

Paranoid Personality Disorder, p. 465
Diff: M, Type: Applied, Ans: a

22.   Theorists explain the paranoid personality disorder as coping with inadequacy. This leads to
       the ideas that people are evil and will attack you if given the chance. These ideas are
       consistent with _____ orientation.
       a. cognitive
       b. behavioral
       c. psychodynamic
       d. humanist-existential

Paranoid Personality Disorder, p. 465
Diff: H, Type: Applied, Ans: d

23.   According to recent research, if a person living in the United States is distrustful of both local
       TV news and the government, that type of person is:
       a. rare: such distrust defines those with paranoid personality disorder.
       b. rare: such distrust defines those with schizotypal personality disorder.
       c. uncommon: distrust of government, but not distrust of local TV, defines those with
           avoidant personality disorder.
       d. common: most people in the United States distrust both the local TV news and the
           government.

Personality and the Brain: The Case of Phineas Gage, pp. 463, 466 (Box 16-1)
Diff: H, Type: Applied, Ans: c

24.   After suffering severe brain trauma, Phineas Gage appeared not to care about his friends and
       coworkers, and developed wild, grandiose plans he later had to abandon. These symptoms are
       most similar to the symptoms of which of the following personality disorders?
       a. obsessive-compulsive
       b. antisocial
       c. schizoid
       d. avoidant

Personality and the Brain: The Case of Phineas Gage, p. 466 (Box 16-1)
Diff: M, Type: Applied, Ans: c
25.   "Even our negative emotions help us survive. For example, aren't our suspicions often justified?" Most likely someone with a _____ theoretical perspective made this statement.
   a.   cognitive
   b.   psychodynamic
   c.   evolutionary
   d.   sociocultural

Schizoid Personality Disorder, p. 467
Diff: M, Type: Applied, Ans: a
26.   One similarity of those experiencing paranoid personality disorder and those experiencing schizoid personality disorder is that they tend:
   a.   not to have close ties to others.
   b.   to distrust others.
   c.   to be described by others as arrogant and angry.
   d.   not to score well on typical intelligence tests.

Schizoid Personality Disorder, p. 467
Diff: H, Type: Factual, Ans: d
27.   The schizoid personality disorder differs from paranoid personality disorder in that:
   a.   those with schizoid personality disorder seek close affiliations with others, while those with paranoid personality do not.
   b.   paranoid personality disorder is treatable only through drug therapy; schizoid personality can be treated with psychotherapy.
   c.   women are more likely to have schizoid personality disorder than paranoid personality disorder; the opposite is true for men.
   d.   those with schizoid personality disorder desire to be alone; those with paranoid personality are alone because of suspiciousness.

Schizoid Personality Disorder, p. 467
Diff: M, Type: Applied, Ans: a
28.   Wes has always been a loner. He has never much cared for being with other people. He does not form relationships easily. He appears to be without emotion. Wes may be exhibiting the _____ personality disorder.
   a.   schizoid
   b.   paranoid
   c.   histrionic
   d.   narcissistic

Schizoid Personality Disorder, p. 467
Diff: E, Type: Factual, Ans: d
29.   The theorist who describes the schizoid personality disorder as arising from coping with parental rejection by avoiding relationships represents the _____ theoretical orientation.
   a.   cognitive
   b.   behavioral
   c.   existential
   d.   psychodynamic

Schizoid Personality Disorder, p. 467
Diff: M, Type: Applied, Ans: c

30.   An individual diagnosed with schizoid personality disorder reports having a great deal of
        difficulty figuring out how others feel, and as a child had difficulty developing adequate
        language skills. These findings would make the most sense to a theorist with which
        background?
        a.   psychodynamic
        b.   sociocultural
        c.   cognitive
        d.   biological

Schizoid Personality Disorder, p. 467
Diff: E, Type: Factual, Ans: a

31.   The theorist who describes schizoid personality disorder as arising from an inability to
        perceive effectively what is going on in the environment, including emotions, reflects the
        _____ theoretical orientation.
        a.   cognitive
        b.   behavioral
        c.   existential
        d.   psychodynamic

Schizoid Personality Disorder, p. 467
Diff: M, Type: Applied, Ans: a

32.   Cognitive theorists believe that because of their difficulty scanning the environment,
        perceiving accurately, and picking up emotional cues, those with schizoid personalities
        develop _____ very slowly.
        a.   language and motor skills
        b.   secondary sex characteristics
        c.   allergies and other medical problems
        d.   thinking disorders

Schizoid Personality Disorder, p. 467
Diff: H, Type: Applied, Ans: b

33.   A person who is least likely to be affected by criticism or praise from other people is one
        suffering from the _____ personality disorder.
        a.   avoidant
        b.   schizoid
        c.   paranoid
        d.   obsessive-compulsive

Schizoid Personality Disorder, p. 468
Diff: H, Type: Applied, Ans: b

34.   There is a new game called "Moods" where one acts out the mood listed on a card. Being
        encouraged to play this game is most like the treatment _____ might use for those with
        schizoid disorders.
        a.   psychoanalytic therapists
        b.   cognitive therapists
        c.   behavioral therapists
        d.   biological therapists

Schizoid Personality Disorder, p. 468
Diff: M, Type: Factual, Ans: b

35. The type of therapy that generally provides the least help for those with schizoid personality disorder is:
    a. behavioral.
    b. drug.
    c. cognitive.
    d. None of the other alternatives provide help for those with schizoid personality disorder.

Schizotypal Personality Disorder, p. 468
Diff: H, Type: Applied, Ans: d

36. When Selina sees a report of a train wreck on television, she thinks that it is a sign that she should not take the train to work the next day. She takes the bus instead. If she has a diagnosable personality disorder, it is most likely:
    a. schizoid personality disorder.
    b. avoidant personality disorder.
    c. paranoid personality disorder.
    d. schizotypal personality disorder.

Schizotypal Personality Disorder, p. 468
Diff: M, Type: Applied, Ans: b

37. A belief that the news anchor on CNN is giving one important messages about one's behavior reflects:
    a. bodily illusions.
    b. ideas of reference.
    c. passive-aggressive disorder.
    d. word salad.

Schizotypal Personality Disorder, pp. 468-469
Diff: H, Type: Factual, Ans: b

38. All of the following characterize schizotypal personality disorder except:
    a. digressive conversation.
    b. backward masking.
    c. ideas of reference.
    d. bodily illusions.

Schizotypal Personality Disorder, p. 469
Diff: M, Type: Factual, Ans: d

39. Digressive and vague language with loose associations accompanied by attention and concentration problems are characteristic of:
    a. schizoid personality disorder.
    b. avoidant personality disorder.
    c. paranoid personality disorder.
    d. schizotypal personality disorder.

Schizotypal Personality Disorder, p. 469
Diff: E, Type: Factual, Ans: b
40.   The disorder that appears to be most closely related to the schizotypal personality disorder is:
       a. anxiety.
       b. schizophrenia.
       c. obsessive-compulsive disorder.
       d. narcissistic personality disorder.

Schizotypal Personality Disorder, p. 469
Diff: H, Type: Factual, Ans: d
41.   A person who does poorly on a task called backward masking is most likely to be
       experiencing:
       a. schizoid personality disorder.
       b. paranoid personality disorder.
       c. borderline personality disorder.
       d. schizotypal personality disorder.

Schizotypal Personality Disorder, p. 469
Diff: H, Type: Factual, Ans: d
42.   The schizotypal personality disorder appears to be associated with:
       a. reduced levels of serotonin in the brain.
       b. reduced levels of dopamine in the brain.
       c. increased levels of serotonin in the brain.
       d. increased levels of dopamine in the brain.

Schizotypal Personality Disorder, p. 469
Diff: H, Type: Applied, Ans: a
43.   A client being treated for schizotypal personality disorder must show up for therapy
       appointments on time, dress appropriately, and complete some social skills training. Most
       likely the theoretical orientation of the therapist is:
       a. behavioral
       b. community.
       c. biological.
       d. partial hospitalization.

Schizotypal Personality Disorder, p. 469
Diff: M, Type: Applied, Ans: d
44.   Which of the following disorders is most responsive to drug therapy?
       a. avoidant personality disorder
       b. schizoid personality disorder
       c. paranoid personality disorder
       d. schizotypal personality disorder

Antisocial Personality Disorder, p. 470
Diff: E, Type: Factual, Ans: b
45.   The personality disorder that is most often associated with criminal behavior is the:
       a. histrionic personality disorder.
       b. antisocial personality disorder.
       c. borderline personality disorder.
       d. narcissistic personality disorder.

Antisocial Personality Disorder, p. 470
Diff: h, Type: Applied, Ans: d
46. A friend of yours says, "A 15-year-old high schooler accused of shooting several classmates received a diagnosis of antisocial personality disorder." Your most accurate reply would be:
    a. "Yes, that kind of behavior often is associated with that diagnosis."
    b. "I don't think so; those with that diagnosis seldom engage in criminal activity."
    c. "Yes, and I'll bet that wasn't the only diagnosis, either."
    d. "No; the kid is too young for that diagnosis."

Antisocial Personality Disorder, p. 470
Diff: M, Type: Factual, Ans: b
47. Compared with those with "odd" personality disorders, those with "dramatic" personality disorders:
    a. are more likely to wear odd assortments of clothing.
    b. are more common in prison populations.
    c. avoid social contacts.
    d. seldom express emotion.

Antisocial Personality Disorder, p. 471
Diff: M, Type: Applied, Ans: b
48. Ben set up an elaborate scheme to mine gold in the Rockies. He had a large town meeting and made a presentation of his stock. The shares were only $5 each, and everyone could afford them. He showed pictures of the mine and explained how the company expected to gross $100 million each month. As it turns out, he was a terrific con artist who had made several "successful" proposals such as this in towns across America in the last couple of years. He is most likely suffering from:
    a. paranoid personality disorder.
    b. antisocial personality disorder.
    c. narcissistic personality disorder.
    d. obsessive-compulsive personality disorder.

Antisocial Personality Disorder, p. 471
Diff: H, Type: Factual, Ans: c
49. Which of the following statements is not generally true of those with antisocial personality disorder?
    a. They lie very frequently.
    b. They are careless with money, and often do not pay their debts.
    c. They care for no one's safety, except theirs and their children's.
    d. They think their victims deserve what happens to them.

Antisocial Personality Disorder, p. 471
Diff: E, Type: Applied, Ans: b
50. Sarah respects none of society's boundaries and is insensitive to other people, frequently violating their rights. She does not consider the consequences of her actions. She experiences:
    a. schizoid personality disorder.
    b. antisocial personality disorder.
    c. histrionic personality disorder.
    d. schizotypal personality disorder.

Antisocial Personality Disorder, p. 471
Diff: H, Type: Applied, Ans: c
51.   A friend says to you, "He must have antisocial personality disorder; look how careful he is about his own well-being, but how careless he is about others' safety." Your most accurate reply would be:
   a.   "You're right; those are classic characteristics of antisocial personality disorder."
   b.   "You're partly right; most people with antisocial personality disorder are careful about the safety of family members."
   c.   "You're partly right; most people with antisocial personality disorder are careless about their own safety, as well as the safety of others."
   d.   "You've got it backwards; most people with antisocial personality disorder are careless of their own safety, but show at least some concern for others' safety."

When Life Imitates Art, p. 472 (Box 16-2)
Diff: M, Type: Applied, Ans: d
52.   A recent movie details the activities of a serial killer who was subsequently diagnosed with antisocial personality disorder. Should law enforcement agencies worry about the possibility of "copycat" killings following the movie's release?
   a.   no, because copycat killings almost never occur in reaction to movies
   b.   no, because copycat killers don't copy those who are diagnosed with a personality disorder
   c.   only if the movie gets a poor review
   d.   yes

Antisocial Personality Disorder, p. 472
Diff: E, Type: Factual, Ans: a
53.   The person most likely to be diagnosed with antisocial personality disorder is:
   a.   a white American man.
   b.   a white American woman.
   c.   an African American man.
   d.   an African American woman.

Antisocial Personality Disorder, p. 472
Diff: M, Type: Factual, Ans: b
54.   The person most likely to abuse alcohol probably experiences _____ personality disorder.
   a.   no
   b.   antisocial
   c.   narcissistic
   d.   dependent

Antisocial Personality Disorder, p. 472
Diff: H, Type: Factual, Ans: d
55.   The two childhood disorders that have been related to later antisocial personality disorder are:
   a.   depression and withdrawal.
   b.   schizophrenia and bipolar disorder.
   c.   mental retardation.
   d.   conduct disorder and attention–deficit hyperactivity disorder.

Antisocial Personality Disorder, p. 473
Diff: E, Type: Factual, Ans: d
56.   The absence of parental love results in emotional detachment and the use of power to form relationships. This is most like a _____ explanation of the development of antisocial personality disorder.
       a.   cognitive
       b.   biological
       c.   behavioral
       d.   psychodynamic

Antisocial Personality Disorder, p. 473
Diff: M, Type: Factual, Ans: b
57.   The fact that children learn antisocial behavior by modeling parental conflict and aggressiveness provides support for:
       a.   psychodynamic theory.
       b.   behavioral theory.
       c.   both psychodynamic and behavioral theories.
       d.   neither psychodynamic nor behavioral theories.

Antisocial Personality Disorder, p. 473
Diff: H, Type: Applied, Ans: a
58.   A young boy is constantly told by his parents to "Be a man!" whenever he is in conflict with friends. In turn, his parents themselves often act aggressively toward each other, and toward him. The theorist who would be *best* able to explain an adult diagnosis of antisocial personality disorder for this boy would be:
       a.   behavioral.
       b.   cognitive.
       c.   biological.
       d.   psychodynamic.

Antisocial Personality Disorder, p. 473
Diff: M, Type: Factual, Ans: c
59.   Giving in to a child's refusal to comply with a parental request may inadvertently reinforce stubborn and defiant behavior, setting the scene for the development of antisocial personality disorder. This is most like a _____ explanation of the development of antisocial personality disorder.
       a.   cognitive
       b.   biological
       c.   behavioral
       d.   psychodynamic

Antisocial Personality Disorder, p. 473
Diff: H, Type: Applied, Ans: b
60.   "What's the big deal? I just don't understand why that matters to you. Why can't you just do what I do?" This quote provides evidence that most strongly supports the _____ explanation for antisocial personality disorder.
       a.   behavioral
       b.   cognitive
       c.   psychodynamic
       d.   biological

Antisocial Personality Disorder, p. 474
Diff: H, Type: Applied, Ans: b

61.   If you wanted to write a book about a fictional character who is a "typical" example of antisocial personality disorder, you might have the character exhibit all of the following except:
   a.   incessant lying.
   b.   periods of very high anxiety.
   c.   persistent violation of others' rights.
   d.   lack of conscience after committing crimes.

Antisocial Personality Disorder, p. 474
Diff: H, Type: Applied, Ans: a

62.   Which of the answers would complete the following sentence to support the idea that alcohol use and antisocial personality disorder are related because of their "risk taking" aspects. Drug users with personality disorders often say they use drugs for:
   a.   recreational reasons.
   b.   pain relief.
   c.   raising their inhibitions.
   d.   developing better social relationships.

Antisocial Personality Disorder, p. 474
Diff: H, Type: Applied, Ans: d

63.   Assume a study of prison inmates diagnosed with antisocial personality disorder shows that they generally experience less anxiety than other people when they lie or "con" others. This outcome would most strongly support which theoretical position?
   a.   behavioral
   b.   psychodynamic
   c.   cognitive
   d.   biological

Antisocial Personality Disorder, p. 474
Diff: E, Type: Factual, Ans: b

64.   Researchers and clinicians have had little or no success in treating _____, regardless of the treatment approach taken.
   a.   histrionic personality disorder
   b.   antisocial personality disorder
   c.   dependent personality disorder
   d.   obsessive-compulsive personality disorder

Antisocial Personality Disorder, p. 474
Diff: E, Type: Factual, Ans: b

65.   Of the following, the most difficult personality disorder to treat appears to be the:
   a.   histrionic personality disorder.
   b.   antisocial personality disorder.
   c.   dependent personality disorder.
   d.   obsessive-compulsive personality disorder.

Antisocial Personality Disorder, p. 474
Diff: H, Type: Factual, Ans: a
66.   Which of the following statements is most accurate regarding antisocial personality disorder?
      a.   Most who have it are not treated, and most who are treated are not helped much.
      b.   Most who have it are not treated, but most who are treated are helped substantially.
      c.   Most who have it are treated, but most who are treated are not helped much.
      d.   Most who have it are treated, and most who are treated are helped substantially.

Borderline Personality Disorder, p. 474
Diff: M, Type: Applied, Ans: b
67.   Keira has an unstable self-image, major mood shifts, and is prone to depression and impulsive behavior. She most likely should be diagnosed as having a:
      a.   histrionic personality disorder.
      b.   borderline personality disorder.
      c.   depressive personality disorder.
      d.   narcissistic personality disorder.

Borderline Personality Disorder, p. 475
Diff: H, Type: Applied, Ans: a
68.   "There's nothing out there for me. I can't stand other people, and I can't stand myself, either. I'm just really mad right now." Such a statement would most likely be made by someone with which personality disorder?
      a.   borderline
      b.   antisocial
      c.   narsissistic
      d.   paranoid

Borderline Personality Disorder, p. 475
Diff: H, Type: Applied, Ans: a
69.   "That personality disorder has become so common, I encounter it almost every day that I see more than a few clients." Most likely, this clinician is talking about which personality disorder?
      a.   borderline
      b.   antisocial
      c.   schizoid
      d.   avoidant

Borderline Personality Disorder, p. 475
Diff: H, Type: Applied, Ans: c
70.   Everyone else is enjoying the warmth of the early spring day except one college student, who seems irritable, even angry. Yesterday, when it was cold and dreary, the same student seemed unusually excitable. This student's behavior is most similar to that of someone with which personality disorder?
      a.   obsessive-compulsive
      b.   narsissistic
      c.   borderline
      d.   antisocial

Borderline Personality Disorder, pp. 475-476
Diff: H, Type: Applied, Ans: a

71. "Yell a lot, let your anger out; you'll be less aggressive a lot sooner," says the therapist at a workshop. In real life, the person most likely to do what the therapist suggests would be a:
   a. woman, but her aggressiveness would not diminish quickly.
   b. woman, and her aggressiveness would diminish quickly.
   c. man, but his aggressiveness would not diminish quickly.
   d. man, but his aggressiveness would diminish quickly.

Borderline Personality Disorder, p. 476
Diff: H, Type: Applied, Ans: d

72. Transported to the hospital after a suicide attempt, a man is later admitted to the hospital's psychiatric wing. Most likely, if the man is diagnosed with a personality disorder, it will be:
   a. paranoid.
   b. avoidant.
   c. narcissistic.
   d. borderline.

Borderline Personality Disorder, p. 476
Diff: H, Type: Applied, Ans: b

73. The client is making practically no progress in therapy, and expresses several symptoms similar to those of someone with bipolar disorder. The client has been diagnosed with a personality disorder; most likely, the disorder is:
   a. dependent.
   b. narcissistic.
   c. schizoid.
   d. schizotypal.

Borderline Personality Disorder, p. 476
Diff: M, Type: Applied, Ans: b

74. The client is doing reasonably well in therapy, and expresses several symptoms similar to those of someone with social phobia. The client has been diagnosed with a personality disorder, most likely, the disorder is:
   a. dependent.
   b. avoidant.
   c. borderline.
   d. schizoid.

Borderline Personality Disorder, p. 476
Diff: M, Type: Factual, Ans: d

75. Studies of those diagnosed with borderline personality disorder show that:
   a. less than half attempt suicide, and almost none succeed.
   b. less than half attempt suicide, but over 5% succeed.
   c. over half attempt suicide, but almost none succeed.
   d. over half attempt suicide, and over 5% succeed.

Borderline Personality Disorder, p. 476
Diff: E, Type: Factual, Ans: a

76.   What is a common reason for the hospitalization of people with borderline personality disorder?
       a.   They may attempt suicide or otherwise hurt themselves.
       b.   They finally cannot care for themselves.
       c.   They voluntarily ask for hospitalization, out of desperation.
       d.   They are so afraid of leaving their homes that they suffer social paralysis.

Gambling and Other Impulse Problems, p. 477 (Box 16-3)
Diff: M, Type: Factual, Ans: d

77.   The most common impulse-control disorder is:
       a.   pyromania.
       b.   trichotillomania.
       c.   intermittent explosive disorder.
       d.   pathological gambling.

Gambling and Other Impulse Problems, p. 477 (Box 16-3)
Diff: E, Type: Factual, Ans: b

78.   One who sets fires primarily for the pleasure or tension relief the fire setting provides is a(n):
       a.   arsonist.
       b.   pyromaniac.
       c.   trichotillomaniac.
       d.   kleptomaniac.

Gambling and Other Impulse Problems, p. 477 (Box 16-3)
Diff: E, Type: Factual, Ans: b

79.   The frequent failure to resist the impulse to steal is called:
       a.   pyromania.
       b.   kleptomania.
       c.   a personality disorder.
       d.   pathological gambling.

Gambling and Other Impulse Problems, p. 477 (Box 16-3)
Diff: E, Type: Applied, Ans: c

80.   Bertha pulls her hair out of a spot on the top of her head. She appears to be bald there. This is a symptom of an impulse control disorder called:
       a.   pyromania.
       b.   kleptomania.
       c.   trichotillomania.
       d.   intermittent explosive disorder.

Borderline Personality Disorder, p. 478
Diff: H, Type: Factual, Ans: c

81.   The person most likely to exhibit strong symptoms of borderline personality disorder is:
       a.   a young adult man.
       b.   a middle-aged man.
       c.   a young adult woman.
       d.   a middle-aged woman.

Borderline Personality Disorder, p. 478
Diff: M, Type: Factual, Ans: c

82.   The fact that those diagnosed with borderline personality disorder often were neglected, rejected, or sexually abused as children is best predicted by which view?
       a. cognitive
       b. biological
       c. psychodynamic
       d. sociocultural

Borderline Personality Disorder, p. 478
Diff: H, Type: Applied, Ans: d

83.   Gort's parents never quite liked him. They probably did not want children in the first place. He just was not accepted. It was clear early in school that he had a low opinion of himself. He also did not know how to interact with the other children. Now he cuts himself and has been to the ER several times. This is a description of the possible development of:
       a. histrionic personality disorder.
       b. avoidant personality disorder.
       c. schizoid personality disorder.
       d. borderline personality disorder.

Borderline Personality Disorder, p. 478
Diff: H, Type: Applied, Ans: c

84.   A therapist treating a client diagnosed with borderline personality disorder worked out the following analysis. The parents probably did not want children in the first place. The child just was not accepted. The child developed low self-esteem, dependency, and an inability to copy with separation. The therapist's theoretical orientation is probably:
       a. behavioral.
       b. biological.
       c. object relations theory.
       d. cognitive-behavioral theory.

Borderline Personality Disorder, p. 478
Diff: M, Type: Factual, Ans: c

85.   A biological cause implicated in borderline personality disorder is:
       a. enlarged ventricles.
       b. reduced levels of dopamine.
       c. decreased levels of serotonin.
       d. elevated levels of acetylcholine.

Borderline Personality Disorder, p. 478
Diff: H, Type: Applied, Ans: c

86.   A little girl has been discovered to be the victim of sexual abuse. When she becomes an adult, the probability that she will be diagnosed with borderline personality disorder is:
       a. slightly lower than it would be for people in general.
       b. about what it would be for people in general.
       c. substantially higher than it would be for people in general, although still well under 50%.
       d. substantially higher than it would be for people in general, and well over 50%.

Borderline Personality Disorder, p. 479
Diff: H, Type: Applied, Ans: d

87.   A friend asks your advice about the best therapy to use for treating borderline personality disorder. Your best answer is:
    a.   "They all work about equally well—that is, not very well at all."
    b.   "If you're going to use a psychodynamic approach, avoid relational therapy."
    c.   "Using drugs is a safe, effective way to treat the disorder."
    d.   "Research suggests that dialectical behavior therapy is the most effective."

Borderline Personality Disorder, p. 479
Diff: E, Type: Factual, Ans: a

88.   Which of the following have sociocultural theorists suggested as a cause for the emergence of borderline personality disorder?
    a.   rapid social change
    b.   traditional family structures
    c.   clinging and dependent parents
    d.   nontraditional family structures

Histrionic Personality Disorder, p. 480
Diff: M, Type: Applied, Ans: c

89.   When the seat belt light in DiDi's car stays on for a few extra seconds, she bursts into tears. She always craves attention and reacts to even the smallest event with an elaborate show of emotion. She probably could receive a diagnosis of:
    a.   obsessive personality disorder.
    b.   antisocial personality disorder.
    c.   histrionic personality disorder.
    d.   narcissistic personality disorder.

Histrionic Personality Disorder, p. 480
Diff: M, Type: Applied, Ans: a

90.   A person constantly strives to be the center of attention, yet the ideas the person so eloquently expresses are usually shallow and changeable. If this person were diagnosed with a personality disorder, it most likely would be:
    a.   histrionic.
    b.   borderline.
    c.   antisocial.
    d.   obsessive-compulsive.

Histrionic Personality Disorder, p. 480
Diff: H, Type: Applied, Ans: b

91.   A "doctor" in a TV drama suggests using antidepressant medication in the treatment of borderline personality disorder. Based on the most current research, you know:
    a.   that is really good advice: antidepressants can be very helpful in treating borderline personality disorder.
    b.   that is mediocre advice: use of antidepressants for borderline personality disorder may help, but may increase suicidal tendencies.
    c.   that is bad advice: antidepressants have no real effect on symptoms of borderline personality disorder.
    d.   that is really bad advice: antidepressants in fact may increase the severity of the symptoms of borderline personality disorder.

Histrionic Personality Disorder, p. 481
Diff: M, Type: Applied, Ans: d
92.   Historically, which of the theoretical orientations seems the most gender-biased in its
       explanation of the development of histrionic personality disorder?
       a. cognitive
       b. behavioral
       c. sociocultural
       d. psychodynamic

Histrionic Personality Disorder, p. 481
Diff: H, Type: Factual, Ans: b
93.   The highest percentage of people with which of the following personality disorders would
       probably seek treatment on their own?
       a. borderline
       b. histrionic
       c. antisocial
       d. narcissistic

Histrionic Personality Disorder, p. 481
Diff: E, Type: Applied, Ans: b
94.   The type of therapist most likely to try to help people diagnosed with histrionic personality
       disorder to believe they are not helpless, and to teach them better thinking skills, is:
       a. psychodynamic.
       b. cognitive.
       c. sociocultural.
       d. behavioral.

Narcissistic Personality Disorder, p. 482
Diff: M, Type: Applied, Ans: b
95.   "I am the greatest!" a famous boxer declared loudly and often. Had he in fact acted
       throughout his adult life as though he were the greatest, the most appropriate personality
       disorder diagnosis would be:
       a. histrionic.
       b. narcissistic.
       c. antisocial.
       d. impulse-control.

Narcissistic Personality Disorder, p. 482
Diff: E, Type: Factual, Ans: c
96.   The personality disorder that is characterized as undying love and admiration for oneself is:
       a. borderline.
       b. histrionic.
       c. narcissistic.
       d. schizotypal.

Narcissistic Personality Disorder, p. 482
Diff: E, Type: Applied, Ans: b

97.   Ty is fairly handsome, but not as handsome as he thinks he is. He doesn't give a hoot about anyone but himself and is sure that everyone around him feels the same way. He is most likely experiencing:
       a.   schizoid personality disorder.
       b.   narcissistic personality disorder.
       c.   schizotypal personality disorder.
       d.   obsessive-compulsive personality disorder.

Narcissistic Personality Disorder, p. 482
Diff: M, Type: Applied, Ans: a

98.   The "flower children" of the 1960s and 1970s have sometimes been called the "me" generation, reflecting the supposed self-centered individualism of the time. If this is true, a sociocultural theorist would predict a larger than usual percentage of which kind of personality disorder among the aging "me" generation?
       a.   narcissistic
       b.   antisocial
       c.   obsessive-compulsive
       d.   dependent

Narcissistic Personality Disorder, p. 483
Diff: H, Type: Factual, Ans: d

99.   A teenager whose actions and thoughts are often self-centered is as:
       a.   likely as an adult to be diagnosed with narcissistic personality disorder (if male).
       b.   likely as an adult to be diagnosed with narcissistic personality disorder (if female).
       c.   likely as an adult to be diagnosed with narcissistic personality disorder (female or male).
       d.   unlikely as an adult to be diagnosed with narcissistic personality disorder (male or female).

Narcissistic Personality Disorder, p. 483
Diff: M, Type: Factual, Ans: a

100.   Behavioral and cognitive theorists propose that people who develop narcissistic personality disorder may have been treated:
       a.   too positively in early life.
       b.   too negatively in early life.
       c.   either too positively or too negatively in early life.
       d.   ambiguously and neglectfully in early life.

Narcissistic Personality Disorder, p. 483
Diff: H, Type: Applied, Ans: a

101.   A person exhibits many of the symptoms associated with narcissistic personality disorder. That person is most likely to be:
       a.   male and the oldest child in his family.
       b.   female and the oldest child in her family.
       c.   male and the youngest child in his family.
       d.   female and the youngest child in her family.

Narcissistic Personality Disorder, p. 483
Diff: H, Type: Applied, Ans: a

102.   You might suspect an "era of narcissism" is approaching for a country when:
   a.   there is increasing emphasis on self-expression and competitiveness.
   b.   preferences in women's and men's clothing undergo substantial shifts.
   c.   there is a decline in materialism and individualism.
   d.   the sale of "inspirational" DVDs, books, and tapes suddenly increases.

"Anxious" Personality Disorders, p. 484
Diff: E, Type: Factual, Ans: a

103.   The personality disorders that generally are most responsive to psychotherapy are:
   a.   anxious
   b.   dramatic
   c.   odd
   d.   All these alternatives are about equally responsive to psychotherapy.

Avoidant Personality Disorder, p. 484
Diff: H, Type: Applied, Ans: c

104.   Like those with paranoid personality disorder, those with avoidant personality disorder usually:
   a.   are very sensitive to criticism.
   b.   avoid close relationships.
   c.   are very sensitive to criticism and avoid close relationships.
   d.   are indifferent to criticism and seek out close relationships.

Avoidant Personality Disorder, p. 484
Diff: E, Type: Factual, Ans: b

105.   A person who is inhibited in social situations, feels inadequate, and is very sensitive to criticism may be experiencing:
   a.   paranoid personality disorder.
   b.   avoidant personality disorder.
   c.   histrionic personality disorder.
   d.   narcissistic personality disorder.

Avoidant Personality Disorder, p. 484
Diff: E, Type: Applied, Ans: b

106.   Elena can't seem to establish social ties because she is afraid of being embarrassed or appearing foolish. She is easily hurt by criticism and is not willing to go into unfamiliar situations. She may be experiencing:
   a.   paranoid personality disorder.
   b.   avoidant personality disorder.
   c.   histrionic personality disorder.
   d.   narcissistic personality disorder.

Avoidant Personality Disorder, p. 484
Diff: M, Type: Factual, Ans: b

107.   Avoidant personality disorder seems most closely related to:
   a.   schizophrenia.
   b.   social phobias.
   c.   mania.
   d.   eating disorders.

Avoidant Personality Disorder, p. 484
Diff: H, Type: Applied, Ans: b

108.   If a person primarily fears close social relationships, one would most appropriately conclude that the person is experiencing:
      a.   social phobia.
      b.   avoidant personality disorder
      c.   both social phobia and avoidance personality disorder.
      d.   a personality disorder from the dramatic cluster.

Avoidant Personality Disorder, p. 485
Diff: M, Type: Factual, Ans: b

109.   According to psychodynamic theorists, an important factor in the development of avoidant personality disorder is:
      a.   an early sense of guilt.
      b.   early experiences of shame.
      c.   lack of development of trust.
      d.   an inability to express anger.

Avoidant Personality Disorder, p. 485
Diff: M, Type: Factual, Ans: b

110.   Clinicians are most likely to use which explanations for the development of avoidant personality disorder?
      a.   cognitive and biological
      b.   cognitive and psychodynamic
      c.   sociocultural and psychodynamic
      d.   sociocultural and biological

Avoidant Personality Disorder, p. 485
Diff: H, Type: Applied, Ans: c

111.   A client being treated for avoidant personality disorder must increase the number of social contacts per day—defined as people greeted with at least the phrase, "Hello. How are you doing?"—in order to later engage in some desired activity. Most likely, the therapist has which theoretical background?
      a.   psychodynamic
      b.   cognitive
      c.   behavioral
      d.   sociocultural

Avoidant Personality Disorder, p. 485
Diff: M, Type: Applied, Ans: c

112.   Group therapy is particularly useful in the treatment of avoidant personality disorder primarily because group therapy:
      a.   allows those in the group to see that others have avoidant personality disorder, too.
      b.   involves an eclectic combination of theoretical approaches.
      c.   provides practice in social interactions.
      d.   requires attendance at therapy sessions.

Avoidant Personality Disorder, p. 485
Diff: M, Type: Factual, Ans: b
113. Cognitive therapy for avoidant personality disorder focuses on:
      a. providing practice in social behaviors in a group setting.
      b. increasing the client's tolerance of emotional discomfort and building up his or her self-image.
      c. providing social skills training and exposure treatment that requires clients to gradually increase their social contacts.
      d. helping patients uncover the origins of their symptoms and resolve the unconscious conflicts that may be operating.

Dependent Personality Disorder, p. 485
Diff: E, Type: Factual, Ans: c
114. A person who has an excessive need to be taken care of and is clingy is most likely to qualify for a diagnosis of:
      a. paranoid personality disorder.
      b. histrionic personality disorder.
      c. dependent personality disorder.
      d. narcissistic personality disorder.

Dependent Personality Disorder, pp. 485-486
Diff: H, Type: Applied, Ans: c
115. "Someone's head resting on my knee,/Warm and tender as he can be,/Who takes good care of me,/Oh wouldn't it be lovely?/Lovely, lovely, lovely, lovely…" are the approximate lyrics of a song from the musical *My Fair Lady*. These lyrics most closely reflect symptoms of which personality disorder?
      a. narcissistic
      b. avoidant
      c. dependent
      d. schizotypal

Internet Dependence: A New Kind of Problem, p. 486 (Box 16-4)
Diff: H, Type: Applied, Ans: c
116. A friend spends hours each day in chat rooms, and seems to rely increasingly on the approval and advice of "cyberfriends." In fact, your friend finds it harder and harder to leave the chat rooms; they control your friend's every decision. This behavior pattern is most similar to that of people with which of the following personality disorders?
      a. antisocial
      b. narcissistic
      c. dependent
      d. avoidant

Dependent Personality Disorder, p. 487
Diff: E, Type: Applied, Ans: c
117. A high school student asks a guidance counselor, parents, and friends for suggestions before deciding on a college to attend, and on an academic major. This student's behavior is:
      a. typical of those with dependent personality disorder.
      b. typical of those who will develop dependent personality disorder.
      c. normal for those in high school.
      d. reflective of an anxiety disorder, not of dependent personality disorder.

Dependent Personality Disorder, p. 488
Diff: E, Type: Factual, Ans: c

118. If parents excessively reinforce clinging and punish attempts at independence, the result might be the development of:
    a. paranoid personality disorder.
    b. borderline personality disorder.
    c. dependent personality disorder.
    d. narcissistic personality disorder.

Dependent Personality Disorder, p. 488
Diff: H, Type: Applied, Ans: b

119. A child who is severely criticized for acting independently, and who is praised for doing exactly what parents say to do, later develops dependent personality disorder. The therapist who would be *least* surprised by this outcome would have which theoretical orientation?
    a. sociocultural
    b. behavioral
    c. cognitive
    d. psychodynamic

Dependent Personality Disorder, p. 488
Diff: M, Type: Factual, Ans: d

120. Assertiveness training would be most often effective in the treatment of which personality disorder?
    a. obsessive-compulsive
    b. antisocial
    c. borderline
    d. dependent

Dependent Personality Disorder, p. 488
Diff: H, Type: Applied, Ans: d

121. "Be loyal to your family" was what the child heard all the time, along with "You shouldn't—and can't—do it on your own, so don't even try." A behaviorist would say this kind of upbringing would be most likely to produce which of the personality disorders in the child, when he or she reached adulthood?
    a. narcissistic
    b. antisocial
    c. avoidant
    d. dependent

Obsessive-Compulsive Personality Disorder, p. 489
Diff: M, Type: Applied, Ans: b

122. The TV show *Monk* features a detective who is very seldom happy, has few good friends, has a very rigid order and way in which he must do things, and who frequently has difficulty making up his mind about what to do. If he were diagnosed with a personality disorder, most likely, it would be:
    a. narcissistic.
    b. obsessive-compulsive.
    c. schizotypal.
    d. narcissistic.

Obsessive-Compulsive Personality Disorder, p. 489
Diff: E, Type: Applied, Ans: a

123.   The TV show *Saturday Night Live* once featured a skit involving an "Anal Retentive
        Carpenter," who had to keep all his tools and work materials in just the "right" places,
        arranged "just so." He was very anxious any time tools and materials were not just as he
        wanted them. The most appropriate diagnosis for the carpenter would be which personality
        disorder?
        a. obsessive-compulsive
        b. borderline
        c. histrionic
        d. impulse-control

Obsessive-Compulsive Personality Disorder, p. 489
Diff: E, Type: Applied, Ans: d

124.   Jim is such a perfectionist that he is unable to finish anything. He is governed by rules and
        details. Jim might be experiencing:
        a. avoidant personality disorder.
        b. antisocial personality disorder.
        c. dependent personality disorder.
        d. obsessive-compulsive personality disorder.

Obsessive-Compulsive Personality Disorder, p. 490
Diff: H, Type: Factual, Ans: d

125.   Obsessive-compulsive personality disorder is most common among:
        a. unemployed women.
        b. women with jobs.
        c. unemployed men.
        d. men with jobs.

Obsessive-Compulsive Personality Disorder, p. 490
Diff: M, Type: Factual, Ans: b

126.   Psychodynamic theorists explain obsessive-compulsive personality disorder as a fixation at
        the _____ stage.
        a. oral
        b. anal
        c. phallic
        d. genital

Obsessive-Compulsive Personality Disorder, p. 490
Diff: E, Type: Applied, Ans: d

127.   "It is obvious that this case of obsessive-compulsive personality disorder arises from an early
        childhood fixation." Which type of psychologist would most likely have made that
        statement?
        a. behavioral
        b. cognitive
        c. sociocultural
        d. psychodynamic

Obsessive-Compulsive Personality Disorder, p. 490
Diff: H, Type: Factual, Ans: c
128. Those diagnosed with obsessive-compulsive personality disorder appear more responsive to which kinds of therapy?
      a. cognitive and biological
      b. psychodynamic and biological
      c. psychodynamic and cognitive
      d. biological and behavioral

What Problems Are Posed by the DSM-IV-TR Categories?, p. 491
Diff: H Type: Applied, Ans: a
129. All of the following are problems in the use of the DSM-IV-TR to diagnose personality disorders except:
      a. the criteria are so restrictive that several categories rarely, if ever, are used.
      b. people who act very differently may require the same diagnosis.
      c. there is considerable overlap of symptoms across many categories.
      d. sometimes the diagnostician must try to figure out *why* a person does something.

What Problems Are Posed by the DSM-IV-TR Categories?, pp. 491-492
Diff: M, Type: Factual, Ans: d
130. Which of the following disorders in DSM-III-R was dropped from DSM-IV-TR because it was considered a single trait rather than a cohesive disorder?
      a. sadistic personality disorder
      b. impulsive personality disorder
      c. self-defeating personality disorder
      d. passive-aggressive personality disorder

Are There Better Ways to Classify Personality Disorders?, p. 492
Diff: H, Type: Applied, Ans: d
131. "Let's try to figure out where clients fall on several key personality traits, rather than using a dichotomous classification system." Someone saying this would most likely favor which approach to classifying personality disorders?
      a. the traditional DSM-IV-TR approach
      b. a psychodynamic approach
      c. a cognitive-behavioral approach
      d. a dimensional approach

Are There Better Ways to Classify Personality Disorders?, pp. 492-493
Diff: H, Type: Applied, Ans: a
132. "The client scores low on extroversion and agreeableness, but high on neuroticism. Looks like schizoid personality disorder to me." The therapist being quoted is using what instrument to make the diagnosis?
      a. the "Big Five" personality test
      b. "supertrait" theory
      c. a 200-statement test, with each statement rated on a 1 to 7 scale
      d. a "dichotomizing" test

FILL-IN QUESTIONS

Personality Disorders, p. 461
Diff: E, Type: Factual, Ans: traits

1. The persistent and consistent personality characteristics with which we react to and act upon our surroundings are often called personality _____.

Personality Disorders, p. 461
Diff: E, Type: Factual, Ans: personality disorders

2. A pattern of inflexible and maladaptive personality traits that impair social or occupational functioning and cause intense distress are indicative of _____.

Personality Disorders, p. 462
Diff: E, Type: Factual, Ans: comorbidity

3. If two disorders tend to occur together, we call the relationship _____.

Paranoid Personality Disorder, p. 464
Diff: M, Type: Factual, Ans: paranoid (or odd)

4. Suspicion is a major symptom of _____ personality disorder.

Paranoid Personality Disorder, p. 464
Diff: E, Type: Factual, Ans: paranoid

5. A primary characteristic of _____ personality disorder is interpreting the motives of others as hostile.

Schizoid Personality Disorder, p. 467
Diff: M, Type: Factual, Ans: schizoid

6. Individuals who are detached and reclusive, with no interest in developing relationships, experience _____ personality disorder.

Schizotypal Personality Disorder, p. 468
Diff: M, Type: Factual, Ans: schizotypal

7. John experiences ideas of reference and bodily illusions. Most likely, John has a _____ personality disorder.

Schizotypal Personality Disorder, p. 469
Diff: E, Type: Factual, Ans: antipsychotics (or neuroleptics)

8. The drugs most likely to be used to treat the schizotypal personality disorder are _____.

Antisocial Personality Disorder, p. 470
Diff: E, Type: Applied, Ans: antisocial personality

9. Lev has a lifelong history of misconduct, including vandalism, fighting, and failing to meet normal social responsibilities. He fits the description of someone with _____ disorder.

Antisocial Personality Disorder, p. 472
Diff: E, Type: Applied, Ans: antisocial

10. A con artist is most likely to suffer from a(n) _____ personality disorder.

Borderline Personality Disorder, p. 475
Diff: M, Type: Factual, Ans: borderline
11. Swinging in and out of depressed, anxious, and irritable states is characteristic of the _____ personality disorder.

Gambling and Other Impulse Problems, p. 477 (Box 16-3)
Diff: M, Type: Factual, Ans: impulse (or impulse control)
12. Kleptomania, pyromania, and compulsive gambling are considered disorders of _____ rather than personality.

Gambling and Other Impulse Problems, p. 477 (Box 16-3)
Diff: E, Type: Factual, Ans: pyromania
13. The deliberate setting of fires to achieve intense pleasure or relief is known as _____.

Gambling and Other Impulse Problems, p. 477 (Box 16-3)
Diff: E, Type: Factual, Ans: kleptomania
14. The recurrent failure to resist the impulse to steal is known as _____.

Histrionic Personality Disorder, p. 480
Diff: M, Type: Factual, Ans: histrionic
15. Marcel has extremely exaggerated emotional reactions to events. He may be demonstrating a _____ personality disorder.

Narcissistic Personality Disorder, p. 483
Diff: M, Type: Factual, Ans: narcissistic
16. A person who was overly indulged by his or her parents, received excessive, unconditional parental valuation, and was not required to follow rules or develop self-control is at risk for developing _____ personality disorder.

Avoidant Personality Disorder, p. 484
Diff: M, Type: Applied, Ans: avoidant
17. Social phobias may be related to _____ personality disorder.

Dependent Personality Disorder, pp. 485-486
Diff: M, Type: Applied, Ans: dependent
18. Willa cannot do anything on her own. She needs to consult on the smallest decision. She is constantly in need of praise to validate her work and is overly sensitive to any rebuff. She will do almost anything to please others. She may be experiencing _____ personality disorder.

Obsessive-Compulsive Personality Disorder, p. 489
Diff: E, Type: Factual, Ans: obsessive-compulsive
19. The characteristic of perfectionism and a striving for control are associated with _____ personality disorder.

Obsessive-Compulsive Personality Disorder, p. 490
Diff: M, Type: Factual, Ans: anal
20. According to the psychodynamic view, obsessive-compulsive personality is related to fixation during the _____ stage.

ESSAY QUESTIONS

"Odd" Personality Disorders, p. 463
Diff: E, Type: Factual

1. What are the most important differences between the odd and the dramatic personality disorders? You should include examples of at least one specific disorder per category as examples to support your answer.

"Odd" Personality Disorders, p. 465
Diff: M, Type: Applied

2. Why is psychotherapy so often ineffective in treating the odd personality disorders? What suggestions, based on evidence, might you make to maximize the chances of helping someone with an odd personality disorder?

Antisocial Personality Disorder, p. 470
Diff: H, Type: Applied

3. One of the most common—and certainly most troubling—of the personality disorders is antisocial personality disorder. First, define antisocial personality disorder. Second, outline other behavior patterns with which this disorder is associated. Finally, suggest a course of treatment for someone suffering from this disorder.

Antisocial Personality Disorder, pp. 470-480
Diff: M, Type: Factual

4. Please outline the similarities and differences of antisocial and borderline personality disorders, being sure to mention why each seems so resistant to any form of psychotherapy.

Antisocial Personality Disorder, p. 477
Diff: M, Type: Applied

5. What are the general characteristics of impulse-control disorders? Using pathological gambling as an example, show how impulse-control disorders differ from personality disorders, and what therapeutic approaches seem to be most effective with impulse-control disorders.

Histrionic Personality Disorder/Narcissistic Personality Disorder, pp. 480-484
Diff: H, Type: Applied

6. From the viewpoint of either a psychodynamic or a cognitive psychologist, differentiate histrionic and narcissistic personality disorders, say how they originate, and suggest possible treatments for them.

"Anxious" Personality Disorders, pp. 484-490
Diff: H, Type: Applied

7. Why does the DSM-IV-TR need separate anxious personality disorders? Aren't they simply more severe forms of anxiety disorders? Please justify the use of anxious personality disorders, either by describing how obsessive-compulsive personality disorder differs from obsessive-compulsive disorder, or by describing how dependent personality disorder differs from depression.

Internet Dependence: A New Kind of Problem, pp. 486-487 (Box 16-4)
Diff: M, Type: Applied

8.   Some psychologists have claimed that "Internet dependence" is a new variety of personality disorder, while others say it more closely resembles an impulse-control or substance-related disorder. What do you think? First, describe important characteristics of Internet dependence. Second, say how, based on those characteristics, you would classify Internet dependence.

No specific topic, No specific page
Diff: M, Type: Factual

9.   List the three clusters of personality disorders and the specific disorders that make up each cluster.

No specific topic, No specific page
Diff: H, Type: Applied

10.   Psychodynamic *theories* often seem to do a good job of explaining the existence of personality disorders, yet psychodynamic *therapies* often do not work particularly well with personality disorders. How can this be? One way to start answering this question would be to focus on a particular personality disorder, describing the disorder, then the possible treatment, from a psychodynamic perspective.

Possible answers should focus on common "symptoms" of personality disorders—such as lack of trust, lack of impulse control, any rapid mood swings—which psychodynamic theories can explain, but which stand in the way of virtually any therapy having a chance to be effective.

CHAPTER 17

Disorders of Childhood and Adolescence

MULTIPLE-CHOICE QUESTIONS

Childhood and Adolescence, p. 498
Diff: M, Type: Factual, Ans: a
1. Surveys show that _____ is a common experience for close to half of all children in the United States.
    a. worry
    b. depression
    c. anxiety
    d. substance abuse

Childhood and Adolescence, p. 498
Diff: M, Type: Applied, Ans: b
2. "Old age isn't just faded adulthood, but an important, separate stage of life." This statement fits well with the stage theory proposed by:
    a. Freud.
    b. Erikson.
    c. Beck.
    d. Jung.

Childhood and Adolescence, p. 498
Diff: M, Type: Factual, Ans: a
3. Compared to teenagers of a couple of generations ago, today's teens are:
    a. less trusting.
    b. less sensitive.
    c. more affectionate toward their families.
    d. generally unhappy.

Childhood and Adolescence, p. 498
Diff: E, Type: Factual, Ans: d
4. Childhood disorders for which there are no direct adult counterparts are:
    a. disruptive disorders.
    b. anxiety disorders.
    c. mental retardation.
    d. elimination disorders.

Childhood and Adolescence, p. 498
Diff: E, Type: Factual, Ans: c

5.   Compared to girls, boys are:
     a.   less likely to commit suicide.
     b.   more likely to be well adjusted.
     c.   more likely to have a diagnosable psychological disorder.
     d.   somewhat less likely to have a diagnosable psychological disorder.

Oppositional Defiant Disorder and Conduct Disorder, p. 499
Diff: M, Type: Applied, Ans: c

6.   Nellie is openly hostile toward her parents. She argues with them constantly and will not do anything they say. They cannot control her. The diagnosis she is most likely to receive is:
     a.   conduct disorder.
     b.   juvenile delinquency.
     c.   oppositional defiant disorder.
     d.   attention-deficit/hyperactivity disorder.

Oppositional Defiant Disorder and Conduct Disorder, p. 499
Diff: H, Type: Applied, Ans: d

7.   Xavier will not obey his mother. When threatened with punishment, he swears, throws things, and threatens to break everything in the house. His outbreaks seem to be restricted to his parents, but he is almost completely unmanageable. This is an example of:
     a.   conduct disorder.
     b.   juvenile delinquency.
     c.   childhood schizophrenia.
     d.   oppositional defiant disorder.

Oppositional Defiant Disorder and Conduct Disorder, p. 499
Diff: H, Type: Factual, Ans: b

8.   Boys and girls have about the same percentage chance of being diagnosed with:
     a.   oppositional defiant disorder if they are prepubertal.
     b.   oppositional defiant disorder if they are postpuberty.
     c.   conduct disorder if they are prepuberty.
     d.   conduct disorder if they are postpuberty.

Oppositional Defiant Disorder and Conduct Disorder, p. 499
Diff: H, Type: Applied, Ans: c

9.   A child has repeatedly engaged in shoplifting and in hitting neighborhood pets with rocks. The child frequently is aggressive, and has engaged in an increasing number of fights. The most reasonable diagnosis for this child is:
     a.   oppositional defiant disorder.
     b.   attention-deficit/hyperactivity disorder (ADHD).
     c.   conduct disorder.
     d.   antisocial personality disorder.

Oppositional Defiant Disorder and Conduct Disorder, p. 499
Diff: M, Type: Applied, Ans: a

10.   Bertie is extremely aggressive. She is always fighting with her peers and is frequently very cruel to them. She never tells the truth when a lie will do. Her most likely diagnosis is:
   a.   conduct disorder.
   b.   juvenile delinquency.
   c.   passive-aggressive disorder.
   d.   oppositional defiant disorder.

Oppositional Defiant Disorder and Conduct Disorder, p. 499
Diff: H, Type: Applied, Ans: b

11.   A two-year-old child is evaluated as "noncompliant" by a preschool teacher. Most likely, that child's level of noncompliance at five years of age will be:
   a.   higher, whether the child is a girl or a boy.
   b.   lower, whether the child is a boy or a girl.
   c.   higher is the child is a boy, lower if the child is a girl.
   d.   higher if the child is a girl, lower if the child is a boy.

Oppositional Defiant Disorder and Conduct Disorder, p. 502
Diff: H, Type: Applied, Ans: d

12.   A child has been diagnosed with conduct disorder, but was not previously diagnosed with oppositional defiant disorder. This situation is:
   a.   very common; the two disorders are not related to one another.
   b.   common; although the disorders are related, less that 10% of those diagnosed with conduct disorder were earlier diagnosed with oppositional defiant disorder.
   c.   not very common; almost half of those diagnosed with conduct disorder were earlier diagnosed with oppositional defiant disorder.
   d.   uncommon; over 80% of those diagnosed with conduct disorder were earlier diagnosed with oppositional defiant disorder.

Oppositional Defiant Disorder and Conduct Disorder, p. 502
Diff: M, Type: Applied, Ans: c

13.   A child sneaks out of the home every now and then, and goes through the neighborhood breaking lawn decorations and scratching car paint. These behaviors most closely fit which pattern of conduct disorder?
   a.   overt-destructive
   b.   overt-nondestructive
   c.   covert-destructive
   d.   covert-nondestructive

Oppositional Defiant Disorder and Conduct Disorder, p. 502
Diff: M, Type: Applied, Ans: d

14.   At a parent-teacher conference, a child's parents are astounded to learn that their son has been showing up late for school, despite leaving home with more than enough time to get to school. This behavior most closely fits which pattern of conduct disorder?
   a.   overt-destructive
   b.   overt-nondestructive
   c.   covert-destructive
   d.   covert-nondestructive

Oppositional Defiant Disorder and Conduct Disorder, p. 502
Diff: H, Type: Applied, Ans: b

15.   "That kid is pleasant enough, but will lie about practically anything, even things that don't
       seem to matter much." This behavior most closely fits which pattern of conduct disorder?
       a.   overt-destructive
       b.   overt-nondestructive
       c.   covert-destructive
       d.   covert-nondestructive

Bullying: A Growing Crisis?, p. 503 (Box 17-2)
Diff: H, Type: Applied, Ans: a

16.   Perhaps the biggest problem facing school administrators who try to deal with bullying is
       that:
       a.   so many students are involved in bullying incidents, it's hard to tell who is dangerous.
       b.   they really don't care, since bullying is such an unusual occurrence in most schools.
       c.   there is a very real possibility that the bullies will attack them, as well as their student
             victims.
       d.   students really don't rate bullying as a serious problem.

Oppositional Defiant Disorder and Conduct Disorder, p. 503
Diff: M, Type: Applied, Ans: a

17.   "Relational aggression" is a term used to describe a pattern of aggression most common
       among:
       a.   girls diagnosed with conduct disorder.
       b.   boys diagnosed with conduct disorder.
       c.   boys diagnosed with oppositional defiant disorder.
       d.   girls diagnosed with oppositional defiant disorder.

Oppositional Defiant Disorder and Conduct Disorder, p. 503
Diff: H, Type: Applied, Ans: b

18.   When a child is diagnosed with two disorders, which of the following statements is most
       strongly supported by research findings?
       a.   Boys diagnosed with conduct disorder are more likely than girls diagnosed with conduct
             disorder to also be diagnosed with ADHD.
       b.   Girls diagnosed with conduct disorder are more likely than boys diagnosed with conduct
             disorder to also be diagnosed with ADHD.
       c.   Depressive symptoms usually occur before conduct-disorder symptoms.
       d.   Conduct-disorder symptoms usually occur before ADHD symptoms.

Oppositional Defiant Disorder and Conduct Disorder, p. 503
Diff: H, Type: Applied, Ans: b

19.   Carl is a terrible bully. He is very aggressive and repeatedly takes advantage of his "friends."
       He will say anything to get his way or try to stay out of trouble. Recently he was arrested for
       vandalism and ended up getting probation. He will most likely be labeled as displaying:
       a.   conduct disorder.
       b.   juvenile delinquency.
       c.   passive-aggressive disorder.
       d.   oppositional defiant disorder.

Oppositional Defiant Disorder and Conduct Disorder, p. 503
Diff: M, Type: Applied, Ans: a
20. A 16-year-old has just been arrested for the third time for shoplifting. He would most likely
     be labeled a(n):
     a. juvenile delinquent recidivist.
     b. juvenile delinquent.
     c. adult criminal recidivist.
     d. adult criminal.

What Are the Causes of Conduct Disorder?, p. 504
Diff: E, Type: Factual, Ans: c
21. Conduct disorder has most often been associated with:
     a. genetic or hormonal predisposition.
     b. a history of child abuse.
     c. poor parent-child relationships.
     d. poverty.

How Do Clinicians Treat Conduct Disorder?, p. 504
Diff: M, Type: Applied, Ans: a
22. A 10-year-old has a diagnosable conduct disorder. The approach most likely to succeed
     would be to:
     a. begin therapy at once.
     b. wait to see if the child outgrows the problem.
     c. wait until the child is into puberty, since therapy is most effective then.
     d. wait until the child is postpuberty, since therapy is most effective then.

How Do Clinicians Treat Conduct Disorder?, p. 504
Diff: M, Type: Factual, Ans: a
23. The failure of parental supervision is associated with:
     a. conduct disorder.
     b. school phobia.
     c. attention-deficit/hyperactivity disorder.
     d. childhood depression.

How Do Clinicians Treat Conduct Disorder?, p. 504
Diff: H, Type: Applied, Ans: c
24. In effect, parents learn to do behavior therapy with their children diagnosed with conduct
     disorder—targeting and rewarding desired behaviors, for instance—in an intervention called:
     a. parent-interaction therapy.
     b. video tape modeling.
     c. parent management training.
     d. family-consequence sensitization.

How Do Clinicians Treat Conduct Disorder?, p. 504
Diff: H, Type: Applied, Ans: c
25. "My seven-year-old needs to get help for conduct disorder. What do you recommend?" asks a
     friend. Of the following alternatives, your best answer is:
     a. "Video tape modeling works especially well with elementary school children."
     b. "Treatment foster care is best, if the program is well-established."
     c. "Parent management training should work best."
     d. "Parent-child interaction therapy would be my recommendation."

Child Abuse, p. 505 (Box 17-3)
Diff: H, Type: Applied, Ans: a

26.   Of the following, the child at greatest risk for experiencing physical abuse would be a:
       a.   physically disabled nine-year-old boy.
       b.   physically disabled nine-year-old girl.
       c.   middle-socioeconomic group nine-year-old girl.
       d.   middle-socioeconomic group nine-year-old boy.

Child Abuse, p. 505
Diff: H, Type: Applied, Ans: b

27.   You read a case study about a ten-year-old girl from a poor background who was sexually
       abused. This case is:
       a.   common; girls from poor backgrounds are the most common victims of sexual abuse.
       b.   fairly common; girls, regardless of their socioeconomic group, are the most common
             victims of sexual abuse.
       c.   uncommon; girls from wealthy backgrounds are the most common victims of sexual
             abuse.
       d.   very uncommon; boys from wealthy backgrounds are the most common victims of sexual
             abuse.

Child Abuse, p. 505
Diff: M, Type: Applied, Ans: d

28.   If there were several Parents Anonymous groups in a city near you, you could be sure that in
       that city:
       a.   children diagnosed with conduct disorder, and who were abusing alcohol, were receiving
             help.
       b.   children diagnosed with conduct disorder, and who were abusing alcohol or any other
             drug, were receiving help.
       c.   parents whose children were physically or verbally abusing them were receiving help.
       d.   parents who were themselves child abusers were receiving help.

Child Abuse, p. 505
Diff: E, Type: Applied, Ans: d

29.   Tamara's parents are down on her all the time. When they are not criticizing her, they ignore
       her. This is an example of:
       a.   punishment.
       b.   sexual abuse.
       c.   parental discipline.
       d.   psychological abuse.

Child Abuse, p. 506
Diff: M, Type: Factual, Ans: d

30.   Although U.S. teenagers constitute about 14% of the population, they make up more than
       25% of all of the following categories except:
       a.   murderers.
       b.   perpetrators of violent crimes.
       c.   victims of violent crimes.
       d.   embezzlers.

Child Abuse, p. 506
Diff: M, Type: Factual, Ans: c
31.   The least effective way to deal with conduct disorder is:
    a.   prevention programs.
    b.   teaching children how to deal with their anger.
    c.   having them live in juvenile training centers.
    d.   through family intervention.

Child Abuse, p. 506
Diff: M, Type: Applied, Ans: d
32.   A child is receiving problem-solving skills training as a treatment for conduct disorder. You can be reasonably sure that:
    a.   stimulant drug (e.g. Ritalin) administration is recommended, but not required.
    b.   the child is a preschooler.
    c.   the child is female.
    d.   the techniques used are cognitive behavioral.

Child Abuse, p. 506
Diff: M, Type: Applied, Ans: a
33.   "Will that program really help? I keep hearing bad things about how kids act once they leave." Based on research, the person who said this would be most accurate if she or he were expressing reservations about:
    a.   a juvenile training center.
    b.   treatment foster care.
    c.   problem-solving training.
    d.   an Anger Coping and Coping Power Program.

Child Abuse, p. 507
Diff: H, Type: Applied, Ans: c
34.   A preadolescent child who has not received a clinical diagnosis participates in a program designed to stop the development of an antisocial pattern of behavior. Most likely, that program is:
    a.   the Anger Coping and Coping Power Program.
    b.   one that involves the use of stimulant drugs such as Ritalin.
    c.   Scared Straight.
    d.   Parents and Children Anonymous.

DSM Checklist, p. 508 (Table 17-2)
Diff: H, Type: Applied, Ans: c
35.   A child's distracting behaviors occur only in a school setting, and include failure to follow instructions and finish work, answering questions before they have been completed, and a lot of seat squirming and fidgeting. Could ADHD be a diagnosis of this child?
    a.   Yes, it could be a diagnosis.
    b.   No; the child's symptoms started at too young an age.
    c.   No; the child's symptoms occur in only one setting.
    d.   Yes, it could be, but only if the fidgeting is distracting to others.

Attention-Deficit/Hyperactivity Disorder, p. 508
Diff: M, Type: Factual, Ans: a

36.   Generally speaking, as children diagnosed with ADHD enter adulthood, the number of them who continue to have ADHD:
    a.   decreases, and symptom severity decreases as well.
    b.   decreases, although symptom severity remains the same among those diagnosed ADHD.
    c.   decreases, although symptom severity among those diagnosed ADHD increases.
    d.   stays the same, although symptom severity decreases.

Attention-Deficit/Hyperactivity Disorder, p. 508
Diff: H, Type: Factual, Ans: b

37.   Among other things, a diagnosis of ADHD must include a total of at least:
    a.   18 symptoms, lasting at least 6 months.
    b.   12 symptoms, lasting at least 6 months.
    c.   18 symptoms, lasting at least 12 months.
    d.   12 symptoms, lasting at least 12 months.

Attention-Deficit/Hyperactivity Disorder, p. 508
Diff: H, Type: Applied, Ans: d

38.   A child who has been diagnosed with ADHD frequently disrupts the class to such a degree that the teacher can no longer conduct instruction. This kind of problem behavior is:
    a.   very unusual; many diagnosed with ADHD have trouble learning, but almost none exhibit serious behavior problems.
    b.   unusual; only about 20% diagnosed with ADHD exhibit serious behavior problems.
    c.   common; about half of those diagnosed with ADHD exhibit serious behavior problems.
    d.   the norm; over three-quarters of those diagnosed with ADHD exhibit serious behavior problems.

Attention-Deficit/Hyperactivity Disorder, p. 508
Diff: M, Type: Applied, Ans: d

39.   Pat does not follow what the teacher is doing and has difficulty focusing on the task at hand. His behavior in class is disruptive because he cannot sit still. He gets poor grades in school. These symptoms indicate:
    a.   a conduct disorder.
    b.   school phobia with acting out.
    c.   dyslexia with childhood anxiety.
    d.   attention-deficit/hyperactivity disorder.

Attention-Deficit/Hyperactivity Disorder, p. 508
Diff: E, Type: Factual, Ans: a

40.   Attention-deficit/hyperactivity disorder is more common in _____ than _____.
    a.   boys; girls
    b.   girls; boys
    c.   adolescents; children.
    d.   adults; children

Attention-Deficit/Hyperactivity Disorder, p. 508
Diff: H, Type: Applied, Ans: c

41.   Several decades ago, a child had a great deal of difficulty keeping on task in school. Not only did the child frequently roam around the classroom and talk to others, the child frequently squirmed around while at a desk. At the time, the child was diagnosed as suffering from "minimal brain damage," today's likely diagnosis would be:
    a.   oppositional defiant disorder.
    b.   conduct disorder.
    c.   ADHD.
    d.   mental retardation.

What Are the Causes of ADHD?, p. 509
Diff: H, Type: Applied, Ans: a

42.   A parent of an infant asks what you would recommend specifically to reduce the chances of the infant developing ADHD. Research-based responses would include:
    a.   "Make sure your kid doesn't watch too much TV."
    b.   "Try to control your child's sugar intake."
    c.   "Many food additives can lead to ADHD."
    d.   All of the above alternatives are research-based and accurate.

What Are the Causes of ADHD?, p. 509
Diff: H, Type: Applied, Ans: c

43.   Compared to adults, children are:
    a.   more likely to take drugs for attention problems, although their use is decreasing.
    b.   more likely to take drugs for attention problems, and the use of drugs is remaining constant.
    c.   more likely to take drugs for attention problems, and the use of drugs is increasing.
    d.   about equally likely to take drugs for attention problems, and the use of drugs is increasing.

How Is ADHD Treated?, p. 509
Diff: E, Type: Factual, Ans: a

44.   The drug Ritalin is classified as a:
    a.   stimulant.
    b.   depressant.
    c.   tranquilizer.
    d.   antidepressant.

What Are the Causes of ADHD?, pp. 509-510
Diff: M, Type: Factual, Ans: a

45.   The two most common treatments for attention-deficit/hyperactivity disorder have been:
    a.   behavioral and drug therapies.
    b.   group therapy and sociotherapy.
    c.   behavioral and group therapy.
    d.   insight therapy and cognitive therapy.

What Are the Causes of ADHD?, pp. 509-510
Diff: E, Type: Applied, Ans: d

46.   Recent research suggests that the most effective ways to treat ADHD are:
       a.   psychodynamic therapy and drugs.
       b.   gene therapy and psychodynamic therapy.
       c.   behavioral therapy and gene therapy.
       d.   drugs and behavior therapy.

How is ADHD Treated?, p. 510
Diff: M, Type: Applied, Ans: c

47.   "What should I look for in an effective ADHD treatment program?" a friend asks. Your best
       answer among the following alternatives is:
       a.   "Psychodynamic therapy works best, with or without drugs."
       b.   "Cognitive therapy outperforms even Ritalin."
       c.   "Drugs work best."
       d.   "Drugs, combined with behavior therapy, work best."

Ritalin: Chemical Straightjacket or Miracle Drug?, pp. 510-511 (Box 17-4)
Diff: M, Type: Factual, Ans: c

48.   In terms of Ritalin consumption per person, the greatest increase in Ritalin use in the United
       States occurred in the:
       a.   early 1980s.
       b.   late 1980s.
       c.   early 1990s.
       d.   late 1990s.

How is ADHD Treated?, pp. 510-511
Diff: M, Type: Factual, Ans: b

49.   Most Ritalin manufactured each year is used by:
       a.   girls in the United States.
       b.   boys in the United States.
       c.   girls outside the United States.
       d.   boys outside the United States.

How is ADHD Treated?, p. 511
Diff: H, Type: Applied, Ans: b

50.   "I'm concerned about Ritalin use; its possible effects on children's growth, and its increasing
       heart-attack risk in hypertensive adults" an acquaintance worries. Your best reply, based on
       the most recent research is:
       a.   "Don't worry—the latest studies pretty much rule out those problems."
       b.   "You're right to worry—and we need more research to quantify the risk."
       c.   "You need to be concerned about growth effects in kids, but not heart-attack risk in
             adults."
       d.   "You need to be concerned about heart-attack risk in adults, but not about growth effects
             in kids."

How is ADHD Treated?, p. 511
Diff: H, Type: Applied, Ans: a

51. A friend has been receiving both stimulant medication and behavior therapy for ADHD and the treatment program has been reasonably effective. As your friend approaches adulthood, the best thing to do would be to:
   a. continue the present treatment program.
   b. gradually stop treatment; the symptoms almost always fade away in adulthood.
   c. continue only the behavior therapy; drugs are relatively ineffective with adults.
   d. continue only the stimulant medication; behavior therapy is relatively ineffective with adults.

How is ADHD Treated?, pp. 510-511
Diff: H, Type: Applied, Ans: d

52. A child diagnosed with ADHD displays comorbidity, and receives both stimulant medication and a form of behavior therapy. According to research, the comorbidity is most likely:
   a. a conduct disorder.
   b. an anxiety disorder.
   c. either a conduct disorder or an anxiety disorder.
   d. both a conduct disorder and an anxiety disorder.

The Sociocultural Landscape: ADHD and Race, p. 511
Diff: H, Type: Applied, Ans: c

53. Compared to white American children, African American and Hispanic American children with similar levels of activity and attention problems are:
   a. about equally likely to be assessed for ADHD, but less likely to be diagnosed with ADHD.
   b. about equally likely to be assessed for ADHD, but more likely to be diagnosed with ADHD.
   c. less likely to be assessed for ADHD, and less likely to be diagnosed with ADHD.
   d. less likely to be assessed for ADHD, but more likely to be diagnosed with ADHD.

The Sociocultural Landscape: ADHD and Race, p. 511
Diff: M, Type: Applied, Ans: a

54. Compared to white American children, African American and Hispanic American children with similar levels of activity and attention problems are:
   a. less likely to be diagnosed with ADHD, and less likely to receive effective treatment.
   b. less likely to be diagnosed with ADHD, but more likely to receive effective treatment.
   c. about equally likely to be diagnosed with ADHD, but less likely to receive effective treatment.
   d. more likely to be diagnosed with ADHD, but less likely to receive effective treatment.

The Sociocultural Landscape: ADHD and Race, p. 512
Diff: H, Type: Applied, Ans: b

55. When asked, a parent says, "Why does my kid have ADHD? I guess it's in the genes." Given this very limited information, your research-based guess would be that the parent is:
   a. African American, and more likely than most to seek treatment for the child.
   b. white American, and more likely than most to seek treatment for the child.
   c. African American, and less likely than most to seek treatment for the child.
   d. white American, and less likely than most to seek treatment for the child.

The Sociocultural Landscape: ADHD and Race, p. 512
Diff: M, Type: Applied, Ans: d
56.   Of the following parents, the ones least likely to have children who receive effective treatment for ADHD are:
   a.   white Americans with private health insurance.
   b.   African Americans with private health insurance.
   c.   white Americans who are Medicaid-insured.
   d.   African Americans who are Medicaid-insured.

The Sociocultural Landscape: ADHD and Race, p. 512
Diff: E, Type: Applied, Ans: d
57.   Of the following alternatives, the one least likely to contribute to inequities between African Americans and white Americans in receiving long-acting stimulant drug treatment for ADHD is:
   a.   economic factors.
   b.   social bias.
   c.   stereotyping.
   d.   differences in drug tolerance.

Enuresis, p. 512
Diff: M, Type: Applied, Ans: d
58.   A 3-year-old child is wetting the bed at night. The bed wetting apparently is beyond the child's control. The best diagnosis is:
   a.   enuresis.
   b.   encopresis.
   c.   oppositional defiant disorder.
   d.   no diagnosis, in this case.

Enuresis, p. 512
Diff: E, Type: Applied, Ans: a
59.   Joey has been wetting his bed since he was a baby. He is 10 years old now. As a result, he will not stay over at his friend's house or go to camp. His condition is called:
   a.   enuresis.
   b.   encopresis.
   c.   conduct disorder.
   d.   noctural emission.

Enuresis, pp. 512, 514
Diff: M, Type: Factual, Ans: c
60.   Which of the following statements is most accurate regarding enuresis and encopresis?
   a.   Both occur most commonly at night.
   b.   Both occur most commonly during the day.
   c.   Enuresis occurs most commonly at night, encopresis during the day.
   d.   Enuresis occurs most commonly during the day, encopresis at night.

Enuresis, p. 513
Diff: M, Type: Applied, Ans: c
61.   A child awakens suddenly to the sound of a bell, and heads for the bathroom. Most likely the child is receiving:
    a.   psychodynamic therapy for enuresis.
    b.   psychodynamic therapy for encopresis.
    c.   behavioral therapy for enuresis.
    d.   behavioral therapy for encopresis.

Enuresis, p. 513
Diff: M, Type: Applied, Ans: d
62.   One useful approach to treating enuresis employs:
    a.   insight therapy.
    b.   stimulant drugs.
    c.   operant conditioning.
    d.   classical conditioning

Enuresis, p. 513
Diff: H, Type: Applied, Ans: a
63.   A child is awakened during the night, goes to and uses the toilet, and receives a sticker and praise from a parent. Later in the week, accumulated stickers may be turned in for a highly desired toy. This child is undergoing:
    a.   dry-bed training for enuresis.
    b.   dry-bed training for encopresis.
    c.   bell-and-battery therapy for enuresis.
    d.   bell-and-battery therapy for encopresis.

Encopresis, p. 514
Diff: H, Type: Applied, Ans: b
64.   A diagnostician says, "I'm reasonably sure there's a hereditary factor for this disorder, especially since your uncle had the same disorder." This statement would be least accurate regarding:
    a.   conduct disorder.
    b.   encopresis.
    c.   enuresis.
    d.   autism.

Encopresis, p. 514
Diff: H, Type: Applied, Ans: c
65.   "I knew right after we got home from the hospital that our kid had a problem," the parent said. Unless the parent is using 20-20 hindsight, the child's diagnosis most likely is:
    a.   mental retardation.
    b.   ADHD.
    c.   autism.
    d.   enuresis.

Encopresis, p. 514
Diff: H, Type: Factual, Ans: a
66. Which of the following disorders of childhood and adolescence is most common?
    a. conduct disorder
    b. encopresis
    c. ADHD
    d. mental retardation

Encopresis, p. 514
Diff: M, Type: Factual, Ans: d
67. The most common and successful treatments for encopresis are:
    a. medication and family therapy.
    b. behavioral and family therapy.
    c. bell and pad system.
    d. behavioral and medical treatments.

Pervasive Developmental Disorders, p. 515
Diff: M, Type: Applied, Ans: a
68. The child most likely to show the *first* symptom of autistic disorder would be a:
    a. boy under 3 years old.
    b. girl under 3 years old.
    c. boy over 5 years old.
    d. girl over 5 years old.

Pervasive Developmental Disorders, p. 515
Diff: H, Type: Applied, Ans: b
69. A female child is diagnosed with autism. Later, as an adult, she is unable to hold a job and has very limited communication skills. Her case is:
    a. very rare; most people diagnosed with autism are males, and their symptoms usually diminish substantially by early adulthood.
    b. uncommon; most people diagnosed with autism are males, and their symptoms usually remain severe into adulthood.
    c. uncommon; most people diagnosed with autism are females, and their symptoms usually diminish substantially by early adulthood.
    d. common; most people diagnosed with autism are females, and their symptoms usually remain severe into adulthood.

Pervasive Developmental Disorders, p. 516
Diff: H, Type: Applied, Ans: b
70. Assume that you are alone in a room with a child suffering from a disorder of childhood. If you didn't know what the child's diagnosis was, what behavior of the child's might start to convince you that the disorder is autism?
    a. The child argues defiantly with parents.
    b. The child is not responsive to other people.
    c. The child screams uncontrollably when separated from parents.
    d. The child is very active, and finds it difficult to stay on task.

Pervasive Developmental Disorders, p. 516
Diff: H, Type: Applied, Ans: d

71.   When a child with autism says "You want a drink" when he really means that he wants a drink, he is displaying:
    a.   self-stimulatory behavior.
    b.   delayed echolalia.
    c.   limited imagination.
    d.   pronominal reversal.

Pervasive Developmental Disorders, p. 516
Diff: E, Type: Applied, Ans: a

72.   The mockingbird gets its name from the fact that it often imitates the call of other birds, without conveying any particular message. A human who imitates others' speech without really communicating most likely would be diagnosed with:
    a.   autism.
    b.   ADHD.
    c.   mental retardation.
    d.   oppositional defiant disorder.

Pervasive Developmental Disorders, p. 516
Diff: E, Type: Factual, Ans: a

73.   One speech problem displayed by many autistic children is that they repeat everything said to them. This is called:
    a.   echolalia.
    b.   neologism.
    c.   nominal aphasia.
    d.   pronominal reversal.

Pervasive Developmental Disorders, p. 517
Diff: H, Type: Applied, Ans: d

74.   Ralphie is autistic and does not like much variation in his life. He puts his toys on a shelf in a particular order and throws a tantrum if his mother moves any of them. Any one of several trivial changes in his daily routine can set him off. This is an example of:
    a.   overstimulation.
    b.   stimulus over selectivity.
    c.   a self-stimulatory behavior.
    d.   a perseveration of sameness.

Pervasive Developmental Disorders, p. 517
Diff: E, Type: Applied, Ans: d

75.   When a child with autism jumps, flaps her arms, twists her hands and fingers and makes unusual faces, the child is engaging in:
    a.   self-injurious behavior.
    b.   self-communication behavior.
    c.   self-motor behavior.
    d.   self-stimulatory behavior.

A Special Kind of Talent, p. 517 (Box 17-5)
Diff: H, Type: Applied, Ans: d
76.   A person diagnosed with autism listens to a piano piece at a concert. Later at home, the person plays the piano piece without the music, and without making a mistake. This behavior is best described as:
a.   perseveration of sameness.
b.   repetitive and rigid behavior.
c.   delayed echolalia.
d.   savant skill.

Pervasive Developmental Disorders, p. 518
Diff: H, Type: Applied, Ans: a
77.   A friend asks you for a nearly foolproof way to find out if someone has been diagnosed with autism or with Asperger's disorder. Your best answer among the following would be:
a.   "Try to talk with the person; if he or she converses well, it's probably Asperger's."
b.   "Check for delayed echolalia; that's much more common in Asperger's."
c.   "Does he or she have many adaptive skills? Adaptive skills predict autism.
d.   "If the person is a 'rule person [boy]' it's probably autism."

Pervasive Developmental Disorders, p. 518
Diff: H, Type: Applied, Ans: d
78.   A person diagnosed with Asperger's disorder is extremely curious about why other people think what they think, and has zero tolerance for others' occasionally illogical thinking. According to one classification system (with apologies for sexist language), the term for this individual would be:
a.   emotion boy.
b.   rational boy.
c.   rule boy.
d.   logic boy.

Pervasive Developmental Disorders, p. 518
Diff: H, Type: Applied, Ans: d
79.   "It is possible, even probable, that 'refrigerator parents'—cold, rejecting, rigid—caused this disorder." This is a reasonable statement about the cause of many cases of:
a.   autism.
b.   Asperger's disorder.
c.   both autism and Asperger's disorder.
d.   neither autism nor Asperger's disorder.

Pervasive Developmental Disorders, p. 519
Diff: M, Type: Factual, Ans: b
80.   According to one psychological view of autism, the inability to take another's perspective is not developed in autistic children. This ability is called:
a.   egocentrism.
b.   a theory of mind.
c.   social awareness.
d.   metacognitive knowledge.

Pervasive Developmental Disorders, p. 519
Diff: M, Type: Factual, Ans: a

81.   Most recent research has provided evidence that the primary causes of autism include:
    a.   brain abnormalities.
    b.   personality characteristics of the parents.
    c.   social status.
    d.   environmental stress.

Pervasive Developmental Disorders, p. 519
Diff: H, Type: Factual, Ans: d

82.   Research has shown that, during infancy and early childhood, autistic children are more likely to:
    a.   have parents who divorce than are "normal" children.
    b.   be raised in a family with financial difficulties than are "normal" children.
    c.   have old, rejecting parents.
    d.   None of the answers are true.

Pervasive Developmental Disorders, p. 519
Diff: E, Type: Factual, Ans: c

83.   Recent studies show that autistic children are more likely than other children to have abnormalities in which section of the brain?
    a.   cerebral cortex
    b.   corpus callosum
    c.   cerebellum
    d.   hypothalamus

Pervasive Developmental Disorders, p. 520
Diff: M, Type: Applied, Ans: c

84.   A therapist works with an autistic child, providing praise and a small spoonful of ice cream whenever the child imitates a specific sound the therapist makes. The therapist is using what type of therapy?
    a.   communication training
    b.   community integration
    c.   behavioral therapy
    d.   play therapy (a form of psychodynamic therapy)

Pervasive Developmental Disorders, p. 520
Diff: M, Type: Applied, Ans: a

85.   Studies of the use of behavioral techniques in the treatment of autism have shown that behavioral techniques can produce:
    a.   long-term gains in school achievement and intelligence test performance.
    b.   only short-term gains in school achievement and intelligence test performance.
    c.   long-term gains in school achievement, but only short-term gains in intelligence test performance.
    d.   only short-term gains in school achievement, but long-term gains in intelligence test performance.

Pervasive Developmental Disorders, p. 520
Diff: E, Type: Factual, Ans: b

86.   Recent work has revealed that the most effective treatment for autism has been the use of:
       a.   drug therapy.
       b.   behavioral therapy.
       c.   educational therapy.
       d.   psychodynamic-humanistic therapy.

Pervasive Developmental Disorders, p. 521
Diff: M, Type: Applied, Ans: c

87.   A child with autism points to a picture of a fork in order to say, "I want food." This child is using:
       a.   a self-communication device.
       b.   a token economy system.
       c.   an augmentative communication system.
       d.   an integrative motor system.

Pervasive Developmental Disorders, p. 521
Diff: H, Type: Applied, Ans: c

88.   A child diagnosed with Asperger's disorder leans to make choices, and learns that rules are
       not necessarily rigid. Facing change and being flexible are other parts of the therapy. Most
       likely, the child is experiencing:
       a.   simultaneous communication therapy.
       b.   child-initiated interaction therapy.
       c.   cognitive social integration therapy.
       d.   mainstreaming.

Pervasive Developmental Disorders, p. 521
Diff: H, Type: Applied, Ans: b

89.   "What is over there?" asks the child, pointing to a distant object; "Does it belong to you?" the
       child asks the therapist. The therapist answers the child in detail, and praises the child's
       efforts at communication. Most likely, the child is receiving:
       a.   child-initiated interactions training for Asperger's disorder.
       b.   child-initiated interactions training for autism.
       c.   cognitive social integration therapy for Asperger's disorder.
       d.   cognitive social integration therapy for autism.

Mental Retardation, p. 522
Diff: E, Type: Applied, Ans: d

90.   Fred has an IQ of 65 and cannot do school work. He lives on the streets by begging, is
       usually dirty, and is always hungry. He would probably be labeled:
       a.   normal.
       b.   dyslexic.
       c.   schizophrenic.
       d.   mentally retarded.

Mental Retardation, p. 522
Diff: M, Type: Applied, Ans: c

91.   Quentin is 25, has an IQ of 60, and never did well at schoolwork. However, now he lives on
       his own, has a job, and is able to perform the routine chores of life. He would not be
       considered mentally retarded because:
       a.   he is too old.
       b.   his IQ is not low enough.
       c.   he has adequate adaptive functioning.
       d.   his condition was not diagnosed before the age of 18.

Mental Retardation, p. 522
Diff: H, Type: Applied, Ans: c

92.   Intelligence test results should not be the only things used to determine mental retardation,
       because intelligence test scores:
       a.   are not positively correlated with school performance.
       b.   lack reliability.
       c.   don't indicate level of adaptive behavior.
       d.   lack validity.

Mental Retardation, p. 523
Diff: E, Type: Applied, Ans: d

93.   If you knew that a child had recently been administered the Vineland and AAMR, you could
       be reasonably sure the childhood disorder being tested for was:
       a.   savant syndrome.
       b.   separation anxiety disorder.
       c.   enuresis.
       d.   mental retardation.

Reading and 'Riting and 'Rithmetic, p. 524 (Box 17-6)
Diff: E, Type: Factual, Ans: a

94.   A reading proficiency level that is much lower than would be expected based on the measure
       of general intelligence is called:
       a.   dyslexia.
       b.   perceptual deficit disorder.
       c.   expressive language disorder.
       d.   mixed receptive/expressive language disorder.

Reading and 'Riting and 'Rithmetic, p. 524 (Box 17-6)
Diff: M, Type: Applied, Ans: b

95.   Seth does well in some school subjects. However, the only way that he can read is slowly,
       one word at a time. He must direct his gaze with his index finger. Even with great effort, he
       makes many errors and has poor comprehension. This is a description of:
       a.   aphasia.
       b.   dyslexia.
       c.   echolalia.
       d.   word blindness.

Reading and 'Riting and 'Rithmetic, p. 524 (Box 17-6)
Diff: M, Type: Factual, Ans: c

96.   The specific symptoms associated with dyslexia include:
       a.   strikingly impaired mathematical skills.
       b.   having difficulty comprehending and expressing language.
       c.   an impairment of the ability to recognize words and to comprehend what is being read.
       d.   extreme and repeated errors in spelling, grammar, punctuation, and paragraph
            organization.

Reading and 'Riting and 'Rithmetic, p. 524 (Box 17-6)
Diff: H, Type: Applied, Ans: d

97.   Selina displays normal behavior and intelligence, but she does not seem to be able to explain
       her actions and intentions as well as you would expect. If the deficit is severe enough, she
       might be diagnosed with:
       a.   dyslexia.
       b.   a perceptual deficit.
       c.   attention-deficit/disorder.
       d.   an expressive-language disorder.

Reading and 'Riting and 'Rithmetic, p. 524 (Box 17-6)
Diff: E, Type: Factual, Ans: c

98.   Ian has received the diagnosis of developmental coordination disorder. You would expect
       that he would have a problem:
       a.   expressing himself in speech.
       b.   reading a sentence from a book out loud.
       c.   buttoning his shirt and dressing in general.
       d.   listening to a teacher explain how to do a mathematics problem.

Mental Retardation, p. 525
Diff: M, Type: Factual, Ans: a

99.   Mild mental retardation is most common in which socioeconomic class?
       a.   lower
       b.   middle
       c.   upper
       d.   Mild mental retardation is about equally common across socioeconomic classes.

Mental Retardation, p. 525
Diff: M, Type: Factual, Ans: d

100.   About what percentage of those diagnosed with mental retardation fall in the DSM-IV-TR
       "mild retardation" category?
       a.   less than 10%
       b.   25%
       c.   55%
       d.   85%

Mental Retardation, p. 525
Diff: M, Type: Factual, Ans: d
101.   Early home intervention programs for those in the "mild" retardation category:
    a.   provide little help for children because of parental resistance.
    b.   improve overall functioning, but not later school performance.
    c.   do not improve overall functioning, but do improve later school performance.
    d.   improve both overall functioning, and later school performance.

Mental Retardation, p. 525
Diff: E, Type: Factual, Ans: b
102.   Most cases of mild retardation seem to be related to:
    a.   inherited traits.
    b.   sociocultural and psychological factors.
    c.   fetal alcohol syndrome.
    d.   organic brain syndrome.

Mental Retardation, p. 525
Diff: M, Type: Applied, Ans: b
103.   Isabelle was born into a very poor family. Her mother and father were barely able to sustain themselves. They had below-average IQs. Isabelle's nutrition and health care were never very good. She is at risk for:
    a.   autistic disorder.
    b.   mild mental retardation.
    c.   attention-deficit/disorder.
    d.   severe mental retardation.

Mental Retardation, p. 525
Diff: E, Type: Factual, Ans: b
104.   The most consistent and important difference between retarded and nonretarded people is that a retarded person:
    a.   is more sensitive.
    b.   learns more slowly.
    c.   has a tendency toward belligerence.
    d.   suffers from an organic brain syndrome.

Mental Retardation, p. 525
Diff: M, Type: Applied, Ans: c
105.   Biological factors appear *not* to be the most important causes of which level of mental retardation?
    a.   profound
    b.   moderate
    c.   mild
    d.   Biological factors are the most important causes of all of the above.

Mental Retardation, pp. 525-526
Diff: M, Type: Applied, Ans: b
106.   The percentage of individuals at the four levels of mental retardation from mild to profound:
    a.   increases steadily as the intelligence level decreases.
    b.   decreases steadily as the intelligence level decreases.
    c.   stays about the same as the intelligence level decreases.
    d.   is highest for the "moderate mental retardation" level.

Mental Retardation, p. 526
Diff: H, Type: Applied, Ans: d

107. If one knew nothing more than that the person with mental retardation also had extensive and severe medical problems and physical handicaps, the best estimate of that person's level of mental retardation would be:
    a. mild.
    b. mild or moderate.
    c. moderate or severe.
    d. severe or profound.

Mental Retardation, p. 527
Diff: E, Type: Factual, Ans: a

108. Most diagnosed cases of Down syndrome are of the _____ type.
    a. trisomy 21
    b. mosaicism
    c. age-related
    d. translocation

Mental Retardation, p. 527
Diff: M, Type: Applied, Ans: b

109. Paula is moderately retarded, and has a small head and flat face. She also has short fingers. Her condition seems to be:
    a. PKU.
    b. Down syndrome.
    c. Tay-Sachs disease.
    d. fragile X syndrome.

Mental Retardation, p. 527
Diff: M, Type: Factual, Ans: a

110. The most common of the identified chromosomal causes of Down syndrome is:
    a. trisomy 21.
    b. mosaicism.
    c. translocation.
    d. PKU.

Mental Retardation, p. 527
Diff: H, Type: Applied, Ans: a

111. An infant is diagnosed with a biological disorder. As the infant ages, its physical and mental conditions deteriorate steadily so that the infant loses vision and motor control, and at the age of 3, the child dies. Most likely, the child was suffering from:
    a. Tay-Sachs disease.
    b. Down syndrome.
    c. fragile X syndrome.
    d. phenylketonuria (PKU).

Mental Retardation, p. 527
Diff: M, Type: Factual, Ans: a
112.   If a pregnant woman wishes to avoid having a child with fetal alcohol syndrome (FAS), what
        should she do?
        a.   avoid drinking alcohol, since no safe level of drinking while pregnant has been
              established
        b.   avoid only binge drinking, since only binge drinking is associated with FAS
        c.   drink no more than the equivalent of one ounce of alcohol per day
        d.   drink no more than the equivalent of two ounces of alcohol per day

Mental Retardation, p. 527
Diff: E, Type: Applied, Ans: d
113.   Hanna could not metabolize phenylalanine properly when she was born. She is displaying:
        a.   cretinism.
        b.   hydrocephalus.
        c.   Tay-Sachs disease.
        d.   phenylketonuria (PKU).

Mental Retardation, p. 527
Diff: M, Type: Factual, Ans: b
114.   Which of the following do phenylketonuria and Tay-Sachs disease have in common?
        a.   Both can be detected at birth and treated.
        b.   Both are caused by a double recessive gene.
        c.   Both are metabolic defects involving an amino acid.
        d.   People of Eastern European Jewish ancestry are at increased risk for both.

Mental Retardation, p. 527
Diff: E, Type: Factual, Ans: a
115.   An iodine deficiency in the diet of a pregnant woman may lead to a condition in which the
        baby has a dwarflike appearance and a defective thyroid gland. This disorder is called:
        a.   cretinism.
        b.   encephalitis.
        c.   Down syndrome.
        d.   Tay-Sachs disease.

Mental Retardation, p. 528
Diff: E, Type: Applied, Ans: a
116.   At the end of the year the criteria for remaining in the state school changed, and Henry was
        simply released into the community. This is an example of:
        a.   deinstitutionalization.
        b.   a normalization program.
        c.   an example of mainstreaming.
        d.   an example of special education.

Mental Retardation, p. 528
Diff: E, Type: Factual, Ans: b
117.   Anoxia, one possible source of mental retardation, involves brain damage resulting from:
        a.   ingestion of lead-based paint.
        b.   lack of oxygen during or after delivery.
        c.   poisoning from pesticides or fertilizer nitrates.
        d.   seizures induced by inhalants or automobile exhaust fumes.

Mental Retardation, p. 528
Diff: E, Type: Factual, Ans: d

118.   In poor inner-city neighborhoods, children sometimes eat paint that is flaking off walls. This
        can lead to mental retardation because of:
        a. meningitis.
        b. encephalitis.
        c. microcephaly.
        d. lead poisoning.

Mental Retardation, p. 529
Diff: M, Type: Factual, Ans: a

119.   Most children with mental retardation live:
        a. at home.
        b. in "normalization" residences.
        c. in relatively small, county-run institutions.
        d. in relatively large, state-run institutions.

Mental Retardation, p. 529
Diff: M, Type: Factual, Ans: d

120.   Nations that pioneered "normalization" in the treatment of mental retardation include:
        a. the United States and Canada.
        b. the former Soviet Union and China.
        c. Japan and Great Britain.
        d. Denmark and Sweden.

Mental Retardation, p. 529
Diff: M, Type: Applied, Ans: b

121.   Glenda is in a facility for the mentally retarded. She gets up in her apartment, dresses, and
        goes to the dining room, where she orders breakfast off a menu. She goes to work in a
        sheltered workshop. At the end of the day she goes home to her apartment and cleans up for
        dinner. This arrangement is part of:
        a. deinstitutionalization.
        b. a normalization program.
        c. mainstreaming.
        d. special education.

Mental Retardation, p. 529
Diff: E, Type: Applied, Ans: b

122.   Fredrick is in public school, but he is grouped with other low-IQ children like him. He and
        his classmates have a specially designed program that is different from that of the other
        children in the school. This is most likely an example of:
        a. mainstreaming.
        b. special education.
        c. deinstitutionalization.
        d. a normalization program.

Mental Retardation, p. 529
Diff: E, Type: Applied, Ans: b

123.   The technique that is often used to teach individuals with mental retardation is:
    a.   cognitive.
    b.   behavioral.
    c.   humanistic.
    d.   mainstreaming.

Mental Retardation, p. 529
Diff: E, Type: Applied, Ans: b

124.   Self-help and communication skills of the mentally retarded are improved most often by the use of:
    a.   psychodynamic therapy.
    b.   behavioral techniques.
    c.   mainstreaming.
    d.   drug and hormonal interventions.

Mental Retardation, p. 530
Diff: M, Type: Factual, Ans: c

125.   Which of the following is true about people with mental retardation?
    a.   Only about 10% of those with mental retardation marry.
    b.   After training, many people with severe mental retardation can hold jobs in the community.
    c.   Socializing, sex, and marriage are difficult issues for mentally retarded people.
    d.   All of the answers are true.

FILL-IN QUESTIONS

Oppositional Defiant Disorder and Conduct Disorder, p. 502
Diff: H, Type: Factual, Ans: overt-destructive

1.   The pattern of conduct disorder involving overt aggression and "in-your-face" confrontation is called _____ pattern.

Oppositional Defiant Disorder and Conduct Disorder, pp. 503-504
Diff: E, Type: Factual, Ans: juvenile delinquent (or recidivist)

2.   Fifteen-year-old Glen has run afoul of the law several times. He has even spent time in a juvenile detention center. The system is likely to label him a _____.

Child Abuse, p. 505 (Box 17-3)
Diff: E, Type: Factual, Ans: psychological

3.   Child abuse that includes severe rejection, coercive and/or punitive discipline, ridicule, and unrealistic expectations is _____ abuse.

Child Abuse, p. 505
Diff: E, Type: Applied, Ans: child abuse (or psychological abuse)

4.   Ned's parents are always criticizing him. They rarely pay any attention to him at other times. This is an example of _____ abuse.

Child Abuse, p. 505
Diff: E, Type: Factual, Ans: child sexual

5.   When a child is used as an object of gratification for adult sexual desires, it is known as
      _____ abuse.

Attention-Deficit/Hyperactivity Disorder, p. 507
Diff: E, Type: Factual, Ans: attention-deficit/hyperactivity disorder

6.   The disorder in which children attend very poorly to tasks, behave impulsively, and are
      excessively overactive is known as _____.

Attention-Deficit/Hyperactivity Disorder, pp. 507-508
Diff: E, Type: Applied, Ans: attention-deficit/hyperactivity disorder

7.   Martin is a nice little boy, but he cannot sit still in his first-grade class. He does not seem to
      be able to follow what the teacher is doing, and his academic performance is not very good.
      Most of his time is spent in motion. He is displaying _____.

Enuresis, p. 512
Diff: E, Type: Factual, Ans: enuresis

8.   The technical term for bed wetting in children after the age of 5 is _____.

Enuresis, p. 512
Diff: E, Type: Factual, Ans: enuresis

9.   Your 8-year-old child wets the bed, accidentally, 20 times a month. He suffers from the
      elimination disorder called _____.

Encopresis, p. 514
Diff: M, Type: Factual, Ans: encopresis

10.   Bed wetting is more common than involuntary defecation, otherwise known as _____.

Pervasive Developmental Disorders, pp. 515-516
Diff: E, Type: Factual, Ans: unresponsive (or aloof)

11.   One characteristic of autism is that the child is socially _____.

Pervasive Developmental Disorders, p. 516
Diff: E, Type: Factual, Ans: echolalia

12.   Children with a diagnosis of autism often parrot sentences or phrases spoken by others,
      copying the accent or inflection but not understanding the meaning. This phenomenon is
      called _____.

Pervasive Developmental Disorders, p. 516
Diff: E, Type: Applied, Ans: echolalia

13.   Terry is autistic. When his teacher asks, "Do you want candy?" Terry responds, "Do you
      want candy?" This particular communication problem is referred to as _____.

Pervasive Developmental Disorders, p. 518
Diff: M, Type: Factual, Ans: Asperger's disorder

14.   A child who has many of the interpersonal deficits of autism, but who has adequate command
      of language and reasoning skills, is more likely to be diagnosed with _____.

Mental Retardation, p. 522
Diff: E, Type: Factual, Ans: mental retardation

15.   A person with a diagnosis of _____ displays significantly subaverage general intellectual functioning, concurrent deficits or impairment in adaptive behavior, and develops these symptoms before the age of 18.

Mental Retardation, p. 523
Diff: M, Type: Factual, Ans: adaptive functioning (or adaptive behavior)

16.   The Vineland and the AAMD scales were developed to assess _____ as part of the diagnosis of mental retardation.

Reading and 'Riting and 'Rithmetic, p. 524 (Box 17-6)
Diff: M, Type: Applied, Ans: disorder of written expression

17.   A sixth-grade student makes extreme and repeated errors in spelling, grammar, punctuation, and paragraph organization. You have a strong suspicion that the student suffers from _____.

Reading and 'Riting and 'Rithmetic, p. 524 (Box 17-6)
Diff: M, Type: Factual, Ans: dyslexia

18.   The learning problem that affects reading alone is _____.

Reading and 'Riting and 'Rithmetic, p. 524 (Box 17-6)
Diff: M, Type: Factual, Ans: phonological disorder

19.   The failure to make correct speech sounds receives the diagnosis of _____.

Reading and 'Riting and 'Rithmetic, p. 524 (Box 17-6)
Diff: E, Type: Factual, Ans: stuttering or stutter

20.   The disruption of the normal fluency in speech is a condition known as _____.

Reading and 'Riting and 'Rithmetic, p. 524 (Box 17-6)
Diff: E, Type: Factual, Ans: dyslexia

21.   A common specific development disorder involves the impairment in a child's ability to recognize words and to comprehend written language. DSM-IV-TR labels this a developmental reading disorder, but the more common name is _____.

Mental Retardation, p. 527
Diff: E, Type: Factual, Ans: amniocentesis

22.   The test for chromosomal abnormalities in which fluid is drawn from around the fetus is called _____.

Mental Retardation, p. 527
Diff: M, Type: Factual, Ans: PKU (or phenylketonuria)

23.   Children with _____ cannot metabolize phenylalanine properly.

Mental Retardation, p. 527
Diff: M, Type: Factual, Ans: Tay-Sachs disease

24.   The congenital disorder that is especially common among those of Eastern European Jewish ancestry is called _____.

Mental Retardation, p. 527
Diff: E, Type: Factual, Ans: fetal alcohol syndrome
25.   When mothers drink excessive amounts of wine, beer, or hard spirits during pregnancy, their children may be born with serious problems that include mental retardation, low birth weight, slow development, and irregularities in the face or limbs. This condition is called _____.

Mental Retardation, p. 527
Diff: M, Type: Factual, Ans: cretinism
26.   Too little prenatal iodine results in _____ in the newborn.

Mental Retardation, p. 528
Diff: M, Type: Factual, Ans: anoxia
27.   Too little oxygen during birth is called _____.

Mental Retardation, p. 529
Diff: E, Type: Factual, Ans: normalization
28.   The Scandinavian program of the 1960s and 1970s in which mentally retarded people were offered living and working conditions similar to those found in mainstream society, including flexible routines, personal independence, and economic freedom, is called _____.

Mental Retardation, p. 529
Diff: E, Type: Factual, Ans: special education
29.   In _____, children with mental retardation are grouped together in a separate, specially designed educational program.

Mental Retardation, p. 529
Diff: M, Type: Factual, Ans: Mainstreaming
30.   _____ places children with mental retardation in regular classes with nonretarded students.

Mental Retardation, p. 529
Diff: H, Type: Applied, Ans: token economy programs
31.   Operant conditioning programs designed to provide reinforcement for a wide variety of adaptive behaviors and often used to treat institutionalized people with mental retardation and schizophrenia are called _____.

Mental Retardation, p. 530
Diff: M, Type: Applied, Ans: Dating skills programs
32.   _____ are designed to provide people with mental retardation opportunities to socialize with others and normalize their romantic relationships.

Mental Retardation, p. 530
Diff: M, Type: Factual, Ans: Sheltered workshops
33.   _____ provide protected and supervised workplaces for people with mental retardation.

ESSAY QUESTIONS

Childhood and Adolescence, pp. 498-499
Diff: M, Type: Applied
1. Please provide some compelling evidence that children aren't simply "small adults," and that some separate diagnostic categories are necessary for children.

Oppositional Defiant Disorder and Conduct Disorder, p. 499 ff
Diff: M, Type: Factual
2. What are important criteria for differentiating oppositional defiant disorder and conduct disorder? What are some major ways of dealing with these disorders, or keeping them from occurring in the first place?

Attention-Deficit/Hyperactivity Disorder, p. 507 ff
Diff: H, Type: Factual
3. Attention-deficit/hyperactivity disorder (ADHD) has received quite a bit of attention in recent years. Why? What are the symptoms of ADHD that make it so troublesome, and what forms of therapy seem to work best with it? Be sure to address the Ritalin controversy in your answer.

Elimination Disorders, pp. 512-514 ff
Diff: H, Type: Applied
4. Why should we be concerned with childhood disorders such as enuresis and encopresis? After all, they nearly always "go away" by the time the children reach adulthood, don't they? Please provide data-backed reasons why these disorders need to be treated in childhood.

Pervasive Developmental Disorders, p. 515 ff
Diff: M, Type: Factual
5. What are the distinguishing characteristics of autistic disorder (autism)? Why is the disorder so difficult to treat, and what forms of therapy seem to work the best?

Pervasive Developmental Disorders, p. 515 ff
Diff: M, Type: Factual
6. How are autism and Asperger's disorder similar? How are they different? How would the best treatments for each differ, if at all?

Pervasive Developmental Disorders, pp. 520-521
Diff: H, Type: Applied
7. An acquaintance of yours says, "Why bother trying to treat autism? When you consider the time and the cost involved, is it really worth it?" How would you defend recent expensive, time-consuming efforts to treat autism? Please provide specific examples to support your answer.

Mental Retardation, p. 525 ff
Diff: H, Type: Applied
8. The fact that rates of mild mental retardation vary considerably across socioeconomic groups (highest rates in lowest socioeconomic groups), while rates of other levels of mental retardation do not, strongly implies that factors other than biological ones are at work in the development of mild mental retardation. What might those nonbiological factors be? What should psychologists suggest as appropriate interventions to lessen the incidence of mild mental retardation in lower socioeconomic groups?

Mental Retardation, pp. 525-526
Diff: M, Type: Applied

9.   Describe a typical person with each of the four levels of mental retardation.

Mental Retardation, p. 526 ff
Diff: M, Type: Applied

10.   Assume that a married couple in their 20s wishes to minimize the risk of mental retardation in their children. What are some things they should and should not do?

Mental Retardation, p. 528 ff
Diff: M, Type: Applied

11.   What are the arguments for and against the institutionalization of those with moderate, severe, and profound levels of mental retardation? Be sure to include treatment possibilities in your answer.

Mental Retardation, pp. 530-531
Diff: M, Type: Factual

12.   How can opportunities for personal, social, and occupational growth be increased for the mentally retarded? Be sure to discuss work and love issues.

CHAPTER 18   Disorders of Aging and Cognition

MULTIPLE-CHOICE QUESTIONS

Disorders of Aging and Cognition, p. 536
Diff: E, Type: Factual, Ans: c

1. The most feared psychological problem among the elderly is:
   a. stress.
   b. loss of sexual function.
   c. Alzheimer's.
   d. alcoholism.

Old Age and Stress, p. 536
Diff: E, Type: Factual, Ans: d

2. The percentage of the U.S. population aged 65 and older today is:
   a. about 4%.
   b. about 7%.
   c. about 10%.
   d. about 13%.

Old Age and Stress, p. 536
Diff: E, Type: Applied, Ans: a

3. An individual seeking help from a geropsychologist is most likely:
   a. elderly.
   b. mentally retarded.
   c. suffering from enuresis or encopresis.
   d. receiving play therapy.

Depression in Later Life, pp. 537-538
Diff: M, Type: Applied, Ans: d

4. Which of the following would be at greatest risk for depression?
   a. an older man living alone
   b. an older woman living alone
   c. an older man in a nursing home
   d. an older woman in a nursing home

Depression in Later Life, p. 538
Diff: M, Type: Applied, Ans: d

5.   Particular risk factors associated with depression in the elderly includes all of the following except:

     a.   increased suicide risk.
     b.   increased death rates due to illness.
     c.   increased health problems.
     d.   increased financial problems.

Sleep and Sleep Disorders among the Old and Not So Old, p. 538 (Box 18-1)
Diff: M, Type: Factual, Ans: b

6.   Why is REM sleep referred to as paradoxical sleep?

     a.   The person is asleep but can hear what is happening.
     b.   It resembles both deep sleep and wakefulness.
     c.   It only happens when a person is severely sleep deprived.
     d.   It only happens in children.

Sleep and Sleep Disorders among the Old and Not So Old, p. 538 (Box 18-1)
Diff: E, Type: Factual, Ans: a

7.   Dyssomnias are:

     a.   sleep disorders.
     b.   sexual dysfunctions.
     c.   substance abuse disorders.
     d.   psychotic disorders.

Sleep and Sleep Disorders among the Old and Not So Old, p. 538 (Box 18-1)
Diff: H, Type: Factual, Ans: c

8.   Which of the following is a parasomnia?

     a.   narcolepsy
     b.   insomnia
     c.   sleepwalking
     d.   breathing-related sleep disorder

Sleep and Sleep Disorders among the Old and Not So Old, p. 538 (Box 18-1)
Diff: M, Type: Applied, Ans: d

9.   If a person was experiencing insomnia and breathing-related sleep disorder, your best guess would be that this person was a(n):

     a.   child.
     b.   teenager.
     c.   young adult.
     d.   elderly person.

Sleep and Sleep Disorders among the Old and Not So Old, p. 539 (Box 18-1)
Diff: M, Type: Factual, Ans: a

10.   Children are more likely than the elderly to experience:

     a.   sleep terrors.
     b.   insomnia.
     c.   breathing-related sleep disorder.
     d.   circadian rhythm disorder.

Depression in Later Life, p. 539
Diff: H, Type: Factual, Ans: c

11. Which of the following is true about the rate of suicide among the elderly?
    a. Older people are less likely than young people to commit suicide.
    b. The rate of suicide declines from the elderly to the very elderly.
    c. The highest suicide rate is for men over the age of 85.
    d. The overall suicide rate among the elderly is about the same as that for younger people.

Depression in Later Life, p. 539
Diff: M, Type: Factual, Ans: a

12. Regarding treatment of depression in the elderly, studies show that:
    a. drug treatments may need to be altered because drugs are broken down differently in the body.
    b. individual and group therapies are rarely used.
    c. electroconvulsive shock therapy is the treatment of choice.
    d. no therapy is effective more than about half the time.

Anxiety Disorders in Later Life, p. 540
Diff: M, Type: Factual, Ans: a

13. What is the relationship between age and anxiety in the elderly?
    a. As age increases, the rate of anxiety disorders increases.
    b. As age increases, the rate of anxiety disorders decreases.
    c. As age increases, the rate of anxiety disorders increases, then decreases.
    d. There is no relationship between age and anxiety disorders.

Anxiety Disorders in Later Life, p. 540
Diff: M, Type: Applied, Ans: c

14. To date, research shows that anxiety among the elderly is related to:
    a. specific experiences.
    b. losses.
    c. health.
    d. drinking.

Anxiety Disorders in Later Life, p. 540
Diff: M, Type: Applied, Ans: b

15. An elderly individual is suffering from agoraphobia. The form of therapy that person is least likely to receive is:
    a. drug.
    b. psychodynamic.
    c. cognitive.
    d. Drug, psychodynamic, and cognitive therapies are used about equally often.

Anxiety Disorders in Later Life, p. 540
Diff: M, Type: Factual, Ans: b

16. The class of drugs most often used to treat anxiety disorders in the elderly is:
    a. tricyclics.
    b. benzodiazepines.
    c. tetrahydroaminoacridines.
    d. serotonin reuptake inhibitors.

Substance Abuse in Later Life, p. 540
Diff: M, Type: Factual, Ans: b

17. As people age, the incidence of alcohol abuse and other forms of substance abuse:
     a. increases.
     b. decreases.
     c. remains the same.
     d. frequently appears for the first time.

The Oldest Old, p. 541 (Box 18-2)
Diff: M, Type: Factual, Ans: d

18. Studies of the "oldest old" show that compared to those in their 80s and early 90s, the oldest old are:
     a. less agile.
     b. less healthy.
     c. less clear-headed.
     d. more agile, healthier, and clear-headed.

Substance Abuse in Later Life, p. 541
Diff: M, Type: Factual, Ans: d

19. Elderly men are more likely than younger men to _____ related to drinking.
     a. engage in secretivity
     b. socially withdraw
     c. black out
     d. be hospitalized

Substance Abuse in Later Life, p. 541
Diff: M, Type: Factual, Ans: a

20. Those who begin unhealthy drinking patterns later in life typically begin as a response to:
     a. negative events and pressures of growing older.
     b. medication side effects.
     c. a desire to fit in with the peer group.
     d. pressure from their teenage grandchildren.

Substance Abuse in Later Life, p. 541
Diff: E, Type: Applied, Ans: c

21. A particular problem often found more prominently in the elderly that is related to substance abuse is:
     a. alcoholism.
     b. drinking in reaction to negative life events.
     c. misuse of prescription drugs.
     d. use of detoxification.

Psychotic Disorders in Later Life, p. 542
Diff: M, Type: Factual, Ans: b

22. Among the elderly, psychotic cognitive symptoms are usually due to:
     a. schizophrenia.
     b. delirium and dementia.
     c. delusional disorders.
     d. depression.

Psychotic Disorders in Later Life, p. 542
Diff: H, Type: Applied, Ans: c

23.   The case of John Nash, Nobel prize winner and schizophrenic, illustrates _____, which is
       often found in the elderly who have been schizophrenic.
       a.   an increase in symptoms
       b.   a decrease in the ability to complete cognitive tasks
       c.   improvement in one's social and work skills
       d.   the emergence of schizophrenia for the second time

Psychotic Disorders in Later Life, p. 542
Diff: E, Type: Factual, Ans: a

24.   An elderly person who develops false beliefs that are not bizarre is most likely suffering
       from:
       a.   delusional disorder.
       b.   disorders of cognition.
       c.   memory problems.
       d.   sleep disorder.

Psychotic Disorders in Later Life, p. 542
Diff: M, Type: Applied, Ans: a

25.   An elderly person who believes falsely that others are conspiring against her, cheating, or
       spying on her and behaves in angry, irritable, and depressed ways is exhibiting:
       a.   a delusional disorder.
       b.   a cognitive disorder.
       c.   delirium.
       d.   acute anxiety.

Disorders of Cognition, p. 542
Diff: E, Type: Applied, Ans: b

26.   A 65-year-old in otherwise very good health typically will experience occasional:
       a.   dementia.
       b.   memory difficulties.
       c.   delusions.
       d.   hallucinations.

Disorders of Cognition, p. 543
Diff: E, Type: Factual, Ans: b

27.   A clouding of consciousness that develops over a short period of time and can often be
       reversed if its underlying cause can be found is called:
       a.   dementia.
       b.   delirium.
       c.   delusional disorder.
       d.   cognitive mapping.

Disorders of Cognition, p. 543
Diff: H, Type: Applied, Ans: b

28.   An 80-year-old individual has been functioning normally, but now has an infection.
      However, over the course of a few days, the person shows increasing confusion, and
      consistently misinterprets what others are trying to communicate. The most probable
      diagnosis for this condition would be:
      a.   dementia.
      b.   delirium.
      c.   schizophrenia.
      d.   substance abuse.

Disorders of Cognition, p. 543
Diff: M, Type: Factual, Ans: c

29.   The criteria for the diagnosis of dementia include:
      a.   lack of personality disturbances.
      b.   evidence that there is no organic involvement.
      c.   impairment in both memory and other areas of cognition.
      d.   personality disturbances without impairment in short- and long-term memory.

Disorders of Cognition, p. 543
Diff: M, Type: Applied, Ans: b

30.   Rosa has difficulty remembering even where she is going. Maintaining friendships is
      difficult, and she loses her temper because she cannot remember things. Her health has been
      deteriorating and she is clumsier than she was three years ago. She appears to be suffering
      from:
      a.   delirium.
      b.   dementia.
      c.   normal aging.
      d.   Korsakoff's syndrome.

Disorders of Cognition, p. 543
Diff: E, Type: Factual, Ans: b

31.   Alzheimer's is a brain _____ while stroke is a brain _____.
      a.   injury; disease
      b.   disease; injury
      c.   infection; disease
      d.   poisoning; infection

Disorders of Cognition, p. 543
Diff: M, Type: Factual, Ans: b

32.   Alzheimer's is named for the first person to _____ the disease.
      a.   suffer from
      b.   identify
      c.   fund research in
      d.   write a novel about

Disorders of Cognition, p. 543
Diff: M, Type: Factual, Ans: a
33.   A 65-year-old is about what percent likely to be suffering some form of dementia?
      a.   less than 5%
      b.   5%
      c.   10%
      d.   over 15%

Disorders of Cognition, p. 544
Diff: E, Type: Factual, Ans: c
34.   The most frequent cause of irreversible dementia in the elderly is:
      a.   vascular.
      b.   Parkinson's disease.
      c.   Alzheimer's disease.
      d.   congestive heart failure.

Disorders of Cognition, p. 544
Diff: M, Type: Applied, Ans: d
35.   Which of the following statements is most accurate regarding Alzheimer's disease?
      a.   It is progressive and usually starts before age 45.
      b.   It is familial and starts before age 45.
      c.   It is familial and starts after age 80.
      d.   It is progressive and most often starts after age 65.

Disorders of Cognition, p. 544
Diff: H, Type: Applied, Ans: a
36.   The typical pattern of Alzheimer's for the patient is:
      a.   denial, anxiety, withdrawal, dependency.
      b.   denial, anger, bargaining, acceptance, hope.
      c.   denial, projection, regression.
      d.   denial, acceptance, reemergence, reinforcement.

Disorders of Cognition, p. 544
Diff: M, Type: Factual, Ans: a
37.   Early symptoms of Alzheimer's disease include:
      a.   denial of symptoms.
      b.   anger about symptoms.
      c.   indifference to symptoms.
      d.   anxiety or depression about symptoms.

Disorders of Cognition, p. 544
Diff: E, Type: Applied, Ans: c
38.   Your elderly grandfather is deteriorating. At first he seemed only mildly forgetful, but lately he has had trouble recalling the names of close relatives and cannot remember where he is. He used to be very loving and patient, but now he is irascible and very unpleasant at odd moments. This condition is getting worse. He is probably experiencing:
      a.   presenile delirium.
      b.   mental retardation.
      c.   Alzheimer's disease.
      d.   stroke-induced dementia.

Disorders of Cognition, p. 545
Diff: H, Type: Applied, Ans: c

39.   With Alzheimer's, physical health usually:
       a.   declines at the same rate as mental health.
       b.   declines more rapidly than mental health.
       c.   declines less rapidly than mental health.
       d.   remains good until the person dies.

Disorders of Cognition, p. 545
Diff: E, Type: Factual, Ans: b

40.   Alzheimer's disease is diagnosed on the basis of:
       a.   neurofibrillary tangles and senile plaques evident in a CAT scan.
       b.   neurofibrillary tangles and senile plaques evident at autopsy.
       c.   neurofibrillary tangles and senile plaques evident through psychological testing.
       d.   neurofibrillary tangles and senile plaques evident after ingesting medication.

Disorders of Cognition, p. 545
Diff: H, Type: Factual, Ans: b

41.   What are neurofibrillary tangles?
       a.   tangled neurons in the brain
       b.   twisted protein fibers in the brain
       c.   plaque deposits in the brain
       d.   spinal cord deterioration

Disorders of Cognition, p. 545
Diff: M, Type: Factual, Ans: c

42.   Older individuals with Alzheimer's disease differ from older individuals without Alzheimer's
       disease in that they:
       a.   have neurofibrillary tangles in hippocampal and other brain cells.
       b.   form senile plaques between cells in some areas of the brain.
       c.   have an extraordinary number of neurofibrillary tangles.
       d.   have no senile plaques.

Disorders of Cognition, p. 545
Diff: E, Type: Factual, Ans: a

43.   Sphere-shaped deposits of a certain molecule in spaces between neurons in the hippocampus
       in individuals with Alzheimer's disease are called:
       a.   senile plaques.
       b.   neural plaques.
       c.   beta-amyloid proteins.
       d.   neurofibrillary tangles.

Disorders of Cognition, p. 545
Diff: E, Type: Factual, Ans: c

44.   The molecules that are found in sphere-shaped deposits in spaces between neurons in the
       hippocampus in individuals with Alzheimer's disease are called:
       a.   senile plaques.
       b.   neural plaques.
       c.   beta-amyloid protein.
       d.   neurofibrillary tangles.

Disorders of Cognition, p. 546
Diff: M, Type: Applied, Ans: c

45. A person who has Alzheimer's although there is no family history of the disease is said to be experiencing:
     a. nongenetic Alzheimer's.
     b. familial Alzheimer's.
     c. sporadic Alzheimer's.
     d. atypical Alzheimer's.

Disorders of Cognition, p. 546
Diff: M, Type: Applied, Ans: a

46. The best evidence we have to date suggests that Alzheimer's is transmitted genetically in families that:
     a. transmit mutations of certain protein producing genes.
     b. have many members with the sporadic form of the disease.
     c. have no members with the disease, but transmit genetically recessive traits.
     d. do not have a clear history of the disease.

Disorders of Cognition, p. 546
Diff: M, Type: Factual, Ans: c

47. Research on the cause of Alzheimer's disease has led to the conclusion that:
     a. the hereditary component explains the onset of the disease.
     b. at least five different chromosomes have been found to be related to Alzheimer's disease.
     c. there appears to be a significant hereditary component, but this does not fully explain its onset.
     d. there is little or no evidence of a genetic component to Alzheimer's disease, but there may be a viral cause.

Disorders of Cognition, p. 546
Diff: M, Type: Applied, Ans: a

48. A person who can grasp material immediately as it is presented, but who cannot remember it long-term, has difficulty with:
     a. consolidation.
     b. retrieval.
     c. working memory.
     d. sporadic memory.

Disorders of Cognition, p. 546
Diff: E, Type: Factual, Ans: b

49. A person who has difficulty remembering how to use a key is having trouble with:
     a. declarative memory.
     b. procedural memory.
     c. working memory.
     d. sporadic memory.

Disorders of Cognition, p. 546
Diff: E, Type: Factual, Ans: a

50.   A person who can't remember when Christmas is has trouble with:
      a.   declarative memory.
      b.   procedural memory.
      c.   working memory.
      d.   sporadic memory.

Disorders of Cognition, p. 546
Diff: H, Type: Applied, Ans: a

51.   If a person had Alzheimer's disease, one would be most likely to find:
      a.   an excess of 42 amino acids.
      b.   an excess of all amino acids.
      c.   an excess of beta-amyloid proteins.
      d.   a deficit in the production of amino acids.

Disorders of Cognition, p. 546
Diff: H, Type: Applied, Ans: b

52.   A person who has an excess of plaques due to Alzheimer's would be likely to have:
      a.   excessive cell growth.
      b.   cell breakdown and death.
      c.   a loss of amino acid production.
      d.   mutations of the cells of the eye.

Disorders of Cognition, p. 546
Diff: H, Type: Applied, Ans: c

53.   A person with the sporadic version of Alzheimer's would be likely to have:
      a.   a family history of Alzheimer's.
      b.   genetic transmission of mutated genes.
      c.   defects of chromosomes 1, 14, 19, and 21.
      d.   no relatives with the disorder.

Disorders of Cognition, p. 546
Diff: H, Type: Applied, Ans: d

54.   Which of the following is *not* a possible memory deficit?
      a.   an inability to retrieve stored information
      b.   an inability to consolidate new information
      c.   intact short-term memory but long-term deficits.
      d.   getting information into long-term memory without the use of short-term memory

Disorders of Cognition, p. 546
Diff: H, Type: Applied, Ans: a

55.   A person who is going through the alphabet trying to recall the name of someone quite well-known to the person is engaging in:
      a.   retrieval.
      b.   consolidation.
      c.   working memory.
      d.   procedural recovery.

Disorders of Cognition, p. 547
Diff: H, Type: Applied, Ans: b
56.   Someone with difficulty transforming short-term memory into long-term memory is most
      likely to have problems in the:
      a.   prefrontal lobes.
      b.   diencephalon.
      c.   temporal lobes.
      d.   hippocampus.

Disorders of Cognition, p. 547
Diff: M, Type: Applied, Ans: a
57.   You would suspect a problem in the _____ for someone experiencing difficulty with short-
      term memory.
      a.   prefrontal lobes
      b.   temporal lobes
      c.   diencephlon
      d.   occipital lobes

Disorders of Cognition, p. 547
Diff: M, Type: Applied, Ans: b
58.   You would suspect a problem in the _____ for someone experiencing difficulty with long-
      term memory.
      a.   prefrontal lobes
      b.   temporal lobes
      c.   diencephlon
      d.   occipital lobes

Disorders of Cognition, p. 547
Diff: M, Type: Factual, Ans: d
59.   Depletion of the neurotransmitter acetylcholine has been implicated as a:
      a.   treatment of schizophrenia.
      b.   cause of Huntington's chorea.
      c.   treatment for Parkinson's disease.
      d.   critical factor in Alzheimer's disease.

Disorders of Cognition, p. 547
Diff: M, Type: Applied, Ans: c
60.   You would suspect a problem in the _____ for someone experiencing difficulty with
      transforming information from short-term memory to long-term memory.
      a.   prefrontal lobes
      b.   temporal lobes
      c.   diencephlon
      d.   occipital lobes

Disorders of Cognition, p. 547
Diff: M, Type: Factual, Ans: a
61.   When new information is acquired and stored in memory, _____ are produced.
      a.   proteins
      b.   neurons
      c.   plaques
      d.   fibrillary tangles

Amnestic Disorders: Forgetting to Remember, p. 548 (Box 18-3)
Diff: H, Type: Applied, Ans: b

62. A client suffers from severe problems in remembering recent information, and has increasing difficulty using ordinary language and other cognitive skills. The resulting diagnosis probably will be:
   a. amnestic disorder.
   b. dementia.
   c. Korsakoff's syndrome.
   d. concussion.

Amnestic Disorders: Forgetting to Remember, p. 548 (Box 18-3)
Diff: M, Type: Factual, Ans: c

63. An individual with retrograde amnesia:
   a. has trouble learning new information.
   b. can learn new information but does not recall old semantic information.
   c. can learn new information but does not recall events of the past.
   d. has trouble with both learning new information and recalling old information.

Amnestic Disorders: Forgetting to Remember, p. 548 (Box 18-3)
Diff: M, Type: Factual, Ans: c

64. People with amnestic disorders:
   a. almost always experience retrograde and anterograde amnesia.
   b. almost always experience retrograde amnesia; sometimes experience anterograde amnesia.
   c. sometimes experience retrograde amnesia; almost always experience anterograde amnesia.
   d. sometimes experience retrograde and anterograde amnesia.

Amnestic Disorders: Forgetting to Remember, p. 548 (Box 18-3)
Diff: M, Type: Factual, Ans: c

65. An individual who demonstrates a severe anterograde amnesia may still demonstrate evidence of:
   a. short-term memory.
   b. new memories.
   c. verbal skills.
   d. new acquaintances.

Amnestic Disorders: Forgetting to Remember, pp. 548-549 (Box 18-3)
Diff: H, Type: Factual, Ans: c

66. Tomas has a normal IQ, but demonstrates complete impairment of new learning. He also confabulates when asked to provide information about recent events. Tomas most likely is suffering from:
   a. Pick's disease.
   b. Alzheimer's disease.
   c. Korsakoff's syndrome.
   d. Creutzfeldt-Jakob disease.

Amnestic Disorders: Forgetting to Remember, p. 549 (Box 18-3)
Diff: M, Type: Factual, Ans: b

67.   What would the removal of both temporal lobes most likely cause:
       a.   severe retrograde amnesia.
       b.   severe anterograde amnesia.
       c.   both retrograde and anterograde amnesia.
       d.   minimal memory dysfunction that recovers within a year.

Amnestic Disorders: Forgetting to Remember, p. 549 (Box 18-3)
Diff: H, Type: Applied, Ans: d

68.   A soccer player is kicked in the head and suffers a concussion, although the player does not
       lose consciousness. The soccer player probably will experience:
       a.   memory loss that is permanent.
       b.   memory loss that lasts for three to six months.
       c.   memory loss that lasts less than three months.
       d.   no memory loss.

Amnestic Disorders: Forgetting to Remember, p. 549 (Box 18-3)
Diff: M, Type: Factual, Ans: b

69.   About what fraction of severe head injuries result in some permanent memory and learning
       problems?
       a.   1/4
       b.   1/2
       c.   3/4
       d.   virtually all

Dementia, p. 548
Diff: M, Type: Factual, Ans: d

70.   Elevated levels of _____ in the brains of some Alzheimer's patients has led to the search for
       a heavy metal cause of the disease.
       a.   lead
       b.   iron
       c.   calcium
       d.   zinc

Dementia, p. 548
Diff: M, Type: Factual, Ans: b

71.   Recent research suggests that excessive levels of zinc in the brain:
       a.   protect against Alzheimer's.
       b.   trigger plaque formation.
       c.   produce too much RNA.
       d.   prevent protein production.

Dementia, p. 548
Diff: H, Type: Applied, Ans: b

72.   When an autoimmune response occurs, the body attacks:
       a.   foreign substances found in the tissue.
       b.   its own tissue.
       c.   medications intended to treat some disease.
       d.   rogue cells likely to become malignant.

Dementia, p. 548
Diff: M, Type: Factual, Ans: d

73. Which of the following diseases is caused by a virus?
    a. Pick's disease
    b. Alzheimer's disease
    c. Korsakoff's syndrome
    d. Creutzfeldt-Jakob disease

Dementia, p. 548
Diff: H, Type: Applied, Ans: c

74. Of the following, the most legitimate conclusions that can be drawn about animal studies about the impact of zinc on the production of beta-amyloid protein is that:
    a. eating contaminated animals may cause Alzheimer's.
    b. people with Alzheimer's need more zinc.
    c. zinc may act as a toxin and damage the brain.
    d. the negative effects of zinc are offset by aluminum.

Dementia, p. 548
Diff: H, Type: Applied, Ans: d

75. The fact that Alzheimer's disease resembles Creutzfeldt-Jacob disease suggests that Alzheimer's may be caused by:
    a. eating contaminated beef.
    b. genetic mutations on certain genes.
    c. autoimmune dysfunction.
    d. a virus.

Dementia, p. 549
Diff: E, Type: Applied, Ans: b

76. A 74-year-old man has experienced a very sudden decrement in attention, language production, and memory. CT scans show localized damage to specific areas of the brain. He has a history of cardiovascular disease. His diagnosis would most likely be:
    a. Alzheimer's disease.
    b. multi-infarct dementia.
    c. presenile-type dementia.
    d. Creutzfeldt-Jakob disease.

Dementia, p. 549
Diff: E, Type: Applied, Ans: c

77. Quincy suddenly developed a short-term memory problem and only two months later had problems speaking. Six months after that he lost speech and hearing, and the left side of his face became paralyzed. Each change in functioning was abrupt. He probably is suffering from:
    a. Alzheimer's disease.
    b. Huntington's chorea.
    c. multi-infarct dementia.
    d. Creutzfeldt-Jakob disease.

Dementia, p. 549
Diff: H, Type: Applied, Ans: b
78.   A person quite suddenly begins to show specific cognitive impairment; the person has
       difficulty speaking, yet other cognitive functions appear normal. Most likely, that person is
       experiencing:
       a.   Creutzfeldt-Jakob disease.
       b.   vascular dementia.
       c.   mercury poisoning.
       d.   Huntington's disease.

Dementia, p. 549
Diff: M, Type: Factual, Ans: a
79.   Which of the following diseases involves degeneration of the frontal and temporal lobes?
       a.   Pick's disease
       b.   Alzheimer's disease
       c.   Korsakoff's syndrome
       d.   Creutzfeldt-Jakob disease

Dementia, p. 550
Diff: H, Type: Applied, Ans: b
80.   Lucille experienced severe mood, personality, and movement changes. She most likely has:
       a.   Alzheimer's disease.
       b.   Huntington's disease.
       c.   Korsakoff's syndrome.
       d.   Creutzfeldt-Jakob disease.

Dementia, p. 550
Diff: H, Type: Applied, Ans: a
81.   An individual suffering from a neurological disorder shows no evidence of infection or
       poisoning, but experiences tremors, rigidity, and unsteadiness. The most probable diagnosis
       is:
       a.   Parkinson's disease.
       b.   Alzheimer's disease.
       c.   Huntington's disease.
       d.   Creutzfeldt-Jakob disease.

Dementia, p. 550
Diff: M, Type: Factual, Ans: c
82.   Dementia is also associated with:
       a.   gonorrhea.
       b.   genital herpes.
       c.   AIDS.
       d.   genital warts.

Dementia, p. 550
Diff: H, Type: Applied, Ans: a
83.   Someone who has AIDS is also at risk for developing:
       a.   dementia.
       b.   Creutzfeldt-Jacob disease.
       c.   Alzheimer's.
       d.   Pick's disease.

Dementia, p. 550
Diff: H, Type: Applied, Ans: b
84.   If you had a PET scan at a relatively young age, to predict your likelihood of developing Alzheimer's, you would be most disturbed to find:
    a.   a high level of hippocampus activity.
    b.   reduced hippocampus activity.
    c.   normal levels of zinc.
    d.   very few plaques.

Dementia, p. 550
Diff: H, Type: Applied, Ans: c
85.   If you have an unusually high level of AB42 beta-amyloid protein in your blood, you are more likely:
    a.   to be protected from Alzheimer's.
    b.   to develop Pick's disease.
    c.   to develop Alzheimer's.
    d.   to respond well to treatments for brain disease.

Dementia, p. 550
Diff: M, Type: Applied, Ans: c
86.   Psychotherapy would be least likely to be successful in treating which of the following disorders among the elderly?
    a.   depression
    b.   substance abuse
    c.   dementia
    d.   anxiety disorders

Dementia, p. 550
Diff: E, Type: Factual, Ans: a
87.   Which treatment has been most promising and most commonly used with dementias?
    a.   drug therapy
    b.   group psychotherapy
    c.   individual psychotherapy
    d.   cognitive-behavior therapy

Dementia, p. 550
Diff: E, Type: Factual, Ans: b
88.   The theoretical perspective currently receiving the most focus for the treatment of dementias is the _____ perspective.
    a.   cognitive
    b.   biological
    c.   behavioral
    d.   psychodynamic

Dementia, pp. 550-551
Diff: H, Type: Factual, Ans: c
89.   The drug tacrine acts through:
    a.   inhibiting serotonin reuptake.
    b.   increasing the amount of dopamine.
    c.   blocking the breakdown of acetylcholine.
    d.   decreasing the amount of available acetylcholine.

Mad Human Disease?, p. 551 (Box 18-4)
Diff: H, Type: Applied, Ans: a
90.   Recently, the FDA banned those who had spent more than six months total time in Great
      Britain from the early 1980s to the mid-1990s from donating blood in the United States,
      because of the still-unconfirmed possibility that a form of "mad cow disease" might be in
      their blood from eating tainted meat. If humans could contract mad cow disease, they would
      have symptoms similar to those of:
      a.   Creutzfeldt-Jakob disease.
      b.   Alzheimer's disease.
      c.   meningitis.
      d.   lead poisoning.

Mad Human Disease?, p. 551 (Box 18-4)
Diff: M, Type: Factual, Ans: a
91.   Creutzfeldt-Jakob disease is most similar to:
      a.   dementia.
      b.   depression.
      c.   anxiety.
      d.   insomnia.

Mad Human Disease?, p. 551 (Box 18-4)
Diff: M, Type: Factual, Ans: b
92.   Creutzfeldt-Jakob disease has been related to which of the following?
      a.   insomnia
      b.   mad cow disease
      c.   in vitro fertilization
      d.   aging

Dementia, p. 551
Diff: M, Type: Applied, Ans: c
93.   The most accurate of the following statements is that drug therapy at least can help slow
      down the progression of Alzheimer's disease:
      a.   in all patients treated with the disease.
      b.   only in patients with severe forms of the disease.
      c.   in patients treated early in the course of a milder form of the disease.
      d.   in no one; drug therapy doesn't work for Alzheimer's disease.

Dementia, p. 551
Diff: H, Type: Applied, Ans: d
94.   Especially since 2004, there is greater hope for Alzheimer's patients with severe forms of the
      disease due to:
      a.   the development of a treatment that breaks up plaques.
      b.   surgical intervention to remove damaged areas of the brain.
      c.   therapy that doubles the life expectancy for patients.
      d.   a drug that affects glutamate and improves cognition.

Dementia, p. 552
Diff: H, Type: Applied, Ans: a

95.   If all a woman wanted was to reduce her risk of developing Alzheimer's, she should:
    a.   take estrogen for years after menopause.
    b.   reduce estrogen before and after menopause.
    c.   avoid taking Motrin for menstrual discomfort.
    d.   take male sex hormones after menopause.

Dementia, p. 552
Diff: H, Type: Factual, Ans: b

96.   In order to control occasional pain and inflammation, a person uses an over-the-counter drug containing ibuprofen. Interestingly, recent research shows that person also may be reducing the risk of contracting which disease?
    a.   Creutzfeldt-Jakob disease
    b.   Alzheimer's disease
    c.   Huntington's disease
    d.   Parkinson's disease

Dementia, p. 552
Diff: M, Type: Factual, Ans: c

97.   Cognitive and behavioral treatments for those experiencing Alzheimer's disease:
    a.   retard the progressive course of the disease.
    b.   eliminate cognitive but not physical impairments.
    c.   help improve the quality of life for patients and family.
    d.   eliminate the physical but not the cognitive impairments.

Dementia, p. 552
Diff: E, Type: Factual, Ans: c

98.   One of the most frequent reasons for the institutionalization of Alzheimer's patients is:
    a.   to provide more sophisticated medical treatments.
    b.   to provide increased opportunities for employment.
    c.   because caregivers are overwhelmed.
    d.   for better rehabilitation services.

Dementia, p. 552
Diff: H, Type: Applied, Ans: b

99.   Of the following, which is the most likely to lead to hospitalization for an Alzheimer's patient?
    a.   a familial cause for the disorder
    b.   the caretaker being overwhelmed
    c.   the patient does not want to live at home
    d.   the patient's pet interfering with care.

Dementia, p. 553
Diff: E, Type: Factual, Ans: a

100.   Which of the following is an example of a sociocultural approach to treating Alzheimer's?
    a.   day-care facilities
    b.   behavior modification
    c.   medication
    d.   psychotherapy for caregivers

Issues Affecting the Mental Health of the Elderly, p. 553
Diff: E, Type: Factual, Ans: b

101.   The term "double jeopardy" describes people who may develop psychological problems
       because they are:
       a.   old and female.
       b.   old and members of an ethnic minority.
       c.   young and members of an ethnic minority.
       d.   physically ill and members of an ethnic minority.

Issues Affecting the Mental Health of the Elderly, p. 553
Diff: M, Type: Factual, Ans: c

102.   Triple jeopardy, as an issue affecting the mental health of the elderly, refers to:
       a.   depression, anxiety, and substance abuse.
       b.   dementia, delirium, and substance abuse.
       c.   being old, a minority member, and a woman.
       d.   discrimination, poor long-term care, and poor medical care.

Issues Affecting the Mental Health of the Elderly, p. 553
Diff: E, Type: Factual, Ans: a

103.   Sources of discrimination in the mental health care of the elderly include:
       a.   language barriers that interfere with medical and mental health care.
       b.   need for care in a skilled facility.
       c.   lack of good quality wellness programs.
       d.   combination of substance abuse and depression.

Issues Affecting the Mental Health of the Elderly, p. 553
Diff: M, Type: Factual, Ans: c

104.   A partially supervised apartment, a senior housing complex for mildly impaired elderly
       people, and a nursing home with round-the-clock care are all examples of:
       a.   health-maintenance facilities.
       b.   wellness programs.
       c.   long-term care.
       d.   double jeopardy facilities.

Issues Affecting the Mental Health of the Elderly, p. 553
Diff: M, Type: Factual, Ans: a

105.   The percentage of the elderly population living in nursing homes at any given time is about:
       a.   5%.
       b.   15%.
       c.   25%.
       d.   35%.

Issues Affecting the Mental Health of the Elderly, p. 554
Diff: H, Type: Applied, Ans: b

106.   Which of the following is the most likely to be said by an elderly person regarding long-term
       care?
       a.   "I'm glad I saved enough for this."
       b.   "I've known lots of people who got better and came home."
       c.   "I'm worried about how my life will change."
       d.   "I can't wait for all the interesting new activities I'll be able to do."

Issues Affecting the Mental Health of the Elderly, p. 554
Diff: H, Type: Applied, Ans: d

107.   If you do things during your life that promote physical and psychological well-being, you are engaging in a _____ approach to aging.
   a.   preventative
   b.   medical
   c.   conditional
   d.   health-maintenance

Issues Affecting the Mental Health of the Elderly, p. 554
Diff: H, Type: Applied, Ans: b

108.   If a young person is taking a health-maintenance approach to aging, the person would be:
   a.   buying long-term care insurance.
   b.   doing things that promote physical and mental health.
   c.   avoiding negative life events.
   d.   being sensitive to cultural differences among people.

"You Are the Music, While the Music Lasts," p. 555 (Box 18-5)
Diff: E, Type: Factual, Ans: a

109.   Oliver Sachs finds that music can help elderly people:
   a.   move.
   b.   speak.
   c.   compose pieces.
   d.   draw.

"You Are the Music, While the Music Lasts," p. 555 (Box 18-5)
Diff: M, Type: Applied, Ans: c

110.   If you walked in on Oliver Sachs working with elderly people, you wouldn't be surprised to see them:
   a.   sleeping deeply.
   b.   having sex.
   c.   dancing.
   d.   writing poetry.

Putting It Together, p. 556
Diff: H, Type: Applied, Ans: a

111.   Those of us who do *not* develop Alzheimer's will nevertheless benefit from Alzheimer's research because:
   a.   memory and cognition are central to life.
   b.   ways to prevent Alzheimer's are likely to be developed in the next year or two.
   c.   we should all be taking drugs to prevent Alzheimer's.
   d.   treatments for Alzheimer's are enormously successful.

Putting It Together, p. 556
Diff: H, Type: Applied, Ans: b

112.   All of the following are suspected causes of Alzheimer's except:
   a.   abnormal neurotransmitter activity.
   b.   bacterial infection.
   c.   immune system dysfunction.
   d.   genetic factors.

Putting It Together, p. 556
Diff: H, Type: Factual, Ans: c

113.   It is estimated that as many as _____ percent of the elderly could benefit from mental health services, but only _____ percent receive them.
   a.   10; 1
   b.   20; 10
   c.   50; 20
   d.   60; 30

Putting It Together, p. 556
Diff: M, Type: Factual, Ans: d

114.   The misuse of prescription drugs by the elderly is a form of _____ disorder.
   a.   anxiety
   b.   depressive
   c.   schizophrenic
   d.   substance abuse

Putting It Together, p. 556
Diff: H, Type: Applied, Ans: d

115.   If an elderly person was found to have dementia, your best guess about what was causing it would be:
   a.   infection or alcoholism.
   b.   accident or drug overdose.
   c.   carbon monoxide or other chemical poisoning.
   d.   Alzheimer's or vascular problems.

Putting It Together, p. 556
Diff: H, Type: Factual, Ans: a

116.   Among the proposed causes of Alzheimer's are all of the following except:
   a.   concussion or other brain injury.
   b.   genetic factors.
   c.   slow-acting infections.
   d.   toxicity from zinc or aluminum.

Putting It Together, p. 557
Diff: H, Type: Factual, Ans: d

117.   Which of the following is not one of the key issues in addressing mental health among the elderly cited in your textbook?
   a.   problems of racial and ethnic minority groups
   b.   poor long-term care options
   c.   need for health maintenance by young adults
   d.   poverty among the elderly

Putting It Together, p. 557
Diff: H, Type: Applied, Ans: c

118.   If someone asked you about the effectiveness of treatment for Alzheimer's you would have to say:
   a.   "Drug treatment alone, without cognitive and behavioral therapies, is the best."
   b.   "The current focus is more on the patient than the patient's family."
   c.   "Even the best treatments have only limited success."
   d.   "There is really no way to improve the lives of Alzheimer's patients."

Putting It Together, p. 557
Diff: H, Type: Applied, Ans: d

119. Which of the following is *least* likely to be a focus of those interested in the problems of old age in the coming years?
      a. the issues of elderly members of minority groups
      b. inadequacies in long-term care
      c. the need for health-maintenance by young people
      d. finding ways for the oldest of the old to be as healthy as those just younger than they are

FILL-IN QUESTIONS

Old Age and Stress, p. 536
Diff: E, Type: Factual, Ans: geropsychology

1. The field dedicated to the mental health of the elderly is _____.

Depression in Later Life, p. 537
Diff: E, Type: Factual, Ans: depression

2. The most common mental health complaint of the elderly resulting from a loss is _____.

Substance Abuse in Later Life, p. 541
Diff: M, Type: Factual, Ans: misuse of prescription drugs

3. An often unintended substance abuse problem in the elderly, exacerbated by overprescribing is _____.

Psychotic Disorders in Later Life, p. 542
Diff: M, Type: Factual, Ans: delusional disorder

4. A kind of psychotic disorder in which individuals develop beliefs that are false but not bizarre is called _____.

Disorders of Cognition, p. 542
Diff: H, Type: Factual, Ans: dementia; delirium

5. The leading cognitive disorders among the elderly are _____ and _____.

Disorders of Cognition, p. 543
Diff: M, Type: Factual, Ans: dementia

6. The organic mental syndrome marked by impaired cognitive functioning in such areas as memory, abstract thinking, and judgment is called _____.

Disorders of Cognition, p. 543
Diff: M, Type: Factual, Ans: Delirium

7. _____ is an organic mental syndrome marked by sudden onset and characterized by a clouded state of consciousness in which a person has great difficulty concentrating and focusing attention.

Disorders of Cognition, p. 543
Diff: M, Type: Applied, Ans: dementia

8. Theodore has difficulty remembering even where he is going. Maintaining friendships is difficult, and he easily becomes angry when he cannot remember things. His health has not been as good as it was, and he is more clumsy than he was three years ago. He is most likely suffering from _____.

Disorders of Cognition, p. 543
Diff: E, Type: Factual, Ans: dementia

9.   Alzheimer's disease is considered a _____ .

Disorders of Cognition, p. 545
Diff: H, Type: Factual, Ans: neurofibrillary tangles; senile plaques

10.   Examples of structural changes in the brain associated with Alzheimer's and diagnosed through autopsy are _____ and _____ .

Disorders of Cognition, p. 547
Diff: M, Type: Factual, Ans: amygdala; hippocampus

11.   The two most important memory structures contained in the temporal lobes are the _____ and the _____ .

Disorders of Cognition, p. 547
Diff: H, Type: Factual, Ans: acetylcholine, glutamate

12.   The neurotransmitters _____ and _____ are important in forming memory protein.

Amnestic Disorders: Forgetting to Remember, p. 548 Box 18-3
Diff: M, Type: Applied, Ans: retrograde

13.   A lack of memory for events that occurred before the event that caused the amnesia is called _____ amnesia.

Amnestic Disorders: Forgetting to Remember, p. 548 Box 18-3
Diff: M, Type: Applied, Ans: anterograde

14.   After a blow to the head, Albert is unable to make any new memories. Albert is demonstrating _____ amnesia.

Amnestic Disorders: Forgetting to Remember, p. 548 Box 18-3
Diff: M, Type: Factual, Ans: thiamine

15.   A deficiency of the vitamin _____ is involved in Korsakoff's syndrome.

Amnestic Disorders: Forgetting to Remember, p. 548 Box 18-3
Diff: M, Type: Factual, Ans: Korsakoff's syndrome

16.   Prolonged alcohol abuse is related to _____ .

Disorders of Cognition, p. 549
Diff: H, Type: Factual, Ans: frontal; temporal

17.   Pick's disease involves degeneration of the _____ and _____ lobes.

Disorders of Cognition, p. 550
Diff: M, Type: Factual, Ans: Huntington's disease

18.   Children of people with _____ have a 50% chance of developing the disorder.

Disorders of Cognition, p. 553
Diff: M, Type: Applied, Ans: sociocultural

19.   Day-care and assisted living facilities are examples of the _____ approach to treatment for dementia.

Issues Affecting the Mental Health of the Elderly, p. 554
Diff: H, Type: Factual, Ans: wellness (or health maintenance)

20.   Medical scientists agree that young people should take a _____ approach to their own aging.

ESSAY QUESTIONS

Old Age and Stress, p. 537
Diff: M, Type: Factual

1.   Psychological problems of the elderly can be divided into two groups, those that are unique to them and those they share with other age groups. Discuss disorders of these two groups; be sure to indicate how disorders that occur in persons of all ages are nevertheless different in the elderly.

Psychotic Disorders in Later Life, p. 542
Diff: H, Type: Factual

2.   Describe delusional disorder in the elderly. How does it differ from other psychotic disorders? What are some of the presumed causes of the disorder?

Disorders of Cognition, p. 543 ff
Diff: H, Type: Applied

3.   Trace the common pattern of development of Alzheimer's from its initial stage until the person dies.

Disorders of Cognition, p. 543 ff
Diff: M, Type: Factual

4.   Alzheimer's disease is of increasing concern in our aging society. What are the symptoms of Alzheimer's disease? What are possible causes of the disease? What treatment would you recommend for those suffering from Alzheimer's disease?

Disorders of Cognition, p. 546 ff
Diff: M, Type: Factual

5.   Your choice: Either describe in detail the brain structures important in memory, *or* describe in detail the chemical changes that occur in the brain when memories are formed.

Disorders of Cognition, p. 549 ff
Diff: M, Type: Factual

6.   Please define and differentiate the following forms of dementia: vascular dementia, Creutzfeldt-Jakob disease, and Parkinson's disease.

Disorders of Cognition, p. 552 ff
Diff: H, Type: Factual

7.   Often, behavioral and cognitive therapies are used in the treatment of dementias such as Alzheimer's disease, even when there is no possibility of a cure. If the disease is progressive and incurable, of what use are such treatments? Please defend the use of behavioral and cognitive therapies in such situations.

Disorders of Cognition, p. 552 ff
Diff: H, Type: Applied

8.   Caregiving can take a heavy toll on the close relatives of people with dementia. Discuss who the caregivers are, what special challenges they face, and the treatments/programs that have been developed to make life easier for them.

Issues Affecting the Mental Health of the Elderly, p. 553
Diff: M, Type: Applied

9.   The elderly face issues of discrimination within our society. What are some sources of discrimination against the elderly, and what are effective ways of dealing with those types of discrimination.

Issues Affecting the Mental Health of the Elderly, p. 554
Diff: H, Type: Applied

10.   Given the importance of a health-maintenance or wellness approach to aging, discuss some important steps you would advise young people to take in order to avoid mental health problems as they age.

CHAPTER 19 Law, Society, and the Mental Health Profession

MULTIPLE-CHOICE QUESTIONS

Law, Society, and the Mental Health Profession, p. 560
Diff: H, Type: Applied, Ans: a

1. A forensic psychologist would be likely to do all of the following except:
    a. write legislation to regulate the practice of psychology in the courts.
    b. testify in criminal or civil proceedings.
    c. research questions pertinent to trials.
    d. profile serial killers.

Psychology in Law: How Do Clinicians Influence the Criminal Justice System?, p. 560
Diff: M, Type: Applied, Ans: c

2. Interactions between mental health professions and the legal field involve all of the following except:
    a. the use of mental health professionals to help courts assess the stability of people accused of crimes.
    b. courts, on the advice of mental health professionals, forcing some people to enter treatment, even against their will.
    c. courts forcing some people to become mental health professionals, even against their will.
    d. providing protection for the rights of patients.

Psychology in Law: How Do Clinicians Influence the Criminal Justice System?, p. 560
Diff: M, Type: Applied, Ans: a

3. Courts ask for mental health professionals to help determine if defendants are:
    a. responsible for the crimes they commit and capable of defending themselves in court.
    b. telling the truth or covering for someone else who really committed the crime.
    c. able to serve as their own counsel (lawyer) and educated regarding the law.
    d. in need of medical treatment in testing.

Psychology in Law: How Do Clinicians Influence the Criminal Justice System?, p. 560
Diff: M, Type: Factual, Ans: b

4. If a court decides that a defendant is mentally unstable, the defendant will:
    a. never be tried.
    b. not be punished in the usual way.
    c. spend the rest of his or her life in jail.
    d. be committed to a mental hospital for the rest of his or her life.

Psychology in Law: How Do Clinicians Influence the Criminal Justice System?, p. 560
Diff: H, Type: Applied, Ans: d

5.   Defendants who are actively hallucinating and experiencing delusions during the time of their trials are most likely to be:
        a.   judged not guilty of the crime by reason of insanity.
        b.   judged not guilty of the crime due to severe mental instability.
        c.   committed for treatment until they improve enough to be released.
        d.   committed for treatment until they improve enough to defend themselves.

Psychology in Law: How Do Clinicians Influence the Criminal Justice System?, p. 560
Diff: M, Type: Applied, Ans: b

6.   Defendants who were acting irrationally and in disordered ways when they allegedly committed the crimes are most likely to:
        a.   be judged to be faking or using a legal loophole to get out of their crime.
        b.   be judged not guilty by reason of insanity.
        c.   be committed to a mental hospital until they are able to defend themselves.
        d.   fail to rely on testimony of mental health professionals.

Psychology in Law: How Do Clinicians Influence the Criminal Justice System?, p. 560
Diff: H, Type: Applied, Ans: c

7.   A person who has been criminally committed has been:
        a.   found guilty of a crime but mentally ill.
        b.   found guilty of a crime but developmentally disabled.
        c.   accused of a crime and in need of mental health treatment.
        d.   accused of a crime and unable to cooperated in mental health treatment.

Psychology in Law: How Do Clinicians Influence the Criminal Justice System?, p. 560
Diff: H, Type: Applied, Ans: d

8.   Defendants can be criminally committed if they are judged to be mentally unstable:
        a.   at the time of the crime but not at the time of the trial.
        b.   at the time of the trial but not at the time of the crime.
        c.   both at the time of the trial and at the time of the crime.
        d.   All the answers are true.

Psychology in Law: How Do Clinicians Influence the Criminal Justice System?, p. 560
Diff: H, Type: Applied, Ans: a

9.   Which of the following people would never have to stand trial for a crime he or she might have committed?
        a.   one judged not guilty by reason of insanity
        b.   one judged mentally unstable at the time of the trial
        c.   one unable to assist in his or her defense at the time of the trial
        d.   one who had experienced criminal commitment

Psychology in Law: How Do Clinicians Influence the Criminal Justice System?, p. 560
Diff: M, Type: Factual, Ans: d

10.   One important issue in the relationship between the legislative and judicial systems and the mental health profession is:
        a.   determining guilt for a crime.
        b.   determining whether to prosecute.
        c.   investigating the details of certain crimes.
        d.   regulating aspects of mental health care.

Psychology in Law: How Do Clinicians Influence the Criminal Justice System?, p. 560
Diff: M, Type: Factual, Ans: d

11.   What must be true before a person may be tried for a crime and potentially found guilty?
       a.   The person must have normal intelligence.
       b.   The person must be a citizen of the United States.
       c.   The person must not act in a bizarre way in court.
       d.   The person must be capable of helping to defend him or herself in court.

Psychology in Law: How Do Clinicians Influence the Criminal Justice System?, p. 560
Diff: E, Type: Factual, Ans: a

12.   Who makes the final decision as to whether or not a person may be tried by the judicial
       system?
       a.   the courts
       b.   a panel of psychiatrists
       c.   a panel of psychologists
       d.   a court-appointed psychologist or psychiatrist

Psychology in Law: How Do Clinicians Influence the Criminal Justice System?, p. 560
Diff: E, Type: Factual, Ans: d

13.   If a person accused of a crime is found not guilty by reason of insanity, he or she is
       committed to a psychiatric facility for treatment. This is called:
       a.   2 PC.
       b.   incarceration.
       c.   civil commitment.
       d.   criminal commitment.

Psychology in Law: How Do Clinicians Influence the Criminal Justice System?, p. 560
Diff: E, Type: Applied, Ans: b

14.   Len killed a man in a fit of rage. His voices told him that the man was about to destroy the
       Earth and the man must be stopped. Len is likely to be sent to a mental institution because:
       a.   no crime was committed.
       b.   he was mentally unstable at the time of the crime.
       c.   a person who commits such a crime must be insane.
       d.   he was mentally unstable at the time of the trial and unable to defend himself.

Psychology in Law: How Do Clinicians Influence the Criminal Justice System?, p. 560
Diff: E, Type: Applied, Ans: d

15.   Merv got into a fight and killed his opponent. When he went to trial, he had a mental
       breakdown. He did not know where he was and had hallucinations. He was unable to answer
       questions. He is likely to be sent to a mental institution because:
       a.   he had a mental disorder.
       b.   no crime was committed.
       c.   he was mentally unstable at the time of the crime.
       d.   he was mentally unstable at the time of the trial and unable to defend himself.

Psychology in Law: How Do Clinicians Influence the Criminal Justice System?, p. 560
Diff: E, Type: Applied, Ans: a

16. If someone was interested in pursuing a career in a field that combined mental health and the legal and judicial systems, you should direct that person toward:
    a. forensic psychology.
    b. behavioral neuroscience.
    c. medical science.
    d. neurology.

Criminal Commitment and Insanity during Commission of a Crime, p. 561
Diff: M, Type: Factual, Ans: c

17. The definition of "insanity" used in legal cases was written by:
    a. psychologists.
    b. criminologists.
    c. legislators.
    d. judges.

Criminal Commitment and Insanity during Commission of a Crime, p. 561
Diff: M, Type: Applied, Ans: b

18. In using the insanity plea, the burden of proof to prove sanity or insanity ordinarily rests with the:
    a. court.
    b. defense.
    c. prosecution.
    d. legislature.

Criminal Commitment and Insanity during Commission of a Crime, p. 561
Diff: M, Type: Factual, Ans: a

19. The version of the insanity defense that declares that a person cannot be held responsible for his or her actions if they were the result of mental disease or mental defect is called the:
    a. Durham test.
    b. M'Naghten rule.
    c. organic deficiency test.
    d. irresistible impulse test.

Criminal Commitment and Insanity during Commission of a Crime, p. 561
Diff: M, Type: Applied, Ans: a

20. Tony killed the guy he was fighting with. At his trial he claimed that he did not know what he was doing because he was drunk. Under which "insanity" standard might he be found not guilty be reason of insanity:
    a. Durham test.
    b. M'Naghten rule.
    c. organic deficiency test.
    d. irresistible impulse test.

Criminal Commitment and Insanity during Commission of a Crime, p. 561
Diff: M, Type: Factual, Ans: a

21.   The Durham test judges a person not to be criminally responsible if he or she has acted:
   a.   under the influence of a mental disease or mental defect.
   b.   under a compulsion or an irresistible impulse to act.
   c.   without the knowledge of the nature of the act or actions were wrong.
   d.   lacking the ability to conform his or her conduct to the requirements of law, as a result of mental disease or defect.

Criminal Commitment and Insanity during Commission of a Crime, p. 561
Diff: M, Type: Applied, Ans: d

22.   Rex beat the guy to within an inch of his life. In court Rex claimed that he was forced to do it. He just exploded. He was not in control of himself. Under which "insanity" standard might he be found not guilty by reason of insanity?
   a.   Durham test
   b.   M'Naghten rule
   c.   organic deficiency test
   d.   irresistible impulse test

Criminal Commitment and Insanity during Commission of a Crime, p. 561
Diff: M, Type: Applied, Ans: a

23.   Pat, who was drunk as a skunk, got into a bar fight and killed his opponent. Which legal test would most likely be used to find him not guilty by reason of insanity?
   a.   Durham test
   b.   ALI guidelines
   c.   M'Naghten rule
   d.   irresistible impulse test

Criminal Commitment and Insanity during Commission of a Crime, p. 561
Diff: H, Type: Applied, Ans: a

24.   The burden of proof in an insanity case is usually:
   a.   on the defense attorneys to prove the defendant is insane.
   b.   on the prosecution attorneys to prove the defendant is sane.
   c.   on the defense for federal cases and on the prosecution for most state cases.
   d.   on the defense for most state cases and on the prosecution for federal cases.

Criminal Commitment and Insanity during Commission of a Crime, p. 561
Diff: H, Type: Applied, Ans: c

25.   Which of the following situations would fit the criteria of insanity established by the M'Naghten rule?
   a.   a person experiencing a mental disorder at the time of the crime
   b.   a person who did not know right from wrong at the time of the crime
   c.   a person who did not know right from wrong and was experiencing a mental disorder at the time of the crime.
   d.   None of the answers is true.

Criminal Commitment and Insanity during Commission of a Crime, p. 561
Diff: H, Type: Applied, Ans: c

26.   Suffering from headaches, alcoholism, and ulcers would make one eligible for an insanity defense under the:
       a.   M'Naghten rule.
       b.   irresistible impulse test.
       c.   Durham test.
       d.   American Law institute test.

Criminal Commitment and Insanity during Commission of a Crime, p. 561
Diff: H, Type: Applied, Ans: b

27.   If a man walked in on his wife in bed with his best friend and killed the friend and the wife in a fit of "passion," that man would be eligible for an insanity defense under the:
       a.   M'Naghten rule.
       b.   irresistible impulse test.
       c.   Durham test.
       d.   American Law Institute test.

Criminal Commitment and Insanity during Commission of a Crime, p. 561
Diff: H, Type: Applied, Ans: c

28   If a person experiencing severe paranoid delusions committed a crime while saying, "I know this is wrong and I shouldn't be doing it," that person would be eligible for an insanity defense under the:
       a.   M'Naghten rule.
       b.   irresistible impulse test.
       c.   Durham test.
       d.   American Law Institute test.

Criminal Commitment and Insanity during Commission of a Crime, p. 561
Diff: H, Type: Applied, Ans: d

29.   If a paranoid schizophrenic commits murder and either is not able to understand that murder is wrong or is not able to control his or her actions and follow the law, that person would be eligible for an insanity defense under:
       a.   the Durham test.
       b.   the American Law Institute test.
       c.   the irresistible impulse test.
       d.   All the answers are true.

Criminal Commitment and Insanity during Commission of a Crime, pp. 561-562
Diff: E, Type: Factual, Ans: c

30.   Which of the following cases caused the uproar and outrage that led to a return to the M'Naghten rule in determining insanity?
       a.   Sirhan Sirhan's assassination of Robert F. Kennedy
       b.   Oliver North's indictment in the Iran-Contra scandal
       c.   John Hinckley's attempted assassination of Ronald Reagan
       d.   A Bulgarian zealot's attempted assassination of Pope John Paul II

Criminal Commitment and Insanity during Commission of a Crime, p. 562
Diff: H, Type: Applied, Ans: a

31.   In response to a recommendation by the American Psychiatric Association, current federal practice is most like the:
    a.   M'Naghten rule.
    b.   irresistible impulse test.
    c.   Durham test.
    d.   American Law Institute test.

Criminal Commitment and Insanity during Commission of a Crime, p. 562
Diff: M, Type: Applied, Ans: a

32.   Which of the following is most likely to be acquitted by reason of insanity?
    a.   a schizophrenic who is white
    b.   a substance abuser who is a woman
    c.   an older person who commits a nonviolent crime
    d.   a person who has never been hospitalized for mental illness or arrested

Criminal Commitment and Insanity during Commission of a Crime, p. 562
Diff: H, Type: Applied, Ans: b

33.   Criticisms of the insanity defense point to all of the following except that:
    a.   in a given case, the testimony of clinicians is often not in agreement.
    b.   clinicians are biased to assume that people have free will and are responsible for their actions.
    c.   clinicians are trying to evaluate the defendant's state of mind during a time that has long past.
    d.   the insanity defense allows dangerous people to escape punishment.

Criminal Commitment and Insanity during Commission of a Crime, p. 562
Diff: E, Type: Factual, Ans: b

34.   The most common diagnosis of those found not guilty by reason of insanity is:
    a.   depression.
    b.   schizophrenia.
    c.   bipolar disease.
    d.   sociopath or psychopath.

Criminal Commitment and Insanity during Commission of a Crime, p. 562
Diff: M, Type: Factual, Ans: a

35.   The most common (and perhaps the most serious) objection to the insanity plea is that:
    a.   dangerous people go free.
    b.   people get jail rather than treatment.
    c.   it shortens the time that a guilty person must "serve."
    d.   it prevents the punishment of people with mental disorders.

Criminal Commitment and Insanity during Commission of a Crime, p. 562
Diff: H, Type: Applied, Ans: a

36.   About what percentage of defendants in the United States are found not guilty by reason of insanity in a typical year?
    a.   .25%
    b.   1%
    c.   25%
    d.   40%

Criminal Commitment and Insanity during Commission of a Crime, p. 564
Diff: M, Type: Factual, Ans: a

37.   Some states have adopted a verdict of "guilty but mentally ill." The sentence that must be given to those so convicted is:
       a.   jail with treatment if necessary.
       b.   prison with mandatory treatment.
       c.   jail and treatment until sane and then release.
       d.   hospitalization and treatment until sane and then release.

Criminal Commitment and Insanity during Commission of a Crime, p. 564
Diff: M, Type: Factual, Ans: c

38.   Currently in the United States, patients who are criminally committed to a mental hospital can be released:
       a.   only after they have been hospitalized an amount of time equal to the time they would have spent in prison.
       b.   only when they are judged to be no longer dangerous.
       c.   when they are no longer considered insane.
       d.   after they have spent time in a halfway house.

Criminal Commitment and Insanity during Commission of a Crime, p. 564
Diff: M, Type: Applied, Ans: a

39.   If a mentally ill person committed murder, was convicted and sent to prison, but was also given treatment while in prison, that person probably lived in a state that had a _____ option.
       a.   guilty but mentally ill
       b.   guilty with diminished capacity
       c.   not guilty by reason of insanity
       d.   guilty by reason of insanity

Criminal Commitment and Insanity during Commission of a Crime, p. 564
Diff: M, Type: Applied, Ans: b

40.   If a mentally ill person committed murder, but was convicted of committing manslaughter, that person probably lived in a state that had a _____ option.
       a.   guilty but mentally ill
       b.   guilty with diminished capacity
       c.   not guilty by reason of insanity
       d.   guilty by reason of insanity

Criminal Commitment and Insanity during Commission of a Crime, p. 564
Diff: M, Type: Factual, Ans: d

41.   In which of the following defenses is mental instability considered a mitigating circumstance in a crime?
       a.   guilty but dangerous
       b.   guilty but mentally ill
       c.   guilty by reason of insanity
       d.   guilty with diminished capacity

Criminal Commitment and Insanity during Commission of a Crime, p. 564
Diff: H, Type: Factual, Ans: b

42. In the case of *Foucha v. Louisiana*, the Supreme Court ruled that the only acceptable basis for determining the release of hospitalized offenders is whether or not they are still:
    a. mentally ill.
    b. insane.
    c. dangerous.
    d. unable to assist with their defense.

Criminal Commitment and Insanity during Commission of a Crime, p. 564
Diff: H, Type: Factual, Ans: a

43. Recently states have begun to abolish their sex offender laws. Among the reasons they are doing this is:
    a. racial bias can affect the application of the law.
    b. courts are becoming more sensitive to the rights of sex-offenders.
    c. the public wants sex offenders to have more rights.
    d. clinicians are better able to predict who is sexually dangerous.

Criminal Commitment and Insanity during Commission of a Crime, p. 566
Diff: M, Type: Factual, Ans: b

44. Many states have a category of "mentally disordered sex offenders," which assigns moral responsibility to the offender. This category, which is related to the insanity defense, is based on the premise that:
    a. most sex offenders suffer from schizophrenia.
    b. sexual offenses, such as pedophilia, reflect an underlying mental disorder.
    c. sex offenders should receive treatment rather than punishment, because their crimes are so offensive to society.
    d. sexual offenses are difficult to prove, and requiring a guilty verdict would allow too many offenders to avoid punishment.

Criminal Commitment and Insanity during Commission of a Crime, p. 566
Diff: H, Type: Applied, Ans: c

45. One difficulty with the mentally disordered sex offender classification is that:
    a. it fails to protect sex offenders from the abuse they often receive in prison.
    b. it does not allow for treatment in a mental health facility for sex offenders.
    c. racial bias appears to affect who is given this classification.
    d. it allows sex offenders to escape a criminal record.

Criminal Commitment and Incompetence to Stand Trial, p. 566
Diff: M, Type: Factual, Ans: c

46. A person who is accused of a crime cannot be convicted if he or she is mentally unstable either at the time of the crime or at the time of the trial. *Competence to stand trial* is important to ensure that the person:
    a. knows whether he or she is guilty.
    b. may argue coherently on the witness stand.
    c. understand the charges and can consult with counsel.
    d. can show the jury his or her state of mind at the time of the crime.

Criminal Commitment and Incompetence to Stand Trial, p. 567
Diff: H, Type: Factual, Ans: c

47.   The majority of criminals institutionalized for psychological treatment in the United States are there because:
       a.   they were judged mentally incompetent.
       b.   they were judged not guilty by reason of insanity.
       c.   prison officials decided they needed treatment.
       d.   their trials resulted in "hung" juries.

Civil Commitment, p. 568
Diff: M, Type: Applied, Ans: d

48.   Civil commitment is for a person who:
       a.   has committed a crime but is judged not guilty by reason of insanity.
       b.   has committed a crime but is judged not able to tell right from wrong.
       c.   has voluntarily sought treatment for mental problems.
       d.   refuses treatment others think he or she needs.

Civil Commitment, p. 568
Diff: H, Type: Applied, Ans: d

49.   A person who had a serious mental illness and was in need of treatment could, nevertheless, not be civilly committed unless that person was also:
       a.   a danger to him or herself.
       b.   a danger to others.
       c.   a danger to his or her parents.
       d.   a danger either to self or to others.

Civil Commitment, p. 568
Diff: E, Type: Factual, Ans: c

50.   The process of forcing certain individuals to undergo mental health treatment is called:
       a.   police power.
       b.   *parens patriae.*
       c.   civil commitment.
       d.   emergency commitment.

Civil Commitment, p. 568
Diff: M, Type: Factual, Ans: b

51.   The aspect of state responsibility that promotes and protects the interests of individuals even from themselves is called:
       a.   police power.
       b.   *parens patriae.*
       c.   civil commitment.
       d.   emergency commitment.

Civil Commitment, p. 568
Diff: M, Type: Factual, Ans: a

52.   The aspect of state responsibility that promotes and protects the interests of individuals from dangerous people is called:
       a.   police power.
       b.   *parens patriae.*
       c.   civil commitment.
       d.   emergency commitment.

Civil Commitment, p. 568
Diff: M, Type: Factual, Ans: b

53.   The principle of *parens patriae* (parent of the country) permits the state to make decisions that promote an individual's best interest. It has been used to support the process of:
    a.   police power.
    b.   civil commitment.
    c.   criminal commitment.
    d.   guilt by reason of insanity.

Civil Commitment, p. 568
Diff: M, Type: Applied, Ans: c

54.   *Parens patriae* refers to the state's rights to make decisions that are in the individual's best interest, and to the idea that police power gives the state the right to protect society from harm. These two principles have been used to support:
    a.   the use of the insanity defense.
    b.   the process of criminal commitment.
    c.   the process of involuntary commitment.
    d.   the use of the diminished-capacity defense.

Civil Commitment, p. 568
Diff: M, Type: Applied, Ans: a

55.   Iris has had a diagnosis of schizophrenia. She mutters a lot about being possessed. Lately, she has been carving her arm with a knife. You think that she requires treatment before she hurts herself any more. The authorities have a right to commit her based on the principles of:
    a.   *parens patriae.*
    b.   *habeas corpus.*
    c.   *in loco parentis.*
    d.   *politico parentis.*

Civil Commitment, p. 568
Diff: M, Type: Applied, Ans: d

56.   If parents go to a mental health professional and seek to have their son committed, and the mental health professional agrees and involuntarily commits the son without a hearing or the opportunity for the son to contest the decision, we know that the son is probably:
    a.   experiencing a minor rather than major mental disorder.
    b.   also developmentally disabled.
    c.   experiencing repeated mental problems.
    d.   a child.

Civil Commitment, p. 568
Diff: M, Type: Factual, Ans: b

57.   In *Addington v. Texas*, a young man fought being involuntarily committed, arguing that the standard for showing that a person is mentally ill was unclear and unfair. As a result, the standard for committing a person was revised to:
    a.   a "reasonable possibility" of mental illness.
    b.   "clear and convincing" proof that the individual is mentally ill.
    c.   "preponderance of the evidence" that the person is mentally ill.
    d.   proof "beyond a reasonable doubt" that the individual is mentally ill.

Civil Commitment, p. 568
Diff: M, Type: Factual, Ans: a

58. In *Addington v. Texas*, a young man fought being involuntarily committed, arguing that the standard for showing that a person is mentally ill was unclear and unfair. This case resulted in the courts setting a standard that commitment:
     a. requires clear and convincing proof.
     b. must be necessary to avoid danger to others.
     c. must be necessary beyond a reasonable doubt.
     d. must be necessary to relieve the family of the burden to treat.

Civil Commitment, p. 569
Diff: M, Type: Applied, Ans: d

59. In an emergency, if a person is clearly suicidal or homicidal because of hallucinations and delusions, that person can be involuntarily committed by:
     a. the person's parents.
     b. a mental health professional in the emergency room.
     c. the police.
     d. two physicians.

Civil Commitment, p. 569
Diff: H, Type: Factual, Ans: b

60. The standard for "clear and convincing proof," according to the U.S. Supreme Court is:
     a. total certainty.
     b. 75% certainty.
     c. equivalent to "beyond a reasonable doubt."
     d. equivalent to "near-total certainty."

Civil Commitment, p. 569
Diff: H, Type: Applied, Ans: a

61. In the past, people with mental disorders were less likely than those without mental disorders to commit violent or dangerous acts. Why do we think that is?
     a. Many more were hospitalized in the past than are now.
     b. The newer antipsychotic drugs do not control violence as well as older drugs did.
     c. Fewer people with mental disorders are living in the community now than in the past.
     d. Those with less severe mental disorders are showing an increase in violence these days.

Civil Commitment, p. 569
Diff: E, Type: Factual, Ans: d

62. Temporary commitment in an emergency situation is possible if:
     a. the family requests it.
     b. both parents request it.
     c. the M'Naghten rule is applied.
     d. two physicians certify it (the two-physician certificate—"2 PC").

Civil Commitment, p. 569
Diff: M, Type: Applied, Ans: b

63. What is the basis for making a 2 PC determination to commit on an emergency basis?
     a. The patient must be violent.
     b. The patient must be a danger to self or others.
     c. The patient must be a child.
     d. The patient must be involved in a criminal proceeding.

Civil Commitment, p. 570
Diff: H, Type: Factual, Ans: d

64.   Monahan's research on the relationship between violent behavior and severe mental disorder shows that:
   a.   people with severe mental disorders are much less likely to commit violent acts than those without mental disorders.
   b.   there is no difference between those with and those without severe mental disorders in the rate of violent acts.
   c.   people with severe mental disorders are much more likely to commit violent acts than those without mental disorders.
   d.   people with severe mental disorders are somewhat more likely to commit violent acts than those without mental disorders.

Civil Commitment, p. 570
Diff: M, Type: Factual, Ans: d

65.   What proportion of mental patients assault another patient during hospitalization?
   a.   4%
   b.   12%
   c.   15%
   d.   25%

Civil Commitment, p. 570
Diff: M, Type: Factual, Ans: d

66.   What is the rate of assault for people who display a substance-abuse disorder?
   a.   4%
   b.   12%
   c.   15%
   d.   25% or more

Civil Commitment, p. 570
Diff: H, Type: Applied, Ans: b

67.   Which of the following is true about dangerousness and mental disorders?
   a.   Today the rate of violent behavior among those with mental disorders is not different from the rate among those without mental disorders.
   b.   People with substance abuse disorders are more likely to have assaulted others than those with a mental disorder.
   c.   Those with schizophrenia are more likely than those with any other mental disorder to assault others.
   d.   During the time they are hospitalized, no more than 10% of those with mental disorders assault others.

Civil Commitment, p. 570
Diff: H, Type: Applied, Ans: d

68.   How good are mental health professionals at predicting dangerousness?
   a.   They are better at accurately predicting long-term than short-term risks of dangerousness.
   b.   They tend to overestimate the likelihood that a patient will be violent.
   c.   They are wrong more often than they are right when predicting long-term violence.
   d.   All the answers are true.

Civil Commitment, p. 571
Diff: H, Type: Applied, Ans: b
69.   If you encountered someone convicted of a violent criminal offense, you could legitimately also expect to find that the person:
   a.   is schizophrenic.
   b.   is a substance abuser.
   c.   is clinically depressed.
   d.   is also a sex offender.

Civil Commitment, p. 571
Diff: M, Type: Factual, Ans: b
70.   Which of the following is a criticism of civil commitment?
   a.   Too many dangerous people are allowed on the streets.
   b.   The therapy offered to people committed in civil proceedings may not be effective.
   c.   The current civil commitment procedures allow people who should be convicted of crimes to go free.
   d.   Effective therapy is denied people because they do not recognize the need and they cannot be committed.

The Separation of Mind and State, p. 571 (Box 19-2)
Diff: M, Type: Factual, Ans: c
71.   John Brown and Abraham Lincoln were labeled by some as "insane" because of their views on:
   a.   women's rights.
   b.   prohibition.
   c.   slavery.
   d.   prison reform.

Civil Commitment, pp. 571-572
Diff: H, Type: Applied, Ans: d
72.   Those who believe civil commitment should be abolished would be most likely to disagree with which of the following?
   a.   Judgments of dangerousness are so inaccurate that they should not be used to deprive someone of liberty.
   b.   There is a danger that civil commitment might be used to control or punish political dissidents.
   c.   People who are involuntarily committed often do not respond well to treatment.
   d.   We should rely more on psychiatrists and psychologists and less on the legal system to make decisions about commitment.

Civil Commitment, p. 572
Diff: H, Type: Applied, Ans: b
73.   Which of the following statements most accurately reflects current trends in civil commitment?
   a.   Many people who could be described as "social deviants" (drug addicts, check bouncers, counterculture adherents) are committed.
   b.   During the 1960s and 1970s, commitment regulations and standards were made stricter.
   c.   Today more people are institutionalized through civil commitment than ever before.
   d.   States are currently moving to make commitment regulations and standards even stricter.

Civil Commitment, p. 572
Diff: H, Type: Factual, Ans: c
74.   The *Wyatt v. Stickney* decision forced state hospitals to provide:
      a.   care in a mental patient's home community.
      b.   public advocates for mental patients.
      c.   more social action and physical exercise for mental patients.
      d.   periodic review of treatment plans and progress for mental patients.

Protecting Patients' Rights, p. 572
Diff: E, Type: Factual, Ans: a
75.   In the case of *Wyatt v. Stickney*, the U.S. Supreme Court ruled that people who have been involuntarily committed have a right to:
      a.   treatment.
      b.   a hearing.
      c.   a fair trial.
      d.   a periodic review of their status.

Protecting Patients' Rights, p. 572
Diff: M, Type: Factual, Ans: c
76.   The case of *O'Connor v. Donaldson* resulted in the ruling that:
      a.   parents cannot commit adult children.
      b.   there must be a six-month limit on involuntary commitments.
      c.   a person who is not dangerous cannot be held if he or she can survive in freedom.
      d.   involuntary commitment requires the certificates of two psychiatrists, not two physicians.

Protecting Patients' Rights, p. 573
Diff: M, Type: Factual, Ans: c
77.   In recent years, public advocates for those with mental disorders have turned their attention to the rights of _____ to receive treatment.
      a.   mental patients in hospitals
      b.   medical patients in hospitals
      c.   mental patients in the community
      d.   nursing home residents

Protecting Patients' Rights, p. 573
Diff: E, Type: Factual, Ans: b
78.   The focus of the Protection and Advocacy for Mentally Ill Individuals Act of 1986 was to:
      a.   force the release of long-term committed people.
      b.   set up an advocacy system for patients problems.
      c.   assure the right of patients to refuse any and all treatment.
      d.   require institutions to provide specific treatments for committed individuals.

Protecting Patients' Rights, p. 573
Diff: E, Type: Factual, Ans: c
79.   The recent cases that have increased the patient's right to refuse treatment have focused largely on the right to refuse:
      a.   psychotherapy.
      b.   civil commitment.
      c.   biological treatments.
      d.   to participate in any form of treatment at all.

Protecting Patients' Rights, p. 574
Diff: M, Type: Applied, Ans: d

80. If a patient is assigned to a community mental health center inpatient facility instead of a mental hospital, the decision makers are applying the principle of:
    a. minimum wage.
    b. aftercare.
    c. community residence/group home.
    d. least restrictive environment.

Protecting Patients' Rights, p. 574
Diff: M, Type: Applied, Ans: a

81. Patients who perform work in mental institutions, particularly private institutions, are guaranteed _____ for that work.
    a. minimum wage
    b. aftercare
    c. community residence
    d. least restrictive environment

Protecting Patients' Rights, p. 574
Diff: M, Type: Applied, Ans: c

82. A group home is an example of :
    a. minimum wage.
    b. aftercare.
    c. community residence.
    d. least restrictive environment.

Protecting Patients' Rights, p. 574
Diff: H, Type: Applied, Ans: c

83. A patient in a mental hospital would probably have the least success when trying to refuse:
    a. psychosurgery.
    b. electroconvulsive shock.
    c. medication.
    d. All of the answers are equally hard to refuse.

Protecting Patients' Rights, p. 574
Diff: H, Type: Applied, Ans: a

84. Which of the following is an example of the way patients' rights might interfere with patients' recovery (that is, an example of a time when patients' rights are not good for the patients)?
    a. The right to refuse medication means that patients might harm themselves or others.
    b. Payment for work done enhances token economy programs.
    c. The right to refuse medication helps lower treatment costs.
    d. Our present state of knowledge does not justify overriding patients' decisions.

Law in Psychology,: Malpractice Suits, p. 575
Diff: H, Type: Factual, Ans: b

85. "Litigaphobia" and "litigastress" refer to:
    a. patients' fear that they will be sued.
    b. clinicians' fear that they will be sued.
    c. patients' fear that they will be abused.
    d. clinicians' fear that they will be assaulted.

Law in Psychology,: Malpractice Suits, p. 575
Diff: E, Type: Factual, Ans: c

86.   An important current distinction between psychologists and psychiatrists that is changing
       is that:
       a.   psychologists use mental tests and psychiatrists do not.
       b.   psychologists do psychotherapy and psychiatrists do not.
       c.   psychiatrists may prescribe drugs and psychologists may not.
       d.   psychologists may order biological treatments and psychiatrists may not.

Law in Psychology,: Malpractice Suits, p. 575
Diff: H, Type: Applied, Ans: c

87.   One outcome due to the rise in malpractice suits related to hospitalization, based on actual
       hospitalization statistics, is that:
       a.   patients are likely to be released after less time in the hospital.
       b.   patients will be treated by only one therapist, rather than a team.
       c.   patients will be less likely to be released from the hospital.
       d.   fewer students will go into forensic psychology.

Law in Psychology: Professional Boundaries, p. 575
Diff: H, Type: Applied, Ans: d

88.   Compared to past years, these days:
       a.   there are more distinct lines between the work of psychologists and psychiatrists.
       b.   psychologists have less authority than in previous years.
       c.   only psychiatrists can admit people to psychiatric hospitals.
       d.   some psychologists are able to prescribe psychiatric medication.

Psychology in Law: Jury Selection, p. 576
Diff: H, Type: Applied, Ans: a

89.   Which of the following questions is an attorney most likely to ask his or her jury specialist?
       a.   What approach should I take in order to get the jury on my side?
       b.   Is my client competent to stand trial?
       c.   Is eyewitness testimony accurate, according to psychological research?
       d.   Should my client get sole custody of the children?

Psychology in Law: Psychological Research of Legal Topics, p. 576
Diff: M, Type: Applied, Ans: c

90.   Research indicates that eyewitness testimony is:
       a.   highly reliable.
       b.   better for fleeting and unexpected events.
       c.   impaired by events of the crime.
       d.   not subject to the introduction of misinformation.

Psychology in Law: Psychological Research of Legal Topics, p. 577
Diff: M, Type: Factual, Ans: d

91.   Which of the following is *not* true about profiling?
       a.   Profile information needs to be combined with other more compelling clues.
       b.   Profiling is based on traits shared by those who commit particular kinds of crimes.
       c.   Profiling can be inaccurate.
       d.   Profiling is realistically portrayed on most television shows.

Psychology in Law: Psychological Research of Legal Topics, p. 577
Diff: H, Type: Applied, Ans: b

92.   Imagine that a witness says he or she is absolutely certain that the defendant is the one who committed the crime. What is the most likely true about the witness's certainty?
        a.   The witness is more accurate than someone who is only fairly sure.
        b.   The jury will be more likely to believe the certain witness.
        c.   We don't know, because the impact of certainty on accuracy has not yet been studied.
        d.   Regardless of their level of certainty, eyewitnesses are remarkably accurate.

Serial Murderers: Madness or Badness?, p. 578 (Box 19-3)
Diff: M, Type: Factual, Ans: c

93.   What is the mental state of most serial killers?
        a.   They are legally insane.
        b.   They are usually psychotic.
        c.   They suffer from mental disorders but are not legally insane.
        d.   They are legally sane and do not suffer from any mental disorders.

Serial Murderers: Madness or Badness?, p. 578 (Box 19-3)
Diff: M, Type: Factual, Ans: a

94.   Frequently, when a serial killer comes to trial, he or she makes the insanity plea. What usually happens?
        a.   They are usually found guilty.
        b.   They are usually found guilty but mentally ill.
        c.   They are usually found not guilty by reason of insanity.
        d.   They are usually found guilty with diminished capacity.

Serial Murderers: Madness or Badness?, p. 578 (Box 19-3)
Diff: M, Type: Applied, Ans: d

95.   Which of the following is least descriptive of serial killers?
        a.   They are men.
        b.   They typically move from place to place with no ties to a community.
        c.   They like media attention and are fascinated by police work.
        d.   They are of less than average intelligence.

Serial Murderers: Madness or Badness?, p. 578 (Box 19-3)
Diff: H, Type: Applied, Ans: b

96.   Why is the plea of not guilty by reason of insanity generally unsuccessful for serial killers?
        a.   Their crimes are motivated by their sexual fantasies.
        b.   They know what they are doing and that it is wrong.
        c.   They do not have mental disorders.
        d.   They do not benefit from mental health service.

Serial Murderers: Madness or Badness?, p. 578 (Box 19-3)
Diff: H, Type: Applied, Ans: c

97.   Which of the following best fits the profile of a serial killer?
        a.   They typically have a strong conscience and have high regard for societal customs.
        b.   They are fearful of getting caught.
        c.   They were generally abused as children—sexually, physically, and emotionally.
        d.   They have very few fantasies.

What Ethical Principles Guide Mental Health Professionals?, p. 579
Diff: H, Type: Applied, Ans: b

98.   If a psychologist wanted to write a newspaper column on mental health issues in the community, the psychologist would need to do which of the following in order to comply with professional ethical standards?
   a.   Psychologists can't give advice in newspapers, only face to face.
   b.   The psychologist would need to make sure the advice was based on sound research.
   c.   The psychologist would have to be supervised by a psychiatrist who oversaw the work.
   d.   The psychologist could not give information about medication in the articles.

What Ethical Principles Guide Mental Health Professionals?, p. 579
Diff: E, Type: Factual, Ans: d

99.   The APA code of ethics states that sexual relationships between a psychologist and client are:
   a.   permitted if both parties agree.
   b.   permitted as soon as treatment ends.
   c.   prohibited only for therapeutic purposes.
   d.   prohibited under almost all circumstances.

What Ethical Principles Guide Mental Health Professionals?, p. 579
Diff: H, Type: Applied, Ans: c

100.   A psychologist wanted to accept a client with whom he had previously had a sexual relationship. According to ethical guidelines, the psychologist:
   a.   would have to wait to see the woman until two years after the last time they had sex.
   b.   would need to be especially sensitive, but could proceed.
   c.   couldn't see the patient.
   d.   could see the patient only if he were supervised by a woman therapist.

What Ethical Principles Guide Mental Health Professionals?, p. 579
Diff: H, Type: Applied, Ans: c

101.   If Dr. Phil were a psychologist (he is not), would he be ethically allowed to offer advice to people on television?
   a.   No, psychologists can only offer advice to people who are on-going clients.
   b.   No, psychologists can offer advice in newspapers, but not on television.
   c.   Yes, as long as he bases his advice on appropriate psychological practice.
   d.   Yes, as long as he also sees the person for follow-up therapy.

What Ethical Principles Guide Mental Health Professionals?, p. 579
Diff: H, Type: Applied, Ans: d

102.   If you are the typical therapist, you:
   a.   have had a sexual relationship with at least one client.
   b.   have never been sexually attracted to a client.
   c.   have had a sexual relationship with a client you were not attracted to.
   d.   have been sexually attracted to a client but not had a sexual relationship with a client.

What Ethical Principles Guide Mental Health Professionals?, p. 579
Diff: H, Type: Applied, Ans: a

103.   Imagine that you are a therapist working on the U.S.–Mexican border but don't speak
        Spanish. What is proper ethical behavior for you?
        a.   acknowledge your limitations and seek further training
        b.   pretend to be knowledgeable so as not to upset your clients
        c.   ignore the potential influence of culture and language because the basic concerns of all
             people are the same
        d.   continue to practice as you were originally taught

What Ethical Principles Guide Mental Health Professionals?, p. 579
Diff: H, Type: Applied, Ans: b

104.   Which of the following disorders would you be most likely to find in a person who was
        receiving therapy because of previously experiencing sexual misconduct from another
        therapist?
        a.   sexual dysfunction
        b.   depression or posttraumatic stress disorder
        c.   schizophrenia
        d.   generalized anxiety disorder

What Ethical Principles Guide Mental Health Professionals?, p. 580
Diff: M, Type: Applied, Ans: d

105.   Which of the following is the greatest?
        a.   The number of therapists who report having sex with a patient.
        b.   The number of therapists who probably do have sex with a patient.
        c.   The number of therapists who fantasize about a patient.
        d.   The number of therapists who are sexually attracted to a patient.

What Ethical Principles Guide Mental Health Professionals?, p. 580
Diff: H, Type: Applied, Ans: b

106.   A therapist who broke confidentiality with a patient without the patient's consent because of
        fears that the person would harm someone else was acting according to the ethical principle
        of:
        a.   confidentiality.
        b.   duty to protect.
        c.   right to treatment.
        d.   compassionate concern.

What Ethical Principles Guide Mental Health Professionals?, p. 580
Diff: M, Type: Applied, Ans: a

107.   Psychologists are ethically bound to keep material about their patients confidential except:
        a.   when someone is in danger.
        b.   when writing up a case study for a journal article.
        c.   when discussing the case as part of a college class.
        d.   when discussing the patient with a spouse.

What Ethical Principles Guide Mental Health Professionals?, p. 580
Diff: H, Type: Factual, Ans: b

108.   A landmark California court case, *Tarasoff v. Regents of the University of California*, dramatically affected the right to confidentiality between client and therapist. This case led to the conclusion that:
    a.   confidentiality may not be broken if there is a clear danger to an identifiable person.
    b.   a therapist must break the obligation of confidentiality if there is a clear danger to a specific identifiable person.
    c.   confidentiality must not be broken simply to protect a person who may be in close proximity to an intended victim.
    d.   a therapist must break the obligation of confidentiality if there is the potential that the person may hurt someone, even if a particular victim has not been identified.

What Ethical Principles Guide Mental Health Professionals?, p. 580
Diff: E, Type: Factual, Ans: c

109.   The current code of ethics declares that therapist should break confidentiality even without the client's consent:
    a.   never.
    b.   only when the client might cause self harm.
    c.   when the client or another person is threatened.
    d.   when it is deemed necessary to protect another person's property.

What Ethical Principles Guide Mental Health Professionals?, p. 580
Diff: H, Type: Applied, Ans: c

110.   If a therapist has a client who is threatening to kill another person, the therapist must inform that other person because of the ethical principle of:
    a.   confidentiality.
    b.   right to know.
    c.   duty to protect.
    d.   sunshine.

Bringing Mental Health Services to the Workplace, p. 581
Diff: H, Type: Applied, Ans: d

111.   If you were an air traffic controller and your employer required you to attend a seminar on dealing in healthy ways with stress, you would be receiving:
    a.   individual therapy.
    b.   an employee assistance program.
    c.   health maintenance insurance.
    d.   a problem-solving seminar.

Bringing Mental Health Services to the Workplace, p. 581
Diff: M, Type: Applied, Ans: b

112.   In the workplace, psychological problems are estimated to contribute most to:
    a.   absenteeism.
    b.   industrial accidents.
    c.   work terminations.
    d.   promotion denials.

Bringing Mental Health Services to the Workplace, p. 581
Diff: E, Type: Factual, Ans: d
113. Which of the following is most likely to influence job performance in terms of accidents, damage, and absenteeism?
    a. depression
    b. anxiety disorders
    c. psychotic disorders
    d. substance-related disorders

Bringing Mental Health Services to the Workplace, p. 581
Diff: E, Type: Applied, Ans: b
114. If you were having marital problems that were affecting your work and your employer made mental health service available to you to deal with those problems, your employer would be providing you with:
    a. services mandated by law.
    b. an employee assistance program.
    c. a peer review system.
    d. a stock ownership plan.

Bringing Mental Health Services to the Workplace, p. 581
Diff: M, Type: Applied, Ans: c
115. Peter is having trouble coping with his financial problems and is getting depressed about them. He seeks out someone at his company who helps by counseling employees on such issues and tries to intercept problems before they get out of hand. Peter is seeking help from:
    a. stress-reduction seminars.
    b. problem-solving seminars.
    c. an employee assistance program.
    d. an outpatient counseling center.

The Economics of Mental Health, p. 581
Diff: H, Type: Applied, Ans: a
116. Today, the cost of direct mental health services is mostly paid by:
    a. individual patients and their private insurance companies.
    b. the Medicaid and Medicare programs.
    c. the military.
    d. a combination of federal programs.

The Economics of Mental Health, p. 582
Diff: E, Type: Factual, Ans: a
117. The type of system that many health insurance companies have set up to try to curtail expenses associated with providing treatment is referred to as:
    a. a managed care program.
    b. a private insurance company.
    c. an employee assistance program.
    d. a health maintenance organization.

The Economics of Mental Health, p. 582
Diff: H, Type: Applied, Ans: c

118.   A therapist who was worried that patients would receive less costly short-term care rather than more promising long-term treatment, would have treatment monitored by an insurance employee rather than a therapist, and would have confidential treatment reports read by others, is concerned about:
   a.   employee assistance programs.
   b.   stress inoculation treatment.
   c.   managed care programs.
   d.   problem-solving seminars.

The Economics of Mental Health, p. 583
Diff: H, Type: Applied, Ans: b

119.   The rise of managed care programs for treating mental disorders has resulted in:
   a.   a focus on maintaining confidentiality at all costs.
   b.   a preference for short-term rather than long-term improvement.
   c.   less detail about the patient being shared with fewer insurance employees.
   d.   return of treatment decisions to the therapists rather than to the insurance companies.

The Person within the Profession, p. 584
Diff: H, Type: Applied, Ans: c

120.   Imagine that you are a therapist treating another therapist for a disorder. What is the therapist most likely to exhibit?
   a.   a physical problem caused by stress
   b.   a suicide attempt
   c.   depression or anxiety
   d.   sexual dysfunction

The Person within the Profession, p. 584
Diff: E, Type: Factual, Ans: b

121.   A recent national mental health survey of psychotherapists found that more than three-quarters of them reported being in therapy themselves at least once, and that they:
   a.   are likely to seek therapy because they feel inadequate.
   b.   seek therapy for the same problems that affect other people.
   c.   are more likely to seek help for depression than are other people.
   d.   experience more anxiety disorders than other people because they feel obligated to appear well adjusted.

Therapists Under Attack, p. 585 (Box 19-5)
Diff: H, Type: Applied, Ans: d

122.   If you become a therapist and are like the majority of therapists, you will:
   a.   never feel threatened by a patient and never experience emotional distress yourself.
   b.   never feel threatened by a patient but feel depressed or anxious nevertheless.
   c.   be attacked by a patient and consequently feel anxious and depressed.
   d.   feel threatened by a patient and also experience emotional distress.

Putting It Together, p. 585
Diff: H, Type: Applied, Ans: a
123. Which of the following is the most accurate conclusion one can draw about the mental health field?
      a. Mental health professionals are gaining respect in society.
      b. What mental health professionals know and can do outweighs what they do not know and cannot do.
      c. There is more isolation of the branches of mental health disciplines, and less cooperation across disciplines.
      d. Interconnectedness among various social institutions inevitably works to the advantage of patients.

Putting It Together, p. 585
Diff: H, Type: Applied, Ans: b
124. All of the following are examples of ways in which social institutions limit a person's mental health care except:
      a. health maintenance organizations that limit the number of treatment sessions one can have.
      b. legal protection of patients' rights and confidentiality.
      c. labels applied by the legal system that stigmatize a person.
      d. insurance companies that decide which treatment is best for a particular person.

Putting It Together, p. 586
Diff: H, Type: Applied, Ans: c
125. According to our legal system, what is necessary for a person to be punished for a crime?
      a. The person must be free from all diagnosable mental illnesses.
      b. The person must be of at least average intelligence.
      c. The person must be judged responsible for his or her actions and capable of cooperating with the defense.
      d. The person must be able to understand the legal proceedings and be able to express their objection to mistakes made by the prosecution.

Putting It Together, p. 586
Diff: H, Type: Applied, Ans: d
126. Imagine that you are an attorney and that your client has been sentenced to prison with the proviso that he or she will also receive psychological treatment. Your client has received a verdict known as:
      a. innocent by reason of insanity.
      b. guilty with diminished capacity.
      c. criminally insane.
      d. guilty but mentally ill.

Putting It Together, p. 586
Diff: H, Type: Applied, Ans: a
127. If you were interested in a securing a civil commitment for someone you cared about, you would have to show clearly that the person:
      a. was dangerous.
      b. had tried but not benefited from therapy.
      c. did not have a substance abuse problem causing the disorder.
      d. had schizophrenia or antisocial personality disorder.

Putting It Together, p. 586
Diff: H, Type: Applied, Ans: b

128.   Thanks to recent court emphases, mental patients who are hospitalized are guaranteed the right to:
    a.   be employed.
    b.   receive treatment or be allowed to refuse treatment.
    c.   attend college.
    d.   live independently.

FILL-IN QUESTIONS

Psychology in Law: How Do Clinicians Influence the Criminal Justice System?, p. 560
Diff: E, Type: Applied, Ans: criminal

1.   Ken was judged to be insane during the course of his trial. His was a _____ commitment.

Psychology in Law: How Do Clinicians Influence the Criminal Justice System?, p. 560
Diff: E, Type: Factual, Ans: responsible; capable (or competent)

2.   Mental health practitioners are often called upon in criminal proceedings to comment as to whether a person is _____ for his or her crimes and _____ of defending himself or herself in court.

Psychology in Law: How Do Clinicians Influence the Criminal Justice System?, p. 560
Diff: E, Type: Factual, Ans: criminal commitment

3.   A person who is found to be mentally unstable either at the time of the crime or at the time of the trial is generally sent to an institution for treatment in a process called _____.

Criminal Commitment and Insanity during Commission of a Crime, p. 561
Diff: M, Type: Factual, Ans: M'Naghten rule

4.   The requirement that a person must know the difference between right and wrong in order to be convicted of a crime is known as the _____.

Criminal Commitment and Insanity during Commission of a Crime, p. 561
Diff: M, Type: Factual, Ans: Durham test

5.   The notion that a person was not guilty by reason of insanity if the unlawful act was the product of a mental disease or defect was known as the _____.

Criminal Commitment and Insanity during Commission of a Crime, p. 561
Diff: M, Type: Factual, Ans: irresistible impulse

6.   Dissatisfaction with the M'Naghten rule led to another interpretation that focused on whether the defendant was able to control his or her actions. This was known as the _____ test.

Criminal Commitment and Insanity during Commission of a Crime, p. 562
Diff: M, Type: Factual, Ans: schizophrenia

7.   Today the most frequent diagnosis of defendants who are acquitted of a crime by reason of insanity is _____.

Criminal Commitment and Insanity during Commission of a Crime, p. 564
Diff: H, Type: Factual, Ans: diminished

8.   Dan White, who killed two prominent San Francisco politicians in 1978, pleaded a version of the insanity defense that portrayed his mental instability as an extenuating circumstance. This is called pleading "guilty with _____ capacity."

Civil Commitment, p. 568
Diff: E, Type: Factual, Ans: civil

9.   Generally, people can be committed to a mental hospital against their will if a judgment is made that they are mentally ill and gravely disabled. If no criminal act is involved, the procedure is called _____ commitment.

Civil Commitment, p. 568
Diff: M, Type: Factual, Ans: civil commitment

10.   When a person is considered to be in need of treatment and is dangerous to himself or herself, the person may be involuntarily placed in a mental health facility through the process of

_____.

Civil Commitment, p. 568
Diff: H, Type: Factual, Ans: child (or minor)

11.   A _____ who exhibits bizarre and dangerous behavior may be committed involuntarily without a hearing.

Civil Commitment, p. 569
Diff: H, Type: Applied, Ans: two-physician certificate (or "2 PC)

12.   You are a physician in the emergency room when the police bring in a young man screaming, "Boffo told me to kill all of them, even the pretty ones." You are sure there is an underlying psychological disorder and that this young man is dangerous, so you grab another physician to have the young man committed against his will. This will be a _____ commitment.

Civil Commitment, pp. 569-570
Diff: M, Type: Factual, Ans: dangerousness

13.   One criticism of civil commitment procedures centers around the accuracy of the assessment of _____.

Protecting Patients' Rights, p. 572
Diff: H, Type: Factual, Ans: *Wyatt v. Stickney*

14.   In the case known as _____, a federal court ruled that the state was constitutionally obligated to provide therapy for individuals who had been civilly committed. This case supported the individual's right to treatment.

Protecting Patients' Rights, p. 573
Diff: M, Type: Factual, Ans: biological

15.   The debate over the right to refuse treatment has focused primarily on _____ treatments.

Law in Psychology: Professional Boundaries, p. 575
Diff: M, Type: Factual, Ans: prescribing medication

16.   There has been much debate about permitting psychologists to carry out one of the few remaining activities that has until now been restricted to psychiatrists, that is, _____.

Serial Murderers: Madness or Badness?, p. 578 (Box 19-3)
Diff: M, Type: Factual, Ans: low
17. Serial killers frequently employ the insanity plea during their trials. The general level of success of this plea for them has been _____.

Bridging Mental Health Services to the Workplace, p. 581
Diff: M, Type: Factual, Ans: employee assistance programs
18. Programs frequently run by employers that seek to provide aid for moderate problems before they cause serious reactions in their employees are called _____.

The Economics of Mental Health, p. 582
Diff: M, Type: Applied, Ans: managed care
19. Before therapy could begin, the therapist had to submit her plan for therapy to the insurance company for approval. Her client was approved for eight one-hour sessions. This insurance company is part of a _____ program.

The Person within the Profession, p. 584
Diff: H, Type: Factual, Ans: 84
20. About _____% of therapists surveyed reported having seen a therapist for treatment themselves at least once.

ESSAY QUESTIONS

Psychology in Law: How Do Clinicians Influence the Criminal Justice System?, p. 560
Diff: M, Type: Factual
1. There are two reasons for a person to be criminally committed for treatment. Describe them.

Criminal Commitment and Insanity during Commission of a Crime, p. 561
Diff: H, Type: Applied
2. Provide an example of a situation that would lead to a finding of not guilty by reason of insanity under each of the following: M'Naghten rule, irresistible impulse test, Durham test, American Law Institute test (four examples in all).

Criminal Commitment and Insanity during Commission of a Crime, pp. 562, 564
Diff: H, Type: Applied
3. Discuss at least three distinct criticisms that have been leveled at the insanity defense and how proponents of the insanity defense have answered these criticisms.

Civil Commitment, p. 568
Diff: M, Type: Applied
4. What is the difference between criminal and civil commitment?

Civil Commitment, pp. 568-569
Diff: H, Type: Factual
5. Outline the procedures for civil commitment involving a child, an adult, and an emergency situation with an adult.

Civil Commitment, pp. 569-570
Diff: H, Type: Applied

6.   Describe at least three research results that support the idea that those with severe mental disorders are dangerous.

Civil Commitment, pp. 571-572
Diff: H, Type: Applied

7.   Imagine that you are a defense attorney arguing against civil commitment for your client. Based on text material, describe three different reasons you could give the judge for not committing your client.

Protecting Patients;' Rights, pp. 572-573
Diff: H, Type: Applied

8.   Based on law established and interpreted by the U.S. Supreme Court, list the major rights to treatment that mental patients have.

Protecting Patients;' Rights, pp. 572-574
Diff: H, Type: Applied

9.   Discuss one right that mental patients have. Tell how that right might both protect their interests and interfere with their treatment.

Serial Murderers: Madness or Badness?, p. 578 (Box 19-3)
Diff: H, Type: Applied

10.   Outline a profile (that is, descriptors) of a typical serial killer.

What Ethical Principles Guide Mental Health Professionals?, pp. 579-580
Diff: H, Type: Factual

11.   List and briefly explain the major points in the professional ethical standards for psychologists as they apply to clinical work.